SCHOOLCRAFT COLLEGE LIBRARY

3 3013 00142170 4

W9-CBK-025

WITHDRAWN

The Modern Art of Chinese Cooking
by Barbara Tropp

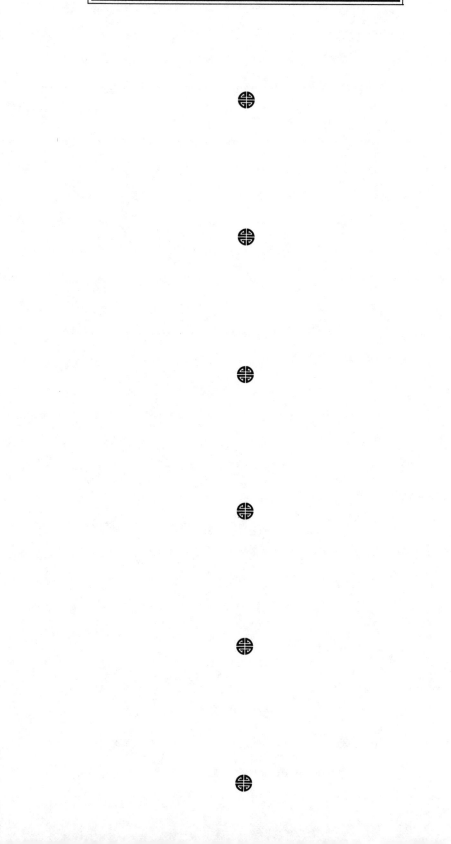

The Modern Art of Chinese Cooking
by Barbara Tropp

Including an unorthodox
chapter on East-West desserts and
a provocative essay on wine
by Gerald Asher

Design
The Office of Michael Manwaring

Illustration
Bill Chiaravalle

Photography
Allan Rosenberg

William Morrow and Company, Inc.
New York   1982

Library of Congress Cataloging in Publication Data

Tropp, Barbara.

The modern art of Chinese cooking.

Includes index.

1. Cookery, Chinese.   I. Title.

TX724.5.C5T685 1982   641.5951   82-8143

ISBN 0-688-00566-7   AACR2

◆

Printed in the United States of America

2 3 4 5 6 7 8 9 10

TO

Po-fu
who awoke my appetite

Harvey
who sculpted my taste

and

James and Lucy Lo
who taught me how to cook

I t is impossible to acknowledge sufficiently all the help that has gone into the pages of this book. A note from a student, a call to a fellow cook, a recipe given by a Chinese granny as she fed me from her crock of homemade pickles—each has been incorporated into a fabric for which others supplied many of the finest threads.

Of the many that helped, these are but a few:

The Chinese community of Princeton, New Jersey, and the Department of East Asian Studies of Princeton University fed me with food, knowledge, and poetry for many years. My life was enriched there. James and Lucy Lo, scholar-cooks of remarkable sensibility, taught me much of what I know, and my gratitude and affection for them are immeasurable. The Hu family of Rumson, New Jersey, let me play in the kitchen of their restaurant, a brave and daring thing at the time.

Carl Sontheimer gave me my first opportunity to write about Chinese cooking. Barbara Kafka, my first editor, inspired me and encouraged me, and has been a trusted mentor and valued friend. James Beard said at the outset to keep a set of measuring spoons by the typewriter, which was some of the best advice I ever got.

When I moved west, San Francisco welcomed me with open arms, and I am indebted to many of the talented cooks who live here: Jan Weimer, Marion Cunningham, and Flo Braker have given detailed answers to questions in realms of cooking where I know little and they are experts. Diane Dexter and Jay Perkins provided scientific stuffing wherever needed to give body to the technique notes. Bill Shurtleff of The Soyfoods Center lectured me on soyfoods. Margaret Fox, Jane Helsel, Donna Nordin, and Michael James shared recipes. Michael and his partner, Billy Cross, invited me to cook for The Great Chefs of France at The Robert Mondavi Winery, experiences that broadened my horizons and taught me to love cold Chinese noodles with Champagne. Jim Nassikas, president of the Stanford Court Hotel, lent me a shelf in the hotel refrigerator when this book was getting under way and then installed me in his secretary's office when my typewriter broke down the night before it was due. Debbie Slutsky and Clay Wollard put their talent to work in my kitchen. Gary Jenanyan and Mary Jane Drinkwater supplied warmth and ice cream recipes. Oona Aven tested, tasted, and ate most everything in the dessert chapter, and a little more besides. Rosemary Manell was a storehouse of knowledge whenever I tapped on the door. My friends at Greens said, "Stop worrying. Chop faster!" and taught me lessons more valuable than how to hold a chef's knife.

Edward Schafer, Agassiz Professor of Oriental Languages and Literature at the University of California at Berkeley, supplied Chinese notes on kiwi fruit, ginger, and *sorbet*. His book, *The Golden Peaches of Samarkand*, and the hefty volume to which he contributed, *Food in Chinese Culture*, have been treasure troves into which I've dipped again and again.

Gerald Asher, one of my first friends in San Francisco, made a gift of his essay on wine and the wine suggestions following the recipes that I am honored to include here. His wonderful book, *On Wine*, contains more of his adventures with wine and Chinese food.

Susan Lescher, my agent, took on this book in the days of its infancy and nurtured it with an encouragement that mattered greatly. Maria Guarnaschelli, my editor, pushed it through to completion with an intensity that bettered it. I thank her for her trust. John Guarnaschelli snatched the pages from his wife's desk and became my official long-distance tester. Lois Bloom ran around New York City's Chinatown in search of the best.

Finally, for the physical beauty of this book, I am indebted to other hands: Michael Manwaring and his talented staff supplied the design. Bill Chiaravalle did the illustrations, elevating my pots and pans to works of art. Allan Rosenberg took the photographs that appear on the jacket, while Sandra Griswold stood by with patience and tweezers to arrange every last carrot cube. They are a skilled group of professionals with whom it has been a privilege to work, and I thank the people at William Morrow for allowing us to collaborate.

T his is the book I needed when I first set out to cook, armed with little but a good palate and a wide experience of eating wonderful Chinese foods. It is designed for someone who thirsts to know *why* something does or doesn't work in the kitchen. Someone who is fascinated as I am by the alchemy of cooking and the process whereby one transforms raw meat and vegetables into cooked things of a different order. It is also designed for someone who wants to learn to *taste* and to cook from instinct and the sort of freedom one gains from a thorough understanding of the range of Chinese flavors.

This is a romantic cookbook, in that it is filled with the poetry, philosophy, and art that are an inseparable part of the world of Chinese cooking. But it is also a thorough-going, practical workbook—a primer of trustworthy recipes, reliable techniques, solid information about tools, and lots of good, down-to-earth kitchen sense. I have learned through years of teaching that my students need both: food for the spirit as well as food for the belly, and an understanding of the roots of a culture in order to be able to cook its food.

Perhaps most of all, this book is my mirror. It is not a comprehensive record of a civilization or an encyclopedia of a cuisine, but rather the reflection of one person's studies, taste, vision, and style, and of a life that is lived happily between East and West. It reflects my very classic Chinese insistence on precision cutting, fresh ingredients, and clear-tasting foods that are unhampered by the tyranny of sugar, cornstarch, salt, ketchup, and chemicals that dominates many Chinese kitchens in the West. And at the same time, it reflects my very modern Western insistence on food that is practical and healthy as well as enticing, adaptable to an active lifestyle where the cook is often a breadwinner with obligations and passions beyond the kitchen. The result is an unusual blend of fresh snow peas and food processors, cassia blossoms and ice-cream makers, and classic Chinese foods and California wines—a comfortable yin-yang balance of East and West that nourishes me well.

Because this is primarily a teaching book, I have organized the chapters with a view to *creating Chinese cooks*, even more than with a view to explaining Chinese history, regional cooking styles, or themes in Chinese eating. The book begins with philosophy, moves through techniques, and then moves on to food. It follows my belief that when you set out to master Chinese cooking it is Chinese philosophy that is your foundation, Chinese cooking techniques that supply the bricks and the mortar, and the delicious food that follows is then the natural result and the crowning glory. Without philosophy to give it shape, Chinese food is shallow. Without technique, it falls apart. It is like a special house that one cannot hope to build from the pinnacles down.

In constructing the individual chapters, I have tried to combine things that are helpful to consider together. For example, eggs and tofu are presented as a pair because they each satisfy a vegetable yearning, and both modern Americans and traditional Chinese look for reasons of economy and taste to this middle ground between vegetable and meat protein. Noodles, dumplings and springrolls appear in one chapter because in food terms noodle doughs and dumpling and springroll wrappers are the same thing, and a Chinese cook handles them and judges their texture and doneness in quite the same way. Bread, buns, and rice were wedded together because in the Chinese world rice on the one hand and breads and buns on the other are the flip side of the same coin—the staple starch of a Chinese meal depending upon whether the cook is from the north or the south. We are so thoroughly indoctrinated in the West into thinking that to eat a Chinese meal requires a bowl of white rice that I wanted to dramatize what is a traditional option by talking about rice, breads, and buns in the same breath. It is there to remind you that you *do* have a choice when the menu planning is underway and you stop to think, "Now, what can I serve that is going to sop up all this good Chinese sauce . . . ?"

In designing a book whose primary purpose is to teach, it appears that some very attractive things about Chinese cooking might be lost. Where is the history, the folklore, the differences between north and south and Hunan and Szechwan? And what about those little eats called *dim sum*? Well, they are all here, interwoven like brightly colored threads, popping out here and there between directions on steaming and the how-to's of flipping a noodle nest. There are detours to teahouses and occasional steps backward in time, but for the most part my choice has been to take you in through the kitchen door and to introduce you to China amidst the clatter of pots and pans and the thunk-thunk of chopping. That is where one really learns to cook.

The
Philosophy
of
Chinese
Cooking

烹調的哲理

YIN AND YANG IN CHINESE CULTURE

The ancient Chinese philosophy of *yin*—that which is feminine, dark, and yielding—and *yang*—that which is contrastingly masculine, bright, and hard—underlies the whole of Chinese culture. It is not a hard law or a vigorous system as the old philosophers present it, but rather a general appreciation of dualities and a faith that harmony arises from the proper blending of opposites. To that way of thinking, the world is not a matter of irreconcilable opposites, but one of *complementary pairs.*

A preoccupation with yin and yang is evident in all the traditional Chinese arts. The archetypal Chinese landscape painting with its solid mountain looming alongside a low-flowing evanescent stream, the classic poetic couplet with its mirror images like

> *a long plume of smoke rises above the plain*
> *while a round sun sets over the river*

and the no-less-typical Chinese stir-fry of brown beef tossed with green broccoli are each manifestations of yin and yang. Streams and mountains, fire and smoke, and meat and vegetables are all yin-yang pairs. And for the artists of China, through the centuries, the task was to bring them together in harmony.

Yin and yang are not unrelated, but *inter-related,* as the ancient symbol shows. There is a fluid S shape dividing this world, and always a dot of one thing emerging in the space of the other. While the tension of opposition pulls them apart and defines each as unique, yin and yang invariably mesh and intertwine, like oil and vinegar in a salad, each accruing some special drama by virtue of contrast with the other.

the symbol for the ancient, fluid
partnership of *yin* and *yang,* sometimes
seen as two fish swimming head to tail

When yin and yang are in balance, and opposites are in harmony, the world sings sweetly. When they are out of whack—when one overshadows the other to too great an extreme—there are earthquakes, divorces, revolutions, eclipses, and culinary disasters! Thus, the Chinese painter carefully juggles rocks and rivers in a composition, the Chinese chef balances sweet and sour in a sauce, and the Chinese politician of whatever dynasty or age does *tai-chi* in the morning before he goes to the office, and writes poetry after work. Chinese habitually arrange and perceive their world, whether it is defined by the contents of a wok or the governing of a nation, according to the ideal of yin in balance with yang. The Chinese world is a traditionally inclusive one, where opposites are welcomed together in dynamic duality.

YIN AND YANG IN THE CHINESE KITCHEN

Every Chinese chef, from the simple Taiwanese peasant who stir-frys in a single wok by the roadside to the fastidiously trained banquet chef in charge of a Peking duck restaurant catering to a thousand, works unconsciously or consciously according to the culinary rules of *yin* and *yang.* It is not a hard and fast law of exacting combinations, like the one which binds Japanese macrobiotic cooking, but rather a gentle intuition and a visual and sensory confirmation of what does and doesn't go together. It may not even be known by name, but it is *inbred* in the culture. The roadside cook habitually combines white, salted chicken and green, sugar-sweet snow peas in a simple stir-fry and serves it alongside a bowlful of steamed rice. The banquet chef, in a different setting, orchestrates a majestic dinner featuring platters of crunchy mahogany duck skin, tender beige duck meat, crisp and chilled green scallions, steaming soft and white mandarin pancakes, and unctuous purple-black hoisin sauce. Each of them plans a meal where *flavors, textures, colors, food types,* and *cooking methods* are presented in conspicuous juxtaposition. This is the unvarying rule of the Chinese kitchen, wherever it be and no matter how humble or grand.

I must emphasize, however, that yin and yang is an *unconscious* mode for most Chinese. A Chinese cook puts poultry and greens together because it *feels* right, or wraps a sharp-tasting scallion and a sweet sauce in a neutral pancake because it is traditional and automatic. When I once suggested to Po-fu, my initiator in the realms of appetite, that yin and yang were beautifully presented in a dish sitting before us, he looked at me as if I were insane—an addled student of too much poetry. Yet it is there without question in every real Chinese dish, in the composition of every properly put together Chinese meal, and in the every move of a traditional Chinese cook.

In the realm of Chinese seasonings, yin and yang reveals itself in classic partnerships like sweet (sugar) and sour (vinegar), soy sauce and rice wine, ginger and scallion, salt and Szechwan peppercorns. It is also behind more subtle pairings, like the habit of combining chili with a touch of sugar. Chili used alone presents a singular, overriding taste that registers harshly on just one part of the tongue. It is too yang. Add but a pinch of sugar (yin), and the taste becomes rounder, fuller, more complex. The result is a fiery full flavor, instead of just fire.

In the composition of a Chinese dish, yin and yang means a *purposeful pairing of opposites.* Pork sausage is classically teamed with chicken or a green or white vegetable, where there are vivid color and texture foils for the chewy, rose-colored meat. Similarly, a salad of greens would not exist in China, but in its place would be a cold-tossed dish mixing multicolored heaps of shredded carrots, slivered snow peas, and grated red radish. Even when making a purely meaty dish—say, a stewed duck—the Chinese hand is ever ready to mix yin and yang. The duck skin is crisped to a deep brown in hot oil before stewing to make it stand apart in color and texture from the flesh.

The yin-yang principle extends still further to Chinese menu planning. Any dinner of ten stir-frys, ten spicy dishes, or ten sweet and sour sauces is so out of balance from the Chinese perspective as to cause an eclipse! The rule is dynamic contrast: pair a stir-fried crisp green with a stewed, soft brown meat. Juxtapose a mild, steamed vegetarian dish with a spicy deep-fried fish. Balance a labor-intensive, caloric showpiece with a simple, slimming dish. If you want to do a dish that must be made on the spot, include it in a menu with one that can be done in advance. Intersperse a meal of fiery Hunan and Szechwan specialties with a few deliberately mild dishes so that your palate can appreciate the excitement of the heat in contrast to the subtlety of the other seasonings. Choose cooling foods in the hot months and warming foods in the winter months. Or, plan a simple meal when you're hassled and a more complicated one when you're calm. If you keep yin and yang consciously in mind, you will never plan a meal that will overtax the cook, bore the guests, or drive them into an early grave from the effects of too much salt, sugar, chili, or oil.

YIN AND YANG ON THE CHINESE TABLE

Yin and yang is a conspicuous if automatic part of Chinese food presentation, whether it be the scattering of a few scallion rings in some clear soup bought at a market stall, or a kaleidoscopic progression of dishes at a colorful banquet spread. The rule is again one of *lively contrast.* Serving a brown chicken in an equally brown bowl shows off neither the chicken nor the bowl, whereas the same chicken put on a celadon plate and rimmed with red radish fans and deep green coriander *looks* exciting. Likewise, a batch of white steamed buns proffered up on a white platter looks ho-hum dull, but line the dish with a red napkin and the buns suddenly appear jazzy.

It is a simple system. Garnish white noodles with scallion greens. Garnish green beans with scallion whites. If you are serving two brown dishes and a red one, put the red in the center to highlight the browns on either side. And so on and so forth, making simple but thoughtful efforts to make the food look lively in a yin-yang way.

Even the actual chewing, if you are to do it in Chinese fashion, follows a yin-yang rhythm. The Chinese way is to sample a bit of savory meat, then a bit of cooling spinach, then a bit of spicy fish, then a bit of sweet pickled cucumber, then a crunchy nugget of radish, and so on, going from dish to dish. Eating in this manner is lively and healthy. There's no rush for a grossly sweet dessert, for one's tongue has sampled bits of sweetness all along, and no ignoring of those healthy greens because they are an inseparable part of a whole intriguing *medley* of tastes.

Given their pleasure in contrasts, the Chinese habit in everyday dining is to present the full assortment of dishes at once, putting four or five dishes simultaneously on the table in a fashion that baffles most Westerners accustomed as we are to eating in courses. If serving in discrete courses is more your style (as it is for slower-paced Chinese banquets where the dishes emerge from the kitchen one by one in a slow, stately procession meant to encourage the flow of wine), you should still remember yin and yang. Plan a crunchy dish first, followed by a soft-textured dish, or a mildly seasoned entrée before a spicy main course. Alternate the colors of the different courses. Serve stir-fried dishes in alternation with steamed or stewed dishes, so you don't need to dash madly to the kitchen at every turn and your guests have the experience of several textures and techniques.

Similarly, if the Chinese custom of putting a cluster of contrasting dishes in the center of the table so that everyone can reach in and help themselves is not to your liking or well suited to your table, be it overly long, populated by wineglasses, or round in shape but lacking the spinning lazy Susan that makes the communal Chinese custom practical for even large groups, by all means serve the food in individual portions but still with an eye to yin and yang. Garnish each guest's plate with a bit of contrasting color. Or, present three cold appetizers together on the individual plates in an arrangement to best contrast their colors and shapes. The principle remains the same and so does the effect, in spite of a difference in style.

To my mind, yin and yang is the very best sort of philosophy—a system you can ponder endlessly, but one you can also *see* and one you can *eat*. It is a simple but powerful tool in the hand of any aspiring Chinese cook. You cannot cook without it if you want to create *real* Chinese food, and you will cook better with it no matter what your cuisine.

The Art of Cutting: The Chinese Cleaver

刀法

Exacting knife work is fundamental in a Chinese kitchen. In a cuisine where things tend to sear immediately and cook quickly, food must be cut evenly in order to cook evenly. The thin slices, the thread-like julienne strips, and the carefully squared cubes and chunks that occupy the largest part of a Chinese cook's efforts each require a uniform precision. Chinese dishes are unforgiving of sloppy or erratic cutting, and the Chinese eye is equally critical of imperfection on the plate. A hair-fine tangle of julienned ginger crowning a steamed fish will encourage gasps, sighs, and toasts, whereas a stir-fry of lumpily cut, unevenly cooked bits will inspire silence.

As a glorification of necessity, Chinese writers through the ages have waxed eloquent on the art of cutting. One of China's earliest philosophers, the abundantly witty Taoist sage Chuang Tzu, immortalized Cook Ting, a butcher in the palace kitchen (here translated by Burton Watson):

> At every touch of his hand, every heave of
> his shoulder, every move of his feet, every thrust
> of his knee—ZIP! ZOOP! He slithered the knife
> along with a zing, and all was in perfect rhythm,
> as though he were performing the dance of the Mulberry
> Grove, or keeping time to the Ching-shou music.

Centuries later in the Tang, the art of the knife became a popular leitmotiv in the poetry of China's Golden Age. The pure-white slices of fresh fish produced by a cleaver moving faster than the eye could see were "snowflakes." Shreds of golden carp were "silver threads" upon a plate. So deft were the knife moves and so fragile-thin the resulting slivers that one chef's dinner was snapped up by a passing wind and transformed into a bevy of butterflies! Or so the poets, laboring hungrily over their verses, would have us believe.

Poetry notwithstanding, a Chinese cleaver is the very heart of a Chinese kitchen, and its proper use is one of the greatest pleasures of cooking "in Chinese." Whether the cutting edge is that of a two-pound butcher's cleaver or a comparatively dainty vegetable cleaver, one must know the tool and its nature intimately to use it masterfully, "in perfect rhythm."

I was given my first Chinese cleaver by Po-fu at age twenty-three and did not venture to pick it up until age twenty-five. At that time, I had wielded nothing more imposing than a butter knife in my sheltered kitchen pokings and had no one to show me what to do with a discernibly sharp cleaver.

It was actually a child-size cleaver. The handle was scalloped, like the handle grips on a tricycle, and the blade was a short one by Chinese standards, with a grinning camel imprinted on the side. I whacked it on some chicken bones to dull it, then used it occasionally when I thought I'd like to show off.

One morning I woke up, decided that enough slow, shoddy, dull cutting was enough, and rode the bus to New York Chinatown and returned with ten pounds of cleavers. I infiltrated several Chinese restaurants, watched hawk-like in any kitchen where a cleaver was in swing, and doggedly (camel-like?) set about teaching myself how to use it. I found little help in books and more guidance from principles that I had learned in *tai-chi** and Chinese calligraphy—balance, relaxation, restful concentration.

_____

* *Tai-chi* is a set of slow, stylized movements evolved from the ancient Chinese system of healing and maintaining the body through the proper balance of yin and yang. A cook is a *tai-chi* dancer, I like to think, whether at the cutting board or in front of the stove—moving rhythmically and economically and arriving at an outward harmony of movement through an inner focus on the task.

At age thirty-two, I use a cleaver the same way I practice these other arts—with some grace, some surety, and an occasional little wobble. It feeds me, inspires me, and is thoroughly rewarding in the practice. If you have never picked one up, you should try! What follows is here to help you.

THE ANATOMY OF A CHINESE CLEAVER

For all practical kitchen purposes, a Chinese cleaver is a three-part tool.

The first part, and the most crucial, is the 8–9-inch long *blade* consisting of a sharp *cutting edge*, a dull, flat *top edge*, and two *broad sides*. The blade as a whole may be thick or thin as it rises from the cutting edge, strikingly heavy or relatively light, depending upon whether it is designed to whack heartily through bones or to sliver young ginger into gossamer threads. If properly balanced, the blade will fall front end first swiftly to the board when the cleaver is held loosely by the handle, indicating that the weight of the blade alone will accomplish a significant part of the chopping.

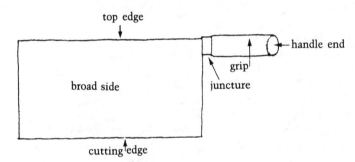

The cutting edge, always razor-sharp, may be curved to a slight or greater degree or be rigidly straight, the profile to depend upon its use. A cleaver whose lifework is to dismember chickens must be curved and pointed at the tip to work into every joint and crevice, whereas a blade destined to cut mostly vegetables will require a straight edge to best meet the board.

The top edge may be broad or narrow, about ¼ inch wide on a bone-breaking cleaver or ⅛ inch wide on a cleaver designed for boneless tasks. Its primary use is to serve as an occasional pounder. On a bone-breaking cleaver, the blade will sometimes be turned over to shatter a bone and expose the marrow-rich interior. On a lightweight cleaver, the top edge is used for lightweight work—pounding a head of garlic to break it into cloves or gently pounding a tough piece of meat to tenderize it.

Either broad side of the blade serves as a flattener and a scooper-upper. As a flattener, it will smash scallion nuggets, spreading the fibers and releasing the juice, spank a garlic clove and free the skin, or slap a slice of chicken to uniform thinness. In its handy role as a scooper-upper, the broad side of the blade will carry cut things to the wok and discarded things to the sink, and be the envy of every narrow French blade in town.

The second and next important part of the anatomy of a Chinese cleaver is the 3½-inch-long *handle* consisting of a *grip* and a *blunt handle end*.

The grip is most commonly made of wood, though it is sometimes made of metal, and is variously smooth and lacquered, coarse and unfinished, squared or round. Like the steering wheel of a car, it is the device one grips to make the thing "go," and it must feel good and sit comfortably in one's hand if it is to be of good use.

The blunt handle end is sometimes smooth, and othertimes made ugly and bumpy by a nail or thick metal staple. The end functions as a mini-mallet, smashing a coin of fresh ginger to break the fibers and bring its juices to the surface or pounding some Szechwan peppercorns to a coarse and pungent powder.

The final part of a cleaver's anatomy is *the juncture* between the handle and the blade. In a heavyweight Chinese cleaver designed for butchering, where one grips the handle close to the end, there may be no juncture at all or simply a narrow metal ring. In a lightweight cleaver, however, where one's hand grasps equal parts of handle and blade, the juncture will come in direct contact with the soft belly of the palm. The metal sheath may be smooth or sharp, straight or cantilevered, and will radically affect the ease with which the cleaver may be used for close chopping.

TRADITIONAL TYPES OF CHINESE CLEAVERS

There are three basic types that define rather neatly the different tasks of a traditional Chinese cook. These are not necessarily the exact cleavers you will want or need in your kitchen, but they will introduce you to the types of specialty cleavers used by a professional Chinese chef.

Heavyweight Butchering Cleaver
The largest Chinese cleaver, the guillotine of the kitchen, is a heavyweight, broad, thick-bladed monster designed for no-nonsense chores like chopping through pork and beef bones. It is likely the very model used by Chuang Tzu's Cook Ting to cleave his thousand palace-bred oxen into bits. The handle is deeply grooved for a secure grip and tapers to a narrow, ringlike juncture, emphasizing that one wields such a cleaver by holding the handle near the end. The blade is a merciless 1¾ pounds heavy, 8 inches long, 4½ inches broad, and ¼ inch thick at the top—sheer muscle for banging with no subtlety intended.

I purchased this cleaver before I discovered that butchers in the United States have nifty electric saws with which they will happily slice bones to neat bits with no charge to the customer. Before that discovery, I used my butcher's cleaver to split spare-ribs crosswise into nuggets and to cut up heavy bones for stock. I now treasure it as a museum piece. It would be overkill for the lighter bone-chopping tasks that are part of everyday cooking.

heavyweight Chinese butcher's cleaver designed for chopping beef and pork bones

side view of blade: relatively thick right down to the cutting edge

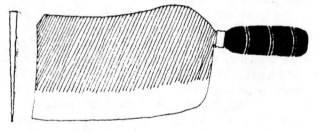

Heavyweight Poultry Cleaver
An interim weight and shape en route to the more everyday Chinese cleaver is the type designed especially for cutting poultry. The pointy tip and generously curved, long blade are perfectly shaped to work into every joint of a duck or chicken, slitting a neat line around the thigh, cleaving a whole breast in two, or splicing a neck at just the appropriate

spot. Like the contours of the bird, the contour of the blade is curved, easing the back and forth rocking that is basic to dismembering poultry. The handle is ridged and narrows to a ringlike juncture, as befits the stationary end-of-handle grip with which one chops through poultry bones. The cleaver weighs a hefty 1½ pounds, and the blade is an elegant 9 inches long, 3 inches wide, and ¼ inch thick at the top. It is heavy enough to cut cleanly through poultry bones with no worry about nicking the blade, yet compact and long enough to be turned inside the narrow cavity of a duck.

I purchased this cleaver when I was still a fledgling chopper, much miffed because my lightweight cleaver had become nicked and scallop-edged in the course of chopping chicken bones. A differently shaped cleaver that was less weighty could accomplish the bone-chopping as well, but I enjoy the specialty shape and the extra dexterity it affords me. I still use it to dismember poultry before cooking, though its weight is unduly cumbersome for chopping already-cooked birds.

heavyweight Chinese cleaver designed
for dismembering chicken and duck and
chopping through poultry bones

side view of blade: too thick for fine
slicing and too thin for heavyweight
bones

Lightweight Cleaver for Vegetables and Boned Meats

The everyday, must-have tool of a Chinese cook is a relatively lightweight cleaver (relative, that is, to the bone-choppers above), heavy enough to accomplish most of the work of slicing through vegetables and boned meats by virtue of its own weight, yet thin and tapered enough in the blade to cut paper-thin slices and fine julienne threads. It is called a "vegetable cleaver" in Chinese, but its use extends far beyond the vegetable realm to include anything without bones. The handle is usually evenly thick from end to end, and the juncture between handle and blade is often wide and pronounced, allowing one's hand to grip both the blade and the handle above the juncture and thus command with precision the thrust and angle of the blade. The contour of the edge is either fully straight or slightly curved at the ends, the former specialized for straight slicing and the latter flexibly suited for both straight slicing and rock-mincing. A cleaver of this everyday variety weighs about ¾ pound, and sports a blade that is about 8 inches long, 3¼–4 inches broad and only ⅛ inch wide across the top.

I cannot chop properly without this cleaver and carry it with me most everywhere I go. There is nothing to replace it in the world of Western knives for sheer versatility. It accomplishes about 90 percent of a Chinese cook's chores and, once accustomed to the benefits of the size and weight, you will find it difficult to use anything else.

lightweight everyday Chinese vegetable cleaver designed for cutting vegetables and boned meats; cutting edge may be absolutely flat or slightly rounded

side view of thin, finely tapered blade

MUST-HAVE EVERYDAY CLEAVERS

There is no such thing as an all-purpose cleaver, at least in the Chinese world. A cleaver that will crack bones deftly lacks the thinness and finesse required for fine work. Conversely, one that will julienne hair-fine threads of ginger will nick if made to chop a bone.

While you do not need all three of the specialty cleaver types described above, for homestyle Chinese cooking and the preparations described in this book you will need two cleavers. The first is a heavy, general-use, *bone-chopping cleaver*, and the second is a relatively lightweight cleaver with a thin blade described as a *Chinese vegetable cleaver*.

Heavyweight Bone-Chopping Cleaver

For cutting through bones, both raw and cooked, you will need a thick-bladed cleaver that weighs 1–1¼ pounds.

If you are looking for a bone-chopping cleaver, you have several choices. Best, in my opinion, is to go to a sizable Chinatown and specifically to a Chinese hardware store or the kitchenware counter of a large grocery and get an inexpensive cleaver that looks in profile much like the everyday Chinese vegetable cleaver pictured above, but which has a discernably *thicker blade*. There are several styles of this type of cleaver on the market, and the one I favor has a wooden handle and a dull finish blade that will not rust. The handle is notched for easy gripping, and the blade is honed about ¼ inch from the edge. When you hold this cleaver loosely in your hand, the tip should fall immediately downward if it is properly weighted. This cleaver will feel awkwardly heavy in your hand, like a hatchet you might use for chopping firewood.

my general bone-chopping cleaver: a thicker and broader blade than my everyday vegetable cleaver, the same general shape without the subtleties of design

Another choice, if you already have one, is to use a *Western cook's cleaver* of the sort pictured on page 25. While it does not have the dimensions of a heavyweight Chinese cleaver, it will accomplish the job of chopping bones. If you do not already have one, do not buy it for Chinese purposes. You get a lot of style for a lot of money, but the task can be done better for a third of the price.

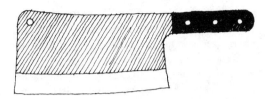

heavyweight Western cook's cleaver: good for chopping through bones, but lacks the length and width of the Chinese model

    A third choice is to use a cheap Chinese-made cleaver that has proved uncomfortable or unsatisfactory for lightweight work and that you are now willing to see nicked or otherwise abused in the assault on bones. This is an especially comfortable option if you are ready to move on to a top-quality, everyday vegetable cleaver of the type described below and do not want to banish the old one, unused, to a far corner of the kitchen.

Lightweight Chinese Vegetable Cleaver

For all chopping chores *aside* from splitting bones, you will need a relatively lightweight cleaver of the everyday design described and illustrated above on page 24, with a blade that is only ⅛ inch wide at the top and tapers quickly to a superfine thinness. I have used at least a dozen different cleavers of this sort, and my favorite, by far, is the American-made *Dexter Chinese chef's knife*, preferably the "super stainless" model and definitely the full-size model with a blade that is 8 inches long. The stainless blade is made from high-carbon steel, which gives it the best of both worlds—the no-stain beauty and ease of stainless, partnered with the fine sharpening and holding qualities of carbon. The contour of the blade is likewise a perfect blending, combining the straightness required for long slices and the slightly rounded edges that facilitate rock-mincing. The handle is a beautifully finished, evenly round wooden barrel with a smooth, nail-free end. The juncture is a smooth brass glove ¾ inches wide, comfortably tapered to meet the blade. Furthermore, the blade rises from the juncture with a subtle, slightly rounded angle, making it possible to use for hours on end with no injury to a tender palm. I am in *love* with this tool and have seen no finer East or West. In a market that is glutted with ill-made Chinese cleavers, this is *the* lightweight cleaver to get if you do not already have one, or the first to consider buying if yours needs replacing.

my own favorite Chinese vegetable cleaver: *Dexter's full-size Chinese chef's knife* with an 8-inch super stainless blade

"LITTLE" AND "LESSER" KNIVES

In a Chinese kitchen, there are great or big knives *(da-dao)*, and little or lesser knives *(syao-dao)*. The big knives, great in weight and in the variety of tasks they will accomplish, are the cleavers. The little knives, lesser in size and range of service, are either narrow, extremely light cleavers or Western-style paring knives. They are the knives responsible for carving the dragon on the winter melon, turning an icicle radish into a chrysanthemum, peeling ginger, stringing celery, and other such minutiae as would make a hefty cleaver look like overkill.

The very lightweight cleaver that qualifies as a "lesser" knife looks much like an everyday Chinese vegetable cleaver except for its discernibly narrow blade, usually 2–2¼ inches across. The blade is very thin from top to bottom, and consequently it is very light in the hand. The profile is also reminiscent of a Japanese chef's knife, but whereas the latter is a major tool in a Japanese kitchen and has a thick, finely weighted blade of immaculate construction, the Chinese narrow cleaver is typically unweighted and feels flimsy. These knives are appealingly light and unintimidating if you are a newcomer to cleavers, but their very lack of weight and width severely undermines their usefulness. Do not get one *in place* of an everyday vegetable cleaver.

narrow, extremely light Chinese cleaver,
designed solely for small tasks

My own choice instead of the cleaver above is to use a Western-style paring knife as my "lesser" blade. For those few tasks where my everyday Chinese vegetable cleaver seems needlessly large—such as peeling fresh water chestnuts and deveining shrimp—the paring knife functions perfectly while taking up little room. The one I use is a Swiss-made Victorinox stainless paring knife with a 3-inch long blade and a humble plastic handle. It is a fraction of the price of other "lesser" knives I have bought in the past, and I recommend it heartily if you do not already own a good little knife.

a wonderfully serviceable "lesser" knife

SHARPENING A CHINESE CLEAVER

I am continually amazed to discover how many people feel more comfortable with a dull knife. It is as if sharpening a knife were difficult—which it is not—or as if a properly sharp knife might suddenly jump from your hand to cut you—which it won't! The fact of the matter is that keeping a knife sharp is very easy, and that using a sharp knife makes the chopping go significantly *faster* with significantly *better* results. You will see this for yourself if you experiment even once with a newly sharpened knife. Moreover, if you *are* cut with a sharp knife, the cut will heal cleanly and quickly. I know that is not a pleasant thought, but it is nonetheless one more reason to *keep your knives sharp.*

Having experimented with a wide variety of stones, steels, and gizmos, I have settled on a classic, round *12-inch sharpening steel* as the everyday tool to keep my cleavers razor-sharp. It is a ½-inch thick, tapered baton of finely ridged chromed steel, attached to a deeply ridged wooden handle. The handle is topped by a ring, which allows me to hang it within arm's reach of my cutting surface. That's my reminder to sharpen my cleaver or "lesser" knife regularly, with 6–8 strokes of the steel before each day's use. With this system, I never need to have my cleavers sharpened professionally (though I do confess I wear out a steel about once every 16 months).

a round, 12–14-inch sharpening steel

Owing to the size and weight of a Chinese cleaver, the method for using a steel differs from that normally seen in a Western kitchen. Instead of holding the steel out in the air and sharpening the knife on a horizontal plane, the steel is planted tapered tip down on a secure, no-slip surface, and the cleaver is drawn down and across the abrasive steel in a vertical movement. This allows the weight of the cleaver itself to do most of the work of sharpening and has the secondary advantage of being far safer than the Western method, because the blade moves away from your hand. I use the same stance with my "lesser" Western knives and find it equally easy and efficient.

There are four things to keep in mind if you are new to using a sharpening steel. One, the angle of the blade to the steel should be *20°*. Less, and you will be slapping the blade instead of sharpening it. More, and you will be rounding and dulling the edge. Two, be sure to stroke the blade with *conviction*, first on one side of the steel then on the other, several times back and forth until the edge feels keen. A too-gentle stroke will offer nothing in the way of edge-sharpening abrasion. Three, draw the *full length* of the blade across the steel with each stroke, sharpening the total edge and not just a part of it. Finally, check the edge by gently *tapping* your finger along it from end to end. If it is not razor-sharp after a good ten strokes, then it is likely that you have sharpened it unevenly. Try a few strokes on one side of the steel only, and see if that brings the edge up to sharpness. I, for instance, seem to always stroke lighter on the right side of the steel, and habitually compensate by stroking a few extra times on the left side.

the practical way to sharpen the full edge of a cleaver with a steel, letting the weight of the blade do most of the work

proper 20° angle of the blade against the sharpening steel

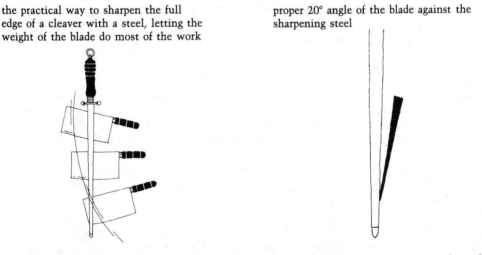

If you are dutiful in using a steel before or after each day's cutting, less than a dozen strokes will keep your lightweight vegetable cleavers in top form. Bone-breaking cleavers may require professional sharpening once a year or so, but steady use of a steel will keep them serviceably keen.

STORING A CHINESE CLEAVER

Given a properly sharp cleaver, you must take extra care to store it so both you and the cleaver are out of harm's way. I know of two systems that work well.

The first is the one I use in my own kitchen, a slotted wooden rack that attaches to the far side of my work table, out of traffic's way, and holds the cleavers handle side up for easy access. These racks are easily found in kitchenware shops or stores carrying butcher blocks.

The second system is the one I use on the road, which is very adaptable for the kitchen. It is a protective sleeve for the cleaver, easily made out of heavyweight cardboard or leather that you stitch securely shut on three sides. With the sleeve in place, protecting both you and the edge of the blade, the cleaver can be safely kept in a drawer.

Two safe ways to store a cleaver

in a heavy cardboard or leather sleeve, open at one end and securely stitched or stapled shut on the other three sides

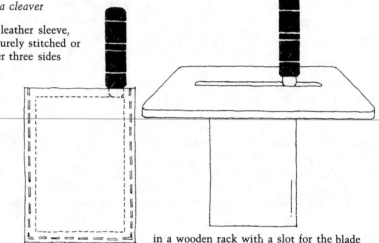

in a wooden rack with a slot for the blade

A magnetic rack, in my experience, is simply unreliable for Chinese cleavers. On two occasions I have seen cleavers fall without warning from double-bar, super-strong magnetic racks, and one time should have been enough.

CUTTING SURFACES

The traditional mate for a Chinese cleaver is a *cross-section of a hardwood tree*, and a handsomer, more honest-looking object is hard to imagine gracing a kitchen. Even the huge ones stationed behind every Chinatown deli counter—greasy from countless ducks and sunk deep in the middle from a zillion cleaver blows—exude a nobility that makes any other chopping block seem pedestrian.

The standard, home-size chopping block is about 16 inches in diameter and 6 inches thick. To prevent it from splitting, it must be seasoned soon after buying with a liberal rubbing of linseed oil or fresh corn or peanut oil, as much as the wood will drink up. Thereafter, clean it after each use with a sponge or cloth wrung out in plain hot water, and as needed with several scrapings of a *metal pastry scraper* or a spatula to remove any buildup of food particles or grease. *Do not* soak the board in water or apply any soap or detergent to it. Both will damage the wood by significantly weakening the fibers. If the top gets gunky or tacky, layer it thinly with kosher salt and let it sit overnight to drink up any blood or grease, then scrape it clean the following morning. A scrubbing with a solution of vinegar, water, and baking soda is also useful as an occasional deodorizer. The same care goes for any unfinished wooden cutting surface, be it a butcher-block table or a homely wooden cutting board.

traditional Chinese chopping block:
cross-section of a hardwood tree

metal pastry scraper for cleaning

     A less traditional cutting surface, but the one I use in my kitchen for everything except pastry-making (for which I like wood), is an *acrylic cutting board*. This is not glass, ceramic, or sleek plastic—all of which will damage your knives—but a high-density rubber-like plastic with some give for your knife and a tiny hatchwork "tread" that works nicely to grip the food. These boards never smell, split, or require scraping, and the thicker ones will not warp. They do not damage knives and will clean up nicely with soap and water and an occasional, stain-removing once-over with a stiff, metal-bristle brush. In the eyes of many, they have no style, but their use in my opinion far outweighs their unexotic looks. I know of no other surface on which I can bone chicken, dismember ducks, clean fish, and chop vegetables in quick succession with no more required than a quick trip to the sink to give each item a clean surface. These boards are available cheaply in any large Chinatown, at about one-third the cost charged by a Western kitchenwares store. As with any cutting surface, the bigger the better as far as I'm concerned. Get the largest board your counter will allow.

a practical, everyday cutting
board made of white acrylic
with a raised "tread" on
the surface

metal-bristle brush
for cleaning

A Note for Tall and Small Choppers
The first and last word on cutting surfaces is *height*—namely, theirs and yours. Regardless of what you choose to cut on, your hands should be able to rest flat on top of the cutting surface with your elbows gently bent. This is what is required for maximum chopping speed *and* maximum comfort.
     Smaller people (like myself), about five feet tall, generally need a surface 34–35

inches from the ground, whereas my tall cook-friends six feet and over report their cutting surfaces to be about 38 inches high. Ultimately, it will depend on the length of your arms; however, all "non-average" types should be forewarned that the average Western kitchen is not scaled to allow you to work your best.

If you must work in a kitchen ill-suited to your height, you can still work comfortably by making the necessary adjustments. Short people can wear suitably high heels for chopping or build platforms or stand on top of a box. (I have done all three, sometimes two at a time.) Tall people can boost the height of a cutting board by putting *it* on top of an ample platform made of books, other chopping boards, or a heavy box. No matter how you manage it, chopping at a height appropriate to *your* height is crucial to speed and comfort.

CORRECT CLEAVER POSTURE

Whenever I teach others how to use a Chinese cleaver, my first words are invariably those of my Chinese calligraphy and *tai-chi* masters: *RELAX!* In Chinese, the word is *soong* 鬆. The character shows the ideograph for "hair" over the ideograph for "pine tree," pictorially combining what is soft and flowing with what is naturally and effortlessly erect.

Let your shoulders sink down. Let your elbows sink down. Don't lock your knees. *Let go* of the enormous effort required to keep the body tense. Allow your fingers to curve gently around the handle and the blade, so the weight of the cleaver is free to do most of the work of chopping. Then, take a deep, slow breath clear down to your belly, so the spine inflates, the body stands straight on its own, and fills with a subtle energy.

If your body is relaxed, the *chi* (one's natural energy) will flow to the hand. The mind's attention will focus easily on the board, and the knife will move faster and find its mark without strain.

BASIC CLEAVER HOLDS: GRAND-SLAM CHOPPING VERSUS CLOSE-CHOPPING

A cleaver is essentially the same as a baseball bat when it comes to how one grips it. For a "home run," when brute power and slam are required, one moves back on the handle. The force concentrates in the heave of the shoulder and the elbow, and the hand's job is to receive that force through a relaxed but secure grip on the blade. In this kind of *"grand-slam chopping"* the work is done by the upper arm and the blade, with no particular guidance from the fingers. This is the hold with which one breaks bones, dismembers poultry, and hack-minces large cubes of meat.

On the other hand, when one wants to "punt" the ball or drive it to a particular point on the infield or, in chopping, when finesse, control, and exactitude are required, the hand moves closer up on the handle, and in the case of chopping grasps part of the blade. The palm rests over the juncture between the handle and the blade, and the fourth and fifth fingers curve around the grip. The thumb rests straight on one side of the blade, while the second and third fingers curve gently toward the palm on the other side of the blade. This is the *"close-chopping hold,"* where there is almost no movement from the shoulder and most of the vitality comes from the *wrist*. The fingers have the responsibility of controlling, guiding, and "steering" the blade, and the chopping itself is an equal collaboration between the weight of the blade and the directives of the fingers. This is the hold one uses for slicing, shredding, and rock-mincing, and for close, decorative work.

There are subtle variations on these two holds, but they are the basic ones from which all the others stem.

Two basic cleaver holds

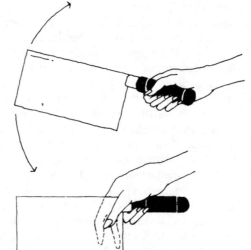

"grand-slam chopping" for cleaving bones and whack-mincing; hand gripping the handle alone and the action centered in the shoulder and elbow

"close-chopping" for slicing, dicing, rock-mincing, and decorative work; hand gripping both handle and blade, action stemming from the wrist

CUTTING TECHNIQUES: FOR THE LIGHTWEIGHT CHINESE VEGETABLE CLEAVER

Simple Slicing

Slicing with a cleaver occurs mainly on two planes: horizontal and vertical. The Chinese character for "slice" (*pien* 片), itself images the idea. One special style of vertical slicing is diagonal slicing.

For horizontal slicing, when you are holding the knife *parallel* to the board, the technique required for greatest safety and control is one that I've dubbed *"flying fingers."* In this posture, your cutting hand holds the cleaver parallel to the cutting surface in the close-chopping hold, with the fingers carefully guiding the blade. Your free hand anchors the food to the board, pinning it down with the midsection of your closely-joined middle three fingers while your palm, thumb, pinkie, and the tips of the middle fingers all arch upwards and "fly" out of reach of the advancing blade. If every part of the hand except for the small portion required to anchor the food to the board is "flying," there is *no way* you can be cut by the blade. When extra control is needed to pin down a particularly small or slippery piece of food, simply rock the pinning fingers forward.

Horizontal slicing is the way to cut a chicken breast crosswise into broad slabs, the way to cut some pieces of meat against the grain, and the way to cut a too-thick round of zucchini into two evenly thin slices.

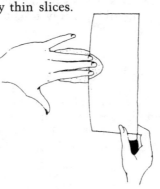

"flying fingers" anchoring a piece of chicken breast for horizontal slicing

For *vertical slicing*, when the knife is perpendicular to the board, the technique required for greatest safety and efficiency is one I call *"curved knuckles."* The five finger-tips of your free hand join together and curve inward in unison toward the palm, and the side of the blade balances against the third and fourth knuckles, which serve as a retreating barrier for the cleaver. So long as the fingertips remain curved under, there is *no way* they can be cut by the descending blade.

In this arrangement, the nail-covered portion of the fingers are responsible for holding the food in place on the board. If the item to be cut is something long and slim like a single carrot, then the fingers will join closely together and the thumb will stretch back to help push the carrot forward into the path of the advancing knife. On the other hand, if the task is to cut a cluster of carrot sticks, then the fingers will be spread a bit as the thumb and pinkie grasp the cluster gently by the sides.

Whatever the posture, the anchoring hand must be *relaxed* and hold the food only *lightly* against the board because its job is to move backward as the knife advances with each new slice. The fingers stay curved under, the knuckles remain as a supportive barrier for the blade, and the nails skirt lightly along the length of the object being cut.

It is a smooth, fluid movement when put into practice, designed to give you maximum speed with a minimum of tension and effort, and a precision control over the thickness or thinness of the slice. A *paper-thin slice* is obtained by a minimal movement, and a *thick slice* from a discernible movement of the knuckles and the fingers moving backward.

Vertical slicing is the way to cut a cucumber into perfectly even thick or thin rounds, and the way to cut meat or vegetables into slices or shreds.

"curved knuckles" bracing the knife for vertical slicing through miniature green Chinese cabbage

For *diagonal slicing*, the knife is again perpendicular to the board and the technique is again "curved knuckles." The slices can be long oblongs or short ovals depending on the angle of the knife across the thing to be cut, and thick or paper-thin depending on the retreating movement of your knuckles behind the blade.

Diagonal slicing is primarily the way to cut cylindrical vegetables into oblong coins.

Roll-Cutting
An intriguing variation of simple diagonal slicing is roll-cutting, a specialty cut applied to long, dense cylindrical objects like asparagus and carrots and also to long, thin squashes and Chinese eggplant. The aim is twofold: To achieve a greater surface area for quick-cooking and penetration of seasonings and to provide some intrigue and fun for the tongue.

To roll-cut a cylindrical vegetable, first make a diagonal slice near the stem end and discard the stem. Be alert to the angle. A too-sharp one will yield a skinny tip that will turn flabby upon cooking or marinating, and too slight an angle is not as attractive. Next, roll the object a quarter to a third of a turn away from you, then slice again at a similar angle 1½ inches farther down. Continue rolling and slicing until the whole object has been reduced to evenly long segments with diagonally cut ends (except in the case of asparagus, where one end should sport a nice purple tip). The ends will *not* be neatly parallel if you have roll-cut properly. They will be splayed out, slightly awkward looking, and feel witty on the tongue.

roll-cut lengths of asparagus: irregular ends cut at a not too-sharp or too-slight angle

Simple Shredding: The "Straight-Stack Method" for Block-Like Foods

To cut block-like foods—a slab of pressed tofu or a piece of flank steak, for example—into ⅛–¼-inch thick shreds requires combining *horizontal* and *vertical* slicing in a simple two-step sequence.

Step #1 is to slice the food horizontally with "flying fingers." Step #2 is to stack the slices neatly in an *upright pile*, then cut the stack vertically into shreds using "curved knuckles." For ¼-inch thick toothy shreds, make both the horizontal and vertical cuts at even ¼-inch intervals. For ⅛-inch thin "matchstick" shreds, make both series of cuts precisely ⅛ inch apart. If the resulting shreds are too long, gather them together, then cut them crosswise to the desired length.

This method is best at producing the standard shreds that are appropriate to stir-frys, soups, and cold salads requiring body.

simple shredding of a cake of tofu: slice horizontally, stack, shred vertically

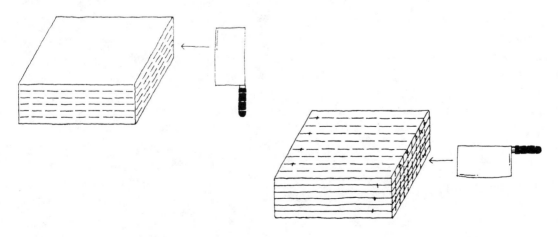

Simple Shredding: The "Step Method" for Cylindrical Objects and Hair-Fine Shreds

When the item you are shredding—say, a cucumber or a carrot—is not wide enough to give you an attractively long shred if you slice it into rounds and use the straight-stack method described above, then the trick is to slice it *on the diagonal* into oblong coins and shred these longer coins into longer shreds. It would be tedious to make small, straight stacks of the coins and shred them one by one, so the solution is not a straight, upright stack but a *step-like arrangement* whereby you can spread the slices in an overlapping pattern across your cutting surface and shred them in one continuous movement. It is a compromise position—not as fast as if you were able to stack the whole pile upright, but certainly not as slow as shredding them one by one or in small discrete groups.

Chinese cooks rely on this method for most of their shredding. Not only for commonly shredded cucumbers and carrots, but also for the uncommonly fine shreds of things like ginger that one frequently sees garnishing Chinese dishes. The step method gives incredible control to cut hair-fine shreds (called "threads," in Chinese); without the need to keep your fingers tense enough to manage an upright stack of slices, the subtle drawing back of the fingers bracing the blade is far easier to command.

To shred a cylindrical item like a carrot: First cut it on the diagonal into even oblong coins, cutting thicker coins for a thicker shred or thinner coins for a thinner shred. If you want *long* shreds, angle the knife on a sharper diagonal; the length of the slice will equal the length of the shred.

Once the carrot is sliced, push the coins together in the original carrot shape to straighten them, then spread them into a neat, step-like arrangement. You may spread them by patting with your fingers, or use the broad side of the cleaver to the same effect. Once the arrangement is set, use "curved knuckles" to shred the coins lengthwise at the desired intervals—$\frac{1}{32}$ inch for a needle-fine shred, $\frac{1}{16}$–$\frac{1}{4}$ inch for thicker shreds.

cutting a cylindrical object (a carrot)
into shreds: cut diagonal coins, push
together in original shape to straighten,
spread in step-like arrangement, shred
lengthwise

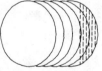

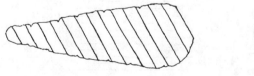

To fine-shred a rectangular item like a piece of ginger: First cut the ginger into a neat rectangle by cutting off the skin and knobby ends. Slice vertically *along the longest side* with "curved knuckles." Push the slices together in the original block to even them, then spread them in a neat, overlapping step-like arrangement. Shred along the length of the slices into fine or finest slivers with "curved knuckles," modulating the fineness of the shred with a greater or lesser moving back of the knuckles supporting the blade.

cutting fresh ginger into fine shreds: reduce the ginger to an easily shredded rectangle, slice vertically along longest side, spread slices in step arrangement, shred lengthwise

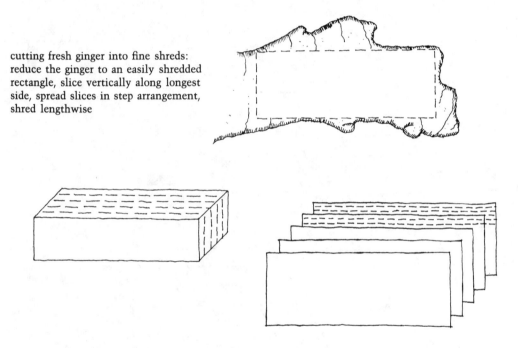

Once you get the hang of it, this step method produces gasp-inspiring results (how did you ever get the ginger *that* thin!) with little time and effort. If you begin with a neatly staggered arrangement, and keep both the retreating hand and the cleaver hand fully *relaxed*, you can reduce a hefty carrot or enough ginger for four big fish to a heap of hair-fine threads in only 2–3 minutes.

Precision Cubing and Dicing
Cutting an exacting cube or a precise, tiny dice with a Chinese cleaver is a simple, speedy procedure involving three steps.

Step #1 is to slice the object horizontally with "flying fingers." Step #2 is to stack the slices, then cut them vertically along the *longest* side with "curved knuckles." (This produces stick-like shreds.) In step #3 you gather the shreds together, turn them *or* the cleaver ¼ turn (90°), then cut vertically into cubes with "curved knuckles." The resulting cubes may be ½ inch square or ⅛ inch square, all depending on the width of your slices. For a perfect cube of whatever size, you need to cut at *precisely the same width* through all three steps.

to cube a rectangular object like a cake of tofu: a horizontal slice followed by two vertical slices at right angles

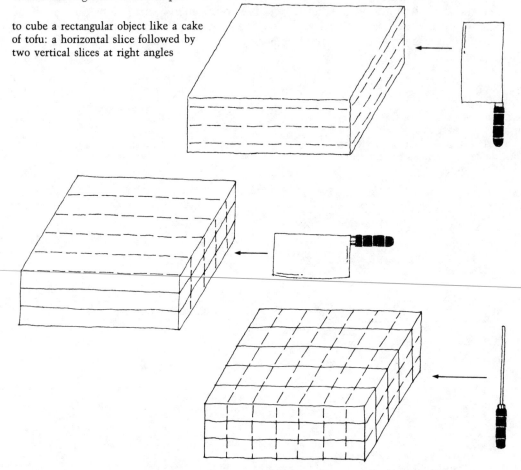

This method works perfectly to cube any block-like object that sits without wobbling on the board—anything from a neat rectangle of fresh tofu to a less-neat piece of raw or cooked meat.

To dice small or cylindrical objects such as water chestnuts or whole carrots one follows the same principle but with a bit of adjustment to make things easier.

To cut a peeled water chestnut into a neat, peppercorn-size dice: Hold the flat ends of the water chestnut between your thumb and first finger, rounded end touching the board. Using a cleaver or paring knife, cut the water chestnut into even, coin-like slices a scant ¼ inch thick. Stack the coins neatly, grasp the sides of the stack between the thumb and first finger, then slice lengthwise into even strips a scant ¼ inch wide. As the last step, turn the pile *or* the blade 90° and cut the strips crosswise at scant ¼-inch intervals to obtain neatly diced, peppercorn-size bits. The result is a perfect size dice for a water chestnut when it is mixed into a purée for dumplings or meatballs or used in a stir-fry: small enough to feel good on your tongue and go "crunch" between your teeth, and not so big as to be obtrusive or look clunky.

to dice a round object like a water
chestnut: slice coins, stack, shred, cut
shreds crosswise

This is the same technique one uses to mince large cloves of garlic or nuggets of
ginger to a tiny square mince, cutting at 1/16-inch intervals, when the texture or look of a
sauce demands very tiny cubed bits.

To cut a carrot into a tiny dice: Cut a lengthwise sliver from the carrot and turn
it on the new flat side so it will sit without rolling. Cut a second lengthwise sliver from
one of the round sides, discard it, then cut the carrot lengthwise into slices 1/4 inch thick.
Stack the slices neatly on the second squared side and cut lengthwise into sticks 1/4 inch
wide. Finally, turn the pile *or* the blade 90°, then cut the sticks crosswise at even intervals into a 1/4-inch dice. To be absolutely precise and have no half-rounded cubes in the
end, you could begin by slivering off all four sides to produce a conveniently rectangular
carrot, but two is enough for me, so long as it lies obediently on the board.

to dice a carrot: square two sides at
right angles, slice lengthwise, stack, cut
into sticks, cut sticks crosswise

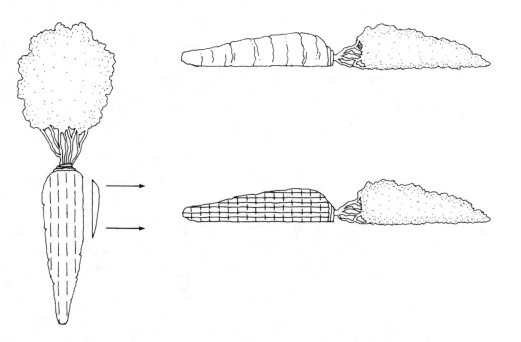

Rock-Mincing: Cutting Hard Things to Small Irregular Bits

When mincing is to serve a flavor purpose primarily and exacting shape is not important to the eye or the tongue, ingredients are quickly rock-minced to a pile of small, irregular particles.

The first step is to reduce the item to a coarse chop. Large items are best broken down through *dicing*, as described above. Smaller items, like a clove of garlic or a nugget of ginger may be simply *smashed* with the broad side or handle end of a cleaver to ready them for mincing.

Rock-mincing is a simple matter of letting the weight of the cleaver do the work, and guiding the blade to rock evenly up and down over the food. First, steady the far end of the blade with your three joined middle fingers. There's no need to forcefully grasp the blade and waste energy. You simply need to steady it with a relaxed hand. Then, grip the handle near the blade with your other hand, holding it in a relaxed close-chopping hold with your thumb and first finger touching the blade lightly to guide it. The steadied tip of the blade should meet the board, and the other end should be raised an inch or two above the food.

Once the cleaver is poised, the trick is to let it rock freely up and down and back and forth over the food. The tip remains in almost the same place throughout the process, while the handle moves back and forth in an arc to evenly cover all the food. Periodically, as the food scatters outward, pause to scrape it back into a concentrated pile with a push of the blade. Level the pile if you need to with the side of the blade, then continue rock-mincing as before. The periodic pile-making insures that the bits get rejumbled and therefore evenly minced.

Keep the hand that grasps the handle *relaxed*. Let the blade drop down entirely on its own weight, then lift it lightly on the heels of the natural rock upward. With a relaxed hand, it is a speedy, rhythmic business, and one of the most satisfying and pleasurable of all the cleaver's dances.

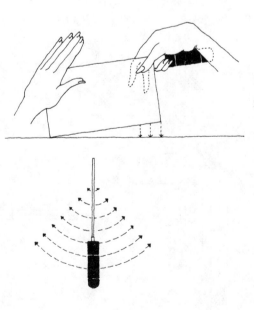

proper cleaver hold for rock-mincing: three joined fingers lightly steadying the blade, the other hand grasping the handle near the blade, guiding it in the upswing and letting it fall of its own weight

a top view of rock-mincing: far tip of the blade held stationary, and handle moving back and forth in an arc over the food

Precision Mincing: Cutting Hard Things to a Teeny-Tiny Square Dice
Mincing is often the extension of precision dicing in an exacting Chinese kitchen, where a square mince of infinitesimal cubes is considered delightful on the tongue and a treat for the eye. In the minced topping for a fish, for instance, the play of precise, nubbly bits against the smooth fish flesh is thought to be far more engaging, in a yin-yang drama of textures, than an irregular mince or mash of things afloat indistinguishably in a sauce.

Sauce ingredients like garlic and ginger and garnishes such as Smithfield ham are thus often given this precision treatment. The technique is quite simple, the approach differing slightly with the shape of the object to be minced.

To square-mince a rectangular object, like a finger-length of ginger or a block of Smithfield ham, reduce it to a cluster of fine, squared shreds, between ¹⁄₁₆ and ⅛ inch thin, as illustrated above (page 35). Grasp the shreds together in a neat bunch, hold the blade 90° to the cut ends, then cut crosswise at tiny intervals to mince.

To square-mince a roundish object, like a fat clove of garlic or a nugget of fresh ginger, dice it as you would a water chestnut (page 37), but make the slices mere slivers and the final dice mere bits. What you have after, in the end, is a minuscule dice.

This technique requires more time than rock-mincing for sure, but it can be incredibly satisfying to those alerted to the fine nuances of texture and is honored in cutting circles as a true sign of cleaver expertise.

reducing squared shreds to a minuscule
square mince, by cutting crosswise with
"curved knuckles"

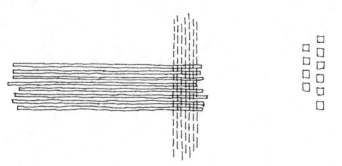

**Whack-Mincing and Puréeing Raw Meat and Fish: Double-Cleaver Work
(That Can be Done with a Single Cleaver)**
When faced with a pile of raw, cubed meat, raw shrimp or fish in need of chopping or puréeing, a Chinese cook will traditionally hold identical cleavers in each hand, then set about whacking the food to reduce it to the desired mince or paste. This is a true dance to drumbeats, the knives moving in fast staccato rhythm, first one, then the other, with the cook often shifting back and forth and around the food to whack it evenly from all sides. It is as exciting as a congo rhythm, to the ears and body both, and I have a positively hard time restraining myself from hooting and whooping whenever I'm chopping with two cleavers.

Two cleavers diminish the mound twice as fast, but one cleaver may also do the job. The method, with one tool or two, is to march the blade back and forth, up and down over the surface of the food pausing periodically to scoop it up and turn it over in order to redistribute it—until you have chopped, minced, or mashed it evenly.

Primary to this technique is to let the shoulders and elbow relax and sink down and turn the work over to the *wrist*. To grasp the cleaver correctly, the thumb rests on top of the blade to steady and direct it, while the remaining four fingers curve securely around the grip (making this a variation on "grand-slam chopping" described above). Raising the cleaver is accomplished with an upward flick of the wrist, then the wrist relaxes to let the blade drop. If you can relax the wrist entirely and do only the work required to raise the blade, you can whack-mince without tiring.

This is the cutting technique whereby one "polishes" the surface of store-bought ground meat to expose new surface area, chops large cubes of meat to reduce them to an intriguingly irregular, fresh grind, and purées raw meat or fish to a smooth paste.

the proper hold for whack-mincing:
thumb on the blade for control, wrist
poised to flick up then relax and let the
blade fall of its own weight

Chinese Techniques: Stir-Frying

炒

S tir-frying is what has earned Chinese cooking its name in the West. The galloping pace, the exhilarating sizzle, and the dramatically brief whirl of arms, spatula, and ingredients have so captivated the Western imagination that we think of stir-frying, wrongly, as the whole of Chinese cooking. Rightly, we find it exciting and appetite-inspiring. The shape of the wok, the deftness of the stir-fry cook, and the look and crunch of the slivers and crisp things decanted in one dazzling sweep onto the plate have made stir-frying the sports car of the world of cooking. For hours one can watch a professional Chinese cook in action (in Chinese, one says "in performance"), and feel it is the next best thing to a day at the races.

Stir-frying as a kitchen technique is the product of a labor-rich, fuel-poor country. Add together the many Chinese hands ready to chop, the few Chinese twigs or lumps of Chinese coal available to burn, and a never-ending quantity of oil capable of being heated to hellishly hot degrees, and one arrives at stir-frying. The whole of the operation can be understood from this commonsense perspective. Why a round wok? Because its round shape best conducts the heat generated by a fire built within a cylindrical pit designed to contain the precious fuel. Why such slivering and thin-slicing? Because things cook more quickly, seared in seconds on account of being small. Why a round-edged spatula? To meet with exactitude the contours of a round pot. Why the use of peanut, cottonseed, soybean or corn oil? Because they heat to high temperatures without burning. On and on one can provide simple yet accurate answers to the "mysteries" of stir-frying, poking holes in the mystique that surrounds it as thickly and deceivingly as the San Francisco fog.

Yet the fact is that stir-frying *is* exotic to the Western cook. It requires a different distribution of labor, a different way of looking at texture, a more demanding precision when cutting, and a different set of cooking instincts than we are used to or inherit as Western cooks. But that's about the whole of it! As I have learned myself in kitchens that produced the best Chinese food I have ever eaten, one can stir-fry beautifully in a flat-bottomed aluminum pot perched on a tin foil-covered electric coil. There are no special tools required beyond those typically found in a Western kitchen. Organization, careful timing, and caring tasting are more important to successful stir-frying than lickety-split speed. To assume otherwise is to fall for the "myth" of stir-frying. If you are cooking in a Chinese restaurant, yes, you *do* need immense woks, raging fires, and an ability to toss 5 pounds of shrimp into the air in 5 seconds with a flick of one wrist—*and* have them land back in the pot. Just like if you are working in a Western restaurant, you need 20-gallon stockpots, the speed to butcher a saddle of lamb in a flash, and the strength to slide 50 pounds of whatever into an oven without taking yourself with them! But this is the world of restaurant cooking, and the realities of excellent, traditional home-cooking are comfortingly another matter.

Tools for Stir-Frying 用具	The tools required for successful stir-frying are few, simple, and cheaply acquired—if they aren't already in your kitchen. One needs a heavy, capacious, even-heating pot with a surface that is friendly to oil, a lid to cover it, and a long-handled something to toss the food about. Everything else is secondary.

The pot must be heavy, lest the oil burn too quickly and the food scorch or stick, though "heavy" is a relative term. (I learned to stir-fry in my grandmother's aluminum stockpots, and while I learned the lesson well, it was a trial by fire and an accomplishment *in spite of* the tools.) Heavy like copper or lead is overdoing it. Heavy like spun steel, cast iron, or the sort of heavy-gauge, professional-weight cookware now sold widely in kitchenware shops is just right.

Capacious is a requirement in order to have the freedom to flip and toss things about, so they sear without stewing and you can tackle a pound of Chinese cabbage without having half of it wind up on the floor.

Even-heating means even-cooking, and you cannot stir-fry well in a pot that remains half-cold or in a warped pot with hot spots.

Friendly to oil defines a sort of happy meshing that occurs between some metals and oil, whereby a pot will drink up a slight amount of oil and let the rest glaze its surface smoothly, thereby forming a patina and letting the food skid freely about. Spun steel, cast iron, and Calphalon are all friendly surfaces. Teflon, on the other hand, is not. Its whole purpose in life is to do away with oil and reduce it to a humiliating puddle in a corner of the pot.

As for the lid, it may be flat or domed, made of most any material, and sometimes even overhang the pot. Its mission is to keep steam inside the pot, and however this is achieved is fine.

The long-handled something may be a metal or wooden spatula, or a long, broad-bowled spoon that is heatproof. It should be sufficiently long to keep your hands away from the heat and flared enough at the cooking end to thrust the food quickly and efficiently about.

Beyond these elementary specifications, the base line for deciding the best tools for stir-frying is what kind of stove you own.

If you are stir-frying over gas, you may use a *round*-bottomed wok, though you don't necessarily need one. The round contours of a wok are embraced naturally by the climbing fingers of flame, so the whole pot heats evenly—and therefore usefully—almost up to the rim. However, you can get equally good heat distribution on gas with a *flat*-bottomed pan and may use it with equally good results.

If you are stir-frying over electric burners or a flat surface like Corningware, on the other hand, you need a *flat*-bottomed wok or a flat-bottomed Western pan and will get best results from nothing else. The flat coils are designed to be met by a flat cooking surface and if you stand a round-bottomed wok on a flat coil you wind up with a "hot spot"—one burning spot in the middle about the size of a silver dollar—while the rest of the pot remains tepid to cold. In my opinion, trying to stir-fry on an electric stove with a round-bottomed wok is like trying to walk across town on toe shoes. It has a certain drama and charm, but is rather inefficient given the realities of a flat surface. You'll get where you wanted to go in any event, but slowly and probably painfully, in spite of looking "exotic."

Having demoralized half my audience, let me be insistent. The fun and satisfaction of stir-frying lies mostly in the results—the actual edible, chewable item. If you could chew a wok, then electric stove owners would have something to bemoan, but if you can produce a delectable stir-fry in a humbly flat skillet or a flat-bottomed wok, then who cares?

WOKS

Wok is the Cantonese word for "pot," specifically a round-bottomed vessel beautifully suited for the sliding-slipping-flipping movements of stir-frying. A *round-bottomed wok* is designed for *gas* specifically. It is the style of wok that is used in China on account of fire, gas, or propane being all there is now or ever was. A *flat-bottomed wok* may be used on gas, but it is specifically designed for *flat electric coils*. Electric stove owners should use only a flat-bottomed wok for stir-frying, if they wish to use a wok at all. There is some loss of depth and unbridled movement owing to the flat base, but the rounded contours of the sides are still beautifully harmonious with the actions of stir-frying. Moreover, the flat bottom has a "plus" of greater stability; you never have to worry about a flat-bottomed wok tipping over. If you own a round-bottomed wok and have an electric stove, you may still use the round-bottomed wok for *deep-frying*, as described on page 75.

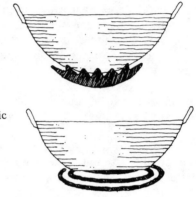

round-bottomed wok designed for gas stoves

flat-bottomed wok designed for electric stoves

An *electric wok*, in my estimation, is nearly useless for real stir-frying. The heating unit is located on the bottom, so as happens when you put a round wok on a flat coil, you wind up with a hot spot—and not much else. An electric wok, if you're stuck with one, may be used to some advantage for steaming or deep-frying providing the heat range is high enough, but when it comes to stir-frying, it's an uphill, slow, and demoralizing battle, and I'd sooner stir-fry in a big tin pail.

The first issue in purchasing a wok is material. *Spun steel* is the metal traditionally used for making woks in China, and the centuries-old model, in my opinion, still works the best. It is a good heat conductor that is simultaneously heavy enough to heat oil quickly without burning it and is light enough to maneuver easily on the stove. The semi-porous nature of spun steel allows it to develop an even "patina"—the glossy, part-imbedded finish of oil, which makes a well-seasoned wok shine like a black gemstone and permits the food to slide easily over the surface with a minimum of fresh oil. Spun steel, furthermore, is hardy. It is shaped on a spinning template to make it so. You may rinse it out immediately for the next dish with no fear of its warping, go at it with a spatula without worrying about the finish, and bang it around as much as you like with no thought of its chipping or scratching. Spun-steel woks are also *cheap*. They are cheap when you buy them from a Western supplier, and usually half as cheap again when you purchase them from a Chinese dealer. For about ¼ the price of one copper mail-order wok from a spiffy Western kitchenwares company, you can buy two spun-steel woks, and use one for stir-frying and the other for deep-frying, content in the knowledge that your two humble traditional models will serve you better and last longer than the jazzed-up modern.

You will now find many other materials being used to make woks in this country, all designed by Western manufacturers eager to jump on the Chinese cooking bandwagon. None have shaken my recommendation of spun steel. *Stainless* is too light; things burn in it easily and it will not develop a proper patina. Its appearance in a wok is an invention on the part of people who know we like to keep our pots clean, but don't know very much about stir-frying. *Copper* is unnecessarily heavy. It is difficult to maneuver in the way stir-frying often calls for one to tilt and turn the pot, it will not develop a proper patina, and one can't put it immediately under water to be cleaned without its warping. Its use in a wok has more to do with the prejudices of Western cooks and notions of prestige than with any understanding of the Chinese art of stir-frying. *Calphalon* is also, in my opinion, needlessly heavy and expensive in a wok. It is a superb material for stir-frying in a flat pot, but not in a wok. *Teflon* is ridiculous. Stir-frying in Teflon is like trying to boil an egg in a steamer; the nature of the cooking vessel is inimical to the task.

With the material settled, the next question is the *diameter* of the wok. A *14-inch wok* is my recommendation for every standard stovetop. A smaller wok may be less of an encroachment on neighboring burners, but it limits the amount and type of thing you can stir-fry with ease, and while a 12-inch wok may initially seem more manageable, the extra inches of freedom to flip and toss the food about will make stir-frying a lot more pleasant, and probably more successful. With that in mind, you may go to a *16-inch wok* if you have a professional range whose gas output is capable of heating it to the rim, but this larger size will not heat properly on a home stove.

In considering diameter, whatever the stove, also take into account *depth*. Some woks are decidedly deeper than others, so if you can't spread *out* owing to nearby burners or a wall alongside your stovetop, then you may be able to expand vertically to get the capacity you need.

Design is the next consideration, and in woks this is mostly a matter of *handles*. The traditional model has either two metal ears or only one metal arm, depending on what province you're from, but the modern vintage with one wooden arm and either a metal or wooden ear opposite is superb for stir-frying. It eliminates the need to work with a potholder or mitt, and gives you wonderful leverage for tilting the pot. I have had one for eight years (dating from before they figured out that the heavier wooden ear was required to perfectly balance a wooden arm), and it is still my favorite wok for stir-frying, in spite of its coy habit of being always slightly tipped.

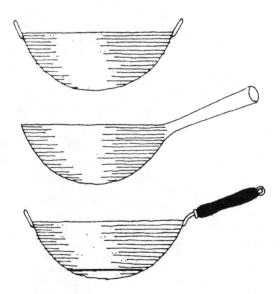

round-bottomed wok with two metal ears (good for stir-frying, though requires potholder or mitt; excellent for deep-frying); an up-dated model is available with 2 wooden ears, eliminating the need for a potholder

round-bottomed wok with one all-metal arm (used in restaurants for the most part by well-skilled cooks who flip the contents with one hand)

round- or flat-bottomed wok best-suited for home-style stir-frying, with one wooden arm and one wooden or metal ear

Cleaning and Seasoning a Spun-Steel Wok

Having purchased a wok, one is now faced with the issue of cleaning and seasoning it—removing the layer of machine oil or grease that is left on by the manufacturers of traditional woks as a protection against rust, and applying a more permanent layer of oil, called a *patina*, that will "season" the metal so it will not rust thereafter, thereby making it into a more efficient cooking surface by permitting you to stir-fry with a minimum of oil.

To clean a newly purchased *wok*, give it a thorough going-over, inside and out, with soap and an abrasive. This is just about the only time you should soap and scour your wok. You may need to use a *bit* of soap after a bout of deep-frying something like a triple batch of walnut-dredged chicken slices that has left the wok coated with an overly thick film of grease. And, you may need to scour it thoroughly again and reapply a new patina if the original one becomes gummy or interferingly uneven on account of improper cleaning or an ineffective heat source that heats the wok only partway up the sides. However, as a general rule to protect the wok and make you a better stir-fry chef, *never, after applying a patina, soap or scour your wok.*

To clean a seasoned wok after cooking, take it promptly to the sink, flush the inside with *plain hot water* and *wipe* it out with an un-soaped sponge, a sink rag, or a long-handled scrubber with soft, thin bristles. The soft sponge will dislodge any clinging bits of food and the hot water will get rid of all the excess grease, while leaving the precious patina intact. I am so emphatic about the benefits of a well-developed patina that I do not recommend using even the traditional Chinese rattan scrub brush in the average Western kitchen. The baby patina on a wok used only several times a week is usually too thin to withstand any amount of scratching. If you *do* attack your wok with abrasives and soap out of conditioning or habits appropriate to your other pots, you will rob it of its patina and insure that it leads a rusty, ineffective life. Food will stick to it, you will use more oil than is needed in stir-frying, and no one will be happy but my grandmother (who thrice-scrubbed even the bottom of her pots).

yes!

un-soaped sponge

scrubber with soft, thin bristles

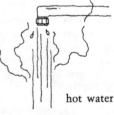

hot water

no!

soap

Chinese scrubber of thick-bristled, stiff rattan

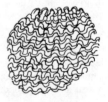

abrasive metal scrubbing pad

Once the wok is shiny-clean and thoroughly scoured of grease for the first and preferably the only time in its life, you must proceed immediately to apply a patina to the inner surface. The outside of the wok will blacken on its own from the heat, but the inside is up to you.

To patina a wok for the first time, or to re-patina a wok that has rusted, been scoured out by an overzealous friend, or otherwise raped of its smooth black surface:

Step #1: Clean the wok, if new, with soap and an abrasive to remove every trace of the oil applied by the manufacturer, as described above. If the wok has been used and needs refinishing, work over the surface with an abrasive and soap, as much as required to smooth it and remove any rust.

Step #2: Set the wok over high heat until it is hot enough to evaporate a bead of water on contact. If you are seasoning a round-bottomed wok, remove the grid from the burner and put the wok directly on top of the gas jet, so the flame will heat the pot *fully* to the rim. This heating step is crucial. It opens the "pores" of the metal and enables it to drink up the oil. If your own stove does not have the power required to heat the wok fully to the rim, consider applying the patina on a friend's stove that is hotter than your own.

Step #3: Dunk a wadded lint-free rag or a thick clump of dry paper towels into fresh corn or peanut oil, then wipe the oil-soaked cloth evenly all around the inside of the hot wok, from the crown to the very center, slowly and deliberately driving the oil into the metal. The oil will begin to smoke and the center of the wok will begin to blacken, and that is exactly what you want. When the metal is no longer drinking in any oil, turn off the heat, rub the oil once or twice more into the surface, then wipe off the excess oil with the cloth and put it aside. As the metal cools, the superficial oil will "congeal" in tiny rivulets on the surface, and may be wiped away. Let the wok cool 10 minutes or overnight, as convenient, before continuing.

Step #4: Reheat the wok over high heat until hot enough to sizzle a bead of water on contact. Repeat Step #3, using fresh oil and the same rag or a fresh one, disregarding the smoke and driving the oil evenly into the metal from the rim to the center of the wok. Let the metal cool as before, then repeat the heating and oiling process one or two more times before using the wok. Immediately after the last application, wipe the metal clean of excess oil with a dry paper towel, so the surface will be smooth and not gummy when it cools. At this point, there will be a black, burned-looking area in the center, which will darken further and creep upwards to the rim as the wok is used and the patina is reinforced.

Step #5: After stir-frying in the wok for the first time, rinse the wok out *immediately* with hot water, using a soap-free sponge or rag to gently dislodge any clinging food particles. Do *not* use soap or an abrasive from this point on, or you will break down the patina. Wipe the wok dry, reheat it over high heat until hot enough to evaporate a bead of water on contact, then repeat Step #3. Wipe off excess oil with dry paper towels so it will not become tacky, let the wok cool, then store it until the next use. Store it in such a way that nothing can scratch the patina.

Step #6: Repeat Step #3 after each use of the wok, until it develops an evenly black patina with a striking, soft sheen. Repeat Step #3 whenever the patina needs reinforcing, through overzealous cleaning or too little use. If you have an inefficient stove, such that the topmost portion of the wok never gets sufficiently hot to blacken, run to the same friend's house periodically to treat your wok to the hotter flame.

Wok Maintenance

Once the patina has been set, keeping a wok "running smoothly" is a simple business. Probably the most important thing to remember is to *clean it almost immediately after using, while the metal is still hot.* This is particularly important when the wok is new, or if you like to stir-fry, as I do, with a modicum of oil. As the metal cools and the food particles stick, cleaning requires more time and is harder on the patina. While the metal is hot it is a mere 5-second job—a rush under hot water and a few "swooshes" with an un-soaped sponge—easy to do just before the dish is served or while a friend carries it to the table.

Once cleaned, the wok should be *thoroughly dried over high heat* before storing. My usual tactic is to shake it dry, then return it to the still-warm burner while I enjoy my dinner. Then, just before putting it away, I fire the metal over high heat to evaporate any water and open the pores of the metal, and wipe the inside evenly with a bit of oil to reseal the patina.

Storing a wok properly is part of its maintenance. The requirements are minimal: Keep it in a *dry* spot and away from things that may scratch the surface. Hang it on a wall or prop it on a shelf, nested in a wok ring to keep it still.

WOK COVERS

The traditional wok cover is made of lightweight aluminum, shaped like a dome, and topped by a small, heatproof knob. A variation on the standard design is a plateau-shaped dome, which affords more outward spread but less height. I tend to favor the plateau-shape because it better accommodates chickens and the like for smoking (page 90), but for stir-frying either shape will serve you well. I do avoid using lids that have a curved strip of metal or wood for the handle. Metal gets hot and one then needs a potholder or mitt to lift the lid, and the wooden arch seems unnecessarily bulky and heavy. I like a simple, small, and sturdy knob one can reach for without thinking.

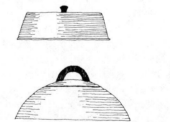

domed wok lids with knob handles

plateau-shaped lid with knob handle

domed or plateau-shaped lid with arched
wood or metal handle

The most important requirement of the cover is that it be *½ inch smaller than the diameter of the wok.* Thus for a 14-inch wok, one needs a 13½-inch cover. Any smaller, and it limits the capacity of the wok. Larger, and it will not cover the wok tightly.

A wok cover will not require a patina or any special treatment, beyond as frequent a washing as your conscience or kitchen partner dictates. Its job is to contain the steam in the latter stages of some stir-frying, so the demands on it are simple.

WOK RINGS

A frequent adjunct to the wok is a metal ring or collar, designed to support a round-bottomed wok so that it sits securely above the flame without tipping. A flat-bottomed wok does not require a ring. Its flat base insures that it will not tip.

The standard and most flexible design is a *dual-diameter ring*, 10 inches across on one side, 8 inches across on the other, standing 2¼ inches high. The ring may be turned either way. The ideal arrangement is *flared side up*, to permit a greater spread of heat to the wok. However, the jet, grid, or coil over which the ring must fit is frequently too wide for the 8-inch side, and requires that the ring be turned narrow side up, in order for the ring to sit squarely on the stove. Because this limits the heat spread, the best alternative if you are in the latter situation is to spend the few dollars (if that) to purchase a *single-diameter ring*, and get the needed 10- or 11-inch spread both top and bottom. It is no fun to have to stir-fry on a wobbly wok or one that is not giving you the most heat your stove can turn out.

dual-diameter wok ring:

ideal position with wide side up

single-diameter rings

limiting position with narrow side up

Whatever the diameter, the ring must be made of a sturdy metal able to withstand high heat, and must be pierced in such a way as to allow the air to enter so the flame is not stifled. The best design for my taste is a line of 1-inch holes around the ring, which gives you clear peepholes through which to monitor the flame. A less preferable design is the "tooth-top" model (shown above), which lets the air through but limits your view.

Most important is that the ring be *high enough to raise the bottom of the wok just above the jet or coil*. Too low a ring and the wok will receive no support and tip regardless, wobbling like a neck in a too-big collar. Too high a ring and the wok will be well-supported but raised too far from the flame, preventing it from heating quickly and uniformly.

When stir-frying over gas in a round-bottomed wok, I frequently use *no ring* at all. Some gas jets, once the burner grid has been removed, are perfectly contoured to support a wok with maximum exposure to the flame. On other gas stoves, the grid itself may be turned upside-down to provide an improvised collar that will support the wok perfectly. Both of these ring-less improvisations are usually *limited to stir-frying*. They are frequently too dangerous for deep-frying, where one needs absolute, trustworthy support, but for stir-frying it can be a marvelous way to obtain high, quick heat.

three good arrangements for a round-bottomed wok over a gas flame:

proper distance with a ring

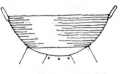

wok supported by an inverted burner grid

wok balanced directly on the gas jet with no ring

WOK SPATULAS AND SCOOPS

For the actual stirring, tossing, and flipping of food in a round or flat-bottomed wok, the single required and best tool is a *rounded metal wok spatula* with a flared, shovel-like end to match the contours of the wok. The handle should be long enough to keep your hand comfortably far from the heat and permit good leverage for flipping, but not so long as to make you stand 2 feet away from the stove. The flared shovel end should be broad enough to cover a large area of the surface in one sweep, but not so broad that it will not fit snugly into every corner of the wok. For a 14-inch wok, a good size wok spatula is one with a 10–11-inch handle and a 4-inch wide shovel end. For a 16-inch wok, a 12-inch handle and a 5-inch wide shovel are best.

Whatever the size, the wooden plug at the end of the handle should be firmly nailed or glued in place. Nothing is more aggravating—and unfortunately more common—than a handle end that keeps falling off.

It is also preferable that the shovel and the handle be fashioned from *one continuous piece* of metal. This lengthens the life of the spatula and makes it easier to clean.

rounded metal wok spatula

Similar measurements and design standards apply to the *broad-bowled Chinese metal scoop* that is often used in tandem with or sometimes instead of the spatula. A restaurant chef will typically use one or two scoops alone for stir-frying, using the scoop to reach for liquids and seasonings arrayed in pots or bowls alongside the stovetop, then relying on the rounded side to push the food against the metal, the lip to scrape and toss it about, and the bowl of one or two scoops to lift the food from the wok. For a home cook, the scoop is simply an adjunct to the spatula. The spatula does the stirring, tossing, and flipping, while the scoop gets called in at the end to help "scoop" the finished dish from the wok to the waiting plate. For years, I didn't own a scoop and did all my stirring and decanting with a spatula. I still prefer this system for its simplicity, but will enlist a scoop when stir-frying for a mob or when using a 16-inch wok—in other words, whenever the extra "hand" seems useful.

broad-bowled Chinese metal scoop

Shovels and scoops are traditionally made of *spun steel*, and this is the only material I will buy. The stainless variety seems unpleasantly light and flimsy, and somehow not "honest" in my hand. Spun-steel implements will gradually develop a patina on their own. They need not be soaped or scoured as a rule, and should be left lightly oiled, especially if used infrequently. I hang them on nails, within easy reach just above the stove, by driving a sturdy metal tack partway into the top of the plug.

WESTERN FLAT-BOTTOMED POTS FOR STIR-FRYING

A wide variety of Western pots work beautifully for stir-frying. *All* of them work better than an electric wok, and all will work better on an electric coil than a round-bottomed wok. To judge which pot will function most capably is first a question of material and second a question of size.

In my experience, metals best suited for stir-frying in a flat-bottomed pot are *spun steel, Calphalon, heavy-gauge aluminum with a stainless steel coating,* and *cast iron.* If it were only a question of material, and not money or what's on hand, I would probably choose in that order. All have good to excellent oil behavior, and what the stainless-coated aluminum lacks in ability to develop a patina or seasoning, it makes up for in good heat conduction and good weight.

For stir-fry recipes involving about 1–1½ pounds of food, where the food will not fill the pan more than halfway, a large *12–14-inch skillet* made from any of the above metals is extremely serviceable. Ideally, it should have *gently sloping sides* to encourage the sliding and tossing of the food, as many paella pans and skillets do. A skillet with *straight sides* may be used almost as easily, but requires a bit more attention when stir-frying to be certain to get the spatula or spoon into every corner.

different styles of 12–14-inch skillets (including a paella pan on the left) suitable for stir-frying

If you do not have such a large skillet, or if the bulk of the item—let's say Chinese cabbage—does not permit it to fit in the skillet with plenty of extra room to toss it about, then look to a deeper pot to solve the problem. A *wide and deep sauté pan, a Dutch oven,* or a *broad stockpot* made of any of the metals mentioned above will work perfectly, so long as the pot is *at least 10 inches in diameter and no more than 5–6 inches deep.* Any narrower and the food tends to pile up and stew, rather than quickly cook; any taller, and it is difficult to toss and flip the food properly. This makes both a high-sided saucepan or marmite and a tall stockpot decidedly *bad* choices.

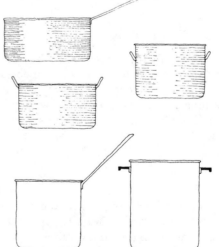

3 good choices for stir-frying:

a deep and wide sauté pan

a wide and shallow Dutch oven

and a broad, shallow stockpot

2 terrible choices for stir-frying:

a saucepan (sometimes called a marmite if it has 2 small handles) that is too tall and too narrow

a professional-type stockpot that is too tall and too narrow

Especially when stir-frying in greater quantity, you must expand *outward in dimension* and not upward in height when it comes to choosing a pot. On several occasions I have been forced to use narrow, tall pots when cooking in Western restaurant kitchens where they are standard equipment, and each time I have watched helplessly while my painstaking preparation turned to sog and mush.

STIR-FRYING IMPLEMENTS FOR WESTERN POTS

My first choice when stir-frying in a flat Western pot is to use *a straight-edged wooden spatula with a gently curved paddle.* The wood is kind to the surface of the pot and the shape is good for getting into corners and flipping things about. In this way, it is more flexible and feels better in my hand than a straight-edged metal spatula. Look for one made from smooth hardwood with a *tapered edge* and a paddle that does not have slits in it.

wooden spatula with a gently curved paddle

My second choice is a *long-handled spoon with a broad bowl.* I here prefer metal to wood, as the bowls are generally broader and deeper and the thin edge is better for scraping the food from the surface. The handle should be at least 10 inches long and the bowl at least 3 inches long and 2 inches across, though an inch or two larger in either direction is best.

long-handled metal spoon with a broad bowl

CHOPSTICKS FOR STIR-FRYING

While I like to stir-fry with a minimum of tools, I never stir-fry without a pair of *wooden chopsticks* at my side, either the standard 10-inch table size or the 17–19-inch cooking length (illustration, page 79). These simple implements are perfect to lift up a single sliver or cube of something when tasting, and are wonderfully adept at arranging the finished food on the plate. The Chinese sort with the square top and round bottom are easier for me to manipulate than the more graceful, stiletto-like Japanese type, but this is mostly a matter of habit.

OIL CONTAINERS

Stir-frying is an oil-based happening, so it stands to reason that a good oil container will function well to help you on your way. If you attempt to pour the 2–4 tablespoons oil required for most dishes straight from a gallon jug, you're hoisting too much weight and losing too much control over the amount that winds up in the pan. I have two alternative oil containers, both mentioned here with the affection one reserves for discoveries made in the aftermath of near-disasters.

My original solution to the oil crisis was a *tin camp pot with a ladle* stuck in it. The pot had a helpful wire handle and could fit easily between the burners on my stove, besides reminding me of the little oil pails that were a fixture of most every kitchen in Taiwan. The ladle allowed me to see exactly how much oil I was putting into the pot *before* it got there, which was a giant step on the road to producing non-greasy food. I recommend the system heartily.

lightweight pail outfitted with a ladle

In recent years, I have opted for a more chic container (as life becomes more sophisticated in spite of me). It is a 24-ounce Perrier *bottle outfitted with a plastic pour spout* from the neighborhood liquor store, and I suspect a more unlikely combination would be hard for Mr. Perrier or Ms. Chivas-Regal to imagine. The bottle fits my (small) hand precisely, being easy to lift and invert, while the spout lets out a steady stream of oil somewhere between a trickle and a gush. A Perrier bottle's worth of oil lasts a conveniently long while, and when it runs out I simply use a funnel to refill it from the economical gallon jug. The bottle may be whichever sort your hand picks out as best, but the spout top is hard to beat.

a pour-bottle that fits easily in your hand, topped with a liquor pour spout

PAPER TOWELS

A much-admired French cooking friend of mine once proclaimed that a French kitchen (specifically his French kitchen, I suppose) would go on the rocks without a constant supply of linen towels. Well, a Chinese kitchen (specifically mine) *runs* on paper towels.

A big wad of paper towels near at hand when you're stir-frying is an indispensable helpmate. If you have too much oil in the pot, you can wipe it out. If too much soy comes gushing out of the bottle into the pan, you can blot it up. In the middle of stir-frying, if you should discover that the stir-fried whatever is swimming in oil, push the whatever to one side, press a wadded towel in the pan, then stir the towel gently until the oil is mopped up. The system may sound silly, but I have seen people look far sillier trying to tip a wok to drain it of excess oil or running across the kitchen to the sink to pour the unwanted oil out. Overdoing the oil is an all too common problem, and some nearby paper towels are a friendly, efficient solution.

The
Stir-Frying
Process

炒的方法

THE QUESTION OF "BIG HEAT"

Probably the single biggest issue in stir-frying—and the primary cause, along with the wok, of the mystique surrounding it—is the need for *high heat* ("big heat," in Chinese). I have stir-fried on all kinds of stoves, from a raging restaurant monster to a dying home electric, and on surfaces ranging from pristinely invisible Corningware to the lumpy coils of a beat-up hot plate, and as much as I may need to wrestle with any of them, as long as I can work over *unmitigated high heat* I can stir-fry successfully. Once the heat is there—fierce and scorching hot—you can lower it or move the pan off the burner to reduce the temperature in the pot. But *without a steady source of truly high heat with which to begin, stir-frying is next to impossible.* Things wilt in the pan on account of being cooked through before they're seared, precious liquids are lost as food sweats instead of sizzles, and seasonings do not bind and penetrate properly but simply slosh around. High heat is essential!

On most home stoves, it is no problem to obtain the high heat necessary for proper homestyle stir-frying. (If you intend to stir-fry for 50 over a home stove without doing it in five stages you *will* have a problem, but for more on that subject turn to the endnote on page 58.)

The average electric stove has at least one large coil capable of generating a requisitely fierce heat, and if the coil is not functioning well, it's time to call a serviceman or choose a stewed dish.

The average gas stove varies considerably in the amount of heat it will generate, but on most models (excepting some very modern ones) it is very easy to adjust the height of the flame with the turn of one screw. The gas company people in any city in which I've lived have always been happy—if not somewhat mystified—to raise the flame to my specifications, namely *as high as it will go while remaining mostly blue.* It takes but a phone call and a few minutes, and if the stove is the right kind you can have one if not all of your burners adjusted to provide all the heat the stove can produce.

"Big heat," however, is only the initial stage in the stir-frying process. In homestyle stir-frying, where one is working without the split-second reflexes and recipe formulas of the trained restaurant chef, there is a *standard progression from high to medium-high to relatively low heat,* and that is true for most of the recipes in this book. *High heat* functions to heat the metal, heat the oil, and sear the food, locking the flavors and juices in. *Medium-high heat* allows time for the food to be seasoned and steam-cook to near-doneness, whether from its own heat or from liquids that have been added to the pot. *Low heat* (which is relative to the searing heat with which the process begins and does not necessarily correspond to the "low" setting on your stove) is the time when one adjusts the seasonings, binds the liquids if required, and tastes and adjusts once more before the food leaves the pot. In the times needed to stir-fry one dish versus another, the progression may be very clear or it may be telescoped into the space of 2–3 minutes. Clearly visible or not, one quickly becomes accustomed to the rhythm of a fast-paced beginning that tapers off at the end, and the need to adjust the heat or adjust for the heat accordingly.

On a gas stove, the adjustment of heat from high to lower degrees is easily and immediately enacted with a turn of the dial. Gas is a very *supple* heat. It is or it isn't there, in whatever degree you wish it to be with one simple twist of your wrist.

On an electric stove, it is harder to adjust heat to quick demand and it is impossible to change temperatures in an instant, as stir-frying often requires. Electric is stubborn and slow. A hot coil stays hot for a long time after you've changed the setting, and it takes seeming ages for a cold coil to heat to fierceness. The solution many people offer is to set one coil on "high" and one on "low," and then move the pan back and forth between them. I find this unnecessary. A pot appropriate for stir-frying will retain enough heat on its own so that one can *slide it off the coil to create a lower or "low" heat, then return it to the coil when more intense heat is desired*, using the interim time to reduce the setting if you need to cool the coil. This is the system that works best for me. It avoids the discomfort and possible danger of another hot burner and simplifies one's focus.

STIR-FRYING WITH THE FIVE SENSES

Whether gas or electric, a round-bottomed wok or a flat Western pan, I hold staunchly to the opinion that stir-frying is primarily a matter of using one's senses—hearing, sight, smell, touch, and taste—and that it is the tuning into and exploitation of these senses that makes for successful stir-frying (and a lot of other things, as well). One stir-fries with one's *eyes*—judging the precise moment when a slivered vegetable is glossed evenly with oil, seared a deeper color, and ready to receive a sprinkling of salt or sugar. One stir-fries with one's *nose*—sensing through smell when scallion and ginger have "exploded into fragrance" (*bao-syang*, in Chinese), releasing their essences into the oil, and thereby transforming the oil into a flavor medium as well as a cooking medium for what next goes into the pot. One stir-fries with one's sense of *touch* and texture—touching oil-glossed walnuts with a hand to see if they are hot enough to caramelize the sugar waiting to be sprinkled over them, or sampling a noodle with your tongue and teeth to see if it has become soft enough to be served. One stir-fries with one's sense of *taste*—tasting whatever is being cooked at all possible junctures to gauge the balance of flavors in the pot and achieve exactly the taste you're after. Most important, one stir-fries with the *ears*—for it is the ears that know best the heat of the pot! The ears hear the sizzle of water on properly heated metal and then can correctly judge the pot ready to receive the oil. The ears hear the searing sizzle of one sliver of meat in the oil and then know with surety that the oil is hot enough to begin cooking. And, it is the ears that know when a higher heat is required because they hear a silence instead of a sizzle. In becoming an accomplished stir-fry cook, one becomes a veritable Pavlovian dog. Responding to that auditory sizzle and learning to manipulate the heat and the pot to its rhythm is the essence of the stir-fry dance.

I insistently stress the senses because as cooks and people we too often forget that these are our *best tools*, far better than any timer or measuring device or cookbook one can buy. Don't look at your watch. Don't even look at the recipe after a while. At least not as a primary judge. Stir-fry with an eye riveted to the pot, the oil, and what's being cooked, as you add the ingredients one by one to the pan. Stir-fry by smelling, tasting, and touching if necessary, relying on all these wonderfully accurate sensory gauges to determine timing and fine-tune the dish. Above all, stir-fry by listening, using what I call a "merry sizzle" to tell you when the heat is properly high. No sizzle, no happy sound, and it's time to raise the heat or move the pot back onto the coil. Too riotous or firecracker-like an explosion, and it's possible the heat is too high or the pot is too dry and one needs to lower the heat or move the pot from the coil.

You can artificially isolate the jobs of each sense, but the dance, in fact, is a meshing of them all. They are your best friends, those five senses, and you can't stir-fry without them. Any one of them, used to the full, will serve you better than a copper wok.

THE STIR-FRY PROCESS: STEP BY STEP THROUGH THE DANCE

Step #1 The first step in stir-frying is *organization*. After chopping, marinating, and combining all you possibly can—that is, doing everything short of the actual cooking—line up the ingredients systematically *within arm's reach* of the stove. Stir-frying doesn't give you time to vault across the kitchen to retrieve the bottle of soy sauce from its niche. The dance is too fast. Build an extra shelf above the stove, set up a card table, a snack table, or an overturned box next to you or behind you, buy a small trolley-table on wheels, whatever, have a surface within reach of your stove where you can station everything you'll need. Then, put a serving plate to warm in a low oven. It's not an affectation (though I used to think so), it's useful! A warm plate will keep food *warm*, and that wonderful dash of chicken fat or oyster sauce which makes that stir-fry of Chinese vegetables extraordinary will congeal to an unappetizing blob if decanted onto a cold plate.

Step #2 Once you are organized, *turn on the "big heat."* Arrange the ring for the wok if you'll need one, turn the gas jet or electric coil up to its highest setting, then put the pot on to heat. Have a tiny glass of liquid nearby for the next step.

Step #3 When you sense the metal is hot or see the patina beginning to smoke, *test the pot with a bead of water*. If it sizzles and hisses and evaporates immediately on contact, then the metal is sufficiently hot to receive the oil. If the water sits there coldly, bubbles bemusedly, or sizzles only shyly, then the pot is not hot enough. Retest until the water evaporates immediately on contact, and only then are you and the pot ready to proceed.

Step #4 Once the pot is properly hot, *add the oil and swirl the pot to glaze it with the oil*, so far as the amount of oil allows. If you are using a wok, add the oil in a necklace around the rim so it will coast down and partly coat the sides en route to the center. Whether you need to glaze only the bottom or both the bottom and the sides of the pan will be partly a matter of the pot and partly a matter of the food to be stir-fried. In a wide skillet most of the stir-frying occurs on the bottom, whereas in a wok the lower half of the sides see equal action owing to the size and contours of the base. Vegetables will most times not stick to an unglazed side, but marinated meat surely will. Experience will teach you what is required, but in general you should glaze as much surface as the designated amount of oil permits.

Step #5 Once the pot is glazed, *test the heat of the oil with a single piece of whatever is to go into the pot first*—a bit of minced ginger, a sliver of broccoli stem, a slice of marinated chicken, a drop of beaten egg. If the oil sizzles merrily, rimming the item with a cluster of white bubbles—searing whatever you've added without scorching or browning it—then the oil is properly hot. No sizzle means the oil is not hot enough. A fierce sizzle accompanied by a visible browning or blackening means the oil is too hot. In that case, turn gas heat off entirely or move the pan from the electric coil to allow the metal and the oil to cool. Remove the singed victim from the oil, retest with a new bit or sliver, then proceed when you have the right sizzle.

Step #6 When the oil is properly hot, add the first thing to be stir-fried to the pan. In many cases, that will be one or more *aromatics* ("fragrant ingredients," in Chinese)—ginger, scallion, garlic, chili, Szechwan peppercorns—those things that infuse the oil with flavor and sometimes color, so that the primary ingredient is then stir-fried not in a plain oil but in a freshly seasoned one. Regulate the heat to maintain a gentle sizzle, so the fragile aromatics *foam without browning*, lowering the gas or moving the pot from the coil if required to lower the oil temperature. Stir the aromatics in small circles or push them back and forth, to infuse them evenly. *When the fragrance is pronounced* ("exploded," in Chinese), the infusion is complete and you can proceed.

Step #7 When the aromatics are infused in the oil, if this step was necessary, then *add the main ingredient(s) to the pot.* Stir-fry briskly to glaze it evenly with oil, maintaining a "big heat" to sear its surfaces and seal the juices in. Adjust the heat so the item *sizzles without scorching,* lowering the gas or moving the pan off the coil if you need to lower the temperature of the oil. Toss, flip, stir, and chop at the ingredient as its shape and texture requires, so that its surfaces are exposed quickly and evenly to the hot oil.

Step #8 As you stir-fry, *check the amount of oil in the pan with your eye,* right from the beginning and again as you add each new ingredient. If there is too much oil in the pan, that is, more than is needed to glaze the item and provide the pot with a lightly glossed surface over which the food can skid, push whatever you are stir-frying to the side and quickly wipe out the excess with a dry paper towel. If the pot on the other hand is too dry, and the food is sticking or scorching against dry metal, then push the food aside and quickly dribble in the needed amount of oil from the empty side of the pan, so the oil heats on the metal before it comes in contact with the food. As you make the oil adjustments, lower the gas or move the pot from the coil as needed so the ingredients do not scorch. Make the adjustment without dallying, then promptly restore the heat or return the pot to the coil to maintain a merry sizzle.

Step #9 Once the primary ingredient is evenly glossed and seared, *add the seasonings*—sugar, salt, soy sauce, or whatever is called for in the recipe. At this time, you may need to lower the heat to protect the food from scorching and to give yourself the extra seconds to season the food. Work swiftly, but do not hesitate to pull the pan from the heat to momentarily "stall" the cooking. The food will continue to cook from the heat of the pan for a good 20 seconds or so, and in fact you will still be "cooking" over high to moderately high heat on account of the heat being generated by the metal alone. Once the seasonings are added, stir-fry briskly to coat the food, returning the pot to the heat as soon as possible and using the sizzle to determine further heat adjustments.

Step #10 When the seasonings have been added and blended, a number of things are possible as the next step in the process.

—One, the dish may already be *texture-cooked to doneness by the stir-frying alone,* and be ready to decant onto the waiting plate. A simple stir-fry of thin vegetables, seasoned only with a dash of salt and wine, for instance, would be cooked through to proper tender-crispness in minutes and require no further cooking. In this case, the job remaining is to turn off the heat and get the food onto the plate *quickly,* lest it overcook from the heat of the pan.

—Or, as a second possibility common when stir-frying a chunky vegetable or something that will best absorb seasonings through a liquid medium, a single liquid or a combination of liquids is added to the pot in order to *steam-cook the food to doneness.* In this case, the liquids are added and blended with several quick stirs, the heat is adjusted to maintain a steady simmer, then the pot is covered. When the food has partly or entirely absorbed the liquid and has been softened or seasoned in the bargain, the lid is removed, the seasonings are adjusted, and the food is removed swiftly to the waiting plate. In steam-cooking, the primary concerns are proper heat and accurate timing. If the heat is too low, the food will stew to mush; too high and it will scorch against a dry pan. You need a steady simmer under the cover, and a watchful eye sometimes aided by tasting to judge when just enough liquid has been absorbed.

Step #11 When the food is cooked to doneness, the last step is to *taste for the proper balance of seasonings,* and make whatever adjustments your tongue determines are necessary. I typically turn off the gas or move the pot from the coil, and taste-adjust the dish off the heat, using no heat other than that which is generated by the pan itself.

This gives me the time to be particular about an extra dash of soy sauce or whatever. This is also the moment when I fold in the finishing sprinkle of sesame oil or the occasional cornstarch binder. Working off the heat helps to insure that the food will not overcook.

I insist upon these *careful last seconds*. It is very often the difference between a bad dish and a good one, or a good dish and an exceptional one. One cannot dally and one must be decisive, but the heat being off "takes the heat off" the cook!

Step #12 The dish is done, scraped quickly from the pot, and mounded or spread evenly on the waiting warm plate. If the stir-frying was properly executed, there should be *no excess oil on the plate and no excess oil left in the pan*, meaning that all that was used was the amount required to gloss and sear the food. Pause briefly to *arrange the dish prettily* before bringing it to the table. In a few seconds' time, you can pull up a sliver of green here and there, turn a bell pepper shiny side up, mound the chicken attractively, or do whatever is needed to accentuate the appeal of the dish, and then wipe the plate clean of any oil- or soy-spattered edges. These last touches are like ending a dance gracefully, with a twirl instead of a thud. They make the dish beautiful and arouse people's appetites to eat what you have labored to cook.

Having quickly neatened the dish, *rush it to the table*. Most stir-fried foods are best eaten while they are fragrant, fresh-looking, and steaming-hot—offering their invitation to the nose, the eye, and the belly.

AN ENDNOTE ON STIR-FRYING IN QUANTITY

Cooking in quantity is a surprisingly different dynamic than cooking for a small group of 4–8, and nowhere does one discover this more quickly than when trying to triple or quadruple one's favorite stir-fry. One cannot simply double or triple many ingredients (that is, salt for seasoning or liquids for steam-cooking) and expect good results. Of equal discouragement, one cannot put double or triple the amount of food in the same pot and expect it to cook in the same way or time, producing the same texture.

A 14-inch wok or a deep 12–14-inch skillet will accommodate double of most of the recipes in this book. For greater amounts, or to be absolutely certain of the results, *stir fry in batches*. Above all, *do not put more in the pot than your stove can sizzle quickly and convincingly*.

As a general rule when stir-frying a double recipe, do not double the salt or the water or chicken stock used to flavor and steam-cook the single recipe. *Begin with only the single amount of salt and 1½ times the steam-cooking liquids*, then adjust from there by tasting and watching the pot.

Chinese Techniques: Steaming

蒸

S teaming is surely one of the most-used, straightforward, and energy-saving of Chinese cooking techniques. With a pot of water, a reliable heat source, and a platform by which to raise whatever one is steaming above the crest of boiling water, one has a beautifully simple means by which to cook the most plebeian or grandiose of Chinese dishes. On the more humble side of things edible, steaming is the way to cook one's daily rice or steam one's daily bread or buns. At Chinese gastronomy's more complex extreme, steaming is the means by which to cook a whole, celebratory, pumpkin-size winter melon—hollowed out and filled on the inside with a colorful variety of meats and vegetables, and "embroidered" (as the Chinese would say) on the outside with an intricate knife-carving of a mythological dragon chasing the sun. And in the middle, one finds something like a steamed whole fish, its skin slit deep with score marks and the flesh drizzled with wine and seasonings. Steamed only minutes, it is simple but admirable, understated yet memorable—the easiest and most noble method by which to cook a fresh fish.

In the everyday Chinese kitchen, mine among them, steaming is a trustworthy, practical, and as-creative-as-you-like method by which to put food on the table. It is not dramatic (like stir-frying), messy (as deep-frying can often be), comforting (like stewing), or terribly demanding of space, time, or attention. Steaming is what I call *no-hands cooking*. Put a dish in the steamer and you are then free to stir-fry, deep fry, or simply dream away the time until dinner. Once you have mastered the knowledge of how much water is needed in the pot, or as I do, have learned to choose an outrageously large pot in which you can boil copious amounts of water without needing to even *think* of having to replenish it, you may dance around the block while your supper gets cooked.

Tools for Steaming

用具

The first issue in steaming food is to assemble *useful tools for steaming,* and of these there is a wide variety all worth considering. None is expensive, and some are as cheap as several tin cans and a tin pot. Whether you're a student with only pennies and a closet to cook in, or a householder with billions and an automated kitchen, assembling the tools you'll need is an easy endeavor.

If I had only one steaming device to recommend, it would be the modern *aluminum steamer set.* This is a stack of sheer practicality that includes, from bottom to top: one large stockpot for holding water, 2 perforated steaming tiers for holding the food, and one dome-shaped lid for holding the steam inside the pot.

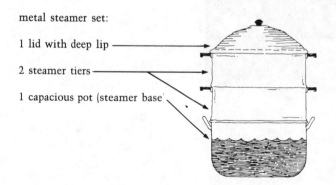

metal steamer set:

1 lid with deep lip ——

2 steamer tiers ——

1 capacious pot (steamer base)

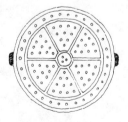

bottoms-up view of perforated metal steamer tier

In a good metal steamer set, quality is a matter of *design* more than of money or materials. The best ones I know are made in Taiwan of cheap, lightweight aluminum, come in 11-, 13-, and 15-inch diameters, and sell for less than the price of a single, fancy saucepan. The pot should hold at least 1½ gallons, capacious enough so you never need to worry about replenishing the steaming water. The steamer trays should be sturdy, not flimsy, so they will support a whole, hefty bird on a heavy plate without buckling. The flat surface of the trays should be liberally and evenly perforated with small, pea-size holes to allow the steam to jet up all around and to permit you to steam dozens of tiny dumplings directly on the tray without having to worry that they'll half-slip through the holes. The cover should have a high, smooth dome and a deep "lip" around the inside of the rim. The sloping dome causes the water droplets which condense inside the lid to slide directly down to the rim, where they are caught in the lip. Covers designed with a plateau-like top or covers that are simply flat will send the water raining down on the food.

Once you have such a set, you have more things than you think. The pot is ideal for a multitude of everyday kitchen jobs, from boiling up pasta to hard-boiling eggs, and can be used like most big pots as a capacious mixing bowl. The steaming tiers with their sturdy handles make excellent colanders, and may also be used as serving trays for glasses and carry-alls for whatever needs lugging about. The stack even "folds up" for easy storage. If you put the pot inside the topmost steaming tier, then invert the cover inside the pot, the dimensions are reduced by half and you have a very stowable item!

metal steamer set in "nesting position,"
ready to store

All in all, I am fairly wild about these contraptions. They are honestly simple and practical, easy to clean and virtually indestructible. But what about alternatives?

For the aesthetically and traditionally minded, certainly the choice steaming tool is the *bamboo steamer*. These are beautiful and practical, simultaneously *objets d'art* and *batterie de cuisine*, without which a traditional Chinese kitchen would seem soulfully lacking. Woven by hand of bamboo, and traditionally put together with bamboo nails and bamboo lacings, the bamboo steamer serves several functions and has several advantages. The shallow dome-shaped bamboo lid absorbs water, so one never needs to worry about condensation sprinkling down on the food. The woven steamer tiers are simultaneously cooking tools and serving pieces. Unlike a metal steamer, the bamboo one may be brought to the table with a flourish, garnished with leaves or left beautifully bare. The tiers double as fruit baskets, serving trays, and wall decorations. Hung simply on a nail, the bamboo tiers and lid stay exposed to light and air, resisting any tendency to mildew and looking gorgeous in the bargain, with their simple, clean lines and beautiful woven geometries.

bamboo steamer lid

bamboo steamer tier

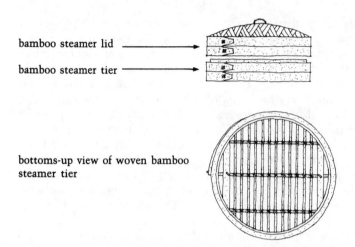

bottoms-up view of woven bamboo
steamer tier

Side by side with their advantages, bamboo steamers have several disadvantages, not insurmountable but worth knowing. They are by nature prone to mildew, burning, and falling apart, and hence must be stored properly in reach of air and light, placed on the stovetop beyond the range of flames, and chosen with an eye to construction. They must be washed carefully, with only hot water and a stiff brush, then dried carefully. A bamboo steamer is expensive relative to a metal one, and is furthermore only half as deep. It is more adaptable to the steaming of small items than to the steaming of a high-breasted chicken, a plate of tall pears, or a wheel of high-puffed steamed bread. While the lid goes some way toward accommodating larger items, and one may occasionally find deep bamboo steamers, the bamboo steamer is limited, as beautiful things, alas, many times are.

Bamboo steamers do not typically come in ready-made sets, so the first issue is what to get. To begin, buy two steaming tiers and one lid. Even if one tier seems enough at the outset, you will soon be wanting another. Most recipes involving small items like dumplings require two tiers to steam the whole batch simultaneously, and whereas a fish needs only one tier on which to steam, what about a place for those buns or leftover rice you may wish to serve with it? In my kitchen, steamers are like potholders: one is ridiculous, two are sufficient, and usually I'm capable of finding good use for three or four.

Diameter is the next question. Choose either a 12-inch or 14-inch steamer, depending upon your stove and your needs. A stove whose burners are arranged close together will accommodate a 14-inch steamer only at the expense of losing 1 or more neighboring burners, so you are in that case better off building *up* with more tiers than building *out* with inches. If, on the other hand, you've an army to feed, long fishes waiting to be steamed, or burner space to spare, then the larger size may be what you require.

Regardless of size, look closely at *construction.* Many of the bamboo steamers now coming out of Asia are shoddily and shamefully constructed. (The ancient steamer-makers who lived down the road from me in Taipei would weep and roll their eyeballs if they could see what has become of their craft!) Wire is now used in binding the steamers, and often the rusting sort at that, nails poke out here and there, and the material being used is flimsy enough to be mistaken for the sort used to build model airplanes. An honest, serviceable bamboo steamer should be heavy in the hand, made mostly if not entirely of bamboo, and look and feel like it will last a lifetime. The lid should be tightly and meticulously woven, and should be crowned by a sturdy loop-handle that will accommodate two fingers. The woven steamer rack should sit securely in its round frame, and not wiggle or jiggle when you tug on it. The tiers and the lid should fit rather snugly together. If there is a lot of shimmy-shammying from side to side, then it's likely that the steam will escape when the water is bubbling beneath it. Check also for any tiny holes in the wood. Those holes mean worms, and discovering a colony of them when you put the steamer to use is interesting but not terribly amusing.

Once armed with the perfectly made, carefully chosen bamboo steamer, you still need a vessel capable of holding boiling water on which to perch it. There are several possible arrangements, some more serviceable than others.

The traditional arrangement, which I like least, is to put the steamer inside a wok of a slightly larger diameter, so the metal comes up in a 1- or 2-inch wide collar around the lower tier. My strongest objection to this system is that it robs the wok of its hard-won patina, and simultaneously robs the cook of the freedom to leave the stove. (Neither of these a problem in the usual Chinese household, where the patina was reinforced thrice daily and the cook never did leave the stove!) The capacity of the average wok requires that one remain vigilant to replace the water that steams away, a job which is mostly hassle and guesswork. In addition, the width of the wok oftentimes encroaches on needed burner space, not to mention that using the wok as a steaming vessel robs the cook of the wok! The one time I do use a wok in preference to another vessel for steaming is when I am steaming a giant fish and my 20-inch restaurant-size wok is all that will hold it. Bar those rare occasions and rare fishes, a wok is never a steaming vessel in my kitchen.

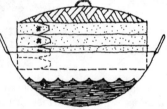

the traditional arrangement: bamboo steamer tier and lid seated in a wok

My own heretical preference, tried and proven through the years, is to use a large, lightweight, and preferably cheap stockpot as the base for a bamboo steamer. This can be your grandma's aluminum stockpot that lies ignored in the basement, one you can purchase cheaply from a hardware store, or simply a pot pulled from your kitchen shelf. It should be deep, so you can fill it to the gills with water and never even have to *think* of replenishing it. It should be about ½ inch smaller in diameter than your steamer, so the steamer, no matter how tall it grows, will sit securely on top. It should be lightweight, so it will heat quickly and stand to be moved easily, if necessary. And it should be *cheap*, so that if you do run out of water and the bottom burns hideously dry, it can be roughly scrubbed clean or tossed out without incurring great damage to your pocket or your honor.

bamboo steamer sitting directly atop uncovered stockpot

A variation on this theme, involving the modest purchase of a flat, metal, and circular *perforated Chinese steaming tray*, is to put the metal tray on top of the stockpot, and then pile the steamer tiers on top of the tray. The tray makes a stable base for the steamer, especially useful when the diameter of the stockpot is exactly that or just a bit larger than the diameter of the steamer.

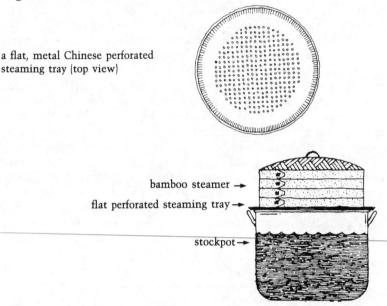

a flat, metal Chinese perforated
steaming tray (top view)

bamboo steamer →

flat perforated steaming tray →

stockpot →

There is yet another way of using a bamboo steamer, and that is to perch it atop a *metal* steamer. This, in fact, is what I do most often in my own kitchen, where I have both sorts of steamers and frequently juggle them in combination. Sometimes, I simply borrow the metal pot as the base for the bamboo steamer when the one matches the other and there are no handles in the way. At other times, I put the bamboo tier on top of one or two of the metal tiers. This is useful either when a protruding handle gets in the way of the bamboo tier balancing directly atop the pot, or when I need a full array of steaming racks, some for steaming small items, and others for steaming larger items in a deeper space. Steamers are to the kitchen what modular book shelves are to the study, a flexible way to rearrange space imaginatively to suit your needs.

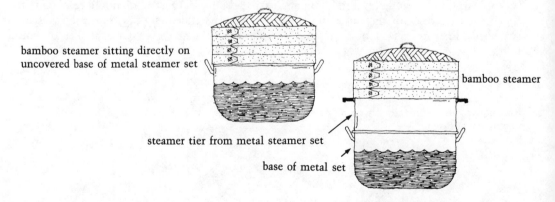

bamboo steamer sitting directly on
uncovered base of metal steamer set

bamboo steamer

steamer tier from metal steamer set

base of metal set

Now to the question of *improvising a steamer.* You don't have or you don't want to purchase a metal steamer set or a bamboo steamer. You want to tackle some of these recipes *right now*, so what do you do? There are several possibilities, all more or less workable, many using things snatched from one's usual cache of kitchen objects.

Most primitive and capable of being erected over a campstove is the partnership of *one large pot and several tin cans*, the cans emptied of contents and with both ends cut away. The pot must be wide enough to hold whatever you are steaming with room to spare, and the cans must be tall enough to hoist the dish you are steaming at least ¾ inch above the water. The two typical combinations are a stockpot outfitted with tall cans, or a roasting pan outfitted with short cans, the choice depending upon the size of the thing to be steamed. For instance, a plump chicken requiring an hour of steaming would do best in a stockpot with an ample amount of water beneath it, while a long fish that will steam to doneness in minutes can better recline in a roaster and requires only a shallow bit of water. Being a bad one for balance, I prefer 3 cans to the usual recommended 2, or the conscription of one large can on the order of the sort which holds vegetable shortening. With this system, you need to put the cans in the pot and hold them in place with a dish *prior* to adding boiling water to the pot, or else they will be washed askew by the bubbling of the water.

stockpot–tin can steamer

roasting pan–tin can steamer

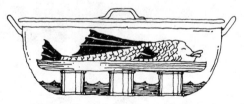

Owing to this, I encourage the consideration of one of two helpful items, cheaply bought in a Chinese hardware store or in many Oriental markets, and bound to ease the life of any steam-it-yourselfer. Both provide a single, stable steaming base for an improvised steamer, with no need to worry about float-away cans.

The first, designed expressly for this purpose, is a *long-legged steaming trivet*, a simple rack or arrangement of metal bars permanently attached to 4 tall legs. Designed to be put into a wok, it may also be used in a stockpot (preferably, in my thinking, for the reasons stated above). Be sure it is sturdily made! My first resembled a squashed grasshopper when it collapsed on its maiden voyage under the weight of a plump duck. The longer the legs and broader the platform, the better, as you can thus fill the steamer with more water and balance the dish you are steaming more securely on top.

non-collapsible Chinese metal steaming
trivet with 4 tall legs

Another stable alternative to the set of tin cans is an ordinary *wok ring* or *wok collar*, the ring of metal that comes with many wok sets and may be easily and inexpensively purchased on its own. Here, as with the trivet, you have a dual-function item. The ring will raise whatever you are steaming several inches above the water, and concurrently support the dish on its crown. The higher the wok ring the better, to permit more water for steaming, and one with a dual-diameter may prove most flexible in supporting both big and little dishes.

dual-diameter wok ring or collar

inverted wok ring used as steaming base
for improvised stockpot steamer

wok ring used as steaming base for
improvised wok steamer

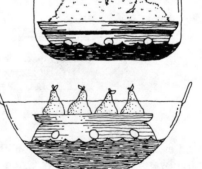

Whatever the propper-upper, the choice lid for any of these improvised steamers is a *dome-shaped wok lid* or an *overturned metal bowl*. The dome shape causes the water that condenses on the inside of the lid to skid down the sides free and clear of the food, instead of raining down on top of it. Another choice, and a last resort, is to line a flat lid with a cloth towel, so the cloth absorbs the moisture from the steam. In this case, be careful to bring the towel up in some fashion around the lid, securing it with pins or string, so there's no chance for it to drape down around the pot and catch on fire.

Three other tools are worth mentioning to improvisers, here in the order of their relative worth.

The first is the flat metal *perforated Chinese steaming tray*, already pictured (page 64). This pizza-pan type of contraption may be put on top of a stockpot or inside a wok, with the plate or thing to be steamed laid on top, then covered with a dome-shaped lid. It is a lot of function for the price and can be very useful indeed. It permits you to fill the wok or pot with the maximum amount of water.

a perforated Chinese steaming tray in its traditional position in a wok, allowing maximum water below

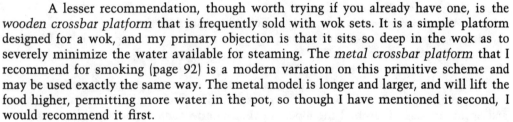

A lesser recommendation, though worth trying if you already have one, is the *wooden crossbar platform* that is frequently sold with wok sets. It is a simple platform designed for a wok, and my primary objection is that it sits so deep in the wok as to severely minimize the water available for steaming. The *metal crossbar platform* that I recommend for smoking (page 92) is a modern variation on this primitive scheme and may be used exactly the same way. The metal model is longer and larger, and will lift the food higher, permitting more water in the pot, so though I have mentioned it second, I would recommend it first.

simple crossbar of wood with interlocking, take-apart bars

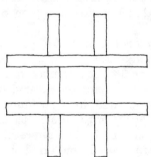

A final possibility for on-the-spot improvisation is the *collapsible metal steamer basket* that became a standard item in Western kitchens a decade or so ago. If you have the sort with a permanent pin in the middle, it is adequate for steaming a limited number of dumplings or buns. If the pin screws out, then you can balance a plate on top, though frequently with some peril. The short legs require you to stint on water and the basket shape severely limits the capacity and type of things you steam, but it is a possibility nonetheless.

Western-made collapsible steamer basket

**The
Steaming
Process**

蒸的方法

Now that you are outfitted with a steamer of one sort or another, the thing to get down to is the actual process—how it works, the step by step of steaming, and some useful tools to help you on your way.

The first issue is to locate a *reliable heat source*. The obvious choice is the stovetop, but I often find it convenient at a large dinner to steam away from the stove on a hot plate that I can plug in most anywhere. This frees the stove for other cooking, and so long as the hot plate is outside the range of roving children or animals, I'm perfectly content to let it do its business on top of the washer, in a bedroom, on the porch, wherever.

Once the heat source is chosen, the next issue is the *boiling water* on which the whole process depends. It is the general rule to bring the water in the steaming vessel to a gushing boil *before* the food to be steamed goes in—thereby searing the food immediately, as opposed to slowly heating it to a sweat—and this is the ideal. However, sometimes with an improvised steamer, you may first have to position the food in the steamer and then pour the boiling water around it, to prevent the platform from otherwise sloshing away. In any case, be certain to have plenty of boiling water at hand, either directly in the pot and/or bubbling in a kettle alongside if you will need to replenish the steamer. Having extra water already boiling means minimal interruption of the steaming process if you are forced to replenish the pot.

What is important when filling the vessel is not to let the water touch the food or the dish or tier on which it is steaming. Add as much water as possible to lessen or eliminate the need to replenish, but leave *at least a ¾-inch clear space* between the top of the water and the bottom of the rack or plate.

Equally important is that the plate on which you are steaming be *at least 1 inch smaller in diameter* than the diameter of the steaming vessel, so the steam can rise easily and evenly up and all around the food. For the same reason, the lid should not touch or hover too closely above the food. If things are to steam properly, they need room in which to steam.

Something to put the food on is the next (if it wasn't the first) question, and the answer will depend largely on the item to be steamed. Some things like dumplings, which have no sauce, may be put directly on an *oiled bamboo or metal steamer tier*, or on an *oiled plate* if you are working with an improvised steamer that lacks a rack-type platform. There are several variations on this direct steaming method—wet cheesecloth, blanched Chinese cabbage leaves, squares of parchment paper, or beds of oiled pine needles all being possibilities with greater or lesser degrees of lyricism—but the primary issue is that the food does not stick to the rack, and I find oiling the rack itself the easiest and often most attractive solution.

Other things, like fish—which are first drizzled or rubbed with seasonings and will render precious juices as they steam—require steaming in a heatproof shallow bowl, deep enough to contain the juices yet flat enough to allow for an even absorption of seasonings. My first choice in this case is a *heatproof Pyrex pie plate*. They come in many sizes, in both diameter and depth, and are conveniently unobtrusive if one wishes to serve in them. A fish steamed in a Pyrex dish inside a bamboo steamer may be brought directly to the table, with the pretty bamboo lattice still visible through the glass. Sometimes a *flat heatproof plate* will do where there's little juice, and sometimes a *cookie rack* is needed inside the pie plate to hold the item above its juice, but in general have a Pyrex pie plate on hand and you've a most valuable tool in which to steam things. A second choice would be a heatproof gratin dish, whose shape is restricted but particularly suited to steaming a whole fish.

So here the water is at a rolling boil and the item is properly readied to be deposited in the steamer, and there arises the question of how to approach all that steam barehanded. Don't!! For any work at all around steam, use and treasure a pair of *elbow-length cooking mitts.* These are not the sort that end at your wrist. What is needed are gloves that will come clear to the elbow, to protect both your hands and your upper arms. The thicker, the better, in my opinion. Steam, while it's clear and innocent-looking, can leave a nasty, painful burn, and no amount of improvising with towels, potholders, or last year's long prom gloves will protect you like a sturdy, well-padded pair of elbow-length mitts.

long, padded, elbow-length cooking mitts

Mitts, in my opinion, are a necessity, but what is handy if you want an additional tool is a *Chinese steamer-retriever.* This ingenious device is a simple set of metal "arms," which expand to reach around an item, then contract to grasp it tightly. It is ideal when you need to pull a plate or bowl from a steamer, the only catch being that the dish must have a *lip* by which the steamer-retriever can grasp it.

Another possibility when it comes to retrieval is to hook a series of strings under and around the dish, then knot them at the top so you have a *string sling* by which to lower and raise the dish into the steamer. I am a poor knot-maker at best, and would sooner use mitts or the metal retriever than rely on strings, but the possibility should not be forgotten if you've no other tool at hand.

homemade string-sling

Chinese steamer-retriever with open-and-close metal arms

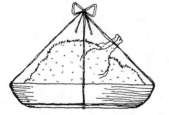

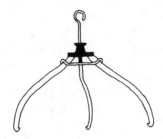

If the first issue is to get the thing into the steamer and the last is to yank it out, then mention must still be made of the interim when one is frequently required to *lift the lid*—to check or replenish the water, to baste the food, or to check it with one's eye, a knife, or a chopstick for doneness. As a crucial safety consideration, remember to lift the lid *away* from you, and to resist any impulse to stick your face into the pot. Peer discreetly from a distance, poke and baste, or refill as you must, then return the cover as soon as possible. Lift the lid *at an angle* rather than pulling it away entirely, to cause less of an interruption to the steaming. With a metal steamer set, make sure the angle is slight or lift the lid straight up, lest the water collected neatly in the lip go spilling over the food. Whatever the steamer, the rule is to uncover it slowly, discreetly, away from you, and as infrequently as possible.

lifting the steamer lid at an angle away from you (bamboo steamer atop metal steamer base)

STEP BY STEP THROUGH THE STEAMING PROCESS

Having danced all around the steaming process to explore every nook and cranny, here in summary are the basic steps to steaming the Chinese way.

Step #1 Bring as much water as the steaming vessel can hold to a *gushing boil* over high heat, remembering that the water must not be allowed to touch the food or the plate on which it is steaming.

Step #2 Add the food to the steamer (either in its dish or placed directly on an oiled rack), protecting your hands and upper arms with long mitts, and positioning the dish in the vessel so that the steam can circulate freely and evenly all around it.

Step #3 Reduce the heat, if directed in the recipe, to maintain a *steady* but less vigorous steam.

Step #4 Cover the steamer tightly, so a minimum of steam escapes. A bit of escaped steam is a good reassurance that all's well below, but a big gush means a hole in the steamer or a careless stacking job.

Step #5 Leave the mitts on top of or alongside the steamer, where you will remember to use them. Be certain they are not within reach of flames or an electric coil.

Step #6 When it's time to uncover the steamer to replenish the water or to check or remove the food, lift the lid slowly away from you and keep your face away from the steam. Work quickly, either to interrupt the process as little as possible or to retrieve the food as soon as it's done. Wear mitts to protect yourself, and remove the food if you need to with the help of a metal steamer-retriever or a well-constructed string-sling.

Step #7 Once the food is retrieved, turn off the heat, lest the pot burn dry.

ENDNOTES ON STEAMING LEFTOVERS

One of steaming's most useful functions is to reheat foods, quickly and easily, in a way that is economical of heat and space. Last night's leftovers may steam underneath, on top of, or alongside tonight's brand new supper, and the two removed simultaneously for serving.

One never has to worry about foods drying out in steaming, but reheated foods may go limp if they were crisp to begin and may increase in liquid content if the bowl is not covered. About the first, one can do nothing—if a hot, soft leftover snow pea seems more appealing than a crisp, cold one, then plunk it into the steamer to reheat it. However, one can halt an increase in liquids by *covering the bowl tightly.* Last night's fish will thus not have its sauce diluted, or the day-before-yesterday's *Buddha's Feast* won't wind up in a watery pool. You may use foil or you may resteam food in a covered heat-proof dish, of which there are some very pretty, inexpensive sorts available in Oriental stores. Dumplings, steamed buns, and the like need not be covered, as the dough can absorb moisture repeatedly and suffer no fate worse than fluffiness.

AND A NOTE ON TALL STEAMERS

If you are cooking for a mob and have cause to stack a pile of steamers on the order of the great Dr. Seuss cat who walks about under a mountain of hats, then you may question how the bottom layer will steam relative to the top. If the heat source is strong enough to generate a healthy steam clear to the top, then the top story and the bottom story will steam to doneness in the same time, and there will be no need to rotate them. If the heat source is weaker, then *stack up the steamers only so far as the gush of steam permits.* There is nothing worse than food that is left to sweat slowly away in a weak puff-puff of steam. If the heat source on which the process depends only generates enough steam for two layers, then stack them no higher!

Chinese Techniques: Deep-Frying

炸

T o me, deep-frying is one of the most intriguing processes common to the Chinese kitchen. Most times, the hot oil functions as a cooking medium—transforming shrimp balls, walnut-dredged chicken slices, meatballs of finely minced pork, or the like into edible foods by heating them through and cooking them to doneness, surrounded by a nonpermeable heat shield that seals in the juices and nutrients. Other times, and to me the most fascinating, deep-frying functions as a way to give already cooked foods or foods that need no cooking to begin a particular and compelling texture—crisping the skin of a tea-smoked duck, or embossing a crunchy edge on the flesh of anise-soaked peanuts. In a few instances, the deep-frying even *precedes* the cooking, as in the case of a fish whose skin is crisped from head to tail in oil before it is then steam-cooked to doneness in a sauce. Whatever the motive, there is always a specialness associated with a deep-fried dish. The lips anticipate a certain delectable brittleness and the tongue expects a hot juiciness that is nowhere as enticing as with deep-fried foods.

Deep-frying has a bad name in the West. I am constantly surprised to discover that even my good-cook friends think of deep-frying as messy, dangerous, hideously caloric, or wasteful of oil—and then proceed to roast a grease-spitting duck for hours in an oven, fry a pound of vegetables in ¼ pound of butter, or bury a platter of fresh fruit under a blanket of whipped cream! We are creatures of habit and prejudice, in the kitchen no less than elsewhere, and in our culture we tend not to separate *grease* from *oil*.

Much of deep-frying is, in fact, spatter-free, and what does land on the stovetop in more dramatic frying may be wiped clean in seconds with nothing more complicated than hot water, providing that one pounces while the metal is hot and the oil is fresh. Hot oil *is* dangerous, without doubt, but in my experience not any more so than having to poke in and out of a hot oven, basting a bird, turning it, and balancing a pan of rendered fat. Deep-frying is, moreover, the least caloric way of cooking with oil. A vegetable that is sautéed in butter or stir-fried in oil will pick up more oil, and hence calories, than the same item properly deep fried. Furthermore, the oil for deep-frying may be recycled and reused not merely one but many times, and who can say that for a pound of butter?

Mostly, it is the yin-yang foundation of Chinese cooking that insures that deep-frying is healthful for the eater and practical for the cook. Unlike our own American habit of pairing deep-fried chicken with deep-fried potatoes, alongside buttered vegetables or buttered hot bread, a Chinese cook working consciously or (more typically) unconsciously from a yin-yang sense of "rightness" will pair a deep-fried dish with a steamed dish or dishes that exclude or severely limit oil. Thus, a deep-fried duck is customarily served with a steamed bun or mandarin pancake, and a steamed vegetable and a soup. A deep-fried dish is regularly partnered by steamed, not fried, rice. Or, deep-fried peanuts will be presented as a before-dinner nibble in the company of pickled cabbage or vinegared cucumbers. The person eating the dish then experiences a wonderful variety and balance of textures and flavors without suffering an overload of oil, while the cook can concentrate on frying just that one item in the context of less dramatic and less demanding dishes. When seen from the Chinese perspective—whether that of the person in the kitchen or the person seated at the table—deep-frying is sane, exhilarating, and marvelously satisfying.

WOKS

Nowhere is a Chinese wok more valuable than when deep-frying. The contours of a wok afford maximum surface area for frying with a minimum amount of oil, allowing one to deep fry a whole chicken, for example, in about ⅔ the oil required to fill a flat Western pot. The wok creates a broad surface on which any number of small items can float and turn freely, wonderfully visible and easily retrieved from the oil. There is no reaching or peering deep into the pot, as is typical with a Western deep fryer.

a comparison: deep-frying in a wok gives
you the same surface area for frying
with only ⅔ the oil required for a flat-
bottomed deep fryer

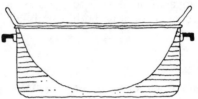

A *flat-bottomed wok* is especially useful for deep-frying on account of its very stable built-in base, and I will frequently enlist one even on my gas stove. The only time I use a round-bottomed wok, in fact, is when I am deep frying a particularly plump whole chicken that might appreciate the extra depth.

A *round-bottomed wok* is the traditional Chinese choice, in any event, and may be used for deep-frying over gas *or* electric heat. The oil will take longer to heat over electric, given the mismatch of the round-bottomed pot and the flat coil, but it is nonetheless one way for electric stove owners to use a round-bottomed wok if they already own one.

The crucial issue when using a round-bottomed wok for deep-frying is to insure that it sits securely on the burner, with no chance of tipping or being tipped. Most times that requires a *wok ring*, though on gas stoves an overturned burner grid will frequently provide the same support, while allowing the wok to sit somewhat closer to the flame (illustration, page 49).

An *electric wok* can be used successfully for deep-frying if the thermostat is reliable and will heat the oil to an unquestionable 425°. The electric model has the advantage of freeing the stovetop for other uses, but it has the disadvantage of heating very slowly. I tend to dislike these contraptions in any event, but if you are stuck with one, this is perhaps a way to make use of it.

WESTERN POTS FOR DEEP-FRYING

Western vessels specifically designed for deep-frying are rather limited for Chinese cooking owing to their more restricted shapes. It is difficult to fry a whole anything, a plump chicken or duck, or a nobly long fish, in a Western basket-type fryer or in an electric skillet or deep fryer, though any of these may be used profitably for frying discrete, small items like shrimp balls.

In a Western-equipped kitchen where I have no recourse to a wok, I typically turn to a *large Dutch oven* (illustration, page 51) for deep-frying "whole anythings," and to a *very wide and deep skillet* (illustrations, page 51) for frying smaller items. The biggest consideration when choosing a frying vessel is the size of the pot vis-à-vis the size or number of things to be fried. The pot must be broad enough and deep enough to accommodate whatever is to be cooked, with plenty of room left over to let it enter and exit easily and be turned over if required. Secondarily, it helps for the pot to be heavy. Otherwise, the oil tends to smoke and burn more freely once heated to a high degree.

In spite of the frugal instinct to use a Western pot already in one's possession, my hearty recommendation is still to purchase a flat-bottomed wok for deep-frying. In terms of versatility and economy, both regarding oil and its own price, there is nothing to beat it.

OIL THERMOMETERS

Chinese cooks do not use oil thermometers. Deep fryers of long experience, they rely on experience to gauge the heat of the oil, typically putting a corner or piece of whatever they're deep frying into the oil to test its heat, or sometimes using a favored divining tool—a scallion nugget, a piece of steamed bread, or a wooden chopstick, all of which will sizzle in hot oil owing to the moisture trapped within.

I use an oil thermometer because it is easy and reliable and makes me feel secure. The one I favor is the Taylor-made *dial-type deep-fry thermometer with a kettle clamp* attached to its 5½-inch long metal spike, which I can clamp to the side of the wok and forget about. I don't need to hold it and it will sit there unbudging and register the oil temperature throughout the frying process, requiring nothing of me but a watchful eye when I deign to cast it one (which is often). My only gripe is that this particular model registers only to 400°, but that is enough to make it an extremely useful helpmate.

a clamp-on dial-type deep-fry
thermometer, with the clamp pushed to
the top so the bottom of the spike will
submerge deeper (and register better) in
the hot oil

The mercury-filled flat thermometers, which are more accurate and register temperatures to a higher degree, are not as good a companion to a wok. They are awkwardly long, and when clipped in place are fully capable of bursting if the temperature of the oil climbs too high.

CHINESE MESH SPOONS

Long, super-light, and beautiful to look at, these are among the most serviceable tools in a Chinese kitchen, and of indispensable aid in deep-frying. An intricately woven wire web-bowl at the end of a slender but sturdy bamboo handle, a *Chinese mesh spoon* is at once the implement that deposits the food in the oil, turns it about, fishes it from the pot, and holds it briefly above the oil to "drip-dry." You cannot burn yourself on the handle, oil cannot collect in the open-weave bowl, and the diameter of the bigger spoons makes it easy to support a whole, hefty chicken with a single tool and a single hand—all impossible tasks for the average Western slotted spoon. A Chinese mesh spoon is a tool of a thousand uses, for a cook of most any persuasion.

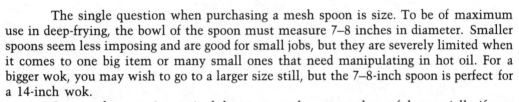

a large Chinese mesh spoon

The single question when purchasing a mesh spoon is size. To be of maximum use in deep-frying, the bowl of the spoon must measure 7–8 inches in diameter. Smaller spoons seem less imposing and are good for small jobs, but they are severely limited when it comes to one big item or many small ones that need manipulating in hot oil. For a bigger wok, you may wish to go to a larger size still, but the 7–8-inch spoon is perfect for a 14-inch wok.

One mesh spoon is required, but two can be extremely useful, especially if you are more adept with a spoon than with either chopsticks or tongs. Deep-frying small items is most comfortable if made a two-hand job—one hand to scoop the items as they are done from the oil, and one hand to hold a large spoon or strainer in which to deposit them and let them drain briefly above the oil—and a spoon in either hand (or chopsticks or tongs in the plucking hand, and a spoon in the receiving hand) is a very relaxed way to get the job done. It eliminates the franticness of repeatedly turning from the pot to deposit things on a tray to drain, and allows the cook's focus to remain on the pot, where it belongs. For this sort of *two-spoon system*, the retriever spoon may be a smaller mesh variety (4–5 inches in diameter), and still function capably.

two-spoon retrieval system, viewed from above a wok

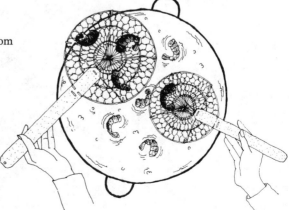

Two mesh spoons also come in handy when retrieving something long like a big fish, or something awkwardly large like a flattened duck, or anytime when the extra leverage seems helpful or necessary.

two-spoon support for retrieving a whole
fried fish

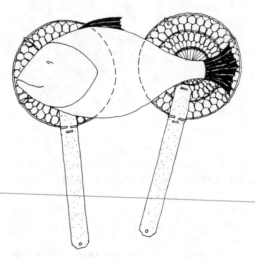

OIL SKIMMERS

An *oil skimmer* is a delicate object in comparison to a mesh spoon, a dainty dragonfly in the world of kitchen objects. It is a 5-inch circle of very fine mesh at the end of a thin, 9-inch wire handle, which looks most at home plucking the perfect tempura shrimp from a tiny wok at the behest of a serenely silent Japanese cook.

lightweight, fine-mesh metal skimmer

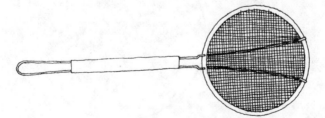

In the more free-wheeling arena of Chinese deep-frying—where the food is generally bigger, the pot broader, and the cook's demeanor less controlled—skimmers are of only occasional use. I employ them when I am frying things coated with crushed nuts or seeds and need to dredge the oil periodically of tiny bits of debris that if left to collect through a lengthy frying will lower the oil temperature and significantly deepen its color. The skimmer is thus an especially useful tool when you are frying coated things in batches; for single recipes, you probably won't need it.

Do not be tempted to use the light skimmer *in place* of a large Chinese mesh spoon. In addition to its delicacy the fine mesh collects oil too readily, and the food will not drain as well.

COOKING CHOPSTICKS AND WOODEN TONGS

Wooden cooking chopsticks, measuring 16–19 inches long, are as good as having two extra-long heatproof fingers when you're deep-frying small items. If you are agile enough to use them, or have the patience to practice a bit, the long sticks will deposit food in the oil, pull frying stuck-together items apart, turn things over, and pluck the finished food from the oil with the deftness of a hungry heron after a fish. If you are using cooking chopsticks for the first time, it may seem as cumbersome as the first time you wore hiking boots, but it is a tool well worth getting used to.

The very thin, slender, Japanese cooking chopsticks are not as serviceable for Chinese deep-frying as are the thicker Chinese-made sort with its square top and round bottom. My hands, at least, appreciate the extra bulk when manipulating bulkier foods. The pair, which for years has been my favorite, measures 16 inches long and ¼ inch in diameter at the round tip.

long, wooden Chinese cooking chopsticks, with square and round (heaven-earth) ends

stiletto-like wooden Japanese cooking chopsticks, round at both ends

If you are not comfortable with chopsticks, you are better off using one of two alternatives. The first is a pair of *wooden tongs*. I find them somewhat awkward, inflexible, and too uncomfortably close to the oil, but they are heatproof and serve some people well. A better alternative, to my mind, is a Chinese mesh spoon, whether it has a small bowl that can retrieve only one or two things at a time, or a larger one with which you can make a grand sweep.

wooden tongs

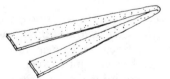

LADLES FOR DEEP-FRYING

In deep-frying large single items, one can usually eliminate the need for turning them by ladling hot oil continuously over the top as they fry. Nothing is better suited for the job than a *long-handled Chinese metal scoop* (illustration, page 50), the sort that is a common adjunct for stir-frying. The bowl should be 3½–4 inches across for greatest efficiency in scooping and spreading the oil.

PAPER TOWEL DRAINS

There is nothing worse than oily food, and even when food is deep fried properly—in such a way that the food repels the oil instead of drinking it up—it must be drained well after leaving the oil in order to taste perfect. Holding the item briefly above the oil to "drip-dry" is often the first step, but the job is really accomplished by putting the food aside on an *absorbent paper drain.* In my more ardent conservationist days, I used newspapers and brown bags, but neither works as well as the paper towels I now depend upon.

As the first step in deep-frying anything, arrange 2 or 3 layers of paper towels on a heatproof tray, using as many layers and trays as the food will require, then position it within easy reach of your stovetop. A baking sheet and sometimes a large plate will do for large single items, but my first choice when frying numerous small things is a *light-weight aluminum jelly-roll pan* (a baking sheet with ½–1-inch tall sides), or a large aluminum baking pan. Given the walls, you can shake the tray back and forth, the food will roll about and blot itself dry, and you've accomplished the important in two seconds' time. Furthermore, the tray can go in the oven—towel liner and all—if it's necessary to briefly hold the food before serving or in between frying batches.

my usual deep-fry set-up: 2 or 3 layers of two-ply paper towels neatly folded in the bottom of a rectangular jelly-roll pan, with a Chinese mesh spoon and cooking chopsticks in readiness on top

OIL STRAINERS

To filter and recycle oil that has been used for deep-frying, you'll need a *large, fine-mesh strainer,* or some *finely woven cotton cheesecloth,* or preferably both.

The strainer should be of the finest mesh available, to sift the oil of even fine particles of food. The one I use is stainless and quite expensive, but is head and shoulders above the common hardware store variety for the fineness of the mesh. It also helps for the strainer to have a hook opposite the handle end, so it will balance securely on a pot or bowl while you pour the oil through it.

fine-mesh metal strainer with long handle and hook opposite to balance it over a pot or bowl

In conjunction with the strainer, I filter the oil through several layers of cheese-cloth, not the stretch sort which is so common nowadays, but the old-fashioned, flat-weave, all-cotton variety commonly sold 4 square yards to a bag. Double or triple the cheesecloth to multiply its crumb-catching ability, then cut off as much as you need to fit into the strainer with a safe overhang of 1–2 inches. The cheesecloth will trap all the teeny-tiny things afloat in the oil and most of the residue that falls to the bottom. It will make a coarser mesh strainer serviceable, and a fine mesh strainer even more effective. Do *not* wet the cheesecloth (as is usually done in soup straining, for instance, to expand the cotton and tighten the weave); the oil will pick up the moisture and spatter upon reheating.

The Deep-Frying Process 炸的方法

STAGES OF HEATING OIL

Hot oil is the arena and the essence of Chinese deep-frying, and to know how it behaves is crucial if you are going to cook with it, man-ipulate it, and make it produce wonderful food.

Corn or peanut oil travels visibly through several stages as it heats, each appropriate for frying certain foods as opposed to others, and regardless of whether one is using a deep-fry thermometer, it is meaningful and important to be able to recognize the stages with your eye.

The first stage is what I call the *"slow-fry"* stage. This is the first significant stage of heating, when there is rapid movement just below the surface of the oil—swirls and ripples that are easy to see against the black patina of a well-seasoned wok—but the oil is not yet sufficiently hot to be shimmering or be covered by a haze. This is the stage at which one can deep fry or precook a limited number of food types: whole nuts, which require a gentle heat in order not to dry out or burn, or slices of marinated chicken or fish to be "velveted" as a preliminary to stir-frying, where you want to flavor-seal and oil-coat them on the outside without cooking them through.

The slow-fry stage corresponds to 275° on a deep-fry thermometer. Food put into oil at this temperature will sink to the bottom and bubble relatively slowly.

As the oil becomes hotter and the movement of the molecules more rapid, the surface of the oil shimmers and then becomes covered by a light but distinct haze. The *light-haze stage* (called cooking over "little heat" in Chinese), is conducive for the frying of delicate, fragile-fleshed foods like shrimp, and thinly sliced and coated foods like wal-nut-dredged chicken slices, or sesame seed-coated slices of fish. The oil at this stage is hot enough to bring the moisture inside the food to a near-boil—thus setting up the proper oil-water repulsion that enables food to cook without absorbing oil—yet the oil is not hot enough to burn or dry out such delicate or thin items. This makes it ideal also for the brief frying of marinated slices of beef and pork that will later be stir-fried to doneness in a sauce.

The light-haze stage corresponds to 350°–375° on a deep-fry thermometer. The lower end of this stage, when the oil is shimmering and the thermometer reads 350°, is the temperature at which one deep-fries smaller items like shrimp balls, springrolls, meatballs, and slices of marinated meat. The upper end of the stage, when the light haze is more apparent and the thermometer reads 375°, is the temperature at which one many times puts a whole or half a chicken or duck into the oil. A sample of food put into the oil at the appropriate temperature will come to the surface within 3–5 seconds, surrounded by a crown of small white bubbles. Most deep-frying occurs at this stage.

As the oil heats further, the light haze becomes thicker. This is the *dense-haze stage* (cooking over "big heat" in Chinese), just before the oil begins to smoke. At this temperature, the oil is hot enough to fry large items like a whole fish or fowl—things with enough bulk to retain their inner moisture—whereas oil this hot would singe or toughen smaller, thinner, or more fragile foods. This is also the stage at which a web of dry bean or rice noodles will puff and curl instantly into a "nest."

The dense-haze stage corresponds to 400°–425° on a deep-fry thermometer. A sample of food put into the oil at this temperature will rise immediately to the surface ringed and covered with white bubbles.

DEEP-FRYING WITH THE SENSES: USING ONE'S EYES

Just as one's ears are of consummate usefulness in stir-frying, one's eyes are invaluable when deep-frying. The eyes gauge rightly the heat of the oil before the food goes in—checking for ripples, haze, and smoke. Once a sample of the food to be fried is slipped into the oil, it is again the eyes that judge the oil to be properly hot, monitoring the speed with which the dab or bit of whatever returns to the surface, and checking for bubbles or burning. Most important, it is the eyes that know far better than any stopwatch or written recipe when the food is ready to be taken from the oil—nuts and nut coatings should be light brown, as they will continue to darken after leaving the pot from their own internal heat; sliced things and small items will float perceptibly higher on the surface of the oil, their raw moistness no longer weighing them down; the score marks of a frying fish will reveal the flesh near the bone to be pearly white. All this is perceived by the eyes. Trust them when deep-frying, before anything else.

DEEP-FRYING A WHOLE ANYTHING

Probably the single most terrifying moment in the life of a fledgling Chinese cook is when said fledgling is faced with a wok-full of near-smoking hot oil, a long or large whole something like a fish or a duck, and the need to get the one into the other. The first time I had occasion to deep-fry a foot-long fish, I stood rooted before the stove like one struck dumb, with the fish dangling by its tail clenched in my hand, for so long that the kitchen was inundated with smoke before I decided to give up and steam it instead.

In recognition of primitive terror and with fond thoughts of a Chinese woman I knew who would regularly pitch a 5-pound fish into an immense wok with the skill of a professional bowler, let me proffer up several suggestions to shrink the inevitable fear.

First, when deep-frying a whole anything it is necessary to *account for the bulk of the item and limit the oil accordingly.* Like putting a fat man into a brimming bathtub, if you fill the vessel full of oil, it will surely runneth over. For most big items, you will be safe if you leave 3–3½ inches clear at the top of the pot.

Second, *count on the oil temperature being lowered immediately and significantly* as soon as the item enters the pot. If you need to fry a duck at 375°, then the oil must be 400° to begin and the heat raised to its highest under the pot.

Third, *expect a lot of bubbling and spattering* and prepare yourself accordingly: Wear a long-sleeved cook's coat or protective shirt, step back from the stove in the first seconds, and hold a large lid as a shield between you and the oil, angling the lid away from you to contain the spattering. Do not *cover* the pot. If you do, the steam will have no escape and the spattering will worsen. The fury always dies down quickly, but preparing yourself for the initial cacophony is more than half the battle.

Fourth, plan clearly a *mode of approach, a strategy* if you will—the safe and hopefully neat way of getting the whole something into the oil.

With a *fish,* the usual tactic is to hold it by the tail in one's hand, then lower it slowly into the oil nose first, wiggling the tail slightly so as to keep the body moving until it has been seared and will not stick to the pot, then letting the fish slip entirely into the oil. To counter the inevitable spattering, I always brandish the fish in one hand and the wok lid-shield in the other (the militant posture of a coward, but a safe and heartening one nonetheless).

In the case of a *duck or chicken,* my strategy is to lower it into the oil balanced securely on a Chinese mesh spoon, the larger the bowl and longer the handle the better. Here, one must be sure to first dip the empty mesh bowl into the oil to heat it through just before picking up the bird, lest the bird adhere to the metal when it enters the oil.

Whatever the approach, the entry speed must be *slow.* Plunking or throwing a whole anything into hot oil is decidedly unwise.

Finally, to avoid having to turn the item, an imposing directive often seen hiding bare of further comment in the forest of a Chinese recipe, use a broad ladle or Chinese scoop to *baste the top of the item continuously and evenly as it fries,* crisping the top skin under a steady wash of hot oil. This was the trick of my bowler-cook friend, and besides being an expert solution to the turning problem, it is a rhythmic way to relax and regain some calmness once the food is in the oil.

RECYCLING DEEP-FRYING OIL

Recycling the oil used for deep-frying—straining it free of food particles and residue, then reusing it for further deep-frying and stir-frying—is a natural activity in a Chinese home kitchen. Recycled oil is called "cooked oil" in Chinese, in contrast to "clear oil," which has never been used, and while its color progressively deepens with use, recycled oil, which is strained meticulously, stored properly, and not used beyond its time, will impart no significant flavor or aroma of its own to new foods. It will *heat somewhat slower, burn somewhat more easily, and color foods a bit deeper,* but the difference at first is slight and when it becomes noticeable that's the signal to begin again with fresh oil.

Step #1 in recycling oil is to *let it cool.* In the interest of safety, avoid decanting hot oil and avoid even moving it if possible. When I am working in a kitchen where space is at a premium and it is necessary to free the stovetop for other uses, I will carefully move the wok-full of hot oil to another room, out of reach of two- and four-legged creatures, and sit it securely on top of an empty pot or wok ring to cool. If you are faced with a wok filled with more than 3 or 4 cups of hot oil, and you absolutely need the wok and must empty it, do so by scooping the oil with a ladle into a second pot or heatproof bowl to cool. Avoid tipping a full wok to drain it, at all costs. It is simply too dangerous.

Step #2 is to *strain the oil meticulously*, removing not only the larger visible bits of debris, but also the infinitesimal, tiny particles suspended in the oil. The ideal straining device is a large, fine-mesh metal strainer lined with several layers of cheesecloth (page 81). The cheesecloth is imperative, and a generous amount of it. The super-strainer is helpful, but so long as you have ample cheesecloth the strainer may be of a coarser mesh. Strain the oil 1 or 2 times as necessary to clean it to the fullest.

Step #3 is to *store the oil airtight in a cool place.* If you do not use oil regularly, the refrigerator may be the best spot. In my kitchen, it sits in a dark cool cupboard kept chilly by the winds off the San Francisco Bay.

Step #4 is to *gauge when the oil is no longer usable and discard it.* My gauge is color. When the oil is brown as opposed to golden, I throw it out. Depending on what I have been frying, that may be after 2 uses or after 20 uses. Two deep-fried fish will darken the oil considerably, whereas 10 pounds of raw peanuts will darken it only a shadow's worth. Use your eyes to tell.

Also, use your nose. Chinese cooks regularly segregate oil used for frying fish and will reuse it only for frying more fish. I have no hard and fast rule. If the oil smells fishy, I will keep it for the next fish or try the raw potato trick (heating the oil with some raw potato chunks thrown in to absorb the smell). If it has been used for shrimp or some delicate water creature that leaves no perceptible odor in the oil, then I don't segregate it.

TIMES WHEN IT IS IMPERATIVE TO USE FRESH OIL, LITTLE-USED OIL, OR OIL THAT IS RESERVED FOR SPECIFIC PURPOSES

Recycled oil may be used for most stir-frying and deep-frying, so long as your eye and nose judge it to be sufficiently clean and golden. It is imperative, however, to use fresh oil or oil that has been used only once in light frying in the following situations, which, if you are a frequent fryer, will justify your keeping a bottle of oil to one side specifically for their use.

Deep-frying noodle nests and raw nuts. The dry bean threads or rice noodles that transform into puffy white "nests" upon frying will absorb any debris in the oil like a magnet, so to keep them pristinely white I keep a quart bottle of oil labeled "nests." The label on the same bottle reads "and nuts," because I use this oil as well for frying raw nuts, another food that colors too deeply and quickly if immersed in oil that has been used for heavy deep-frying. The "nests and nuts" oil may be reused (for them exclusively) for many fryings before it darkens, and needs only occasional straining. Once it darkens, I mix it with an equal amount of fresh oil and add that to my general deep-frying pool.

"Velveting" chicken, fish, and shellfish. The temperatures at which certain foods are velveted in oil as a preliminary to stir-frying are too low to cause the usual repulsion between the item being fried and the oil used to cook it. Hence, the fragile velvet coating tends to discolor, absorb flavors, and even toughen if treated to oil that has been recycled from heavier uses. I generally keep a separate bottle of oil for velveting, straining it through a fine sieve between each use, and then using it for general stir-frying or deep-frying once it has turned darker through repeated heating. If you do not fry as regularly as I do, you can share the same bottle between noodle nests and raw nuts and velveted foods.

Deep-frying nut- and seed-covered foods. Walnuts, almonds, and sesame seeds, which I enjoy using as a crunchy coating for slivers of fish, meat, and poultry, will darken too quickly and deeply if fried in recycled oil that is turning brown. Oil that is still yellow-gold, though used, will work fine, but be on guard that richly colored oil will darken the coatings conspicuously.

Deep-frying shrimp paste. All the delectable goodies made with a seasoned purée of raw shrimp will turn brown-gold rather than rosy-gold if deep-fried in recycled oil that is a shade or two within reach of being discarded. New oil is not imperative, but nearly new oil (such as has deep-fried shrimp before) is.

STEP BY STEP THROUGH THE DEEP-FRYING PROCESS

Deep-frying can be relaxing or harrowing, and most anything in between. Deep-frying discrete, small items like shrimp toast is neat and slow-paced enough to be done in party dress with a posture of calm elegance to match, whereas deep-frying a whole anything can be a chaos of bubbles and spatters as exciting as a football game and requiring almost equally protective garb. Being familiar with the rhythm of the process is the key to mastering it, and the way to stay focused in the face of hot oil.

Step #1 Organize everything you will need within easy arm's reach of the stovetop. That means finding room for a paper towel-lined tray or two (heatproof, if it will need to go into the oven), one or two mesh spoons or a mesh spoon and either long cooking chopsticks or wooden tongs to manipulate the food, and the food to be fried. Put a serving platter in a low oven to warm. Or, if you will need to hold the food in the oven between batches or briefly before serving, set the oven to 325°, arrange the oven rack conveniently, and have the serving platter nearby for quick heating at the last minute.

Step #2 Heat the deep-frying vessel over high heat until the metal is hot enough to evaporate a bead of water on contact, thereby opening the pores of the metal to drink in a bit of oil and help insure that the food will not stick if it comes in contact with the sides or bottom of the pot.

Step #3 Add the oil, then clamp the oil thermometer in place. Add as much oil as is dictated by the bulk of the thing to be fried. A noodle nest will fry easily in only 3–4 inches of oil; a plump chicken with a hefty breast won't be happy and clear of the pot with less than 6–7 inches of oil. If you are in doubt as to the exact amount, add more oil rather than less, as you cannot add extra cold oil to the pot once the frying process has begun. Remember to leave several inches clear at the top of the pot in the case of bulky items or if specified in the recipe, to accommodate the oil the item will displace or the fulsome bubbling which accompanies the frying of some foods.

Step #4 Heat the oil to the degree specified in the recipe, then *adjust the heat* beneath the pot to insure that the temperature does not rise. You may need to further heat the oil once you have tested it or have begun frying, but it should be kept from climbing until you've made the test.

Step #5 Test the oil with a small piece of whatever is to be fried—a dab of shrimp paste or a whole shrimp ball if you're cooking shrimp balls, a chunk of walnut if you're frying walnut-dredged chicken, or a bit of skin tweaked from the tail end of a whole duck or chicken if you're frying a whole bird. Just about the only instance I can think of where you'll have problems getting a small test sample is in the case of a whole fish. Then you lower the nose into the oil and judge from there.

Judge from the reaction of the oil to the food whether the oil is sufficiently hot to begin frying. In most cases, the sample bit should rise quickly to the surface surrounded by a ring of white bubbles. (The fish nose will not rise, but it will bubble.) The bubbles indicate that the oil is hot enough to repel the moisture of the food, whereby the food stands apart from the oil and does not absorb it.

Do not forgo testing the oil. It must be tested with a fresh sample bit each time you fry a large item and between every batch of smaller items, when the oil typically requires several minutes to regain its original high heat. Trust only the test. Trust it above your instincts, and trust it above the thermometer reading.

Step #6 When the test sample indicates the oil is sufficiently hot, add the item to be fried to the oil.

If the item is a large one, a "whole anything": Lower it into the oil slowly, by hand or in the bowl of a Chinese mesh spoon you've preheated by dipping into the frying oil. Expect loud bubbling and spattering and step back from the pot while shielding yourself from spatters with a large lid. If the item does not bubble immediately and vigorously, remove it at once from the oil. Raise the heat, wait for the temperature to climb higher, then retest with the whole item. When the item is successfully bubbling in the oil, raise the heat under the pot to its highest, in order to regain the heat lost when the food entered the oil. Move the item back and forth slowly with the spoon, so it will not be tempted to stick to the pot. Ladle the top of the item evenly and continuously with hot oil to cook the exposed portion to crispness and to avoid having to turn it.

Or, *if you are frying a number of small items:* Drop the first item into the oil about an inch above the surface, using hands or chopsticks as the texture of the item and your own feeling of comfort permits. If it rises to the surface in the seconds specified in the recipe, then proceed immediately to add a second item to the oil. Continue to add the items steadily one-by-one to the oil, so long as the bubbling and quick rising continue, and so long as each new item finds room to float and fry freely on the surface. Drop the items into the oil from different spots, to lessen the likelihood of their clustering together, and if they do stick to one another, split them gently apart with chopsticks or a mesh or wooden spoon. Raise the heat as needed to maintain a merry bubbling, using the bubbles as your primary gauge and paying the oil thermometer only secondary attention. If the bubbling falters, stop immediately adding new items to the oil and raise the heat. If the food, on the other hand, is scorching or drying, remove what remains in the oil and quench the heat. Wait several minutes, retest the oil with a fresh sample, then restore the heat and resume frying once the bubbling is right. Spin or turn the items slowly as they fry, to insure even coloring and cooking.

Step #6 *Remove the food from the oil when its color and position on the surface indicate that it is done,* that is, cooked through but still moist.

Most things will continue to darken and cook from their own internal heat and should be pulled from the oil when a shade or two *lighter* than desired. This is particularly the case with fragile items like shrimp, seeds, and nuts, which lose their flavor if they are overly browned. Simultaneously look to the position of the food on the surface of the oil. Food when it has shed enough moisture to be cooked through will float *high* on the surface of the oil. This is especially evident when frying a small batch of items, where the first one that entered the pot will rise to doneness just ahead of its neighbors.

As soon as the position and color are right, remove the item immediately. Remove it sooner than later, if in doubt. Food can always be dropped back into hot oil to refry to doneness, but there is no rescuing or reversing food that has overcooked.

To retrieve a "whole anything": Lift the item from the oil carefully, supported and balanced securely on one or two Chinese mesh spoons. Hold it briefly above the oil to "drip-dry," then tilt it carefully, if needed, to drain the cavity of oil. Transfer the item to the towel-lined tray, then blot the sides and top dry with paper towels.

To retrieve small individual items: Pull the items one-by-one from the oil, as soon as you judge them by color and position to be done, with chopsticks, tongs, or a Chinese mesh spoon. Do not wait to retrieve things in batches. To avoid having to continuously turn and deposit things on the paper-towel drain, hold a large Chinese mesh spoon or strainer stationary in one hand above the oil and use it as a catch-all for the individual items you pull from the pot. When the spoon or strainer is full, then quickly turn and transfer the cooked items to the paper towels to drain. As you become accustomed to deep-frying many small things at one time, work at slipping a raw item into the oil on the heels of every cooked item you retrieve, frying continuously, in other words, instead of in isolated batches. As you deposit food on the paper-towel drain, scatter it in a single layer and shake the tray gently to blot up excess oil. Switch to a new tray and new toweling if the first tray becomes crowded or oil-soaked.

Step #7 If you need to fry in batches, or if you need to double deep-fry, then it is necessary to pause, retest the oil with a fresh sample and often raise the heat to bring the oil to the original high temperature before continuing the frying. The retesting and possible reheating are crucial. If the oil is not properly hot, the second batch of food will be greasy or the half-cooked food will not crisp in the second frying.

If you must wait more than several minutes for the oil to reheat, or you are frying in batches but feel you must serve the food at one time, keep the fried items hot in a 325° oven. Do not hold them in the oven more than 5–10 minutes, or they will diminish in flavor and increase in oiliness.

Step #8 Serve fried foods as soon as possible after draining. Deep-fried foods invariably wilt, deflate, and become unappealing as they cool. Holding them in the oven more than several minutes is certain death to their original fresh beauty! Some foods— like shrimp balls—cannot be eaten immediately on account of being burning-hot, but should be *presented* immediately while they are full-blown and at their prettiest.

A deep-fried whole chicken or duck is the only exception to the rule, at least in my kitchen. The bird will shatter if chopped immediately and must first cool at room temperature for about 5 minutes before it can be cut cleanly.

Step #9 Once the oil has cooled, strain, bottle, and store it as described above, for use in future stir-frying and deep-frying.

ENDNOTE ON GETTING BURNED

Any cook who really *cooks* gets burned at least occasionally, and it is very useful whether you're baking, sautéing, stir-frying, or deep-frying to know what to do if you collide with a hot pot or are spattered by hot oil.

The first and immediate step is to cool the skin, as quickly as possible. Ice is then

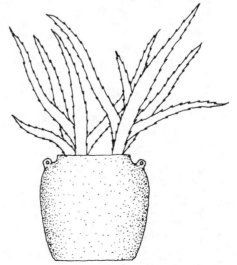

an aloe plant, with its prickly, stubby, gel-filled leaves—a plant that thrives in water or simple potting soil and needs only occasional watering

the first thing to turn to. Once the skin has cooled down, the next step is to cover it with something soothing. I have an aloe plant on my kitchen windowsill, given to me years ago by a student, and if I burn myself I break off a fat leaf, slit it open to expose the gel, then apply the soothing goo to the burn. Vitamin E or vitamin A and D, squeezed from a vitamin capsule or a tube, or in cream form, is another healer. An oil-based skin ointment specifically for burns or diaper rash is also good. At least *one* of these dressings should be located within a minute's sprint of your stove.

Minor accidents are part of any active kitchen and preparing for them insures they will not become major, and somehow even seems to prevent them.

Chinese Techniques: Smoking

燻

S moked foods are a regular, and in some provinces an everyday, feature of the Chinese diet. Tea-smoked chickens are standard fare in Peking, camphor-smoked ducks a proud specialty of Szechwan, and no Hunanese with an ounce of regional pride will fail to recount (at length!) the treasury of densely smoked foods for which Hunan is famed—the hams, spareribs, liver, eggs, duck tongues, duck webs, soybeans, and endless variety of major and minor nibbles that have been transformed in the crucible of many a family's smoking room. Smoked foods in China are traditionally listed in the category of "foods to make the wine go down," so well do they serve to spark the appetite and tease the tongue.

Historically, smoking was a method of food preservation closely akin to drying. Nowadays on a Chinese menu it primarily denotes a style of *flavoring*—a dusky, succulent, complex excitement of tastes that adds a finishing touch to already cooked foods. Rather than a long, elaborate process involving a specially constructed room or chest where temperatures rise high and long enough to cook, flavor, and preserve raw food, this simpler style of stovetop smoking is a short process designed solely to season and to color. In the brief span of 20–30 minutes, and in the uncomplicated small space of a sealed pot, an already steamed fowl or fish is permeated by smoke and turned a deep mahogany brown.

The smoking agents may vary but are commonplace: tea leaves, sugar, rice, fragrant wood, or wood by-products. The method itself is as simple as turning on a burner. In fact, there is nothing at all formidable about smoking foods. It is only the flavor, that incredible taste mingled with aroma, that is ineffable and wonderfully complex.

What this means to the home cook is that the sensual pleasures of smoked chicken, smoked duck, and smoked fish are well within the reach of even a klutsy kitchen person. If you can steam food, line a pot, and turn on the heat to start some sugar burning, you needn't go to Szechwan to savor a smoked duck. All that is required is a plump fresh bird or fish (one that is fat as opposed to very lean will taste best), a fair amount of tin foil, a heavy pot, and an eager appetite. As for a smoky kitchen—given an open window and even a half-hearted breeze—what lingers for a mere hour and is gone thereafter is so exquisite a scent that it should be bottled and advertised in *Vogue*.

Tools for Smoking

用具

POTS FOR SMOKING

When I first began searching for recipes for Chinese smoked foods, the few writers on the subject seemed divided into two camps: those who would smoke things in an oven above a metal pan of charcoal, wood, or whatever, and those who relied on "an old pot." Being of the old pot school myself and noting also that those of pot inclination were the Old Guard, homestyle Chinese cooks I most admired, I followed their humble route. It is the one I still stick to.

The old pot best suited for smoking is most any heavy pot with a lid, capacious enough to contain whatever you are smoking with a good 4 inches to spare above and below, and at least 2 inches' clearance all around. The pot must be *heavy*, as it will be heating over moderately high heat for upward of 30 minutes with nothing liquid inside it, and a thin pot would buckle or worse under the assault. Old is considered desirable, as the heat and smoke will stain the metal to some degree and will remove the patina from a wok, but a newish pot, so long as it is not a showpiece, is certainly eligible for the job.

My smoking set is the 14-inch *flat-bottomed spun-steel wok* I use for deep-frying, partnered with a *plateau-shaped wok lid*. The shape of the wok and lid accommodates the plumpest chickens with ease, and both are able to tolerate rough treatment. Spun steel is wonderfully hearty and unmindful of the heat, and I find it little bother to reapply the patina after smoking. Because it functions primarily as a deep-frying vessel, the patina on this wok is not crucial. If it were a matter of smoking in a wok I used daily for stir-frying, emblazoned with a much-loved, years-old patina, I would probably pause before using it for smoking and buy another wok. In other words, if you have a wok especially for deep-frying, use that; if you are only an occasional stir-fryer with one wok, then borrow it to smoke in and reapply the patina; or, if you stir-fry regularly and value the patina on your wok, then consider buying a second wok for deep-frying and smoking. Spun-steel woks are so inexpensive when bought from a Chinese source that I don't feel it a betrayal to my own innate sense of frugality to recommend the purchase of such a useful tool.

a shape and weight beautifully suited for smoking: a flat- or round-bottomed spun-steel wok with a plateau-shaped lid

A *round-bottomed wok* will function just about as well as a flat-bottomed wok for smoking. Extra care must be taken to strew the smoking ingredients evenly over the bottom, but that's about the only difference. A round-bottomed wok should be balanced on a wok ring, gas jet, or overturned burner grid (illustrations, page 49), and brought as close to the heat as possible.

If you do not have a wok, a *Dutch oven* made of a heavyweight metal like cast iron is ideal, though any *heavyweight stockpot* large enough to accommodate the food and strong enough to withstand being heated empty of liquids will do.

The lids for any of these pots needn't be heavy, but must not encroach upon the food. If a dome-shaped lid is unavailable and needed, you may fashion a "tent" of heavy-duty foil to get the required height.

TIN FOIL

To line the pot and the lid, and to prevent the smoking ingredients both from caramelizing onto the pot and discoloring it, you will need a generous amount of tin foil, preferably heavyweight. The shiny side of the foil should always be facing *up*, that is, away from the pot and the lid, so it will best reflect the heat.

The ideal sort is one that has appeared rather recently, marketed in 18-inch wide rolls by Reynolds Wrap under the name "EXTRA HEAVY for freezing and cooking." One layer of this stiff, hardy stuff will do the trick. Otherwise, use two layers of *heavy-duty tin foil*, or three or four layers of the everyday thin variety, called "regular weight." If in doubt, use *more* layers rather than fewer, especially to line the pot. The lid is where you can get by with only a single layer as the concern here is discoloration, not caramelization.

SMOKING RACKS

To support the food to be smoked 1½–2 inches above the smoking ingredients, you will need a rack able both to support the food and to withstand the heat that will build inside the pot.

If you are smoking in a wok, the ideal tool is a Chinese-made *collapsible four-bar rack*, which looks like a tic-tac-toe grid when fully opened, and closes to an easily stowable 13 inch length. The four bars are each ½ inch wide and 10 inches long, joined at the points of overlap with small metal fastenings. *Metal* is preferable to bamboo. The traditional bamboo rack looks terribly pretty at first, but the edges that come in contact with the pot get increasingly singed and shorter with each use. The hefty, interlocking wooden bars that are often prepackaged in wok sets (illustration, page 67) will not burn so badly, but they are usually too small to raise the food high enough above the smoking mixture.

Chinese-made collapsible four-bar metal rack

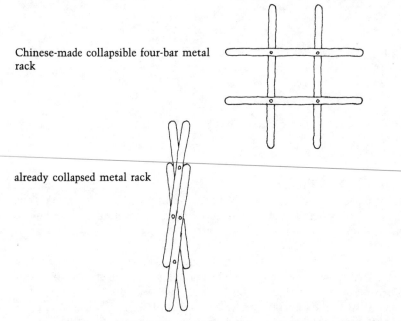

already collapsed metal rack

If you are smoking in a wok and do not have the collapsible grid, you may try two alternatives: The best of the two is a *round or oval metal cooling rack*, the sort used for cooling cookies. It will not burn, is unimpeachably stable, and the smoking residue will wash off easily with an abrasive. For a 14-inch wok, the round rack must be 11–12 inches in diameter, and the oval rack 12 × 8½ inches, in order to lift the food sufficiently high above the smoking mixture.

round metal cooling rack

oval metal cooling rack

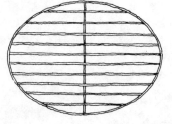

The lesser choice is a primitive arrangement of *four wooden chopsticks,* each 10–10½ inches long, and spread as far apart as needed to form a stable support system. Be sure they are the heftier, square-topped Chinese sort, and expect them to scorch at the tips.

improvised chopstick rack

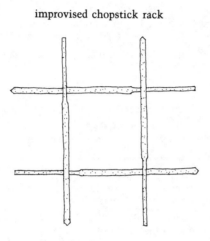

If you are smoking in a flat Western pot with straight sides, you will need *a rack with legs,* either improvised or built-in, and a surface spread big enough to support the food and small enough to fit easily into the pot. A simple system is to place any of the racks recommended above on *several empty tin cans.* The cans should be thoroughly clean and have both ends cut out, so the smoke rises through them as well as around them, and they should be of sufficient number and arranged in such a way as to support the rack with maximum stability. Short cans will best fit a shallow pot, whereas tall cans may be helpful in a deeper pot to raise the food higher and make it easier to turn and retrieve.

Dutch oven for smoking with short cans to support rack

stockpot for smoking with tall cans to support rack

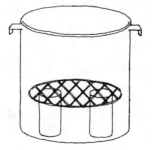

**The
Smoking
Process**

燻的方法

Smoking foods in order to flavor and color them is a simple matter of stationing them in an enclosed space over a mixture of fragrant combustibles that will smoke instead of blaze. The enclosed space should be sealed tightly to prevent the smoke from escaping. The heat should be intense enough to combust the mixture in the first place and then keep it happily puffing. The smoking mixture should have enough substance to burn for about 30 minutes, and possess enough fragrance to scent and flavor the food intriguingly. And that's about it!

SMOKING INGREDIENTS

Traditional Chinese smoking materials include hickory, camphor, and cypress woods, raw rice, peanut shells, black and jasmine tea leaves, brown sugar, and a host of specialty items ranging from pine needles to cassia bark to fruit peels. The wood and the sugar create the smoke by combusting, the rice comes into play by fueling the mixture, and the aromatics, including the wood, the tea, and the specialty spices, create the fragrance.

My standard home-smoking mixture is based on almost equal parts brown sugar, raw rice, and dry black tea leaves. The sugar may be light brown or dark brown or a combination of the two, the rice may be white or brown but preferably talc-free, and the tea is whatever my nose judges to best complement the food. I sometimes use perfumed Chinese teas—rose black and litchi black primarily, both too highly perfumed for me to drink with pleasure, but perfect as a scent for smoked chicken. Other times I use Western spice blends flavored with orange rind and cinnamon. Depending on mood and menu, I will enrich the mixture with Szechwan peppercorns, home-dried orange or tangerine peel, dried apple or peach skins, or crumbled cinnamon sticks or pieces of Chinese cassia bark. You may elaborate on the basic trio of rice, sugar, and tea as playfully as you like, so long as you use only dry ingredients and don't overload the pot.

HEAT FOR SMOKING: HOW TO KNOW WHAT'S HAPPENING IN THE POT

To start the smoking mixture burning is no problem, though it can take upwards of 10 minutes over high heat if the pot is properly heavy and your stove is not the mightiest. Given a healthy stovetop, usually 4–6 minutes are required to start the sugar burning and to send aloft the first delicate whiffs of smoke, then about 2 minutes more for the dainty whiffs to turn into convincing puffs. At this point one covers the pot and the process begins in earnest.

Once the cover is in place, two things are crucial. One is to insure that the smoke is contained within the pot in order to do its job. Two is to adjust the heat to maintain a *steady puff of smoke*—not a trickle that will not do anything at all, and not a burning cloud that will scathe the food harshly, but a steady smoke somewhere in the middle.

My solution to both problems begins with a generous 4–5-inch overhang of tin foil around the rim of both the pot and the lid. Once I clamp the lid on the pot, I then crimp the two hems of foil loosely shut, all but for one small spot, the "escape hatch." It is a very simple system whereby the smoke is well contained yet one can still gauge its force through the escape hatch. Too thin an escaping wisp or none at all is the signal to raise the heat; too churning a smoke barreling through the hatch is the signal to lower it. *A broad, ribbony stream of smoke* is exactly what is needed. It is your best indication that the heat is just right.

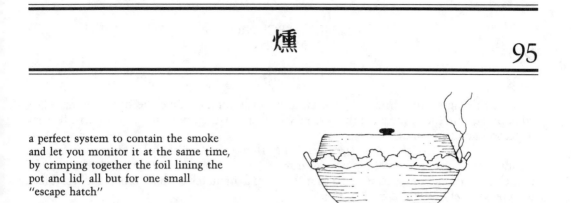

a perfect system to contain the smoke
and let you monitor it at the same time,
by crimping together the foil lining the
pot and lid, all but for one small
"escape hatch"

USING THE SENSES: JUDGING DONENESS

The eyes are one's most important tool when smoking. It is the eyes that judge the heat to be properly intense during the process, and it is the eyes that judge by the color of the food whether it is sufficiently smoked.

Depth and evenness of color are the best indications of when something has smoked long enough to be flavorful. If a smoked chicken is pale in color, it will be pale in flavor, no matter how long it has smoked. The exterior of a well-smoked item should be rich brown to deep mahogany brown, depending on the strength of flavor you like, and in the case of poultry it should be evenly colored top, bottom, and all around. It may not be necessary to turn the food over midway through the process, or it may be necessary to turn it over an odd number of times, all depending upon the food, the intensity of the smoke, and even the contours of the pot. Use your eyes to know when the process is complete.

SMOKY KITCHENS

Recipes in English for smoked Chinese foods almost always include grandmotherly shriekings about the smoke that will linger long after the last smoked duck wing has disappeared. Rubbish!

If you smoke 15 muscle-bound chickens in one night in one small kitchen, as I have had occasion to discover, then, yes, the house will fairly reek and so will you. However, if you smoke only one or two items at a time, then quickly dispose of the caramelized smoking ingredients and the foil that lined the pot, what lingers is only an ephemeral, ethereal incense.

To insure that the kitchen and the house stay smoke-free, begin by crimping the foil shut as directed. Create some ventilation and as much as comforts you by opening doors and windows and turning on fans. When you are done smoking, uncover the pot near an open window or outside on the porch. But most of all, *dispose of the burnt ingredients and foil at once*. Then what remains to haunt you is just the memory of a great meal.

STEP BY STEP THROUGH THE SMOKING PROCESS

Step #1 Line the pot and the lid with a generous amount of tin foil, so that the interiors are completely covered and there is an overhang of 4–5 inches of foil around the rims of both the pot and lid. Take special care to line the pot and particularly the *bottom* of the pot thickly and well, using 3–4 layers of regular-weight foil, 2 layers of heavy-duty foil, or a single layer of "extra heavy" foil. If in doubt, use more rather than fewer layers, to prevent the ingredients from caramelizing onto the metal. Leave the overhanging edges sticking out instead of pressing them neatly back against the pot, so that they will be easy to grasp and crimp shut.

Step #2 Mix the smoking ingredients thoroughly and lightly with your fingers, blending the sugar and breaking up any lumps. Spread the mixture evenly in the bottom of the pot without compacting it, so that it covers a diameter of about 8 or 9 inches. Place the pot securely over the cold burner.

Step #3 Oil the top of the rack thoroughly with Chinese or Japanese sesame oil or corn or peanut oil, so the food will not stick to it. Arrange the rack securely in the pot, lifted at least 1½ inches above the top of the smoking mixture. Center the food on the rack, breast side up for a chicken or duck. If the food is forced to come in contact with the sides of the pot, put a small piece of oiled parchment at the point of contact lest they adhere upon heating.

Step #4 Turn the heat to high, and wait for the mixture to begin smoking convincingly. It can take upwards of 10 minutes. Two or three thin wisps is *not enough.* Wait until several ribbons of smoke rise in different corners of the pot, and only then put the lid in place. Crimp the foil loosely shut with fingers, chopsticks, or tongs, or press it shut with the back of a wooden spoon or spatula, leaving an inch-wide "escape hatch" through which you can monitor the intensity of the smoke. Seal the foil securely enough to insure a minimum loss of smoke, but not so tightly that it will be hard to open without tearing, as you may need to reseal it later on.

Step #5 Adjust the heat to maintain a steady leak of ribbony smoke from the escape hatch, which may mean leaving it alone or reducing it, all depending on the power of your burner. Set a timer according to the recipe, then check every several minutes to insure that the smoke remains constant. If it falters, raise the heat, adjusting it as your eye dictates.

Step #6 When the time is up, turn off the heat, and wait the required minutes while the smoking continues from the heat of the pot. Remove the pot to an airy spot, if practical. Loosen the foil, then lift the lid slowly *away* from you to avoid being hit by escaping smoke. Blow the smoke away if needed to clear your view, then *judge the food for proper color.* It should be evenly a rich brown, light to dark mahogany according to the degree of intensity you like. If the food is too hot to check barehanded, lift it carefully with a clean, dry cloth. Be aware that whole ducks or chickens will have a cavity partly filled with hot juice.

Step #7 If the food requires turning over to color it evenly or additional smoking to color and flavor it more deeply, *sprinkle an additional 4 tablespoons brown or white sugar* around the edges of the burnt smoking mixture in order to regenerate the smoke. Return the uncovered pot to high heat, wait for the mixture to smoke *convincingly,* then replace the cover. Crimp the foil shut, monitor the escaping smoke, and adjust the heat as before to maintain a steady puff. Repeat the process as many times as is needed to get the right depth and evenness of color, adding sugar each time to refuel the smoke.

Step #8 When your eye judges the color to be right, *free the food gently from the rack* and transfer it carefully to a waiting plate. If you have smoked a chicken or duck, tilt the cavity over the pot to drain it of juices.

Step #9 Before doing anything else, *immediately dispose of the tin foil and smoking ingredients,* wrapping the one tightly in the other. Put it outside the house or wrap it airtight, to contain the burnt odor.

Step #10 Proceed to gloss the food with sesame oil or cook it further, as the recipe directs.

Chinese Techniques: Sand-Pot Cooking

沙鍋

Whereas deep-frying, stir-frying, steaming, and smoking may all seem foreign to the average Western kitchen, cooking food in a squat, cozy, crockery pot seems less so. It is a comforting feeling seeing such a pot on a stove. One feels secure, at home, nestled in. One can slip vicariously into the pot and be warmed, like a child with a blanket over his head.

In much the same way as stew pots and crock pots the world over, the purpose of a Chinese sand pot is to cook large or chunked things slowly, in an environment where they retain a special moisture and pick up a dramatic depth of flavor. In China, the ingredients bound for the sand pot are often first deep-fried, stir-fried, or pan-fried to set the exterior with a distinctive texture and color. However, once in the pot, their business is to sit and stew, bubbling gently, developing flavors and gravies leisurely, and exuding a heartening perfume to seduce all who walk by.

Earthenware pot cookery is ancient in China—among the oldest of all vessel-enclosed cooking methods—but its appeal is thoroughly modern. It is energy-saving of both fuel and human energy, freeing the cook for other jobs, or freeing the cook to play.

Tools for Sand-Pot Cooking

用具

CHINESE SAND POTS

Chinese "sand pots" or "sandy pots" earn their Chinese name because their exterior is off-white and sandy in texture, left unglazed to conduct the heat with maximum efficiency. They come in a variety of sizes and shapes, all striking and all remarkably inexpensive. Of greatest service is the *squat-bellied sand pot*, with a sandy, unglazed exterior and a smooth, fire-glazed interior ranging in color from milk chocolate to a deep chocolate brown.

The squat sand pot is commonly available in two designs: the first, with one long, protruding sandy handle, and the other equipped with two small, glazed, and loop-like handles. Both sorts have close-fitting lids, left sandy on the inside to absorb steam

Chinese sand-pot designs: all for stovetop use (Chinese have no ovens), made from the same combination of sand and clay, with an off-white, sandy-textured, unglazed exterior for best heat conduction, and a smooth, glazed interior to contain moisture

the one-handle, squat-bellied Chinese sand pot

the loop-handle, squat-bellied Chinese sand pot

a squat-bellied sand pot with one long and one loop handle, reinforced with protective wire during cooking, and usually glazed brown on the outside for extra strength and good looks. The lids are variously domed or plateau-shaped, but all of them have a small steam hole pierced close to the rim.

The design you choose is mostly a matter of taste, as the contours and construction of the two are nearly identical. The one-handle model bears the stamp of tradition. It is also available bounded by a protective wire brace, which is highly recommended if you are the sort who bangs things around. (Naturally enough, this is the design used in restaurants.) The two-handle design is a shade more elegant, perhaps, and fits easily onto a table for serving. In my house, I have both.

Size is a more important consideration. Smaller pots with a 1-quart capacity and 7½-inch diameter are cozily suited for stewing garlic (page 118) and black mushrooms (page 290), and for reheating leftovers. The largest size, with a 5-quart capacity and 12-inch diameter, will accommodate a whole duck (page 166). An intermediate 3-quart size with a 10-inch diameter, is just right for embracing a stew of chicken and chestnuts (page 156) or a double batch of spareribs (page 202). I have all three sizes (the trio bought for under $25 in San Francisco's Chinatown), and enthusiastically recommend getting at least two. If you must restrict yourself to one pot only, the 3-quart size is the one to get.

Before buying a sand pot, check it carefully for cracks. A Chinese dealer will ritually fill the pot you've chosen with water, then put it on top of newspaper to test for leaks. If your dealer isn't tradition-minded, then give the pot a thorough eye-balling.

Once purchased, I have never bothered to season or seal these pots in any way. I wash them out with hot water to remove the dust of Kiangsi province (where they are made now, as they have been for centuries), then promptly use them, and if they season themselves through use, I wouldn't be surprised. I use the pots with great care, heating them slowly and always with ample liquid inside, but beyond that I have never found any special treatment necessary.

Moreover, if the pot should crack through to the inside glaze, the crack may heal itself. (Cracks restricted to the outer sandy surface are inconsequential, though a sign to treat the pot with extra tenderness.) I have one large sand pot that leaked a bit through a crack in the bottom at a time when I had no choice but to cross my fingers and reuse it immediately to stew a second duck. The crack sealed itself shut in the second stewing and has never opened since. Which is to say, don't dispose of a cracked pot until you have heated it with a bit of sauce inside (my instinct says to make it a very rich, sweet sauce) and seen if it would mend.

Cleaning a sand pot is a simple matter of hot water and some gentle wiping with a barely soaped sponge. Abrasives will be injurious to both the glaze and the semi-porous sandy finish, so don't use them.

Most important, dry the pot literally to the core after washing, either by leaving it to sun-dry for several hours with the lid beside it turned sandy side up, or by putting the pot and the lid in an oven for an hour or two with the pilot on. A damp sand pot kept in a dark place will mildew. If it does, simply wash it out, but be sure to sun-dry or oven-dry it thoroughly before storing.

IMPLEMENTS FOR SAND POTS

Spoons and spatulas used for sand-pot cooking should be made of *wood*, to best protect the glazed surface inside the pot. Chopsticks are also very helpful, whether to redistribute the contents while they're stewing, or to arrange them prettily in the pot just before serving.

FLAME TAMERS AND ASBESTOS PADS

On a *gas* stove with a very flexible heat control, you may put a sand pot directly on top of the burner grid with little risk of its cracking. If the gas stove does not allow for fine, supple gradations of heat, or if you are cooking on an *electric stove*, then you should put an isolating Flame Tamer or asbestos pad between the pot and the coil or flame. These are inexpensive, 8-inch disks of pierced metal or metal-rimmed asbestos, usually equipped with a rubber-coated handle of heavy-duty wire. There is also a heavier, handle-less model that looks like a metal Frisbee and is somewhat more expensive. Whatever the variety, the heat-taming barrier insures a gentle, diffuse heat under the sand pot and safeguards it against cracking.

heat-tamer pad of asbestos or metal with handle

the pad in place under a sand pot and on top of a burner grid or coil

SUBSTITUTE WESTERN POTS

Though a Chinese sand pot could, in fact, be legitimately called an earthenware or clay pot, I have translated it literally from the Chinese to emphasize that it is very different from the clay-pot cookers now so fashionable in the West. In looking for a substitute for a sand pot, *do not* use a Schlemmertopf-type pot made of unglazed clay. It cooks on a different principle that eschews oil and extra liquids, and will produce disappointing and unattractive results if used for a sand-pot recipe. Also, *do not* use any earthenware pot with a leaded glaze. To eat the food cooked in one will poison you.

As a serviceable and aesthetic substitute for a sand pot, you may use an earthenware pot with a fully glazed interior and an unglazed exterior that is designed for stovetop use. Gorgeous specimens are available from the ateliers of known and unknown potters here and abroad, and the Chinese sand pot rivals them only in cheapness. Check before using one to make sure that the glaze is lead-free.

Also serviceable is any heavy, covered casserole designed for stovetop cooking, be it enamelware, Corningware or cast iron. They will cook with a different speed and give somewhat different results than you would get with a sand pot, but all of them will do a capable stewing job. Of the bunch, I prefer the homey, cast-iron model, preferably with a glass lid. It cooks slowly and well, and conveys some of the spirit of the Chinese pot when brought to the table.

Be forewarned, however, that in the final analysis a Chinese sand pot is *inimitable*. It has a cooking rhythm, a look, and a centuries-old aura all its own, and it is well worth having for the very humble price.

The Process: Cooking in a Chinese Sand Pot 沙鍋用法	*WARNING: HOW TO CRACK A SAND POT* A Chinese sand pot will crack if it is put onto heat empty of liquid. It must be at least ¼–⅓ *full of liquid* when you put the pot on the stove.

A sand pot will also crack if it is exposed to sudden, drastic changes in heat. Have the pot at *room temperature* and put it on a *cold burner* to begin. Raise the heat slowly underneath it, beginning with *low* to warm the pot, then proceeding to *medium* to bring the liquids to a bubble. Do not remove the pot to a cold or wet surface until it has cooled to room temperature.

Finally, a sand pot will crack if you drop it! The side handles and the knob on the cover will get blazing hot even if the pot is set over low heat, so remember to check and move it only with the help of pot holders or mitts.

PRELIMINARY SEARING IN METAL

Because texture is so vital a feature of food to the Chinese tongue, a one-dimensionally soft stew holds no attraction—except if you're toothless. On this account, and also owing to the Chinese appreciation for the flavor of oil, it is rare that something is put into a sand pot to stew without first being seared in oil, through either pan-frying, stir-frying, or deep-frying in a metal skillet or wok able to tolerate high heat. The oil colors, flavors, and firms the food, and also locks in the juices prior to stewing. Thus, a duck that is first pot-browned over high heat to crisp the skin will not turn flabby or look anemic when stewed. The double-treated bird acquires a double dimension: the skin textured and richly colored from frying in oil, and the flesh dramatically tenderized through slow cooking in liquid.

A Chinese cook would not blot the oil-seared food before transferring it to the sand pot, but you may do so if you like. I go by instinct, gauging the tastes of my guests and the amount of oil in the accompanying dishes. If I am using simple boiled noodles or steamed bread to partner the sand-pot dish, then a bit of "good grease" (the flavorful sort) is as welcome as a dollop of butter in another culinary setting.

STEP BY STEP USE OF A SAND POT

A Chinese sand pot is a tool foremost and not a cooking technique *per se*, but there is a certain progression one follows in order to cook with it successfully.

Step #1 Have the sand pot at *room temperature*, no colder, to begin. If you are taking the pot from the refrigerator to reheat leftovers stored within, be certain to bring it to room temperature prior to heating, lest the bottom crack with a sudden change of heat.

Step #2 Once the food, if the recipe directs, has been textured and colored through brief searing in hot oil, it should be layered evenly in the sand pot and covered with the requisite cooking liquids. Large pieces of poultry to be cooked in their skin, such as a whole duck, should be placed in the pot on top of a layer of blanched Chinese cabbage, carrot shavings, scallion segments, or sautéed onions—a vegetable bed that will be a subtle, complementary backdrop—to insure that the fragile skin does not stick to the bottom of the pot.

Step #3 Cover the pot, position it on the burner, then raise the heat to *low*. Keep it at this setting for upwards of 10 minutes, to warm the earthenware. If the stove is electric or is otherwise not capable of fine gradations of heat, insert a protective heat guard or Flame Tamer between the pot and the burner.

Step #4 Once the lower portion of the outside of the pot is warm, raise the heat to *medium* to bring the liquids to a simmer. Be patient, do not stir the contents, and leave the pot covered.

Step #5 When steam escaping through the lid reveals that the liquids are fully bubbling, reduce the heat to low to maintain a steady, weak simmer. The sandy exterior of the pot is a superb heat conductor, so it is likely that you will need to reduce the heat to its *lowest* setting. Baste or stir the food gently to shower it evenly with liquid, then cover the pot and set a timer according to the recipe.

Step #6 Stir or baste the food occasionally to redistribute the liquids and the placement of food in the pot, replacing the cover securely each time. Monitor the heat carefully to maintain a steady, gentle simmer, and do not be surprised if you need to turn the heat progressively *lower* to prevent boiling.

Step #7 Once the food is done cooking, remove the pot to a surface that is capable of absorbing the heat. Do *not* transfer the hot pot to a wet or cold surface or it will crack. Place it on a wooden or woven trivet, or on a thick cloth or bamboo mat. One or two thick pot holders or a folded kitchen towel will also do for less elegant presentation, so long as they are dry.

Step #8 Use the sand pot as a serving vessel, opening the lid at the table to unleash the aroma and set peoples' appetites stirring. Keep the pot covered for second helpings. Store leftovers, if you like, directly in the pot, but be sure to bring the pot to room temperature before reheating.

"Little Dishes": Nuts, Relishes, & Appetite Arousers

小碟子

◆

◆

"Little Dishes" are the beginning, the grand and delightful overture, to a traditional Hunanese meal. They are little plates of goodies—nuts, relishes, pickles—meant to stimulate the appetite and arouse every taste bud to happy anticipation of the meal ahead. Like overtures of a musical sort, they should present a medley of colors and textures and rouse the eaters to a pleasurable attention. The Chinese character for "little dishes" looks much like the character for "butterflies," and the right assortment of "Little Dishes" is indeed much like a field of butterflies—lively, glimmering with color, and a lighthearted thing.

I was taught many of these "Little Dishes" by my old and foodwise Hunanese mentor, James Lo, who often chided me that in Hunan such recipes were guarded as family secrets and never divulged to a daughter lest she marry outside the family and tell them to her mother-in-law. I remained safely single, so Mr. Lo divulged more. Whenever I would stop by, at mealtime or in between, I would be presented with the latest of his experiments—a chopstick full of this pickle, that nut, or those vegetables from the Lo's garden—each pulled from its own special bowl or jar, until I had a string of dishes before me of wonderfully different and delectable tidbits. They were, for me, a gastronomic playground, and I would nibble away completely content.

I have adopted the Hunanese habit as my own and rarely offer a meal to guests without at least two or three of these treats as starters. The Hunanese fashion is to present a kaleidoscopic array of about as many little dishes as there are eaters, but I find that a small number chosen with an eye to contrasting color and texture and presented on appealing little plates does the perfect job of inciting curiosity, inspiring conversation, and chasing the pre-dinner wine or Champagne down every welcoming throat.

| **Fire-Dried Walnuts or Pecans**
羅家核桃 | It was my literary friend and mentor, James Lo, who first delighted me with these walnuts, and I have been delighting people with them—and their pecan cousins—ever since. These nuts have a beguiling texture and an irresistible gloss of caramelized salt and sugar that make them almost universal favorites. ◆ These are not the heavily candied walnuts one finds in Hunanese restaurants. Rather, they are refined, elegant sweetmeats, just perfect for greeting guests. |

You may soak and dry the nuts days in advance, but to serve them warm and freshly caramelized is the ultimate seduction.

TECHNIQUE NOTES:
Soaking the walnuts or pecans in boiling water removes much of their natural bitterness. (Taste the soaking liquid to experience it first-hand!) More important, it gives them, once they are dry, a marvelously rich, plush texture that cannot be had otherwise.

If you are shelling your own walnuts and want perfect, unbroken halves, use a hammer and aim at the *smooth* side of the shell. This goes against instinct but conforms to walnut anatomy.

I like to buy walnuts already shelled so I can see that they are plump, and prefer buying them in a health-food or specialty store where the turnover is quick and I can taste what I am buying. If you are not permitted to taste a sample then insist on smelling the nuts. One good whiff will tell you if they are fresh and sweet or stale and rancid. To store all nuts and prevent their oil content from turning rancid, bag them airtight in plastic and keep them in the freezer.

Yields about 2 cups nuts, enough to serve 10–15 as a light munch preceding or during a meal.

INGREDIENTS:

> *½ pound (2 cups) plump and perfect walnut or pecan halves*
> *2 teaspoons fresh corn or peanut oil*
> *½ teaspoon coarse kosher salt*
> *2 tablespoons sugar*

Soaking and drying the nuts:
Put the nuts in a heatproof bowl. Cover with boiling water, then soak for 30 minutes. Drain, pat dry, then spread evenly on a large jelly-roll pan or baking pan lined with a triple thickness of paper towels. If you are doing a double or triple recipe, arrange the nuts on two pans.

Dry 30 minutes in the middle section of a preheated 300° oven. Turn the tray, reduce the heat to 250°, then check at 10-minute intervals and remove the nuts from the oven when they are almost entirely dry, with just a kernel of moistness at the core. Test nuts from several spots on the tray to be sure. If you are not proceeding immediately to caramelize them, put the nuts in a shallow bowl to cool, stirring occasionally. Once cool, the nuts may be bagged airtight and kept for 2 days before continuing.

Caramelizing the nuts:
Heat a wok or heavy skillet over moderate heat until hot. Add the oil, swirl to coat, then add the nuts. Stir gently with a wooden spoon or wooden spatula until they are evenly glossed with oil and feel warm to the touch. Lower the heat immediately if the nuts begin to scorch.

Sprinkle the salt over the nuts, stir gently to mix, then slowly sprinkle in the sugar, a tablespoon at a time, until you have a sweetness to suit you. The taste should be lively and sweet, with a hint of salt. Stir constantly while adding the sugar, and break off any caramelized bits that cling to the spoon, stirring them back into the nuts when you are done. The whole process will take about 3–4 minutes, and the salt and sugar will melt and adhere to the nuts.

Serve the nuts hot or cool, either as an hors d'oeuvre or as a pleasantly sweet diversion during a meal, piled in a bowl with the prettiest pieces on top.

Cooled nuts may be bottled airtight and stored in a cool place for up to 2 weeks.

MENU SUGGESTIONS:
I usually reserve these nuts for a more elegant meal, when the mood is special and the flavors of the other foods are refined rather than bold and spicy. They are excellent on their own, or make a pretty trio served alongside *Cold-Tossed Celery in Garlic Vinaigrette* (page 116) and *Soy-Dipped Red Radish Fans* (page 114). Do not serve them when a nut coating or a nutty sauce will follow. To pair them with a wine, try a California white wine or Champagne.

<table>
<tr><td>

Mongolian Fried Peanuts

油炸花生

</td><td>

While some Chinese archaeologists have identified entombed morsels as peanuts, it is the general consensus that peanuts were introduced to China in the mid-sixteenth century, relatively late in her culinary history. Whatever their antiquity, it is a sure fact that the humble peanut became wildly popular among Chinese, as much so as that other New World import, tobacco.

</td></tr>
</table>

♦ North Chinese, in particular, have a penchant for peanuts. Boiled in seasoned water and sometimes roasted, they typically appear at the beginning of a meal, alongside a plate of pickled cucumbers and one of cold noodles. ♦ This is my favorite peanut dish, learned from a broad-faced Mongolian cook. It is very simple to prepare and utterly addictive. If you are a calorie-counter, eat them roasted. If you couldn't care, bring them to full glory by frying. Small Valencia peanuts are especially good in this dish, but any red-skinned peanut will do.

TECHNIQUE NOTES:
To achieve the perfect balance of crunchy texture and full flavor, it is essential not to overcook the nuts, either in the oven or in the oil. They should be dry, but with a kernel of moistness at the core; crisp, but not hard.

Makes 1½ cups peanuts, enough to serve 10–15 as a light munch preceding a meal.

INGREDIENTS:

>   *½ pound (1½ cups) raw, red-skinned peanuts*
>
>   *To infuse the peanuts:*
>   *1 heaping tablespoon Szechwan brown peppercorns*
>   *1 heaping tablespoon star anise*
>   *1 heaping tablespoon coarse kosher salt*
>   *⅛ teaspoon sugar*
>   *2½ cups water*
>
>   *3–4 cups fresh corn or peanut oil, or oil for deep-frying nuts (page 84)*
>   *coarse kosher salt to taste*

Seasoning the nuts:
Discard any rotten or blemished nuts. Combine the peppercorns, anise, salt, sugar, and water in a medium-size saucepan. Bring to a boil over high heat, stir, then reduce the heat to maintain a steady simmer. Cover the pot tightly, simmer 5 minutes, then add the peanuts. Stir to combine, replace the cover, then cook 5 minutes more. Turn off the heat and let the peanuts steep in the covered pot for 10–12 hours.

Roasting the nuts:
Drain the nuts in a colander (do not run them under water), then pat dry with paper towels. Spread the nuts evenly in a large jelly-roll pan or baking pan lined with a triple

thickness of paper towels, and discard the anise. If you are making a double or triple batch, spread the nuts on 2 trays. Bake in the middle section of a preheated 350° oven for 30 minutes, shaking the tray occasionally to redistribute the nuts. Rotate the tray, reduce the heat to 300°, then check at 10–15-minute intervals until the nuts are almost entirely dry, with a touch of moistness at the core. Taste-test peanuts from different parts of the tray to be sure.

Remove the nuts from the oven, and put them in a shallow bowl to cool. Stir occasionally, and discard the peppercorns when they are cool enough to be removed with your fingers.

The nuts can be fried immediately, or left overnight. If you like them roasted, eat them now while warm.

Frying the nuts:
Have ready a tray lined with a double thickness of paper towels, a Chinese mesh spoon or metal strainer, a large, absorbent brown paper bag, and about ½ teaspoon coarse kosher salt.

Heat a wok or deep, heavy skillet over moderate heat until hot. Add the oil and heat to the slow-fry stage, 275° on a deep-fry thermometer. Reduce the heat to low, then add the peanuts to the oil. They will hardly bubble. Fry 4–7 minutes, depending on the size of the nuts, until they turn golden. Stir constantly and slowly while frying. Do not allow the oil temperature to rise. And do not let the nuts brown. They will continue to cook from their own heat after leaving the oil.

Scoop the nuts from the oil with the spoon or strainer, hold them briefly above the oil to drain, then spread them on the towel-lined tray. Shake the tray to blot up excess oil, then pour the nuts into the paper bag. Close the bag, gently turn and shake it to blot up the last oil, then add salt to taste and gently shake the bag again to distribute the salt. The nuts will stay warm for a while in the bag, if you wish to hold them briefly.

Eat the peanuts immediately or when cool, as an hors d'oeuvre, or placed in small bowls on the table as a diversion during a meal.

Once cool, the nuts will keep for 2 weeks, stored in an airtight jar.

MENU SUGGESTIONS:
These are ideal openers for an informal meal of cold foods. I often serve them alongside *Sweet and Tangy Cucumber Pickles* (page 110) or *Hot and Sour Chinese Cabbage Hearts* (page 112) to precede or accompany a meal of noodles or dumplings. Their rustic character makes them wonderful for munching with beer.

Maltose-Glazed Cashews

糖酥腰果

This is an extremely pretty and appealing Cantonese dish of lightly sweet, crystalline cashews—"nuts with waists," as they are called in Chinese. The glaze is made with maltose, the same subtle, golden sweetener that characterizes the skins of Peking and Cantonese ducks. When it hardens, the nuts are like jewels. ◆ Maltose is readily available in Chinese markets. If you cannot get it, substitute the variety of malt syrup sold in health-food stores or a mild-flavored honey. The results will not be as special but are still very good. ◆ Whole blanched almonds are also excellent done this way. They will brown more quickly than the cashews, in about 3 minutes.

TECHNIQUE NOTES:
Maltose is cantankerously stiff and sticky. To pry it loose, dip a sturdy metal spoon in

boiling water until hot, then scoop quickly into the maltose.

For choosing and storing raw nuts, see TECHNIQUE NOTES, page 105.

Yields about 1⅔ cups nuts, enough to serve 10–15 as a diversionary nibble before or during a meal.

INGREDIENTS:

> ¾ cup water
> 3 tablespoons sugar
> 2 tablespoons maltose (page 553)
> ½ pound (1⅔ cups) raw whole cashews
> 3 cups fresh corn or peanut oil, or oil for deep-frying nuts (page 84)

Caramelizing the nuts:
Combine the water, sugar, and maltose in a small, heavy saucepan. Bring to a boil over moderately high heat, stirring to dissolve the sweeteners. Boil undisturbed for 1 minute. Add the nuts, swirl the pan to coat them, then reduce the heat to maintain a steady simmer. Simmer 6–7 minutes, swirling the pan occasionally to coat the nuts, until there are only 2 tablespoons syrup left in the pan.

Frying the nuts:
While the nuts are cooking, heat a wok or deep, heavy skillet over high heat until hot. Add the oil and heat to the slow-fry stage, 275° on a deep-fry thermometer. Adjust the heat so the temperature doesn't rise. Have an unlined jelly-roll pan or baking pan and a pair of chopsticks or two wooden spoons within reach.

Once the nuts are done, scoop them from the syrup with a Chinese mesh spoon or drain them in a fine-mesh strainer or metal colander. (Save the remaining caramel, if you like, for glazing ham or poultry.) Add the nuts to the heated oil. They will barely bubble. Fry for about 8 minutes, stirring constantly, until the cashews turn a deep golden brown.

Scoop the nuts at once from the oil with a Chinese mesh spoon or metal strainer, deposit them in the unlined pan, and separate them immediately with the chopsticks or the handles of the wooden spoons. While the nuts are warm, they stick to each other like glue. Once cool, they harden like glass.

When the nuts are fully cool and crisp, blot them with paper towels to absorb the excess oil. If you are not serving them immediately, store them in a cool dry place to keep them crisp.

The cashews are best freshly made. Leftovers may be refrigerated in a dry, air-tight jar.

MENU SUGGESTIONS:
The cashews are lovely on their own, or partnered with *Sweet and Crunchy Red Bell Pepper Cubes* (page 115) and *Cold-Tossed Celery in Garlic Vinaigrette* (page 116) for an assortment of "Little Dishes." The taste of maltose is a nice complement to poultry, so think of them when the menu features chicken or duck. These nuts are also lovely with a dry sherry, at any time of day or night.

**Sweet
and Tangy
Cucumber
Pickles**

糖醋小黄瓜

This is a bright and crunchy Hunanese pickle, full of tart sweetness and full of fire. Its celadon gleam and brisk crispness will enliven a whole array of foods, from cold Chinese noodles to leftover roasts to a hamburger freshly sizzling from the grill. ◆ Choose absolutely firm cukes, solid feeling from tip to tip. I prefer the common, seeded sort for this condiment, though you may also use the smaller variety of Kirby pickling cucumber. ◆ For garlic lovers, you may add a touch of garlic. In that case, reduce the sugar as directed to highlight the garlic bite. ◆ Unlike what we are accustomed to calling "pickles" in the West, these Hunanese nibbles require no lengthy cooking or curing. Salt the cukes before going to bed, take 5 minutes to cook them the next morning, then they are ready to eat that night. The process is completely unintimidating, and the results are delicious.

TECHNIQUE NOTES:
Salt, as it is used here, is a firming agent. Salting a vegetable leaches water from the tissues and strengthens the cellular structure, making the vegetable crisp and crunchy. Fine table salt typically contains iodine and anti-caking agents, including sugar, which can cause discoloration and leave an acrid taste behind. When salting vegetables or meats for Chinese cooking, use only coarse kosher salt, which is a pure salt without additives and has a uniquely mild, unobtrusive taste.

The role of sugar in classic Chinese cooking (desserts excepted) is usually that of a flavor enhancer rather than an overt sweetener. Its job is to call forth the "fresh" (hsyen) qualities inherent in foods and to accentuate the character of other spices. In this pickle, the sugar enlarges the hotness of the chili and dramatizes the tang of the vinegar. Without the sugar, the pickle tastes flat.

To strip a cucumber quickly of its peel, use a spatula-type cheese slicer. It cuts the peeling time in half.

Yields 1 cup, enough to serve 6–8 as a crunchy nibble.

INGREDIENTS:

> *1½ pounds very firm cucumbers with seeds (to yield ¾ pound peeled and seeded), or ¾ pound seedless cucumbers*
> *1 teaspoon coarse kosher salt*
>
> *For stir-frying the pickle:*
> *2½ teaspoons corn or peanut oil*
> *⅛ teaspoon dried red chili flakes*
> *1 teaspoon finely chopped fresh garlic (optional)*
> *1 tablespoon thin (regular) soy sauce*
> *2–3 tablespoons sugar (for garlic pickles), or 4–6 tablespoons sugar (for pickles made without garlic)*
> *1 scant tablespoon cider vinegar*

Cutting and salting the cucumbers:
Trim the ends off the cucumbers, and peel the cucumbers if waxed.

If they need seeding, cut the cucumbers in half lengthwise, then cut each half crosswise into even segments about 2½ inches long. Remove the seeds using a teaspoon or tablespoon whose bowl matches the contour of the seed bed, cradling the cucumber in one hand while scooping the seeds out with the other. Then, turn the spoon upside-down, and scrape out any pulpy ribs or watery flesh. The watery pulp must be removed if the pickles are to be crunchy. Cut the seeded cucumber "boats" lengthwise into thin strips ¼ inch wide.

If you are using seedless cucumbers, cut them lengthwise into long, thin spears ¼ inch wide, then cut crosswise into strips 2–2½ inches long.

Put the cut cucumbers in a glass or stainless bowl. Toss well with the salt to mix, then seal and let stand at room temperature 6 hours or overnight, tossing occasionally. If you wish to hold them a bit longer, refrigerate after several hours to retard the salting process.

Squeezing the cukes and stir-frying the pickle:
Drain the salting liquids. Gently press the excess water from the cucumbers by clasping them a handful at a time between your palms. Press firmly; do not wring. The vegetable should still be moist and firm when you are done.

Have the cucumbers and the stir-frying ingredients all within easy reach of your stovetop.

Heat a wok or heavy skillet over high heat until hot enough to evaporate a bead of water on contact. Add the oil, swirl to coat the pan, then reduce the heat to medium-low and add a chili flake or two. When the pepper begins to sizzle, add the remaining pepper (and the garlic), and adjust the heat so it sizzles gently without scorching. If the chili burns, wipe the pan clean and begin anew. When the mixture is aromatic, in 3–6 seconds, add the cucumbers and toss briskly to glaze, adjusting the heat to maintain a lively sizzle. When the cukes are evenly glossed, in about 30 seconds, add the soy, sugar, and vinegar, then stir until the sugar is dissolved and the liquids are steaming. Taste for desired sweetness and adjust if required. The sauce should sparkle with a zesty hotness, though expect it to grow spicier as it sits. Raise the heat for about 15 seconds to bring the liquids to a boil, then scrape the mixture immediately into a glass or stainless bowl.

Press the cucumbers gently under the liquid, then let them sit at room temperature until cool, stirring occasionally. For best flavor, chill several hours or overnight before serving.

Serve the cucumbers chilled or at room temperature in a bowl of contrasting color or in individual dip dishes alongside each plate. Dribble a bit of the juices on top to gloss the pickles and give them some extra, sweet fire.

Store refrigerated in an immaculately clean glass jar with a tight-fitting lid. The pickles keep nicely 1–2 weeks and will grow in hotness over the first 2–3 days.

MENU SUGGESTIONS:
The bright taste of these pickles makes them a good preliminary to a meal of spicy and smoked foods, like *Orchid's Tangy Cool Noodles* (page 356) and *Tea and Spice Smoked Chicken* (page 158). They are also perfect with steamed or baked buns, and with dumplings. Serve them on their own, or as part of a trio including *Hot and Sour Chinese Cabbage Hearts* (page 112) and *Soy-Dipped Red Radish Fans* (page 114). With hamburgers, they're splendid.

Hot and Sour Chinese Cabbage Hearts

酸辣白菜心

Recipes abound for the chilled and tangy white cabbage pickle that northern Chinese so enjoy, the Chinese relative of the well-known Korean *kim-chee*. This one is unique for using only the very crisp ribs and core of the cabbage. Its distinctive taste comes from the combination of numbing Szechwan peppercorns and spicy fresh ginger, and its unusual texture is a result of the way the cabbage is cut. ◆ Choose the variety of Chinese cabbage that is entirely light white-green in color, with evenly broad leaves wrapped tightly around one another (page 536). Pick a head for the same qualities by which you would judge good lettuce—firm, densely packed leaves, and an overall moist, fresh appearance. Don't worry if there are only giant heads available. The outer leaves will keep for 2 weeks or more, sealed airtight in a plastic bag and refrigerated, and can be put to delicious use in *Spicy Buddha's Feast* (page 299), *Stir-Fried Chinese Cabbage with Sweet Sausage* (page 309), and *Baby Lion's Head Casserole* (page 209). ◆ Pickle-type dishes like this are a boon when you are expecting company. You can salt the cabbage overnight, cook it within minutes the next day, then let it chill in the refrigerator for a full day before eating.

TECHNIQUE NOTES:
Curious though it may seem, this sort of Chinese cabbage comes in "male" and "female" forms. It is not visible from the outside, but you will see it as soon as you cut off the base. If the cabbage is a "male," the base will be a single large disk comprised of tightly overlapping pieces of cabbage. If it is a "female," then the base will be a central disk surrounded by several smaller ones. At the core of the "male" is a single miniature cabbage. At the heart of the "female" is a whole family of tiny cabbages decked around a central core. (Who imitates whom, I wonder?)

Cut the bases of the "male" into pie-shaped wedges, ¼–½ inch wide. They will spread a bit, like fans. With your knife held parallel to the board, cut the "female" bases into thin coins ⅛ inch thick. Leave the coins joined where possible to form cloud-like clusters. Leave the tiny cabbages uncut. With this little bit of attention, the mundane cabbage becomes special, intriguing to the eye and interesting on the tongue.

For the alchemy of salting vegetables to crisp them, see TECHNIQUE NOTES, page 110.

Yields about 1½ cups, enough to serve 8–10 with an assortment of cold dishes.

INGREDIENTS:

> *1½–2 pounds Chinese cabbage (to yield ¾ pound heart and ribs)*
> *1½ teaspoons coarse kosher salt*
>
> *For stir-frying the cabbage:*
> *1 tablespoon corn or peanut oil*
> *¼ teaspoon Szechwan brown peppercorns*
> *2 teaspoons finely minced fresh ginger*
> *¼ teaspoon dried red chili flakes*
> *1½ teaspoons thin (regular) soy sauce*
> *2–3 tablespoons sugar*
> *1½ teaspoons cider vinegar*

Cutting and salting the cabbage:

Cut a thin slice off the very bottom of the cabbage, so that the base is clean and white. Discard this first slice and any wilted leaves. Make your next slice ½–¾ inch farther up the base, reserving the thick disk and arranging the freed leaves in a neat pile. Continue slicing off a thick base disk and stacking the leaves until you reach the cabbage core or heart.

Cut the heart into 1-inch pieces. Leave any tiny cabbages intact. Cut the base disks into wedges or coins, as described in TECHNIQUE NOTES above. Starting with the innermost leaves, trim away any flaccid edges and cut the crisp white ribs crosswise into bands a scant 1 inch thick and 1½–2 inches long. Cut until you have ¾ pound base, heart, and rib pieces. Bag the outer leaves and trim for use in other dishes.

Put the cut cabbage in a glass or stainless bowl. Sprinkle with salt, toss well to mix, then cover and let stand 6 hours or overnight at room temperature, tossing occasionally. If you wish to hold the cabbage a bit longer before cooking, refrigerate after several hours to retard the salting process.

Squeezing and stir-frying the cabbage:

Drain the salting liquid, then rinse the cabbage briefly with cold water. Squeeze the cabbage gently between clasped palms, a handful at a time, to remove excess water. Press; do not wring. The cabbage should still be firm and moist when you are done. Put the cabbage and the stir-frying ingredients within reach of your stovetop.

Heat a wok or large, heavy skillet over high heat until hot enough to evaporate a bead of water on contact. Add the oil, swirl to coat, then reduce the heat to low and add 1 peppercorn to the pan. When it begins to sizzle, add the remaining peppercorns, the ginger, and chili flakes, adjusting the heat so they sizzle without scorching. (If they burn, wipe the pan clean and begin again with fresh ingredients.) Stir the mixture until fully fragrant, about 10 seconds, then add the cabbage to the pan and stir briskly to combine, fluffing the cabbage to separate it as you stir. Add the soy, sugar, and vinegar, and stir until the mixture is blended and the liquids are hot, 1–2 minutes. Taste the liquid for the desired blend of sweet and spicy, adjust if necessary, then scrape the mixture into a glass or stainless bowl. Let cool, stirring occasionally.

For best flavor, chill 24 hours before serving. Serve well chilled, in a shallow bowl of contrasting color to show off the pretty white-gold of the cabbage or in individual dip dishes alongside each place setting. Gloss the cabbage with a bit of juice, and arrange a peppercorn or several chili flakes on top as an accent.

The cabbage keeps well, tightly sealed and refrigerated in an immaculately clean jar, for about one week. Flavor peaks in spiciness on the second day.

MENU SUGGESTIONS:

These pickled cabbage hearts go equally well with informal and formal foods. They are wonderful accompaniments to cold dishes such as *The Five Heaps* (page 361) and *Bong-Bong Chicken* (page 133), and are also good with hot dishes like *Velvet Pork Pie with Szechwan Pickle* (page 189) and *Golden Egg Dumplings* (page 328). I frequently serve them as a trio with *Fire-Dried Walnuts or Pecans* (page 105) and *Soy-Dipped Red Radish Fans* (page 114).

Soy-
Dipped
Red
Radish Fans

涼拌紅蘿蔔

This is the Chinese version of our radish "roses," a delicate fan of crisp radish that unfolds in a zestily flavored sauce rather than in ice water. Beautiful looking and delicious, they are excellent as an edible garnish, a wine-chaser hors d'oeuvre, or a crunchy, colorful addition to any meal. ◆ The best radishes are those sold with their green, leafy tops intact. Choose them fat, firm, and unblemished, and store in a misted plastic bag until ready to use. ◆ Radish fans are best made 8–24 hours in advance, though if you're in a hurry you may use light brown sugar to season them instead of white. That quickens the marinating process somehow, though the radishes then become quite strong the next day.

TECHNIQUE NOTES:
For a fast, foolproof method of cutting fans, put a pair of wooden chopsticks flat on a cutting surface, then place a radish between the thinner (round) ends. (Most Chinese chopsticks have one round and one square end, emblematic, some say, of heaven and earth.) Pinch the thick ends of the chopsticks together, as illustrated, so the radish is held in the V-shaped wedge. Put your hand on top, simultaneously anchoring the chopsticks and grasping the radish, then cut the radish as directed. The chopsticks will prevent the knife from slicing through the fans—an altogether neat trick.

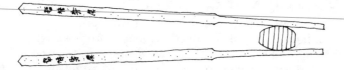

For "salting" a vegetable with salt and sugar, see TECHNIQUE NOTES, page 117.

Serves 2–3 as a nice munch, 4–6 as a smaller nibble.

INGREDIENTS:

> *1 dozen large, pretty red radishes*

> *Salting ingredients:*
> *½ teaspoon coarse kosher salt*
> *½ teaspoon sugar*

> *Seasonings:*
> *2 teaspoons thin (regular) soy sauce*
> *3–4 teaspoons brown or white sugar, to taste*
> *¼ teaspoon Chinese or Japanese sesame oil*
> *⅛–¼ teaspoon hot chili oil*

Slicing and salting the radishes:
Trim the root and stem ends of each radish neatly, so that any green is cut away and the two ends are stark white. (If the radishes aren't perfectly fresh and hard, plump them for several hours or overnight in the refrigerator in a bowl of cold water.)
To cut the radishes into fans, hold the radish clamped between a pair of chopsticks as described above in TECHNIQUE NOTES. With a sharp, thin-bladed knife make a series of cuts 1/16 inch apart across the width of the radish, cutting down to the chop-

sticks, until the top is cut like a fan. (If your fingers get in the way when you near the end, turn the radish around and complete the cuts.)

Toss the radishes in a glass or stainless bowl with the salt and sugar, then put aside for 45 minutes at room temperature, tossing occasionally.

Seasoning the fans:
Whisk the seasonings until blended and slightly thick, tasting for desired sweetness. Put aside to develop for 10 minutes.

Drain the radishes, then squeeze several at a time between your palms to extract excess liquid. Press; do not wring. Put the radishes in a clean dry bowl, then scrape the seasonings on top and toss well to mix. For best flavor, marinate 5–6 hours at room temperature or overnight in the refrigerator, to give the seasonings time to penetrate and enlarge. Toss occasionally while marinating, or place the radishes fan side down in the liquid for even absorption.

Serve chilled. Press gently with your fingers to spread the fans, and present them on a plate or in a bowl of contrasting color, with a bit of the sauce drizzled on top.

The radishes keep 2–3 days, sealed and refrigerated, and grow a bit stronger if you store them in the sauce.

MENU SUGGESTIONS:
The crunch and color of the radish fans make them a perfect garnish for dishes like *Orchid's Tangy Cool Noodles* (page 356), *Master Sauce Chicken* (page 153), *Tea and Spice Smoked Chicken* (page 158), and *Tea and Spice Smoked Fish* (page 256), or any of the mildly spiced cold noodle dishes. For picnics, they are ideal tote-alongs with *Marbelized Tea Eggs* (page 325) or *Master Sauce Eggs* (page 327). As openers for a meal, I like the radishes with a chilled, dry white wine, either alone or in tandem with *Fire-Dried Walnuts or Pecans* (page 105). Try them also with vodka or gin-based drinks—a good Martini or an ice-cold glass of vodka.

Sweet and Crunchy Red Bell Pepper Cubes
糖醋紅椒

This is a simple, crunchy "pickle" of bell pepper cubes marinated in a light dressing of soy sauce, sugar, and rice vinegar. Its bright color and clean, fresh taste would make it a welcome addition to a barbecue, a simple dinner, or a Chinese feast starring a constellation of "Little Dishes." I much prefer red to green bell pepper, but you may do this dish with either, or even mix the two, if you wish. ◆ This dish is a good discovery if you like or need to cook ahead. The peppers require 2 full days to reach their flavor peak, so you can stash them in the refrigerator and forget about them until it's time to eat.

TECHNIQUE NOTES:
When shopping for bell peppers, look for ones with vivid color, unbroken skin, and a uniform firmness. When cutting them, take care to remove any fleshy white ribs with a sharp paring knife. If the peppers are firm and the ribs are carefully removed, you are assured of a crunchy pickle.

For the use of coarse kosher salt to transform vegetables to a special crispness, see TECHNIQUE NOTES, page 110.

Yields 2 cups pepper cubes, enough to serve 4–8 as a cold dish, 10–15 as a cold nibble with a host of other dishes.

INGREDIENTS:

> ¾ pound firm, unblemished red bell peppers
> 1 teaspoon coarse kosher salt

Seasonings:
> 2 teaspoons thin (regular) soy sauce
> 2 teaspoons unseasoned Chinese or Japanese rice vinegar
> 1 tablespoon sugar

Cutting and salting the peppers:
Wash and carefully dry the peppers. Cut each pepper lengthwise into fourths, then remove the cores, seeds, and ribs. Use a sharp paring knife to trim the area around the stem so that the fruit is uniformly red. Cut into ¾-inch cubes.

Put the pepper cubes into a clean glass or stainless bowl. Sprinkle with salt, toss well to mix, then cover and let stand at room temperature 6 hours or overnight. Stir occasionally to redistribute the cubes in the liquid.

Marinating the peppers:
Combine the soy, vinegar, and sugar, stirring well to dissolve the sugar. Drain the peppers thoroughly (do not rinse or press them), then place in a dry bowl or in an immaculately clean glass jar with a tight-fitting lid. Scrape the seasonings on top, toss well to mix, then let the peppers stand 1–3 hours at room temperature. At least once an hour, stir the peppers or rotate the jar to redistribute the seasonings.

Refrigerate 2 full days, stirring occasionally. The peppers will then be at peak flavor and ready to eat.

Serve the peppers chilled, heaped prettily in a bowl of contrasting color, or in small dip dishes alongside each plate. Just before serving, top with some of the seasoning liquids to give them a nice sheen.

The peppers will retain their flavor and texture upwards of a week, refrigerated and sealed airtight.

MENU SUGGESTIONS:
I typically serve the pepper cubes alongside one of the green "Little Dishes," such as *Sweet and Tangy Cucumber Pickles* (page 110) or *Cold-Tossed Celery in Garlic Vinaigrette* (page 116). When there's time, complete the trio with *Maltose-Glazed Cashews* (page 108). Alone, try the peppers with *Stir-Fried Beef with Silky Leeks* (page 214), or *Beef and Broccoli on a Bird's Nest* (page 219).

**Cold-Tossed
Celery in
Garlic
Vinaigrette**

凉拌芹菜

If you have stared helplessly in Chinese restaurants at dishes loaded with forlorn, economic squiggles of stir-fried celery, then here is a dish to restore your confidence in *real* Chinese cooking. It is a crunchy, lightly spiced "pickle," as much at home at a Western barbecue as on a Hunan table. For celery-haters like myself, it is a revelation. ♦ Buy only pale green-white celery, with smooth, full ribs, fresh tips, and delicate, tender leaves. If you have other uses for celery, purchase two heads and use only the hearts and innermost ribs for the pickle. For best flavor, make the pickle 4–6 hours in advance. Like all "Little Dishes," this one requires little work and is delightfully light and novel.

TECHNIQUE NOTES:

Instead of using coarse kosher salt alone, it is a good idea to salt acrid vegetables like celery and radishes with a mixture of salt and sugar. The sugar eliminates any bitterness and leaves no taste of its own behind. For the alchemy of salting vegetables, see TECHNIQUE NOTES, page 110.

Yields 3 cups, enough to serve 6 as a crunchy addition to a cold meal, 8–10 as part of an assortment of "Little Dishes."

INGREDIENTS:

> 2 pounds young, firm celery, lighter rather than darker green (to yield 1 pound after trimming or 5 cups raw celery fingers)

Salting ingredients:
> 1 teaspoon coarse kosher salt
> ½ teaspoon sugar

Seasonings:
> 1 tablespoon plus 2 teaspoons thin (regular) soy sauce
> 2 tablespoons sugar
> 2 tablespoons Chinese or Japanese sesame oil
> 1½ teaspoons unseasoned Chinese or Japanese rice vinegar
> ¼–½ teaspoon hot chili oil
> 1–1½ teaspoons freshly minced garlic

Cutting and salting the celery:

Cut off the base of the celery, then wash and dry the individual stalks. Use only the tender inner stalks which are pale white-green. On the larger ribs, cut off the flared bottom and the tough band where the main stalk joins the leafy upper crown. If the crown has a nice central stalk and pretty, tender leaves, then trim the end of the stalk and cut it where it joins the leaves, to yield a finger-size stalk and 2 leafy branches. The smaller, innermost stalks will not need trimming; simply divide the leafy crown from the base.

String the outside of the larger ribs by catching the strings at the end of the rib with your knife and pulling up to release them. (As a double check, repeat the process from the other end.) The tender innermost ribs will not need stringing.

Cut the stalks into 2½-inch lengths, then cut lengthwise into pinky-size strips ⅜ inch wide. Put the celery fingers and leaf clusters in a glass or stainless bowl, then toss with the salt and sugar. Let stand at room temperature for 40 minutes, tossing occasionally.

Seasoning the celery:

Whisk the seasonings by hand until the sugar dissolves and the mixture thickens slightly, then put aside to develop for 10 minutes.

Drain the celery, rinse with cool water, then spread on a lint-free towel and pat dry. Put the celery in a clean dry bowl, and scrape the seasonings on top. Toss well, seal, and marinate at room temperature 1–2 hours, or refrigerate 3–4 hours for best flavor. Toss frequently while marinating to distribute the seasonings.

Serve slightly chilled, in a shallow bowl or in individual dip dishes alongside each place setting. Dribble a bit of the vinaigrette on top, and unfold several of the leaf clusters for a pretty presentation.

The celery is at its crunchy best within hours of marinating. Any leftovers may be drained and refrigerated. They will be limp, but still tasty, the next 1–2 days.

MENU SUGGESTIONS:
This pickle has a certain elegance, and I like to serve it with pretty, refined dishes like *Pearl Balls* (page 187), *Smoked Tea Duck* (page 169), or *Steamed Whole Fish with Seared Scallions* (page 248). It is particularly nice paired with *Soy-Dipped Red Radish Fans* (page 114), and will accompany anything from steak to pasta tossed with fresh herbs and oil.

Mongolian Stewed Garlic

紅燒蒜頭

This is a condiment for garlic lovers and sensualists only!—a glossy, gem-like heap of individual garlic cloves, turned creamy and mahogany brown by a rich stewing sauce. It was inspired by tales of a dish eaten by a friend in the home of a princely Mongolian living in Taiwan. ◆ To make it, you will need very fresh, hard garlic of the more delicate rose-hued variety, and a light, unsalted stock that can be made easily at home from chicken bones (page 446). Otherwise use water, and, if the garlic is old or green at the core, don't do the dish at all. Tinned stock and bad garlic give medicinal results. ◆ This is a no-hands, no-work bit of cooking. The garlic stews on its own for hours and will keep for a week or more.

TECHNIQUE NOTES:
Cooking unpeeled garlic over long slow heat works a miracle of transformation. The normally hot-tasting garlic becomes sweet and creamy smooth. The heat must be very gentle for the magic to occur. Medium or high heat will turn the garlic bitter.

Yields 1 cup richly seasoned garlic, enough to serve 8–16 as a condiment to highlight other foods.

INGREDIENTS:

> 4–5 very large, rock-hard heads of garlic, with huge cloves and a rose-hued skin, or enough smaller heads to yield 45–50 fat, firm cloves (do not use "elephant" garlic)
> 2½ tablespoons black soy sauce
> 3 tablespoons Chinese rice wine or quality, dry sherry
> ½ cup light, unsalted chicken stock or water
> 2–3 tablespoons finely crushed golden rock sugar (page 570)

Preparing the garlic:
With your fingers, carefully pull apart the heads of garlic, separating the individual cloves from the rooty base. Remove most of the papery, white outer peel, leaving intact and unbroken the thicker, rose-hued skin which encases each clove. Do not use any cloves that are soft, bruised, or half-peeled.

Stewing the cloves:
Combine the soy, wine, and stock in a Chinese sand pot or a small, heavy pot that will hold the garlic snugly. Bring the liquids to a steaming, near-simmer over low heat, then add the cloves, and stir to combine. Stew the mixture 5–10 minutes, scatter in the sugar, and stir to dissolve. Cover the pot, check after several minutes, and adjust the heat to

maintain a steamy, near-simmer with few or no bubbles. Cover and stew the garlic 3½ hours. Lift the lid occasionally to check that the liquids are not boiling, and at the same time swirl the pot to coat the cloves with sauce.

When done, remove the lid partway and let the cloves sit for 2 or more hours before eating, swirling the pot occasionally to distribute the sauce.

Serve the cloves tepid or at room temperature, in the sand pot or in a small bowl to show off their rich color, or in individual dip dishes alongside each plate. Just before serving, spoon on a bit of sauce.

To eat the garlic, crush a clove lightly against the roof of your mouth. Let the creamy pulp dissolve on your tongue, then discard the peel.

Cool, the garlic may be refrigerated for a week or more in an airtight glass jar. Rotate the jar occasionally to distribute the sauce. Leftover sauce is excellent on cold noodles, or as a garlic-tinged accompaniment for meats or dumplings.

MENU SUGGESTIONS:
To my taste, the garlic is best on its own with one or two other dishes in a simple, rustic supper. Try it with another sand-pot dish like *Mountain Stew* (page 254) and a gutsy vegetable like *Dry-Fried Szechwan String Beans* (page 297). Do not, however, pass up the chance to eat the garlic with a hunk of French bread and some tasty cheese, and a glass of good wine to wash it down.

Anise-Spiced Soybeans

醬汁黃豆

Soybeans have achieved a somewhat besmirched reputation in this country as a "health(y) food," but Chinese consider them in their whole form to be a fun food—texture-rich little nuggets to enjoy with wine or with an assortment of cold snacks. ◆ Those who like the strong taste of anise will love this dish. It is another of the Lo's "Little Dishes," a hill of cold, sauced, *al dente* soybeans that makes an unusual accompaniment to many meals. ◆ Start the soybeans 2 nights in advance for best flavor. Soaking and simmering the beans is what I call "no-hands cooking," requiring almost no time and a minimum of attention.

SHOPPING NOTES:
I buy soybeans in 1-pound plastic bags in Chinatown markets, where they are almost always picked over before packaging. If you buy them in a health-food store, look for them to be blond, clean, and round, and once home pick them over carefully and discard any damaged beans or little pebbles.

Yields 1½ cups, enough to serve 8–12 with an assortment of "Little Dishes."

INGREDIENTS:

½ *cup dried whole soybeans*

To season the beans:
1 *whole star anise (equal to 8 individual points)*
1 *tablespoon thin (regular) soy sauce*
2–3 *tablespoons sugar*

Soaking and simmering the beans:
Pick over the soybeans carefully, discarding any that are bruised, blackened, or shriveled.

Cover with 3 cups cold water and soak overnight. The beans will swell as they soak.

Discard any empty shells or beans floating on the surface, then drain the soybeans. Put them in a small, heavy pot and cover with cold water to come 2 inches above the beans. Bring to a boil, reduce the heat to maintain a steady simmer, and simmer 5 minutes.

Drain, then rinse the beans and the pot with cold water to remove any scum. Return beans to the pot and add cold water just to cover. Bring to a near-boil over high heat, reduce the heat to maintain a simmer, and add the anise, soy, and sugar to the pot. (Leave the star anise whole for a decoration when serving.) Stir to dissolve the sugar, then cook uncovered, stirring frequently, until the sauce is reduced by half and is slightly thick, 15–20 minutes. When nearly done, taste for desired sweetness and adjust if necessary to achieve a rich blend of soy, sugar, and anise flavors.

Cooling and serving the beans:
Remove the pot from the burner. Cover loosely, and swirl the pot frequently while cooling to distribute the sauce. When thoroughly cool, discard any loose shells and scrape the mixture into a clean glass jar or bowl. Seal tightly and refrigerate a full day for best flavor.

Serve at room temperature or slightly chilled, mounding the beans in a bowl of contrasting color or serving them in individual dip dishes alongside each place setting. Arrange the star or several individual points on top for color, then pour the sauce evenly over the beans. Eat with chopsticks, if you wish to test your skill, or with a small spoon if you're less patient and greedy for the sauce.

The soybeans keep 4 days, sealed and refrigerated. Flavor peaks on the second day.

MENU SUGGESTIONS:
The soybeans are shown to best advantage if juxtaposed with other "Little Dishes" of bold color and flavor, like *Soy-Dipped Red Radish Fans* (page 114) and *Sweet and Tangy Cucumber Pickles* (page 110). They are an informal munchie, best followed by noodles, dumplings, or cold dishes.

Sweet and Sour Green Tomato Pickle

甜酸青蕃茄

According to my friends and culinary mentors, the Lo's, Chinese did not see tomatoes until the 1930's. Tomatoes were used green and were valued for their refreshing tartness—that quality of *swan*, or flavorful sourness, which is one of the Five Flavors of classic Chinese cuisine. ◆ Here, in a cold pickle, the green tomatoes are delightfully crunchy and alive with vinegar. There is a whiff of garlic and just enough sweetness to offset the sour. It is a perfect dish for late summer, when the garden is brimming with tomatoes and the red ones have lost their charm. ◆ Begin 2 days in advance of serving.

TECHNIQUE NOTES:
Keeping the garlic cloves whole scents the tomatoes without giving them a strong garlic taste. Using white sugar in the initial salting eliminates the bitterness of the unripe fruit; brown sugar in the marinade gives the pickle a good depth of flavor.

Yields 2 cups.

INGREDIENTS:

> 1 pound medium-size green tomatoes (about 4)

> To salt the tomatoes:
> 1 tablespoon coarse kosher salt
> 1 teaspoon sugar

> Seasoning ingredients:
> 1 tablespoon plus 1 teaspoon cider vinegar
> 1 tablespoon plus 2 teaspoons packed light brown sugar
> 2 medium cloves garlic, stem end removed, lightly smashed and peeled

Cutting and salting the tomatoes:
Twist off the stems, then wash, dry, and shine the tomatoes. Cut each one into 8 or 9 wedges. For attractive wedges, begin by cutting the tomato in half lengthwise through the stem. Then, cut wedges always to the side of the stem mark, so that in the end only 2 or 3 wedges bear a blemish. Cut these off with a neat diagonal slice. This is prettier and easier than coring the tomatoes.

Put the wedges in a glass or stainless bowl, sprinkle with the salt and white sugar, and toss well. Cover and let sit at room temperature for 12 hours, tossing occasionally.

Marinating the pickle:
Whisk the vinegar and brown sugar to dissolve the sugar, and set aside. Drain the tomatoes, rinse briefly with cool water, then spread on a lint-free towel to blot up excess moisture. Transfer the tomatoes to an immaculately clean glass jar with a tight-fitting lid, then stir the vinegar mixture and scrape it into the jar. Add the garlic, seal the jar, and turn it to distribute the seasonings. (Don't worry if the liquids seem skimpy; they will triple after an hour.)

Put the jar on its side, and let the tomatoes marinate at room temperature for 6 hours, turning the jar occasionally to distribute the liquids. Then, refrigerate 24 hours before serving, turning the jar periodically.

Serve the wedges whole, or cut each wedge into 2 or 3 thinner wedges ¼ inch thick. Heap in a small bowl, or arrange in a pretty spiral pattern on a plate of a contrasting color and spoon a bit of juice on top.

The tomatoes will stay crunchy 4–5 days, refrigerated in the jar. Color and flavor are best on the first and second days.

MENU SUGGESTIONS:
I love this pickle served alongside *Coriandered Chicken Salad with Mustard Sauce* (page 131), *Ma-La Cold Chicken* (page 129), *Cold Duck Salad with Two Sauces* (page 164), and *Springrolls with Dijon Mustard Sauce* (page 389)—anywhere the cold tomatoes and spicy mustard sauce can work their magic together. It is also an excellent accompaniment to *Tea and Spice Smoked Fish* (page 256), an all-American grilled burger, or a salad plate of cold roast beef.

Poultry: Chicken & Duck

鷄鴨

◆

◆

Chicken or duck is the everyday king of the Chinese table, and lest I ever forget it there was always at least one clucker or quacker strutting and scratching within eye's distance or earshot when I lived in Taipei. If it wasn't the family hen, then it was the neighbor's chickens, the poultry man's ducks, or a sisterhood of chicks wiggling full tilt down some dirt alleyway after their mother. Peasants on the bus I took to school rode along with live chickens pinned between their knees, the man down the street raised Peking ducks, and Po-fu, the gourmet head of our household, kept me in tow on his regular rounds of the poultry markets looking for the plumpest black chickens—succulent birds with black skin and black bones—that would keep him young and keep me pretty (or so he always said). By the end of my years in Asia, I had a strong appreciation for the everyday grandeur of poultry in the Chinese world and had eaten of it plentifully.

My taste for poultry has only grown greater, and while the world I now live in is far from the one in which a village headman would regularly kill a chicken then cook it in honor of me and my Chinese hiking friends when we would arrive hungrily at his door, I still go as far as necessary to find and buy fresh-killed birds. On this I feel very strongly. I will drive thirty minutes out of my way to get fresh-killed poultry in a Chinatown market rather than purchase the bird that has been sitting for days wrapped in cellophane in the supermarket down the street. Tasting has taught me the difference, and I have spoiled myself. Likewise, I never buy frozen poultry and will not freeze it before cooking. Again, my taste has shown me the huge gap between a bird that is juicily fresh and one that is dry and less succulent from even a brief stay in the freezer, and so long as poultry remains my passion I refuse to do it harm.

HOW TO CHOOSE FRESH CHICKENS AND DUCKS   Whether it is a whole bird or parts, I judge fresh poultry by the moist look of the skin, the plump fullness of the flesh, and the lack of any odor. Whenever possible, I buy the whole bird with all its appendages intact, for in addition to liking to use the neck, feet, and wingtips in stock, I can better judge the healthy freshness of the bird by looking at it top to toe. Dry or bruised skin, sunken flesh, pools of bloody liquid, or clumps of ice in the cavity are my warning signs. If I see them, I don't buy the bird.

CLEANING FRESH POULTRY   If you buy a fresh-killed chicken or duck in a Chinese or other ethnic market, it will be sold to you eviscerated but with the head and feet left on. Removing the appendages, storing what's useful for stock, and cleaning the bird is a simple matter of about 5 or 10 minutes. What you'll need is a sturdy, large cutting board (I prefer the thick white plastic sort [page 29] for the thoroughness with which you can clean it), a sturdy cleaver or chef's knife with a thick blade designed for chopping through bones, and the following game plan.

First lay the chicken or duck on its back, centered on the board. Stretch out the neck, then lop it off at its base with one hearty chop. Chop off and discard the head, discard the neck skin, chop the neck into inch-long pieces, and reserve them in a plastic bag for making stock. Next pull the wing out from the body and chop off the wingtip at the V-shaped joint where it joins with the rest of the wing. Repeat with the second wing, then bag the tips with the neck pieces. (Some people like to gnaw on the wingtips, and if you are one of them by all means don't cut them off. I prefer to gnaw other parts, so I confine the wingtips to the stock bag.) Finally, remove the feet and the tail. To remove the tail, it's easiest to raise the legs by the feet—just as if you were powdering a baby's bottom—then lop off the tail with one stroke of the blade. The feet should be whacked off at the knee joint, then the feet and tail bagged for stock. (One note of caution: When you go to make stock, don't use too many feet lest the stock become gummy. About 2 feet per 3–4 pounds of bones will give you all the gelatin it needs.) At this point, stow the bag in the freezer until you have accumulated enough parts to make stock (see recipe page 446).

Now you are ready to clean the inside of the bird. While cleaning the cavity of a duck or chicken, my policy is to remove everything that will come out with a tug of my fingers. The first things to be removed are the fat sacs on either side of the tail, which are even larger in fresh chickens than in ducks, and which I save for rendering (see below). Next, unlike most Western cooks I've talked to, I remove the kidneys—the reddish, liver-textured masses that you must dig out with your fingers and/or the point of a small knife—that lie nestled above the tail on either side of the backbone. Most cooks leave the kidneys in, but it is my feeling that they are the first things to deteriorate if you must store the bird before cooking and that their presence mars the flavor of a sauce and the texture of the final dish. For most all Chinese recipes, where the bird is marinated inside as well as outside and one is meant to chew happily on the bones, I just don't want them there. After the kidneys, I remove any membranes, vessels, bloody bits, or unidentifiable oddments dangling in the cavity or clinging to the walls. I leave in most of the fatty deposits around the neck region so they can help keep the bird moist in cooking, but everything else comes out. When I am done, I want to be left looking at a cavity that is clean and white-looking down to the bones. Once I am satisfied, I flush the cavity clean with cold water.

Finally, come the refinements. I inspect the cavity for any lingering blood clots, trim the neck and tail regions of a duck of some of its overload of fat, then go over the outer skin and pluck it free of any large feather shafts that remain. A careful patting inside and out with paper towels or a clean, lint-free kitchen towel, and the bird is ready for marinating, cooking, or storing.

I also use this same interior clean-up method when working with whole chicken breasts, that is, I scrupulously remove any bloody clots or loose membranes, then rinse the breasts briefly with a flush of cold water. My philosophy is that it doesn't harm the chicken and only improves the quality of the stock or dish to which it's being added.

STORING WHOLE BIRDS OR POULTRY PARTS IN THE REFRIGERATOR There's a great trick for keeping chicken fresh for days in the refrigerator that I learned from my food authority friend, Jan Weimer. The trick is to take the whole cleaned bird or chicken breasts and wrap them in a clean, dry, lint-free kitchen towel before stowing them in a plastic bag and putting them in the refrigerator. The towel absorbs any blood or liquid that leaches from the chicken, and the chicken or duck (or squab, turkey, or whatever) stays fresh far longer than if left to sit in its own juice. It is a wonderful method, well worth the price of having to launder a kitchen towel!

BONING CHICKEN BREASTS If you value the freshness of the chicken breast you are about to eat and have fallen prey to the healthy addiction to homemade chicken soup, then you will always bone chicken breasts yourself. It takes only minutes, is a simple process to learn, and the reward is meat you know to be fresh and some tasty trimmings for the stockpot, in addition to the money saved for your few minutes' labor.

I begin with whole breasts—two individual breasts that are joined at the top by the wishbone and farther down by a V-shaped keel bone, and are covered by a single large piece of skin. The first step is to rip the skin off with one good tug and discard it. Then, I turn the breast over and tug loose and discard any bloody membranes clinging to the bony cavity formed by the breasts.

Step #2 is to put the breast on a cutting surface flesh side down and cut through the hard and dark colored top of the keel bone with the tip of a strong, sharp knife or cleaver, so that you can flatten the breast with your hands and lay it flat on the board for easy boning.

(From this point on, different cooks exhibit different styles. Here is mine—a combination of a bit of knife work and a better bit of yanking.)

Step #3 in my method is to put the flattened breast bony side down and to run a knife along the length of the keel bone to one side to sever the piece completely. At this point, I have two individual breasts, one still attached to the keel bone.

Step #4 centers on freeing the keel bone. I put the breast half with the keel bone attached bony side down, then use the knife to cut along the length of the keel bone to detach it from the meat. Once the cut is neatly made, I put the knife down and work mostly with my thumbs to slip them between the meat and the bony cage and move them about beneath the flesh to release it. When I feel that it is freed, then I just yank the meat free—carefully yet firmly—so that the main breast piece comes off with the tubular fillet still attached.

Step #5 is to bone the other breast piece in the same manner, skipping the knife work necessitated by the keel bone. Now one is left with two and possibly four pieces of breast meat: the two triangular main breast pieces and the two tubular fillets, which may or may not have come free from the breast in the course of boning. The bones all go into the plastic bag for making stock.

Step #6 is to gently separate the fillets from the main breast pieces if they are still joined, then remove and discard the white, glove-like membrane clinging in whole or part to the fillets. Discard as well any bits of membrane adhering to the breasts. Locate the tip of the thick white tendon that pokes out from the top of the fillet, then lay the fillet tendon side down on the board. Grasp the tendon tip with a dry towel, and, holding your knife on a gentle angle between the towel and the fillet and *almost* but not quite touching the board, pull on the tendon with the towel, pulling it free of the meat. The trick is to use the knife to hold the meat in place so it is not dragged along with the tendon and to *not* cut the tendon with the knife. It's a quick and easy business once you have the knack of it, and you shouldn't let one or two failures discourage you from perfecting this little trick.

When the tendons are zipped free and discarded, the only thing left to do is neaten the main breast pieces. Spread them flat on the board and use your knife to trim away any blood clots, veiny or membranous pieces, and fatty lozenges at the periphery of the meat. What you want are two neat triangular breast pieces that feel perfectly smooth and soft to the touch. All the trimmings go into the stock bag so that nothing is lost.

This is all there is to boning a chicken breast—a 3- to 5-minute operation once you become proficient, one that rewards you with four beautifully trimmed and plump pieces of chicken instead of the raggedy boned breasts sold so dearly in stores.

THE CHINESE WAY TO RENDER CHICKEN AND DUCK FAT   I am not a fan of duck fat in any form and regularly give it away to pâté-making friends, but I love the lushness that a dollop of chicken fat gives to a pan-fried scallion bread or a simple stir-fry of greens and so always arrange to have some handy in the freezer.

Poultry fat needs to be *rendered* in order to be a smooth and successful cooking agent. That is, it needs to be melted in such a way as to separate the pure fat from any skin, connective tissues, or excess moisture. The Chinese way is simply to cube the fat, place it in a heatproof bowl, then steam it over high heat until the clear fat melts away from the rest. The liquid fat should be strained through cheesecloth, whereupon it will keep in the refrigerator for at least a week or may be frozen indefinitely. (Because it is a fat, it never gets very hard even when frozen, and I just scoop it out of the freezer container as I need it.) As for the bits left behind, you can discard them or, if you like cracklings, you can fry them up in a skillet until dark and crispy and then eat them in a salad, in a soup, or simply as is.

CUTTING UP A WHOLE BIRD CHINESE-STYLE   When you are faced with a whole cooked chicken or duck and the question is how to cut it for serving, the answer will differ if you are Chinese, Western, or—like me—something in between. In the West, we typically carve poultry from the bone, and any bone lovers are exiled to the kitchen to vent their passions in private. In China, the norm is to chop the entire bird, bones included, into small rectangular pieces that can be managed with chopsticks and then to reassemble them into the shape of the original bird. The head is anchored in place and the tail is arranged perkily at the appropriate end. In addition to being tricky to master, the final picture isn't, to Western eyes, terribly attractive.

My own Chinese-style method is a slight variation from the tradition, which would offend no one, I suspect, but aficionados of poultry heads and tails. What is required is a sturdy cutting board, a relatively heavy cleaver designed for chopping through bones, and the chutzpah to whack heartily and happily through some rather thick bones.

First allow the bird to cool slightly if it is fresh from the pot or smoker. Even 5 minutes' rest will permit the flesh to firm somewhat so that the meat cuts cleanly and you can do a neat job. If you are forced to cut the bird while it is very hot, have a bowl nearby to retrieve any juices and do not be discouraged if some of the pieces are not perfect.

Begin by putting the bird breast side up on the board. Run your knife carefully all around the hump of the leg where it meets the side of the bird, cutting neatly through the skin and into the flesh. When the knife meets the bone all around, then pull the leg back to expose the joint and cut through the joint to free the leg.

Once the legs are severed from the body, turn the bird over and remove the wings in the same fashion.

Turn the bird breast side up, then with a swift blow chop cleanly through the keel bone, dividing the breast in two from the neck to the tail cavities. (If the bird is very hot or your courage lacking, you may approach this in a slower but more familiar manner, by using the knife to make a clean cut down to the bone then cutting through the bone with poultry shears or sturdy scissors.) Gently pull the breast halves apart to expose the backbone, then chop cleanly along one side of the backbone to sever the body in two. Remove the backbone entirely by chopping cleanly along its other side, then discard or reserve it, as you like. (The backbone too may be removed with a shears or scissors, though if you practice with a cleaver it becomes a quick and easy operation.) Finally, place each body half cut side down on the board, then feel with the knife where the rib cage ends and cut each half lengthwise in two.

Now, you are ready for the final chopping that makes the bird easy to eat with chopsticks. Chop each drumstick into three pieces, then reassemble them in their original shape and put the two legs at one end of your serving platter. (Chop heartily, with no hesitation, and the bone will sever cleanly.) Chop the wings into two pieces where they meet at the elbow joint, then reassemble them as well and place at the opposite end of the platter. As for the four body pieces, chop them each crosswise into pieces about ¾ inch wide. (Again, whack heartily and without reluctance and the knife will chop cleanly through the bone.) Then arrange these pieces in between the wings and the legs, keeping them for the most part in their original line but placing the prettiest pieces on top and concealing the less successful bits beneath.

When you are done, push the pieces gently together so the bird mounds nicely on the platter, wipe the rim, then garnish any bald or unimpressive spots with sprigs of fresh coriander.

The same chopping scheme, minus the arranging, is how you chop a whole raw chicken for cooking.

Mostly, chopping poultry is a matter of the proper spirit. A glass of wine or a moment of Zen concentration will usually speed you on your way.

Ma-La Cold Chicken

麻辣雞絲

I discovered this jewel in a tiny, unpretentious restaurant on one of my interminable food treasure hunts through San Francisco's Chinatown. It is a playful variation on a classic Szechwanese cold dish, a lovely example of the art of yin and yang. Striking and light enough for a *nouvelle cuisine* dinner, it also makes a satisfying lunch. ◆ *Ma-La* means "numbing and spicy," the qualities of the Szechwan peppercorns and red chili infused in the oil. The oil or either sauce will alone make the chicken memorable. As a threesome, they are devastatingly good. ◆ Cucumber traditionally partners cold chicken, but this dish deserves something special. I use thin asparagus or Chinese longbeans, fresh tiny snow peas, tender string beans, or "clouds" cut from broccoli stems (page 220). Blanch the vegetable until tender-crisp, then chill to set the color. ◆ With the chicken and sauces on hand, this is a 5-minute dish. Without the sauces, you can prepare it in 1 hour. Everything may be refrigerated overnight for easy assembly the next day.

TECHNIQUE NOTES:
It is a traditional Chinese practice to cook a whole chicken by submerging it in a potful of boiling water, then immediately turning off the heat, covering the pot, and leaving the chicken to "cook" until the water cools. The result is a supremely juicy bird and a nifty bit of "no-hands" cooking. I have adapted the method here for cooking chicken breasts for cold chicken salads, further infusing the water with some scallion, ginger, and Szechwan peppercorns to give a hint of flavor to the chicken. The presence of the aromatics also seasons the poaching liquid, which I strain and reduce after extracting the chicken to make a delicious chicken stock for use in soups and stir-frys. I call this method "no-poach chicken," and it is your surest route to tender, juicy breast meat. Please note that only impeccably *fresh* chicken will do here. Frozen chicken will always be comparatively mediocre when cooked, whatever the method.

There is a marvelous quality to warm oil freshly infused with seasonings, and it is a Chinese commonplace to drizzle such oils over chicken. Make *Ma-La Oil* just before serving so it is still warm and aromatic when eaten.

Serves 2–3 as a main course, 4–6 as part of a multicourse meal.

INGREDIENTS:

>   *1½ pounds fresh whole chicken breasts, with skin on and bone in*
>   *1 quarter-size slice fresh ginger*
>   *1 thin whole scallion, cut into 3-inch lengths*
>   *⅛ teaspoon Szechwan brown peppercorns*

1 pound pencil-thin asparagus, woody ends snapped off, or ¾ pound Chinese
    longbeans, trimmed and cut into 3-inch lengths
scant ½ teaspoon Chinese or Japanese sesame oil

For making Ma-La Oil:
2½ tablespoons Chinese or Japanese sesame oil
2½ tablespoons fresh corn or peanut oil
1 rounded tablespoon thin-cut green and white scallion rings
2 nickel-size slices fresh ginger, lightly smashed
¼ teaspoon Szechwan brown peppercorns, twigs removed
⅛–¼ teaspoon dried red chili flakes
¾ teaspoon thin (regular) soy sauce

⅓–½ cup Dijon Mustard Sauce (page 475)
⅓–½ cup Chinese sesame sauce of your choice (page 471 and 472)

Preparing "no-poach" chicken:
Rinse the chicken briefly under cool water, and remove any blood clots that might mar
the stock. Fill a small, heavy pot that will hold the chicken snugly with enough cold
water to cover it by 2 inches. Spank the ginger and scallion with the handle end or broad
side of a Chinese cleaver or chef's knife to spread their fibers and bring their juices to the
surface, then add them to the cold water with the Szechwan peppercorns.
    Cover the pot and bring the water to a rolling boil over high heat. Turn off the
heat, add the chicken, poking it beneath the liquid with a wooden spoon, then replace
the cover.
    Leave the chicken in the covered pot for 2 hours. If more convenient, you may
leave it in the pot until the water is completely cool. (Once the 2 hours are up, the water
will not be hot enough to further cook the chicken.)
    Remove the chicken from the liquid. At this point, it may be refrigerated 1–2
days before using, sealed airtight. If you wish a light unseasoned stock, ideal for use in
stir-frys and soups, strain the poaching liquid then reduce it over moderate heat by about
two-thirds or until tasty. "No-poach chicken stock" may be kept in the refrigerator up to
a week, or frozen indefinitely.

Slicing the chicken:
Remove the skin, then remove the meat carefully from the bone in one piece. Separate
the fillets from the main breast pieces and remove the membranes covering them. Use a
small, sharp knife to cut off any cartilage clinging to the main breast pieces. Make an
incision and remove the tendon from the fillets.
    With a sharp, thin-bladed Chinese cleaver or chef's knife, cut the breast pieces
and fillets crosswise on a diagonal *against* the grain into thin strips ¼ inch wide. Keep
each piece of chicken intact after cutting, so that you can transfer it to the bed of greens
in a neat, pretty pattern.
    If you are working in advance, put the chicken aside on a plate or baking sheet
and seal it airtight with plastic film. I prefer to cut the chicken just in advance of assembling the salad, but it will keep nicely in the refrigerator overnight if it is more convenient to work in advance. Bring to room temperature before using.

Preparing the vegetable:
Roll-cut, blanch, and chill the asparagus as directed on page 288. For Chinese longbeans,

blanch for 1 minute in boiling, unsalted water to cover, then drain immediately under cold running water to stop the cooking and set the color. Pat the vegetable thoroughly dry. Chill until serving, overnight if desired.

Making the seasoned oil:

Just before assembling the salad, put the 2½ tablespoons each of sesame and vegetable oils in a small pot and swirl to combine. Add a single scallion ring, then heat over moderate heat until the scallion sizzles. Let it sizzle 5 seconds, then remove the pan from the heat. Add the scallion rings, ginger, peppercorns, and red chili flakes, then swirl the oil to mix. If the ingredients burn rather than sizzle, then the oil was too hot and you must begin again with fresh oil and seasonings. Put the pot of seasoned oil aside to develop while you assemble the salad, and cover the pot to keep the oil warm.

Assembling the salad:

Just before serving, toss the chilled vegetables with ¼–½ teaspoon sesame oil and arrange in a bed on a large plate of contrasting color. Arrange the chicken evenly on top, leaving a border of green showing underneath. Remove the ginger from the oil, then whisk in the soy. Spoon the oil to taste over the chicken, scattering bits of the chopped seasonings on top. Place mustard sauce at one end of the platter and sesame sauce at the other. If you are using *Sweet and Silky Sesame Sauce* (page 472), thin it, if needed, to a smooth pouring consistency.

Invite the guests to help themselves to salad and to some of each sauce. I love taking a bite of first one and then the other. The contrasts are delightful.

Leftover salad is good cold. Leftover *Ma-La Oil* may be refrigerated, for use on cold noodles, cold meats, or Western salads. Strain the oil before storing to insure clarity. Serve at room temperature for fullest flavor, and add a pinch or two of *Roasted Szechwan Pepper-Salt* (page 476) if you wish.

MENU SUGGESTIONS:

This is a good meal on its own, for a luncheon or light dinner, accompanied by a big California Chardonnay and followed by *Glacéed Orange Slices* (page 487).

Coriandered Chicken Salad with Mustard Sauce

芥末雞絲

This refreshing cold platter with its zesty combination of chicken and mustard is part-Chinese, part-French, part-California, and pure delicious. It is a real appetite-arouser, a favorite among my Chinese friends. With its clean taste and good looks it makes a lovely centerpiece for a buffet, a colorful start for a sit-down dinner, or a light and portable one-dish lunch. ◆ This is a practical, economical choice for entertaining. The chicken may be prepared a day in advance, and the mustard sauce made weeks ahead. The platter can be arranged hours before serving, then stored in the refrigerator until the guests arrive. The recipe may be multiplied indefinitely should you be expecting a crowd.

TECHNIQUE NOTES:

The way to make ice-chilled chicken in north China was to grab the bird from the boiling pot, then run outside and throw it down the well. With one good splash, the meat contracted and the juices gelled, producing a vibrantly textured chicken with the moistness locked in. It is great fun to do. Use a big bowl of ice cubes if you don't have a well.

For recognizing ripe tomatoes, the surest judge is your nose. Ripe tomatoes *smell* sweet, and only a sweet-smelling tomato *tastes* truly good.

Serves 2–3 as a main course, 4–6 as part of a multicourse meal.

INGREDIENTS:

> 1¾–2 pounds fresh whole chicken breasts, with skin on and bone in (to yield 3–3½ cups shreds)

> *For cooking the chicken:*
> 2 nickel-size slices fresh ginger
> 1 thin whole scallion, cut into 3-inch lengths

> *Salad ingredients:*
> ½ pound firm sweet-smelling tomatoes (prettiest to use 3–4 small), or ½ pint firm sweet-smelling cherry tomatoes
> 1 large red bell pepper
> ½ pound firm seedless cucumbers, or 1 pound firm cucumbers with seeds
> 1 bunch fresh picture-perfect coriander
> 2 teaspoons freshly toasted sesame seeds (page 565)

> *Dijon Mustard Sauce (page 475)*

Cooking and ice-chilling the chicken:
Rinse the breasts and put them in a heavy pot that will hold them snugly. Lightly smash the ginger and scallion to spread the fibers and bring the juices to the surface, then add them to the pot with enough cold water to come 3 inches above the chicken. Bring to a rolling boil over high heat, reduce to maintain a steady simmer, and simmer the chicken uncovered for 25 minutes. About 3 minutes before the chicken is done, fill a large bowl with 2–3 trays of ice cubes and enough cold water to cover the chicken.

Once the chicken is done, remove it from the pot with a Chinese mesh spoon or tongs and plunge it immediately under the ice. Chill, submerged, for 15 minutes. Drain and pat dry.

If you like, the simmering liquid may be strained and reduced by two-thirds for use as a light stock. For a richer stock, add some chicken bones to the pot and simmer the mixture for an hour or so.

Shredding the chicken:
Discard the skin, then remove the meat from the bone in as much of one piece as possible. Remove the thin membranes encasing breast and fillet, and discard any tendons or fat. By hand, shred the meat with the grain into strips 2 inches long and pencil-width (see TECHNIQUE NOTES, page 135). If you need to work in advance, the shredded chicken may be sealed airtight and refrigerated overnight. Bring to room temperature before serving.

Slicing the vegetables:
Slice the vegetables just before assembling the salad, so they are fresh and perky when served.

Cut larger tomatoes in half lengthwise, then core. Place cut side down, then cut across the width into slices a scant ¼ inch thick. If you are working with very large tomatoes, cut the slices in half lengthwise to make them manageable. Cut cherry tomatoes in half lengthwise to one side of the stem, then slice off the stem mark. If the cherry tomatoes have pretty stems, leave a few of the stems intact for color.

Cut the pepper in half lengthwise, and remove core, seeds, and ribs. Place cut side down, then cut across the width into thin slices ⅛ inch thick.

Trim the cucumbers and peel them if they are waxed. Seed, if necessary. Cut the cucumbers into strips, half circles, or seeded arcs.

Cut off the lower stems of the coriander, just above where they are tied. Wash the sprigs in cold water, pat or spin dry, then discard any imperfect leaves. Chop the leaves and upper stems coarsely into ¾-inch bits.

Assembling the salad:
Toss the chicken with the sesame seeds, then divide the chicken into 2 mounds and arrange them at opposite ends of a large, round platter. Arrange the vegetables in separate wedge-like mounds around the platter, so that you have an alternation of red-green-white, looking like a very colorful pie. Fan the vegetables, fluff the coriander leaves, and put the prettiest specimens on top. Once assembled, the platter may be tightly sealed and refrigerated 2–3 hours prior to serving.

Serve at room temperature or slightly chilled, with a bowl of the mustard sauce. Invite each participant to choose, toss, and dress his or her own salad fixings.

Unsauced leftovers keep 2–3 days refrigerated. Bottled and refrigerated, the sauce keeps indefinitely.

MENU SUGGESTIONS:
This platter stands easily on its own as a one-dish luncheon or light dinner, accompanied by a California Sauvignon Blanc or Fumé Blanc.

> **Bong-Bong Chicken**
>
> 棒棒雞

Bong-bong means "club-club," a description of the pounding process that gives this cold chicken its special softness. Satisfying and filling, this is Szechwanese fare at its earthy best—simple to prepare, complexly flavored, and gutsily good. ◆ The classic formula calls for sesame sauce and shredded mung bean sheets to accompany the chicken. I find peanut sauce equally tasty and bean threads (glass noodles) easier to handle. Cucumber is a traditional variation for color and crunch. ◆ This is great party or picnic food. Cheap and easy, it can be made in quantity, well in advance.

TECHNIQUE NOTES:
To achieve its special character, the chicken must be bashed lightly—not to flatten it, but to spread the fibers. A lightweight rolling pin does the job perfectly. The blunt end of a cleaver handle is a good second choice.

Serves 2–3 as a main course, 4–6 as part of a multicourse meal.

INGREDIENTS:

> 1½ *pounds fresh whole chicken breasts, with skin on and bone in, cooked the "no-poach" way (page 129)*

> *Toppings (choose one):*
> ½–⅔ *cup Chinese sesame sauce of your choice (pages 471 and 472)*
> ½–⅔ *cup Spicy Szechwan Peanut Sauce (page 473)*

> *Salad bases (use one or both):*
> 1½–2 *ounces bean threads (glass noodles)*
> ¾ *pound very firm seedless cucumbers, or* 1½ *pounds very firm cucumbers with seeds*

> *Optional garnish:*
> 3–4 *tablespoons fresh coriander leaves, coarsely chopped*

Cutting and clubbing the chicken:
Skin and bone the cooked chicken, keeping the meat in as much of one piece as possible. Separate fillet and main pieces. Discard any membranes, tendons, or hard spots. Cut the meat against the grain into strips ¼ inch wide. With a rolling pin, lightly club each strip in 2 or 3 places to separate the fibers and loosen the meat. Be gentle with the delicate fillets. Pull the strips into 2 or 3 pieces; they should come apart easily. Tightly sealed, the chicken may be refrigerated overnight.

Preparing the salad base:
Soak the noodles until soft and silky, as directed on page 533, then cut into 3–4 inch lengths.
  Cut off the tips of the cucumbers. Peel and seed, if necessary. To remove seeds, cut the cucumbers in half lengthwise, then scoop out the seeds with a small spoon. Cut the cucumbers into thin strips, which is traditional, or into small arcs, which is a pretty treatment for seeded cucumbers.
  If you are working in advance, the noodles may be drained and left at room temperature. The cucumbers may be sealed airtight and refrigerated up to several hours.

Assembling the dish:
Drain the noodles thoroughly so they will not dilute the sauce. Spread the noodles on a large platter, then layer the cucumbers and chicken on top. For a nice presentation, choose a platter of contrasting color, and arrange the layers so that each is rimmed by a border of the one underneath. Just before serving, pour thin streams of sauce over the chicken; do not smother it. Garnish with the coriander, if desired, and serve a bowl of sauce alongside. Invite each guest to dress and toss his or her own portion.
  Unsauced and ungarnished, the dish may be sealed and refrigerated for an hour before serving. The salad may be served slightly chilled, but the sauce should be at room temperature for peak flavor.
  Unsauced leftovers will keep 1–2 days, refrigerated and sealed airtight. For a change, try dressing them with *Dijon Mustard Sauce* (page 475).

MENU SUGGESTIONS:
This is a gutsy dish, most at home in the company of simple foods with striking flavors, such as *Strange Flavor Eggplant* (page 295) and *Orchid's Tangy Cool Noodles* (page 356). For a luncheon, I often star it on its own surrounded by a colorful assortment of "Little

Dishes." To accompany the chicken, try a light red wine with bite—a California Gamay Beaujolais or a Beaujolais.

| Master Sauce Chicken Salad with Tea Melon 茶瓜拌雞絲 | This is one of my warm-weather favorites, my personal contribution to the American phenomenon known as Chinese chicken salad. It is a dish of contrasts. The blond chicken is rich with master sauce, the orange carrots sparkle with vinegar, and the gold tea melon is chewy and satisfyingly sweet. For a summer meal, it is perfect. ◆ Tea melon is a crisp, cucumber-type vegetable that comes packed in syrup. It has a unique, silky texture and a beautiful, gold-hued trans- |

lucence. If you cannot get to a Chinese market to buy it, substitute 1–2 tablespoons finely slivered stem ginger in syrup, for sweetness with a slight bite. ◆ This is a good dish for large-scale entertaining. It can be made in huge batches, is very economical, and requires little labor, most of which can be done 1–3 days in advance. If you have a food processor, a chunk of the work is done in seconds.

TECHNIQUE NOTES:
"Hand-torn chicken" is the Chinese name for most cold, shredded chicken dishes. It is a traditional technique, dating from an age when people had time and a real interest in the pleasures of the palate. The irregular strips soak up sauces or allow them to cling, and feel just delightful on the tongue. The effect is precisely that of hand-torn lettuce.

To shred speedily, use the tips or nails of your thumb and third finger, and begin near the edge of the meat. Keep your hand and wrist relaxed and shred as if you were plucking harp strings.

Serves 4–5 as a main course, 6–10 as part of a multicourse meal.

INGREDIENTS:

> *Salad ingredients:*
> *2½–2¾ pounds fresh whole chicken breasts, with skin on and bone in (to yield about 5 cups shredded chicken)*
> *master sauce (page 154) almost to cover (about 5–6 cups)*
> *1½ pounds sweet-tasting carrots, trimmed and peeled (to yield 6 cups shredded carrots)*
> *⅛ cup drained tea melon (page 580)*
>
> *Seasonings:*
> *6 tablespoons Chinese or Japanese sesame oil*
> *3½–4½ tablespoons unseasoned Chinese or Japanese rice vinegar*
>
> *Optional garnish:*
> *sprigs of fresh coriander*

Stewing and shredding the chicken:
Rinse the breasts under cold water, remove any bloody clots, then put aside to drain. Put the master sauce in a heavy pot that will hold the breasts snugly in one layer and bring to a boil over moderate heat. If you do not have enough sauce to come ¾ of the way up the chicken, then replenish as directed on page 155. Slip the chicken skin side down into the hot liquid, then baste it well while the sauce returns to a boil. Reduce the heat to main- tain a gentle simmer, cover the pot, and simmer 20 minutes. Check the simmer and baste

the chicken every 5–10 minutes. Turn once, after 10 minutes.

Remove the pot to a cool burner, turn the chicken again skin side down, then let it steep in the covered pot 1½–2½ hours, basting frequently. The longer the chicken steeps, the richer the flavor. Remove the chicken from the sauce, put it aside to cool, then strain the sauce to remove any impurities. Both the chicken and sauce may be sealed separately and refrigerated up to a full day before proceeding.

Remove the chicken skin in one piece and trim the fatty edges and underside to make a neat rectangle of uniform thinness. Cut the skin into long, thin slivers, enough to yield about ⅔ cup. Remove the meat from the bone in one piece, then gently separate the fillets and discard any membranes, tendons, or fat. Shred the meat lengthwise and with the grain by hand into thin strips about 2 inches long and pencil width. Toss the chicken lightly with 3 tablespoons sauce to moisten, then toss again with 2–3 tablespoons more sauce, enough to flavor the chicken richly without making it soupy. Combine the chicken with some or all of the julienned skin. It imparts a delicious silkiness. If you are working in advance, the sauced chicken may be sealed airtight and refrigerated overnight.

Preparing the carrots and tea melon:
Shred the carrots in a food processor or by hand. Toss them thoroughly with the sesame oil, rubbing with your hands to distribute the oil among the shreds. Toss again lightly with rice vinegar to taste. The carrots should be slightly sharp, to balance the richness of the chicken.

Julienne the tea melon into long, thin threads ⅛ inch thick. Cover with syrup until ready to use. The carrots and tea melon may be sealed separately and refrigerated overnight. Before serving, toss the carrots to redistribute the seasonings and drain off any excess liquid.

Assembling the salad:
Just before serving, arrange the carrots in a wide, full ring around a serving platter of contrasting color. Mound the chicken in the center, then scatter the tea melon decoratively on top. Drizzle on ¼–½ teaspoon syrup if you have a sweet tooth, and garnish with sprigs of fresh coriander, if you like.

Serve at room temperature or slightly chilled. Present the salad colorfully intact, then toss at the table or invite each guest to choose and toss their own portion.

Leftovers keep 1–2 days, refrigerated.

MENU SUGGESTIONS:
This is a good, light meal on its own, well accompanied by a California Chenin Blanc or French Vouvray. To expand the menu, add an assortment of "Little Dishes," *Soy-Dipped Red Radish Fans* (page 114) and *Sweet and Tangy Cucumber Pickles* (page 110) being two good choices.

Hoisin-Explosion Chicken

醬爆雞丁

This is the first stir-fried dish I ever attempted, and it is an ideal place to begin if you are new to a Chinese kitchen. Subtly sweet and rich, with a classic contrast of velvety chicken, slippery-crisp vegetables and crunchy nuts, it combines every technique you need to know to produce elegant, restaurant-style stir-frys. ◆ The taste explosion that makes this dish so appealing is a multi-regional affair. Hoisin is a predominantly north Chinese condiment, chili is a Szechwanese touch, while wine used as it is here is an Eastern taste. ◆ Use bamboo shoots only if they are white, crisp, and exceedingly clean-tasting. Otherwise, substitute straw mushrooms, black mushrooms, or a double amount of bell pepper. ♦ This is an excellent mid-week dish, a good choice for a one-dish dinner, or a party of guests with divergent tastes. All the preparation, save the final 5–10 minutes of cooking, may be done in advance.

TECHNIQUE NOTES:
Blanching cut and specially marinated chicken in oil or water prior to stir-frying is a technique common to Chinese restaurant kitchens. The 20-second bath tenderizes the chicken remarkably, hence the process has been dubbed "velveting" in English. Velveted chicken is half-cooked, will not stick to the pan, and needs almost no oil when stir-fried. Therefore, the resulting dish is grease-free and done in a flash. It is an absolutely distinctive and practical method, well worth adopting at home.

Oil-velveted chicken is firm and plush; water-velveted chicken is soft and bouncy. The oil texture has great character, while the water process is attractively easy and clean. Choose the one that suits you best.

Velveting in advance either way will rob the meat of its lushness; however, the meat may be marinated a full 1½ days prior to velveting. My general practice is to marinate the chicken overnight. This gives the meat the opportunity it needs to soak up the marinade and swell to a juicy fullness, and gives me the chance to work in advance. If you rush the marinating process, much of the liquid will be left behind when the chicken is velveted, and neither you nor the meat will reap its benefits.

If you are sensitive to the great taste of good chicken, you will always use fresh as opposed to frozen; however, with velveting it is a *must*. Frozen chicken will not work. The plush texture that is the signal beauty of velveting cannot be had with meat that has been frozen.

For the components of a velvet marinade, see TECHNIQUE NOTES, page 145. For shallow-frying nuts, see TECHNIQUE NOTES, page 107.

Serves 3–4 as a main course, 5–8 as part of a multicourse meal.

INGREDIENTS:

> *1 pound skinned and boned fresh chicken breast, carefully trimmed of membranes, cartilage, and fat (weight after trimming; equal to about 2 pounds with skin on and bone in; see page 126 for easy, 5-minute boning)*

> *For marinating the chicken:*
> *1 large egg white*
> *1 tablespoon Chinese rice wine or quality, dry sherry*
> *1 teaspoon coarse kosher salt*
> *1 tablespoon cornstarch*

> *3–4 cups fresh corn or peanut oil, or oil for deep-frying nuts (page 84)*
> *⅓–½ cup whole blanched almonds, cashews, or hazelnuts*
> *1 medium red bell pepper*
> *1 medium green bell pepper (to yield 2 rounded cups red and green pepper cubes)*
> *6 ounces whole bamboo shoots (to equal 1 cup wedges)*

Aromatics:
   2 teaspoons finely minced fresh garlic
   1 scant tablespoon finely minced fresh ginger
   1 tablespoon finely minced green and white scallion
   ⅛–¼ teaspoon dried red chili flakes (optional)

Liquid seasonings:
   2½–3 tablespoons hoisin sauce
   1½ teaspoons Chinese rice wine or quality, dry sherry
   2 teaspoons thin (regular) soy sauce

For velveting the chicken:
   3–4 cups fresh corn or peanut oil (nut-frying oil from above may be used)
   or
   4 cups water plus 2 teaspoons corn or peanut oil

   3 tablespoons corn or peanut oil, for stir-frying

Cubing and marinating the chicken:
Trim the chicken of fat and membranes. You should have 1 pound after trimming. Spread it flat, then cut into cubes ¾–1 inch square. (If you are new to stir-frying, choose the larger size. It will be good insurance against overcooking the chicken if you are a bit slow in getting it out of the pan.)
   Mix the marinade ingredients until smooth and thick, in the work bowl of a food processor fitted with the steel knife or in a blender. Process a full 30–60 seconds to achieve a rich consistency. Scrape the marinade over the chicken, toss well with your fingers to coat and separate the cubes, then seal the mixture airtight and refrigerate 8 hours to 1½ days to set the marinade and infuse the chicken with its flavors. The longer the chicken marinates, the better the texture and taste in the end.

Shallow-frying the nuts:
Heat a wok or heavy skillet over high heat until hot. Add the oil, then heat to the slow-fry stage, 275° on a deep-fry thermometer. Reduce the heat so the temperature will not rise. Have a paper towel-lined plate or baking sheet within easy reach of your stovetop.
   Add the nuts to the oil, then stir slowly and continually until they turn pale brown, about 5 minutes. Do not allow them to get too dark, as they will continue to turn a shade or two darker from their own heat after leaving the oil. Remove the nuts in one sweep with a Chinese mesh spoon or heatproof strainer, then put aside on the plate to drain. Shallow-fried nuts may be bottled airtight and kept in a cool place for several days before using.

Preparing the vegetables and sauce ingredients:
Core, seed, and de-rib the peppers, removing any trace of white from the ribs or stem end. Cut the peppers into 1-inch cubes. You should have 2 rounded cups. Once cut, the peppers may be refrigerated overnight in a lightly misted plastic bag. Blot dry before stir-frying to prevent the skin from blistering.
   Blanch the bamboo shoots in plain boiling water to cover for 10 seconds, then drain and refresh under cold running water. Cut lengthwise into spears ¼ inch thick, then crosswise into wedges 1 inch long. Once cut, the bamboo shoots may be refrigerated overnight, covered with cold water. Drain well before using.
   Combine the minced aromatics on a small saucer, alongside the chili flakes if

you are using them. Combine the hoisin sauce, wine, and soy sauce in a small bowl, stirring to blend. If you are working in advance, seal the aromatics airtight and refrigerate until use, up to several hours.

Velveting the chicken:

Velveting in oil: Have the chicken, a large Chinese mesh spoon or a large heatproof strainer to retrieve the chicken from the oil, and a bowl in which the spoon or sieve can nest and allow the chicken to drain alongside your stovetop. Heat a wok or a deep, heavy skillet over high heat until hot. Add the oil and heat to the slow-fry stage, 275° on a deep-fry thermometer. Reduce the heat or turn it off entirely so the temperature does not rise. (If the oil is too hot, the chicken will turn yellow and tough.) Stir the chicken to loosen the cubes, then slide them smoothly and carefully into the oil. Stir slowly and poke at the chicken with chopsticks or a wooden spoon to help separate the cubes (do not despair if some insist on sticking together) until they are 90 percent white, about 20 seconds. At that point, scoop the chicken from the oil in one batch using the spoon or sieve. If you are in any doubt, scoop them out sooner rather than later, lest they overcook in the oil. Retrieved at the right time, the cubes will be 90–95 percent white, cooked on the outside but still raw on the inside. Hold the chicken briefly above the oil to drain, then nest the spoon or sieve in the waiting bowl to allow any excess oil to drip off.

Once velveted, the chicken should be stir-fried at once. If you need the frying pot for stir-frying, carefully decant the oil into a heatproof bowl or pot. Once cool, it may be strained, bottled and stored for future velveting or frying. If you do not need the frying pot, let the oil sit until cool before handling it.

Velveting in water: Station a metal colander in the sink, and have the chicken and a large, flat plate within reach of your stovetop. Bring the greased water to a simmer in a large saucepan, then reduce the heat to maintain a bare simmer whereby the water ripples and rolls more than bubbles. (Too fast a simmer, and the chicken loses its coating and toughens.) Stir the chicken to loosen the cubes, then slide them into the water. Stir very gently to separate the cubes in the water, then allow them to cook until they are 90 percent white, about 20 seconds. At that point, drain them immediately into the waiting colander. If you are in any doubt, drain the chicken sooner rather than later. Properly velveted, it will be 90–95 percent white on the outside and still raw on the inside. Shake to remove excess water, then spread the chicken in a single layer on the waiting plate. Once velveted, the chicken should be stir-fried immediately.

Stir-frying the dish:

Combine the peppers and bamboo shoots in a heatproof bowl. Have the velveted chicken, nuts, vegetables, aromatics, combined liquid seasonings and 3 tablespoons of corn or peanut oil all within easy reach of your stovetop. Put a platter of contrasting color in a low oven to warm.

Heat a wok or deep, heavy skillet over high heat until hot enough to evaporate a bead of water on contact. Add 2 tablespoons oil, swirl to glaze the bottom of the pan, then reduce the heat to medium-high. When the oil is hot enough to sizzle one piece of bell pepper, add the cubed peppers and the bamboo shoots to the pan. Stir-fry briskly until the vegetables are evenly glossed with oil and heated through, about 1 minute, adjusting the heat so they sizzle without scorching. Remove the vegetables promptly to the waiting bowl, return the pan to the heat, then add the remaining tablespoon of oil and swirl to glaze the pan.

When the oil is hot enough to sizzle one bit of the minced aromatics, add them to the pan, nudging the chili flakes in last if you are using them. Stir until fully fragrant,

15–20 seconds, adjusting the heat so they foam without browning. Give the liquid seasonings a stir, add them to the pan, and stir to combine. Raise the heat slightly to bring the mixture to a simmer, then add the chicken and vegetables. Toss rapidly to cook the chicken through, coat it with the sauce, and reduce the sauce slightly so it clings to the meat, about 20–30 seconds. Turn off the heat. Quickly taste the sauce and adjust with a bit more hoisin sauce if a sweeter taste is desired. Fold in the nuts with a few fast sweeps, then decant the mixture onto the heated platter. Pause briefly to turn some of the peppers bright side up on top, and serve.

Leftovers may be rewarmed in a steamer set over high heat or in the oven, covered tightly. The vegetables lose much of their crispness, but the taste is still delicious.

MENU SUGGESTIONS:
This dish is wonderfully satisfying in combination with *Ham and Egg Fried Rice* (page 405) or *Celery and Pork Thread Fried Rice* (page 406) for a simple supper, along with a Fumé Blanc or Sauvignon Blanc with good body.

Tung-An Chicken

東安子雞

Tung-An is a county in Hunan, and this dish has all the beauty of refined Hunanese cuisine: It is pungent yet subtle, complexly flavored without masking the primary good taste of chicken. It is an easy dish to turn out, perfect for the beginning cook, and a paradise for the lover of pungent, saucy stir-frys. ◆ The original version calls for a whole young chicken and fresh red chili threads. I find whole breasts and dried red chili flakes far easier to use, and I make up for the visual loss by adding plush strips of black mushroom. The breasts must be from small young chickens for the dish to be good. ◆ The chicken may be cooked a day in advance. The rest of the dish can be assembled and cooked within 30 minutes.

TECHNIQUE NOTES:
Parboiling then water-chilling the chicken gives it a supple texture and a strikingly clean taste. It also means that the dark sauce will slide off the chicken, leaving it a lovely ivory-white.

Adding the vinegar to the sauce last keeps its zing intact. It is neither boiled off nor compromised by the flavors of the other ingredients.

Serves 2 as a main course, 3–5 as part of a multicourse meal.

INGREDIENTS:

1½ pounds fresh and tender chicken breasts, with skin on and bone in

For parboiling the chicken:
2 nickel-size slices fresh ginger
1 thin whole scallion, cut into 3-inch lengths

For stir-frying the chicken:
2½–3 tablespoons corn or peanut oil
4 medium or 2 large Chinese dried black mushrooms
1 teaspoon Szechwan brown peppercorns, twigs removed
1 tablespoon finely julienned fresh ginger threads, cut hair-thin
2 thin or 1 hefty whole scallion(s), cut into 2½-inch lengths
¼ teaspoon dried red chili flakes

Sauce ingredients:
  ½ cup rich, unsalted chicken stock
  2 tablespoons thin (regular) soy sauce
  1 tablespoon Chinese rice wine or quality, dry sherry
  1½ teaspoons sugar
  1 teaspoon coarse kosher salt
  1½ teaspoons unseasoned Chinese or Japanese rice vinegar

  1 teaspoon cornstarch dissolved in 1 tablespoon cold chicken stock
  ½ teaspoon Chinese or Japanese sesame oil

Parboiling the chicken:
Rinse the breasts under cold running water and remove any bloody clots. Smash the ginger and scallion lightly to release their juices, and put them with the breasts in a small, heavy pot to hold the chicken snugly. Add boiling water to cover, return the liquids to a boil over high heat, then reduce the heat to maintain a steady simmer. Simmer the breasts 10 minutes. Remove the chicken immediately from the pot with a Chinese mesh spoon or a slotted spoon, and spray with cold water to stop the cooking. Reserve the cooking liquid. Use it to empty your freezer of bones and make stock (page 446). The chilled chicken may be sealed airtight and refrigerated overnight. Bring to room temperature prior to cooking.

Other preparations:
Soak the mushrooms in cold or hot water to cover until fully soft and spongy, 20 minutes to an hour. Snip off the stems, rinse under running water to dislodge any sand trapped in the gills, then cut the caps into long strips ⅛ inch wide.

Roast the peppercorns in a dry skillet over medium heat, stirring for about 1 minute until they are fragrant and begin to smoke. Crush to a coarse consistency with the end of a cleaver handle, or in a mortar.

Cut whole chicken breasts in half to one side of the keel bone. Leaving the skin in place, remove the meat in as much of one piece as possible. (You may discard the chicken skin, if you wish, but it is customary in this dish to leave it on.) Separate the fillets from the main pieces, and remove any membranes, fatty lozenges, and the tough tips of the tendons. (Much of the meat will be red; at this stage it is only partially cooked.) Slice the meat crosswise, against the grain, into strips ½ inch wide. Cut long strips into 1½–2 inch lengths.

Cut the scallion segments lengthwise into slivers ⅛ inch thick, and combine in a small dish with the ginger threads and red chili flakes.

Combine the stock, soy, wine, sugar, and salt, stirring to dissolve the sugar.

Preparations may be completed several hours in advance. Seal the ingredients airtight, and bring to room temperature before cooking.

Stir-frying the dish:
About 10 minutes before serving, have all the ingredients and a Chinese mesh spoon or slotted spoon within easy reach of your stovetop. Put a serving dish of contrasting color in a low oven to warm.

Heat a wok or large, heavy skillet over high heat until hot enough to evaporate a bead of water on contact. Add the oil, swirl to coat the pan, then reduce the heat to medium-high. When the oil is hot enough to gently sizzle a pinch of peppercorn, add the peppercorns and let them sizzle until fragrant, about 5 seconds. Adjust the heat as necessary to prevent scorching. Add the scallion, ginger, and red chili flakes and stir until the fragrance is pronounced, 10–15 seconds. Add the mushrooms, toss to combine, then add the liquids to the pan and raise the heat to bring the mixture to a gentle simmer, stirring. Add the chicken, stir gently until it turns 95 percent white, then remove it promptly with the slotted spoon to the heated serving dish. Move quickly, lest the chicken overcook in the liquid.

Add the vinegar to the simmering sauce, stir, then taste for a good balance of sharp and sweet. True to Hunan taste, it should be on the sharp side. Lower the heat, stir the cornstarch mixture to recombine, then add it to the pan, stirring until the sauce thickens and becomes glossy, 5–10 seconds. Pour the sauce evenly over the chicken and sprinkle the sesame oil on top. Serve immediately, while pungent and aromatic.

Leftovers make an excellent cold topping for a salad of mixed greens or shredded carrots dressed with sesame oil and rice vinegar. Like all dishes made with chili, expect this one to be hotter the second time around.

MENU SUGGESTIONS:
I love this dish on its own for a simple supper, with *Silver and Gold Thread Rolls* (page 419) or a bowlful of *Everyday Chinese Rice* (page 400) to soak up the sauce and in season some *Cold-Tossed Asparagus with Sesame Seeds* (page 288) to munch on between mouthfuls. To accompany the chicken, try a white Burgundy, Meursault, Pouilly-Fuissé, or an oaky (as opposed to fruity) California Chardonnay.

| Hot
| and Sour
| Hunan
| Chicken

酸辣雞球

If *Tung-An Chicken* personifies Hunan's urban refinement, then this is its sassy country cousin. Dressed up with green zucchini rounds and orange carrot coins, here is a chicken that is unabashedly gutsy. I love eating it in the summer, when I can shop for the ingredients right in the garden. ◆ This is a simple dish to make. The chicken can be marinated a day or more in advance, and the whole dish assembled and served within 15 minutes. ◆ Characteristically, this kind of country dish calls for a whole, bone-in chicken, cut into small chunks. However, substituting boneless breasts gives it a nice touch of class and feeds the stockpot besides.

TECHNIQUE NOTES:
This recipe illustrates the technique for slicing and cooking vegetables of differing firmness. The carrots are cut half as thin and cooked twice as long as the zucchini, so in the end they will be equally tender-crisp. I love the carrots extra-crunchy—probably a reaction to the years in Po-fu's house when the near-toothless elders demanded near-soggy vegetables. If you like carrots a bit softer, stir-fry them an additional 15–20 seconds prior to adding the zucchini.

For velveting chicken, see TECHNIQUE NOTES, page 137.

Serves 3–4 as a main course, 5–8 as part of a multicourse meal.

INGREDIENTS:

> ¾ *pound skinned and boned fresh chicken breast, carefully trimmed of membranes, cartilage, and fat (weight after trimming; equal to 1 pound 6–8 ounces with skin on and bone in; see page 126 for easy, 5-minute boning)*

For marinating the chicken:
  1 large egg white
  1 tablespoon Chinese rice wine or quality, dry sherry
  1 teaspoon coarse kosher salt
  1 tablespoon cornstarch

  ¾–1 pound firm young zucchini, trimmed
  ½ pound carrots, trimmed and peeled

Aromatics:
  1 walnut-size nugget fresh ginger
  4–5 large cloves garlic, stem end removed, lightly smashed and peeled
  2 tablespoons Chinese salted black beans (page 561)
  ¾ teaspoon dried red chili flakes

  4 tablespoons corn or peanut oil, for stir-frying

Liquid seasonings:
  ½ cup unsalted chicken stock
  2½ tablespoons thin (regular) soy sauce
  2 tablespoons Chinese rice wine or quality, dry sherry
  2½ tablespoons white vinegar
  ¼ teaspoon sugar

For velveting the chicken:
  3–4 cups corn or peanut oil
  or
  4 cups water plus 2 teaspoons corn or peanut oil

Binder:
  1 tablespoon cornstarch dissolved in 1½ tablespoons cold chicken stock

Slicing and marinating the chicken:

Spread the meat flat on a cutting surface and cut it into 1-inch squares. Holding your knife parallel to the board, cut the thickest squares in half through the middle (using the "flying fingers" technique detailed on page 31), so that the pieces are of a relatively even thickness and will cook to doneness at the same time.

Blend the marinade ingredients until smooth and thick in the work bowl of a food processor fitted with the steel knife or in a blender. Process for a full 30–60 seconds to achieve a rich consistency. Combine the chicken and marinade in a small bowl, stirring with your fingers to coat and separate each slice. Seal airtight and refrigerate 6–8 hours or up to 1½ days, to permit the chicken to absorb the marinade. The longer it marinates, the more tender and flavorful it will be.

Other preparations:

Slice the zucchini into ¼ inch thick rounds. Slice the carrots into diagonal coins ⅛ inch thick. Sliced, the vegetables may be sealed and refrigerated in an airtight plastic bag for several hours before stir-frying.

Mince the ginger and garlic in the dry work bowl of a food processor fitted with the steel knife. Add the black beans, then process with one or two on-off turns to chop them coarsely. Alternatively, mince and chop the ingredients by hand. Set aside on a small saucer with the chili flakes. If you are working in advance, seal the saucer airtight and refrigerate the aromatics.

Combine the stock, soy, wine, vinegar, and sugar in a small bowl. This may be done hours ahead and the liquids left at room temperature or refrigerated.

Velveting the chicken:
About 10–15 minutes in advance of serving, velvet the chicken in water or oil, following the instructions on page 139.

Stir-frying the dish:
Have the velveted chicken, the vegetables, the minced aromatics and liquid seasonings, the oil for stir-frying, and the cornstarch mixture at hand.

Heat a wok or a deep, heavy skillet over high heat until hot enough to evaporate a bead of water on contact. Add 4 tablespoons oil, swirl to coat the pan, then wait until the oil is hot enough to sizzle 1 bit of minced garlic. Reduce the heat to medium-high, then add the aromatics to the pan, nudging the chili in last. Adjust the heat so they foam without browning. Stir until fully fragrant, about 15 seconds, then add the carrots. Stir briskly to separate the coins and coat them evenly with the oil and seasonings, then continue to stir-fry until they are slightly wilted or curly-looking around the edges, about 1 minute and 15 seconds in all. Add the zucchini and stir-fry briskly for 1 minute, separating the slices and mixing them with the carrots. Fold in the chicken with several quick stirs, then pour the combined liquids evenly over the top. Raise the heat to bring the liquids to a boil, stir 4–5 seconds to combine, then level the ingredients in the pan. Reduce the heat to maintain a steady simmer and cover the pan. Cook for 2 minutes. Remove the cover, test a zucchini slice for the desired crispness, and cook several seconds more if needed. Lower the heat to medium. Stir the cornstarch mixture to recombine it, then pour it evenly over the ingredients. Stir in wide sweeping motions for about 5 seconds, until the sauce thickens and becomes glossy.

Remove the mixture to a heated serving platter or shallow bowl. Arrange several of the carrot and zucchini coins on top to highlight the dish, then serve at once.

Leftovers are wonderful at room temperature, with a nice hunk of crusty bread to soak up the sauce. You may also steam the remainders in a covered bowl over high heat until hot, though the vegetables will lose their crunch. Like all dishes with chili flakes, expect this one to be hotter on the second day.

MENU SUGGESTIONS:
This is a colorful one-dish meal when accompanied by *Pan-Fried Scallion Breads* (page 435) or *Everyday Chinese Rice* (page 400). Add a California Zinfandel and I, for one, would be thoroughly content.

Lettuce- Wrapped Spicy Chicken 松子雞絲	I call this dish "the poor man's minced squab," in homage to the renowned Cantonese dish from which it is derived. The chicken version is a fraction of the labor and cost and is equally tempting and more fearlessly seasoned. It is a wonderfully versatile dish, appropriate for a festive occasion or a quiet dinner for two. ◆ Yin-yang contrast is the key to its beauty. The chicken should be steaming hot and glossily white, and the lettuce a chilly bright green. When you

wrap one inside the other, you taste spice, cool, crisp, hot, and tender all at once. ◆ Chinese chili sauce is ideal here. Its light oil base keeps the chicken white and provides just the right blend of subtlety and spice. Do *not* use hot bean paste; it would overshadow the chicken. Lacking the chili sauce, substitute a sprinkling of fresh chili threads cut hair-thin or ¼–½ teaspoon dried red chili flakes, and add them to the pan with the ginger. ◆ This is an excellent dish for a party. You may do everything short of the actual cooking up to 1½ days in advance, then stir-fry and serve the dish within 5 minutes.

TECHNIQUE NOTES:

If you concentrate on *undercooking* this dish, then you will not overcook it. The chicken threads cook through in a minute, so you must move quickly to add the chili, nuts, and binder. Aim to remove the chicken from the pan while the meat is still slightly pink inside, and it will cook to perfection from its own heat just as you set it on the table.

When boneless chicken is cut for stir-frying, it is treated to a special marinade: salt and wine season it, egg white gives it a plush, glossy coating, and cornstarch binds the marinade and seals in the juices. The longer the marinating period, the better for taste and texture. I prefer to leave it for a full day whenever possible. To combine the marinade ingredients, I use the food processor. It produces an unsurpassedly light, smooth marinade, which is worth having to wash the work bowl. If you do not have a processor, use a blender. In either case, process the mixture for a full 30–60 seconds to achieve a rich consistency that will cling to the chicken. If neither machine is available, put the marinade ingredients in a medium bowl, adding the cornstarch last so it will not stick to the bottom, then whisk until smooth and thick. Because beating increases the volume of the marinade, it will appear to be an excessively large amount when you pour it over the chicken. With 8–36 hours' refrigeration, however, the chicken will absorb most if not all of the marinade and become more tender and flavorful in the process. As a final word on velvet marinades, please note that the recipe calls for 1 large egg white. That is exactly *2 tablespoons* of egg white, which is contained in 1 grade "large" egg. If you are using larger than "large" eggs, you must measure out the egg white carefully before adding it to the marinade. Otherwise, the excess egg white will not incorporate properly with the other ingredients and will hang from the chicken like an unpleasantly chewy bit of skin when it is velveted.

Serves 3–4 as a main course, 6–8 as part of a multicourse meal.

INGREDIENTS:

> ¾ *pound skinned and boned fresh chicken breast, carefully trimmed of*
> *membranes, cartilage, and fat (weight after trimming; equal to 1 pound 6–8*
> *ounces with skin on and bone in; see page 126 for easy, 5-minute boning)*

For marinating the chicken:
  1 large egg white
  1 teaspoon coarse kosher salt
  1½ tablespoons Chinese rice wine or quality, dry sherry
  2 teaspoons cornstarch

  ½ ounce bean threads (glass noodles)
  8–16 perfect lettuce leaves, curly-edged red variety recommended
  3–4 cups fresh corn or peanut oil, for deep-frying the bean threads

For stir-frying the chicken:
  4–6 tablespoons corn or peanut oil
  1½ teaspoons finely minced fresh ginger
  1½–2 teaspoons Chinese chili sauce (page 537)
  1½ teaspoons cornstarch dissolved in 1 tablespoon cold water or cold chicken
  stock
  ¼ cup coarse-chopped walnuts, toasted pine nuts, or freshly toasted chopped
  almonds

Shredding and marinating the chicken:
Separate the fillets from the main breast pieces, remove membranes and tendons, then seal each piece of meat individually airtight in plastic wrap. Spread the pieces on a flat tray or plate, press gently to flatten, then chill in the freezer until rigid enough to be sliced neatly. Check frequently; timing will vary depending on the freezer. Do not freeze the chicken solid, which would injure its texture and taste.

When the meat is firm enough to slice neatly, remove the first piece from the freezer. Holding your knife parallel to the board, cut it through the middle into even slices ⅛ inch thick, then stack the slices and cut them crosswise, against the grain, into even shreds ⅛ inch thin. Cut the longer shreds into 1½–2 inch lengths. Repeat with the remaining pieces of chicken. (If you are new to this style of shredding, read about "flying fingers" and "curved knuckles" on pages 31 and 32. Once you get the knack, it is a 4-minute job to shred a whole breast with Chinese-style precision.)

Blend the marinade ingredients until smooth and thick in a food processor or blender. Process 30–60 seconds to achieve a rich consistency. Pour the marinade over the chicken, then stir well with your fingers to coat and separate the slices. Cover and put aside at room temperature, stirring occasionally, until the chicken is supple. Then seal the mixture airtight and refrigerate it for at least 1 hour, to set the marinade and infuse the chicken with its flavors. If you like, the chicken may be left to marinate for 1½ days.

Frying the noodle nest:
Use sturdy scissors to cut the dry noodles into 4–5-inch lengths, then pull the individual strands apart inside a large paper bag so they do not fly all over the kitchen. Have the noodles, a paper towel-lined tray, a large mesh or slotted spoon, and a pair of chopsticks or wooden tongs alongside your stovetop.

Heat a wok or large skillet over high heat until hot. Add oil to a depth of 2 inches or more, then heat to the dense-haze stage, 400° on a deep-fry thermometer. Turn off the heat so the oil does not burn. Test the oil with a single noodle. If it curls and puffs instantly, then the oil is ready.

Add half the noodles to the oil, wait for a split second while they puff, then quickly turn the nest over to puff the other side. Press the nest lightly into the oil for only an instant to insure that every strand is fried, then swiftly remove the nest to the tray to drain. Repeat with the remaining noodles. Fry them as speedily as possible, so they do not get oily. Once drained, break the noodles into bits with your fingers.

The noodles may be fried up to 1½ days in advance. Store them in a paper bag, or keep them in the oven with the pilot lighted if your kitchen is humid.

Once the oil cools, strain, bottle, and refrigerate it for frying nuts or noodle nests.

Preparing the lettuce:
Up to a day in advance of serving, wash, dry, and trim the lettuce of any coarse stems or imperfections. If you are working ahead, leave the leaves slightly damp. Stack them in order of size, then refrigerate wrapped in a damp tea towel or in a plastic bag lined with damp paper towels.

An hour or two before serving, dry the lettuce and arrange it in a flowerlike spiral on a large plate or lightweight serving tray. Start with the larger leaves on the outside, then work the smaller leaves into a cluster in the middle, putting the lettuce heart in the very center as a decoration. Bag the tray or cover it with a slightly damp cloth and refrigerate it until the moment of serving.

Stir-frying the chicken:
About 15–20 minutes in advance of serving, spread the noodles on a large serving platter and place in a low oven to warm. Have the chicken and all the ingredients for stir-frying within easy reach of your stovetop. Stir the chicken to loosen the shreds.

Heat a wok or heavy skillet over high heat until hot enough to evaporate a bead of water on contact. Add 4 tablespoons oil, swirl to coat the pan, then reduce the heat to medium. When the oil is hot enough to sizzle one bit of ginger, add the ginger. Stir to diffuse it in the oil, adjusting the heat so it foams without browning. When it is fully fragrant, about 10 seconds, add the chicken to the pan.

Stir-fry briskly *just* until the chicken turns white, dribbling in more oil from the side of the pan if the chicken is sticking. Be sparing with the oil, and if you add too much, wipe it away with a paper towel. As soon as the chicken turns white, reduce the heat to low, then fold in the chili sauce with a few quick stirs. Taste, and add more chili if desired.

Quickly stir the cornstarch mixture to recombine it, then pour it evenly over the chicken. Stir until the mixture becomes glossy and slightly thick, 3–4 seconds. Mound the chicken in the center of the noodle nest, then sprinkle with the nuts.

Serve the chicken immediately, accompanied by the platter of chilled lettuce.

Eating a lettuce-leaf package:
Invite each guest to take a lettuce leaf and fill it with a dollop or two of the chicken mixture. To eat it in traditional Chinese style, wrap the lettuce in a tube-like cylinder around the chicken with the help of your chopsticks. Hold the package shut at the far end with chopsticks and at the close end with the thumb and first finger of your other hand, then daintily steer it into your mouth to take a bite.

If you are happy using your fingers and don't care about elegance, then eat it American-style. Roll the lettuce around the filling, crimp the cylinder shut at both ends with your fingers, then eat it like a hot dog.

Leftovers are good cold, or resteamed in a tightly covered bowl until hot. Either way, they are slightly oily, extra-spicy, and superb for midnight munching.

MENU SUGGESTIONS:
This is a satisfying meal when paired with *Velvet Corn Soup* (page 460), or a festive first course in a dinner. *Pearl Balls* (page 187) would follow nicely, as would *Steamed Whole Fish with Seared Scallions* (page 248). To serve with the chicken, choose a Gewürztraminer or a light and fruity rosé.

Walnut Chicken Slices

核桃雞片

This is *real* Cantonese cooking—a rich and superbly textured dish without a bit of the glop or goo we associate with Cantonese cooking in America. The chicken is soft and succulent, the chopped nut coating is crisp and flavorful, and the touch of roasted pepper-salt cuts any trace of oil. It is an elegant way to begin a meal and has for years been one of my favorites. ◆ The deep-frying must be done at the last minute, but the remaining preparation may be done leisurely, days ahead. ◆ This is a great dish for entertaining. It doubles or triples beautifully.

TECHNIQUE NOTES:
Chilling the slices prior to frying helps the breading adhere. The egg white dries slightly, making a better "glue" for the nuts. However, if a lot of nuts fall off in frying, remove them with a fine-mesh skimmer. Too much debris in the bottom of the pot will lower the oil temperature and turn it shades darker, making it difficult to fry the slices with proper speed and set them with a good color.

Yields about 50 slices, enough to serve 6–8 as part of a multicourse meal, or about 15 as an hors d'oeuvre (not bad for ¾ pound of chicken!).

INGREDIENTS:

>   *¾ pound skinned and boned fresh chicken breast, carefully trimmed of membranes, cartilage, and fat (weight after trimming; equal to 1 pound 6–8 ounces with skin on and bone in; see page 126 for easy, 5-minute boning)*
>   *⅔–1 pound shelled walnuts*
>
>   *For marinating the chicken:*
>   *1 large egg white*
>   *1 tablespoon Chinese rice wine or quality, dry sherry*
>   *1½ teaspoons coarse kosher salt*
>   *2 tablespoons cornstarch*
>
>   *5–6 cups fresh corn or peanut oil, for deep-frying*
>   *Roasted Szechwan Pepper-Salt (page 476)*

Slicing the chicken:
Separate the fillets from the main breast pieces, if you have not already done so, and

remove membranes and tendons. Cut the chicken into rectangular pieces about 1½ inches long and 1 inch wide. Do not worry about having irregularly shaped pieces. Holding your knife parallel to the board, anchor the meat with the "flying fingers" technique described on page 31, and cut the thicker rectangles through the middle into 2 or 3 rectangles a scant ¼ inch thin. Using the broad side of the cleaver or knife, gently smack and flatten any slices that are thicker at one end.

Marinating the chicken:
Blend the marinade ingredients until smooth and thick in the work bowl of a food processor fitted with the steel knife or in a blender. Process the mixture a full 30–60 seconds to achieve a rich consistency.

Combine the chicken and marinade in a small bowl, stirring with your fingers to separate and coat the slices. Seal airtight, and refrigerate 1–36 hours to set the marinade and flavor the chicken. The longer it marinates, the softer and more flavorful it will be.

Chopping the nuts and dredging the chicken:
Chop the nuts in the food processor or by hand, 1 cup at a time, until peppercorn-size. Sift through a colander to remove the nutty "dust."

Spread a layer of nuts about ¼ inch deep in the bottom of a baking dish or large pie plate. Stir the chicken to redistribute the marinade, then arrange the slices almost next to one another on top of the nuts. Pour another ¼-inch layer of nuts evenly over the chicken, then press on the nuts with joined fingers to help them adhere. Transfer the slices in a single layer to a wax paper-lined tray or plate. Repeat until all the chicken slices have been coated. Put sheets of wax paper between the layers of coated slices. Seal airtight and refrigerate the slices for 1–8 hours before frying.

Extra nuts may be bagged and frozen for future use.

Frying the chicken slices:
About 15–20 minutes in advance of serving, preheat the oven to 250°. Line a jelly-roll pan or baking pan with a double thickness of paper towels. Have the lined pan and cooking chopsticks or a Chinese mesh spoon within easy reach of your stovetop.

Heat a wok or a deep, heavy skillet over high heat until hot. Add the oil, then heat to the light-haze stage, 350° on a deep-fry thermometer. Adjust the heat so the temperature does not rise, then remove the chicken from the refrigerator. Test the oil with one slice of chicken. If it comes to the surface within 2–3 seconds wearing a crown of white bubbles, the oil is ready.

Fry 10–15 slices at a time, slipping them into the oil one by one, in close succession, so long as the bubbles continue to surround each new slice and they all have room to float. Adjust the heat as required to maintain a steady 350° temperature. When the slices are cooked through, in about 1 minute, the nuts will be gold and the slices will float visibly high on the surface of the oil. Remove them promptly as they fry to doneness, retrieving them one by one from the oil and transferring them to the towel-lined tray to drain. Do not allow the coating to turn brown in the oil, as the nuts will continue to turn a shade or two darker from their own heat while the slices drain.

Between batches, put the tray in the oven to keep the slices warm, and shake the tray occasionally to even the slices and blot up the excess oil. Retest the oil with each new batch, and wait several minutes if needed for the oil to regain its original temperature. If you are frying a double or triple recipe, pause once or twice to dredge the oil of nuts.

Once all the chicken is fried, transfer the slices to a heated platter and sprinkle them lightly with pepper-salt. A dip dish of pepper-salt may be nested attractively in the center or alongside, for those who want an extra dash.

Straining the oil:
After the oil cools, strain it twice through several layers of cheesecloth. Even so, a dark scum will settle to the bottom of the oil when stored. When you next use it, discard this portion and wipe or wash the container clean.

Any leftovers are good snack food when served at room temperature. If reheated, they grow a bit oily, but will still be snapped up.

MENU SUGGESTIONS:
This is a perfect appetizer with which to launch a good bottle of white wine or Champagne and a party meal. As part of an elegant supper, pair it with *Clear-Steamed Flounder with White Pepper* (page 250) and *Shrimp, Leek, and Pine Nut Fried Rice* (page 408). Try the chicken also in the company of a good Italian white wine—a Soave or Orvieto.

Paper-Wrapped Chicken

紙包雞

I first saw these mysterious parcels of chicken at a dinner given by some arty young Chinese friends. Everyone reached right in with their chopsticks to deftly unwrap the paper and exclaim over the tender, aromatic treat inside. Everyone, that is, except me! I was then a vegetarian, and while I was stupid not to abandon my principles on the spot and grab some of that chicken, the smell and look of it were enough to urge me to become a born-again carnivore. ◆ Clear, sturdy cellophane that will not melt in hot oil is the ideal wrapping. The brand I use is Clearphane "transparent film gift wrapping," usually found in the dusty corners of old-fashioned drug and stationery stores. Be sure to test what you buy *before* you set about wrapping the packages. ◆ Less pretty but still serviceable is parchment paper. Like the cellophane, be sure to pleat it sharply at every seam so the package will not unfold when fried.

TECHNIQUE NOTES:
Sesame oil does the dual job of flavoring the chicken and keeping it from sticking to the paper. Do not use too much, lest the chicken be overpowered or the package become hard to crease closed.

Serves 6–9 as part of a multicourse meal, 18 as a single hors d'oeuvre.

INGREDIENTS:

>   1 pound skinned and boned fresh chicken breast, carefully trimmed of membranes, cartilage, and fat (weight after trimming; equal to about 2 pounds with skin on and bone in; see page 126 for easy, 5-minute boning)

> For marinating the chicken:
> 1 tablespoon thin (regular) soy sauce
> ½ teaspoon coarse kosher salt
> 1 teaspoon sugar

¼ teaspoon freshly ground white pepper
1 tablespoon Chinese rice wine or quality, dry sherry

For garnishing the packages [choose one set of garnishes, or cut the ingredients in half and decorate some of the packages one way and some of the packages the other way]:
6 medium Chinese dried black mushrooms
18 strips flavorful boiled or smoked ham, 1½ inches long, ⅛ inch thick, and ¼ inch wide (equal to about 2 ounces uncut ham)
½ cup green peas, blanched until tender-crisp if fresh, thoroughly defrosted if frozen
or
1 Chinese pork sausage (page 541)
18 perfect coriander leaves

For wrapping the packages:
18 5-inch squares of heavy-duty clear cellophane
2–3 tablespoons Chinese or Japanese sesame oil

6–8 cups corn or peanut oil, for deep-frying

Slicing and marinating the chicken:
Slice the chicken into thin rectangles as directed on page 148.
    Combine the marinade ingredients in a shallow bowl, then add the chicken and stir well with your fingers to separate and coat the slices. Put aside for 30 minutes, stirring occasionally. For fuller flavor, seal airtight and refrigerate overnight.

Preparing the garnishes:
For the first set of garnishes, cover the mushrooms with cold or hot water, and soak until fully soft and spongy, 20 minutes to an hour. Drain, rinse to remove any sand trapped in the gills, then gently squeeze out the excess moisture. Snip off the stems with scissors, then cut each cap lengthwise into 3 strips.
    And/or, for the second set of garnishes, cut the sausage on a diagonal into 18 thin coins, each ⅛ inch thick. Just before wrapping the packages, steam or simmer the coins until the fat turns soft and translucent, 10–12 minutes.

Wrapping the packages:
Line up the sesame oil, cellophane squares, garnishes, and chicken slices. Stir the chicken to redistribute the marinade. Have a plate or tray nearby to hold the finished packages.
    Following the illustration on page 152, put a cellophane square in front of you turned to form a diamond. With your fingers, spread an even film of sesame oil over the entire face of the cellophane. For garnish #1, place a strip of ham horizontally just above the center of the diamond. Put a strip of mushroom below the ham, black side down. Just below the mushroom, make a string of 4–5 peas. For garnish #2, put a slice of sausage alongside a coriander leaf in the center of the diamond; put the leaf dark green side down. Place two or three slices of chicken directly on top of the garnishes in a rectangular pattern. If you have several skimpy or odd-shaped pieces, then overlap them to form a neat rectangle. (For proper wrapping, the filling should now be positioned ⅓ above and ⅔ below the midline of the diamond.)

Bring the point of the cellophane closest to you up and over the filling. Crease sharply just below the chicken. Bring the two side points over the filling, crossing one another. Align these overlapping flaps so the sides of the package form right angles with the base. Run your nail along the two sides to crease them sharply. Fold the bottom third of the package, that is the part containing the chicken, up and over, so the package looks like an envelope with the top flap open. Finally, tuck the flap as far as it will go into the envelope between the chicken and the two crossed sides, then crease it sealed just above the chicken. You should now have a neat rectangular package, about 2½ inches long and 1¼ inches wide. Run your nail along each edge to sharpen the folds.

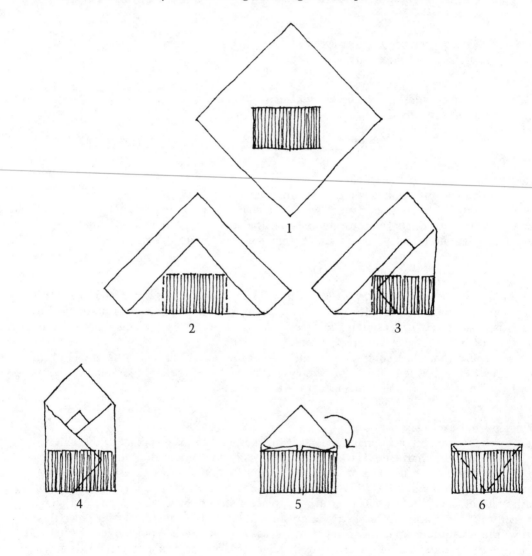

If you are not successful, practice the folds with a 5-inch square of empty paper until you have mastered the shape, and then try it with the chicken. It is easy, once you understand the method.

The finished garnish #1 packages may be refrigerated on the uncovered plate or tray for several hours. Bring to room temperature before frying. Garnish #2 packages must be fried at once while the sausage is soft.

Frying the packages:
About 15–20 minutes before serving, heat a wok or deep-frying vessel over high heat until hot. Add the oil and heat to a moderate 325° on a deep-fry thermometer, when rapid swirls are visible just below the surface of the oil. Have the chicken, a tray lined with a double thickness of paper towels, and cooking chopsticks, wooden tongs, or a mesh spoon all within easy reach of your stovetop. Adjust the heat so the oil temperature does not rise.

Test the oil with one package. If it rises to the surface in 3–4 seconds surrounded by tiny white bubbles, the oil is ready.

Fry 5–8 packages at a time, slipping them slowly into the oil one by one, checking to see that each rises quickly to the surface surrounded by bubbles and has room to float. Turn the packages gently once or twice as they fry. Remove from the oil after 2–3 minutes, when the chicken has turned white and had an extra minute to exchange flavors with the garnishes and sesame oil. Stand the packages on end on the toweling to drain, then fry the remaining packages. Retest the oil with each new batch, and wait several minutes if needed for the oil to regain its original temperature.

Serve the packages as soon as they are all fried, arranged in a swirl or in overlapping rows on a heated platter of contrasting color, garnish side up. Invite everyone to open his or her own package, with chopsticks or fingers as desired. If you have oiled the paper sufficiently, the envelope will open easily and the chicken and garnishes will cleave together as one delectable morsel.

MENU SUGGESTIONS:
This is an elegant, novel way to open a dinner of refined tastes. *Steamed Whole Fish with Seared Scallions* (page 248), *Steamed Winter Melon with Ham* (page 315), and *Shrimp, Leek, and Pine Nut Fried Rice* (page 408) would be one nice menu to follow, accompanied by a dry Alsatian Riesling or California Johannisberg Riesling.

| Master Sauce Chicken

滷雞 |

North Chinese kitchens harbor the smells that are most dear to me and among them is invariably that of a potted chicken, simmering slowly in a rich soy brew. It is a dish that requires almost no work to produce, and at the end of several heavenly scented hours you are left with a sublime chicken and an inspired master sauce from which you can create any number of homey, tempting dishes. ◆ Master sauces can be simple or complex. An average home cook combines wine, soy, sugar, and anise, while the restaurants of old Peking purported to begin with no less than twenty ingredients, passed as a secret from chef to apprentice. My recipe offers a bit of both worlds. You may blend the primary ingredients for a full-flavored, simple sauce, or add the optional aromatics for a more complex brew. Go out of your way to find Chinese golden rock sugar (page 570). It contributes a soft, inimitable sweetness and a lovely sheen. If you cannot find it, substitute about 2 tablespoons sugar to taste. ◆ This chicken is good hot from the pot, tepid, or at room temperature. Leftover meat may be shredded and used in *Master Sauce Chicken Salad with Tea Melon* (page 135), or in any impromptu salad. ◆ Master sauce will keep indefinitely in the freezer and grows better with use. It is the base for *Master Sauce Eggs* (page 327), *Carnelian Carrot Coins* (page 289), and *Master Sauce Mushrooms* (page 290). In your Western repertoire, it will enrich most anything meaty, from brisket to grilled pork.

TECHNIQUE NOTES:
Be diligent about basting the chicken. The repeated basting imparts a rich color and penetrating flavor, not to be had otherwise.

Serves 4–5 as a main course, 6–10 as part of a multicourse meal.

INGREDIENTS:

> *3½–4 pound perfectly fresh chicken, fresh-killed best (weight after removal of head, neck, feet, wingtips, tail and fat sacs)*

> *Primary sauce ingredients:*
> *2½ cups water*
> *2 cups thin (regular) soy sauce (read the cautionary note regarding brands on page 568)*
> *⅓ cup Chinese rice wine or quality, dry sherry*
> *4–5 quarter-size slices fresh ginger*
> *12 individual points star anise (equal to 1½ whole stars)*
> *2 ounces Chinese golden rock sugar, crushed (equal to ⅓ cup smashed bits)*

> *Optional aromatics:*
> *1 thin scallion, cut into 3-inch lengths*
> *1 tablespoon crumbled Chinese cassia bark (page 534), or 1½-inch cinnamon stick, broken into bits*
> *1 thumb-size piece home-dried orange or tangerine peel (page 557), blanched in plain simmering water for 10 minutes and drained*

> *¼–¾ teaspoon Chinese or Japanese sesame oil*

Simmering the chicken and setting the color:
Clean the chicken thoroughly as directed on page 125.

Choose a heavy pot that will hold the chicken snugly and allow it to be turned. Spank the ginger and scallion to release their juices, then add them to the pot with the water, soy, wine, anise, and optional aromatics. Do *not* add the sugar at this time.

Bring the ingredients to a boil over moderately high heat, then ease the chicken into the pot, breast side up. While waiting for the liquids to return to a boil, baste the chicken continuously with a large spoon to set the color and tighten the skin. Continue basting for several seconds after the boil is reached, then reduce the heat to maintain a gentle simmer and cover the pot. Simmer 20 minutes. Uncover the pot twice during this initial cooking to check the simmer and baste the bird.

Turn the chicken over, being careful not to tear the skin. One reliable method is to anchor a long cooking chopstick or wooden spoon in the cavity while turning the bird by its neck bone with a mitted hand. Scatter the sugar evenly around the chicken, swish the sauce to dissolve the sugar, then baste continuously for 1 minute. Cover the pot and simmer 20 minutes more, basting the chicken thoroughly at 10-minute intervals.

Steeping to deepen the flavors of the chicken and the sauce:
Move the covered pot to a cool burner and let the chicken steep for 1½ hours. Baste the chicken several times as it steeps, replacing the cover each time to retain the heat.

Turn the chicken over, with the same care as before. Baste it thoroughly, replace the cover, and steep 30 minutes more, again basting at 10-minute intervals.

Glossing and serving the chicken:
Gently remove the chicken to a plate, then tip the plate over the pot to drain the cavity of sauce. Transfer the chicken to a cutting board and let it cool several minutes. Rub the sesame oil between your palms, then smooth it evenly over the chicken to give it fragrance and sheen. Don't miss the spots under the wings and thighs.

Serve the chicken hot, tepid, or at room temperature. To retain its moistness, cut just before serving, either Chinese-style (page 128) or in a fashion to suit you. Present the chicken on a platter of contrasting color. Hide any chopping failures or skinless bits under a mound of the prettiest breast pieces, then surround with the wings and drumsticks. Moisten with a few spoonfuls of the heated sauce and garnish, if desired, with sprigs of fresh coriander or clusters of red radish fans (page 114).

Leftover chicken is best at room temperature or gently reheated with a bit of the master sauce.

Storing and replenishing the master sauce:
Strain the sauce through several layers of damp cheesecloth, discard the seasonings, then refrigerate up to one week or freeze indefinitely for future use. Leave a small amount of chicken fat in the sauce. It will lend its sheen and rich goodness to the next thing you cook.

If the sauce diminishes and you do not want to start from scratch with a whole chicken, then use 2–3 pounds chicken breasts. Add to the sauce that remains more of everything you started with, but substitute a light, unsalted chicken stock for water and use only 2–3 slices of ginger. Keep to the original proportions given in the recipe and follow the cooking procedure on page 135. As you cook it, taste the replenished sauce for the proper balance of sugar, soy, and wine, and adjust if needed.

MENU SUGGESTIONS:
This is wonderful picnic, patio or buffet food, best accompanied by colorful cold dishes such as *Dry-Fried Szechwan String Beans* (page 297), and *Orchid's Tangy Cool Noodles* (page 356). If you are serving the chicken hot, try it with *Red Bell Pepper with Garlic and Coriander* (page 314) and *Everyday Chinese Rice* (page 400), or *Shanghai Vegetable Rice* (page 402), for a homey, satisfying dinner. Partner the chicken with a light California Zinfandel or a Beaujolais or Gamay Beaujolais with personality. Or, try a Bardolino or a white Zinfandel or other Blanc de Noirs, depending on mood and menu.

| Casseroled Chicken with Smoky Chestnuts 紅燒栗子雞 | Itinerant chestnut vendors filled the streets of Taipei in winter, animating the alleyways with their calls and the sweet, dusky perfume of roasting chestnuts, stirring in me memories of Fifth Avenue and the winters of my childhood. While Chinese, like New Yorkers, love munching them plain, a good many chestnuts find their way into poultry stews such as this one. Warming, satisfying, and seductively hinting of wine, it is a lovely dish at any time of year. ◆ I like the |

dried variety of chestnuts found in Chinese markets. They are extremely easy to use, smoked and fragrant unlike the Italian ones, and available year round. Fresh chestnuts should be roasted or toasted before inclusion in the stew, and I offer the following recipe from a 1936 volume entitled *The Chinese Cookbook: 300 Very Fine "Number One Good" Recipes . . . First Class Food* by Mr. M. Sing Au.

Sand-Roasted Chestnuts
Half fill a frying pan with sand, and heat over hot fire. Put in a handful of raw chestnuts. If sand is real hot, it will require about 15 minutes to cook the chestnuts. [NB: *Stir the chestnuts constantly. Over gas, you may use a wok.*]

Like most stews, this one is best made in advance and left to sit for a day or more before eating. The flavors develop, the aroma intensifies, and a good dish becomes extraordinary.

TECHNIQUE NOTES:
Deep-frying the chicken before potting it serves two ends. One, it turns the meat a lustrous mahogany-gold. Two, it firms the texture to a resilient chewiness, what the Chinese call "locking up" the meat. It is a distinctive touch, well worth the extra step.

Serves 4 as a main dish, 6–8 as part of a multicourse meal.

INGREDIENTS:

> brimming ½ cup dried Chinese chestnuts, or 1 cup freshly roasted chestnuts, peeled
> 3½–4 pound perfectly fresh chicken, fresh-killed best (weight after removal of head, neck, feet, wingtips, tail and fat sacs)

> For marinating the chicken:
> 2 medium whole scallions, cut into 3-inch lengths
> 3 quarter-size slices fresh ginger
> 5 tablespoons thin (regular) soy sauce (read the cautionary note regarding brands on page 568)

> For stewing the chicken:
> 5 tablespoons Chinese rice wine or quality, dry sherry
> 3 tablespoons packed brown sugar
> 3 tablespoons thin (regular) soy sauce
> 2 cups water or light, unsalted chicken stock

> 6 cups corn or peanut oil, for deep-frying

Soaking the dried chestnuts:
Cover the chestnuts with boiling water and cover the bowl to retain the heat. Soak 3

hours, or overnight. Use a toothpick or bamboo skewer to remove any red skin trapped in the folds, then return the chestnuts to the soaking liquid until ready to use.

Chopping and marinating the chicken:
Clean the chicken thoroughly as directed on page 125. Chop it into bite-size pieces Chinese-style, as directed on page 128. Discard any loose bits of bone that may result from chopping.

Lightly smash the scallion and ginger to release their juices, then combine them in a bowl with the chicken and 5 tablespoons soy sauce. Toss well to distribute the seasonings, then press the chicken flat, seal the bowl airtight, and marinate 3–6 hours at room temperature or up to 24 hours in the refrigerator. Toss occasionally to redistribute the marinade.

Frying the chicken in two batches:
Discard the ginger and scallion. Stir the chicken to loosen the pieces. Have a tray lined with a triple thickness of paper towels and a large Chinese mesh spoon or a deep-fry basket near your stovetop.

Heat a wok or a deep, heavy pot over high heat until hot. Add the oil, leaving 2½ inches free at the top of the pot to accommodate bubbling. Heat the oil to the dense-haze stage, 400° on a deep-fry thermometer.

Dip the mesh spoon or fry basket into the oil to heat it through and prevent the chicken from sticking to the metal. Put one half of the chicken into the spoon or basket, then gently lower it into the oil. The chicken should foam upon contact. If it does not, remove it and wait for the oil to gain the proper temperature.

Stir immediately and gently to separate the pieces, using the rim of the spoon or basket. When the chicken turns a deep brown gold, in a minute or less, remove the pieces in one sweep, and hold them briefly above the oil to drain. Transfer to the towel-lined tray, then give the tray a shake to even out the pieces and blot up the excess oil.

Wait for the oil to regain 400°, then repeat with the remaining chicken. Expect the second batch to brown in less time, about 30 seconds.

Let the oil cool, then strain, bottle, and refrigerate it for future use.

Stewing the chicken:
Combine the stewing ingredients, stirring to dissolve the sugar.

Choose a Chinese sand pot (page 98), or a heavy pot that will hold the chicken snugly. Put the chicken, the drained chestnuts, and the combined stewing ingredients in the pot. If you are using freshly roasted chestnuts, wait until the final 20 minutes of simmering before adding them to the pot.

Bring the liquids to a boil over moderate heat, then reduce the heat to maintain a gentle simmer. If you are using a Chinese sand pot, begin with low heat and raise it gradually to prevent the pot from cracking. (You may also wish to use an asbestos pad.) Stir the contents to distribute the sauce, then cover the pot and simmer 50 minutes. Lift the lid once or twice to check the simmer and stir the stew. When it is done, taste the sauce. It should be smoky and sweet, with an edge of soy and wine. Adjust the seasonings, if necessary, to bring the flavors to fullness.

For best taste, let the stew come to room temperature, then refrigerate it for 1–3 days before eating.

Serving the stew:
If refrigerated, bring the stew to a simmer and heat it through. Carry it from the kitchen

in the covered sand pot or in a heated, covered serving bowl, and lift the lid at the table to inspire everyone's appetite.

Have one or more small bowls available to hold bones. Sucking on bones to unleash their goodness is permissible in the best of Chinese society, so encourage your guests to be traditional.

Leftovers keep well and improve upon reheating.

MENU SUGGESTIONS:
I like this dish best with *Everyday Chinese Bread* (page 410) or *Silver and Gold Thread Rolls* (page 419) to soak up the sauce. Another sauce solution is *Everyday Chinese Rice* (page 400). If a vegetable is wanted, try *Brussels Sprouts with Black Sesame Seeds* (page 313), or *Spinach with Glass Noodles* (page 308). To accompany the chicken, try a Rhône wine—a Châteauneuf-du-Pape or Gigondas.

Tea and Spice Smoked Chicken 燻雞

As a graduate student studying for master's exams and deprived of most of life's sensual pleasures, I became addicted to smoked chicken. This great, northern Chinese treat was made regularly by a broad and beaming Taiwanese woman who ran a mom-and-pop deli not far from Princeton, and while the window advertised "Italian Bangers" and a shelf of pornography magazines lined one wall, I knew that far better than all *those* chickens were the home-smoked ones that lay secreted behind the counter. ◆ When I left Princeton, hunger overcame trepidation and I discovered that smoking chickens on my own was easy and practical, and did not fill the house with smoke. Indeed, I was disappointed. The incense from the smoking spices was so seductive that I wished it would have lingered longer. ◆ Smoked chicken is very easy and leisurely to prepare. The marinating, steaming, and smoking steps require only an hour or less apiece, so this is a great choice for a cook who can steal only a bit of time each day. Begin at least 30 hours before serving, or as much as 3 days in advance, whichever is convenient. ◆ Smoked chicken is delicious hot, tepid, or at room temperature, and is equally at home at a fancy dinner or a picnic.

TECHNIQUE NOTES:
For everything I know about Chinese-style smoking, including techniques and tools, read carefully the section on smoking (page 90). If your pot will not comfortably accommodate a high-breasted chicken, then fashion a dome-shaped lid from several layers of heavy-duty foil, molding them around a large mixing bowl to get the right shape.

Serves 4–5 as a main dish, 6–10 as part of a multicourse meal.

INGREDIENTS:

> *3½–4 pound perfectly fresh chicken, fresh-killed best (weight after removal of head, neck, feet, wingtips, tail and fat sacs)*

> For marinating the chicken:
> *2½–3 tablespoons coarse kosher salt*
> *1–1½ tablespoons Szechwan brown peppercorns*
> *¼–½ teaspoon finely minced home-dried orange or tangerine peel (optional)*

For steaming the chicken:
   2 medium whole scallions, cut into 3-inch lengths
   5 quarter-size slices fresh ginger

For smoking the chicken:
   ¼ cup dry black tea leaves
   ¼ cup packed brown sugar
   ⅓ cup raw rice
   1 tablespoon Szechwan brown peppercorns
   3 whole star anise (equal to 24 individual points)
   ⅛ cup Chinese cassia bark, broken into small bits, or two 2-inch cinnamon
     sticks, broken into small bits

   ¼ cup white or packed brown sugar, for smoking the second side of the
     chicken
   1–1½ teaspoons Chinese or Japanese sesame oil

Marinating the chicken:
Clean the chicken thoroughly, as directed on page 125. Blot it dry inside and out.
    Combine the salt and peppercorns for marinating in a heavy skillet, using the larger amount for a bigger bird or if you enjoy a more intense seasoning. Set the skillet over medium heat and stir constantly until the salt turns off-white, about 4 minutes. The peppercorns will smoke, but adjust the heat as necessary to prevent them from scorching.
    Once the salt is roasted, grind the hot mixture to a coarse powder, in the work bowl of a food processor fitted with the steel knife, processing for about 2 consecutive minutes, or in a spice mill, blender, or mortar. Strain through a fine-mesh strainer to remove the peppercorn husks, then combine with the minced dry peel, if you are using it. (The peel gives the chicken skin a tangy edge of flavor which I love.)
    Rub ⅔ of the spice mixture vigorously over the outside of the chicken, being sure not to miss the spots under the wings and thighs. Rub the remaining ⅓ in the cavity, turning the chicken once or twice so you reach every spot. Put the bird breast side up in a Pyrex pie plate or shallow bowl, cover airtight with plastic wrap, then set it aside to marinate at room temperature for 24 hours. Turn the bird once after 12 hours, then reseal. For a fuller flavor or for convenience, you may refrigerate the bird for an additional 24 hours, again turning it over midway through the time in the refrigerator. Bring to room temperature before steaming.

Steaming the chicken:
(For details on steaming and how to improvise a steamer, see page 60.)
    Drain the accumulated liquids, then place the chicken breast side up in a Pyrex pie plate or a heatproof quiche plate or shallow bowl at least 1 inch smaller in diameter than your steamer. (I marinate and steam the chicken in the same pie plate.) Smash the ginger and scallions with the blunt handle end or broad side of a cleaver or chef's knife to spread the fibers and bring the juices to the surface, then spread ⅓ on the floor of the cavity and ⅔ over the top of the chicken, poking a piece or two of scallion under the wings. This gives the chicken a remarkably clean fragrance as well as a nice bit of flavor.
    Fill the steamer with water to within 1 inch of the steaming rack, then bring to a rolling boil over high heat. Put extra water on to boil if the steamer will need replenishing. Put the plate with the chicken in the steamer, wait briefly for the steam to gush up around the chicken, then cover the steamer and reduce the heat to medium-high. Steam

the chicken for 35–40 minutes, the extra minutes for the bigger bird. After 20 minutes, turn off the heat momentarily (to quench the steam while you work), then slowly lift the steamer lid away from you and remove most of the juices surrounding the bird with a bulb-top baster if the juices are threatening to overflow the bowl. Retain the juices. Then, promptly replace the lid, restore the heat to medium-high, and resume steaming.

Air-drying to crisp the skin:
Once the steaming time is up, turn off the heat and lift the lid very slowly away from you. Wearing long cooking mitts, carefully remove the bowl with the chicken from the steamer, then tilt over the juice bowl to decant the remaining steaming liquids. Remove the scallion and ginger from the top and the cavity of the chicken, using chopsticks to get the pieces lodged in the cavity, then very gently transfer the chicken breast side up to a rack to cool. Put the rack on a tray or plate to catch the drippings and leave the bird to cool and dry for 3 hours or overnight, turning it once midway to insure even drying. Once completely cool, the chicken may be bagged airtight and refrigerated 1–2 days prior to smoking. Bring to room temperature before smoking.

If you don't have time to air-dry the chicken, simply pat it dry inside and out with paper towels, then proceed directly to smoke it. It will still be delicious.

Storing the steaming juices:
Strain the reserved juices through several layers of damp cheesecloth, then refrigerate them. When the fat congeals on top, scrape it off and store the fat and the jellied juices separately in the freezer. Use them for stir-frying Chinese cabbage (page 311), making a smoked chicken noodle soup (page 462), or adding flavor to any simple dish where a seasoned fat or seasoned chicken stock would be appreciated. Be careful when using the juices especially as they are quite salty. I usually combine them with an equal or greater portion of unsalted chicken stock, tasting as I add until I get just the degree of seasoning I want.

Smoking the chicken to flavor and color it:
Prepare the pot, lid, and rack for smoking as directed on page 95. Combine the smoking ingredients, then spread them evenly in the bottom of the pot. Fit the oiled rack in the pot, about 1 inch above the smoking ingredients, then place the chicken breast side up on the rack.

Put the pot over high heat. When the mixture starts to smoke convincingly in 2 or 3 spots, anywhere from 4–10 minutes depending on the stove and the pot you are using, cover the pot securely and crimp the foil loosely shut. Smoke the chicken for 10 minutes, then turn off the heat, and let the chicken rest in the sealed pot for 5 minutes without removing it from the stove. (It will still be smoking inside the pot, from the combusting sugar mixture, the heat of the pot and the residual heat of the burner.)

Once the resting time is up, carefully undo the foil seal and then slowly raise the lid away from you (ideally, with the fan above the stove turned on, near an open window, or out on the back porch). The chicken should be a rich golden to mahogany brown on its breast side. If it is not, then the heat was not intense enough to start the mixture smoking properly, and you should sprinkle an additional 3–4 tablespoons sugar around the edge of the blackened smoking ingredients and repeat the smoking process as outlined above for only half of the smoking and resting times, waiting first to see that the smoke has started in earnest before you cover the pot. If, on the other hand, the top side is nicely golden brown to deep brown—the darker color indicating a more intense flavor—then carefully turn the chicken over, breast side down, on the rack. The bird will be fairly hot, so use mitts or several folded paper towels to protect your hands while turning it. Expect while you turn it that a bit of hot liquid, built up inside the cavity of the bird while it was being smoked, will spill out of the cavity and into the pot, and don't worry about it.

Once the bird is turned, sprinkle the additional 4 tablespoons of white or brown sugar evenly around the edge of the blackened smoking ingredients, then return the un-covered pot to high heat. Wait until the newly added sugar begins to bubble and smoke convincingly in several spots, then replace the cover as before, crimping the foil shut. Smoke the bird on the second side for 5 minutes, then turn off the heat and let it rest in the covered pot on the second side for 3 minutes, extending the time by a few minutes if you learned when smoking the first side that your stove is not as energetic as it might be. When you lift the lid, the bird should be golden brown.

Once the bird is smoked on both sides, remove it carefully to a large plate, hold-ing it evenly so that the juices inside the cavity will empty out onto the plate (where you can enjoy eating them). Wrap up the burnt ingredients in the foil lining the pot and the lid, then dispose of them in a sealed bag or outside of the house. They are the culprits in smelling up the kitchen. Rub the sesame oil between your palms, then smooth it evenly over the outside of the chicken, which should be left breast side up on the plate.

Cutting and serving the chicken:
You may serve the chicken immediately after glossing it, or serve it tepid or at room temperature within a few hours of smoking. Or, you can let the bird cool, seal it airtight, and then refrigerate it for 2 days before eating, serving it at room temperature or sealing it airtight in foil and reheating it in a 400° oven just until hot.

Just prior to serving, cut the chicken Chinese-style (as directed on page 128), or in pieces to suit you. Then transfer to a serving platter of contrasting color, putting the prettiest pieces on top and hiding any tattered edges with colorful clumps of fresh cor-iander or a cluster of red radish fans (page 114). Once cool, it is easy to cut in very neat, clean-edged pieces. If it is hot, expect the chicken juices to run all over the cutting board and move quickly to spill them (they are delicious!) back onto the serving platter. (If they have been left behind after the guests are gone, I lap them up with bread.)

Leftovers should be sealed tightly to preserve their perfume. Eat them reheated or at room temperature, not ice cold, to enjoy the full aroma. They are also excellent shred-ded into a salad of crisp greens and dressed lightly with oil and rice vinegar, or added to a soup (page 462).

MENU SUGGESTIONS:
For a light meal, try pairing the chicken with a simple stir-fried vegetable like *Red Bell Pepper with Garlic and Coriander* (page 314), or with a tossed salad of interesting greens and a light red Bordeaux. As part of a cold buffet, the chicken is excellent in combination with *Peony Blossom Cold Noodles* (page 358) and *Sweet and Tangy Cucumber Pickles* (page 110) or *Hot and Sour Chinese Cabbage Hearts* (page 112).

**Cinnamon
Bark
Chicken**

桂皮雞

I love crumbly cinnamon bark with its distinctive sweet-strong flavor. One day I rubbed a generous amount of it over the skin of a
marinating chicken and—*voilà!*—the scrumptious "Cinnamon Bark
Chicken" was born. It is a variation on *Fragrant Crispy Chicken*, one
of many Szechwanese classics known not for a fiery seasoning, but
for a uniquely interesting texture. This is a chicken whose bite is as
good as its bark. You will want to eat it all, including the delicate,
crispy bones. ◆ Look for cinnamon that is paper-thin and decidedly aromatic. If
you use the thicker sort, then use a 2–2½-inch piece and pulverize it before roasting. ◆ This is a leisurely dish to prepare, good for weekend entertaining. You may marinate the bird overnight, steam it in the morning, then deep-fry and serve it that night.

TECHNIQUE NOTES:
Breaking the breast bone flattens the chicken, making it easier to fry and allowing a more
even penetration of spices during marination and steaming. It is great fun besides.

What may not seem like fun is deep-frying a whole anything. For encouragement,
see page 82. For the technique of double deep-frying, see TECHNIQUE NOTES, page 242.

Serves 3–4 as a main course, 5–6 as part of a multicourse meal.

INGREDIENTS:

> *3½–4 pound perfectly fresh chicken, fresh-killed best (weight after removal of
> head, neck, feet, wingtips, tail and fat sacs)*

> For marinating the chicken:
> *3–3½-inch cinnamon stick, very fragrant, paper-thin variety, crumbled*
> *2½ teaspoons–1 tablespoon Szechwan brown peppercorns*
> *2½–3 tablespoons coarse kosher salt*
> *10–12 individual points star anise (equal to 1 whole star, plus 2–4 points)*

> For steaming the chicken:
> *2 tablespoons Chinese rice wine or quality, dry sherry*
> *3 medium whole scallions, cut into 3-inch lengths*
> *3 quarter-size slices fresh ginger*

> *1½–2 tablespoons thin (regular) soy sauce*
> *6–7 cups corn or peanut oil, for deep-frying*

> Accompaniments:
> *Roasted Szechwan Pepper-Salt (page 476)*
> *Flower Rolls (page 415)*

Marinating the chicken:
Clean the chicken thoroughly as directed on page 125. Pat dry inside and out. Put the
chicken on its back, then press firmly on the breastbone with two hands to break the
bone and flatten the bird.

Combine the ingredients for marinating the chicken in a heavy skillet. (Use the
larger amounts for the bigger bird or if you like a more intense seasoning.) Set over moderate heat and stir until the salt turns off-white and the mixture is fragrant, about 4
minutes. The peppercorns will smoke; do not let them or the cinnamon burn.

Grind the spices continuously for 3 minutes in the work bowl of a food processor fitted with the steel knife, or in a mortar. The anise will not break up completely, so be careful when you rub the chicken not to pierce the skin with the pointy bits. Rub the chicken evenly with the mixture, using ⅔ on the outside and ⅓ in the cavity. Do not miss the spots under the wings and thighs. Put the chicken breast side up in a Pyrex pie plate or shallow bowl, cover loosely with plastic wrap and put aside to marinate 3 hours to overnight at room temperature. Turn the bird once, midway through the marinating.

Steaming the chicken:
(For details on steaming and how to improvise a steamer, see page 60.)
Drain and discard the accumulated liquids. Rub the outside of the bird with the wine, then place it breast side up in a Pyrex pie plate or shallow bowl at least 1 inch smaller in diameter than your steamer. Lightly smash the ginger and scallion to release their juices, then spread ⅔ on top of the chicken and the remainder in the cavity.

Fill the steamer with water to within 1 inch of the steaming rack, then bring to a rolling boil over high heat. Put extra water on to boil if the steamer will need replenishing. Place the bowl in the steamer, wait until the steam begins to gush around the chicken, then cover the steamer. Steam over medium heat 1¾ hours. Every 30 minutes, check the level of the water and remove most of the juices surrounding the chicken, using a gravy-type ladle or a bulb-top baster.

For straining, storing, and using the juices in other dishes see page 160.

Air-drying and coloring the chicken:
Carefully remove the bowl from the steamer, then tilt to decant the remaining juices. Wait a few minutes for the chicken to cease steaming, then discard the scallion and ginger, using chopsticks to retrieve the pieces in the cavity. Brush off the peppercorn, cinnamon, and anise bits, then smooth the soy evenly over the outside of the bird to impart flavor and color.

Gently transfer the bird breast side up to a rack to cool. Put a baking sheet under the rack to catch the drippings, then place the chicken in a drafty place or direct a fan on it, for about 3 hours, or until dry. The chicken may be left to air-dry up to 8 hours. Turn the bird and rotate the rack periodically, to insure even drying.

Double deep-frying the chicken:
Have the chicken, a tray lined with a triple thickness of paper towels, some extra paper towels, a long-handled ladle, and a large Chinese mesh spoon all within reach of your stovetop.

Heat a wok or a wide, deep, heavy pot over high heat until hot. Add the oil, then heat to the upper end of the light-haze stage, 375° on a deep-fry thermometer. Test the oil with a pinch of the chicken skin. If it foams gently within 2 seconds of contact, then the oil is ready. Adjust the heat so the oil temperature does not climb above 375°.

Dip the mesh spoon into the oil to heat it through and prevent it from sticking to the chicken, then lower the bird into the oil on the spoon. Use the ladle to baste the bird continuously as it fries and to move it slowly and constantly so that it does not stick to the pan. When the underside of the bird is golden, after 1½–2 minutes, turn it over gently, bracing the sides with the ladle and the spoon. Continue to baste and move the bird until the other side is golden, about 1 minute. Remove the chicken promptly to the paper-towel drain.

Raise the oil temperature to the dense-haze stage, 400° on a deep-fry thermometer, when a bit of chicken skin foams immediately on contact. Fry the chicken a second time, for only about 15 seconds on each side, until the bird is a rich golden brown. Remove and drain on fresh paper towels.

Serve the chicken whole on a heated serving platter rimmed by the steamed buns and accompanied by small dip dishes of pepper-salt. Do not attempt to carve or chop the bird. It is so crunchy it will shatter. Instead, invite your guests to partake of the bird in the traditional manner, tearing the soft meat from the bones with their chopsticks, dipping it lightly in the seasoned salt, then encasing it in a plush fold of warm bread.

Leftovers are delectable at room temperature.

MENU SUGGESTIONS:
My favorite way to serve the chicken is with *Flower Rolls* (page 415), and *Steamed Winter Melon with Ham* (page 315), followed by *Velvet Corn Soup* (page 460). A good wine would be a red Burgundy, a Côtes du Rhône, or a non-fruity and distinctively full-bodied rosé like a Tavel.

Cold Duck Salad with Two Sauces
涼拌鴨絲

Crisp, crunchy, and wonderfully colorful, this salad is simple enough for a solitary lunch or festive enough for a party. It combines a luxury meat with the most humble and inexpensive of vegetables, a yin-yang duality common in Chinese cuisine. Mustard sauce, a Cantonese accompaniment, gives the salad sparkle. Sesame sauce, a northern touch, gives it depth. ◆ Traditionally, the rich shredded duck is partnered by fresh bean sprouts and blanched, rather bitter, Chinese celery. Western celery hearts with their slight bite mate perfectly with the duck and do not require blanching. The other vegetables, chosen for color, lend easily to variation. Feel free to double one thing if you can't find another. ◆ Much of the preparation may be done a day or more in advance of serving. The finished platter may be assembled several hours ahead.

TECHNIQUE NOTES:
To slice neatly, cooked meat should be thoroughly chilled. The muscle firms, and you can cut clean slices with little effort. For good eating, however, those same slices should be at room temperature or only slightly chilled. The muscle softens, the juices run, and the meat is at its savory best.

Blanching the bean sprouts and snow peas eliminates their grassy taste and sets them with good color. Rushing them under cold water or plunging them into a bowl of ice water immediately after draining stops the cooking and insures that they will be crisp.

Serves 2–3 as a main course, 4–6 as part of a multicourse meal.

INGREDIENTS:

> *½–⅔ pound skinned and boned, roasted or simmered duck meat, carefully trimmed of fat, membranes, and cartilage (to equal 2½–3½ cups shredded meat; for Chinese-style simmering, follow the method on page 176)*

> *Salad ingredients:*
> *¼ pound fresh bean sprouts*
> *½ pound fresh, small snow peas, or 1 medium green bell pepper*
> *1 medium red bell pepper*

3 ounces trimmed inner white celery ribs (to yield 1½ cups matchstick shreds)
¼ pound sweet-tasting carrots, trimmed and peeled (to yield 1 cup shreds)

Dijon Mustard Sauce (page 475)
Sweet and Silky Sesame Sauce (page 472)

Slicing the duck:

Up to a day in advance of serving, skin and bone the duck and remove any fat, membrane, or cartilage. Be fastidious. For a clean cut, chill the meat thoroughly in the refrigerator before slicing.

Flatten the meat with the broad side of a sharp, thin-bladed Chinese cleaver or chef's knife, then slice it crosswise against the grain into thin shreds a scant ⅛ inch thick. If you are working in advance, put the shreds aside neatly on a plate, seal airtight with plastic film, and refrigerate. Bring to room temperature before using.

Preparing the salad ingredients:

Blanch the bean sprouts in plain boiling water to cover for 30 seconds. Drain promptly, then flush with cold running water to chill. If you are doubling or tripling the recipe, plunge the drained sprouts into a bowl of ice water to chill them quickly. Cover with water and refrigerate until use.

String the snow peas from both ends, then slice lengthwise into slivers ⅛ inch wide. Blanch in plain boiling water to cover until deep green, about 10 seconds, then drain promptly and chill as above. Pat dry. If you are working in advance, spread the snow peas on a plate and refrigerate until use, sealed airtight.

Shred the remaining vegetables—peppers, celery, and carrots—just before assembling the salad so they are perfectly fresh. Peppers should be cored, seeded, and the white inner ribs removed with a sharp knife, then slivered lengthwise into strips ⅛ inch wide. Celery hearts do not need stringing; just sliver. Carrots may be shredded in a food processor or, for a finer shred, with a grater.

Just before assembling the salad, swish the bean sprouts to dislodge any green seed cases, drain, and spread on a clean, dry towel to blot up excess water.

Assembling the salad:

Mound the duck shreds in the center of a large platter of contrasting color, then surround the duck with mounds of the cut vegetables, alternating the colors and placing the prettiest slices on top. If you are working in advance, seal the platter airtight and refrigerate it for 1–2 hours. Bring to room temperature before serving, or serve slightly chilled.

Present the salad flanked by bowls of the two sauces. Invite the guests to help themselves to the different salad ingredients and one or both of the sauces, tossing the salad on their plates and mingling the sauces together. Just like the salad ingredients, they are delightfully compatible opposites.

Leftovers keep 1–2 days, sealed airtight and refrigerated.

MENU SUGGESTIONS:

This dish is perfect on its own for a luncheon or light dinner, accompanied by one or more "Little Dishes" (pages 103 to 121) or a salad-type dish like *Cold-Tossed Asparagus with Sesame Seeds* (page 288) or *Carnelian Carrot Coins* (page 289). To accompany the duck, choose a young white wine like a California Chardonnay, or a young and vigorous red wine with a bit of bite—a red Loire wine, Bourgueil or Chinon.

**Wine-
Simmered
Duck**

紅燒鴨

Here, in its cozy casserole, is the first cousin to *Master Sauce Chicken* (page 153), another member of the "red-cooked" clan of soy and wine-simmered meats. Unlike them, this duck requires more wine, longer cooking, and an extremely gentle heat to bring it to full goodness. When done, the meat falls from the bones, lushly permeated by the winy sauce. With the addition of noodles, carrots, and dusky black mushrooms, this is a hearty but elegant one-dish meal, perfect for a winter night. ◆ My recipe requires the duck to be cooked several hours to a full day in advance, so you can enrich the stew pot with the noodles and vegetables. This makes for leisurely preparation, ideal for the working person or the novice cook. As unintimidating as it is delicious, this is a good choice if you have never before cooked a duck.

TECHNIQUE NOTES:
Different regions and cooks each have their own methods for treating the duck before potting it, all designed to tighten the skin and remove some of the fat. Deep-frying, simmering, and searing in oil are the most common. Far better, in my opinion, is the technique put forth by Lilah Kan in her straightforward and energetic book, *Introducing Chinese Casserole Cookery.* The duck is turned in a hot pot lined with a bit of salt and in a mere 15 minutes acquires a crisp skin and exudes close to a cup of fat. It is a simple, unbeatable technique, adaptable for many duck dishes.

To further conquer the problematic duck, Chinese cooks often place it on a small round bamboo mat to prevent the fragile skin from scorching. You can very occasionally find these in Chinatown stores, but I regularly use the carrot ribbons as a replacement. They do the needed job and lend their flavor to the sauce at the same time.

Serves 2 as a one-dish dinner, 3–6 as part of a multicourse meal.

INGREDIENTS:

    *3½–4½ pound duck, fresh-killed best (weight after removal of head, neck,
      feet, wingtips, tail, and oil sacs)*
    1 teaspoon coarse kosher salt
    1 medium carrot, trimmed and peeled (to yield 1 cup packed carrot ribbons)

Sauce ingredients:
    4 hefty or 5 medium whole scallions, cut into 3-inch lengths
    5 quarter-size slices fresh ginger
    2½ whole star anise (equal to 20 individual points)
    *3 tablespoons thin (regular) soy sauce (read the cautionary note regarding
      brands on page 568)*
    3 tablespoons black soy sauce
    1¾ cups Chinese rice wine or quality, dry sherry
    1 cup water
    3½ tablespoons crushed Chinese golden rock sugar (page 570)

Accompaniments:
    6 medium Chinese dried black mushrooms
    ¾ pound carrots, trimmed and peeled (to equal 2 cups coins)

¼–⅓ pound fresh or frozen Chinese egg noodles, ¹⁄₁₆–³⁄₁₆ inch thick
1½ teaspoons Chinese or Japanese sesame oil

Cleaning and de-fatting the duck:

Chop off and discard the wingtips and tail. Remove the oil sacs and any fatty lozenges from around the neck and tail regions, then clean the duck thoroughly, as directed on page 125. Dry the duck extremely well, inside and out, to eliminate splattering. Pierce it all over with the tines of a long cooking fork to encourage the rendering of fat. Have a long-handled spoon, a plate lined with a triple thickness of paper towels, and some extra paper towels alongside your stovetop.

Heat a wok or large, heavy skillet over high heat until hot. Sprinkle the salt evenly in the pan, then wait until it feels hot to the touch. Put the duck in the pan breast side down, then reduce the heat to medium-high as the fat begins to render. Keep the heat as high as possible without causing the fat to smoke. Grasping the neck or leg with kitchen tongs or a mitted hand, move the duck back and forth to brown the breast evenly, then turn the duck on its side. Brown the side, then the back, then the other side, tipping and moving the duck to brown it evenly, all but the spots under the wings and thighs. Pierce the skin repeatedly with the fork, especially around the thighs and shoulders where the fat is concentrated. The whole process will take about 15 minutes and render up to a cupful of dark brown fat. While the duck is browning, the wingtips may scorch. If so, just scrape off the black spots with the tip of a knife before putting the duck in the stew pot.

Turn off the heat, stick the spoon in the cavity, then lift and transfer the duck to the paper towel drain. Pat it dry with the paper towels, inside and out, to remove the oil and salt.

Discard the fat and wash the pan clean, using only hot water if you are using a wok and want this opportunity to enrich the patina. Clean the stovetop now, while the grease is hot and easily wiped away.

Stewing the duck:

Choose a large Chinese sand pot (page 98) or heavy casserole that will hold the duck snugly. If you have a round bamboo mat, wash and dry it well, oil it lightly with corn or peanut oil, and place it in the pot. Or, lacking the bamboo mat, shave the single carrot into long ribbons with a vegetable peeler and clump the ribbons in the bottom of the pot to make a mat 6–7 inches in diameter.

Lightly smash the scallion and ginger to release their juices, then arrange the scallions in the pot as a further cushion. Place the duck on the scallions, breast side down. Combine the ginger, anise, soy sauces, wine and water, and add to the pot. Do *not* add the sugar at this time.

Bring the liquids to a simmer over moderate heat, then reduce the heat to maintain a weak simmer. If you are using a sand pot, begin over low heat to prevent the pot from cracking and use an asbestos pad to obtain an even, gentle heat. Baste the duck, cover the pot tightly, and simmer 1¼ hours, raising the lid periodically to check the simmer and baste the duck.

After 1¼ hours, carefully turn the duck, grasping the neck with tongs or a mitted hand so as not to tear the skin. Push the carrots back underneath the duck as best you can to cushion it. Scatter the sugar into the sauce, swish to dissolve, then baste the duck. Cover the pot and simmer an additional 1 hour, raising the lid periodically to check the simmer and baste the duck with the sauce.

At the end of the simmering time, turn off the heat. Gently remove the duck to a plate, then tip the plate over the pot to empty the cavity of sauce. Strain the sauce through a fine-mesh strainer, pressing down lightly on the scallions, carrot, and ginger to extract their juices. If you have a handy, spouted plastic fat separator, you may remove the fat while it is still liquid. Otherwise, refrigerate or freeze the sauce until the fat congeals, then scoop off and discard every trace of fat. Once the duck cools, refrigerate it sealed airtight, overnight if you wish. Bring it to room temperature 30 minutes before serving.

Preparing the accompaniments:
You may prepare the accompaniments 2 hours to a day in advance of serving the duck.

Soak the mushrooms in cold or hot water to cover until fully soft and spongy. Snip off the stems, rinse the caps to dislodge any sand trapped in the gills, then squeeze the mushrooms gently to remove excess liquid. Cut the carrots on the diagonal into oblong coins a scant ¼ inch thick.

Bring the sauce to a simmer in a heavy saucepan, then taste and adjust if necessary to achieve a good balance of soy, sweet, and wine. Add the carrot coins, reduce the heat to maintain a gentle simmer, then cover the pot and simmer the carrots 30 minutes. Remove the pot from the heat and add the mushrooms to the sauce. Replace the cover and let the vegetables steep in the liquid for 1½ hours. Strain the sauce and put the vegetables and the sauce in separate bowls. If you wish, they may be sealed airtight and refrigerated overnight.

Thoroughly defrost the noodles if they are frozen. Fluff the noodles to separate the strands. Bring a generous amount of unsalted water to a rolling boil over high heat, then add the noodles. Stir to separate, then boil 1–2 minutes, or until they are partly cooked but still underdone. They will simmer to doneness in the sauce. Drain immediately, then rush under cold running water to stop the cooking. Shake to remove excess water, then toss the drained noodles with the sesame oil. If you are working in advance, the noodles may be bagged and refrigerated overnight. Bring the noodles to room temperature before using.

Heating and serving the duck:
Thirty minutes before serving, return the duck breast side up to the casserole in which it cooked and pour the sauce on top. Bring the sauce to a gentle simmer, cover the pot, and cook until the duck is heated through, about 20 minutes. Spread the noodles around the duck and poke them under the sauce. (Extra noodles can be accommodated in the cavity if your pot is not large enough.) Scatter the carrots and mushrooms on top of the noodles, then baste to gloss them with the sauce. Cover the pot and cook 5–10 minutes, until piping hot. Serve the duck in the covered casserole, or remove it carefully to a deep heated serving platter.

Traditionally, the casserole is placed festively in the center of the table, and the participants tear the soft meat from the bones with their chopsticks. For convenience, I set the table with shallow pasta bowls and Chinese porcelain spoons to make the eating easier and help each guest to noodles and accompaniments before inviting them to partake of the duck.

Leftovers are excellent reheated. Surplus sauce may be strained and used in the same way as master sauce (page 153), to cook or enrich vegetables, noodles, or meats.

MENU SUGGESTIONS:
This is a perfect one-pot meal for two, with nothing more required than a Rhône wine or

a rich, soft California Cabernet to accompany it. To flesh out a meal for more company, begin with *Shao-Mai Dumplings* (page 375) and end with *Cassia Blossom Steamed Pears* (page 485) or *Crunchy Almond Tart* (page 516).

<table>
<tr><td>

**Smoked
Tea
Duck**

燻鴨

</td><td>

This is an ethereal duck, traditionally smoked over jasmine tea leaves and pungent camphorwood, and here flavored by the tea in the company of more easily obtained spices. The result is a richly perfumed bird with an incredibly crisp skin, a thin layer of delicately seasoned fat, and a memorably tender flesh. ◆ The transformation from raw duck to smoked duck involves four separate steps, each

</td></tr>
</table>

leisurely, and requiring no particular expertise. Even the deep-frying, the final step that crisps the skin, is a quick, clean, and easy affair. The duck must be started at least 1½ days in advance, but you may begin a full 5–6 days ahead if you wish, making this an ideal dish for weekend entertaining when you have a busy week. ◆ This is a party dish, worthy of a birthday, an honored guest, or a special seduction.

TECHNIQUE NOTES:
Read with care the chapter on smoking (page 90), for detailed information on tools and techniques.

Serves 3–4 as a main course, 5–6 as part of a multicourse meal.

INGREDIENTS:

> 3½–4½ pound duck, fresh-killed best (weight after removal of head, neck, feet, wingtips, tail, and oil sacs)

> For marinating the duck:
> 3 tablespoons coarse kosher salt
> 2 tablespoons Szechwan brown peppercorns
> 1½ teaspoons finely minced, home-dried orange or tangerine peel (page 557)
> 1 teaspoon finely minced fresh ginger

> For smoking the duck:
> ½ cup dry jasmine tea leaves
> ½ cup packed brown sugar, light or dark
> ½ cup raw rice
> 5 finger lengths home-dried orange or tangerine peel, torn into small pieces
> 5 tablespoons Chinese cassia bark (page 534), broken into small bits before measuring, or three 2-inch cinnamon sticks, broken into small bits

> 6–7 cups corn or peanut oil, for deep-frying

Marinating the duck to season it:
At least 1½ days in advance of serving, marinate the duck.

First, remove the oil sacs and clean the duck meticulously, as described on page 125. Then, blot dry inside and out.

Combine the salt and Szechwan peppercorns in a dry, heavy skillet. Put the skillet over moderate heat and stir until the salt turns off-white, about 4–5 minutes. Expect the peppercorns to smoke but do not let them scorch.

Grind the hot mixture to a powder in the dry work bowl of a food processor fitted with the steel knife (processing for 2 minutes continuously), or in a spice mill, blender, or mortar. Strain through a fine sieve to remove the peppercorn husks, then combine with the minced orange peel and ginger.

Rub ⅔ of the mixture evenly over the outside of the duck, including the hidden spots under the wings and thighs, then rub the remaining ⅓ evenly throughout the cavity. Put the duck breast side up in a shallow plate to hold it snugly, cover airtight with plastic wrap, then set aside to marinate 24 hours at room temperature, turning the duck over midway through marination. For a more intense flavor, or if more convenient, the duck may be refrigerated an additional 24 hours and turned an additional time. Bring to room temperature before smoking.

Smoking the duck to flavor, scent, and color it:
Prepare the pot, rack and lid for smoking as described on page 95. Combine the smoking ingredients, then spread them over the bottom of the pot. Fit the rack about 1 inch above the smoking mixture.

Drain the duck of the accumulated liquids, then pat it thoroughly dry, inside and out, with paper towels. Put the duck breast side up on the rack.

Set the uncovered pot over high heat until the smoking ingredients begin to send up thick plumes of smoke in several places, 4–10 minutes, depending on the vitality of your burner and the thickness of the pot. Once you are sure that the process is underway, cover the pot securely and crimp the foil loosely shut (tight enough to keep the smoke in and loose enough so that you can undo it without tearing when it comes time to turn the bird over). Reduce the heat to medium-high, then smoke the duck for 20 minutes. If you see that by lowering the heat the telling plume of smoke seeping from the "escape hatch" has faded to a mere wisp, then restore the heat to high. This will vary from stove to stove.

At the end of 20 minutes, remove the pot from the heat, then carefully undo the foil seal and slowly lift the lid away from you (ideally, near an exhaust fan, an open window, or out on the back porch). The duck should be a deep golden brown. If it is not, indicating that the heat under the pot was too feeble to generate the needed gutsy smoke, then sprinkle an additional ¼ cup sugar around the edges of the smoking ingredients, and repeat the process for 10 minutes over high heat, first waiting until the sugar begins to bubble and smoke convincingly before you cover the pot and begin counting the 10 minutes.

When the bird is a deep golden brown, remove it from the smoker, first tilting it to drain the cavity of the hot liquids that have accumulated during smoking. Then wrap the burnt smoking ingredients in the tin foil lining the pot and the lid and dispose of them promptly. They are the culprits in smelling up the kitchen.

Once the duck is smoked, proceed immediately to steam it.

Steaming the duck to cook it:
(For details on steaming and how to improvise a steamer, see page 60.)

Fit a well-oiled rack into a Pyrex pie plate or heatproof dish large enough to hold the duck and at least 1 inch smaller in diameter than your steamer. Put the duck breast side up on the rack, so it will not steam in its own juices. Bring the water in the steamer to a gushing boil, then add the duck to the steamer. Pause briefly for the steam to rise up around the plate, then cover the steamer and reduce the heat to medium-high. Steam the duck for 1½ hours. Midway through steaming, drain the pie plate of the duck juices rendered during steaming if they threaten to overflow it, using a bulb-top baster.

At the end of 1½ hours, turn off the heat. Let the steam subside for 5 minutes, then slowly lift the lid away from you and uncover the steamer.

Transfer the rack with the duck still on top of it to a baking tray, to catch the drippings as the duck cools, then set the duck aside in an airy place. Pat it dry inside and out with paper towels, and tip the bird every 10 minutes or so for 30 minutes to drain the cavity of juices. For best results, let the duck cool and dry completely before frying. Turn it over midway through cooling so the bottom dries as well.

Once cool, the duck may be fried directly or bagged airtight and refrigerated 2–3 days. Bring to room temperature before frying.

Deep-frying to crisp the skin and turn it deep brown:
About 15–20 minutes before serving, heat a wok or a deep, heavy skillet large enough to hold the duck with room to spare over high heat until hot. Add the oil, leaving about 2½ inches free at the top of the pot to account for displacement by the duck and bubbling. (The drier the duck is, the less bubbling there will be.) Heat the oil to the dense-haze stage, 400° on a deep-fry thermometer, when a bit of duck skin tweaked from the tail region rises instantly to the surface with a crown of white bubbles.

While the oil is heating, ready a baking tray lined with a triple thickness of paper towels to drain the duck after frying. Have the tray, a long-handled heatproof ladle, and a large Chinese mesh spoon or two slotted spoons to retrieve the duck from the oil all within arm's reach. Put a serving platter of contrasting color in a low oven to warm. If you have not allowed the duck sufficient time to cool and dry, have a large wok or pot lid nearby to hold above the pot, angled away from you, to shield yourself from possible spatters. (This sounds terribly foreboding, but be assured that the dramatic fizzle dies down within about 30 seconds after the duck enters the oil.)

Once the oil is properly hot and has been tested with a bit of the duck skin, dip the mesh spoon into the oil to heat it, then lower the duck gently into the oil on the spoon, breast side up. It will bubble on contact. Fry the duck until the skin is a deep brown and feels crisp when you tap it with the ladle, about 5–7 minutes. Keep the heat on high to maintain as close to 400° as possible and use the ladle to baste the top of the duck constantly as it fries. Expect it to bubble heartily and to occasionally spurt oil from the cavity and shield yourself as needed with the lid, holding it above the pot (never covering the pot) and tilted away from you. (Again, this sounds terribly dramatic, but it is not. The bubbles stay nicely in the pot and there are some ducks that do not spurt at all, but it is wise to be forearmed!)

Once the duck is properly brown and crisp, turn off the heat. Lift the duck from the oil balanced securely on the big Chinese mesh spoon, pause briefly to let the excess oil drip back into the pot, then transfer the duck to the paper-towel drain. Tilt the duck to drain the cavity (you can do this above the pot if you have two mesh spoons and hold the duck securely in place between them), then pat the duck dry with paper towels.

Transfer the duck to a chopping board, then let it cool for several minutes to firm the flesh a bit for neater cutting. With a sharp, thick-bladed Chinese cleaver or a carving knife and poultry shears, sever the wings and legs from the body. Next, cut the duck in half lengthwise through the middle of the breast and along one side of the backbone. Remove the backbone, if you like, and discard it or put it aside for gnawing on in private. Cut the two duck halves in half lengthwise, to make 4 pieces, then cut each piece crosswise into rectangular strips about 1 inch wide. It is typical in China to whack the legs crosswise into 2 pieces for eating with chopsticks, but I like to leave them intact for this dish.

Once cut, arrange the duck pieces attractively on the heated platter, with the legs and wings rimming the platter and the prettiest pieces on top. Camouflage the less successfully chopped pieces with sprigs of fresh watercress or coriander, then serve at once, accompanied if you like by *Flower Rolls* (page 415). The idea of this partnership is to enfold a piece of duck and skin in a piece of the warm steamed bread, the bread being the perfect balance for the natural richness and oiliness of the duck.

Leftovers may be refrigerated for several days, sealed airtight. They are savory at room temperature and taste especially good if shredded in a salad of crisp greens.

MENU SUGGESTIONS:
I always serve the duck with *Flower Rolls* (page 415), a simple vegetable like *Steamed Cucumber with Cassia Blossoms* (page 317), or *Chinese Cabbage Hearts with Glass Noodles* (page 311). If a soup is desired, the traditional choice is *Velvet Corn Soup* (page 460). And for an untraditional dessert, try *Pear and Jasmine Tea Sorbet* (page 500) with cookies. A red wine with weight, character, and bite—a Beaujolais growth, like Fleurie, Juliénas, Côte de Brouilly—is a perfect partner to the duck.

Fragrant Crispy Duck

香酥鴨

This is the classic Szechwanese duck, a marvelously crunchy bird, redolent with the aromas of cinnamon, Szechwan brown peppercorns, and star anise. It is my favorite duck dish, one I prefer unhesitatingly to its Peking cousin. To pull some spiced skin and soft meat from the bones and envelop them in a steaming *Flower Roll* (page 415) is truly one of the great sensual pleasures of Chinese dining. ◆ The labor involved is minimal, and may be stretched leisurely over 2 or 3 days. I usually start by massaging the bird with spices a night or 2 before I plan to serve it. Only the frying need be done at the last minute and that is a 5-minute process at most. ◆ This is the first duck dish I ever made. I recommend it enthusiastically to the novice cook and the passionate eater.

TECHNIQUE NOTES:
The preparation of the duck involves four significant stages. Seasoning flavors and firms the bird. Steaming cooks it and renders it almost entirely of fat. Air-drying stiffens the skin, laying the base for it to become superbly crunchy. Deep-frying browns and crisps the skin, gives character to the meat, and crisps the bones, which some claim are the best part of the duck.

The lengthy steaming requires ample water, so use the largest pot possible under your steamer. As the duck steams, be meticulous about siphoning off the rendered fat. This clears the pores to exude still more fat and results in a 99 percent fat-free bird.

For the special crisping technique of double deep-frying, see TECHNIQUE NOTES, page 242.

Serves 3–4 as a main dish, 5–6 as part of a multicourse meal.

INGREDIENTS:

3½–4½ *pound duck, fresh-killed best (weight after removal of head, neck, feet, wingtips, tail and oil sacs)*

For marinating the duck:
   3 tablespoons coarse kosher salt
   2½ tablespoons Szechwan brown peppercorns
   1 teaspoon five-spice powder

For steaming the duck:
   2 tablespoons Chinese rice wine or quality, dry sherry
   5 quarter-size slices fresh ginger
   3 medium whole scallions, cut into 3-inch lengths

For deep-frying the duck:
   1½–2 tablespoons black soy sauce
   ¼–⅓ cup sifted all-purpose flour
   6–7 cups corn or peanut oil

Accompaniments:
   Roasted Szechwan Pepper-Salt (page 476)
   Flower Rolls (page 415)

Preparing and marinating the duck:
Use your hands to pull away and discard the oil sacs that nest to either side of the tail and any fatty lozenges that are lodged around the neck and shoulder region. Clean the cavity and the skin of the duck thoroughly, removing blood, membranes, and quills, as directed on page 125. Cut off and discard the tail. Wash the duck under cool water and pat it carefully dry with a lint-free cloth, both inside and out. Press down on the breastbone with both palms to break the bone and flatten the duck. A flatter duck will season more evenly as it marinates and will be easier to fry.

Put the salt and peppercorns in a dry heavy skillet. (I don't use my wok for this, as the salt would rob the pan of its much-prized patina.) Set the skillet over moderate heat and stir the mixture until the salt turns off-white, about 4–5 minutes. The peppercorns will smoke but do not let them scorch.

Scrape the hot mixture into the dry work bowl of a food processor fitted with the steel knife. Grind the spices 1 full minute, or until they are coarsely ground. Or, grind the mixture in a mortar or blender. Sieve through a fine strainer to remove the peppercorn husks.

Rub ⅓ of the mixture evenly throughout the cavity of the bird. Massage the remaining ⅔ spices evenly over the outside. Really work the spices into the skin. Do not forget the wings and thighs, or the spots under them. Put the duck breast side up in a Pyrex pie plate or shallow heatproof bowl that will hold it snugly yet allow it to lie flat. Cover loosely and set aside to marinate at room temperature 6 hours or overnight. If you wish to keep the bird longer, refrigerate it to retard the marination, up to 2 days. Turn the bird once midway through marinating, to insure even seasoning.

Steaming the duck:
(For detailed instructions on steaming and how to improvise a steamer, see page 60.)
Drain the bowl and the cavity of the duck then rub the wine evenly over the outside of the bird. Place the duck breast side up in a Pyrex pie plate or shallow heatproof bowl whose diameter is at least 1 inch smaller than that of your steamer. Lightly smash the ginger and scallion with the side or blunt handle of a cleaver or heavy knife to release their juices, then spread ⅔ in the cavity and ⅓ evenly over the top of the duck.

Bring as much water as your steaming vessel can hold to a gushing boil over high heat. (Remember to leave an inch free between the water and the rack that will hold the duck.) Reduce the heat to medium and put the bowl on the rack. Cover the steamer and steam the duck over medium heat for 3 hours.

Every 30–60 minutes, turn off the heat to quench the steam and use a bulb-top baster to siphon off the rendered fat and juices surrounding the duck. (The bird will render a lot of liquid in the first 30 minutes. Thereafter, it will render less and not need to be drained as often.) Wear long mitts and lift the steamer lid *away* from you to avoid getting burned, and reserve the liquids and fat for use in stir-frys, sauces, and soup. Check at the same time to replenish the steamer with boiling water if needed, then restore the heat to medium, cover the steamer, and continue steaming the duck.

At the end of 3 hours, turn off the heat and let the steam subside before lifting the lid. Remove the bowl, hold the duck in place with mitted hands, then tilt to drain the remaining juices from the bowl and the cavity. The bird will have rendered more than a cup of fat. Don't worry if it looks bony or sad.

Air-drying the duck:
Let the duck cool 5–10 minutes, then invert it carefully onto a flat rack just as you would a fragile cake, by putting the rack over the bowl, then inverting the bowl and lifting it off the duck. It will be extremely tender, so work carefully. Discard the ginger and scallion, using chopsticks to retrieve the pieces lodged inside the cavity. Lightly blot the skin dry with paper towels.

Put the rack on a baking sheet to catch the drippings, then put the duck in a drafty place for 2–3 hours or direct a fan on it until dry. Blot the skin and turn the duck and the rack periodically to insure even drying. The duck may be left to air-dry up to 8 hours prior to frying.

Coating and deep-frying the duck:
About 15 minutes prior to serving, smooth the soy over the outside of the duck with your fingers. Dry your fingers, then dust the outside of the duck thoroughly with the flour. Blow off the excess. Have the duck, a paper towel-lined plate, some extra paper towels, a large Chinese mesh spoon, a long-handled ladle, and the lid of a wok or large pot all within easy reach of your stovetop.

Choose a wok or a large, heavy pot wide enough to accommodate the duck with 3–5 inches to spare at the sides, so you can turn it easily. Heat the pot over high heat until hot, add the oil, then heat to the upper end of the light-haze stage, 375° on a deep-fry thermometer. Pinch a bit of floured skin from the tail region and add it to the oil. If it rises to the surface within 2–3 seconds wearing a crown of white bubbles, the oil is ready. Adjust the heat so the temperature doesn't rise.

Dip the mesh spoon into the oil to heat it through, so it will not stick to the duck. Put the duck on the spoon, breast side up, and lower it slowly into the oil at arm's length. Hold the lid with your other hand to shield yourself from spatters. The duck should foam immediately upon contact. If it does not, remove it from the oil on the spoon and raise the heat.

Withdraw the spoon from the oil and fry the duck until it is a light, nutty brown, about 2 minutes. Use the ladle to baste the top of the bird continuously with the oil. When brown, use the mesh spoon and the ladle to brace the bird and gently turn it over. Fry the second side until brown, only about 1 minute, then remove the duck to the paper-towel drain.

Double deep-frying for crispness and color:
Heat the oil to the dense-haze stage, 400° on a deep-fry thermometer, when a bit of skin rises immediately to the surface of the oil. Fry the duck a second time, for only 15 seconds on each side, until it turns a deep brown. Remove the duck to fresh paper towels to drain, then blot dry.

Once the oil cools, strain, bottle, and refrigerate it for future frying.

Serving the duck:
Serve the duck immediately on a large heated platter of contrasting color, rimmed by the pretty *Flower Rolls*. Put small dip dishes of the roasted pepper-salt to either side of the platter or alongside each place setting. Do not attempt to carve or chop the duck. It would shatter. The bird is tender enough to be torn apart with chopsticks, and the communal partaking of the duck inspires a delightfully intimate feasting.

To eat the duck, take a piece of skin and meat in your chopsticks. Dip one end lightly in the seasoned salt, then enclose it in a warm fold of steamed bread.

Leftovers are good at room temperature. The brittle bones are wonderful.

MENU SUGGESTIONS:
When I first ate this duck, it was in the company of *Flower Rolls* (page 415), and *Velvet Corn Soup* (page 460), and that is still the way I like it best. Steamed *Winter Melon with Ham* (page 315), *Cassia Blossom Steamed Pears* (page 485), and a smooth, memorable red Bordeaux are all worthy additions to the menu.

Birthday Duck 窩燒鴨

When I was a sophomore at Columbia, suffering through my second year of Chinese, my parents took me for my birthday to an elegant Chinese restaurant in Manhattan's East Village. I had rehearsed my lines for a week, and when we walked through the door I looked brightly at the beautiful Chinese woman facing us and said—in what must have been preposterously bad Chinese—"We are three people. Have you table or not?" The woman beamed and led us to a table, then helped us to order a pressed duck garnished with almonds that I never forgot. It was the first time I had eaten duck, and the first time I had used my fledgling Chinese. ◆ Years later, I spotted a picture of the beautiful woman on the back flap of a cookbook and discovered to my glee that the duck recipe was contained within. The woman was Irene Kuo, and this is my version of "Birthday Duck." ◆ Like most Chinese duck dishes, this one requires several steps that are easily stretched out over 2 to 4 days, though you may do the dish in 1 day if you begin 6–8 hours in advance. The process requires no special equipment and no particular skill, but the result is celestial—a succulent piece of boneless, fat-free duck, surrounded by a brittle-crisp golden coating and drizzled with a sweet and tart pineapple sauce and chopped almonds. The texture is dense and extraordinary. ◆ I have given two methods for boning and pressing the duck, the first being the traditional way and the second being a modern adaptation using a food processor. Using the machine compromises nothing in the way of taste and only saves time, but I wanted to record the traditional method as I often use it. If you like to work in advance, you may also freeze the duck before frying it. The coating retains the moisture, and the final product is almost indistinguishable from the fresh.

TECHNIQUE NOTES:
Like many classic Chinese dishes, the first step in the recipe actually cooks the food and

all the successive steps alter the texture. Thus, the simmering cooks the duck, the steaming cooks the coating which enfolds the duck, and the deep-frying colors and crisps the coating. Pressing loosens the poultry muscle and spreads the fat through the fibers.

Water chestnut powder is often used as a coating for refined and special foods that are to be steamed and then deep-fried. It has a delicacy, a translucence, and a brittleness that are unique. The addition of cornstarch gives the coating body.

Serves 3–4 as a main course, 5–6 as part of a multicourse meal.

INGREDIENTS:

> *3½–4½ pound duck, fresh-killed best (weight after removal of head, neck, feet, wingtips, tail, and oil sacs)*

For simmering the duck:
> *2 tablespoons coarse kosher salt*
> *1 tablespoon Chinese rice wine or quality, dry sherry*
> *3 quarter-size slices fresh ginger*
> *2 medium whole scallions, cut into 3-inch lengths*
> *1½ whole star anise, broken into points (to equal 12 points)*
> *1 thumb-size piece fresh orange or tangerine peel, scraped clean of all white pith, or home-dried orange or tangerine peel (page 557) (optional)*
> *about 10 cups boiling water, to cover*

For coating the duck:
> *3 large egg whites, beaten to a light froth*
> *⅓ cup cornstarch*
> *⅓ cup water chestnut powder*

> *5–6 cups corn or peanut oil, for deep frying*

For the sauce (to yield 1 cup):
> *1 large clove garlic, stem end removed, lightly smashed and peeled*
> *1 teaspoon corn or peanut oil*
> *4 tablespoons sugar*
> *6 tablespoons unseasoned Chinese or Japanese rice vinegar*
> *2 tablespoons thin (regular) soy sauce*
> *2 tablespoons Chinese rice wine or quality, dry sherry*
> *8-ounce can pineapple chunks, preserved in its own juice, no sugar added (to yield ½ cup pineapple purée)*

> *2 teaspoons cornstarch dissolved in 3 tablespoons cold water*

To garnish:
> *⅓ cup freshly toasted chopped almonds*
> *sprigs of fresh watercress*

Cleaning and simmering the duck:
With a heavy cleaver or chef's knife, chop off the neck, wingtips, feet, and tail of the duck, as described on page 125. Using the cleaver or poultry shears, cut through the

center of the breast bone and along one side of the backbone to divide the duck length-wise in half. Remove the fat sacs and clean the duck thoroughly as described on page 126, then pat the duck dry. At this point, the duck may be enfolded in a dry, lint-free towel, bagged in plastic, and refrigerated overnight if you are not ready to continue.

With your hands, twist the legs and wings gently but firmly to break the thigh and shoulder bones and make their removal easier later on. Rub the duck halves well with the salt, inside and out. Sprinkle with wine, then place in a large heavy pot to hold them snugly. Smack the ginger and scallion with the broad side or smooth handle end of a cleaver or chef's knife to spread the fibers and release the juices, then add the ginger, scallion, anise, and orange peel to the pot. Pour in boiling water to cover, bring to a boil over high heat, then reduce the heat to maintain a steady simmer. Cover the pot and simmer the duck for 1 hour, checking after 10 minutes to insure that the liquid is sim-mering and not boiling.

Using a large Chinese mesh spoon, remove the duck halves to a plate to cool. (If you are enamored of duck soup, you may strain and refrigerate the stock, then de-grease, reduce, and season it as you wish.) Once cool, the duck may be refrigerated overnight. (If you are boning it the traditional way, it is easiest to work with when cold.)

Boning and pressing the duck:
For boning and pressing the duck in the traditional manner, work carefully with an atten-tion to remove every bone and joint. First, pull the wings free of the body, tearing away as little skin as possible from the breast. Take off whatever meat you can salvage from the wings and put it aside in a small pile. Remove the backbone and pull off any bits of meat clinging to it, adding these to the pile. Next, use your thumbs to release the rib bones, slipping them between the meat and the membrane which connects the bones, then pull-ing back on the rib cage with your free hand. Finally, twist and extract the leg bones—both the large drumstick and the needle-like small bones—working carefully to keep the meat in as much of one piece as possible. As you remove the bones, pull free and discard any fatty masses, tough tendons, or bony cartilage you discover with your fingers, and put aside any loose slivers of meat. Once the bones are removed (double check that there are none left), use a knife to trim away any tough or rubbery strips of skin from the border of the duck halves, so there is a layer of smooth and unfatty skin covering the duck.

As a last step, slip a finger between the skin and the meat in 2 or 3 places to create several "pockets," and poke the extra slivers of meat inside. It is a painstaking patch job, but is easy once you get the knack, and there's no reason to sacrifice even a sliver of delicious duck! When done, you are left with two boned and trimmed duck halves, each with the skin topping a loose collection of meat, and the worst is behind you.

Transfer the first duck half carefully to a large square of wax paper, using a spat-ula if you like, then push it into a more or less rectangular block with your hands. Neatly fold the paper over the duck on all four sides to form a loose rectangular envelope that will contain the duck while it is being pressed. Repeat with the second duck half and a second piece of wax paper. Put the packages side by side with several inches between them on a flat work surface. Weight evenly under one or more large cutting boards, then pile encyclopedias, stockpots, or other worthy items on top of the boards for a total of about 10 pounds weight. Leave the duck halves for several hours, or until they are fairly compact and about ¾ inch thick. A rush job may be done by pressing down gently but firmly on the board with your upper body weight behind you; this will at least squash the muscle.

If you do not have the time or patience for the traditional method, here is an alternative that produces a round "cake" that needs no pressing or careful wresting free of bones: Tear free the duck skin and put it aside. Remove the bones, fatty masses, tendons, and bits of cartilage, reserving only the duck meat—every sliver of it. Pick through the meat a second time to be sure you have removed every hard or bony bit. Trim away any rubbery pieces of skin, then cut the remaining skin into 1-inch squares. (Do not skimp on the skin; it adds greatly to the savor of the duck.) Cut any large pieces of meat into walnut-size bits. Add the skin to the work bowl of a food processor fitted with the steel knife, and process until finely minced. Add the meat, then process with on-off turns until the mixture is pea-size and still very coarse. Do not overprocess. If you do not have a food processor, mince the skin finely by hand, chop the meat into pea-size chunks, then combine the two in a bowl, stirring lightly in one direction until well blended. Finally, turn the mixture onto a square of wax paper, then shape gently with wet hands into a round, lightly compacted cake evenly ¾–1 inch thick.

Coating and steaming the duck:
(For details on steaming and how to improvise a steamer, see page 60).

Sift the cornstarch and water chestnut powder into a pie plate or shallow bowl. In another shallow bowl, beat the egg whites briskly until foamy. Have the duck and a dry flat heatproof plate that will fit your steamer at hand.

If you are working with two duck halves, unwrap the first one and dip it carefully into the egg whites. Coat it on all sides, handling it gently lest it fall apart, then transfer it to the starch-filled pie plate. Spoon the starch mixture over the top and onto the sides to coat it evenly, then lightly blow off any excess and carefully transfer the coated duck half skin side up to the waiting plate. Repeat with the second duck half, then put it alongside the first piece with at least ½ inch between them. If your steamer is not large enough to accommodate a plate that will hold both halves, then use two plates and steam the duck in two batches or on two tiers. (You may well have egg and starch left over, but it is easier to work with more than with less. The leftover starch mixture may be strained through a fine sieve to remove any ducky bits, bagged, and used for the next duck.)

If you are working with a single duck "cake," dip your hands in the beaten egg white and spread it liberally over the top and sides of the cake. Use a spoon to sprinkle the flour on the top and sides, then lightly blow off the excess. Invert the cake onto the waiting plate, then repeat the process on the uncoated side.

As soon as it is coated, bring the water in your steamer to a gushing boil and steam the duck over medium heat for 30 minutes. During the steaming, the coating will turn somewhat translucent and glossy. If there is a dime-size patch of uncooked starch after 30 minutes, then blow or carefully spoon it off to expose the cooked coating beneath.

Remove the plate from the steamer, blot up any liquid on the plate, then slip the duck carefully onto a second dry plate with the help of a flexible spatula, taking care not to injure the coating and leaving the duck with the original steamed side up. Allow the coating to cool and firm before proceeding to fry the duck.

Once completely cool, the duck may be sealed airtight and refrigerated several days, or frozen several weeks. If you are freezing the duck, be sure that it is double wrapped and that each wrapping is sealed airtight. Defrost the duck in the refrigerator before frying. Whether you refrigerate or freeze the duck, fry it directly from the refrigerator for the crispest possible crust.

Making the sauce:

Drain the pineapple chunks and reserve the juice for another use. Add the pineapple to the work bowl of a food processor fitted with the steel knife or to a blender and process until completely smooth and pale. Combine the sugar, vinegar, soy, and wine, stirring to dissolve the sugar. Add the pineapple purée, then stir to blend, leaving the spoon in the bowl. Put all the sauce ingredients within easy reach of your stovetop.

Heat a small, heavy saucepan over medium heat until hot enough to evaporate a bead of water on contact. Add the oil, swirl to glaze the bottom of the pot, then add the garlic and toss until fragrant, about 10 seconds, taking the pot from the burner and swirling it off the heat if the garlic begins to scorch. Stir the pineapple mixture, then add it to the pan. It will hiss and sputter on contact. Let it come to a simmer, stirring, then stir the cornstarch mixture to recombine and add it to the pot. Stir until glossy and slightly thick, about 15 seconds, then turn off the heat. Taste the sauce and adjust with a bit more sugar if you like a sweeter taste.

Cover the pot and let the garlic sit in the sauce as it cools. If you are not frying the duck within the hour, extract the garlic once cool, then seal and refrigerate the sauce until use.

Deep-frying, slicing, and serving the duck:

Have the cold duck, a large Chinese mesh spoon, tongs or cooking chopsticks, a baking sheet lined with a triple thickness of paper towels, and some extra paper towels all within easy reach of your stovetop. Put a serving platter of contrasting color in a low oven to warm. Discard the garlic if you have not already done so, and set the saucepan alongside your stove.

Heat a wok or large, heavy skillet over high heat until hot. Add the oil, allowing at least 1 inch at the top of the pot to accommodate bubbling. Heat to the upper end of the light-haze stage, 375° on a deep-fry thermometer, when a bit of the coating bobs immediately to the surface.

Immediately slip the duck into the oil, then adjust the heat so the duck fries at 350°, surrounded by a ring of merry bubbles. Fry until deeply golden on both sides, about 5 minutes in all, turning the duck once midway through frying. (If your pan can accommodate both duck halves in a single layer, then add the second half to the oil as soon as the first one bobs to the surface. If not, fry in two batches, remembering to allow sufficient time for the oil to reheat between batches, and testing the oil with a bit of uncooked coating before frying the second piece.) Once golden, remove the duck to the paper-towel drain and use the extra towels to blot the top dry.

Transfer the duck to a cutting board and let it cool and firm for several minutes, to enable you to slice it neatly. In the meantime, bring the sauce to a simmer over medium heat, stirring, then cover the pot and remove it from the heat.

If you have fried two duck halves, cut each crosswise into inch-wide bands, chopping with firm strokes for a clean cut. If you have fried the duck in a single round "cake," then slice it into inch-thick wedges. Transfer the slices to the serving platter, pushing them together in their original shape, then ladle the sauce in several broad bands on top. Sprinkle with almonds, garnish with watercress, and serve promptly. Serve extra sauce in a bowl alongside.

Leftovers are unlikely, but are delicious cold the next day. Leftover sauce may be sealed airtight and refrigerated for several weeks without spoiling. It is very good with simple broiled or grilled chicken.

MENU SUGGESTIONS:
For a truly festive menu, begin the meal with *Pearl Balls* (page 187) or *Shao-Mai Dumplings* (page 375), accompany the duck with *Spinach with Glass Noodles* (page 308) or *Chinese Cabbage Hearts with Glass Noodles* (page 311), and end with *Cassia Blossom Steamed Pears* (page 485) or *Pear and Jasmine Tea Sorbet* (page 500). To accompany the celebratory bird, try a Chenin Blanc with good acidity and a bit of sweetness to it.

Meat: Pork & Beef

肉

◆

◆

The Chinese preference from ancient times has been for vegetable protein as opposed to meat protein, and the sight of a field full of soybeans has traditionally been far more appetite-arousing than a field full of cattle. Records of ancient palace feasts and writings concerning medieval Chinese marketplaces tell us that the Chinese have gladly chewed venison, beef, lamb, dog, horse, donkey, bear, pig, panther, camel, rabbit, and various species of goat, fox, and rodent over the course of their rich history of eating. However, Chinese gourmands have never particularly prized meat in general, and Chinese pharmacologists have held its nutritive value to be rather unimpressive.

Especially difficult for a Westerner to fathom is the paucity of edible beef in China and the lack of enthusiasm with which Chinese regard it. Domestic cattle—oxen and water buffalo—are valued workers on the Chinese scene, and a Chinese farmer would no more approach his prized ox with hungry eyes than would a traditional American plainsman consider eating his horse. History and economics aside, Chinese philosophy has enshrined the patient ox with all the virtues of a calm, gentle, and thoroughly devoted beast, and again—just like Black Beauty or the Lone Ranger's steadfast steed, Silver—who would then think of eating it?

Regardless of cultural preference, beef and most especially pork have won a place at the Chinese table. Beef is most plentiful in north China and in Szechwan, where the nomadic habits of the Mongols and the salt mines of central China either created a practical ground for grazing or such an abundance of draft animals that it became thinkable to slaughter them. The Moslem Chinese, with their dietary taboos against pork, have also done much for the availability of beef in Chinese markets.

Yet pork remains the greatly preferred red meat of China, for reasons of economic practicality and taste. The animal itself has no work potential and is easily fed, and indeed a pig is so central to the Chinese notion of domesticity that the Chinese character for "home" shows a roof with a pig beneath it. Further, pork is considered sweeter and cleaner in taste and smell and far more digestible than beef, with a more appealing color and a more appetizing fat.

And I agree! I, who was raised in a Jewish home on an unflinchingly steady diet of steak and hamburger, cook twenty Chinese pork dishes for every one in which I use beef. I find pork lighter and easier to digest, far more tasty and economical besides, and with a clean-tasting fat that does not coat my tongue.

Mostly, I am impressed with the Chinese cook's treatment of pork and beef, and its adaptability to a modern American diet, what with our growing awareness of the environmental and economic extravagance of red meat and our lessening compulsion to eat so much of it. While I am not yet ready to jump on the bandwagon of strict soybean-eaters, I am loudly enthusiastic about Asian ways with meat and thoroughly convinced of their healthfulness. Stir-fried, stewed, smoked, or steamed, meat is one of the pleasures of Chinese eating and its proper preparation is one of the pleasures of my kitchen.

HOW TO CHOOSE PORK FOR CHINESE COOKING   Pork in general should appear moist and pink if it is fresh. If it is dry, brown, gray, or sitting in a pool of bloody liquid, I don't buy it. I choose my markets carefully and favor those where the demand for fresh pork is sizable, the turnover fast, and the premises scrupulously clean and devoted to freshness. In general, I patronize small, independent butchers and avoid the supermarket scene unless their butchers are exceptional.

PREFERRED CUTS OF PORK   Pork butt with its fat ratio of about 15–20 percent fat to 80–85 percent lean is most successful in my recipes and to my taste. Any fattier is just too fatty for me (though not for many traditional Chinese tongues and in certain special dishes). Any leaner, such as a pork chop or loin, and the meat is generally too lean and not flavorful enough for stir-frying. It should be remembered that the fat that renders during the course of cooking is an integral and very tasty part of the final dish, and that if one uses too-lean pork one winds up needing more oil to cook with and producing a less flavorful dish.

I prefer to buy at markets where I can buy a small piece of pork butt and have it ground on the spot. In a situation where I am forced to buy an entire butt, I think of ways to use it and have some of it put aside for whatever dish I was planning to make and then use the rest of it in a stew (which keeps for days) or something like dumplings (which freeze nicely). I have been caught on rare occasions able only to buy chops, and then I choose them with an eye to a good, thick collar of fat, so I can slice or grind it after boning and make up for the lean.

Pork loin has been specified in those recipes that call for a small amount of pork to be sliced and used in stir-frys that are richly sauced. The small amount makes the use of loin chops practical for most cooks, and the flavors and oils of the sauce in all these cases compensate for the leanness of the meat.

STORING PORK I generally arrange things so that I buy fresh pork on the day in which I will begin to prepare it and find that this approach leads to superior food. If I must refrigerate pork overnight, I discard the butcher's wrap or plastic in which it came and rewrap it in plastic film, then stow it airtight in a plastic bag. Air is the enemy in pork's deterioration, so airtight means fresher longer.

I don't like to freeze pork, finding that much of its sweet goodness pales.

BUYING PREGROUND PORK Much of the preground pork sold in large markets is combined with veal, comprised of unrespectable oddments, or spiced—in other words, not acceptable for Chinese cooking. Be suspicious and query the butcher as to what exactly went into the grinder. Complain loudly if need be, and choose a whole piece of pork butt to be ground on the spot so that you know what you're buying. Except in an ethnic market or small butcher shop where there is a demand for pure and fresh ground pork, always suspect that what is being sold is a mixture.

HOW TO CHOOSE BEEF FOR CHINESE COOKING Beef in general should look moist and reddish-pink as an indication of freshness. If the beef displayed in the meat case is dry, dark, or gray with age or exposure to air, I don't buy it. I tend also to shy away from prepackaged beef and patronize butchers who set their meats out fresh every day and who are readily available to answer questions and make suggestions.

PREFERRED CUTS OF BEEF Flank steak is typically cited in recipes for Chinese stir-frys, but I usually use shoulder cuts and the tenderer parts of the round. Beef terminology is so thoroughly confusing and changes so rapidly from one area of the country to the next and from year to year in the trade that I rely mostly on my eyes and the advice of the butcher when I am choosing one cut from another. Flank steak is good when it is very fresh and meticulously trimmed and when the recipe calls for you to slice it on the diagonal and marinate it prior to stir-frying—all of which ameliorates its native tendency to toughness. Top round is better, however, if you can afford it, and I personally find that the time saved in trimming is alone worth the extra price.

STORING BEEF I treat beef as I do pork; I buy it on the day or just a day before I plan to use it, I remove the store wrapping and seal the beef airtight in plastic, and I keep it cold in the refrigerator until it goes into the marinade or into the pot.

**Crispy
Pork
Balls**

炸肉丸

Meatballs of all types are common throughout China. One finds them steamed, boiled, or fried—in soup (page 448), nested in casseroles (page 209), rolled in rice (page 187), or presented plain. In their simplest presentation they usually feature an intriguing texture and a sprightly dipping sauce, as in this recipe. ◆ The food processor makes these pork balls a one-work-bowl, 10-minute recipe, perfect for a quick hors d'oeuvre or an easy supper. The filling may be done a day in advance and the meatballs shaped and refrigerated hours ahead. The straightforward spatter-free frying should be done at the last minute, so the meatballs are crisp and without a trace of grease.

TECHNIQUE NOTES:
Many cooks make the mistake of adding cornstarch or flour to meatballs, thus stealing the natural juices and dampening the flavors. Here, the egg and sesame oil bind the meat and at the same time add a flavorful moistness, while a thin coating of rice flour seals in the juices. Use the cracker crumb type of rice flour found in health-food stores, not the glutinous sort sold in Chinese markets. It will give the meatballs a delicate, delightfully crisp shell.

The two-heat deep-frying makes the meatballs plush on the inside and crunchy on the outside. The initial minutes at low heat cook the meat through. The final cooking at high heat crisps the shell. It is a gentler process than double deep-frying (page 242), and is especially well-suited for small items like meat balls.

Yields 16 small meatballs, enough to serve 8 as an hors d'oeuvre, 2 as a main course with accompanying dishes.

INGREDIENTS:

½ pound ground pork butt

Seasonings:
1 thin whole scallion, cut into 1½-inch lengths
1 small walnut-size nugget fresh ginger
1 tablespoon finely chopped fresh coriander
several grinds fresh black pepper
2 teaspoons thin (regular) soy sauce
1 teaspoon Chinese rice wine or quality, dry sherry
1 teaspoon Chinese or Japanese sesame oil (increase to 1¼ teaspoon for overly lean pork)
¼ teaspoon coarse kosher salt
1 large egg

2–3 tablespoons rice flour
4–6 cups peanut or corn oil, for deep-frying

Dipping sauce:
Dijon Mustard Sauce (page 475)
or
Coriandered Mustard Sauce (page 476)
or
Sweet and Sour Dipping Sauce (page 478)

Making the meat mixture:

Mince the scallion, ginger, and coriander in the dry work bowl of a food processor fitted with the steel knife, scraping down the bowl as necessary until fine. Add the pork and remaining seasonings, then process until combined. The mixture will be a smooth paste. If you do not have a processor, mince the scallion, ginger, and coriander by hand until fine, then combine with the pork and the remaining seasonings, stirring in one direction to blend. Then turn the seasoned meat out on a board and chop it up and down across the length and width to mince it to a fine texture. Sealed airtight, the mixture can be refrigerated 24 hours.

Shaping the meatballs:

Oil your palms and a teaspoon with a bit of sesame oil or corn or peanut oil, so the meat will not stick to them. Spread the rice flour in a shallow dish. Scoop up 1 rounded tablespoon of the pork mixture with the spoon, then roll it lightly between your palms to form a Ping-Pong-size ball. Roll the ball gently in the rice flour to coat it evenly, then put the finished meatball aside on an oiled plate. Once all the meatballs are shaped, they may be refrigerated up to 2 hours, sealed airtight.

Frying the meatballs:

Have the meatballs, a Chinese mesh spoon or slotted spoon, and a tray lined with a double thickness of paper towels within easy reach of your stovetop.

Heat a wok or heavy skillet over high heat until hot. Add the oil and heat to the light-haze stage, 350° on a deep-fry thermometer, when a bit of meat rises slowly to the surface within 3–4 seconds. Drop the meatballs gently one by one into the oil, frying about 8 at a time. Fry for 3 minutes, separating and turning them. Raise the heat and continue to fry for an additional 2 minutes. In this final frying the oil should climb to 375° and wear a light haze. Remove the meatballs promptly from the oil, hold them briefly above the pot to drain, then put aside on the towel-lined tray. If making a double or triple batch, keep the first batch warm on the tray in a 300° oven while frying the rest.

When the oil cools, strain it through several layers of cheesecloth to remove the flour, and bottle and refrigerate it for future use.

When all the meatballs are fried, arrange them around a dip dish of sauce on a heated serving platter of contrasting color. Spear the meatballs with toothpicks if you are using them as an hors d'oeuvre, and serve immediately.

Leftover meatballs are good cold munchies, whole, or sliced in a salad for lunch.

MENU SUGGESTIONS:

I usually use these meatballs as hors d'oeuvres to precede a light meal featuring dishes such as *Shanghai Vegetable Rice* (page 402) and *Stir-Fried Dancing Crab* (page 271). By themselves, they would be good with a simple vegetable like *Stir-Fried Spinach with Charred Garlic* (page 305), *Red Bell Pepper with Garlic and Coriander* (page 314), or *Chinese Cabbage Hearts with Glass Noodles* (page 311). A light red wine with personality goes well.

Pearl Balls

珍珠肉丸

Light, succulent, and disarmingly pretty, these little meatballs of marinated pork dressed in a mantle of sweet rice charm most everyone who eats them. When I served them to one old China hand, she said they reminded her of the food in Kun-ming, in southwest China, in the 1940s. And that is their special beauty—with their simple elegance and gracefully subtle flavor, *Pearl Balls* exemplify real Chinese cooking at its classic best. ◆ "Pearl balls" in the literary tongue are "porcupine balls" in colloquial slang. Both names refer to the pleasantly glutinous rice that swells around the meatballs as they steam. You can buy it in Chinese markets, where you should also hunt for fresh water chestnuts (page 578). They, as much as anything, make this dish distinctive. If you cannot find them, substitute *jicama*, a large tuber with a crisp white flesh that has the texture although not quite the sweetness of fresh water chestnuts. Only as a last resort use canned water chestnuts, and then only use a brand that is crisp to the bite. ◆ *Pearl Balls* are extremely practical party food. They can be started several days ahead, and then left to steam for hours—off in a corner on a hot plate if you need to free up your stove. They are also very portable. On many a catering job I've nestled the meatballs in the back of the car, piled the steamers up front, and set off with a bit of old China in tow.

TECHNIQUE NOTES:
To achieve its special succulence, the pork mixture is made extremely light with the addition of a generous amount of stock, then steamed for hours—past the point where the meatballs are cooked to the point where the texture transforms. The looseness caused by the liquid makes the mixture tricky to roll. The secret is to roll the meatball along in the rice with the cup of one hand, exactly as if you were rolling a ball of newly fallen snow. Then, nest the rice-studded ball in one palm, and simultaneously lift, rotate, and shape it with the cup of your other hand. It is a bit like the child's game of rubbing your tummy with one hand while patting your head with the other, but the method works beautifully to shape the soft meat.

Yields about 25 meatballs, enough to serve 4–5 as a main course, 6–12 as part of a multi-course meal.

INGREDIENTS:

1⅛ cups sweet (glutinous) rice (page 399)

Meatball mixture:
4 large Chinese dried black mushrooms
6–8 large water chestnuts, fresh best (to yield about ½ cup chopped)
1 walnut-size nugget fresh ginger
1 thin whole scallion, cut into 1½-inch lengths
¾ pound ground pork butt
1 large egg
1 tablespoon thin (regular) soy sauce
1½ teaspoons coarse kosher salt
scant ½ cup unsalted chicken stock

Dipping sauce:
  Garlic-Soy Dip (page 477)

Preparing the rice, mushrooms, and water chestnuts:
Cover the rice with 4 cups cold water. Soak at least 1 hour, or overnight if you wish, stirring occasionally to loosen the talc. Shortly before using, drain the rice in a colander, rinse under cold running water until the water is clear, then put aside to drain. The rice should be moist when you use it. It will adhere more easily to the meat.

Cover the mushrooms with cold or hot water, then soak until soft and spongy, 20 minutes to an hour. Rinse the caps to dislodge any sand trapped in the gills, then snip off the stems with scissors and chop the caps into peppercorn-size bits.

Peel fresh water chestnuts. Drain and blanch canned water chestnuts in plain boiling water for 15 seconds, drain, and rush immediately under cold water until chilled. Chop the water chestnuts into tiny peppercorn-size cubes, by hand to retain their special texture.

The chopped mushrooms and water chestnuts may be sprinkled lightly with water, sealed airtight, and refrigerated overnight.

Making the meat purée:
Mince the ginger and scallion in the dry work bowl of a food processor fitted with the steel knife, scraping down as necessary until fine. Add the pork, egg, soy, salt, and stock, then process with on-off turns until combined. Do not overprocess to a paste. Scrape the mixture into a bowl. It will be very loose. Add the chopped mushrooms and water chestnuts, then stir by hand in one direction to blend. (Stirring in one direction prevents the meat from compacting and keeps it light.)

If you don't have a food processor, mince the scallion and ginger by hand, and chop the pork with one or two evenly weighted knives to reduce it to a fine consistency, as described on page 39. Blend well with the remaining ingredients, stirring briskly in one direction until the mixture coheres.

The mixture may be refrigerated up to 24 hours, with a sheet of plastic film pressed directly on the surface of the meat to form an airtight seal. Stir to recombine before shaping the meatballs.

Assembling the meatballs:
Spread the rice in a thick, even layer in a jelly-roll pan or baking pan. Place the meat mixture, a bowl of cold water, and a teaspoon alongside. If you are steaming the meatballs immediately, liberally oil the bottom of a steaming rack with sesame oil or corn or peanut oil to prevent the rice from sticking to it. If you wish to refrigerate the meatballs several hours or overnight, line a baking sheet with wax paper. Put the prepared steaming rack or baking sheet within reach.

Dip your palms and the spoon in the water so that the meat will not stick to them. Scoop up 1 tablespoon of the meat mixture, roll it in the rice, and gently shape it with your hands as described in TECHNIQUE NOTES. Do not *press* the rice into the meat. You need only to pat and shape the ball to make it adhere. Put the meatball on the rack or lined sheet and continue until the meat is used up, spacing the finished pearl balls 1 inch apart.

If you are refrigerating the meatballs, seal them airtight by bagging the baking sheet in a large plastic bag from the cleaners, or cover loosely with plastic film so the soft meat will not be squashed. Bring to room temperature before steaming and arrange 1 inch apart to allow for the swelling of the rice on a well-oiled steaming rack.

Steaming the meatballs:
(For details on steaming and how to improvise a steamer, see page 60.)

Choose the largest possible vessel to fit under your steamer, to avoid having to refill it frequently during the lengthy steaming. Fill with water to come 1 inch below the rack, then bring the water to a gushing boil over high heat. Reduce the heat to medium-high, then steam the meatballs for 1½–2 hours, replenishing the pot with boiling water as required. About 15 minutes prior to serving, prepare the dipping sauce.

Serve the pearl balls directly in the steamer, if you have an attractive bamboo one. Or, remove the meatballs to a heated serving platter of a color to contrast prettily with the rice. Dribble ⅛–¼ teaspoon of the dipping sauce on top of each meatball before serving. If you wish, garnish the steamer or the platter with some green leaves to highlight the ivory luster of the rice.

To eat the meatballs Chinese-style:
Hold a small porcelain spoon in one hand and chopsticks in the other. Scoop the meatball onto the spoon with the help of the chopsticks, then bring it almost to your mouth on the spoon. Use the chopsticks to lift the meatball and complete the journey. Keep the spoon in place just below, to hold what you can't take in one mouthful and to act as a face-saver or lap-saver should the meatball slip from your grasp.

Leftovers are good resteamed or may be eaten at room temperature if you like cold rice. The rice grows more glutinous with resteaming.

MENU SUGGESTIONS:
For an elegant dinner, serve with any of the steamed fish dishes—*Steamed Whole Fish with Seared Scallions* (page 248), *Clear-Steamed Flounder with White Pepper* (page 250), or *Spicy Steamed Salmon with Young Ginger* (page 252)—and a simple green such as *Spinach with Glass Noodles* (page 308). *Pearl Balls* are also excellent on their own, as an hors d'oeuvre. A light red wine with personality or a good-bodied white goes well.

Velvet Pork Pie with Szechwan Pickle 榨菜蒸肉餅

This is a very common, very simple Chinese dish made most everywhere there is fresh pork and a steamer. The variations are numerous, but the base is always a large, homey patty of smoothly minced pork. To this is added a generally subtle blend of seasonings and some liquid-inspiring ingredient to keep the mixture moist. It is, in fact, the Chinese meat loaf, although lighter and less meaty than our own. ◆ This version is rather jazzy and highly seasoned, spiced by the addition of piquant Szechwan preserved vegetable. It was inspired by Cecilia Chiang's fascinating autobiography, *The Mandarin Way*, which is a treasure trove of classic Chinese tastes. To me, the effect of the preserved vegetable is a lot like adding a slice of good kosher dill pickle to an already inviting hamburger. A little bit goes a long, zesty way. ◆ If the preserved vegetable is unavailable or you don't like its taste, substitute chopped, presoaked dried shrimp or black mushrooms, or blanched, tiny fresh peas, chopped fresh water chestnuts, or minced scallion or chopped Chinese chives. Stir them by hand into the purée just before steaming and add about ¼ teaspoon coarse kosher salt to compensate for the saltiness of the pickle. Or, omit the extras entirely and the pie will still be tasty. The primary thing is that the pork be very fresh. ◆ This is a 4-minute preparation with a food processor, ideal for an evening when you have no energy to cook. Once blended, the purée may be refrigerated overnight, then steamed to succulence in 30 minutes.

TECHNIQUE NOTES:
For the secret to making steamed pork mixtures superbly light, see TECHNIQUE NOTES, page 187. Here, it is the stock more than the timing that is important.

Serves 2 as a main course with a vegetable, 4–6 as part of a multicourse meal.

For the pork mixture:
1 tablespoon well-rinsed, chopped Szechwan preserved vegetable (page 571) (to yield 1 tablespoon chopped pickle)
2 teaspoons finely minced fresh ginger
½ pound ground pork butt
2 teaspoons thin (regular) soy sauce
⅛ teaspoon coarse kosher salt
1 tablespoon Chinese rice wine or quality, dry sherry
1 teaspoon Chinese or Japanese sesame oil (increase to 2 teaspoons for overly lean meat)
½ cup rich, unsalted chicken stock
freshly ground black pepper to taste

To garnish:
several green scallion lengths or Chinese chives (page 538)

Blending the pork purée:
Be certain you have rinsed the preserved vegetable thoroughly to remove the peppery outer coating and pat dry before chopping.

Add the pickle and ginger and remaining ingredients to the work bowl of a food processor fitted with the steel knife, and process until smooth. The mixture should be very loose and smell fresh and sweet with an overtone of sesame oil and a faint whiff of pepper.

If you do not have a food processor, chop the pork with one or two equally weighted knives until completely smooth, as described on page 39. Chop the pickle, mince the ginger until fine, then combine with the pork and the remaining seasonings, stirring briskly in one direction until well blended.

The purée may be refrigerated overnight, with a sheet of plastic film pressed directly on the surface to insure an airtight seal. Bring to room temperature and stir to recombine before steaming.

Steaming the pie:
(For details on steaming and how to improvise a steamer, see page 60.)

Choose a shallow heatproof serving bowl 8–9 inches in diameter. To prevent the pork from sticking, spread a thin film of sesame oil in the bottom of the bowl to cover a diameter of 6½ inches. Add the purée to the bowl, then use a wet spatula to smooth it into a slightly mounded pie, 6½ inches in diameter. Round the edges to form a perfect circle.

For a simple garnish, sprinkle the pie with 1 scant tablespoon chopped scallion or Chinese chives. For a more decorative touch, cut 2 or 3 of the chives or scallion lengths into small curling "branches," as described on page 563. Arrange on top, then press into place with a wet finger. You can also scallop the edges of the pie. It will steam in exactly the shape you give it.

Fill the steaming vessel with a generous amount of water. Bring to a full, gushing boil over high heat, then add the bowl to the steamer. Cover and steam over high heat 30 minutes. Do not lift the lid while the pie is steaming. When done, the edges of the pie will shrink back and lift up from the bottom of the bowl, and the pie will be surrounded by a pool of dark golden juices.

Serve at once. To eat the pie, put the bowl in the center of the table and use chopsticks for communal-style Chinese eating. Or, cut the pie into neat wedges for serving, and top each portion with a ladleful of liquid.

Leftovers keep 2–3 days, refrigerated and tightly sealed. Resteam in a tightly covered bowl until hot, or slice as you would a meat loaf for a cold platter or sandwiches. The cold pie has a firm, silky texture just like that of a good, homemade gefilte fish, so you might even like to try it with horseradish.

MENU SUGGESTIONS:
I enjoy this dish most with a homey assortment of vegetables: *Dry-Fried Szechwan String Beans* (page 297) or *Chinese Cabbage Hearts with Glass Noodles* (page 311) or *Spinach with Glass Noodles* (page 308). Add *Shanghai Vegetable Rice* (page 402) for a fuller menu. To partner this pie, try a German Moselle, a Rhine wine, or a California Johannisberg Riesling.

Four-Spice Pork with Spinach

四味肉絲

Here is my favorite aromatic foursome—ginger, garlic, scallion, and chili—flavoring a simple stir-fry of marinated pork ribbons, velvety spinach leaves, and crunchy spinach stems. It is a nice, light dish on its own or an appealing topping for *Pot-Browned Noodles* (page 366). I enjoy it "nude"—dressed only in the natural pork and spinach juices—but if you wish a richer sauce, an optional one is provided. ◆ The spinach may be blanched and the pork marinated up to a day in advance. The stir-frying takes only 5 minutes.

TECHNIQUE NOTES:
For buying and cutting spinach Chinese-style to take advantage of the sweet roots, see TECHNIQUE NOTES, page 305.

For blanching spinach prior to stir-frying, see TECHNIQUE NOTES, page 306.

Serves 2 as a main dish with noodles or rice, 4 as part of a multicourse meal.

INGREDIENTS:

½ *pound boneless pork loin, trimmed of all fat (weight after trimming)*

To marinate the pork:
2 *tablespoons thin (regular) soy sauce*
1 *teaspoon sugar*
2 *teaspoons cornstarch*

1 *pound fresh spinach, preferably with red stem ends intact*

Aromatics:
2 *tablespoons minced fresh garlic*
2 *tablespoons minced fresh ginger*

2 tablespoons minced green and white scallion
2–3 teaspoons Chinese chili sauce (page 537), or ¼–½ teaspoon dried red chili
flakes

3–4 tablespoons corn or peanut oil

Sauce ingredients (optional):
1 teaspoon thin (regular) soy sauce
1 teaspoon sugar
1 tablespoon Chinese rice wine or quality, dry sherry
1½ teaspoons hoisin sauce
½ teaspoon Chinese or Japanese sesame oil

Preparations:
Hold a sharp knife diagonal to the board, then slice the meat against the grain into thin
slices evenly ⅛ inch thick and about 1 inch wide. Cut the slices crosswise, if necessary,
so they are about 2 inches long. Holding the knife on a diagonal lengthens the slice.

Blend the soy, sugar, and cornstarch until smooth. Toss well with the pork, using
your fingers to coat and separate the slices. Seal airtight, then set aside to marinate 1 hour
at room temperature or several hours to overnight in the refrigerator. Stir once or twice
while marinating to redistribute the seasonings. Bring to room temperature before frying.

Cut, blanch, and chill the spinach, as described on page 306. The blanched spinach may be left at room temperature for several hours or sealed airtight and refrigerated
overnight. Bring to room temperature before frying.

Combine the aromatics in a small saucer.

Combine the sauce ingredients, if you are using them.

Stir-frying the dish:
(If you are using the pork and spinach to crown *Pot-Browned Noodles*, begin stir-frying as
soon as you have flipped the noodles over.)

Have the pork, spinach, aromatics, and sauce mixture all within reach of your
stovetop. Using your fingers, stir the pork to separate the slices and fluff the spinach to
loosen the mass.

About 5 minutes before serving, heat a wok or large, heavy skillet over high heat
until hot enough to sizzle a bead of water on contact. Add 3 tablespoons oil, swirl to glaze
the pan, then reduce the heat to medium-high. When the oil is hot enough to sizzle one
bit of garlic, add the garlic, ginger, scallion, and chili sauce. Stir until frothy and fragrant,
about 10 seconds, adjusting the heat so the aromatics sizzle without browning.

Add the pork and toss briskly to separate and coat the slices. If the meat is sticking, dribble in the additional 1 tablespoon oil from the side of the pan. When the meat is
90–95 percent gray, add the spinach. Toss to blend and heat the spinach through, about 30
seconds. If you are adding the sauce, scrape the combined sauce ingredients into the pan
and raise the heat to bring the liquids to a boil. Toss briefly to combine, then remove
at once to a heated serving platter of contrasting color. Work quickly, lest the meat
overcook.

(If you are using the stir-fry as a topping for the noodles, turn off the heat and
cover the pot briefly if the noodles are not quite done. Once they are browned, mound the
pork and spinach gently on top, leaving an inch of noodles showing all around.)

Leftovers keep 2–3 days, refrigerated, and are savory at room temperature.

MENU SUGGESTIONS:
I cannot resist putting this dish atop *Pot-Browned Noodles* (page 366), with a dish of *Carnelian Carrot Coins* (page 289) or *Red Bell Pepper with Garlic and Coriander* (page 314) alongside. On its own as a simple stir-fry, it would make a good meal in tandem with *Shanghai Vegetable Rice* (page 402) or *Celery and Pork Thread Fried Rice* (page 406). Choose between a California Pinot Noir or Burgundy or a more forceful red wine, depending upon whether you serve the dish "nude" or dressed in a sauce.

| Capital Sauce Pork Ribbons 京醬肉絲 | This is a Peking-style dish (hence the name) of shredded scallion and tender pork tossed in a rich, hoisin-based sauce. It is typically served with *Mandarin Pancakes* (page 439) but is also an excellent topping for *Pot-Browned Noodles* (page 366). The preparation time is short and the process is simple, making this an excellent dish for a novice or a working person who wants a good, warming dinner at the end of |

the day. ◆ Traditionally, this dish consists of a bed of raw scallions with the saucy pork threads heaped on top. It is a classic contrast of crisp, acrid green vegetable with sweet and soft pork, and the mixture works beautifully inside a mandarin pancake. It is, in fact, a first cousin to Peking duck, where the duck meat, scallion frills, and hoisin sauce are wrapped up in a pancake before eating. Used as a crown for noodles, however, I like to vary the treatment. I cut the pork into broader ribbons and stir-fry the scallions in at the end to make it a more fitting, toothsome crown for the noodle pillow. Try it one way with the pancakes and the other way when you've a yen for noodles, and see which you like best. ◆ If you are using the pork as a topping for *Pot-Browned Noodles*, cook side one of the noodles after you have deep-fried the pork, using the frying oil. Once you have flipped the noodles over and started them browning, proceed to stir-fry the pork so the two dishes are done simultaneously. ◆ All the preparations, short of the 10-minute cooking, may be done hours or a day in advance.

TECHNIQUE NOTES:
For deep-frying meat as a preliminary to stir-frying, see TECHNIQUE NOTES, page 215.

When a hoisin-based sauce is the focus of a stir-fry, the sauce is often stirred in the pan over high heat before adding the main ingredient. This causes the sugar in the sauce to caramelize while the alcohol or liquid content is reduced, resulting in a depth and intensity of flavor that could not be achieved if the cold sauce were simply poured over the meat and tossed briefly with it to heat it through.

Serves 3–4 as a main dish with *Mandarin Pancakes, Pot-Browned Noodles*, or an accompanying starch, 6–8 as part of a large, multicourse meal.

INGREDIENTS:

1 pound boneless pork loin, trimmed of all fat (weight after trimming)

To marinate the pork:
2 tablespoons thin (regular) soy sauce
2 tablespoons Chinese rice wine or quality, dry sherry
1 tablespoon water
4 teaspoons cornstarch
½ teaspoon sugar
¼ teaspoon Chinese or Japanese sesame oil

6 hefty or 8 medium whole scallions

Sauce ingredients:
3 tablespoons hoisin sauce
scant 2 tablespoons Chinese rice wine or quality, dry sherry
1½ tablespoons thin (regular) soy sauce
5 teaspoons sugar
¼ teaspoon Chinese or Japanese sesame oil, or sesame-based hot chili oil

4 cups corn or peanut oil, for deep-frying

Preparations:
Cut the pork against the grain into thin slices ⅛ inch thick. Cut each slice against the grain into either thin shreds ⅛ inch thick (the traditional skinny cut for a mandarin pancake filling), or broader "ribbons" ½ inch wide (a nice, toothy cut for a noodle topping). Then, cut the shreds or ribbons into 1½-inch lengths. As you work, gently slap the slices with the broad side of your cleaver to thin and even them if necessary.

In a bowl large enough to hold the pork, mix the soy, wine, water, cornstarch, sugar, and sesame oil until thoroughly blended. Add the pork, toss well with your fingers to coat each slice, then seal the bowl airtight and put the meat aside to marinate for 1–3 hours at room temperature or overnight in the refrigerator. Bring to room temperature before frying.

Trim the scallions of root ends and any wilted greens, then cut them crosswise into 2-inch lengths. Cut each piece lengthwise into quarters or sixths to yield thin shreds a scant ¼ inch wide. Rinse the scallions briefly with cold water to remove any grit, then shake to remove excess water. If you are working in advance, bag the scallions in a plastic bag and refrigerate until use. The scallions will typically curl as they sit, which makes for a pretty effect if you are using them raw.

In a small bowl mix the hoisin sauce, wine, soy, sugar, and sesame oil or hot chili oil. Stir to dissolve the sugar and leave the spoon in the bowl.

Deep-frying the pork:
Have the pork, the remaining ingredients, a large Chinese mesh spoon or a large heatproof strainer or colander set securely over a pot, and a pair of pot holders or pot mitts all within arm's reach of your stovetop. Stir the pork to loosen the slices. If you are not using the pork as a noodle topping, put a serving platter of contrasting color in a low oven to warm.

Heat a wok or deep, heavy skillet over high heat until hot. Add the oil, leaving at least an inch free at the top of the pan to accommodate bubbling, then heat the oil to the light-haze stage, 350° on a deep-fry thermometer, when a single piece of pork rises to the surface in 4 or 5 seconds surrounded by a ring of slow bubbles. Adjust the heat so the oil temperature does not rise (on an electric stove this means turning it off altogether), then slide the meat gently into the oil. It will bubble on contact.

Stir slowly with chopsticks or a wooden spoon to separate the pieces as they fry. After 15 seconds, when the meat is mostly gray to golden, remove it in one quick motion with the mesh spoon, or decant the oil swiftly into the pot topped with the strainer or colander to catch the meat. Work quickly, lest the pork overcook. It should be undercooked when it leaves the oil.

(If you are decanting the oil through the strainer to drain the meat, work carefully and use pot holders or mitts. I far prefer to use my 6-inch wide Chinese mesh spoon to scoop out the meat so I don't need to handle the hot oil. I balance the mesh spoon with the meat in it on top of a bowl so the pork can continue to drain and then turn around to deal with the oil once the pork is safely set aside. If there is enough space free on top of the stove and I have an extra pot for stir-frying, then I do not touch the oil at all until it cools. If space or pots are at a premium, then I decant the oil with care into a heatproof receptacle, so I can reuse the pot. In either case, I stir-fry using the deep-frying oil. Then once the oil cools, I strain it through cheesecloth, bottle it, and store it in a cool place for future use.)

Stir-frying the dish:

Return the drained wok or skillet or a second suitable pot to high heat until hot enough to sizzle a bead of water on contact. Add 1½ tablespoons oil, then swirl to coat the pan. When the oil is hot enough to bubble a drop of the sauce mixture, add the sauce. Stir until fully bubbly, then add the pork. Toss briskly several times to mix and heat the pork through.

If you are using the pork as a filling for *Mandarin Pancakes* and wish to eat it with the raw scallions, remove the pot from the heat. Quickly make a bed of the scallions on the serving platter, then scrape the pork into a mound on top, leaving a skirt of scallion showing all around.

If you are using the pork as a topping for noodles, then add the scallions to the pan once the pork is heated through. Toss briskly to combine until the scallions are heated through, about 10 seconds, then mound the mixture on top of the noodle pillow. The whole stir-frying operation should take less than a minute, and the scallions should still be crisp when they leave the pan.

Serve the dish immediately. It is best when piping hot.

Leftovers are tasty at room temperature and will grow somewhat spicier if you have used chili oil in the dish.

MENU SUGGESTIONS:

I like this dish best as part of a simple meal with *Mandarin Pancakes* (page 439) and a green vegetable such as *Stir-Fried Spinach with Charred Garlic* (page 305). It is also an excellent topping for *Pot-Browned Noodles* (page 366) paired with one of the pickle-like "Little Dishes" (pages 103 to 121). To accompany the pork, try a dry European rosé, like a Tavel (not a fruity California rosé).

Szechwan-Hunan Pork Threads

渝湘肉絲

Until a year or so ago, I thought, like most everyone else I know, Chinese and Westerners both, that the name of this dish was "Fish-Flavored Pork Threads." So-called fish-flavored dishes are a hallmark of Szechwan and Hunan cuisine, and while the Chinese are simply content to write the characters for "fish" (*yu*) and "flavor" (*hsiang*) on their menus and not think much more about it, Chinese cookbooks go to great pains to describe how dishes that clearly have nothing whatsoever to do with fish deserve such a name. Well, they don't! Unless I am too preoccupied with thinking in ancient Chinese, it's a good guess that the word *yu* actually refers to the Yu (Chialing) River of Szechwan and that the word *hsiang* actually refers to the Hsiang River of Hunan. Which means that a century or more ago the original characters were forgotten, and that the *real* name of this dish is "Szechwan-Hunan Pork Threads." ◆ Tricks of Chinese language aside, this is a very simple dish. It is a delicious stir-fry of slivered pork, crunchy tree ears, and dark green broccoli in a light, pungent sauce laced with garlic, ginger, and chili. It has nothing to do with fish and everything to do with the piquant flavors for which Szechwan and Hunan are best known. ◆ All the preparation may be done hours or a full day in advance. The final cooking is a matter of minutes.

TECHNIQUE NOTES:
For deep-frying marinated meat as a preliminary to stir-frying, see TECHNIQUE NOTES, page 215.

Blanching the broccoli prior to stir-frying turns it a deep green and cooks it halfway. The final cooking is accomplished in half the time with only a fraction of the oil.

Serves 2–3 as a main course, 4–5 as part of a multicourse meal.

INGREDIENTS:

½ pound boneless pork loin, trimmed of all fat (weight after trimming)

To marinate the pork:
1 tablespoon thin (regular) soy sauce
1 tablespoon Chinese rice wine or quality, dry sherry
½ tablespoon water
¼ teaspoon sugar
2 teaspoons cornstarch

2 tablespoons tree ears (page 576)
1 pound fresh broccoli with solid stems

Aromatics:
2 tablespoons finely minced green and white scallion
1½ tablespoons finely minced fresh garlic
2 teaspoons finely minced fresh ginger
1–1½ teaspoons Chinese chili sauce (page 537)

Sauce ingredients:
1 tablespoon thin (regular) soy sauce
1 tablespoon Chinese rice wine or quality, dry sherry
1½ tablespoons sugar
2 teaspoons well-aged Chinese black vinegar or balsamic vinegar
¼ cup rich, unsalted chicken stock
½ teaspoon Chinese or Japanese sesame oil

1 teaspoon cornstarch dissolved in 2 teaspoons cold chicken stock
3 cups corn or peanut oil, for deep-frying

Preparations:
Slice the pork crosswise against the grain into even slices a scant ¼ inch thick. Cut each slice against the grain into shreds ¼ inch thick, slapping the meat when necessary with the broad side of your cleaver or knife to thin an overly thick edge or make the meat lie flat. Finally, gather the shreds and cut them crosswise into 1½-inch lengths.

In a bowl big enough to hold the pork, mix the soy, wine, water, sugar, corn-starch, and oil, stirring until smooth. Add the pork and toss well with your fingers to coat and separate the shreds. Seal airtight, then set aside to marinate for up to 3 hours at room temperature or overnight in the refrigerator. The longer it sits, the plusher and more flavorful the pork will be.

Put the tree ears in a small bowl and cover with 1 cup of cool water. Soak until supple, about 20 minutes. (They may be left to soak overnight, if you like.) Drain, flush repeatedly with cold water to dislodge the grit from the forest that comes free of charge with the tree ears, then pick through to discard any very tough or gelatinous bits. Tear, if necessary, into nickel-size pieces, then rinse once or twice more for good measure. Cover with cold water until use, refrigerated overnight if you like. Drain well just before using.

With a small, sharp knife, separate the broccoli flowerets from the main stalk at the point where the thin stems join the stalk. Cut any overly large flowerets in half lengthwise. They need not be dainty, but they should be manageable with chopsticks. Cut off and discard the woody part of the main stalk about ½ inch up from the base, then peel off the tough outer bark with a knife or vegetable peeler to expose the celadon-green flesh beneath. Once peeled, cut the stalk into diagonal coins a scant ¼ inch thick, then shred the coins lengthwise into slivers a scant ¼ inch wide. Put the flowerets in one bowl and the shredded stems in another.

Bring a large pot of plain boiling water to a gushing boil over high heat. Add the flowerets, push them beneath the surface of the water, then count 30 seconds. Add the stems, push them down as well, then count another 30 seconds. Drain the broccoli imme-diately into a colander and flush with cold running water to stop the cooking. Shake off the excess water, then put the broccoli aside to drain. If you are working in advance, put the broccoli on a towel-lined plate, cover the plate, and refrigerate until use, overnight if you like. Bring to room temperature before cooking.

Up to a few hours in advance of stir-frying, combine the scallion, garlic, ginger, and chili sauce in a small saucer. Seal airtight and refrigerate if working in advance. Combine the sauce ingredients, stirring to dissolve the sugar. Stir the cornstarch mixture to combine and leave the spoon in the bowl.

Deep-frying the pork and stir-frying the dish:
Have all the ingredients, a large Chinese mesh spoon or heatproof strainer, and cooking chopsticks or a wooden spoon all within easy reach of your stovetop. Put a serving platter of contrasting color in a low oven to warm. Stir the pork to loosen the pieces.

About 10–15 minutes in advance of serving, heat a wok or a large, heavy skillet over high heat until hot enough to evaporate a bead of water on contact. Add the oil, leaving at least an inch free at the top of the pot to accommodate bubbling. Heat the oil to the light-haze stage, 350° on a deep-fry thermometer, when a single piece of pork rises to the surface in 3–5 seconds surrounded by a slow ring of bubbles. Turn the heat off to prevent the temperature from rising, then gently slide the pork into the oil. Expect it to foam on contact. Stir gently with the chopsticks or spoon to separate the slices and fry for only 15 seconds, when the meat is mostly gray to golden. Extract the pork immediately from the oil with the spoon or strainer, then set the strainer over the bowl in which the pork marinated to allow it to drain. Work swiftly to remove the pork from the oil, ideally in one sweep, lest it overcook. It should be undercooked when it leaves the oil, ready to be cooked through in stir-frying.

Leave the oil undisturbed if you have a second pot for stir-frying, so you can wait until it cools to strain it. Otherwise, carefully decant the oil into a heatproof bowl, then wipe the pot clean with paper towels. Once the oil cools, it may be strained through cheesecloth, bottled, and stored in a cool place for future frying.

Return the wok or skillet to high heat until hot enough to evaporate a bead of water on contact. Return 2 tablespoons of the frying oil to the pan, swirl to glaze the bottom, then reduce the heat to medium-high. When the oil is hot enough to sizzle one bit of garlic on contact, add the combined aromatics to the pan. Stir gently to infuse the aromatics in the oil, adjusting the heat to maintain a merry sizzle without browning the garlic. When fully fragrant, in 10–15 seconds, add the broccoli. Toss briskly to combine and heat through, about 1 minute, adjusting the heat to maintain a merry sizzle and dribbling in a bit more oil from the side of the pot if needed to prevent sticking. When the broccoli is hot to the touch, add the pork and drained tree ears, then toss briskly to combine, about 10 seconds. Splash the sauce into the pan and raise the heat to bring the mixture to a boil, tossing to combine.

Reduce the heat to low, stir the cornstarch mixture to recombine, then add it to the pot. Stir until the liquids turn glossy and slightly thick, 10–15 seconds, then turn off the heat.

Decant the mixture onto the heated serving platter, pausing to arrange it prettily, then serve at once.

Leftovers keep nicely 2–3 days, sealed airtight and refrigerated. They are tasty at room temperature, or, if you don't mind soft broccoli, may be resteamed in a covered bowl over high heat until hot.

MENU SUGGESTIONS:
This is a delicious simple supper paired with *Pan-Fried Scallion Breads* (page 435) or *Shanghai Vegetable Rice* (page 402). For a fuller menu, open the meal with *Spicy Shrimp Fritters* (page 237) or *Shrimp Rolls with Crisp Seaweed* (page 241) and add *Stir-Fried Chinese Cabbage with Sweet Sausage* (page 309) or *Stir-Fried Spinach with Charred Garlic* (page 305). To match the piquant flavors of the pork, try a fruity and light California rosé.

Cassia Blossom (Mu-Shu) Pork

木樨肉

Probably my first real Chinese meal was in a little restaurant in the back of a gas station on Route 1, just outside Princeton. While the husband pumped gas up front, the wife cooked splendid food in the back—either hamburgers and fries for the dazed truckers who wandered in or pot stickers, *mu-shu* pork, and other marvelous everyday Chinese wonders for the band of local Sinophiles who knelt rapturously (and hungrily) at her feet.* I, at the time, was a 1960s-style emotional vegetarian, and for me the magic lady made *pork-less mu-shu* pork. The only one I have had better is this very carnivorous version I now make myself. ◆ *Mu-shu* means "cassia blossom," in lyric reference to the bits of stir-fried egg that dot the dish. It is, in fact, rather a forest in a plate—along with the eggy blossoms are crunchy tree ears and slim lily buds, all in a tangle around the wine-rich slivers of marinated pork. It is a light but very satisfying dish, especially when enfolded in a steaming mandarin pancake. ◆ All the preliminaries may be done up to a day in advance, leaving only the quick stir-frying for last minute.

---

* One of our band led *The New York Times* to the station, resulting in the nice couple becoming very rich in a second, palatial restaurant that featured miserable, steam-table food. Said Sinophile was ostracized to Harvard.

TECHNIQUE NOTES:
For cooking eggs in a stir-fry, see TECHNIQUE NOTES, page 372.
For cutting meat against the grain to tenderize it, see TECHNIQUE NOTES, page 450.

Serves 2–3 as a main course, 4–6 as part of a multicourse meal or mandarin pancake party.

INGREDIENTS:

½ pound boneless pork loin, trimmed of all fat (weight after trimming)

To marinate the pork:
1 tablespoon thin (regular) soy sauce
1 tablespoon Chinese rice wine or quality, dry sherry
1 teaspoon sugar
1 teaspoon cornstarch

30 lily buds (page 552)
¼ cup tree ears (page 576)
4 large whole scallions
4 large eggs
½ teaspoon thin (regular) soy sauce
¼ teaspoon coarse kosher salt
5–6 tablespoons corn or peanut oil

Seasonings:
2–3 teaspoons thin (regular) soy sauce
2 tablespoons Chinese rice wine or quality, dry sherry

Preparations:
Wrap the pork airtight in plastic wrap, then freeze just until rigid enough to slice with precision. Slice the meat crosswise with the grain into slices a scant ¼ inch thick, stack neatly, and slice against the grain into long slivers a scant ¼ inch wide. Cut the slivers crosswise, if needed, so they are about 1½ inches long.

Blend the marinade ingredients until smooth and toss well with the pork, stirring with your fingers to coat and separate the slices. Seal airtight, then put aside for 30 minutes at room temperature or overnight in the refrigerator, stirring midway through marinating. Bring to room temperature before stir-frying.

Soak the lily buds and tree ears separately in cool or warm water to cover until supple, about 20 minutes. (Cover the tree ears generously, with about 3 cups water, as they expand greatly when soaked.) Drain the lily buds, then snip off and discard the hard stem ends. Drain the tree ears, rinse thoroughly several times under cool water to remove grit, then pick them over and discard any especially tough or gelatinous bits. Tear into nickel-size pieces, rinse again, and shake dry. The lilies and tree ears may be refrigerated a full day before using, sealed airtight in plastic.

Cut the scallions into 1½-inch lengths, then cut the white and light green segments in half lengthwise. To hold overnight, seal in a water-misted plastic bag.

Beat the eggs lightly with the soy and salt. Seal and refrigerate, if desired, for several hours.

Stir-frying the dish:
Have all the ingredients, several paper towels, and 2 empty bowls or plates all within

reach of your stovetop. Put a serving platter of contrasting color in a low oven to warm. Stir the pork to loosen the slivers.

About 10 minutes before serving, heat a wok or heavy, 8-inch skillet over high heat until hot enough to sizzle a bead of water on contact. Add 2 tablespoons oil, swirl to glaze the pan, then reduce the heat to medium-high. When the oil is hot enough to puff one drop of egg on contact, pour the egg mixture into the pan. It should puff around the edges immediately. Wait several seconds for the bottom to set, then use a spatula to gently push the cooked portion to the side of the pan, letting the loose egg flow beneath to make contact with the oil. If you are using a flat skillet, tilt it to aid the flow. Adjust the heat so the egg cooks swiftly, but stays soft and does not brown. Continue to push the cooked egg aside until the entire mixture is cooked but still only very loosely set. Scrape immediately into one of the waiting bowls or plates, then break the egg into small bits. The whole process should take about 30 seconds.

Use the towels to wipe the pan clean, then return the wok or a larger heavy skillet to high heat. Add 1½ tablespoons oil, swirl, and reduce the heat to medium-high. When the oil is hot enough to sizzle one scallion nugget, add the scallions to the pan. Toss briskly about 15 seconds to glaze the scallions and explode their fragrance, then splash 1 tablespoon wine into the pan. Wait a second for it to hiss, then immediately add the lilies and tree ears. Stir-fry briskly to combine, about 10 seconds, then scrape the mixture into the remaining bowl or plate.

Wipe the pan clean, return to high heat, and add 2 tablespoons oil. Swirl to glaze the pan. When the oil is hot enough to sizzle one sliver of pork, add the pork. Stir-fry briskly, adjusting the heat so the meat sizzles without scorching, until the meat is 90 percent gray. Return the vegetables and eggs to the pan, stir several times, then sprinkle with soy. Stir to combine, sprinkle with wine and stir again to mix. Turn off the heat. Taste and adjust with a dash more soy or wine, if needed. Work quickly lest the mixture overcook.

Serve immediately, while steaming and aromatic.

Leftovers will keep 2–3 days, refrigerated airtight. Reheat tightly covered in a steamer until hot.

MENU SUGGESTIONS:
This dish is best with its traditional mate, *Mandarin Pancakes* (page 439) and is exciting in the company of *Cold-Tossed Three Threads* (page 303) and *Baby Buddha's Feast* (page 302) as part of a mandarin pancake meal. If you wish a substitute for the pancakes, try the pork with a dish of *Everyday Chinese Rice* (page 400) or better yet *Shanghai Vegetable Rice* (page 402), and end the meal with *Cassia Blossom Steamed Pears* (page 485). If you are serving the pork alone, accompany it with a non-fruity California Chenin Blanc or a Vouvray, to provide a "silken backdrop" to the delicacy of the dish. If you are planning a mandarin pancake party with *Cold-Tossed Three Threads* and *Baby Buddha's Feast* in addition to the pork, choose a white Burgundy or a Chardonnay.

| Hunan
Rice
Crumb
Pork

粉蒸肉 | This is a dish from Hunan, the intriguing province of China which sits just to the west of Szechwan. It is a first cousin to the classic *Szechwan Rice Crumb Beef* (page 221), and no two recipes could better indicate the difference between the two cuisines. Whereas the Szechwanese dish is unabashedly spicy, this one is piquant with an overtone of sweetness. Ginger, garlic, and scallion keep the chili sauce in a comfortable shadow, and the unseasoned rice crumbs high- |

light the native sweetness of the rice and the pork. It is a dish to make you sigh, not to sweat. ◆ The classic Hunanese presentation calls for the pork to be steamed on a bed of fresh yams. Chinese yams come in several varieties, many of which are pale in color and sweetness and taste to me much like chestnuts. I prefer actually the small yams I can buy here, the sort with a coppery skin and moist, deep orange flesh. Left unpeeled and sliced in coins, they are pretty and mate perfectly with the pork. ◆ Preparations for this dish are quick and simple and may be done a day in advance.

TECHNIQUE NOTES:
Just like homemade bread crumbs, there is a vast difference between rice crumbs that one grinds oneself from freshly toasted rice and the sort of powdery stuff sold in Chinese and Japanese markets. These crumbs are fresh tasting and nubbly on the tongue, lively as opposed to dead. I leave them coarse, in the Hunanese manner, which gives an earthiness to the dish.

Serves 2–3 as a main course, 4–5 as a small portion in a multicourse meal.

INGREDIENTS:

>*½ pound boneless pork loin, trimmed of all fat (weight after trimming)*

>*To marinate the pork:*
>*1 teaspoon finely minced fresh garlic*
>*1 teaspoon finely minced fresh ginger*
>*2 teaspoons finely minced green and white scallion*
>*1 tablespoon thin (regular) soy sauce*
>*1 tablespoon Chinese rice wine or quality, dry sherry*
>*1½ teaspoons Chinese chili sauce (page 537)*
>*½ teaspoon sugar*

>*½ cup plus 1 tablespoon raw white rice, short- or medium-grain recommended*
>*½–¾ pound fresh small yams, the variety with a coppery skin, deep orange flesh, and tapered ends*

Preparations:
Cut the pork against the grain into even slices a scant ¼ inch thick. Cut the slices against the grain into ribbons ½ inch wide, then cut the ribbons crosswise if needed into 1-inch lengths.

In a bowl large enough to hold the pork, combine the marinade ingredients, stirring well to blend. Add the pork, then toss well with your fingers to coat each slice. Seal airtight, then set aside to marinate, up to several hours at room temperature or overnight in the refrigerator. The longer the meat marinates, the spicier it will be.

Heat a wok or large, heavy skillet over medium heat until hot enough to sizzle a bead of water on contact. Reduce the heat to low, add the rice to the pan, then stir constantly until pale gold, about 5 minutes. If the rice begins to scorch, move the pot off the burner and continue stirring. Transfer the toasted rice to the work bowl of a food processor fitted with the steel knife and process for 4–5 loud minutes until the grains are about ⅓ their original size, small but not powdery. Alternatively, pulverize the rice in a blender or a mortar.

Pour the rice crumbs over the pork, then toss well to combine. Seal airtight, then let the mixture stand up to several hours at room temperature or overnight in the refrigerator, tossing once or twice to redistribute the crumbs. The rice crumbs will absorb some of the seasonings as they sit and turn reddish when steamed. It is not necessary, however, to let the mixture stand before steaming.

Scrub the yams with a stiff brush under cold water to remove any dirt, then pat dry. Cut crosswise into rounds ¼ inch thick. If you are working in advance, then seal airtight and refrigerate until use, overnight if you like.

Steaming the pork:
(For details on steaming and how to improvise a steamer, see page 60.)

Spread the yams in the bottom of a heatproof plate or pie plate at least 1 inch smaller in diameter than your steamer. Toss the pork to redistribute the crumbs, then layer the pieces evenly on top of the yams, leaving a thin border of yams showing all around. Do not worry if the crumbs do not stick to the pork. Pat half of what falls off in a layer underneath the pork, then pat the other half on top.

Bring the water in the steamer to a gushing boil over high heat, put the plate in place, and cover the steamer. Reduce the heat to medium-high to maintain a strong, steady steam, and steam the pork for 40–50 minutes, until the rice is fully swollen and cooked through and the meat is very tender. You may leave the pork in the steamer set over low heat for an additional 10–20 minutes, and the flavors will only grow fuller.

Serve the pork hot from the steamer. Or, if you like, the dish may be left to cool at room temperature, then sealed and refrigerated several hours or overnight. Resteam over medium-high heat until hot, about 15 minutes. The dish is remarkably durable and does not suffer at all through resteaming.

Leftovers keep nicely up to 3 days and may be resteamed over medium-high heat until hot.

MENU SUGGESTIONS:
This makes a good, simple supper with *Ham and Egg Fried Rice* (page 405). If a vegetable is desired, *Dry-Fried Szechwan String Beans* (page 297), *Spinach with Glass Noodles* (page 308), or *Chinese Cabbage Hearts with Glass Noodles* (page 311) are fine accompaniments. A warm slice of *Steamed Banana Cake with Chinese Jujubes* (page 518) would be a nice ending to the meal. To accompany the pork, try a full-bodied Chardonnay.

Garlic-Stewed Sparerib Nuggets

豆豉排骨

This is one of my cold-weather favorites—a cozy, northern-style potful of sparerib nuggets, garlic, and Chinese black beans, stewed for hours until the meat falls from the bones and the sauce turns rich and ambrosial. It is a very simple dish with an earthy character I find immensely appealing. You may add the optional chili flakes and scallion rings for a central Chinese touch, or include some chunky vegetables—½ pound fresh broccoli flowerets, or ½ pound of roll-cut carrots (page 32)—to make a complete one-pot meal. Either way, it is delicious. ◆ Look for very fresh and meaty spareribs with a rich red color. I like to buy them from a butcher who will show me the whole rack. Otherwise, if you buy them prepackaged, hold the package up to eye level to check what is underneath the top layer of ribs—more meaty spareribs, or simply a hunk of bone—and complain or buy an extra package accordingly. If possible, have the butcher cut the ribs crosswise through the bone into inch-wide strips with an electric saw, so that all you need do at home is to cut the strips into nuggets. You can chop the bones at home with a thick-bladed Chinese cleaver designed for such heavy-duty tasks (page 24), but it is an ear-shattering, neighbor-arousing job. ◆ Like most all stews, this one may be done days in advance and reheats beautifully. It also freezes well, so feel free to double the recipe if you are expecting a long winter.

TECHNIQUE NOTES:
Searing the spareribs before stewing them firms the meat and gives it an extra dimension of texture. In Chinese, one says that the meat is "locked up" (firmed) over high "military" heat, before it is stewed to succulence over a slow "literary" fire. For the same two-step process in other Chinese stews, see *Casseroled Chicken with Smoky Chestnuts* (page 156), and *Mountain Stew* (page 254).

Serves 4–5 as a main course, 6–10 as part of a multicourse meal.

INGREDIENTS:

> 2–2¼ pounds lean, meaty spareribs, trimmed of extraneous fat and meatless bone (weight after trimming), cut crosswise through the bone into 1–1¼-inch nuggets on a butcher's electric saw (see directions below if you need to cut them yourself)
> 2 tablespoons corn or peanut oil

Seasonings:
> 3½ tablespoons Chinese salted black beans (not the variety seasoned with five-spice powder; page 561)
> 5–6 large, hard cloves garlic, stem end removed, lightly smashed and peeled
> 2 tablespoons thin (regular) soy sauce
> 2 teaspoons sugar
> 1 cup hot water

Optional aromatics:
> ½–¾ teaspoon dried red chili flakes
> 3–4 tablespoons thin-cut green and white scallion rings

Preparations:
If you are chopping the spareribs at home, first cut off the flap of lean meat that is usually attached to the upper back of the rack. Trim off any fat, then cut the meat into 1–1¼-inch squares and put them aside. Divide the rack into individual spareribs and trim off extraneous fat. Chop the ribs one at a time through the bone into 1¼-inch nuggets, putting the rib curved side down on a sturdy cutting surface and chopping with a heavy, thick-bladed cleaver designed to chop through bones. Do *not* use your thin-bladed, everyday Chinese cleaver for this task. The bones will nick it badly. To chop, grip the cleaver handle securely and chop forcefully and snappily so the bones cut cleanly without shattering. Keep your free hand safely out of the way, pausing in between chops to straighten the rib if it spins out of place. Once cut, combine with the squares of lean meat.

If your butcher has already cut the rack through the bone into long strips, trim them of extra fat and divide each strip into individual nuggets.

Trimmed and cut, the sparerib nuggets may be sealed airtight and refrigerated up to a full day before stewing.

Making the stew:
If you do not have a spouted plastic fat separator, plan to cook the stew at least 3 hours

prior to serving, in order to chill the sauce and congeal the fat. Otherwise, you may begin cooking as little as an hour in advance of serving.

Chop the black beans coarsely. Do not wash them. The salt on the beans has been counted into the seasonings for the stew. Combine the black beans, garlic cloves, soy, sugar, and water, stirring to dissolve the sugar. Have all the ingredients within easy reach of your stovetop.

Heat a deep, heavy skillet or stockpot over high heat until hot enough to evaporate a bead of water on contact. Add the oil and swirl to glaze the bottom and lower sides of the pot. If you are adding the chili and scallion, test the oil with a single piece of scallion. When it foams, add the chili and scallion to the pan and stir gently until fragrant, 10–15 seconds, adjusting the heat so they foam without scorching. Then add the ribs to the pot. If you are cooking the ribs plain, wait until the oil is hot enough to sizzle a single sparerib nugget, then add the spareribs to the pan.

Toss the ribs briskly until they are no longer pink, about 4 minutes, adjusting the heat so they sizzle heartily without scorching. Give the seasonings a stir and add them to the pot. Raise the heat to bring the liquids to a boil, stirring to coat the ribs. Reduce the heat to maintain a steady simmer, then cover the pot and simmer the spareribs for 40–45 minutes. Lift the lid after several minutes to check the simmer. Stir midway through stewing to redistribute the seasonings.

When done, turn off the heat and remove the pot from the burner. Hold the ribs in place with the lid, then tip the pot to pour the sauce into a heatproof bowl. If you have a fat separator, then degrease the sauce immediately. Otherwise, wait for the fat to rise, skim as much off as possible with a broad, shallow spoon, then refrigerate or freeze the sauce until the fat congeals and you can scoop it off.

Once the sauce is degreased, you may serve the ribs and the sauce directly (heating them together in the covered pot if they have cooled), or refrigerate them up to 3–4 days, sealed airtight.

To reheat the stew, I transfer the ribs and sauce to a Chinese sand pot (page 98), layer the top with roll-cut carrots or chunky broccoli flowerets, then heat it covered over a low heat for 20–30 minutes until the vegetables are tender. I then serve the stew directly from the sand pot. If you do not have a sand pot, reheat the stew over moderate heat in a heavy pot, and serve it in a warm serving bowl of contrasting color.

Set the table with Chinese porcelain spoons or soup spoons so that everyone can drink greedily of the sauce. An empty bowl for bones is also useful. If you are eating the stew Chinese-style, you will suck on the cut ends of the bones and garner every delicious drop of sauce.

Leftovers may be refrigerated for several days and reheated a second time.

MENU SUGGESTIONS:
I like this stew best as the focus of a simple dinner, with a bowl of *Ham and Egg Fried Rice* (page 405) to one side, and maybe *Stir-Fried Spinach with Charred Garlic* (page 305) to the other. It will also go wonderfully well with a crusty loaf of hot garlic bread and a salad of interesting greens tossed with a good vinegar and oil. A big Zinfandel, Petite Sirah, Châteauneuf-du-Pape, or Crózes-Hermitage are the wines to best accompany the spareribs.

**Northern-
Style
Chinese
Roast Pork**

京式叉燒肉

Cantonese delicatessens with their broad and sometimes steamy windows are great street theater for strollers through Western Chinatowns. For hours everyday, there is a double show—ducks and chickens and pork and innards hanging from meat hooks in a crowded array of conceivable and incomprehensible postures, dripping their juices into pans of cooked foods beneath, and the dextrous countermen who wield immense cleavers over round wooden cutting boards that look centuries old. The show is wonderful, but the eats are often not. Red food dye, sugar, ketchup, cornstarch, and a canned fruit cocktail assortment of pineapple and marischino cherries inevitably overwhelm what hours before might have been a decent piece of something. ◆ Here is my version of Chinese roast pork, marinated in an unconventional (perhaps Pekinese?) mixture of scallion, garlic, hoisin, and wine, which is flavorful more than sweet. It is ridiculously simple to make and will provide you with days of Chinese-style cold cuts for nibbling, which is exactly how I like it best. ◆ If you are about to become a roast pork aficionado, then by all means purchase 8 or 10 of the S-shaped meat hooks that are sold cheaply in kitchenware shops. You can improvise with drapery hooks, hangers, and the occasional sturdy giant paper clip, but the official hooks are easiest of all. ◆ Do not be in a hurry for this dish. Give the pork a day or more to marinate and then the wait will have been worth it.

TECHNIQUE NOTES:
Pork butt as opposed to loin is ideal here. The interior and exterior fat of the meat bastes the pork strips as they cook and keep it juicy. The pan of water in the bottom of the oven is a further aid to keeping the meat moist. Its job is to provide steam even more than to catch drippings.

Yields 2–2¼ pounds roast pork, enough to serve 8 nicely as cold cuts or "warm cuts" at a small buffet or lunch, 12 or more as part of a large cold meal or *dim sum* brunch where a few small slices are what is wanted.

INGREDIENTS:

   3 pounds pork butt

To marinate the pork:
   6 medium whole scallions, cut into 2-inch lengths
   8 large cloves garlic, stem end removed, lightly smashed and peeled
   3 tablespoons thin (regular) soy sauce (read the cautionary note regarding
    brands on page 568)
   2 tablespoons Chinese rice wine or quality, dry sherry
   3 tablespoons sugar
   2½ tablespoons hoisin sauce
   2 tablespoons rich unsalted chicken stock
   1 teaspoon Chinese or Japanese sesame oil or Five-Flavor Oil (page 480)

Cutting and marinating the meat:

Cut the pork lengthwise into strips 2–2½ inches wide and 1½ inches thick. Cut each strip crosswise, if needed, into pieces 5–8 inches long. Lay the strips flat in a non-aluminum baking dish large enough to hold them snugly in a single layer. If you do not have a baking dish large enough, use two glass or ceramic pie plates or quiche plates.

In a medium-size bowl mix the soy, wine, sugar, hoisin sauce, stock, and oil, stirring well to blend and dissolve the sugar. With the broad side of a cleaver or heavy knife, smash the scallion lengths and garlic cloves smartly to spread the fibers and bring the juices to the surface. Add the crushed scallion and garlic to the soy mixture, then stir well to blend.

Pour the marinade evenly over the pork, scraping the bowl clean. Tip the pork dish to distribute the marinade into every corner and crevice, then seal the dish airtight with plastic wrap. Put aside to marinate for 3 hours at room temperature, then refrigerate 6–30 hours, the longer the better for flavor. Turn the slices and tip the dish to distribute the marinade every hour for the first 3 hours, and thereafter once or twice as convenient. Bring to room temperature before roasting.

Roasting the pork:

Preheat the oven to 350°. Remove all but one rack and place that rack in the highest position in the oven. Put a large baking pan on the floor of the oven (or add a rack in the lowest position and put the pan on the rack if you have an electric oven), then fill the pan with an inch of boiling water.

Drain the marinade from the pork, discarding the liquid and the garlic and scallion. Put the tip of an S-shaped hook through each strip of pork, at least 1 inch from the end so the weight of the meat doesn't tear the strip from the hook. The placement of the hook must enable the pork to dangle from the hook without touching either the rack above or the water below.

Using pot mitts, hang the strips from the oven rack so that they hang over the drip pan and do not touch one another. Work quickly, so as not to reduce the oven temperature too much.

Roast the pork undisturbed for 45 minutes. Then increase the heat to 450° and roast the pork for about 10 minutes longer to crisp the outside a bit and turn it a rich gold. Use an oven thermometer and your eye to judge when the pork is done, and if you are unsure then take a strip from the oven and test a slice. It should be juicy, not dry, when it is done.

Serving the pork:

The pork is excellent hot, tepid, at room temperature, or cold—any way you like. If you are eating it hot, remove the strips from the oven, remove the hooks, then slice the meat crosswise against the grain with a sharp, thin-bladed cleaver or chef's knife into even slices about ⅛ inch thin. For broader slices, angle the knife away from you as you slice. If you are not eating the pork immediately, then remove the hooks and put the strips in a single layer on a plate to cool.

Traditional cold-cut presentation in China calls for paper-thin overlapping slices fanned out attractively on a large platter, surrounded by a colorful assortment of cold foods all designed for nibbling. If you are a home cook, you can make the platter look pretty and perhaps something like a flower with spiraling petals of different foods. If you are a fancy restaurant chef, you will contrive to make the assorted foods look like a fabulous bird on a flowering branch, with a feathered "wing" of pork slices, a feathered "head" of slivered black mushrooms, and radish-fan "blossoms" adorning the branch.

Roast pork keeps nicely in the refrigerator 4–5 days, wrapped airtight. For best flavor, slice just before eating.

MENU SUGGESTIONS:
As a cold cut, try the pork with *Hot and Sour Chinese Cabbage Hearts* (page 112), or *Sweet and Tangy Cucumber Pickles* (page 110). *Carnelian Carrot Coins* (page 289) or *Cold-Tossed Asparagus with Sesame Seeds* (page 288) are other good partners, with a bowl of *Orchid's Tangy Cool Noodles* (page 356) to round out the meal. As a "warm cut," slice it thinly atop *Shanghai Vegetable Rice* (page 402) or *Ham and Egg Fried Rice* (page 405), and serve with *Brussels Sprouts with Black Sesame Seeds* (page 313) or *Stir-Fried Spinach with Fermented Tofu* (page 306).

Recipes which use the pork are *Pearl's Steamed Egg Custard* (page 335) and *Baked Stuffed Buns* (page 432).

Saucy Potted Pork

醬肉

While the Cantonese roast marinated pork in strips, Chinese of the central and northern coastal provinces, that area that is often called "eastern China," take a large piece of pork, marinate it in a savory rather than a sweet sauce, and then put it in a cozy pot to simmer and steep for hours. The result is a very versatile piece of meat. It may be sliced thickly and eaten hot, alongside rice or a steamed bun, or slivered thinly and enjoyed cold in the company of wine or other cold foods. It is an extremely simple dish to make, with a homey quality that I find irresistible. ◆ My Chinese friends who come from one province as opposed to another one fifty miles away will argue hotly as to what the sauce should taste like. One uses a sweet hoisin, another a saltier hoisin-style paste, and still another throws in a slip of cinnamon stick. My version combines them all in an aromatic sauce that is slightly sweet and tastes of wine. ◆ The longer the pork marinates the better it tastes, so plan to let it sit for a day if you can. The stewing is a simple business, requiring nothing more than an occasional swish with a spoon.

TECHNIQUE NOTES:
For stewing a large piece of meat or a whole bird, use a heavy pot with a tight lid that will hold the meat snugly. The heavy pot insures an even, slow heat; the tight lid keeps the cooking heat in the pot and prevents the sauce from reducing; the cozy quarters insure that the full piece of meat will both take from and give to the sauce.

Serves 4–5 as a main dish alongside a hearty serving of rice or buns, 6–8 as a smaller serving in a multicourse meal.

INGREDIENTS:

> *2 pounds boneless pork loin in one piece*

> *To marinate the meat:*
> *3–4 large cloves garlic, stem ends removed, lightly smashed and peeled*
> *¼ cup hoisin sauce, the sweetish variety with a jam-like consistency (page 550)*

Sauce ingredients:
   1 medium whole scallion, cut into 1-inch lengths
   2 quarter-size slices fresh ginger
   ¼ cup thin (regular) soy sauce (read the cautionary note regarding brands on
      page 568)
   2 tablespoons Chinese rice wine or quality, dry sherry
   1 whole star anise, broken into points (to equal 8 individual points)
   1 thumb-size piece Chinese cassia bark (page 534), or a 1-inch piece of
      cinnamon stick, broken into bits
   1 thumbnail-size piece home-dried orange or tangerine peel (page 557) or fresh
      peel, scraped clean of any white pith (optional)
   2¼ cups boiling water
   3–6 teaspoons crushed golden rock sugar

Marinating the meat:
With the broad side of a cleaver or heavy knife slap the garlic smartly to smash it. Pound to a paste with the cleaver handle or in a mortar and pestle, then mix with the hoisin to blend. Put the pork in a medium bowl, then scoop up the hoisin mixture a tablespoon at a time, and massage it vigorously into the meat with your fingers, turning the meat to massage every corner and using all of the hoisin mixture, for a total of 4–5 minutes of vigorous rubbing.

   Using a spatula, scrape the paste from your fingers and the sides of the bowl, then spread it evenly over the exterior of the pork. Seal the bowl airtight, then put the meat aside to marinate for 3 hours at room temperature followed by 8–24 hours in the refrigerator. The longer the meat marinates the more flavorful it will be. There is no need to turn the meat while it marinates because the seasonings are wrapped around it like a coat.

   Bring to room temperature before cooking.

Cooking the meat:
Transfer the meat to a small, heavy pot with a tight-fitting lid that will hold it snugly. Scrape all of the hoisin mixture into the pot. Smash the scallion and ginger with the broad side or blunt handle end of a cleaver or heavy knife, then add them to the pot with the soy, wine, anise, cassia or cinnamon bark, and the orange peel, if you are using it. Pour the water on top, then set the pot over high heat, scraping any paste from the side of the pot and stirring to blend the sauce mixture as it heats.

   Bring the mixture to a near-boil, then reduce the heat to maintain a steady, bubbly simmer. Stir the sauce, cover the pot, then simmer for 30 minutes. After the first 5 minutes, lift the lid to check that the sauce is simmering as required, then replace the cover.

   At the end of 30 minutes, turn the meat over gently with the aid of two large spoons to avoid piercing the meat. Scatter a tablespoon of the crushed sugar into the sauce, swishing to dissolve it with a chopstick or spoon. Replace the cover, simmer 30 minutes more, then turn off the heat.

   Taste and adjust the sauce, if required, with a further sprinkling of crushed sugar. The taste of the hoisin, soy, and wine you are using will all affect the final balance, so feel free to add more sugar as needed to make the sauce mildly sweet with a pleasant overtone of wine. Stir the sugar to dissolve it and taste carefully after each addition.

Steeping the meat and straining the sauce:
After adjusting the sauce, turn the meat over once again with the help of the spoons, then

cover the pot. Let the meat steep in the covered pot for 30 minutes, during which time the sauce will grow richer and the flavors will further permeate the meat.

If you are serving the pork immediately, pour the sauce through a spouted fat separator to remove the fat. Slice the pork crosswise against the grain into even slices, a scant ¼ inch thick. Arrange the slices in an overlapping pattern on a shallow platter of contrasting color, then spoon the de-fatted sauce over the meat.

Or, for even better flavor, transfer the uncut pork to a bowl that will hold it snugly, pour the sauce on top, then chill thoroughly in the refrigerator before serving. Scoop off the congealed fat, extract the pork, and slice it crosswise against the grain into even slices ⅛ inch thin. If you are eating the pork cold or at room temperature, arrange the slices in an overlapping pattern on a serving plate. Garnish with the congealed sauce (which is delicious), or heat the sauce briefly to turn it liquid and then pour over the pork. If you prefer it hot, then arrange the overlapping slices in a large, heavy skillet, spoon the congealed sauce on top, then cover the pot and bring to a steaming simmer over low heat. Slide the meat and the sauce onto a heated platter and serve at once.

Leftovers keep nicely for up to a week, sealed airtight and refrigerated. The flavors develop well with reheating, as with most any stew-like dish.

MENU SUGGESTIONS:
I like this dish best hot, served with *Flower Rolls* (page 415) or deep-fried *Everyday Chinese Bread* (page 410). To enlarge the menu, add a vegetable like *Stir-Fried Spinach with Charred Garlic* (page 305), *Dry-Fried Szechwan String Beans* (page 297) or *Red Bell Pepper with Garlic and Coriander* (page 314). To accompany the pork, choose a rich wine with good acidity and a bit of bite—a Chenin Blanc with good acidity, a good Vouvray, or a white Anjou.

Baby Lion's Head Casserole

小獅子頭

This is a "big affair" dish in China, a large casserole of giant meatballs and stewed cabbage afloat in a rich broth. The traditional taste is far too rich and bland for me, so I have up-dated the dish to suit my own tongue, using a leaner and spicier pork mixture and shaping the meatballs on a tiny scale. The fanciful Chinese name still holds, but these are baby lion's heads rimmed by a cabbagy mane, and not their mommies and daddies. ◆ I cook this dish in a large Chinese sand pot (page 98), which adds to the succulence of the meatballs and the intrigue of the dish, but any large and heavy casserole will do. The presentation can be cozy or dramatic, depending on the number of the guests and the mood of the meal. It is a pleasantly soupy dish, best served in rice bowls or in shallow pasta plates. ◆ Preparations are extremely simple and may be done a night ahead. The stew should be put on to cook an hour to an hour and a quarter before serving.

TECHNIQUE NOTES:
Stir-frying the cabbage and pan-frying the meatballs prior to stewing heightens their flavor and gives them a special texture. Stewing the meatballs on the bed of cabbage allows the cabbage to pick up all the wonderful meaty flavor while insulating the meat from too direct a heat. The final "umbrella" of whole cabbage leaves bastes the meatballs with a tasty bit of vegetable juice while they cook.

Serves 3–4 as a main dish, 6–8 as part of a multicourse meal.

INGREDIENTS:

> *2–2½ pounds Chinese cabbage, the pale green-white variety with densely
> packed, evenly broad leaves (page 536)*
> *1¼ pounds coarsely ground pork butt (ask your butcher to put it through the
> medium blade of the meat grinder, or chop whole butt by hand with one
> or two cleavers (page 39)*

To season the pork:
> *1–1½ teaspoons finely minced fresh ginger*
> *¼–⅜ teaspoon freshly ground pepper*
> *2 teaspoons coarse kosher salt*
> *2 teaspoons Chinese rice wine or quality, dry sherry*
> *2 teaspoons Chinese or Japanese sesame oil*
> *⅓ cup rich, unsalted chicken stock*

To coat the meatballs:
> *1 tablespoon rich, unsalted chicken stock or cold water*
> *1 tablespoon thin (regular) soy sauce*
> *1 tablespoon cornstarch*
> *⅛ teaspoon freshly ground pepper*

> *about ¾ cup corn or peanut oil*
> *1¼ teaspoons coarse kosher salt, or ½ teaspoon Roasted Szechwan Pepper-Salt
> (page 476)*
> *4 teaspoons Chinese rice wine or quality, dry sherry*
> *2¼ cups rich, unsalted chicken stock*
> *thin (regular) soy sauce and/or coarse kosher salt to taste*

To garnish (optional):
> *1 pound tiny live clams, with tightly closed and unbroken shells*

Preparations:
Cut off the cabbage about ⅜ inch above the base, so the outer leaves fall free. Discard the base and any wilted or ragged leaves, then put aside 3 large leaves to serve as an "umbrella" for the meatballs. Continue in the same manner to cut off the base that joins the cabbage and to free the leaves until the entire cabbage is separated, but do not discard these inner base pieces. Cut them pie-like into thin wedges about ¼ inch thick, then stack 1½ pounds of the innermost leaves and cut them crosswise into thick ribbons 1½ inches wide. Segregate the cabbage into 2 piles, one of crisp base wedges and thick cabbage ribs, and the other of the thin, leafier top portion of the leaves. Rinse the 2 piles and the reserved 3 leaves in cold water, then drain well and pat dry. At this point, the cabbage may be bagged airtight and refrigerated until use, overnight if you like. Leftover cabbage may be bagged in plastic and refrigerated for up to a week, for use in stir-frys.

In a large bowl combine the seasonings for the pork. Once blended, add the pork, then stir briskly in one direction with your hand to combine. Take the pork in one hand and throw it lightly and repeatedly against the inside of the bowl to further blend the mixture and tighten the texture. At this point, the pork may be sealed airtight with a piece of plastic film pressed directly on the surface, then refrigerated up to 24 hours. Bring to room temperature and throw lightly against the side of the bowl 3–4 times before using. The mixture will be soft, not solid.

If you are adding fresh clams to the casserole, scrub them well under cold water, then refrigerate covered with a wet towel until use, up to 12 hours.

Stir-frying the cabbage and pan-frying the meatballs:
About 2–2½ hours in advance of serving, heat a wok or large, heavy skillet or stockpot capable of accommodating the cabbage over high heat until hot enough to evaporate a bead of water on contact. Add 3 tablespoons oil, swirl to coat the pan, then reduce the heat to medium-high. When the oil is hot enough to sizzle a piece of cabbage stem, add the pile of crisp stems and ribs. Stir-fry briskly to glaze the pieces with oil and heat them through, about 1 minute, adjusting the heat so they sizzle merrily without scorching. Add the leafier pile next, stirring to combine, glaze, and heat the mixture through, about 30 seconds. Sprinkle with salt or pepper-salt, toss several times to combine, then sprinkle with wine. Pause a second to allow the alcohol to "explode" in a fragrant hiss, then toss the cabbage twice more quickly and turn off the heat. Remove the cabbage at once to the bottom of a large Chinese clay pot or heavy, 3–4-quart casserole, spreading it evenly to the edges of the pot to form a cushion for the meatballs. Do not worry if the cabbage is glossy with oil; the oil will keep it from sticking to the pot.

Combine the stock, soy, cornstarch, and pepper for coating the meatballs, stirring until smooth and well blended. Forming the meatballs one at a time, scoop up 2 tablespoons of the pork mixture, dip your fingers and palms in the coating liquids, then quickly shape and coat the meatballs in one motion. Put the coated meatballs aside on a large plate about an inch apart. Work quickly and stir the coating mixture occasionally with your fingers to keep it smooth and blended. Also, do not worry if the meatballs look a bit flat. They will cook to soft and succulent ovals more than sturdy, high-rising rounds. When the last meatball is shaped, smooth any remaining coating mixture over the top, then proceed immediately to pan-fry them.

Heat a large, heavy skillet over high heat until hot enough to evaporate a bead of water on contact. Add enough oil to glaze the bottom evenly with a scant ¼ inch oil, then reduce the heat to medium-high. When the oil is hot enough to gently sizzle a single meatball, add the meatballs in quick succession to the pan, starting from the outer edge and working in towards the center (where the metal is typically hottest), and placing the meatballs about ¾ inch apart. Fry in two batches if necessary and do not crowd them so much that you cannot turn them easily. Adjust the heat to maintain a merry sizzle, then pan-fry the meatballs until golden on all sides, about 2–3 minutes, checking the bottoms frequently with a spatula and turning them gently with the spatula, spoon, or tongs. If they are sticking, dribble in a bit more oil from the side of the pan. When nicely browned, transfer the meatballs one by one to the casserole, spreading them evenly on top of the cabbage.

Stewing the casserole:
(If you are using a Chinese sand pot, first read about it on page 98.)
Add the chicken stock to the casserole, then put the 3 reserved cabbage leaves over the meatballs like an umbrella, curving down. Place the pot over low heat if you are using a Chinese sand pot or over moderately high heat if the pot is made of metal, then bring the stock to a lively simmer. If you are using a sand pot, you may raise the heat to medium once the pot and the liquids are hot. Cover the pot, adjust the heat to maintain a slow, steady simmer, then cook the casserole for 1 hour. Check the pot after about 5 minutes to insure the simmer. If you are using a Chinese sand pot, check it once or twice thereafter. The superb heat conduction of the pot may cause the liquid to a boil even over moderate heat, and you may need to lower it as the cooking continues.

If you are garnishing the casserole with clams, add them to the pot after 55 minutes, removing the whole cabbage leaves and scattering the clams among the meatballs.

Replace the cover, raise the heat, and steam-cook the clams vigorously for about 4 minutes. Discard any clams that do not open, then remove the pot from the heat.

Taste the broth and ajdust with thin soy and/or coarse kosher salt, or freshly ground pepper or a dash of pepper-salt as required. If the casserole is ungarnished, it will probably need 2–3 teaspoons of soy and a teaspoon or so of salt. If you have added ham or clams, it may need nothing more.

Serve immediately, portioning the cabbage "manes," the "lion's heads," and the broth and any trimmings into individual heated bowls or shallow plates. If you have made the casserole in a Chinese pot, bring it directly to the table still covered, then lift the lid for the proper effect.

Replace the cover to keep the casserole warm for those who want more. The pot will retain enough heat to keep the mixture warm for about 30 minutes.

Leftovers may be refrigerated 2–3 days, and steamed in a tightly covered bowl until hot. They are still tasty, though not as savory as before.

MENU SUGGESTIONS:
To augment the casserole and sop up the sauce, try *Ham and Egg Fried Rice* (page 405), *Celery and Pork Thread Fried Rice* (page 406), *Shanghai Vegetable Rice* (page 402), or deep-fried *Everyday Chinese Bread* (page 410). Follow with *Glacéed Orange Slices* (page 487), or *Pear and Jasmine Tea Sorbet* (page 500). A California Chardonnay or Alsatian Riesling are good wines to try with the casserole.

Lettuce-Wrapped Oyster Beef

蠔豉牛肉

Chinese, like most other people, have a penchant for wrapping one thing inside another and then eating it. Mandarin pancakes, spring-rolls, dumplings, and lettuce-wrapped dishes such as this one are all part of the passion for wrapping. (From whence this passion stems I do not know, but that it is a matter far more interesting than mere convenience or neatness I am certain. Otherwise, a hot dog without its bun, or *mu-shu* pork without its pancake would not seem so sad, so deprived, and so deliberately dull.) ◆ This is a dish that each diner wraps by him- or herself. The filling is a warm, rich, oystery beef, and the wrapping is a cold and crisp leaf of lettuce. It is a dish for a party, because it's fun, or a dish for dieters, because it's rice-less. When in season, my preference is for romaine lettuce. Its sturdy, thick-ribbed character stands up beautifully to the beef, whereas a more delicate leaf gets over-whelmed.* ◆ The preparation is simple and may be done in advance, with only the 3-minute stir-frying left for last.

TECHNIQUE NOTES:
I find Chinese dried oysters tedious to clean and too strong in flavor to enjoy. I typically substitute smoked oysters, whose smoky taste nicely captures the dusky character of the dried sort and whose soft texture works perfectly in a stir-fry. The substitution is not one to one. It is more like 3–4 ounces of smoked oysters for every 1–2 of dried!

Serves 2–3 as a main dish, 4–6 as part of a multicourse meal, or 8–10 as a light hors d'oeuvre.

---

* Raw lettuce wrappers are of Cantonese origin and of very recent date and are probably a reflection of foreign taste. The Chinese traditionally use human excrement as fertilizer—witness one of my favorite book titles, *Poo-Poo Make Plant Glow*—so raw lettuce (on account of the poo-poo) was a no-no.

INGREDIENTS:

> *½ pound ground top round beef*
>
> *To marinate the beef:*
> *1 tablespoon thin (regular) soy sauce*
> *1 tablespoon Chinese rice wine or quality, dry sherry*
> *1½ teaspoons cornstarch*
> *pinch sugar*
>
> *⅓–½ cup baby lima beans or green peas, fresh or frozen*
> *3–4 ounce can smoked oysters, well drained of packing oil*
> *½–1 tablespoon oyster sauce*
> *12–16 washed and trimmed perfect lettuce leaves, preferably romaine*
> *2 tablespoons corn or peanut oil*
>
> *To garnish (optional):*
> *¼–½ ounce bean threads (glass noodles)*
> *3–4 cups corn or peanut oil*

Preparations:
In the work bowl of a food processor fitted with the steel knife, mix the soy, wine, and cornstarch until smooth. Add the beef and process with several on-off turns to "polish" the texture of the meat and blend it with the marinade. Do not overprocess to a paste. Alternatively, whack-mince the beef with one or two equally weighted knives to loosen its formation and polish the texture. Blend the marinade ingredients until smooth, then combine with the beef, stirring in one direction until blended. Throw the beef lightly several times against the inside of the bowl to compact it.

Seal the beef airtight with a piece of plastic wrap pressed directly on the surface, then put aside to marinate for 20 minutes to several hours at room temperature or overnight in the refrigerator. Bring to room temperature before stir-frying.

Blanch fresh lima beans or peas in plain boiling water for about 4 minutes, or just until tender. Drain immediately, then rush under cold running water until chilled. Shake dry. Simply defrost frozen beans or peas. Either may be refrigerated overnight, sealed airtight.

Mince the oysters by hand. Combine the oysters, beans or peas, and ½ tablespoon oyster sauce in a small dish. Seal airtight until use or refrigerate overnight.

Pat the lettuce dry, then arrange it in a pretty spiral on a serving platter or tray. Cover with damp paper towels or a damp lint-free cloth, then chill thoroughly before serving. For overnight storage, bag the towel-draped tray in plastic.

To make the optional noodle nest, follow the directions on page 146. You may fry the nest up to 1½ days in advance.

Stir-frying the beef:
Have the beef, the oyster mixture, 2 tablespoons oil, the extra oyster sauce, and the broken noodles all within reach of your stovetop. Put a serving platter of a color to contrast with the white noodles and brown beef in a low oven to warm.

About 5 minutes before serving, heat a wok or heavy skillet over high heat until hot enough to evaporate a bead of water on contact. Add the oil and swirl to glaze the pan. When the oil is hot enough to sizzle a bit of beef, add the beef and stir-fry briskly, poking, chopping, and pressing to break it into small bits, adjusting the heat so the meat sizzles without scorching. If the beef sticks, dribble in a bit more oil from the side of the pan.

When the beef is 90 percent gray, add the oyster mixture and stir briskly to combine, and heat the mixture through. Turn off the heat, taste, and adjust with a bit more oyster sauce if needed, stirring to blend. The taste should be pronounced, so it can be savored once the beef is inside the lettuce.

Mound the mixture at once on the heated platter. Sprinkle the noodles evenly around the edge. Serve immediately, accompanied by the lettuce.

Each guest should help him- or herself. The traditional approach is to put a boat-like leaf on one's plate or palm, add a dollop of beef to the middle, wrap or curl the lettuce around the beef, and eat it like a taco. A very neat dish if you're not greedy with the beef and there's not a hole in the lettuce!

Leftovers may be resteamed in a tightly covered bowl until hot.

MENU SUGGESTIONS:
Serve as an hors d'oeuvre before a warming meal of *Steamed Whole Fish with Seared Scallions* (page 248), and *Ham and Egg Fried Rice* (page 405), or alone with the rice for a lighter meal. To accompany the beef, try a young and zesty red wine—a light Zinfandel or a Beaujolais with personality.

Stir-Fried Beef with Silky Leeks

京葱牛肉片

Leeks and beef are most common to the northern reaches of China, where the brisk climate makes hearty, lightly sweet stir-frys such as this one exceedingly popular. In my kitchen it usually appears crowning a pillow of *Pot-Browned Noodles* (page 366), and a more satisfying winter meal I find hard to imagine. Tastewise and visually, it is a striking combination. ◆ If you are making the stir-fry as a topping for the noodles, marinate the beef and parboil the noodles in advance. Deep-fry the beef just before you begin to fry the noodles, then complete the stir-fry while the second side of the noodle pillow browns. Easy to orchestrate, the result is a complete one-dish supper. ◆ You may also pair the beef and leeks with rice, a good crusty loaf, or even oven-browned new potatoes. For an extra saucy dish, perfect with the noodle pillow, double or even triple the sauce ingredients. ◆ The beef and leeks may be sliced and marinated a day in advance. Cooking time requires 10–15 minutes.

TECHNIQUE NOTES:
Deep-frying marinated beef and pork as a preliminary to stir-frying locks in the juices, gives the meat an especially luxurious texture, and cooks it partially through for swift and nonstick stir-frying. The oil must be only *moderately* hot (350°), and the meat must leave the oil *quickly* (15 seconds), or else it will become dry and brittle. For a similar "velveting" process but with chicken, see TECHNIQUE NOTES, page 137. Note, however, that beef and pork *cannot* be velveted in water.

Brown sugar when used in a marinade seems to tenderize and flavor the beef a degree beyond what is possible with white sugar. It was a mistake once made by a cooking magazine when printing this recipe, and I received so many rave letters from readers that I henceforth adopted the "mistake" as a *truc*!

Serves 2 as a main dish in combination with noodles or stir-fried rice, 4 as part of a multicourse meal.

INGREDIENTS:

> ½ pound round steak or flank steak, all fat and tough sinew removed (weight after trimming)

> To marinate the beef:
> 1 tablespoon thin (regular) soy sauce
> ½ teaspoon brown sugar
> 2 teaspoons cornstarch
> 1½ teaspoons corn or peanut oil

> ¾–1 pound leeks, rinsed and trimmed of stem ends, wilted greens, and top 2 inches of green stalk (weight before trimming)

> Sauce ingredients:
> 2 teaspoons thin (regular) soy sauce
> 1 tablespoon Chinese rice wine or quality, dry sherry
> 2 teaspoons brown or white sugar
> 1½ teaspoons hoisin sauce
> ½ teaspoon Chinese or Japanese sesame oil

> 3 cups corn or peanut oil, for deep-frying
> ½ teaspoon coarse kosher salt
> ½ teaspoon white sugar

Preparations:
Hold a sharp Chinese cleaver or chef's knife diagonal to the board and slice the beef against the grain into thin slices evenly ⅛ inch thick. (Holding the knife on a diagonal broadens the slices.) Cut the slices crosswise into pieces about 2 inches long, then spank lightly with the broad side of the knife to tenderize and even them.

Combine the soy, sugar, cornstarch, and oil, whisking until smooth. Toss well with the beef, using your fingers to coat and separate the slices. Seal airtight, then put aside to marinate 1 hour at room temperature or several hours to overnight in the refrigerator. Stir once or twice while marinating to redistribute the seasonings. Bring to room temperature before frying.

Cut the leeks crosswise into 2-inch lengths, then lengthwise into shreds ¼ inch wide. Rinse thoroughly, then shake well to remove excess water. Shredded, the leeks may be bagged airtight in plastic and refrigerated overnight.

Blend the sauce ingredients thoroughly to mix, and leave the spoon in the bowl.

Deep-frying the beef:
Have the beef, cooking chopsticks or a wooden spoon, and a large Chinese mesh spoon or a metal colander set securely over a pot all within arm's reach of your stovetop. Stir the beef to loosen the slices.

About 10–15 minutes before serving (or 20–25 minutes if making the pot-browned noodles), heat a wok or deep, heavy skillet over high heat until hot. Add the oil and heat to the light-haze stage, 350° on a deep-fry thermometer. Adjust the heat so the temperature does not rise, then test the oil with one slice of beef. It should fry slowly, not gustily.

Give the beef a stir, then slide it into the oil. It will disappear under a crown of white bubbles. Stir slowly to separate the slices. After 15 seconds, remove the meat in one quick motion with the mesh spoon, or drain the oil swiftly into the pot with the metal colander. Work quickly, lest the beef overcook.

Reserve the frying oil. What remains after stir-frying may be strained through cheesecloth, bottled, and refrigerated for future use.

(At this point begin frying the noodles with the reserved oil, if you are making *Pot-Browned Noodles*. Proceed to the next stir-frying step as soon as you have flipped the noodles over.)

Stir-frying the beef and leeks:
Have the leeks, salt, sugar, deep-fried beef, and sauce ingredients all within easy reach.

Wipe the wok or skillet clean and return it to high heat until hot enough to evaporate a bead of water. Add 2 tablespoons of the reserved oil and swirl to glaze the pan. When the oil is hot enough to sizzle a leek shred, add the leeks to the pan. Stir-fry briskly to glaze the shreds with oil, about 20–30 seconds, adjusting the heat so they sizzle without scorching. Sprinkle with the salt and sugar, then toss another 30–60 seconds until they are soft.

Add the meat and toss briskly to combine. Stir the sauce ingredients, scrape them into the pan, and stir to mix. Raise the heat for 5–10 seconds to bring the liquids to a boil, stirring briskly all the while.

Remove the mixture to a heated serving platter of contrasting color. Arrange a few green leeks on top for a pretty effect, then serve at once. (Or, if you are using the beef to crown the noodles, turn off the heat and cover the pot briefly until the noodles are ready.)

Leftovers keep 2–3 days, refrigerated, and are tasty at room temperature.

MENU SUGGESTIONS:
My favorite way to serve this stir-fry is atop *Pot-Browned Noodles* (page 366), accompanied by nothing more than a good Burgundy. If you need another dish, try *Red Bell Pepper with Garlic and Coriander* (page 314).

Stir-
Fried
Tangy
Beef

醬爆牛肉片

This is a very simple, meat-and-vegetables stir-fry, the sort of dish one finds in a northern Chinese home or in a simple restaurant or stall by the roadside. Its charm is the mixture of tender beef, crisp vegetables, and a mildly spicy sauce with an undertone of sweetness. ◆ Chinese longbeans, sometimes called "yard-long beans," are sold in bunches of about 2 pounds in Chinese markets and specialty produce stores, tied together at one end like a lively ponytail. They should be slender, crisp, and green, not bumpy and thick-skinned, bitter, or yellow. I always break off a bit and chew on it to check whether it is properly sweet and young. When longbeans are not in season, I use shredded broccoli stems or snow peas or any flavorful, young green bean (the Jersey-grown sort is my favorite, even above the fancy *haricots verts*). ◆ Preparations are quick and easy. The beef may be marinated overnight, if you like, but the whole dish can be put together and served within 20 minutes.

TECHNIQUE NOTES:
In a simple stir-fry involving meat and vegetables, the vegetables are usually stir-fried first, with a light dressing of salt, sugar, and wine to bring forth their flavors. When 85 percent cooked, the vegetables are scraped onto a plate, and then the meat is stir-fried

with the sauce ingredients. When the meat is almost cooked through, the vegetables are returned to the pot and stir-fried briskly with the meat so that they are done at the same time. It is a simple, standard dance in a Chinese kitchen, one that leaves the vegetables tasting and looking strikingly fresh, not weighed down or colored over by a sauce.

Brown sugar is excellent for marinating and saucing heartier dishes of stir-fried beef. It would be too rich and strong for a more subtle meat such as pork, but with beef it is perfect.

Serves 2 as a main dish, 3–5 as part of a multicourse meal.

INGREDIENTS:

> *½ pound round steak or flank steak, all fat and tough sinew removed (weight after trimming)*

> *To marinate the beef:*
> *1 tablespoon thin (regular) soy sauce*
> *½ teaspoon brown sugar*
> *2 teaspoons cornstarch*
> *1½ teaspoons corn or peanut oil*

> *½ pound Chinese longbeans or other sweet, tender green bean*
> *½ pound carrots, trimmed and peeled*

> *Sauce ingredients:*
> *1 tablespoon Chinese rice wine or quality, dry sherry*
> *2 teaspoons brown sugar*
> *2 teaspoons thin (regular) soy sauce*
> *1½ teaspoons hoisin sauce*
> *½ teaspoon Chinese or Japanese sesame oil*

> *For stir-frying:*
> *about 6 tablespoons corn or peanut oil*
> *½ teaspoon coarse kosher salt*
> *¼ teaspoon sugar*
> *2 teaspoons Chinese rice wine or quality, dry sherry*
> *2½ tablespoons water*

> *Aromatics:*
> *2 teaspoons finely minced fresh ginger*
> *⅛–¼ teaspoon dried red chili flakes*

Preparations:
Slice the meat crosswise against the grain into long strips ⅛ inch thick, holding the knife on a diagonal to broaden the slices. Cut the slices into pieces about 1½ inches long, to form domino-size rectangles. Mix the soy, sugar, cornstarch, and oil until smooth, add the beef, and toss well with your fingers to coat each slice. Seal airtight, then put aside to marinate for 30 minutes at room temperature or up to a day in the refrigerator. Bring to room temperature before using.

Cut the tips off the longbeans or green beans, then cut into 2-inch lengths. If the beans are not perfectly sweet, blanch them in plain boiling water to cover for 15–30 seconds depending upon thickness, then drain and run under cold water to stop the cooking. (I almost always do this preliminary blanching. It removes the acrid taste that is a sure feature of most beans and tenderizes the skin if it has any tendency to toughness.)

Cut the carrots on the diagonal into elongated coins a scant ¼ inch thick. Arrange the coins like an overlapping deck of cards, then sliver them lengthwise into long strips a scant ¼ inch thick.

The carrots and beans may be prepared hours in advance, sealed airtight, and refrigerated until use. Mist the carrots lightly or cover them with a damp cloth to prevent them from drying.

Mix the sauce ingredients until smooth, stirring to dissolve the sugar. Leave a spoon in the bowl so you can stir it again just before adding it to the pot.

Stir-frying the dish: ·

Have all the ingredients and a plate or bowl to hold the vegetables within easy reach of your stovetop. Put a serving platter in a low oven to warm.

About 5–10 minutes before serving, put a wok or large, heavy skillet over high heat until hot enough to evaporate a bead of water on contact. Add 2½–3 tablespoons oil, swirl to coat the pan, then reduce the heat to medium-high. When the oil is hot enough to sizzle one bean, add the beans to the pan. Stir-fry briskly to sear and coat with oil, adjusting the heat so they sizzle merrily without scorching. Add the carrots, stir-fry quickly to combine, then sprinkle with salt and sugar. Toss to combine, adjusting the heat if necessary to maintain a lively sizzle, then sprinkle the wine into the pan. Wait a split second for it to "explode" in a fragrant hiss, then stir briskly for several seconds to mix. Add the water to the pan, stir to combine, then raise the heat if needed to bring the liquids to a steaming simmer. Shake the pan to even the contents, cover the pot, and steam-cook the vegetables vigorously for 15–20 seconds. Remove the cover, raise the heat if necessary to evaporate the water, then scrape the vegetables onto the waiting plate or bowl. The whole operation should take about 2 minutes, and the vegetables should still be crisp when they are removed from the pan.

Quickly wipe the pan clean, then return to high heat until hot enough to sizzle a bead of water on contact. Add 3 tablespoons oil, swirl to coat the pan, then reduce the heat to medium-high. When the oil is hot enough to sizzle one bit of ginger, add the ginger to the pan, adjusting the heat so it sizzles merrily without browning. Add the red chili flakes and stir to combine until foamy and fully fragrant, 5–10 seconds. Stir the beef quickly to separate the slices, then add it to the pan, adjusting the heat to maintain a lively sizzle. Stir-fry briskly until 90 percent gray, dribbling in a bit more oil from the side of the pan if needed to prevent sticking. Give the sauce ingredients a stir then add them to the pan. Stir-fry several seconds to blend, return the vegetables to the pot, then stir several seconds more to combine. Scrape the contents onto the heated platter, arrange the longbeans here and there for a pretty effect, and serve at once.

Leftovers, if there are any, keep nicely for several days sealed airtight and refrigerated. I like them best at room temperature, but you may also resteam them in a covered bowl until hot.

MENU SUGGESTIONS:

Serve the beef with *Everyday Chinese Rice* (page 400) or *Pan-Fried Scallion Breads* (page 435) for a simple supper, adding *Stir-Fried Spinach with Charred Garlic* (page 305) if you would like another dish. To partner the beef, choose a Beaujolais growth—a Juliénas or Côte de Brouilly.

Beef and Broccoli on a Bird's Nest

芥蘭炒牛肉

This dish is a pretty landscape of food—a mound of slivered, stir-fried beef with fresh broccoli flowerets and coins cut from the tender stems, all served atop a crispy, white bed of deep-fried bean threads. It is simple to do, yet the appearance is so festive that it should be saved for a special dinner. The seasonings are light, either oyster sauce or a bit of chili, as you wish. ◆ Perfectly fresh broccoli is essential. The flowers should be deep green and packed densely together, and the stems should be smooth and also solid when you look at them from the bottom. The stems are the real beauty of this preparation, so look for thick, columnular ones that will have an attractively irregular and cloud-like shape when peeled. ◆ The broccoli may be trimmed, the meat marinated, and the mock bird's nest fried all a full day in advance of cooking. The final stir-frying takes only 5–10 minutes.

TECHNIQUE NOTES:
The quick way to peel broccoli stems is with a vegetable peeler. However, to keep the irregular bulges and curves that make the stems look cloud-like when they are cut into coins, you must use a small paring knife to carefully strip away the tough, outer bark. It takes patience and time, but I find the results well worth it. If you are short of time or patience, do a fast job with the peeler and reduce the stem to a smooth cylinder. It will still taste delicious, which is most of the point.

This is an "arranged" dish where the meat is shown off separate from the vegetables, the sort of presentation a restaurant would make for a banquet. For the contrasting home style of stir-frying beef and vegetables together, see *Stir-Fried Tangy Beef* (page 216).

Serves 2 as a main course, 3–5 as part of a multicourse meal.

INGREDIENTS:

      1 ounce bean threads (glass noodles) (page 533)
      3–4 cups fresh corn or peanut oil
      ½ pound round steak or flank steak, trimmed of all fat and tough sinew
         (weight after trimming)

    To marinate the beef:
      2 tablespoons thin (regular) soy sauce
      ½ teaspoon white or brown sugar (I use white if I am seasoning the dish with
         oyster sauce, brown if I am seasoning it with red pepper.)
      1½ teaspoons cornstarch
      1 teaspoon corn or peanut oil

      1–1½ pounds fresh broccoli, preferably with thick, solid stems
      about 6 tablespoons corn or peanut oil, for stir-frying
      1 teaspoon coarse kosher salt

½ teaspoon sugar
1 tablespoon Chinese rice wine or quality, dry sherry
3 tablespoons water
1–2 teaspoons finely minced fresh ginger (use lesser amount with oyster
  sauce)
⅛–¼ teaspoon dried red chili flakes, or 1 tablespoon oyster sauce mixed with
  2 teaspoons water

Preparations:

Cut the noodles, fry the noodle nest, and strain the frying oil as described on page 146. Instead of breaking the nest into bits, I like to leave it whole so it looks dramatic. (If you are serving the dish on individual plates, Western-style, make a small noodle nest for each guest's plate; it's no more work and it's very pretty.) The nest(s) may be fried a day in advance, then left at room temperature on a paper-towel-lined tray. If your kitchen is humid, store them in an oven with a lit pilot.

Slice the beef crosswise against the grain into thin slices evenly ⅛ inch thick, holding your knife on a diagonal to broaden the slices. Cut the slices crosswise into pieces 1½ inches long. Blend the soy, sugar, cornstarch, and oil until smooth, then toss with the beef, stirring well with your fingers to coat each slice. Seal airtight and set aside to marinate for 30 minutes to 2 hours at room temperature or up to a full day in the refrigerator. Bring to room temperature before cooking.

Cut the broccoli flowerets from the main stem at the point where the thin stalks join the main stem. (To a Chinese eye, a floweret atop a longish stalk is especially attractive.) If the flowerets are more than two bites large, cut them in half lengthwise. With a sharp paring knife, carefully peel the outer skin from the thin stalks, beginning from the cut end. Cut off the base of the main stem at a 30° angle and remove the thicker outer bark, pulling the bark away after each shallow cut as if stringing celery. As best you can, keep the naturally irregular shape of the stem intact. Cut the peeled stem on the diagonal into elongated coins a scant ¼ inch thick. If you had a cooperatively irregular-shaped stem, the coins will look like "clouds." Cut and peeled, the broccoli may be refrigerated overnight in a lightly misted plastic bag.

Stir-frying the dish:

About 10–15 minutes in advance of serving, have all the ingredients and a bowl to hold the broccoli within easy reach of your stovetop. Put a large serving platter or individual plates of a contrasting color in a low oven to warm. Stir the beef with your fingers to loosen the slices.

Put a wok or a large, heavy skillet over high heat until hot enough to evaporate a bead of water on contact. Add 3 tablespoons oil, swirl to coat the pan, then reduce the heat to medium-high. When the oil is hot enough to sizzle a piece of broccoli, add the broccoli and stir-fry briskly to glaze the pieces evenly, adjusting the heat to maintain a merry sizzle without scorching the vegetable. When glazed, after 30 seconds or so, sprinkle with salt and sugar and toss briskly to coat. Sprinkle the wine into the pan, wait a split second for it to "explode" in a fragrant hiss, then add the water. Stir to coat, shake the pan to even the contents, then raise the heat if required to bring the liquids to a simmer. Cover, then steam-cook the broccoli for 3–4 minutes, until tender but still crisp.

Test a piece to be sure. Raise the heat to evaporate any remaining liquid, then remove the broccoli to the bowl and cover it to keep warm.

Quickly wipe the pan clean and return it to high heat until hot enough to evaporate a bead of water on contact. Add 3 tablespoons oil, swirl to coat the pan, then reduce the heat to medium-high. When the oil is hot enough to sizzle one bit of ginger, add the ginger. Adjust the heat so it foams without browning, then add the chili flakes if you are using them, stirring to infuse the oil with the aromatics. When fully fragrant, in about 10 seconds, add the beef and toss briskly to separate the slices, adjusting the heat to maintain a merry sizzle. When the meat is 90 percent gray, add the oyster mixture if you are using it, stir to combine, and remove the pan from the heat.

Assembling and serving the dish:
Move quickly, lest things get cold. Put the noodle nest(s) on the platter or plates. Distribute the broccoli on top, arranging the flowerets so they face out and leaving a border of noodles showing all around. Finally mound the beef in the center, leaving a border of green around the beef.

Leftovers are good at room temperature or may be steamed in a covered bowl until hot. Discard the noodles, which become mushy.

MENU SUGGESTIONS:
For a small, elegant meal, this dish and *Ham and Egg Fried Rice* (page 405), along with *Velvet Corn Soup* (page 460), would be perfect. For dessert, try *Crunchy Almond Tart* (page 516). A modest Bordeaux will best enhance the beef—a moderate Saint-Emilion or a Côtes de Bourg.

Szechwan Rice Crumb Beef 粉蒸牛肉

Here is a Szechwanese wolf in sheep's clothing—a dish of chili-marinated beef slices steamed in a coating of toasted rice. It is easy and impressive, ideal for the occasional cook, the busy one, or someone new to Chinese cooking. ◆ For do-ahead flexibility, one could not ask for more. The beef may be marinated days in advance, then steamed, refrigerated, and resteamed before serving. Extending the process only tenderizes the beef. Moreover, the food processor will chop the rice—the only real labor involved in an otherwise effortless dish.

TECHNIQUE NOTES:
When choosing prepackaged flank steak, inspect the package where the ends of the meat have been turned under. If you see nothing but fat, choose another package. The meat should look moist and shiny, red rather than brown. Once the meat is home, a good trimming job is required. Spread the steak flat and remove any silvery sinew, lifting it with your fingernails or the point of a sharp knife in order to cut it free. Be fastidious. The sinew is unchewable.

For homemade rice crumbs, see TECHNIQUE NOTES, page 201.

Yields 25–30 slices, enough to serve 2–3 as a main dish, 4–5 as part of a multicourse meal.

INGREDIENTS:

> *½ pound flank steak, trimmed of all fat and tough sinew (weight after
> trimming)*

> *For marinating the beef:*
> *2–3 large cloves garlic, stem end removed, lightly smashed and peeled*
> *⅛ teaspoon coarse kosher salt*
> *½ teaspoon sugar*
> *1 tablespoon thin (regular) soy sauce*
> *1 tablespoon black soy sauce*
> *1 tablespoon Chinese rice wine or quality, dry sherry*
> *1½–2 teaspoons Chinese chili sauce (page 537)*

> *Rice crumb coating:*
> *½ cup plus 1 tablespoon raw rice, short- or medium-grain recommended*
> *½ teaspoon Roasted Szechwan Pepper-Salt (page 476)*
> *⅛ teaspoon five-spice powder (page 544)*

Cutting, chilling, and marinating the beef:
Trim the steak carefully, as described in TECHNIQUE NOTES.

With a Chinese cleaver or chef's knife cut the meat lengthwise into strips about 2 inches wide. Holding the knife on a diagonal to the board, cut the strips crosswise into slices ¼ inch thick. Cutting on the diagonal broadens the slice. With the broad side of the knife, spank each slice gently to even and tenderize it.

Mash the garlic and salt to a paste, then combine with the remaining marinade ingredients. If you are doubling or tripling the recipe, mince the garlic and salt in a food processor fitted with the steel knife, add the remaining marinade ingredients, and process until blended.

Scrape the marinade over the beef, and toss well to combine. Seal airtight and marinate 1–3 hours at room temperature or overnight in the refrigerator.

Toasting the rice and coating the beef:
Put the rice in a wok or heavy skillet and set over medium heat. Stir constantly until it turns pale gold, about 5 minutes, lowering the heat if the rice begins to scorch. Add the rice, pepper-salt, and five-spice powder to the work bowl of a food processor fitted with the steel knife, then process for about 4 loud minutes, until the grains are reduced to ⅓ their original size. Alternatively, pulverize the mixture until coarse in a blender or a mortar.

Pour the rice over the beef, then toss well to mix. Seal airtight and marinate for at least 1 hour at room temperature or up to 1½ days in the refrigerator. Toss once or twice while marinating to redistribute the rice crumbs.

Steaming the beef:
(For details on steaming and how to improvise a steamer see page 60.)

Arrange the slices close together in a single layer on a heatproof serving plate or Pyrex pie plate at least 1 inch smaller than the diameter of your steamer. Sprinkle any loose rice over the beef and press it into place lightly with your fingers. If most of the rice is loose, sprinkle ⅓ of it on the plate before arranging the beef on top, then cover with the remainder.

Bring the water to a gushing boil, then steam the beef over medium-high heat for 40 minutes, until the rice is fully cooked and the meat is very tender. If you are steaming in advance, steam the beef initially for 30 minutes, and resteam for 10 minutes just before serving. The partially steamed beef may be left at room temperature for 1 hour or sealed airtight and refrigerated overnight.

Serve the beef piping hot, directly in the steamer basket or transferred carefully with a spatula to a hot serving plate.

Leftovers keep 1–2 days. They are delicious at room temperature or resteamed until hot, and will grow spicier.

MENU SUGGESTIONS:
For a simple dinner, partner this dish with a cooling vegetable like *Spinach with Glass Noodles* (page 308) or *Stir-Fried Spinach with Charred Garlic* (page 305). *Soup of Many Mushrooms* (page 454) would be a good complement to the meal. To stand up to the spice of the beef, choose a simple Côtes du Rhône or a good California red jug wine.

Curry Crescents

咖喱角

The amalgam of spices known as curry was an Indian import to China, which became popular in a small number of stew-type dishes. My personal favorite is this delectable meat-stuffed pastry, a standard item in the *dim sum* repertoire. ◆ The classic Chinese pastry is superbly flaky, but it is also greasy and requires lengthy kneading and folding of a lard-soaked dough, which is a bit like handling a jellyfish. The food processor pastry called for here is a 3-minute breeze, with a touch of sweetness to enhance the curry. The lard-butter combination yields a wonderful, non-oily crust. ◆ Miniaturists will enjoy making the tiny crescents; less patient types will prefer to shape them larger. For those who can't be bothered at all, the savory stuffing can be eaten alone (page 226). ◆ This is an immensely practical hors d'oeuvre for a party. The dough and stuffing must be made in advance. Uncooked crescents freeze beautifully and can be baked straight from the freezer.

TECHNIQUE NOTES:
Draining and chilling the filling are important to the success of the crescents. Draining removes excess beef fat, which masks flavors and makes the pastry hard to seal. Chilling keeps the dough firm and easy to handle and results in a flakier pastry. Grinding the filling to a fine consistency makes a soft-textured mixture that is easily enclosed.

Makes about forty 3-inch-long crescents, enough to serve 12–20 as an hors d'oeuvre, 8–10 as part of a brunch buffet.

INGREDIENTS:

    Pastry ingredients:
        6 ounces (12 tablespoons) almost-frozen sweet butter, cubed
        2 ounces almost-frozen lard, cubed
        3 cups all-purpose flour
        2 tablespoons sugar
        a pinch salt
        10–12 tablespoons ice water

Filling ingredients:
  3 large cloves garlic, stem end removed, lightly smashed and peeled
  1 large walnut-size nugget fresh ginger
  1 medium whole scallion, cut into 1½-inch lengths
  1 large, firm onion
  2 tablespoons Chinese rice wine or quality, dry sherry
  2 tablespoons thin (regular) soy sauce
  ¼ teaspoon sugar
  1 scant tablespoon cornstarch
  ¾ pound ground top round beef
  3½ tablespoons corn or peanut oil
  3–4 tablespoons curry paste (page 542)
  coarse kosher salt to taste
  2 teaspoons Chinese or Japanese sesame oil

  additional flour, for rolling out the dough

Egg wash:
  1 large egg beaten with 1 teaspoon water

Making and chilling the pastry:
For standard, small-capacity food processors divide the pastry ingredients in half and process in 2 batches. For large-capacity work bowls that can process 3 cups of flour at one time, process it in 1 batch. Add the flour, sugar, and salt to the work bowl fitted with the steel knife and distribute the butter and lard on top. Process with on-off turns until the mixture resembles coarse meal. Do not overprocess. With the machine running add the ice water through the feed tube in a thin, steady stream, stopping the water flow and the machine as *soon* as the dough begins to come together. The dough will look rather dry. You should just be able to press it together with your fingers.

If you do not have a food processor, cut the fat into the combined flour, sugar, and salt until the mixture resembles coarse meal. Slowly add enough ice water, tossing with a fork, until the dough can be pressed together with your hands. Seal and refrigerate or freeze as below.

Press the dough into 2 flat disks, each about 1 inch thick. Wrap separately in wax paper, then refrigerate until firm. The dough freezes perfectly. To freeze, seal the paper-wrapped disks airtight in plastic bags. Defrost to a cold temperature in the refrigerator before using.

Making and chilling the filling:
Mince the garlic, ginger, and scallion in the work bowl of a food processor fitted with the steel knife, scraping down as necessary until fine. Add the onion and process with on-off turns until chopped. Scrape the mixture into a small plate. Return the knife to the work bowl, and process the wine, soy, sugar, and cornstarch until smooth. Add the beef in several clumps around the blade, and process with on-off turns to combine. Alternatively, mince and combine the ingredients by hand.

Have the onion and beef mixtures, the remaining filling ingredients, and a bowl lined with a metal strainer or colander near your stovetop.

Heat a wok or large, heavy skillet over high heat until hot enough to evaporate a bead of water on contact. Add 2 tablespoons oil, swirl to glaze the pan, and reduce the heat to medium-high. When the oil is hot enough to sizzle a bit of beef, add the beef mixture. Stir-fry briskly until the beef is 90 percent gray, using the spatula to break up the clumps of meat, and adjusting the heat to maintain a merry sizzle without scorching the meat. Remove the meat to the strainer to drain. Wipe the pan clean, heat until hot, then add the remaining 1½ tablespoons oil and swirl to glaze. When the oil is hot enough to sizzle a piece of onion, add the onion mixture and stir-fry briskly until the onion turns translucent, lowering the heat if the mixture begins to brown. Add the curry paste, stir, and return the beef to the pan. Reduce the heat to low. Stir to combine, add salt and additional curry to taste, and quickly fold in the sesame oil.

Scrape the mixture into the work bowl of the processor fitted with the steel knife and process with on-off turns until nubbly. Taste and adjust seasonings as needed, adding a bit more sesame oil if the mixture seems dry. It should adhere together neatly in a spoon. If you do not have a food processor, chop the filling to a fine consistency with one or two equally weighted knives and adjust the seasonings after the mixture cools.

Chill the filling thoroughly before using, up to 2 days, sealed airtight.

Shaping the crescents:
Use a 3-inch round cutter for cocktail-size crescents, a 4-inch cutter for larger crescents. Have the cutter, 2 baking sheets, a cup of flour, a small cup of water, the egg wash and a pastry brush, the chilled filling, and a teaspoon measure and fork on your work surface.

Remove one disk of dough from the refrigerator and quickly roll it out on a lightly floured surface until it is ⅛ inch thick. Check for even thickness with your fingertips. Flour the board as necessary, keeping the flour to a minimum. If you are new to dough-making or the kitchen is hot, roll out only half a disk at a time and keep the remainder refrigerated.

Flour the cutter, then cut out as many circles as possible. Press the scraps into a ball, bag, and refrigerate. Work quickly, so the dough stays cold. Using 1 level teaspoon for small circles and about 2 level teaspoons for large circles, place the filling off center in each dough circle. Dip a finger into the water, then run it lightly around the edge of the circle. Fold the dough over to enclose the filling, forming a crescent, then press the moistened edges lightly to seal. Continue until the first batch of circles is sealed, transfer the crescents to a baking sheet, and refrigerate while you roll out, fill, and seal the next batch. Continue until all the pastry, including the scraps, has been used up. Refrigerate the crescents on the baking sheets until thoroughly cold.

Remove the first sheet from the refrigerator, and use the fork to crimp and seal the edge of each crescent. Lightly brush the tops with egg wash for color, then return the first batch to the refrigerator while you crimp and gloss the second batch. When all the crescents have been glossed and refrigerated, gloss a second time and refrigerate until firm. With a toothpick or thin bamboo skewer, make a tiny hole in each crescent to act as a steam vent, just under the rounded fold of pastry to hide it from view.

The crescents may be baked immediately or refrigerated or frozen. If working a day or more in advance, put the baking sheets in the freezer, then bag the crescents airtight as soon as they are hard. Bake stored crescents directly from the refrigerator or freezer.

Leftover filling may be refrigerated for several days or frozen. Use it as a spread or wrap it in lettuce leaves for a delightful cold snack.

Baking the crescents:
Bake on ungreased baking sheets in a preheated 375° oven for about 25 minutes until golden. Frozen crescents will require about 5 minutes additional baking. Turn the sheets

and rotate their placement in the oven after 10–15 minutes to insure even coloring.

Remove the crescents immediately to a towel-lined basket or tray. Cool several minutes and serve.

Leftover crescents are good at room temperature or may be reheated in the oven, wrapped airtight in foil.

MENU SUGGESTIONS:
These crescents make a versatile appetizer preceding a hot or a cold menu. I like them on their own, midday, with a spinach or watercress salad, or alongside a bowl of *Wine-Explosion Vegetable Chowder* (page 452). A full-bodied Chardonnay or a light, straightforward, and mature Napa Zinfandel are the best partners for the crescents. Stay away from fruity or complex wines, which would not be appreciated next to the curry.

Cold
Purée of
Curried
Beef

咖喱牛肉末

This light and zesty dish is a mating of the soft, moist filling from *Curry Crescents* (page 223), and either chilled lettuce leaves, crisp crackers, or bread rounds, as you please. With the lettuce, it is an engaging cold supper for the warm months. Spread on crackers or on thin, toasted rounds of good bread, it is a welcome change from pâté, perfect as an hors d'oeuvre. ◆ While it might be more Chinese to eat the beef hot, I like to chill it overnight to give the flavors time to develop. It will keep well for a week and only improve in flavor—a great boon for busy people like me who don't mind eating the same light dish a few days running. You may even freeze the purée. The curry paste preserves it remarkably well.

TECHNIQUE NOTES:
The curried beef requires a neutral background to show it off. For one of the best, cut a long *baguette* into thin rounds ¼-inch thick. Dry on baking sheets in a low oven, turning the rounds to dry them evenly. Do not let them brown. Cool and store in an airtight tin, where they will keep perfectly for months.

Serves 2 as a main course, 4–8 as part of a multicourse meal, 10–12 as an hors d'oeuvre.

INGREDIENTS:

> *1 recipe curried beef filling (page 224)*
> *16–24 pretty lettuce leaves, butter lettuce especially nice*
> *or*
> *unsalted crackers*
> *or*
> *thin rounds of toasted baguettes*

Making the filling:
Follow the directions on page 224. Cool the mixture, then seal airtight and refrigerate, preferably overnight to develop the flavors. Serve at room temperature or slightly chilled.

Serving the purée:
For presentation as a cold platter, arrange the individual lettuce leaves in an overlapping spiral around the outside of a large platter, then mound the beef in the center. Invite each guest to wrap a dollop of the beef in a lettuce leaf, and eat it taco-style.

As an hors d'oeuvre, spread the curried beef on crackers or bread and arrange attractively on a serving tray. Or, present the toasts and purée in separate dishes and invite the guests to help themselves.

MENU SUGGESTIONS:
This is a versatile, zesty appetizer before a summer meal of cold foods such as *Orchid's Tangy Cold Noodles* (page 356), *Dry-Fried Szechwan String Beans* (page 297), *Scallion and Ginger Explosion Shrimp* (page 233), and *Marbelized Tea Eggs* (page 325). It is also excellent on its own alongside a bowl of *Wine-Explosion Vegetable Chowder* (page 452) or *Soup of Many Mushrooms* (page 454). To accompany the cold beef, try a full-bodied California Chardonnay, or a straightforward, mature Napa Zinfandel.

Fish & Shellfish

海鮮

♦

♦

I t is hard to live for years, as I did, among people from Shanghai and not become thoroughly and completely enamored of fish and shellfish. Shanghai means literally "on the sea," and while the people of this great port metropolis have a striking love for the fruits of the oceans and rivers, Chinese in general view all swimming things as among the finest of edibles. Chinese philosophers and painters have from early times taken the fish as the symbol of freedom and pleasure, and in the Chinese language, the word for "fish" is a homonym for abundance. Thus, scholars filled their ponds with carp, fishermen became icons for painters and sculptors, and the common hungry human felt better for a bite of fish.

Freshness, above all, is prized by the Chinese in their fish cookery, and there is great weight given to both the freshness of the fish when it is bought and the preservation of a fresh, lively taste in cooking. The ideal is to have one's own pond or tank from which to grab the tasty victim, then dash to the pot. Second best is to buy newly caught fish in the market, and the markets of Taipei were testimony to the Chinese insistence upon freshness, with their rows upon rows of multicolored fish and buckets of wriggling seafood, just-dead if not still alive, and the price to go down by half if not sold by noon. I remember seeing live shrimp being eaten in a Shanghai restaurant, the dancing crustaceans washed down by many cupfuls of wine. And there is a passage in an old Chinese gastronomy book that says it is a crime to peek at a steaming fish and let loose any of the precious vapors. The very characters for "shellfish" mean "ocean freshness," and if that's not enough I say, "Buy it fresh and keep it fresh-tasting in cooking," then you will be at the heart of the Chinese notion of fish.

HOW TO TELL IF A FISH IS FRESH   The Chinese preference is for whole fish, and in buying it whole you gain not only the delicious, meaty tidbits around the collar, tail, and cheeks, but also the best means of judging whether or not a fish is just-caught, on the way out, or long gone. Different cooks look for different things, but I go right to the eye and to the gills. If the eye is clear and bright, and the gills are a deep, moist red, then I know the fish is fresh. If the eye is dull and cloudy and the gills are pale rouge, gray, or purple brown, then I don't buy the fish. It's that simple. In an Asian market where the fish are laid out in the open, it is easy to lift up the stiff cheek flap beneath the eye and inspect the gills, and cloths are often pinned around the counter to help wipe the fingers that know how to choose fish. If you are shopping in a Western market where the fish is behind glass and the head often camouflaged with parsley, be insistent upon the fishmonger showing you the eye and gill, and if it's an honest store you'll be obliged.

When it comes to buying fish fillets, fish steaks, headless shrimp or scallops, I look for firm, moist flesh, good color, and a nice clean smell. If the flesh looks battered or dry, if it smells fishy or off, or is left sitting in a pool of watery juice, then I don't buy it. I am also very picky about where I shop. An honest market with access to its own boat or daily shipments, with a firm policy of selling only what's fresh, is what I want. If a store carries dead clams and dull-eyed fish, and the owner is not willing to discuss his stock and the state of the fish, then I don't buy there.

CLEANING A WHOLE FISH   Many people assume that when a competent fishmonger has gutted, degilled, and scaled a fish, that's all there is to it. Not so! If you have bought a fresh whole fish at the market, you must take some time and special care to clean it fully, and here's how.

Begin with the inside of the fish. Look in the head region, and if you see any red remnants of gills then snip them free with scissors and discard them. Look next in the cavity and pull out any loose membranes, tissues, or bloody clots. If there is a smooth, rather tough membrane covering the backbone, either hiding it from view or clinging in a torn sheet to either side of it, then pull or cut it free. This is the air bladder, and it may have been left inflated or burst, but the job is to remove it, for if it bursts during cooking the fish may taste polluted. Once the backbone is exposed, clean it fully of any blood, using the tines of a fork to dislodge any stubborn clots.

Next, turn to the outside of the fish. Snip off with sturdy scissors any unwanted fins. If you need to remove the top (dorsal) fin, pull to fan it fully with your free hand to make the cutting easier. Then, run your fingertips from the tail to the head of the fish, that is, against the grain of the scales, to detect and pull loose any the fishmonger missed. Always suspect that scales will have been left around the fins, collar, and tail and do an extra inspection of these spots.

At this point, I rush cold running water into the cavity and all over the outside of the fish, then hold it up by the tail and give it a good shake. If I need to, I'll give the fish a quick rinse with cold water once during the course of cleaning, but my preference is to expose it to as little water as possible.

STORING FRESH FISH   I make it a point to buy fish on the day I plan to cook it, and try never to hold it even a day. If I am forced to refrigerate fresh fish or shellfish over-night, I first remove it from the plastic or paper it was wrapped in at the market, drain off any liquids, then reseal it airtight with fresh plastic film and/or a plastic bag. It goes into the refrigerator on the coldest shelf and if I am using a cranky ice box or one that isn't very cold then I put the wrapped fish on a rack or tray about an inch above a pan of ice.

As to freezing fish, I never do it. Fatty whole fish such as salmon are said by food friends I trust to freeze perfectly well; however, I have never been so blessed with abundance that I have not been able to cook up and eat whatever has swum through the door on the spot. My attitude—thoroughly in keeping with Chinese tradition—is that if I get a fish too big to eat, I'll stage a spontaneous party rather than consign it to the freezer, and that if I am presented with a fish I do not have the time to cook I will give it in turn to a good-cook friend on the condition that he or she glorify its freshness by eating it that night!

ON AVOIDING FISHY-TASTING FISH   Fresh ginger, scallion, and wine are the classic de-fishers in the Chinese treatment of fish and shellfish. When they are called for in the marination or steaming of fish or shellfish that is their job. They keep the fish fresh tasting by contributing their own particular juices, so however else you may alter a recipe do not exclude them from a dish.

CHINESE COOKING AND REGIONAL AMERICAN FISH   When a Chinese cook is transplanted to American shores it always means discovering what's available locally to supplant the huge variety of tasty and generally tiny fish and shellfish that abound in Chinese waters. With whole fish, especially, finding the right one can be a problem, as many Chinese recipes call for a fish that is about 2–2½ pounds, with a firm, white, meaty flesh.

I have lived East Coast and West, and these are the names I first look at: On the East Coast, bass, porgy, flounder, pompano, and red snapper. On the West Coast, Oregon black cod, the occasional fat perch or flounder, ling cod, and salmon. (Many West Coast Chinese cooks use rock cod, but it is a fish I simply do not like.) In between, there is walleyed pike and redfish and that is the lamentable extent of my firsthand knowledge.

Mostly what I do in looking for the requisite fish is to ask a lot of questions of the fishmonger. The larger number have had no experience whatsoever with Chinese cooking and tend to think in terms of bone structure, ease of filleting, and issues that don't concern a Chinese cook, yet when you clearly state the need for a firm-fleshed, fine and light-tasting, non-oily fish, you will usually get the most appropriate fish in the store.

And a last note to West Coasters: The fish known on the West Coast as sea bass and snapper are not the equivalents of the East Coast fish. They are instead species of rockfish, with the same (to me unappealing) taste of their cousin, rock cod.

A NOTE ON "FRESH" SHRIMP   Most all shrimp sold in our fish markets are frozen on the trawler and delivered to the market frozen. Rarely can I find *fresh* shrimp, meaning shrimp that have survived catching without being entombed in ice. Alert your fish store that you are in search of truly fresh shrimp and take advantage of them whenever and wherever you find them. As for the standard "fresh" shrimp, meaning those frozen when they reach the market, judge their relative freshness by a lack of odor and a glossy shell. Buying them still frozen means they'll be "fresher."

Let me emphasize that here and throughout this book, I am talking about "fresh" shrimp that has been delivered to the market *in the shell*. Shrimp that have been stripped of the shell by the packer and frozen "in the nude" are totally inappropriate to Chinese cooking—lacking most any taste and texture. If your fish market shells them upon thawing, that is one thing, but *never* buy shrimp that are shelled and then frozen. They will not be worth what you pay for them.

Scallion and Ginger Explosion Shrimp 葱薑爆蝦

This is a simple and strikingly seasoned dish of whole shrimp in their shells, filled with the tang of ginger and scallion and richly infused with black soy and wine. It was taught to me by my more-Chinese-than-Chinese friend, Harvey, at a time when I was a rank beginner to cooking and was stir-frying on a hot plate secreted in my dormitory room, using a tin stockpot inherited from my grandmother. ◆ For the dish to shine, the shrimp must be extremely fresh. Inspect them for a firm, intact shell, a moist, full-fleshed appearance, and a clean fresh smell. Color is not an issue. Different waters will variously spawn rose-colored, ivory, blue-gray, or brownish shrimp, all of them good-tasting. Whether they are labeled "prawns," "jumbo," or "large" is also unimportant. The bodies, without tails, should be between 2 and 3 inches long to work best in this particular recipe, but make freshness a priority over size. ◆ This is a dish done in minutes that tastes best once cool. You may make the shrimps up to a day in advance for a full, rich flavor.

TECHNIQUE NOTES:
Chinese will often cook whole shrimp in their shells, a method that traps the natural juices and seasonings within the shell while shielding the delicate flesh from contact with direct heat. Truly special occasions—or truly manic cooks—demand that the shell not be cut at all and the vein removed by inserting a toothpick surgically under the shell. I find it saner to cut down the back of each shell with small embroidery scissors. The vein lifts out neatly, and the shrimp then have a discreetly open door through which to absorb the seasonings.

Serves 2–3 as a main course, 4–8 as part of a multicourse meal.

INGREDIENTS:

> 1 pound fresh "large" shrimp in their shells, tails on (I use shrimp that are
> 2½–3 inches long, about 25–30 per pound; for information on "fresh"
> shrimp, see page 233)

> For stir-frying the shrimp:
> 5 tablespoons corn or peanut oil
> 1 teaspoon coarse kosher salt
> 1 teaspoon sugar
> 1 tablespoon finely minced fresh ginger
> 3 tablespoons finely chopped green and white scallion
> 2 tablespoons Chinese rice wine or quality, dry sherry
> 2 tablespoons black soy sauce

> To garnish:
> about 1 tablespoon freshly chopped scallion

Readying the shrimp:
Spray the shrimp briefly with cool water, then drain. Remove the legs, pulling off several at a time between your thumb and first finger. Bend back and then break off the sharp pincer above the tail. Work carefully, so the body of the shell remains intact. Use small scissors with long, thin blades (embroidery scissors are ideal) to cut through the shell along the back of each shrimp, cutting all the way to the tail. Cradle the shrimp in your fingers while cutting, so as not to dislodge the shell. With the point of the scissors carefully extract the black intestinal vein. If the vein is clear, you needn't bother to remove it.

At this point, the shrimp may be bagged airtight and refrigerated up to 8 hours. Mist the shrimp lightly if the shells have become dry. Uncooked shrimp will deteriorate rapidly at low temperatures, so store them in the coolest portion of your refrigerator (*not* the freezer) and on a rack over a pan of ice if the refrigerator is not very cold.

Stir-frying the shrimp:
Combine the ginger and scallion. Combine the wine and soy. Have the shrimp and the remaining ingredients all within easy reach of your stovetop.

Heat a wok or deep, heavy skillet over high heat until hot enough to evaporate a bead of water on contact. Add the oil and swirl to glaze the pan. When the oil is hot enough to sizzle one bit of ginger, add the shrimp. Stir-fry briskly but gently for about 1 minute, glazing the shrimp evenly with the oil and keeping the shells intact. Regulate the heat so the shrimp sizzle merrily without scorching. Sprinkle evenly with salt and sugar, stir-fry for 30 seconds to coat, then reduce the heat to medium-high. Add the ginger and scallion, and stir-fry gently for about 1½ minutes, until their aromas "explode" in full fragrance. Add the wine and soy and continue to stir gently, until the liquids are reduced by one half, raising the heat if needed to maintain a brisk simmer.

Scrape the mixture into a shallow bowl and let cool at least 30 minutes at room temperature, stirring occasionally, to give the seasonings time to penetrate. For a richer, fuller flavor, let the shrimp marinate 1–2 hours at room temperature, loosely covered, or overnight in the refrigerator, sealed airtight. Stir occasionally while marinating to redistribute the juices. Serve the shrimp tepid, at room temperature, or slightly chilled.

To serve, arrange the shrimp in a flower-like spiral pattern on a large plate of contrasting color. Begin at the edge of the plate and work in toward the center, arranging the shrimp so they all curve in one direction, pointing the tails outward to serve as ready "handles" for your guests. Reserve the smallest shrimp for the center, placing them to-gether in a tiny pinwheel. Scrape the juices evenly on top, and garnish with the scallion.

How to eat shrimp in their shells:
If you are as agile-tongued as most Chinese, you will be able to put the shrimp in your mouth—whole or in pieces, depending on the size of the shrimp, the size of your mouth, and the style of the occasion—wiggle your jaws a bit, then neatly spit out a perfectly intact shrimp shell. If you are a typical novice, you will do a rather bad, mangled job of it, but will have a great time trying. (The only Westerner I have seen do this with real finesse is my friend Harvey, who has been practicing by cracking melon seeds between his front teeth and extracting the seed with his tongue—a favorite Chinese pastime—since he was a child.)

Otherwise, you may suck on the shell to extract the juices—very important!—and then peel it off with your fingers. As host or hostess, encourage a lot of good-eating noise, and pass a plate of hot, steamed towels to the shrimp-eaters.

Leftovers keep 2–3 days, refrigerated and tightly sealed. Do not reheat.

MENU SUGGESTIONS:
Served hot, I like this dish best in the simple company of *Ham and Egg Fried Rice* (page 405) or *Shanghai Vegetable Rice* (page 402). Cold, its perfect partners are *Orchid's Tangy Cool Noodles* (page 356) and *Dry-Fried Szechwan String Beans* (page 297). To accompany the shrimp, try a big California Chardonnay.

Phoenix Tail Shrimp 鳳尾蝦

This is the fried shrimp of China—a whole, shelled shrimp with its red tail left on for a handle, dipped in batter, than deep-fried to a crispy golden brown. The body of the shrimp, slit partway and flat-tened, spreads upon frying to an appealing-looking fan. This is the phoenix tail, one more example of how the Chinese love to lyricize food and elevate it above the merely chewable. ◆ This is a lively, if somewhat unorthodox, rendition of a classic. The sesame seeds impart a nice brittle bit of texture to the coating, and the finely minced scallion and ginger give the batter a special note of flavor and color. Jazzed up in this fashion, they make excellent wine-chasers or hors d'oeuvres. ◆ The shrimp may be marinated and the batter mixed a full day in advance. The deep-frying must be done at the last minute, but it is so fast and neat that you can do it in party dress.

TECHNIQUE NOTES:
Frying the head-end of the shrimp briefly before dropping the shrimp fully in the oil does two things. First, it gives the thickest part of the shrimp a bit of lead time in frying, and second, it encourages the shrimp to curl upwards in a pretty shape reminiscent of a phoe-nix tail.

For letting a flour batter "rest" before using it, see TECHNIQUE NOTES, page 238.

Serves 2 as a main course, 3–4 as a first course to precede a meal, or 5–6 as a preliminary nibble with wine.

INGREDIENTS:

½ pound "jumbo" fresh shrimp in their shells, tails on (I use shrimp that are

3–3½ inches long, that is, 10–12 shrimp per half-pound; for information on "fresh" shrimp, see page 233)

To marinate the shrimp:
2 quarter-size slices fresh ginger
1 medium whole scallion, cut into 2-inch lengths
2 tablespoons Chinese rice wine or quality, dry sherry

For the batter:
½ cup all-purpose flour
½ teaspoon coarse kosher salt
⅓ cup plus 1½ tablespoons water, at room temperature
1 teaspoon double-acting baking powder
2½ teaspoons finely minced fresh ginger
2½ teaspoons finely minced green and white scallion
2½ tablespoons freshly toasted white sesame seeds

For dipping or sprinkling:
Roasted Szechwan Pepper-Salt (page 476)
or
Sweet and Sour Dipping Sauce (page 478)

4–6 cups corn or peanut oil, for deep-frying

Marinating the shrimp and making the batter:
Rinse the shrimp briefly with cool water, then pat dry. Remove the shell carefully with your fingers, beginning at the tail end and leaving the tail and the sharp "stinger" just above it intact. Remove the vein with a neat, shallow cut, or by pushing the flesh at the head end back a bit to expose the end of the vein and then pulling on it gently to extract the vein without cutting (some shrimp can be deveined in this manner with real ease). Using a sharp knife, carefully slit the shrimp all along its *inner* curve, cutting ¾ of the way through the flesh. (This is the opposite of the better-known "butterfly" cut, where the shrimp is cut along the *back* side.) Turn the shrimp cut side down, then tap once or twice gently with the broad side of a light Chinese cleaver or chef's knife to spread and flatten the flesh. You don't want to make it terribly thin; just a light one or two taps will do.

Smash the ginger and scallion with the blunt handle end or broad side of a cleaver or chef's knife to spread the fibers and bring the juices to the surface. Mix with the wine in a small bowl, add the shrimp, and toss well with your hands to distribute the marinade. Seal airtight and refrigerate for 2–24 hours to infuse the shrimp. Stir once if convenient, midway through marinating.

Add the flour, salt, water, and baking powder to the work bowl of a food processor fitted with the steel knife, then process for about 1 minute until thoroughly blended, scraping the bowl down once or twice. Add the finely minced ginger and scallion, then process to combine. If you do not have a food processor, use a blender or a whisk, first blending the flour, salt, water, and baking powder to form a smooth, thick batter, and then stirring in the ginger and scallion. Do not add the sesame seeds at this time, lest they lose their crispness. Scrape the batter into a small bowl, seal airtight, then set aside for 2 hours at room temperature or overnight in the refrigerator to allow the gluten to relax.

Deep-frying the shrimp:

About 30 minutes before serving, drain the shrimp of the wine marinade and discard the pieces of ginger and scallion. Put a baking tray lined with a double thickness of paper towels, a pair of chopsticks or wooden tongs, and/or a Chinese mesh spoon or slotted spoon all within easy reach of your stovetop. Put a serving platter of a color to contrast with the shrimp in a low oven to warm and ready a small dip dish of the pepper-salt. Finally, stir the toasted sesame seeds into the batter. Put the batter and the well-drained shrimp alongside your stovetop.

Heat a wok or deep, heavy skillet over high heat until hot. Add the oil, then heat to the light-haze stage, 350° on a deep-fry thermometer. Adjust the heat so the oil temperature remains stable. Test the oil with a drop of batter. It should rise to the surface within 2–3 seconds, wearing a crown of tiny white bubbles.

Pick up the first shrimp firmly by the tail, then dip it into the batter to coat it all but the tail. Holding it still by the tail, lower the shrimp halfway into the oil. After 5–10 seconds, wiggle it a bit and the "head" will float upwards. When the head is floating high on the surface of the oil with a crown of white bubbles, in another 5 seconds or so, let go of the tail. This is all very safe and easy; your fingers do not touch the oil and there is no big bubbling or spattering to frighten the cook.

When the first shrimp is fully in the oil, repeat the process with a second shrimp, and so on until the first shrimp turns golden. It will take about 2 minutes for the first shrimp to turn a light gold, and you should turn it once or twice while frying to insure even coloring, and then remove it promptly to the paper-towel drain where it will continue to darken a shade from its own heat. Working steadily in this manner, the whole batch can be fried within 10 minutes, and the first shrimp out of the oil will still be hot when the last one is done.

Transfer the shrimp promptly to the serving platter and serve at once. You may sprinkle a bit of the pepper-salt on top, or invite your guests to sprinkle or lightly dip the shrimp in the mixture. Use the pepper-salt sparingly. No utensils are necessary; you can pick up the shrimp by their tails.

Do not arrange to have leftovers. The shrimp are best freshly fried.

MENU SUGGESTIONS:

This is a good beginning to a special meal. Dishes like *Birthday Duck* (page 175), *Shrimp, Leek, and Pine Nut Fried Rice* (page 408), *Steamed Cucumber with Cassia Blossoms* (page 317), and *Velvet Corn Soup* (page 460) could follow for a large banquet. For a simpler meal, partner the shrimp with *Shanghai Vegetable Rice* (page 402) and *Spinach with Glass Noodles* (page 308). To accompany the shrimp, serve a white Bordeaux.

Spicy Shrimp Fritters

金錢蝦餅

One of the joys of eating in Taipei, the capital of Taiwan, is that you can have breakfast at a street stand run by a couple from Hunan, lunch at a simple restaurant where the chef is from Peking, and dinner at a splendid restaurant devoted to the food of Shanghai, all within the space of one short block. Then, either between meals or once you have recovered, you can go around the corner and find a restaurant run by Taiwanese that features shrimp fritters such as the ones that follow. ◆ The indigenous food of Taiwan bears the stamp of long Japanese occupation, and these fritters, like the minced shrimp rolls wrapped in a band of laver (page 241), will remind you of the light and lovely tempura-type dishes of Japan. What gives them a Chinese character is the liberal use of scallions and coriander and chili in the batter. They are well spiced, but not overwhelming, and are a perfect party appetizer. ◆ Interestingly, Diana Kennedy in her wonderful book, *The Cuisines of Mexico*, gives a similar recipe for fritters using dried shrimp. I have experimented using them in this batter, and the results are delicious if not terribly Chinese. If you wish to use dried shrimp, buy the sort that is an inch long (page 565). Soak 1 cup dried shrimp in very hot tap water to cover for 15–20 minutes, until the shrimp taste pleasantly salty and chewy. Then drain, pat dry, and add to the batter. Who knows, around yet another corner in Taipei may have been the vendor I never got to, selling *dried* shrimp fritters. ◆ This is an exceedingly easy dish to prepare. The batter may be made a night ahead if you like, and the frying is clean and undramatic.

TECHNIQUE NOTES:
Allowing the batter to sit after blending permits the gluten in the flour to rest and enables the starch molecules in the flour to absorb more of the water and seasonings, resulting in a tender and tasty fritter. Incorporating the stiffly beaten egg white just before frying insures that the fritter will be light.

Makes about 30 fritters, enough to serve 4–6 as a light meal with a hearty soup, 8–10 as part of a multicourse meal, or more as an hors d'oeuvre.

INGREDIENTS:

> *1 pound medium-size fresh shrimp in their shells (for information on "fresh" shrimp, see page 233)*

For the batter:
1 cup all-purpose flour
1 cup room temperature water
½ teaspoon coarse kosher salt

Seasonings:
1 teaspoon finely minced fresh ginger
3 tablespoons finely chopped fresh coriander leaves and upper stems
⅓ cup finely chopped green and white scallion
1½ tablespoons Chinese chili sauce (page 537)

1 large egg white, beaten until stiff
4–5 cups corn or peanut oil, for deep-frying

Optional garnish:
sprigs of fresh coriander

For dipping:
Roasted Szechwan Pepper-Salt (page 476)
and/or
Coriandered Mustard Sauce (page 476)

Preparations:
Peel and devein the shrimp. Rinse with cool water, pat dry, then chop into tiny pea-size bits.

Put the flour, water, and salt in the work bowl of a food processor fitted with the steel knife or in a blender. Process for 2 minutes, until the mixture is smooth and thick, then scrape the mixture into a medium bowl.

Add the ginger, coriander, scallion, and chili sauce to the batter, stirring well to blend. Add the shrimp, then stir to combine. Seal airtight and allow to sit for 2 hours at room temperature or overnight in the refrigerator. Bring to room temperature before frying.

Frying the fritters:

Just before frying, stir the batter several times, then gently fold in the stiffly beaten egg white until the mixture is well blended. Have the shrimp mixture, a tablespoon, a Chinese mesh spoon or slotted spoon, a pair of chopsticks, and a baking sheet or jelly-roll pan lined with a triple thickness of paper towels all within easy reach of your stovetop. Put a serving platter of a color to contrast prettily with the shrimp in a low oven to warm. Ready the pepper-salt and mustard sauce in small bowls or dip dishes to accompany the platter.

Heat a wok or large, heavy skillet over high heat until hot. Add the oil (if you are using a skillet, pour it ¾ inch deep), then heat to the pre-haze stage, 350° on a deep-fry thermometer, when a drop of batter rises to the surface in 3–4 seconds surrounded by a ring of white bubbles. Adjust the heat so the temperature does not rise.

Stir the batter gently once or twice more to bring the shrimp to the surface, then drop a tablespoon of the batter into the oil. The batter will sink straight to the bottom and take 5–6 seconds to rise. Once the first fritter rises to the surface, drop the next tablespoon of batter into the oil, and so on, frying as many fritters in one batch as have room to float on the surface of the oil. As you work, regulate the heat so the fritters fry at a constant 350°, each rising within 5–6 seconds surrounded by a ring of white bubbles.

Fry until evenly golden, about 1½ minutes total per fritter, turning the fritter over with chopsticks once midway through the frying. Remove the fritters promptly to the paper-towel drain while they are still golden and not yet brown.

If you are frying in batches, remember to allow sufficient time for the oil to regain its original high temperature, retesting the oil with a fresh drop of batter before beginning the second batch. When you get the hang of it, you will probably find it easiest to drop a fresh tablespoon of batter into the oil after each cooked fritter leaves the pot, that is, frying continuously rather than in batches.

Serve promptly, when the fritters are at their just-fried best. If necessary, you may hold the fritters on the paper-towel drain in a 250° oven for several minutes between batches, but any longer and they tend to grow oily. I like to send them to the table freshly made, and then arrive at the table several minutes later with the second batch in hand.

Arrange the fritters on the heated platter, garnished with coriander and accompanied by the dishes of pepper-salt and mustard. Encourage everyone to try the first fritter plain, and then sprinkle the next one with a dash of pepper-salt or a dip in the mustard.

Leftovers are tasty cold if you share the penchant for nibbling on cold fried leftovers. Reheated, they grow oily.

MENU SUGGESTIONS:

This is a lovely, spicy opening for a hot or a cold meal, with Champagne. For a simple meal, try the fritters with *Velvet Corn Soup* (page 460) or *Moslem-Style Hot and Sour Soup* (page 450). For a *dim sum* brunch, serve them alongside *Springrolls with Dijon Mustard Sauce* (page 389), *Soy-Dipped Red Radish Fans* (page 114), *Sweet and Tangy Cucumber Pickles* (page 110), *Curry Crescents* (page 223), and/or any of the dumplings (pages 375 to 389). They are also wonderful with *Orchid's Tangy Cool Noodles* (page 356) and *Peony Blossom Cold Noodles* (page 358) for a hot-weather supper.

Deep-Fried Shrimp Balls

炸蝦球

Classic Chinese shrimp balls are traditionally smooth-textured affairs, made from a paste that one squeezes into balls between one's fist. Here is something different—the same shrimp purée enlivened with ginger and diced water chestnuts that must be rolled with great gentility between greased palms. They are charmingly irregular when fried and very delicious, traditionally shaped or not. ◆ Shrimp balls make wonderful appetite arousers for a sit-down dinner, a stand-up cocktail party, or an all-American barbecue in any posture. They are juicy and velvety, and spiked with just enough fresh ginger to raise them above the ordinary. With a sprinkling of *Roasted Szechwan Pepper-Salt* they become even more special. ◆ Making the shrimp paste takes minutes in a food processor and can be done in advance. Shaping the balls may also be done ahead, but the deep-frying—a simple and neat job—must be done at the last minute.

TECHNIQUE NOTES:
For the role of fresh lard in making shrimp paste, see TECHNIQUE NOTES, page 244.

Yields about 18 shrimp balls, enough to serve 6–8 as an hors d'oeuvre, or 4–6 as part of a multicourse meal.

INGREDIENTS:

> *1 recipe shrimp paste (page 244)*
> *4–6 cups corn or peanut oil, for deep-frying*

> *For dipping:*
> *Coriandered Mustard Sauce (page 476)*
> *or*
> *Roasted Szechwan Pepper-Salt (page 476)*

Preparations:
Make shrimp paste as described on page 244. Refrigerate, if desired, overnight. (I prefer to use it freshly made when the ginger is at its peak sparkle, but the loss is not substantial.)

Up to 3 hours in advance, shape the shrimp balls. Lightly grease a flat dinner plate, your palms, and a teaspoon with corn or peanut oil. Scoop up about 1 tablespoon of the paste with the spoon or scoop, then roll it gently between your palms to produce a walnut-size ball. Transfer it lightly to the plate. Continue to shape balls, oiling the spoon and your palms as needed to prevent sticking.

If you are working in advance, seal the plate airtight with plastic wrap, taking care not to squash the shrimp balls. Bring to room temperature before frying.

Deep-frying the shrimp balls:
Have the shrimp balls, a baking tray lined with a double thickness of paper towels, and a Chinese mesh spoon or slotted spoon all within reach of your stovetop. Put a serving platter in a low oven to warm. Ready the pepper-salt in a small dip dish to be served alongside the shrimp.

About 10–15 minutes prior to serving, heat a wok or deep, heavy skillet over high heat until hot. Add the oil, then heat to the pre-haze stage, 325° on a deep-fry thermometer, when there is a lot of movement just beneath the surface of the oil but a haze has not yet formed. Test the oil with a dab of shrimp paste or one shrimp ball. It should rise to the surface within 2–4 seconds, surrounded by tiny bubbles. Adjust the heat so the temperature does not rise.

One by one, drop the shrimp balls carefully into the oil about an inch above the surface. Fry as many at one time as can freely float on the surface of the oil, adjusting the heat so the oil temperature remains constant and each ball rises quickly to the surface ringed with bubbles.

Fry the shrimp balls until golden and swollen, about 3 minutes, turning them occasionally to encourage even coloring. When they are a half-shade lighter than you wish, remove them with the mesh spoon, hold them briefly above the pot to drain, then transfer them to the paper towels where they will continue to cook and darken a bit from their own heat.

If you are working in small batches or are frying a double recipe, keep the tray in a 325° oven so the shrimp balls remain swollen. As they cool, they deflate.

When all the balls have been fried, shake the tray to blot up excess oil. Arrange them quickly on the heated platter and serve at once, accompanied by the pepper-salt, and toothpicks if you like. Warn your guests to be sparing with the dip; just a touch is sufficient.

Leftover shrimp balls require a special palate to be enjoyed cold. Reheated (as some cookbooks advise), they are abominable.

MENU SUGGESTIONS:
This is a perfect appetizer to open most any meal. As a main course for a simple dinner, pair it with *Old Egg* (page 332), *Hakka Stuffed Tofu* (page 343), *Chinese Cabbage Hearts with Glass Noodles* (page 311) or *Spinach with Glass Noodles* (page 308). The shrimp balls may also be included in a soup (page 463) as a one-bowl meal. For a *dim sum* brunch, serve them with steamed buns (page 422), *Gold Coin Eggs* (page 330) or *Shao-Mai Dumplings* (page 375). To accompany the shrimp balls, choose a not-too-sweet California Johannisberg Riesling or an Alsatian Riesling.

Shrimp Rolls with Crisp Seaweed

紫菜包蝦

These thumb-size logs of deep-fried shrimp paste wrapped around the middle with a band of crispy seaweed remind me of Japan, not because this pretty, very Japanese-looking dish probably originated there, but because it recalls the street workers I watched daily during my summers in Kyoto. They were plumpish men turned red by the sun, who in spite of the intense Kyoto heat wore dark woolen bands around their bellies to protect the spirits which reside in one's middle. ◆ The seaweed is the sort known in Chinese as "purple plant," in English as "laver," and in Japanese as *nori*. It may be bought unseasoned in large folded sheets, but I prefer the Japanese brands that are seasoned with soy sauce and red pepper, then precut into bands and sealed in very Japanese-style packages with a dozen neat compartments and enough wrappers to try one's un-Japanese patience. When deep-fried, this oceany stuff has a potato-chip-like appeal—slightly salty and curiously addictive—not at all what one expects from seaweed. ◆ This is an intriguing appetizer or "sea course," which can be mixed happily with many cuisines. The shrimp paste takes only minutes in a food processor, and the rolls may be shaped in advance. The deep-frying must be done last minute, but is neat enough to be executed in a kimono.

TECHNIQUE NOTES:
When deep-frying a number of small, encrusted items that tend to deflate dramatically upon cooling, Chinese often employ the technique of double deep-frying. The first frying is done at moderately low temperatures (350° or 375°) and is responsible for cooking the food 50 percent through and setting it with a light color. The second frying, done at higher heat to accompany one large single batch, cooks the food to doneness, deepens it to the desired color, and puffs the individual items uniformly just before serving. The technique is also employed with large items, like a whole duck or chicken, when you need to fry it slowly in order to cook it, but want a skin-crisping zap of heat at the end.

For the surprising role of fresh lard, see TECHNIQUE NOTES, page 244.

Yields about 18 shrimp rolls, enough to serve 6–8 as an hors d'oeuvre, or 4–6 as part of a multicourse meal.

INGREDIENTS:

> *1 recipe shrimp paste (page 244)*
> *18–20 strips laver, cut 3½ inches long and 1¼ inch wide, preferably the pre-seasoned sort available in Japanese markets, ajitsuke-nori (page 551)*
> *4–6 cups corn or peanut oil, for deep-frying*

> *For dipping:*
> *Coriandered Mustard Sauce (page 476)*
> *and/or*
> *Roasted Szechwan Pepper-Salt (page 476)*

Preparations:
Make the shrimp paste as described on page 244 and refrigerate, if desired, overnight. (I prefer using it freshly made, when the ginger flavor is keenest, but the loss is small and the convenience may be great.)

Up to 3 hours in advance, shape the shrimp rolls. Lightly grease a flat dinner plate and a tablespoon with some corn or peanut oil. Lay the first strip of laver on your work space. Scoop up 1 tablespoon of the shrimp paste and put it in the middle of the laver band. With your fingers, shape the paste into a stubby log, perpendicular to the length of the band. Wrap the band around the shrimp log so it overlaps itself by ¼ inch, then glue the laver to itself with a thin smear of shrimp paste, thereby sealing the band. Smooth the protruding shrimp paste with your fingers to round the log at the ends, then put the roll on the oiled plate. Do not space the finished rolls too closely together lest they stick.

Once shaped, the rolls may be refrigerated for several hours. Seal the plate airtight with plastic, taking care not to squash the rolls, and bring to room temperature before frying.

Deep-frying the shrimp rolls:
Have the shrimp rolls, two baking trays each lined with a double thickness of paper towels, a pair of cooking chopsticks or wooden tongs, and a large Chinese mesh spoon or a large metal strainer with a handle all within reach of your stovetop. Put a serving platter in a low oven to warm. Ready the accompaniment(s) in small dip dishes to serve with the shrimp.

About 15 minutes before serving, heat a wok or deep, heavy skillet over high heat until hot. Add the oil, then heat to the light-haze stage, 350° on a deep-fry thermometer. Adjust the heat so the temperature does not rise, then test the oil with a bit of shrimp paste or one shrimp roll. If the oil is sufficiently hot, it should rise to the surface within 2–4 seconds, wearing a crown of tiny white bubbles.

Carefully drop the shrimp rolls one by one into the oil about an inch above the surface. Fry in batches of 5–8 or more, continuing to add them so long as the rolls have room to float and each one rises quickly to the surface surrounded by white bubbles. If the bubbling ceases, the oil temperature is too low.

Fry the rolls until only lightly golden, about 1 minute, turning them in the oil to encourage even coloring. Remove them half-done to the first towel-lined tray, then raise the heat to bring the oil temperature to 375°. If you are forced to work in small batches or are cooking a double recipe, keep the tray in a 325° oven, so the rolls stay hot and don't shrivel.

When the oil is at 375°, add all the rolls at one time, keeping the heat high so the addition of so much bulk will not lower the temperature. Fry, turning them, until golden and swollen, 15–30 seconds. Remove them swiftly from the oil in one swoop with the mesh spoon or strainer, and transfer to the fresh towel-lined tray.

Shake the tray to blot up excess oil, then arrange the rolls prettily on the heated platter. Work quickly, lest they deflate.

Serve at once, accompanied by the pepper-salt, and/or mustard sauce. Remind your guests to bite down carefully, as the rolls (like one's belly spirits) stay hot with a band wrapped around them. Also, use dips sparingly. One for each end of the roll is my fashion.

Leftovers are only tolerable cold, and worse reheated, so don't make extra.

MENU SUGGESTIONS:
This is a delicious appetizer served with a big-bodied Chardonnay. It is also a good accompaniment to *Ham and Egg Fried Rice* (page 405), *Dry-Fried Szechwan String Beans* (page 297), or *Spinach with Glass Noodles* (page 308). If you wish to serve the above as a multicourse meal, *Velvet Corn Soup* (page 460) would be an appropriate soup.

Gold Coin Shrimp Cakes

麵包蝦餅

It is uncertain when shrimp toast entered the Chinese repertoire, but what is clear is that they are almost universally bad—anemic-looking slabs of shrimp plastered atop squares of greasy Wonder Bread. Horrors! ◆ Here is the ultimate shrimp toast, a plush purée of colorfully garnished shrimp crowning an oblong slice of crusty French *baguette*. In search of Chinese roots, I gamely tried all manner of Chinese breads, but the French won out, even over San Francisco sourdough. ◆ This is a stunning hors d'oeuvre, a dramatic opener for any meal. The food processor blends the purée in seconds, and the only work is spreading it on the bread. The shrimp toast may be assembled several hours in advance, but fry them at the last minute for full beauty and flavor.

TECHNIQUE NOTES:
For the shrimp toast to fry perfectly, the bread must be dense and dry on the outside, and the puréed shrimp must be pressed solidly and evenly on top. Then the oil has no place to penetrate. The oil must be at a moderate 350°—warm enough to sear the shrimp paste

and cook it through, but not so hot that it browns on the outside while remaining raw in the middle. The oil should be fresh or only lightly used to keep the color of the toast light.

Lard is essential to lighten the paste, as strange as that seems from our modern Western perspective. It contributes no taste, just a smooth, airy, and inimitable texture. Buy it fresh from the butcher (page 551), and store the surplus in the freezer.

Makes 20 shrimp toast, enough to serve 6–12 as part of a multicourse meal, 15–20 as an hors d'oeuvre.

INGREDIENTS:

> 1–2 dense-textured French baguettes (to yield 20–25 oblong slices ½–¾ inch thick)

> Shrimp paste:
> ¾ pound fresh shrimp (for information on "fresh" shrimp, see page 233)
> 6 large water chestnuts, fresh best
> 1 large walnut-size nugget fresh ginger
> 1 medium scallion, white and light green parts only
> 1½ tablespoons minced fresh lard (equals ¾ ounce)
> 2 teaspoons coarse kosher salt
> 1 tablespoon Chinese rice wine or quality, dry sherry
> 1 tablespoon water
> 2 tablespoons cornstarch
> 1 large egg white

> Garnishes:
> 20–25 perfect small coriander leaves or tiny scallion branches (page 563)
> about 2 tablespoons black sesame seeds
> 2–3 tablespoons finely minced Smithfield ham

> 4–6 cups fresh corn or peanut oil, for deep-frying

> Dip sauce:
> 2 tablespoons quality ketchup
> 1 tablespoon plus 1 teaspoon unseasoned Chinese or Japanese rice vinegar
> 1 tablespoon water
> ¼ teaspoon Chinese rice wine or quality, dry sherry

Slicing and drying the bread:
Cut the *baguettes* on a diagonal to yield 20–25 ovals about 3 inches long and ½–¾ inch thick. Use a serrated knife for a clean, neat cut. Discard any slices with holes in them.

Spread the bread on a rack until dry on top, about 2 hours, then flip and dry the other side. If you are in a rush or your kitchen is humid, spread the slices on a baking sheet and dry in a 200° oven, turning them over once the top is dry. Bag airtight in plastic until ready to use, overnight if you wish.

Making the shrimp paste:
Shell and devein the shrimp. Rinse with cool water and drain.

Peel fresh water chestnuts and cut into peppercorn-size bits. Blanch canned water chestnuts in plain boiling water to cover for 15 seconds, then drain immediately and chill under cold running water. Cut as above.

Mince the ginger and scallion in the work bowl of a food processor fitted with the steel knife, scraping down as necessary until fine. Add the shrimp, lard, and salt and mince to a near-paste. Add the wine, water, and cornstarch and process until smooth. Alternatively, mince the ginger and scallion by hand, mince the shrimp to a fine paste with one or two equally weighted cleavers, then combine with the lard, salt, wine, water, and cornstarch, stirring until smooth. (By hand, it will take about 15 minutes.)

Stir in the water chestnuts by hand to preserve their texture. Beat the egg whites until stiff, then fold into the purée, stirring until blended. Press plastic wrap on the surface of the mixture to seal it airtight, and refrigerate until use, overnight if you wish.

Forming the shrimp toast:

Have the shrimp mixture, bread slices and garnishes at hand. Lightly oil a broad, flat knife or metal spatula, so the shrimp will not stick. Slice by slice, mound the shrimp evenly on the bread, using the spatula to press it evenly and firmly all around to form a flat plateau ½ inch high, with smooth, gently sloped sides meeting the edge of the bread. Garnish with a coriander leaf or scallion branch in the middle, a light sprinkle of ham at one end, and a dusting of sesame seeds at the other end. Press lightly with your finger to make the garnishes adhere.

Put the finished slices on a plate or tray. They may be refrigerated, loosely covered, for several hours.

Frying and serving:

About 20 minutes before serving, put the shrimp toast, a tray lined with a double thickness of paper towels, a Chinese mesh spoon, and cooking chopsticks or wooden tongs within easy reach of your stovetop. Combine the dip sauce ingredients and set aside in a small serving bowl. Put a serving platter of contrasting color in a low oven to warm.

Heat a wok or large, deep skillet over high heat until hot. Add the oil, and heat to the light-haze stage, 350° on a deep-fry thermometer, when a bit of shrimp paste floats to the surface within 3–4 seconds. One by one, gently slip the toast shrimp side down into the oil, frying as many as can float freely at one time and adjusting the heat so they rise quickly to the surface surrounded by bubbles. Fry about 4 minutes until the shrimp is reddish-gold, then turn the toast over to lightly brown the bread. Do not overcook the shrimp, which will continue to cook from its own heat after it leaves the oil. Scoop the toasts from the oil with the spoon and put them bread side down on the towel-lined tray. The finished toasts can be kept warm in a 325° oven while the rest are being fried. Do not hold more than 5 minutes in the oven or they will shrivel.

Arrange the shrimp toast on the platter like the petals of a flower with the dish of dip sauce in the center.

Leftovers are tasty for snacking if you enjoy cold fried foods. Do not reheat.

MENU SUGGESTIONS:

I typically serve the shrimp cakes as the start of a special dinner. Delicate foods follow well—*Pearl Balls* (page 187), *Lettuce-Wrapped Spicy Chicken* (page 145), *Clear-Steamed Flounder with White Pepper* (page 250), and *Velvet Corn Soup* (page 460). If the above were all served as one spectacular dinner, *Ginger-Infused Crème Caramel* (page 504) or *Caramelized Apple Slices with Armagnac* (page 490) would be an elegant ending. Partner the shrimp cakes with a big-bodied Champagne, namely a California Blanc-de-Noir, or a big-bodied Chardonnay.

Sesame Fish Slices

芝蔴魚片

While sesame seeds are valued by Chinese cooks mainly as a source of aromatic oil, they are also often used whole—in candies, as a garnish, or as a crisp coating for deep-fried foods. Here, they are absolutely delicious as a brittle crust for thin slices of deep-fried fish. Served alongside is a garlic and ginger-sparked dipping sauce to provide a refreshing lift of color and sweetness. ◆ This is an extremely simple dish with an intriguing, different look. Serve it as an hors d'oeuvre in any setting, or as the first hot course in a Chinese meal. The passing and dipping of the crunchy fish slices is a lovely way to bring a group together. ◆ The fish may be sliced and marinated a day in advance, then coated with the seeds and refrigerated several hours before frying. The frying itself is easy and clean.

TECHNIQUE NOTES:
For tension-free frying, hold a large mesh spoon in one hand above the oil, and a pair of cooking chopsticks, wooden tongs, or a small mesh spoon in the other. As the slices fry to doneness, you can retrieve them with the chopsticks or tongs then deposit them in the large spoon to drain, without having to shift your body or attention to transfer them elsewhere.

Also, with every slice you take from the oil, add another fresh slice to the pot. In that way the oil stays at the same temperature, and the fish cooks evenly. This continual, rhythmic process is easier and quicker than frying in batches.

For refrigerating a coating to help it adhere, see TECHNIQUE NOTES, page 148.

Yields 20–25 slices, enough to serve 4–5 as part of a multicourse meal, 6–10 as an hors d'oeuvre.

INGREDIENTS:

> *½ pound fillet of firm-fleshed, white meat, non-oily fish with a neutral character—sea bass, ling cod, sole, or flounder recommended*
>
> For marinating the fish:
> *1 large egg white*
> *1½ teaspoons fresh corn or peanut oil*
> *2 teaspoons Chinese rice wine or quality, dry sherry*
> *¾ teaspoon coarse kosher salt*
> *1½ tablespoons cornstarch*
>
> *1¼ cups untoasted white sesame seeds*
> *4–6 cups fresh corn or peanut oil, for deep-frying*
> *Sweet and Sour Dipping Sauce (page 478)*

Cutting and marinating the fish:
Lay the fillet flat, run your fingers against the grain, and remove any bones you find with a tweezer or needle-nose plier. Keep your fingers pressed flat against the fish and around the bone when deboning, so the bone pulls free without tearing the flesh (see TECHNIQUE NOTES, page 252). Rinse the fillet with cool water, then pat dry.

Spread the fish flat, then use a cleaver or sharp knife to cut it lengthwise into strips about 2 inches wide. Holding the cleaver on a sharp diagonal to the board, cut each strip crosswise with the grain into slices about ¼ inch thick. Holding the knife on an angle broadens the slice.

Blend the marinade ingredients until smooth and thick, in the work bowl of a food processor fitted with the steel knife, a blender, or by hand. Combine the fish slices and the marinade in a small bowl, stirring with your hands to coat and separate the slices. Seal airtight with plastic wrap, then refrigerate 1–24 hours to set the marinade and infuse the fish with its flavor.

Coating the slices with sesame seeds:

Remove the fish from the refrigerator and stir to distribute the marinade.

Spread half the seeds evenly in a large baking pan or pie plate, then spread the fish slices next to one another in a single layer on top. Sprinkle evenly with the remaining seeds, then press with dry fingers to make the seeds adhere. Arrange the coated slices in a single layer on a wax paper-lined plate or baking sheet, seal airtight and refrigerate the fish 1–4 hours prior to deep-frying. Discard the excess sesame seeds.

Making the sauce and deep-frying the fish:

Make the sauce as directed on page 478. Cover the pot so the sauce stays hot, and put a small sauce bowl and a serving platter of contrasting color in a low oven to warm. Have a tray lined with a double thickness of paper towels, a large Chinese mesh spoon, and a pair of cooking chopsticks or a smaller mesh spoon alongside your stovetop. Remove the fish from the refrigerator.

Heat a wok or deep, heavy skillet over high heat until hot. Add oil to a depth of at least 2½ inches, then heat the oil to the light-haze stage, 350° on a deep-fry thermometer, when a single piece of fish comes to the surface within 3 seconds, surrounded by gently sizzling bubbles. Adjust the heat so the temperature does not rise.

Slice by slice, slip the fish into the oil with your fingers from the side of the pan, frying as many slices at one time as have room to float. Maintain a steady temperature so the slices continue to rise to the surface within several seconds.

The first slice is done when the seeds turn pale gold and the fish floats high on the surface of the oil, in 2–3 minutes. Pluck it from the oil with the chopsticks or small spoon, deposit it in the large spoon, then add a fresh slice of fish to the oil. Continue until you have 5 or 6 slices in the spoon, then spread them on the paper towels to drain.

If you are frying a double or triple batch, dredge the oil of seeds midway through frying and put the paper towel-lined tray in the oven to keep the first batch warm while you fry the remainder. Do not hold the slices in the oven more than 5–10 minutes.

Once all the slices are fried, arrange them on the serving platter around the sauce bowl and scrape the sauce into the bowl. Pass the dish, inviting your guests to help themselves to a crusty slice and dip it in the sauce. In my house, this is finger food, though you may use chopsticks if you wish.

When cool, strain, bottle, and refrigerate the oil for future frying.

Leftover fish slices make good cold nibbles, or may be reheated in a hot oven wrapped tightly in foil. They grow a bit oily with reheating, but will be snatched up nonetheless.

MENU SUGGESTIONS:

The fish slices are a novel appetizer, alone or alongside *Walnut Chicken Slices* (page 148). Dishes to follow might include *Shrimp, Leek, and Pine Nut Fried Rice* (page 408) and *Golden Egg Dumplings* (page 328). *Velvet Corn Soup* (page 460), and a selection of fruit and cookies (pages 493 to 496) would be my choices to complete the menu. For a simple meal, partner the fish slices with *Spinach with Glass Noodles* (page 308). To serve with the fish slices, try a sparkling Loire wine with its clean bubble, or a light Chardonnay, French Chablis, or Pinot Blanc.

Steamed Whole Fish with Seared Scallions 豆豉蒸魚

For simplicity, clarity, and purity of flavor, I can think of nothing more appealing than a perfectly steamed fish. When I am worn out from cooking, eating, or just plain living, it is the dish I always turn to. ◆ You need little else but a splendidly fresh whole fish. Black sea bass, available on the East Coast, is my favorite; flounder, porgy, or walleye pike are other choices. Look for a fish with red gills, clear, bright eyes, and a firm, delicate-tasting flesh. The gills, eyes, and firm flesh are your insurance of freshness, while the neutral character works best with these seasonings. Have the fishmonger remove the scales, fins, guts, and gills, but leave the head and the tail (including the fan-like caudal fin at the end) intact. The fish has no majesty without them. ◆ Readying and steaming a whole fish of this size takes only 30 minutes and requires preparation of only a few ingredients. Like all steamed fish dishes done in a classic Chinese mode, it has a versatile, dual character—wonderfully simple for a cozy dinner for two or equally appropriate as the elegant finale for a banquet.

TECHNIQUE NOTES:
For the fish to steam properly, it should be subject to an intense, steady heat without interruption. Do not lift the lid to peer at it before the time has almost elapsed, and then lift the lid only partway so as not to dissipate the steam. Quickly check the flesh at the base of the score mark (nearest the bone) in the thick midsection of the fish. If it is white and firm, then the fish is done.

The searing of the decorative scallion net is a restaurant touch designed for drama and fragrance. The hot oil singes the scallion and the ginger beneath it in an instant, deepening the color, releasing the aroma, and reducing the flavors to the essence. In intent and effect, it is much like the Western technique of flambéing.

For scoring a whole fish to cook it quickly and efficiently, see TECHNIQUE NOTES, page 260.

Serves 2–3 as a main course, 4–6 as part of a multicourse meal.

INGREDIENTS:

1 whole, extremely fresh fish, sea bass preferred—1½ pounds before gutting, head and tail left on

For seasoning the fish:
2 teaspoons salted Chinese black beans (not the variety seasoned with five-spice powder; page 561)
1 tablespoon thin (regular) soy sauce
1 tablespoon Chinese rice wine or quality, dry sherry
1 teaspoon Chinese or Japanese sesame oil (increase to 2 teaspoons for flounder)
½ teaspoon sugar

½ tablespoon fine julienne threads of fresh ginger, cut 1½ inches long and as thin as possible
1 medium whole scallion, cut into 2-inch lengths
1–1½ teaspoons coarse kosher salt

For the scallion net:
   2 tablespoons corn or peanut oil
   1 medium whole scallion, cut into shreds 2 inches long and 3/16 inch thick

Preparing the fish for steaming:

Thoroughly clean the fish, removing scales, membranes, and blood, as directed on page 231. No matter how good your fishmonger, this double cleaning is crucial. Be especially sure the bladder has been removed, or else the fish can be stained with bitterness. Wash the fish with cold running water inside and out, then pat dry.

Lay the fish flat and score it crosswise at 1-inch intervals, from neck to tail on both sides of the fish, as directed on page 260. Cut to within ¼ inch of the bone for a good penetration of steam and seasonings.

Chop the black beans coarsely. Do not wash them; the salt will contribute to flavoring the fish. Combine the beans, soy, wine, oil, and sugar, stirring well to blend.

This much may be done several hours in advance. Refrigerate the fish, ginger, and scallion, sealed airtight.

Steaming the fish:

(For details on steaming and how to improvise a steamer, see page 60.)

Rub the salt evenly over the fish, inside and out, rubbing into the score marks with your fingers. Lay the fish in a Pyrex pie plate or shallow bowl at least 1 inch smaller in diameter than your steamer, ideally one in which you can serve the fish to avoid having to transfer it. (If the fish is a few inches too large, you can "bend" it to fit: Thick, round fish like bass can be stood on their belly, then curved to fit the dish. In this posture, they must wear the seasonings along their "back," that is, their dorsal side. Flat fish like flounder can have their tails curved over, then threaded or skewered in a graceful arc; you should season them before skewering. Fish steamed in these postures can look very playful and lively.) Stir the liquid seasonings to recombine, then pour evenly over the fish and scatter the ginger threads on top. Crush the thick scallion lengths lightly with the broad side of a cleaver or knife to release their juices, then array over the fish.

Bring the steaming water to a full, gushing boil over high heat. Add the fish to the steamer, cover tightly, then steam over medium-high heat for 12–15 minutes, until the flesh at the base of the score marks in the thickest part of the flesh is white. Do not be surprised at the "natural sauce" the fish renders during steaming, which you will see when you lift the lid. It is absolutely delicious and is meant to be served with the fish.

Searing the scallion net:

When the fish is within several minutes of being done, heat the oil in a small saucepan over low heat, until hot but not smoking. Have the shredded scallion nearby.

As soon as it is done, remove the plate from the steamer. If it is necessary to transfer the fish, slide it with care onto a heated serving platter, along with the sauce. Discard the steamed scallions. Scatter the fresh scallion shreds over the fish, then drizzle the hot oil evenly on top, standing at arm's length from the fish and averting your face. The oil will sputter and hiss in a fragrant explosion.

Serve the fish at once, while the aroma is pronounced. Use the score marks as a convenient way to lift the fish from the bone and save the tender fish cheeks for the guest(s) of honor.

Leftovers can be good to excellent cold, depending on the fish. Bone the fish, cover with the leftover juices, then seal airtight and refrigerate. The sauce will congeal in a tasty aspic, and the fish will turn smooth and slippery once chilled.

MENU SUGGESTIONS:
For a simple but luscious meal, pair the fish with any of the fried rice dishes (pages 404 to 410). If a fuller menu is desired, begin with *Pearl Balls* (page 187) or *Shao-Mai Dumplings* (page 375), and serve *Chinese Cabbage Hearts with Glass Noodles* (page 311) or *Red Bell Pepper with Garlic and Coriander* (page 314) in addition to the rice. *Velvet Corn Soup* (page 460), *Soup of Many Mushrooms* (page 454), or *Chinese Meatball Soup* (page 448) would go well. *Pear and Jasmine Tea Sorbet* (page 500) would be my choice for dessert. To partner the steamed fish, choose either an expansive white wine—a big, white Burgundy, a full-bodied Chardonnay, or a white Hermitage—or try a light red wine, such as a light Côtes du Rhône or Beaujolais.

Clear-Steamed Flounder with White Pepper

清蒸比目魚

A "clear-steamed" fish is one that is steamed without bean condiments, in a clear, clean sauce comprised of soy sauce, wine, and the natural fish juices. Beyond that, the steaming ingredients may be few or many, all depending on the region, the occasion, and most important, the personality of the fish. ◆ This medley of seasonings is especially tailored for the mild-mannered flounder, which needs the punch of pepper and the richness of oil to give it character and class. It is a simple recipe with only three requirements. The first is a superbly fresh whole flounder (or another suitable fish of the same type). Make sure its gills are red and the flesh is firm. Second are whole white peppercorns for grinding a "live" spice. Third is a well-cured Smithfield or Westphalian ham (page 549), with a flavorful fat to make up for the flounder's lean. The fat is essential. If you cannot find the right ham, then use 3 or 4 strips of a good fatty bacon. Lay them whole over the fish and remove before serving. ◆ This dish can be prepared and steamed within 30 minutes, dressed up or down as you like with the addition of a few scallion frills. It is an easy way to eat elegantly at the end of a busy day, and a wonderful dish to turn to when company is expected.

TECHNIQUE NOTES:
For scoring a whole fish, see TECHNIQUE NOTES, page 260. For judging when it is done, see TECHNIQUE NOTES, page 248.

Serves 2–3 as a main dish, 4–6 as part of a multicourse meal.

INGREDIENTS:

> *1 whole, very fresh flounder, 1½ pounds before gutting—thoroughly scaled and gutted, head and tail left on*

To garnish the fish:
> 1 medium whole scallion, cut into shreds about 2 inches long and ⅛ inch
> wide

or

scallion chrysanthemums (page 563)

To season the fish:
> 1 tablespoon thin (regular) soy sauce
> 1 tablespoon Chinese rice wine or quality, dry sherry
> 1 tablespoon Chinese or Japanese sesame oil
> coarse kosher salt, depending on saltiness of ham
> ⅛–¼ teaspoon freshly ground white pepper, to taste
> 2 tablespoons coarsely minced Smithfield or Westphalian ham
> 2 tablespoons coarsely minced fat from ham
> ½ tablespoon fine julienne threads of fresh ginger, cut 1½ inches long and as
> thin as possible
> 1 large whole scallion, cut into 2-inch lengths

Preparing the fish for steaming:
Clean the fish meticulously, as directed on page 231. Rinse with cold water, inside and out, then pat dry.

Score the fish on both sides at 1-inch intervals from collar to tail, as directed on page 260. Cut to within ¼ inch of the bone for a good penetration of seasonings and steam. If you need to work in advance, the scored fish may be refrigerated for several hours before steaming, sealed airtight.

Refrigerating the garnishes:
Put the shredded scallion or scallion flowers in a water-flecked plastic bag. Seal the bag so as to trap a lot of air inside, then shake to mist the scallion with the water. Refrigerate 15 minutes or longer to curl the scallions.

Steaming the fish:
(For details on steaming and how to improvise a steamer, see page 60.)

Combine the soy, wine, and sesame oil, stirring to blend. If the ham is not particularly salty or you are using bacon, sprinkle the fish inside and out with about 1½ teaspoons coarse kosher salt. If the ham is highly seasoned, you will need little or no salt, depending on your taste. (With Smithfield, I use none.) Grind fresh pepper over the fish to taste, then rub the salt and pepper into the score marks with your fingers. Lay the fish white side up in a deep serving plate or Pyrex pie plate at least 1 inch smaller in diameter than your steamer. Pour the liquid seasonings evenly on top, scatter the minced ham and fat over the fish, then sprinkle with the ginger threads. Press the scallion lengths under the side of a cleaver or broad knife to release their juices, then array evenly over the fish.

Bring the steaming water to a full, gushing boil over high heat. Add the plate to the steamer, cover tightly, then steam over medium-high heat 12–15 minutes, until the flesh nearest the bone in the midsection of the fish is firm and white. Do not lift the lid to check the fish until it is almost done, lest you dissipate the steam.

Remove the plate from the steamer, or serve the fish directly in the steamer basket, if you have one made attractively of bamboo. If you need to transfer the fish, do so carefully, sliding it onto a heated platter with the aid of a broad spatula, then rimming it with the sauce. Discard the steamed scallion, then decorate the plate with several scallion flowers or a sprinkling of the curly scallion threads. Serve immediately, while hot and steaming.

Leftovers are excellent cold. Bone the fish, cover it with the sauce, then seal airtight and refrigerate. The juices will gel in a pleasantly peppery aspic, and the flesh will turn smooth and slippery once chilled.

MENU SUGGESTIONS:
The fish may be paired with *Everyday Chinese Rice* (page 400) for a simple menu, or *Shrimp, Leek, and Pine Nut Fried Rice* (page 408) for a more elegant one. *Spinach with Glass Noodles* (page 308), *Chinese Cabbage Hearts with Glass Noodles* (page 311), or *Red Bell Pepper with Garlic and Coriander* (page 314) would be good vegetables to accompany the fish. Other menu possibilities are *Velvet Corn Soup* (page 460) and *Mendocino Lemon Tart* (page 513). To accompany the flounder, choose a light red wine or a big white wine.

Spicy Steamed Salmon with Young Ginger

子薑蒸鮭魚

When I moved to San Francisco, two things caught my eye immediately in the local markets. One was giant fresh salmon, shiny silver on the outside and blazing ruby-red within, like no fish I had ever seen. The other was what in Chinese is called "tender" or "young" ginger, an antler-like root that looks much like the familiar, dark-skinned ginger, but is sheathed in a thin, blonde-gold skin from which sprout beautifully pale pink and green shoots. I quickly took to pairing them in a simple, Hunan-style dish, and a prettier, more delicious steamed fish can hardly be had. ◆ If fresh salmon is not available, substitute any very fresh, firm, white-meat fish with a clean-tasting neutral character. In place of the young ginger, you may use the widely available, thick-skinned fresh ginger. Cut it literally into threads to mitigate its sharpness, and sprinkle it sparingly over the fish. For the ham, choose a strong-cured Smithfield or Westphalian ham, with a flavorful fat to add richness to the fish. ◆ This is an elegant dish. It takes only minutes to prepare and should be the centerpiece of a meal.

TECHNIQUE NOTES:
Boning salmon steaks is easy, given the "bone plan" and the right tool. The "free" bones, which can be removed easily, radiate in a V-shaped wedge from the central bone. Run your finger toward the central bone to find them. Once found, push down on the flesh with two fingers, so the bone pops up in between. Yank it free with a tweezer or a small needle-nose pliers. Your fingers prevent the flesh from tearing, so the bone pulls cleanly away. Do not remove the central bone, any of the bones attached to it, or the skin. These are easily removed after steaming, and will meanwhile hold the fish in shape and help to keep it moist.

Serves 2 as a main dish, 4–5 as part of a multicourse meal.

INGREDIENTS:

>   1 pound fresh salmon steaks, cut ¾ inch thick (substitute any fresh, firm, "neutral"-tasting fish)
>   ⅛–¼ teaspoon Chinese or Japanese sesame oil

For seasoning the fish:

   2 teaspoons salted Chinese black beans (not the variety seasoned with five-
      spice powder; page 561)
   1 tablespoon Chinese rice wine or quality, dry sherry
   1 teaspoon Chinese or Japanese sesame oil
   1 tablespoon minced Smithfield or Westphalian ham (page 549)
   1½ teaspoons minced fat from ham
   2–3 teaspoons finely minced fresh garlic
   ⅛ teaspoon dried red chili flakes
   about ½ tablespoon fine julienne threads of fresh "young" ginger, cut 1½
      inches long and as thin as possible
   1 hefty whole scallion, cut into 2½-inch lengths

Readying the fish:

Scrutinize the fish carefully, and remove any scales or blood. Dislodge any blood left clinging to the backbone with the tine of a fork. Do not wash the fish steaks; dab off any impurities with a damp, lint-free cloth or a wet hand.

Remove the "free" bones as described above in TECHNIQUE NOTES. Leave the backbone, attached bones, and skin in place. If you need to work in advance, you may refrigerate the boned fish for several hours, sealed airtight in plastic.

Steaming the salmon:

(For details on steaming and how to improvise a steamer, see page 60.)

Chop the black beans coarsely. Do not wash them. The salt will contribute to seasoning the fish. Combine the beans, wine, and 1 teaspoon sesame oil, stirring to blend. Let the mixture stand 5–10 minutes to exchange flavors.

Choose a heatproof plate or a Pyrex pie plate at least 1 inch smaller in diameter than your steamer. Oil the bottom lightly with ⅛–¼ teaspoon sesame oil, then put the fish steaks next to one another on the plate, arranged top to bottom for a pretty fit. Sprinkle the ham, fat, garlic, and red pepper flakes over the fish, then pour the black bean mixture evenly on top. Scatter on the ginger threads. Use only a bare sprinkling if the ginger is the stronger, thick-skinned variety. You can be more liberal with the subtle, young type. Lightly press the scallion with the broad side of a knife to release its juices, then distribute evenly over the fish.

Bring the water in the steamer to a full, gushing boil. Put the plate in the steamer, cover tightly, then steam over medium-high heat for 8–11 minutes. Steaks cut ½ inch thick will take 8–10 minutes. Steaks cut ¾ inch thick will take 9–11 minutes. While steaming, do not lift the lid to peer at the fish, lest you dissipate the heat. Check it when the time is nearly up. When properly steamed (to my taste), the fish will still look moist and red, but be neither fleshy nor raw.

Serve the fish promptly if you wish to eat it hot. If you wish to serve it tepid or at room temperature, remove it from the steamer when it is about 1 minute underdone, then let it cook to completion from its own heat.

Just before serving, remove the bones, then pull off the skin in a neat ribbon with the aid of a small knife. Discard most of the scallion, leaving a few nuggets on top for color, or arraying one of the prettier branch-like segments alongside. Serve the fish directly in the steamer basket, or transfer it carefully to heated serving plates with a spatula.

Leftovers keep 1–2 days and are very good cold. The salmon juices gel in a delicious aspic.

MENU SUGGESTIONS:
For a simple menu serve the salmon with either *Everyday Chinese Rice* (page 400) or *Shrimp, Leek, and Pine Nut Fried Rice* (page 408), and *Spinach with Glass Noodles* (page 308), or *Red Bell Pepper with Garlic and Coriander* (page 314). If a fuller menu is desired, begin with *Shao-Mai Dumplings* (page 375), follow the fish with *Chinese Meatball Soup*, (page 448) and end on a refreshing note with *Mandarin Orange Ice Cream* (page 498) or *Glacéed Orange Slices* (page 487), and *Orange-Almond Coins* (page 495). To accompany the salmon, choose a mature red Bordeaux, a soft Burgundy from Côte de Beaune, or a light Pinot Noir.

Mountain Stew

沙鍋魚

I went to Taiwan a great mountain-climbing enthusiast and spent much of my first winter there hauling myself over rain-forest-covered terrain, communing with the spirit of one of my favorite Tang poets, a Buddhist monk named Cold Mountain. Aboriginal villages with tattoo-faced old women dotted the areas where I climbed, and there was always some friendly kitchen—usually that of the village head-man—open to me and my companions. It was on one such trip that I encountered this simple stew of fish and tofu cooked in a Chinese sand pot and was captivated by its straightforward goodness and wonderful mixture of textures. It is a classic dish across China, from Shantung in the northeast to Yunnan in the southwest. ◆ A sand pot is a partially glazed earthenware casserole with a sandy exterior (page 98). It is both cheap and handsome, excellent as a stewing vessel and charming as a serving dish. To substitute, use a deep, heavy skillet or a heavy ironware casserole. ◆ This dish is especially savory when reheated. Like all stews, it is practical to make it a day in advance, or to plan to serve it on two consecutive nights. ◆ The recipe calls for inch-thick fish steaks, cross-sections of fish with the backbone in the middle. You may, of course, cut them yourself from the whole fish.

TECHNIQUE NOTES:
This dish is a classic Chinese study in the transformation of textures. Soaking or briefly simmering cubed tofu in boiling water firms it to a smooth, resilient finish. (It also removes some of the starch that can cloud a broth.) Pan-frying the fish gives body and character to the outside, to contrast with the inside, which grows satiny when stewed. Pairing fish and tofu is by itself an edible pun. The fish loses its fishiness and becomes soft, while the tofu becomes firm and tastes like fish.

For pepper in Chinese dishes, see TECHNIQUE NOTES, page 341.

Serves 3–4 as a main dish, 5–8 as part of a multicourse meal.

INGREDIENTS:

> *4 large or 6–8 medium Chinese dried black mushrooms*
> *3 squares (¾ pound) fresh white tofu, firm variety best (page 323)*
> *1 large carrot, trimmed and peeled (to yield 1 cup carrot coins)*
> *2 pounds fresh fish steaks, cut 1 inch thick from a firm, non-oily, white-meat fish, such as sea bass, ling cod, or walleye pike*
> *3 tablespoons corn or peanut oil*
> *4 medium whole scallions, cut into 2-inch lengths*
> *5 quarter-size slices fresh ginger*
> *3 large cloves garlic, stem end removed, lightly smashed and peeled*

Liquid seasonings:
   1 tablespoon packed light brown sugar
   3 tablespoons black soy sauce
   1 tablespoon Chinese rice wine or quality, dry sherry
   1¾ cups rich, unsalted chicken stock
   1½–2 tablespoons quality Chinese black vinegar, or balsamic vinegar (page
      577)

salt and freshly ground white and black pepper to taste

Preparations:
Soak the mushrooms in cold or hot water until soft and spongy, 20 minutes to an hour. Snip off the stems with scissors, rinse the caps to dislodge any sand trapped in the gills, and put aside.

Cut each square of tofu in half lengthwise, then crosswise into thirds, to yield 6 rectangles per square, or 18 rectangles in all. Cover with a generous amount of boiling water, cover, and soak until it is ready to be added to the casserole.

Cut the carrot on the diagonal into thin oblong coins, 1½ inches long and ⅛ inch thick.

Chop the fish steaks neatly into halves or fourths, to obtain rectangular pieces about 2 inches long and 1½ inches wide. For a clean cut use a cleaver or heavy knife and whack with authority. Remove all scales and traces of blood. Be fastidious; these can ruin the stew. Do not bother to remove the bone at this time. It retains the shape of the fish while cooking and may be easily removed later on.

Pan-frying the fish and the aromatics:
Heat a large, heavy skillet over high heat until hot enough to evaporate a bead of water on contact. Add the oil, swirl to glaze the pan, then wait until the oil is hot enough to gently sizzle a particle of fish. Quickly arrange the pieces of fish side by side in the skillet, then fry for about 4 minutes, or until the bottom is firm. Adjust the heat to maintain a steady sizzle without scorching the fish. If it is sticking, dribble in an additional tablespoon of oil from the side of the pan. When the bottom is firm, turn the fish over carefully with a small spatula, then fry the second side. Expect it to firm more quickly, within 1½–2 minutes. Leaving the oil in the pan, gently remove the fish to the bottom of a sand pot or heavy casserole, arranging the pieces side by side in a single layer.

Lightly smash the scallion and ginger with the broad side or blunt handle of a cleaver or heavy knife to release their juices. Combine the scallion, ginger, mushrooms, carrots, and garlic.

Return the skillet to high heat. When the oil is hot enough to sizzle a piece of scallion, add the combined ingredients. Stir-fry briskly for 2–3 minutes, until the mixture is evenly glossed and the fragrance is pronounced. Scatter the mixture evenly over the fish.

Cooking the casserole:
Combine the liquid seasonings, stirring to dissolve the sugar. Pour evenly over the fish, then bring the liquids to a hearty simmer over moderate heat. If you are using a sand pot, start over low heat and increase to moderate once the liquids are steaming and the pot is warm. Reduce the heat to maintain a gentle simmer, cover the pot, and simmer 15 minutes.

At the end of 15 minutes, drain the tofu carefully. Gently scatter the pieces into the pot, poking them under the sauce and between the fish. Cover, simmer 15 minutes more, then turn off the heat.

Taste the sauce. Add salt and adjust the seasonings as required. The sauce should be an even balance of soy and sweet, laced with a heady aroma of vinegar. Remove the bones, arrange a few mushroom caps and carrot coins brightly on top, then sprinkle with a healthy grind of fresh pepper. Baste briefly to mix the pepper into the sauce and glaze the mushrooms.

Serve the casserole immediately, or—for fuller flavor—let it stand several hours at room temperature or overnight in the refrigerator, then reheat over low heat until gently simmering. If you refrigerate the stew in a sand pot, be sure to bring it to room temperature before reheating, to avoid cracking the pot.

Serve the stew directly in the casserole. Or, transfer it carefully to a heated serving bowl and rush it to the table while the aroma is still pronounced.

MENU SUGGESTIONS:
I like this dish best on its own as a one-pot meal. If a green vegetable is needed, try *Spinach with Glass Noodles* (page 308) or *Dry-Fried Szechwan String Beans* (page 297). To partner the fish, try a robust white wine like an Italian dry Orvieto, or a non-fruity Chardonnay, or a good California white jug wine.

Tea and Spice Smoked Fish

燻魚

This is a very different smoked fish from the sort that we are used to eating in the West. The taste and aroma is very light and herby— with touches of cinnamon, orange or tangerine peel, and Szechwan peppercorns—and the smoking process is a matter of only minutes enacted on a stovetop. Unlike the lengthy smoking-preserving process that seasons whitefish and salmon and involves special woods, smokehouses, or ovens, this is a style of smoking that imparts flavor, color, and fragrance to an already-cooked fish. It is simple enough for a beginning cook and requires nothing more than a suitable "old" pot (page 90), a few sheets of tin foil, and a common collection of tea leaves and spices. ◆ What this dish *does* require is an extremely fresh fish, with a clean-tasting, delicate flesh that is somewhat fatty as opposed to very lean, though you do not want a characteristically oily fish. I have had extraordinary results with Oregon black cod (worth a trip to Oregon or a call to a fish market like Newman's in Eugene that will fly you one), and very tasty results with sea bass. Salmon and pomfret (the latter being the common fish for smoking in Taiwan) are also delicious done this way. Be experimental and, when a whole fish of a suitable size and character is not available, use a cross-section of a larger fish that meets the standards for freshness and flavor. Leave the skins and bones intact but if the cross-section is more than 2 inches thick, cut it in half lengthwise through the backbone, score only the skin side, and steam and smoke it skin side up. ◆ You may begin preparations 3 hours or 3 days in advance of serving, and serve the fish hot, tepid, or at room temperature.

TECHNIQUE NOTES:
Read carefully the section on smoking beginning on page 90, for all the details you will need regarding techniques and tools.

When steaming the fish, be careful not to overcook it and err on the underdone side if at all. The fish will continue to cook from its own heat after it leaves the steamer and will cook a further degree or two from the heat generated in the smoker, so to over-cook it in the beginning will make it dry in the end.

The soy sauce in the marinade functions not only to flavor the fish but to pre-serve its freshness. Left in the marinade for 2 days, it will taste as fresh as when you began. You might remember this if you have a whole fish that you must wait a day or two to cook; lacquer the skin with several layers of soy sauce, covering every part of the fish including the cleaned cavity, then let the soy sauce dry, seal the fish airtight, and refrigerate it.

For scoring a fish Chinese-style, see TECHNIQUE NOTES, page 260.

Serves 3–4 as a main course, 5–8 as part of a multicourse meal.

INGREDIENTS:

1 *extremely fresh, bright-eyed fish, with a firm, delicate-tasting flesh that is not overly lean, 1½–2 pounds before gutting, thoroughly scaled and gutted, head and tail left on*

To marinate the fish:
1½ *tablespoons Chinese rice wine or quality, dry sherry*
4 *tablespoons thin (regular) soy sauce (read the cautionary note regarding brands on page 568)*
1 *tablespoon sugar*
1 *tablespoon coarse kosher salt*
2 *medium whole scallions, cut into 2-inch lengths*
4 *quarter-size slices fresh ginger*

To smoke the fish:
⅓ *cup dry black tea leaves*
⅓ *cup raw rice*
⅓ *cup packed brown sugar, light or dark*
1 *teaspoon Szechwan peppercorns, crushed*
3 *quarter-size pieces Chinese cassia bark, broken into small bits, or a 2-inch long cinnamon stick, broken into small bits*
2 *finger lengths home-dried orange or tangerine peel (page 557), torn into small pieces*

1–1½ *teaspoons Chinese or Japanese sesame oil*

Preparations:
If you are beginning with a whole fish, snip off all the fins but the tail fin with sturdy scissors, then clean the fish meticulously inside and out as directed on page 231. Be sure that you remove all the lingering scales and clean the cavity clear down to the backbone. Flush with cold water, pat dry inside and out, then score the fish from collar to tail on both sides, as directed on page 260.

If you are using the cross-section of a larger fish, remove any scales left on it with a fish scaler or by running your fingers against the grain of the scales and pulling them loose. Clean the backbone and the cavity of any bloody bits or pieces of clinging membrane. Rinse with cold water and pat dry, inside and out. With a sharp cleaver or chef's knife, divide the cross-section lengthwise into 2 pieces along the backbone, then score each skin side at 1-inch intervals along the length of each piece, cutting ¾ of the way to the bone.

Put the whole fish in a Pyrex pie plate or shallow bowl that will hold it snugly and allow it to lie flat. Put the two cross-section pieces of fish in the same type of vessel, each with the skin side facing up.

Marinating the fish:

Combine the wine, soy, sugar, and salt, stirring to blend the sugar. Hit the scallion and ginger with the blunt handle end or broad side of a cleaver or heavy knife to spread the fibers and bring the juices to the surface, then mix them with the liquids. Pour the marinade evenly over the fish, arraying half of the scallion and ginger on top.

Spoon the liquids evenly over the top of the fish and into the score marks, using your fingers to spread the score marks to allow the seasonings to penetrate. If you are using a whole fish, spoon the marinade into the belly cavity as well. Repeat at 15-minute intervals for 1–2 hours, while the fish sits uncovered and at room temperature. If you are using a whole fish, turn it over midway through marinating. (Also, if you are working with a whole fish, do not be surprised if the marinade turns the eyes a striking yellow-green.)

If it is not convenient to proceed to steam the fish directly, you may refrigerate it overnight in the marinade, sealed airtight. Bring to room temperature before steaming.

Steaming the fish:

(For details on steaming and how to improvise a steamer, see page 60.)

Drain the fish and discard the liquids and the ginger and scallion. Oil a rack (preferably one on which you can also smoke the fish to avoid having to transfer it) which will support the fish and fit in your steamer. Set the fish on the oiled rack, then prop the rack on top of a smaller pie plate or shallow bowl, so the fish will drain and not steam in its own juices.

Bring the water in the steaming vessel to a gushing boil over high heat, center the bowl with the rack and the fish on top of it on the steaming tier, then cover the steamer. Steam the fish for about 6–8 minutes, depending on its thickness, until the base of the score mark in the thickest part of the fish is just white or still a very faint shade of pink. Remove the fish promptly from the steamer and transfer it on its rack to a baking sheet to cool, where it will continue to cook a bit from its own heat.

At this point, you may proceed to smoke the fish directly or, if it is more convenient, you may let it cool completely and then refrigerate it overnight, sealed airtight. Bring the refrigerated fish to room temperature before smoking.

Smoking the fish:

Line the pot and lid for smoking as described on page 95. If you are smoking the fish on a rack different from the one used for steaming, oil it liberally and place the fish on top.

Combine the smoking ingredients, then spread them evenly in the bottom of the pot. Put the rack with the fish on it into the pot about 1 inch above the smoking mixture, propping the rack above the smoking mixture if necessary with 2 empty tin cans. If the head or tail of the fish is touching the foil, then put a small piece of oiled parchment paper between them at the point where they touch so the fish will not adhere to the foil when smoked.

Set the uncovered pot over high heat until the sugar begins to bubble and send up thick plumes of smoke in several places, anywhere from 4–10 minutes depending on the vigor of the stove and the thickness of the pot. Only at that point, cover the pot securely and crimp the foil loosely shut. Smoke the fish for 10 minutes, turn off the heat, and let the fish rest in the covered pot on top of the burner for 5 minutes. During this "resting" time, the smoking will continue owing to the combustion of the smoking ingredients, the heat of the pot, and the residual heat of the burner.

At the end of the resting time, remove the pot from the burner (ideally, near an exhaust fan, an open window, or outside on the back porch). Uncrimp the foil, then slowly lift the lid from the pot angling it away from you. If the heat was properly intense, then the smoke will have turned the fish a deep golden brown. If the color seems light, then taste a bit of the fish. If the flavor is pale as well, then sprinkle an additional 3–4 tablespoons white or brown sugar around the edge of the burnt smoking ingredients, return the uncovered pot to high heat, and repeat the process for half of the original time, again waiting for the smoking to begin in earnest before covering the pot.

When the fish is as golden and smoky-tasting as you like, remove the rack from the smoker. Immediately seal the burnt smoking ingredients in the foil used to line the pot and the lid and dispose of them. Smooth your palms with the sesame oil, and gloss the fish evenly on both sides, sliding it carefully from the rack onto a serving platter of contrasting color (heated, if you are serving the fish immediately).

Smoked fish is excellent fresh from the smoker, tepid, or at room temperature. Garnish it prettily with sprigs of fresh coriander or clusters of marinated radish fans (page 114) before serving, and use the score marks to help you lift the fish from the bones. If you are serving a whole fish, do not forget to eat the fish cheeks that lie beneath the eyes; they are particularly sweet and meaty.

Leftovers keep nicely 3–4 days, sealed airtight and refrigerated. If you wish to reheat them, seal airtight in tin foil, then place in a preheated 450° oven for about 10 minutes until hot. The buildup of steam during reheating, if the foil package is sealed properly in a butcher's fold, will moisten the fish appealingly. Leftovers are also excellent at room temperature, especially on a piece of good bread spread with *Coriandered Mustard Sauce* (page 476).

MENU SUGGESTIONS:
I like this fish best served very simply, in the company of *Chinese Cabbage Hearts with Glass Noodles* (page 311). For a fuller menu, begin with an assortment of "Little Dishes"—*Soy-Dipped Red Radish Fans* (page 114), *Hot and Sour Chinese Cabbage Hearts* (page 112), and *Cold-Tossed Celery in Garlic Vinaigrette* (page 116)—and choose one of the rice dishes to accompany the fish if you are eating it hot, or one of the cold noodle dishes if you are serving it at room temperature. *Pear and Jasmine Tea Sorbet* (page 500) is a good choice for dessert. To partner the smoked fish, try an Orvieto or a big-bodied, dry Italian white wine.

| Strange Flavor Fish 怪味魚 | In China, the presentation of a whole fish—either steamed as on pages 248 and 250 or deep-fried as here—traditionally concludes the meal on a bountiful note. "Here is fish" is the homonym for "here is abundance," so everyone leaves the table feeling full of fish and symbolic richness. It is much like ending a meal with a cornucopia of fruit, our own Western emblem of plenty. ◆ This is my favorite |

Chinese fish dish, bar none—a crisp whole fish topped by a vinegar-spiked sauce with bits of garlic, chili, ginger, and scallion. It was the creation of Po-fu's gutsy Shanghai-born wife, who would pitch the fish into the oil with the proficiency of an expert bowler. In her sauce there is no cornstarch to dull the flavors, which are boldly tart, tangy, sweet, and spicy all at the same time—"strange," meaning marvelous, and delicious. If you have never before fried a whole fish Chinese-style, this is an addictive place to begin. ◆ This is a very easy dish, involving more drama than work. Frying the fish takes 5–10 minutes and making the sauce takes an additional 1 or 2. You may pan-fry or deep-fry the fish, as you like. I prefer deep-frying for its speed and the convenience of not having to turn the fish, but you may opt for pan-frying if that seems more comfortable. ◆ The main requirement is a bright-eyed, red-gilled, thoroughly fresh fish with a firm, sweet flesh. I like porgy best. Sea bass, pompano, rock cod, fluke, and flounder also work well with the tangy sauce, though a whole flounder can be a bit cumbersome to fry if you are not equipped with a large wok. For a big crowd, fry two smaller fish rather than one giant one. This is far simpler and makes more sense, unless you have a 24-inch restaurant-size wok, a professional Chinese stove, and a good deal of gumption. ◆ Take the several minutes to chop the topping ingredients by hand. In this dish, the textures are as striking as the taste.

TECHNIQUE NOTES:
Scoring a fish—slicing through the flesh almost to the bone in a series of parallel or crisscross cuts—is a classic Chinese technique designed for fast cooking, good penetration of seasonings, and easy eating. To score a fish properly, use a very sharp large knife or cleaver with a thin blade and hold it at a 45° angle to the backbone, aiming the blade toward the head of the fish. With a single slice, cut from within ½ inch of the dorsal (top) side to within ½ inch of the ventral (bottom) side of the fish, slicing ¾ of the way to the bone. In this fashion make parallel score marks 1¼ inch apart down the entire length of the fish. Make the first cut 1 inch from the collar, and the last cut a full 2 inches above the base of the tail. Then turn the fish over and score the other side. Do not score too closely to the tail, or it will break off as you fry the fish or transfer it to a serving plate.

    Pan-frying or deep-frying a fish always raises the worry of its sticking to the pan, no matter what you coat it with and especially when you fry it, as here, "in the nude." Following these rules works beautifully for me: (1) make sure the pot is blazing hot before it is filled with oil. Several beads of water should evaporate instantly on contact; (2) be sure the oil is smoking hot before the fish is added. You should see a thick, shimmering haze just above the surface; (3) pat the fish thoroughly dry, inside and out, just before frying; and (4) if you are deep-frying the fish, keep it moving slightly while it fries, nudging it gently back and forth or spinning it slowly in a circle with the ladle. With these precautions, it should never stick to the pan.

    For further encouragement when it comes to "Deep-Frying a Whole Anything," see page 82.

Serves 2–3 as a main course, 4–6 as part of a Chinese meal.

INGREDIENTS:

      1 exceptionally fresh porgy, sea bass, pompano, rock cod, or other firm, sweet-
         fleshed white fish, 1½–2 pounds after gutting—thoroughly scaled and
         gutted, head and tail left on
      1 teaspoon coarse kosher salt

Aromatics:
  1 tablespoon finely chopped fresh ginger
  1 tablespoon finely chopped fresh garlic
  2 tablespoons chopped green and white scallion
  1 teaspoon dried red chili flakes

Liquid seasonings:
  2 tablespoons thin (regular) soy sauce
  1½ teaspoons well-aged Chinese black vinegar or balsamic vinegar (page 577)
  2 tablespoons sugar
  ½ cup hot water

  6 cups corn or peanut oil, for deep-frying
  or
  about 1½ cups corn or peanut oil, for pan-frying

Preparations:
Clean the fish meticulously as directed on page 231. Flush the cavity and the outside of the fish clean with cold water, then pat it dry inside and out.

Once cleaned and dried, the fish may be bagged airtight in plastic and stored for up to 24 hours in the coldest part of your refrigerator (*not* the freezer). If your refrigerator is not very cold, put the wrapped fish on a rack directly above a pan of ice. Bring to room temperature before frying.

As much as 1 hour in advance of frying, score the fish from collar to tail on both sides, as described above in TECHNIQUE NOTES. Sprinkle the fish evenly inside and out with the salt, then rub the salt into the cavity and down into the score marks with your fingers.

Put the minced aromatics on a small plate, with the chili flakes off to one side. Combine the liquid seasonings, stirring to dissolve the sugar.

Put a deep serving platter in a low oven to warm. Line a heatproof plate or baking pan with a triple thickness of paper towels. Have the towel-lined tray, the combined seasonings, and a large wok or pot lid alongside your stovetop. For deep-frying, you will need a large ladle and a large Chinese mesh spoon. For pan-frying, you will need a large heatproof spoon or shallow ladle and a broad flexible spatula.

Option 1: Deep-frying the fish:
Choose a large wok or a deep, heavy skillet large enough to hold the fish comfortably with inches to spare. If you are using a wok, make sure it is balanced securely on the stove with a wok ring or overturned burner grid (page 48). Heat the pot over high heat until it is hot enough to evaporate a bead of water on contact. Add the oil, leaving at least 1½ inches free at the top of the pot to accommodate bubbling. Heat the oil to the dense-haze stage, 400° on a deep-fry thermometer. While the oil is heating, pat the fish thoroughly dry, inside and out.

Grasp the fish securely by its tail. Holding the lid in your other hand, carefully lower the fish at arm's length into the oil, gently letting go of the tail once a third of the fish is submerged. If the oil is sufficiently hot, the fish will erupt into bubbles on contact. Use the lid to shield yourself from spatters, holding it just above the pot and slanting it sharply away from you so the steam can escape. As the fish fries, spin it slowly in the oil to prevent it from sticking, and ladle the hot oil steadily and evenly over the top.

Once the bubbling has died down and you can put the lid aside, watch carefully to gauge the moment the fish is done. When properly fried, the score marks will be golden at the top and bright white at the base, in about 3–5 minutes. As soon as you think it is done, lift the fish from the oil on the mesh spoon. Do not overcook the fish or it will be dry. If you pull it out too soon and the inside is still pink, just lower it back into the oil on the spoon.

Hold the fish briefly above the oil to drain, then transfer it to the towel-lined tray and put the tray in the oven while you make the sauce.

If frying a second fish, raise the oven temperature to 225° and wait however long it takes—anywhere from 3–10 minutes—for the oil temperature to regain 400°. It must be smoking hot, or the fish will not be crisp. Dry, fry, and drain the second fish in the same manner. It will take a bit longer to fry.

If possible after frying, do not move the oil and use a heavy skillet and another burner to make the sauce. Pause a minute to wipe the stovetop clean with a damp cloth. It takes only seconds now and becomes a chore later on.

Once the oil cools, strain and bottle it for future frying. Traditionally, oil used for frying whole fish is only reused for fish, but use your nose to judge its fishiness and decide its fate. Oil used for frying a single fish is often perfectly suitable for general frying.

Option 2: Pan-frying the fish:
Choose a large, heavy skillet at least 2–3 inches bigger than the fish, to allow you to turn it with ease. Heat over high heat until hot enough to evaporate a bead of water on contact. Add oil to a depth of ½ inch, then heat until the surface is covered by a dense, shimmering haze and the oil is nearly smoking. While the oil is heating, pat the fish thoroughly dry, inside and out.

Hold the fish securely by its tail. With the lid held in the other hand to shield you from spatters, place the fish in the pan at arm's length. If the oil is sufficiently hot, it will erupt in loud bubbling on contact. Use the lid to contain the spattering, slanting it sharply away from you to allow the steam to escape.

Brown the fish on the first side over high heat for about 2 minutes, reduce the heat to medium-high, and continue to cook it for 3 minutes more. While the bottom is cooking, ladle the hot oil continuously and evenly over the top of the fish. Loosen the fish with the spatula, then carefully turn it over with the help of the spoon. Brown the second side over high heat for about 2 minutes, reduce the heat to medium-high, and cook the fish for 2–3 minutes more. The timing will differ depending upon the thickness of the fish and the heat of the stove, so use your eyes to judge. The fish is done when the outside is brown and crisp, and the flesh visible through the score marks is glossily white and firm. Do not overcook the fish. It should look moist when it leaves the pan.

Carefully lift the fish from the oil, supporting it from beneath with the spatula and spoon. Transfer to the towel-lined tray, then put the tray in the oven while you make the sauce.

If frying a second fish, raise the oven temperature to 225° and dredge the oil of any debris. Raise the heat under the skillet to high, add oil to restore the depth to ½ inch, then wait as long as required for the oil to reach the near-smoking point. Do not put the fish in prematurely, or it will not be crisp. Dry, fry, and drain the second fish in the same manner. Expect the second fish to take slightly longer to cook.

Put the fry skillet aside to cool, and proceed immediately to make the sauce.

Making the sauce:
As soon as the (last) fish is put in the oven, heat a small, heavy skillet over high heat until hot enough to evaporate a bead of water on contact. Add 2 tablespoons of the frying oil, swirl to glaze the bottom, then reduce the heat to medium. When the oil is hot enough to sizzle a bit of garlic, add the garlic, ginger, and scallion to the pan, nudging the chili flakes in last and adjusting the heat so they foam without scorching. Stir until fully fragrant, 20–30 seconds, then stir the liquids and scrape them into the pan. Stir gently, bring to a simmer, turn off the heat, and taste. The sauce should be boldly sweet and spicy, with a tangy edge of vinegar. Adjust, if required, with more sugar to bring out the spiciness.

Quickly slide the fish onto the heated platter. Pour the sauce evenly over the fish, scraping the minced bits on top, then serve immediately.

To eat the fish, use the score marks to help lift the flesh neatly from the bones. Eat all the special morsels—the sweet fish cheeks (which should go to the guest[s] of honor), the soft flesh near the tail, and the succulent bits which cling to the bones. When it is time to flip the fish over, it is traditional that two people do it together with their chopsticks, one turning the head while the other turns the tail.

Leftovers may be boned, covered with sauce, and refrigerated, sealed airtight. They are good chilled, when the juices gel in a spicy aspic and the flesh is slippery-smooth.

MENU SUGGESTIONS:
Silver and Gold Thread Rolls (page 419), *Everyday Chinese Bread* (page 410), or *Everyday Chinese Rice* (page 400) are the appropriate sopper-uppers for the excellent fish sauce and with this and a bottle of good wine I am perfectly content. For a fuller menu, you might add *Golden Egg Dumplings* (page 328), *Spinach with Glass Noodles* (page 308), or *Chinese Meatball Soup* (page 448). A non-fruity French white Chablis, a Meursault, or a French white Burgundy will all partner the fish nicely.

Stir-Fried Spicy Scallops with Orange Peel
陳皮鮮貝

This is a delicious dish, one that combines features from my two favorite Chinese cuisines—Hunan and Shanghai. The Hunan half of the dish is the stir-fry of plush scallops and crunchy water chestnuts, in a pungent sauce dotted with bits of orange or tangerine peel and chili. The Shanghai half is the border of deep-fried spinach threads. They have a wonderful, almost smoky taste, even better to my tongue than the fried seaweed which one finds often in Shanghai dishes and which inspired this spinach variation. ◆ For the dish to shine, the scallops and spinach must be very fresh. I also use fresh or home-dried orange or tangerine peel in preference to the sort sold in Chinese markets, finding it has a better, cleaner flavor. ◆ The scallops should be marinated at least a half day and ideally 1–1½ days to give them time to absorb the marinade. All the remaining preparation, including deep-frying the spinach, may be done a half hour or more in advance. The final stir-frying takes only minutes.

TECHNIQUE NOTES:
To deep-fry perfectly, the spinach must be dry and the oil must be very hot (400°). Fry just to the point when the bubbling around the spinach ceases. Under-fried, it will be apple-green in spots and soggy. Over-fried, it will be brown and burnt-tasting. Experiment with a few threads to know the difference.

Marinating and "velveting" the scallops as a preliminary to stir-frying is a tenderizing process also used for chicken, another fragile flesh. For details, see TECHNIQUE NOTES, page 137. For this dish, I like to velvet the scallops in water.

Note also that the velveted scallops are added to the pan *after* the sauce is simmering and are cooked only long enough to heat them through. This is the opposite of the usual Chinese pattern of stir-frying the primary ingredient with the aromatics and then adding the sauce. It insures that the scallops will not overcook.

Serves 2 as a main course, 4 as part of a multicourse meal.

INGREDIENTS:

> ½ *pound fresh scallops (for a note on "fresh" shrimp that also applies to scallops, see page 233)*

> *To marinate the scallops:*
> 1 *tablespoon egg white*
> 2 *teaspoons Chinese rice wine or quality, dry sherry*
> ½ *teaspoon coarse kosher salt*
> 1 *tablespoon cornstarch*

> 4 *large water chestnuts, fresh best*
> 2–3 *ounces impeccably fresh large or medium-size spinach leaves without stems*

> *Aromatics:*
> 2 *finger lengths home-dried orange or tangerine peel (page 557), or 2–3 thumb-size pieces fresh peel, scraped clean of all white pith (to yield ¾ teaspoon minced soft peel)*
> 2½ *tablespoons finely minced green and white scallion*
> 2 *teaspoons finely minced fresh garlic*
> 2 *teaspoons finely minced fresh ginger*
> ⅛–¼ *teaspoon dried red chili flakes*

> *Sauce ingredients:*
> 1 *tablespoon thin (regular) soy sauce*
> 1 *tablespoon Chinese rice wine or quality, dry sherry*
> 1 *tablespoon unseasoned Chinese or Japanese rice vinegar*
> 1 *tablespoon sugar*
> ¼ *cup rich, unsalted chicken stock*

> 1½ *teaspoons cornstarch dissolved in 1 tablespoon cold chicken stock*
> 3 *cups fresh corn or peanut oil, for deep-frying the spinach*
> 4–6 *cups water plus 1 tablespoon corn or peanut oil, for velveting the scallops*
> 2 *tablespoons corn or peanut oil, for stir-frying*

Marinating the scallops:
Rinse the scallops briefly with cool water, then pat dry. Leave tiny bay scallops whole. Cut large sea scallops in half through the middle to yield two thick coins, then cut each coin crosswise into fourths or sixths to yield chunky bits the size of a bay scallop.

Combine the egg white, wine, salt, and cornstarch, and stir briskly for about 2 minutes, until smooth. (Do not be tempted to use more egg white, or it will cling in skin-like bits to the scallops when fried.)

Put the scallops in a small bowl, scrape the marinade on top, then toss well to combine. There will be more marinade than scallops, but do not worry as the scallops will absorb it. Seal airtight, then refrigerate 8–36 hours. The longer the mixture sits, the plumper the scallops will be and the more marinade they will absorb.

Readying the other ingredients:

Peel fresh water chestnuts. Or, drain and blanch canned water chestnuts in plain boiling water for 15 seconds to remove the tinny taste. Drain immediately and flush with cold water until chilled. Cut the water chestnuts neatly into a tiny dice the size of a pepper-corn. Seal airtight and refrigerate until use, overnight if desired.

Clean the spinach leaves with cool water, then shake or spin dry. If you are working in advance, refrigerate the leaves covered with a damp cloth, overnight if desired.

If you are using home-dried orange or tangerine peel, cover with warm water until soft, about 10 minutes, then pat dry. Mince the softened home-dried peel or the scraped fresh peel finely, to yield ¾ teaspoon. Put the minced peel, scallion, garlic, ginger and red chili flakes side by side on a small saucer. Seal airtight and refrigerate until use, up to several hours.

Combine the sauce ingredients, stirring to dissolve the sugar. Combine the corn-starch mixture in a small bowl and leave the spoon in the bowl. This may be done hours ahead.

Cutting the spinach:

Be sure the spinach leaves are dry and blot up any tiny drops of moisture with a paper towel. Stack ¼ of the leaves shiny side down on your cutting surface, with the bigger leaves on the bottom. Roll up the leaves along the long side, like a carpet, rolling away from you. (The shiny side will be on the outside of the roll. This is to keep the leaves from breaking, by rolling them in the direction in which they naturally curve.) Then use a sharp, thin-bladed Chinese cleaver or knife to cut the roll crosswise into thin slices ⅛-inch thin. (This is called "silken threads" in Chinese, and *chiffonade* in French.) Fluff to separate the strands, put them aside on a plate, then repeat with the remaining leaves. If you are working in advance, you may refrigerate the cut spinach for an hour, sealed air-tight but loosely to prevent crushing.

Deep-frying the spinach and velveting the scallops:

About 30 minutes in advance of serving, arrange the ingredients, a large Chinese mesh spoon or heatproof strainer or skimmer, and a baking sheet lined with a triple thickness of paper towels all within easy reach of your stovetop. Put a serving platter of a color to contrast with the spinach and scallops in a low oven to warm. Stir the scallops to loosen the pieces.

Heat a wok or large, heavy skillet over high heat until hot. Add the frying oil to a depth of 1 inch, then heat until the oil is surmounted by a dense haze, 400° on a deep-fry thermometer. While the oil is heating, bring the water for velveting the scallops to a near-simmer in a large saucepan, stir in the tablespoon of oil, then adjust the heat so the water does not boil. Put a colander in the sink, ready to drain the scallops.

When the oil reaches the dense-haze stage, turn off the heat to prevent the temperature from climbing. Test the oil with a single thread of spinach. It should bubble boldly on contact. Add ⅓ of the spinach threads to the oil (they will disperse immediately as they hit the oil), then fry until the bubbles almost cease, about 5 seconds. Immediately scoop the fried spinach from the oil in one movement, hold it briefly above the oil to drain, then invert the spoon and the spinach with a gentle knock onto the paper towels. It will look hopeless when you scoop it from the oil, but will be gleaming and crisp within seconds after it is turned out onto the tray. Do not blot or handle the spinach once fried, as it is very brittle. Fry the remaining spinach threads in two batches, one after the other so that the oil temperature does not fall.

As soon as the spinach is fried, put the tray aside. If you need to free the frying pot for stir-frying, carefully decant the hot oil into a heatproof bowl or pot, then wipe out the extra oil with a paper towel. Otherwise, let the oil sit until cool, then strain and bottle it for future frying.

Check to see that the water for velveting the scallops is at a superficial simmer, then slide the scallops into the water. They will sink to the bottom. Stir gently with chopsticks or a wooden spoon for 15 seconds, then drain immediately in the waiting colander. The scallops should be only part-cooked when they leave the water. If you are in any doubt, drain them sooner rather than later.

Stir-frying the dish:

As soon as the scallops are drained into the colander, set a wok or large, heavy skillet over high heat until hot enough to evaporate a bead of water on contact. Add 2 tablespoons corn or peanut oil (you can use the frying oil), swirl to glaze the bottom, then reduce the heat to medium-high. When the oil is hot enough to sizzle a bit of scallion on contact, add the minced aromatics to the pan, nudging the chili flakes in last. Adjust the heat so they foam without browning, dribbling in a bit more oil from the side of the pan if the mixture is sticking. Stir gently until fully fragrant, 10–15 seconds, then give the sauce mixture a stir and add the sauce and the water chestnuts. Raise the heat to bring the liquid to a simmer, stirring, then add the scallops. Stir briefly to coat the scallops and heat them through, about 10 seconds, then give the cornstarch mixture a quick stir to recombine it and add it to the pan. Stir until the mixture turns glossy and slightly thick, about 10 seconds more, then scrape the mixture into the center of the heated platter. All of this should be done swiftly, so the scallops are just slightly undercooked when they leave the pan and will cook to perfect doneness from their own heat on the way to the table.

Gently slide or scatter the spinach threads around the border of the platter, then serve the dish at once.

This dish is only good when freshly made and newly served, so do not arrange to have leftovers!

MENU SUGGESTIONS:

For a simple dinner, serve the scallops with *Everyday Chinese Rice* (page 400). If a more elegant menu is desired, pair them with *Shrimp, Leek, and Pine Nut Fried Rice* (page 408), and follow with *Cassia Blossom Steamed Pears* (page 485). To accompany the scallops, choose the biggest Chardonnay you can find.

| **Sesame Scallop Balls** 芝蔴鮮貝球 | Fresh scallops with their plush texture and voluptuously sweet flavor are not common on Chinese tables. Typically, scallops are dried to preserve and intensify their taste, then used as a flavoring, much in the same way as dried shrimp. I, however, cannot resist them fresh, and am often inventing Chinese-spirited dishes to show them off. ◆ This is a quintessential marriage of yin-yang textures—a velvety ball of fresh scallop purée encased in a crispy coating of golden |

sesame seeds. It is done in minutes in the food processor and has an elegance to match its ease. Accompanied by a tart and sweet dipping sauce to offset the richness of the scallops, the dish will make an excellent hors d'oeuvre or an unusual fish course. ◆ I prefer large sea scallops for this recipe. They should smell sweet when you buy them, and look moist and pearly white, with perhaps a faint blush of pink. ◆ This is an excellent dish for entertaining. All the preparations may be done in advance, and the last-minute frying is a very clean and simple business.

TECHNIQUE NOTES:
The eighteenth-century Chinese poet-gourmet, Yuan Mei, wrote in his *Cookery Book* of two kinds of cooking heat: "military fire" for fast frying and "literary" or "cultured fire" for slower cooking. The refined scallop (and shrimp also, in some cases) needs to be deep fried over slow, "cultured" fire in relatively warm oil. High "martial" heat will toughen and ruin the delicate flesh. It is one of the few cases in Chinese cooking where food to be deep fried is allowed to remain *under* the oil for more than several seconds after it enters the pot.

For the technique of double deep-frying, see TECHNIQUE NOTES, page 242.

Chilling the scallops and egg white prior to processing results in a thicker, richer purée. The principle is the same as in making a milk shake.

Yields 16 rich scallop balls, enough to serve 4–6 as part of a multicourse meal, 6–8 as an hors d'oeuvre.

INGREDIENTS:

> *For the purée:*
> ½ *pound chilled fresh scallops (for a note on "fresh" shrimp that also applies to scallops, see page 233)*
> 1½ *teaspoons finely minced fresh ginger*
> 1 *teaspoon Chinese rice wine or quality, dry sherry*
> ¾ *teaspoon coarse kosher salt*
> *several grinds freshly ground white pepper*
> 2 *teaspoons cornstarch*
> 1 *large egg white, chilled*
>
> ¾ *cup untoasted white sesame seeds*
> 6 *cups corn or peanut oil, for deep-frying*
> *Sweet and Sour Dipping Sauce (page 478)*

Making the purée:
Rinse the scallops briefly with cool water. Drain and pat dry.

Add the scallops and ginger to the work bowl of a food processor fitted with the steel knife and process until coarsely minced. Add the wine, salt, pepper, cornstarch, and egg white, then process until completely smooth, scraping down as needed. (Do not heap the cornstarch or pepper on the white top of the blade, lest it cling there and not incorporate.) Scrape the purée into a small bowl.

The scallop mixture may be refrigerated up to 12 hours before shaping the balls. Press a piece of plastic film directly on top of the purée to make an airtight seal.

Shaping the balls:
Spread the sesame seeds on a large plate. Line a baking sheet with a sheet of wax paper. Put 2 tablespoons corn or peanut oil in a small dish. Line up the seeds, tray, oil, purée, and a tablespoon on your work surface.

Coat your palms and the spoon with a bit of oil so the purée does not stick. Scoop up a slightly rounded tablespoon of the scallop mixture with the spoon, then shape it softly into a walnut-size ball between your palms, smoothing the surface with your fingers. Roll it gently in the seeds to coat it on all sides, then shape it again softly in your hands. Put it aside on the waxed paper, then continue to make balls until the purée has been used up, oiling hands and spoon as required. When you are finished, there should be about 16 balls.

The scallop balls may be refrigerated for several hours, wrapped airtight in plastic. Bring to room temperature before frying, still sealed airtight. If exposed to air, the balls will have a somewhat tough crust once fried.

Heating the sauce and frying the scallop balls:
Make the sauce and cover the pot to keep it warm. If you like, this may be done before you shape the balls.

About 20 minutes before serving, put a serving platter and a small sauce bowl of contrasting color in a low oven to warm. Line a baking tray with a double thickness of paper towel. Have the tray, several additional sheets of paper towel, a large Chinese mesh spoon, and the scallop balls all within reach of your stovetop.

Heat a wok or deep, heavy skillet over high heat until hot. Add the oil, then heat to the light-haze stage, 350° on a deep-fry thermometer, when a single sesame seed bobs to the surface within 3 seconds and spins with a trail of tiny bubbles. Adjust the heat so the temperature does not rise.

Add 5 scallop balls to the oil, one by one. They will take about 45 seconds to rise to the surface. After about 15 seconds, nudge them gently with the spoon, so they do not sit too directly on the hot bottom of the pan, then turn them once or twice after they float to the surface. Fry until *pale* gold, about 3–4 minutes, then remove to the paper-towel-lined tray. Do not let the scallop balls turn brown in the first frying. They will cook and color to doneness when fried a second time.

Check that the oil is at 350°, then fry and drain the next two batches. Do not worry if the balls collapse as they cool. They will swell again in the second frying.

Double deep-frying:
Raise the heat to 375°, then add the balls in one batch. Adjust the heat so the temperature does not rise. Fry for about 1 minute, turning the balls with the spoon, until they are swollen and golden brown. Do not let them get too dark or swell so that the coating cracks open. As soon as they are puffed, remove the balls in 2 or 3 quick motions to the fresh paper-towel drain, then shake the tray to blot up the excess oil. Serve at once.

To serve as an hors d'oeuvre, scrape the sauce into the warm bowl, put the bowl in the center of the platter, then cluster the scallop balls around it. Serve as finger food or with small forks, inviting your guests to dip the crispy balls into the sauce.

For table service, use the same presentation. Or, drizzle half the sauce over the scallop balls and serve the remainder in a bowl off to one side for those with a sweet tooth.

MENU SUGGESTIONS:

This is an excellent appetizer to serve with a rich Chardonnay. A dinner of refined dishes such as *Golden Egg Dumplings* (page 328) *and Steamed Winter Melon with Ham* (page 315) would follow beautifully. An appropriate dessert would be *Cassia Blossom Steamed Pears* (page 485).

Stir-Fried Spicy Clams in Black Bean Sauce

豆豉蛤蜊

I love very tiny, tender clams, and when I can get them I treat them (and me) to this simple stir-fry, and pile the meat-filled shells and the heady sauce on a bed of steamed noodles. It satisfies my north Chinese love for noodles and garlic, and my south Chinese appreciation of clams dressed richly in an unctuous black bean sauce. ◆ The accompaniments are all open to change—more or less garlic, more or less chili, depending on mood and menu, and rice, or better yet, a crusty loaf of hot garlic bread instead of the noodles. You may also use *Pot-Browned Noodles* (page 366) to bed the clams. In that case, cook the clams while the second side of the noodle pillow browns. ◆ The central issue here is clams. Buy the smallest ones available—1 inch is perfect, 1¼ inch second best—and be sure the shells are closed or will close upon touching, indicating the clam inside is alive and fresh. (A live clam will often "gasp" for air and open its shell slightly when it has been out of the water a while, but, if it "clams up" when the inner lip is touched with a pencil tip or finger, then you know it still is alive and good to eat.) Unless you are pulling the clams yourself from the water, they usually need no cleaning apart from a simple scrubbing. The ones you buy in markets are typically already cleaned. ◆ All the preparations may be done hours in advance. Steaming the noodles and cooking the clams takes about 15 minutes.

TECHNIQUE NOTES:

I usually do not rinse black beans and simply count their saltiness into the seasonings for a dish. However, I do rinse them when saucing clams. The clams are always sufficiently salty on their own when joined by the soy which colors the sauce.

Steaming noodles that have been part-boiled is something I find very convenient. It gives me a way to do in advance the work that requires attention, namely the parboiling, freeing me to accomplish other tasks once the noodles are in the steamer. It also finishes the noodles with a very appealing texture and a steaming hotness that seems to last longer in the bowl. Do not cook the noodles to perfect doneness in the water, as they will grow somewhat softer when steamed.

Serves 2 as a main dish, 3–5 as part of a multicourse meal.

INGREDIENTS:

⅓–½ pound long, ¹⁄₁₆-inch thin Chinese egg noodles, preferably fresh (for making your own, see page 354)

1–1½ teaspoons Chinese or Japanese sesame oil
½–¾ teaspoon coarse kosher salt
2 pounds tiny, fresh clams with tightly closed, unbroken shells
3–4 teaspoons salted Chinese black beans (not the variety seasoned with five-spice powder; page 561)
2 tablespoons Chinese rice wine or quality, dry sherry

Aromatics:
6–8 large cloves garlic, stem end removed, lightly smashed and peeled
1 walnut-size nugget fresh ginger
2 medium whole scallions, cut into 1-inch lengths
⅛–¼ teaspoon dried red chili flakes, or ½–¾ teaspoon Chinese chili sauce (page 537), or thin-cut rings of fresh yellow chili to taste

2 tablespoons corn or peanut oil

Liquid seasonings:
2–3 teaspoons thin (regular) soy sauce
½ teaspoon sugar
1 scant cup light, unsalted chicken stock

2 teaspoons cornstarch dissolved in 1 tablespoon cold chicken stock
½ teaspoon Chinese or Japanese sesame oil

To garnish:
1 tablespoon freshly chopped green scallion rings, or coarsely chopped fresh coriander leaves

Preparations:
Parboil the noodles in a generous amount of plain boiling water, but pull them from the stove while they are still slightly undercooked. Drain immediately, rush under cold water until chilled, then shake off excess water. Toss with 1–1½ teaspoons sesame oil and ½–¾ teaspoon coarse kosher salt, depending on the amount of noodles cooked, tossing with your fingers to coat and separate the strands. Once boiled, the noodles may be bagged airtight and refrigerated for up to 3 days. Bring to room temperature before steaming.

Scrub the clam shells under running water with a stiff brush. Discard any clams that do not shut quickly when rinsed or any with broken shells. Cover with a wet towel and refrigerate up to 12 hours, if not using immediately.

Rinse the black beans with cool water. Drain, chop coarsely, then combine with the wine. Put aside to plump the beans.

Mince the garlic and ginger in the work bowl of a food processor fitted with the steel knife, scraping down as necessary until fine. Add the scallions, then process until coarsely chopped. Scrape the mixture into a small dish alongside the chili flakes. Alternatively, mince the garlic and ginger until fine and chop the scallions coarsely by hand.

Combine the 2 teaspoons soy, sugar, and stock, stirring to mix. Combine the cornstarch mixture and the sesame oil in a small bowl and leave the spoon in the bowl.

Preparations may be done hours in advance. Refrigerate the aromatics, sealed airtight, and cover the wine mixture.

Steaming the noodles and stir-frying the clams:
(For details on steaming and how to improvise a steamer, see page 60.)

About 30 minutes before serving, spread the noodles in a shallow heatproof bowl. If they are not steaming in the serving bowl, put a serving dish in a low oven to warm.

Bring the water in the steaming vessel to a gushing boil over high heat. Reduce the heat to medium, to maintain a slow but steady steam. Add the bowl to the steaming rack, cover the steamer, and steam the noodles about 10 minutes while you stir-fry the clams.

Have all the ingredients within easy reach of your stovetop. If you are not serving the clams on top of the noodles, put a serving bowl in a low oven to warm.

Set a wok or large, heavy skillet over high heat until hot enough to evaporate a bead of water on contact. Add the oil, swirl to coat the pan, then reduce the heat to medium-high. When the oil is hot enough to sizzle one bit of garlic, add the combined aromatics to the pan, nudging the chili in last. Stir until fragrant, about 10–15 seconds, adjusting the heat so the mixture foams without browning. Add the clams, stir briefly to coat, then splash the wine and beans into the pan. When it "bursts" after 1 second in a fragrant hiss, add the liquid seasonings. Stir to mix, even the clams in the pan, then raise the heat to bring the liquids to a simmer.

Cover the pot and steam-cook the clams at a strong simmer 4–5 minutes, until most all the shells are open. Peek only after 3½–4 minutes, lest you dissipate the heat. (You might also shake the pan once or twice while the clams are cooking. This is supposed to speed the opening of the shells. I don't know if that is so, but it does give the cook something to do, and the sound of the clinking shells is very jolly and appetizing.)

When all or most all of the shells are open—a few usually stay defiantly shut—uncover the pot and reduce the heat to low. Stir and taste the sauce, then adjust with more soy sauce if required. Stir the cornstarch mixture to recombine, then add it to the pan. Stir until the sauce becomes glossy and slightly thick, about 15–20 seconds.

Remove the clams from the heat and pile them on the bed of steamed noodles, with the sauce poured on top, or heap them temptingly in a bowl to be eaten with rice or bread. Garnish with a sprinkling of scallion rings or fresh coriander leaves, then bring to the table along with plenty of napkins and a big, empty bowl for the shells.

As for leftovers, I am not a fan of leftover stir-fried clams and never arrange to have any.

MENU SUGGESTIONS:
It is heretical and unheard of in China, but here in America I know of no better accompaniment to this dish than a tossed salad of fresh greens dressed with a good vinegar and oil. For a more thoroughly Chinese menu, partner the clams with *Stir-Fried Spinach with Charred Garlic* (page 305), *Stir-Fried Spinach with Fermented Tofu* (page 306), or *Red Bell Pepper with Garlic and Coriander* (page 314). A good soup would be *Chinese Meatball Soup* (page 448). To serve with the clams, try the traditional French wine for shellfish, a Muscadet Sèvre-et-Maine.

Stir-Fried Dancing Crab

豆豉炒旁蟹

Any knowing Chinese will buy a crab only when it is alive, kicking, and "dancing." Boxes of the critters arrive twice daily in Chinatowns during crab season, thrashing, spitting bubbles, and clinging tightly to their neighbors' claws, so that when one picks up one's chosen beast (by the *tail* end, that is, farthest from the pincers) it often comes up monkey-style, with a string of hangers-on. ◆ A dead crab, one that is not moving, is a decidedly dull crab. The flesh oxidizes within minutes after death, even inside the shell. The only crab I will use is a live one that I do in myself, by dumping it into boiling water for a quick and speedy end. ◆ This dish is easy and fast to make and an absolute joy to eat, if you are the type who enjoys getting your fingers into the food. To quote Euell Gibbons writing in a similar context about a crab boil dinner, "avoid all attempts at toniness, for the dish is not compatible with swank." ◆ The seasonings for the crab may be readied in advance. Killing, cleaning, and stir-frying take a total of 10 minutes if you're a speedy cleaner.

TECHNIQUE NOTES:
Cleaning a crab is a quick but somewhat messy business, best done over the sink. Turn the just-killed crab belly side up, then tear off the "key" or "apron," which is recessed in the belly. In a female, it is shaped like a wide inverted V. In the male, it is a narrow inverted T. Then, firmly grasp the top shell at the rear end and lift it off, using a bit of oomph if needed. Save any roe and creamy tomalley in the top shell, but discard the soft stomach sac attached to the eyes. Scrub and save the top shell if you want to decorate the dish in the traditional manner.* Discard the sets of feathery gills or "devil's fingers" in the body of the crab, then rinse it of any sand or mud. Proceed immediately to cut and cook it.

Serves 2 as a main dish, 3–4 as art of a multicourse meal.

INGREDIENTS:

> 2 pounds large, emphatically alive crabs—Dungeness on the West Coast, blue crabs on the East

Aromatics:
> 1 tablespoon plus 1 teaspoon salted Chinese black beans (not the variety seasoned with five-spice powder; page 561)
> 2 tablespoons Chinese rice wine or quality, dry sherry
> 3–4 large cloves garlic, stem end removed, lightly smashed and peeled
> 1½ walnut-size nuggets fresh ginger, or 2½ walnut-size nuggets fresh "young" ginger (page 548)
> 2 medium whole scallions, cut into 1-inch lengths
> ⅛–¼ teaspoon dried red chili flakes (optional)

Liquid seasonings:
> ½–1 tablespoon thin (regular) soy sauce
> ¼ teaspoon sugar
> ¾ cup light, unsalted chicken stock

> 2 teaspoons cornstarch dissolved in 1 tablespoon cold chicken stock
> ¼ pound ground pork butt, or 2–3 tablespoons coarsely minced Smithfield ham, 2 parts ham lean plus 1 part ham fat (page 549)
> 3 tablespoons corn or peanut oil

To garnish:
> 1 teaspoon Chinese or Japanese sesame oil
> fresh coriander sprigs

---

*I always find the empty shell a big disappointment in a stir-fry, expecting in a childish way that it should somehow be filled with great lumps of crab. So I discard it.

Preparations:

Keep the crab alive and lively until you are ready to cook it, as described in TECHNIQUE NOTES, page 274.

Up to several hours in advance, coarsely chop the black beans. Do not rinse them. Combine with the wine, then set aside to plump.

Mince the garlic and ginger until fine in the work bowl of a food processor fitted with the steel knife or by hand. Mince the scallion more coarsely, either by adding it to the work bowl and processing with on-off turns once the garlic and ginger are fine-minced, or by hand. Seal airtight until use.

Combine the soy, sugar, and stock, using the lesser amount of soy if you are using the Smithfield ham.

Killing and cleaning the crab:

About 25–30 minutes in advance of serving, bring a large pot of unsalted water to a gushing boil over high heat. Holding the crab by its rear end, drop it into the water. As soon as the legs curl and it stops moving, in about 15 seconds, drain or retrieve the crab with a mesh spoon or tongs. Rinse briefly with a spray of cool water, then proceed immediately to clean it, as described above in TECHNIQUE NOTES.

Once clean, snap off the legs and claws. Crack them lightly with a mallet or the blunt handle end of a cleaver to allow the seasonings to penetrate. With a cleaver or heavy knife, chop the body into 2 or 4 pieces, depending upon the size of the crab. Once cut, proceed immediately to stir-fry it.

Stir-frying the crab:

Have all the ingredients within easy reach of your stovetop. Put a serving platter of con-trasting color in a low oven to warm.

Heat a wok or large, heavy skillet over high heat until hot enough to evaporate a bead of water on contact. Add the oil and swirl to glaze the pan. When the oil is hot enough to sizzle one bit of garlic, add the garlic, ginger, scallion, and optional chili flakes, adjusting the heat so they foam without browning. Stir until fragrant, about 15–20 seconds, then add the pork. Stir-fry briskly until the meat is 90 percent gray, tossing, chopping, and pressing to break it into tiny bits and adjusting the heat to maintain a lively sizzle. If you are using ham instead of pork, simply stir-fry to combine and render some of the fat, about 10 seconds.

Add the crab to the pan, stir 3 or 4 times to combine, then splash in the wine and beans. Stir several seconds to evaporate the alcohol, then add the liquid seasonings. Stir, even the contents of the pan, and raise the heat to bring the liquids to a boil. Cover the pan and steam-cook the crab vigorously for about 3 minutes, or until only ¼ of the liquid is left.

Reduce the heat to low, uncover, and stir. Taste the sauce and adjust with soy or a pinch of sugar if needed. Stir the cornstarch mixture to recombine, and add it to the pan. Stir about 15 seconds, until the sauce thickens slightly and becomes glossy. (By this point, there will be only a bit of liquid left and the cornstarch will serve to bind the meat and seasonings to the crab.) Add the sesame oil, toss to combine, then pile the contents onto the heated platter.

Arrange the mound to show a claw poking out here or there, then crown the dish with a top shell or two or a flourish of fresh coriander. Serve the crab immediately, ac-companied by plenty of napkins and a large empty bowl to hold the shells.

For the Chinese approach to crab-eating, pick up the chosen piece with chop-sticks, and a finger as well if needed for surety. Suck noisily and happily on the shell to savor and glean every bit of sauce, then pull the denuded shell apart with fingers, chopsticks, and teeth, and retrieve and enjoy every crabby bit.

Leftovers (unlikely) are a pale shadow of their original glory, but may be eaten cold.

MENU SUGGESTIONS:
This is a dish that goes well with *Ham and Egg Fried Rice* (page 405) or *Celery and Pork Thread Fried Rice* (page 406), and a simple, slightly sharp green such as *Stir-Fried Spinach with Fermented Tofu* (page 306), *Stir-Fried Spinach with Charred Garlic* (page 305), or *Dry-Fried Szechwan String Beans* (page 297). If soup was desired, *Velvet Corn Soup* (with ham) (page 460) would be my choice. To partner the crab, try a big-bodied white Chardonnay.

Clear-Steamed Crab with Ginger

清蒸旁蟹

According to the ancient Chinese scheme of things that assigns qualities of yin and yang to every member of the food world, crab is considered highly yin, that is, chill-inducing. At the crab-eating parties, which abound in classic Chinese novels (hardly anything in literary China happened in the absence of food), young ladies with colds are banned from the feasting, while old grannies don shawls as the crab is set before them. Ground thistle roots are recommended as the appropriate antidote for those who have downed their crab unthinkingly. It is considered, even today, a very serious business. ◆ To balance the dangers inherent in eating crab in the wrong season, emotional state, or physical condition, Chinese culinary custom has always paired it with very yang (heat-inducing) condiments—ginger, vinegar, and wine. Liken it, if you will, to our own traditional hot fudge sundae—an unconscious but beautiful example of American yin and yang. ◆ Here is the easiest, probably most ancient, and undoubtedly safest Chinese way to cook crab. When old Chinese friends come to visit in crab season (which happily, on the West Coast, often coincides with "young" ginger season), this is all we have—and along with a bottle of wine is all we need—for a simple and extraordinary meal. ◆ The crab must be fresh and kicking when you buy it for this dish, otherwise cook something else.

TECHNIQUE NOTES:
Crab can be kept alive in the refrigerator overnight, by packing it well in wet newspaper or under a mound of wet seaweed. Do not store crab in water. It weakens the flesh.

Serves 2 as a main dish, 3–4 as part of a multicourse meal.

INGREDIENTS:

> 2 pounds large, alive, and kicking crabs—Dungeness on the West Coast, blue crabs on the East

> For steaming:
> 2 teaspoons Chinese rice wine or quality, dry sherry
> 3 quarter-size slices fresh ginger or "young" ginger (page 548)

> Individual dipping sauce:
> ¼ teaspoon finely minced fresh ginger, or a cluster of fine julienne threads of "young" ginger, cut hair-thin

1 tablespoon well-aged Chinese black vinegar or balsamic vinegar (page 577)
1 tablespoon thin (regular) soy sauce
¼ teaspoon Chinese or Japanese sesame oil
a pinch finely chopped fresh coriander leaves (optional)

Preparations:
About 30 minutes before serving, kill, clean, chop, and crack the crab, as described on page 273. Scrub the top shell and reserve it as a cover for the crab during steaming.

Steaming the crab:
(For details on steaming and how to improvise a steamer, see page 60.)

Reserving the top shell, arrange the crab pieces in their original shape—with the legs fanned prettily around the body pieces—on a heatproof plate at least 1 inch smaller in diameter than your steamer. Sprinkle the wine evenly over the crab. Bruise the ginger with the blunt handle or side of a cleaver or heavy knife to release the juices, then array it over the body pieces. Replace the top shell, covering the body meat and the ginger.

Bring the water in the steaming vessel to a gushing boil over high heat, then add the plate to the steaming rack. Cover the steamer and steam the crab over high heat for 15 minutes.

While the crab is steaming, mix the dip in individual dishes. Set the table with the dip dishes, plenty of napkins, and a large empty bowl to hold the discarded shells.

Remove the crab promptly from the steamer. Use chopsticks to retrieve and discard the ginger coins, then replace the top shell. Garnish, if you wish, with sprigs of coriander, then serve the crab straightaway.

To eat crab well, one must do so with gusto, without self-consciousness, and in the pursuit of pure eating pleasure. Fingers, chopsticks, and teeth are all worthy tools in the quest. Proper table manners will only get in the way.

Once the meat is freed from the shell, dunk it in the dip and eat it. That is all there is to this simple dish.

Cold steamed crab is quite good, especially when tossed in a simple green salad and dressed with some of the leftover sauce.

MENU SUGGESTIONS:
In China, it is traditional to eat this dish with nothing more or less than good friends, good wine, and plenty of hot steamed towels. (In Maryland, beer and paper bibs take the place of wine and wet towels, but the spirit is the same.) If there is need to extend the meal beyond simple revel, begin with *Shao-Mai Dumplings* (page 375) and add *Velvet Corn Soup* (with ham) (page 460). Heated Chinese rice wine is excellent with the crab. Or, if you wish a Western wine, try a delicate Moselle or Rhine wine. (Do not choose a Spatlese or Auslese, which would be too sweet and intense for the crabs.)

Dry-Fried Lobster

乾燒龍蝦

Lobsters do not create any special stir in Chinese circles, compared with our love of them in the West. They are common only to a limited coastal region of China, and most shellfish-loving Chinese would far prefer a freshwater crab or shrimp to lobster. For the most part what we see in Chinese restaurants is either dreary or showy—a hacked lobster set awash in a turgid, eggy sauce, which one friend refers to as "low-tide sauce," or a whole steamed monster propped up as a banquet centerpiece with tiny lightbulbs set blinking in the eye sockets. ◆ This Chinese lobster recipe is a different species altogether. It is a zesty Eastern-style stir-fry of pungent aromatics and minced pork, with the lobster added last to steam-cook in the vapors of the vinegar-spiked sauce. The sauce mostly evaporates and clings to the lobster (hence the name of the dish), making this a perfect preparation for those who relish eating with their fingers. ◆ Most important to the success of the dish is the lobster itself. It must be vigorously alive when you buy it, arching its back, waving its claws, and ready to start a ruckus with its neighbors in the tank. A somnolent lobster means a starving lobster, one that has been lingering too long in the tank and is wasting away beneath the shell. ◆ The seasonings for the dish may be readied in advance. Killing, chopping, and cooking the lobster can be done in less time than it takes you to eat it.

TECHNIQUE NOTES:
To get the best taste from a lobster, equal to the price you pay for it, you must take it home alive and kill it yourself. Boil up an ample pot of unsalted water, thrust the lobster in head first, then pull it out as soon as it stops moving, in about a minute. It is simple business, the only way to guarantee that the lobster flesh will be vibrant and not mushy when you cook it.

For storing a live lobster at home prior to killing and cooking it, see TECHNIQUE NOTES, page 278.

Serves 2 as a main course in the company of fried rice, or plain rice and a vegetable, or 3–4 as part of a multicourse meal.

INGREDIENTS:

> *1 emphatically alive lobster, 2–2½ pounds*

> *Aromatics:*
> *5 tablespoons finely chopped green and white scallion*
> *2½ teaspoons finely minced fresh ginger*
> *3 teaspoons finely minced fresh garlic*

> *3 ounces ground pork butt*

> *Sauce ingredients:*
> *2–2½ tablespoons thin (regular) soy sauce*
> *3 tablespoons Chinese rice wine or quality, dry sherry*
> *1½ tablespoons well-aged Chinese black vinegar or balsamic vinegar*
> *1–1½ tablespoons sugar*
> *¼ cup light, unsalted chicken stock*

> *3 tablespoons corn or peanut oil*
> *1¼ teaspoons Chinese or Japanese sesame oil*
> *1 teaspoon well-aged Chinese black vinegar or balsamic vinegar*

Killing, cleaning, and chopping the lobster:
Kill the lobster as described above in TECHNIQUE NOTES. Retrieve it from the water as soon as it is still, within a minute.

Transfer the lobster to a cutting surface and break off the large claws and the little legs. Most Chinese cooks throw the little legs away, but I love to eat them like artichoke leaves, squeezing out the meat between my teeth, and so include them in the dish. With a sturdy cleaver or chef's knife, chop the big claws into four pieces: first chop just below the juncture of the two pincers, then chop about an inch farther down, and finally chop to separate the pincers. Whack heartily so the shell splits neatly, and have a towel on hand to mop up the water that will spill from the lobster. Turn the lobster belly side down on the board, then chop off the head a bit below the eyes and discard. Flip the body over, then chop it lengthwise in half. Extract and discard the white stomach sac in the head region, but save the rich, green tomalley (the liver) and any roe if your lobster is a female. Discard the intestinal tract running down the center of the tail if it is black. Finally, turn the two body pieces shell side up and chop them crosswise into pieces about 2 inches wide. Put all of the claw and body bits in a bowl, including any loose, large shells that will add their color to the dish.

Readying the seasonings:
Either before you kill and chop the lobster or immediately after, ready the other ingredients. Put the aromatics and the ground pork side by side on a small plate, reserving a teaspoon of the scallion for use as a garnish. Combine the sauce ingredients, stirring to dissolve the sugar. Use the lesser amount of sugar to begin, then put the extra within reach of your stovetop for possible addition after you have tasted the sauce.

If you are working in advance, seal the aromatics airtight and refrigerate until use, up to several hours.

Stir-frying the dish:
Stir-fry the lobster as soon as possible after chopping it.

Put all the ingredients within easy reach of your stovetop and put a heated platter or shallow bowl of contrasting color in a low oven to warm.

Heat a wok or large, heavy skillet over high heat until hot enough to evaporate a bead of water on contact. Add the corn or peanut oil, swirl to glaze the pan, then reduce the heat to medium-high. When the oil is hot enough to sizzle one bit of scallion on contact, add the scallion, ginger, and garlic. Stir gently until fragrant, 10–15 seconds, adjusting the heat so the garlic foams without browning, then add the pork to the pan. Toss and poke briskly to combine and break the meat into tiny bits, adjusting the heat so it sizzles without scorching.

When the pork is 90 percent gray, stir the liquids and add to the pan. Raise the heat to bring the liquids to a simmer, stirring, then quickly taste the sauce and adjust if required with a bit more sugar. Keep in mind that the sauce will reduce and the flavors intensify greatly before the dish is done.

Add the lobster and toss briskly to coat. Even out the contents of the pan, adjust the heat to maintain a boil, then cover the pot and steam-cook the lobster vigorously for 2½–3 minutes, until only a bit of sauce is left. Remove the cover, raise the heat, and stir briskly several times to redistribute the seasonings, then turn off the heat and sprinkle the sesame oil and vinegar into the pan. Toss several times to combine, then scrape the lobster and all the saucy bits onto the heated platter. Make a few quick adjustments for a claw or two to stick out prettily here and there, garnish with the reserved scallion, then rush the dish to the table while it is steaming and aromatic.

Eating lobster in Chinese:
Have an empty bowl nearby, chopsticks in hand, and the proper spirit to suck, crunch, lick, and dig as the lobster demands. It is helpful to remember that cheerful eating noise

is a requisite at a Chinese table and that using one's fingers and chopsticks in the interest of getting the food to one's mouth is the happy law. Do not be shy.

Leftovers are unlikely but are quite tasty at room temperature, given a few stirs to distribute the seasonings.

MENU SUGGESTIONS:

For a simple dinner, serve the lobster alongside *Shanghai Vegetable Rice* (page 402), *Ham and Egg Fried Rice* (page 405), or *Everyday Chinese Rice* (page 400). For a fuller menu, add a zesty vegetable like *Dry-Fried Szechwan String Beans* (page 297) or *Red Bell Pepper with Garlic and Coriander* (page 314). *Velvet Corn Soup* (page 460) would be good if a soup is desired. To partner the lobster, choose a big white Burgundy or Chardonnay.

Clear-Steamed Lobster with Scallion Oil

清蒸龍蝦

Lobster, in Chinese, is "dragon shrimp," and nothing to my mind better highlights the voluptuous, grand character of lobster than simple steaming. There is no better way to appreciate lobster's freshness and no easier Chinese way to cook it. A sprinkling of soy, wine, and sesame oil and a scattering of scallion, ginger, and Smithfield ham if you like and the lobster is ready for the steamer. Fifteen minutes and a flourish of seared scallions later, it is ready for the table. ◆ The most important part of this dish is the lobster itself. It must be emphatically alive when you buy it to take it home, looking every regal inch a dragon.

TECHNIQUE NOTES:

If you cannot cook the lobster on the day you buy it, then ask the person at your fish store for some seaweed for holding it in the refrigerator. Packed in a blanket of wet seaweed or wrapped in several layers of wet newspaper, it will stay alive and kicking for a day or more. Remember that a sluggish lobster is a less tasty lobster, so cook it while it's frisky.

Serves 2, with an accompanying dish of fried rice, or a bowl of plain rice and a dish of vegetables.

INGREDIENTS:

> 1 emphatically alive lobster, about 2 pounds
>
> *Seasonings:*
> 1 tablespoon thin (regular) soy sauce
> 1½ tablespoons Chinese rice wine or quality, dry sherry
> 1½ teaspoons finely minced fresh ginger
> 1½ teaspoons Chinese or Japanese sesame oil
> 1 scant tablespoon coarsely minced Smithfield ham, or ¼ teaspoon coarse
>   kosher salt
> 1 thin whole scallion, cut into 2-inch lengths
>
> *To garnish:*
> 1 tablespoon corn or peanut oil
> 2 tablespoons green and white scallion rings, cut ⅛ inch thick

Killing cleaning and chopping the lobster:
Kill, clean, and chop the lobster as described on page 276.

Preparing for steaming:
Assemble the pieces shell side down on a heatproof platter at least 1 inch smaller in diameter than your steamer. The platter should have some depth or width to it to accommodate the seasoning liquids and the juices that will be rendered during steaming, and ideally it should be one on which you can serve the lobster. (If you will need to transfer the lobster to another platter for serving, choose one of contrasting color and put it in a low oven to warm.) It is traditional to rearrange the pieces in the original lobster shape, which is especially pretty if you are using an oval dish in which to steam the lobster. If the plate or your fingers cannot bend to the task, then simply arrange the pieces attractively in a single layer, hugging one another.

Combine the soy, sherry, ginger, sesame oil, and ham or salt in a small bowl, stirring to blend. Smash the scallion lengths lightly with the broad side of a cleaver or heavy knife to bring the juices to the surface. Pour the seasonings evenly over the lobster and scatter the scallion lengths on top. Proceed immediately to steam the lobster.

Steaming the lobster and searing the scallions:
(For details on steaming and how to improvise a steamer, see page 60.)

Bring the water in your steaming vessel to a gushing boil over high heat. (I like to do this while I'm chopping and arranging the lobster, so I don't waste a minute.) Put the plate with the lobster and seasonings in place, cover the steamer tightly, then steam the lobster over high heat for 12–15 minutes, until white and firm. Do not lift the cover while the lobster is steaming lest you dissipate the steam.

When the lobster is within minutes of being done, add the tablespoon of oil to a small saucepan and heat over low heat, taking the pan from the heat if the oil begins to smoke.

Remove the lobster promptly from the steamer, then discard the scallion lengths. Test the heated oil, and when it is hot enough to foam a single scallion ring on contact, add the scallion rings to the pan. Swirl the oil until the scallion is fully foaming and fragrant, several seconds, then scatter the scallion at arm's length over the lobster. Serve immediately, while steaming and aromatic.

Eat the lobster with all the noise and gusto you like, comfortable in the thought that any happy Chinese eating venture assumes a lot of noise. Provide bowls for the shells and napkins or damp cloths for the finger lickers, and don't forget the chopsticks for digging out the meat.

Leftovers are delicious cold, on their own or tossed in a lightly dressed salad of interesting greens.

MENU SUGGESTIONS:
Shanghai Vegetable Rice (page 402) would partner this dish perfectly, followed by *Velvet Corn Soup* (page 460). *Flower Rolls* (page 415) would be a nice alternative to rice and *Steamed Winter Melon with Ham* (page 315) could serve instead of the soup. To accompany the lobster, serve a big white Burgundy or Chardonnay.

Vegetables & Vegetarian Dishes

素菜及蔬菜

◆

◆

Colorful fresh vegetables, cooked lightly and simply with respect to the innate flavor and texture of the plant, have come to be synonymous with Chinese cooking in the West. Contrary to our own habits of cooking vegetables to a uniform softness, choosing one part of the plant in preference to another seemingly less sweet or tender part, or variously paring or puréeing a vegetable down to an anonymous bit of color, the Chinese have a passion for preserving and presenting the original character of the whole plant. Leaves, stems, and roots are all eaten with relish. Flavors are left naturally acrid, bitter, or sweet. Crunchy, gelatinous, smooth, and brittle textures are each prized, while cutting seeks to emphasize the natural lines and hollows of the plant. Artifice and cooking time are kept to a minimum, leaving the vegetable looking and tasting bright and fresh—lively and almost "purified" as opposed to just "cooked."

The Chinese passion for vegetables embraces all manners of plants, whether grown on land, plucked from the sea, or cultivated in marshes, paddies, or ponds. There is no squeamishness or reluctance to eat a tiny chrysanthemum leaf, a tuberous lotus root, or the cheerful green top of a spring onion. Each is valued for its tonic quality, lyricized for its associations, and cooked and eaten with pronounced pleasure. The Chinese scholar sitting in his studio meditating on a carved jade cabbage and the cook in the kitchen cutting, salting, and stir-frying a real cabbage are participants in the same, beneficent vegetable kingdom. Likewise the painter of bamboo, the man who sells fresh shoots in the marketplace, or the hungry woman who sits down to dinner with a bowlful of simply braised bamboo tips. There is something healthy, nurturing, and deeply satisfying about vegetables to the Chinese. It is their *approach* to vegetables that is so special, even more than the particular types of vegetables they cook.

FRESH AS OPPOSED TO CANNED VEGETABLES　　Canned bamboo shoots, water chestnuts, and bean sprouts were the exotic vegetables of my childhood, snuck onto the table by my mother when my mashed-potatoes-loving father wasn't looking, and I have tried on occasion to recall their delight for my adult tongue. I simply can't. Water chestnuts, bamboo shoots and bean sprouts seem foul or at best boring when canned, and bear no resemblance whatsoever to the fresh item. I don't use them. Instead, I substitute fresh and lively produce—*jícama*, blanched sun chokes, or firm apples for water chestnuts, carrots for bamboo shoots, or celery hearts or shredded broccoli stems for bean sprouts—something that will mimic in flavor or texture the quality of the real thing. Occasionally, one finds a canned bamboo shoot that is white and clean-tasting or a canned water chestnut that is crunchy and sweet, but for the most part I disdain cans and spurn exotica for good taste.

JUDGING FRESH VEGETABLES　　Plants rely on and are composed largely of water, hence a vegetable with a firm feel, fulsome look, and lively stem, top or leaf is one I judge "fresh." If a vegetable is withered, wrinkled, or dry—indicating a loss of its natural moisture—then I don't buy it. A limp snow pea, a carrot with wilted greenery, or fresh garlic or ginger that is not plump and rock-hard is too long-gone from its earthy bed. It may be good for some things—a stew or a soup that will extract its flavor through lengthy, slow cooking—but for most Chinese quick-cooking a limp vegetable won't do.

In shopping for vegetables, I favor markets that display their produce in the open, where I can feel it, smell it, and inspect it to within an inch of my nose, if I like. If vegetables are pre-bagged, wrapped in cellophane or otherwise hidden from inspection, I find it as depressing as ordering food in an automat, and I stubbornly avoid one as much as the other.

STORING FRESH VEGETABLES　　Vegetables in general like to be kept cool and moist, and, if I am not cooking vegetables on the day I buy them, I store them in the refrigerator in sealed plastic bags. Scallions, radishes, carrots, and others with leafy tops do best if they are misted lightly with water before bagging, which holds true for thirsty greens like Chinese cabbage and fresh coriander. Vegetables with less porous skins, like cucumbers, eggplant, and zucchini, are best stored dry. Asparagus should be refrigerated standing in an inch of water, garlic keeps best left at room temperature and exposed to the air. There are various such exceptions to the bag, seal, and chill routine. Looking at the vegetable, I find, will tell you what it needs. If after several days it is molding, then it needs more air; if it is withered, then it needs to be kept moister and better sealed, and so on.

　　One thing to avoid is the tendency to refrigerate vegetables without any covering, half-bagged in brown paper, or squashed in a corner in some tangled heap. Another thing to avoid is the habit of keeping them too long. Buy it fresh, keep it fresh, and eat it as soon as you can.

Chinese Crudités
五彩蔬菜

Chinese have little or no attraction to raw vegetables. Partly because of their fascination with transforming the colors and textures of food, partly because of the practice of fertilizing vegetables with "night soil" (human excrement), raw vegetables have played no part in classic Chinese cuisine. Even the poorest of Chinese poets, banished to the tropics with little to do but dapple in rusticity and lyricize its charms, would throw his turnips in boiling water before eating them. To Chinese eyes, the fashionable French habit of preceding a meal with an assortment of raw vegetable *crudités* would seem just that—crude.　◆　Here are *crudités* transformed: raw, dull-colored vegetables turned a deep, rich color and a moist, more appealing texture by a brief steaming or seconds-only blanching in unsalted water. Combined with a zesty trio of Chinese-style sauces, they are a bold and lively appetite arouser, a deliciously different way to open or augment a meal.　◆　You will find a full rainbow of vegetable choices below, allowing you to pick what is best in the market and mix East with West. Any four vegetables will make a dramatic platter, and two or even one sauce may be used if you haven't the time or ingredients for the three. The only instruction is to remember yin and yang, and choose with an eye for different colors, shapes, and textures.　◆　Easily assembled, this dish is bright-tasting, low in calories, and very versatile. Serve it at a luncheon, as an hors d'oeuvre before dinner, or as part of a large buffet. It is eminently portable, whether you are en route to the office or the beach. Everything may be done in advance, including the arrangement of the platter.

TECHNIQUE NOTES:
Blanching vegetables Chinese-style is a quick, deft process, that might better be termed "dipping," it is so brief. The goal is to deepen color and dramatize the intrinsically sweet taste, while leaving the character and the crispness of the vegetable intact. To this end, the immersion takes mere seconds, the vegetables are done in small lots for greatest control, and the water is left unsalted.

　　Four cups of assorted vegetables will serve 2–4 as a cold course, 4–6 as an hors d'oeuvre, or 6–12 as part of a large buffet.

INGREDIENTS:

Choice of Crudités (choose 4 or more, with an eye to variety):

Vegetables best blanched:
   pencil-thin fresh asparagus
   fresh broccoli, with dense, dark green tops and solid stalks
   firm young zucchini
   firm yellow squash
   sweet-smelling large carrots or fresh finger-size carrots
   fresh tender string beans or Chinese longbeans
   fresh young snow peas or sugar snap peas
   canned Chinese baby corn (page 531)
   firm fresh lotus root (do not use canned)
   unequivocally crisp and clean-tasting canned whole bamboo shoots (page 532)

Vegetables best steamed:
   fresh small or medium Brussels sprouts
   fresh cauliflower

Vegetables best raw:
   sweet-smelling red or yellow cherry tomatoes
   unblemished red or green or yellow bell pepper
   firm red radishes with green leaves intact
   firm seedless waxless cucumbers
   fresh celery hearts and inner ribs

Sauces (choose 2 or all 3):
   Dijon Mustard Sauce (page 475), or Coriandered Mustard Sauce (page 476)
   Orchid's Spicy Sesame Sauce (page 471), or Sweet and Silky Sesame Sauce
     (page 472)
   Spicy Szechwan Peanut Sauce (page 473)

Preparing blanched vegetables:
Cut the vegetables for blanching as follows. Once cut, they may be refrigerated overnight, sealed airtight in lightly misted plastic bags.

   Blanching instructions follow the list of vegetables. Blanching times are suggestions based on superbly fresh produce. Test to be sure.

   Asparagus: Snap off woody ends, then roll-cut into nuggets 2 inches long, as directed in TECHNIQUE NOTES, page 288. Blanch 30–40 seconds for pencil-thin asparagus, 50–60 seconds for slightly thicker stalks.

   Broccoli: Cut the tops into flowerets and the stalks into "clouds," as directed in TECHNIQUE NOTES, page 219. Blanch the flowerets 5–10 seconds; clouds 4–5 seconds.

   Zucchini or Yellow Squash: Remove tips, then cut on the diagonal into oblong coins 2 inches long and ¼ inch thick, or cut into rounds ¼ inch thick. Blanch 3–4 seconds.

Carrots: Trim and peel carrots. Cut large carrots in the same manner as zucchini or squash above. Leave finger-size carrots whole. Blanch sliced carrots 10–15 seconds; small carrots 30–40 seconds.

String Beans or Longbeans: Discard tips and cut into 3-inch lengths. Blanch string beans 5–25 seconds, depending upon thickness and texture. Blanch longbeans 15–30 seconds.

Snow Peas or Sugar Snap Peas: Remove tips and string, if mature. Blanch 5–15 seconds, depending on size and thickness of pod.

Baby Corn: Drain. Blanch 5–10 seconds.

Lotus Root: To prevent discoloration, peel and slice immediately before blanching, or hold in cold water. Peel and cut into rounds ⅛ inch thick. Cut large rounds in half. Blanch 20–30 seconds.

Bamboo Shoots: Drain. Cut into long, thin wedges ½ inch thick. Blanch 10–15 seconds.

To blanch the vegetables, bring a generous amount of unsalted water to a boil in one or more large pots, depending upon the number and type of vegetables. Light or similarly flavored vegetables like zucchini and yellow squash may be blanched in the same water, though not at the same time. When sharing the same water, blanch the *sweeter* vegetable first—for example, carrots before broccoli. Put a metal colander in the sink or a Chinese mesh spoon or slotted spoon by the stove, of a size suitable for retrieving the vegetables quickly and in one batch. Or, put the vegetables in a wire basket or colander which can be quickly raised and lowered in the water. Unless you have a very cold faucet which gushes a good amount of cold water, put a bowl of ice water in the sink. It is the safest and surest way to cool the vegetables and keep them crisp.

Blanch only 1–2 cups of vegetables at one time. Immerse in the boiling water, then remove or drain as soon as the color deepens, following the time suggestions above. Exceptions to the color rule are those vegetables that need to cook beyond the point of color change to rid them of a grassy taste (asparagus), or white vegetables, which require cooking to enhance taste and preserve, not change, color (lotus root). Once removed from the boiling water, plunge immediately into ice water or rush under cold water until chilled. Do not overcook the vegetables or dally in draining and chilling them. The point to remember is that the vegetable will continue to cook from its own heat even after it leaves the pot.

Shake off excess water, then spread the vegetables on a lint-free cloth for up to 15 minutes. To hold for a longer period, up to 12 hours, transfer the vegetables from the cloth to a large plate, spreading them in more or less of a single layer, seal airtight, and refrigerate.

Preparing steamed vegetables:
(For details on steaming and how to improvise a steamer, see page 60.)

Brussels Sprouts: Trim off the stem just enough to expose new flesh. Discard any yellow or wilted outer leaves. Steam in a single layer over high heat 7–11 minutes, depending on the size of the sprouts, until a sharp knife can easily pierce the base.

Cauliflower: Break into flowerets and peel stems. Steam over high heat 5–10 minutes, depending on the size of the flowerets, until a knife easily pierces the thickest part.

To steam the vegetables, bring the water for steaming to a gushing boil over high heat. Put the vegetables in a single layer in a heatproof plate or Pyrex pie plate at least 1 inch smaller in diameter than your steamer. Add the plate to the steamer, cover tightly, then steam over high heat *just* until you can pierce the center of the vegetable easily with a sharp knife. Remove the vegetables quickly to a colander, then plunge immediately into ice water or rush under cold water until chilled. Drain, dry, and refrigerate as above.

Preparing raw vegetables:

Raw vegetables are best cut only hours before serving, though very firm ones may be cut a day ahead if you are less fussy or pressed for time. Refrigerate in lightly misted plastic bags, all except tomatoes, which are best stored dry.

Cherry Tomatoes: Leave stems on for decoration. Wash and pat dry.

Bell Pepper: Wash and cut in half lengthwise. Remove core, seeds, and ribs. Cut lengthwise into slivers ½ inch thick.

Radishes: Wash, pinch off wilted outer leaves, and trim off roots.

Cucumbers: Remove tips and cut on the diagonal into oblong coins ⅛–¼ inch thick, or into rounds ⅛–¼ inch thick.

Celery: String the outside of the ribs, if needed. Cut into 2–2½ inch lengths, then cut lengthwise into strips ¼ inch wide. Leave the tender leaf clusters and the hearts intact.

Assembling the platter:

Arrange the vegetables in separate mounds, wagon-wheel fashion around the center of a large platter. Make it beautiful by alternating colors and fanning or overlapping the prettiest slices on top. Serve the sauce in bowls alongside, or work the bowls into the arrangement if the platter permits. The finished platter, minus the sauces, may be refrigerated hours before serving. Fleck the vegetables lightly with water to keep them moist, then seal airtight with plastic wrap.

Alternatively, mound the vegetables prettily on individual plates, then arrange them flower-style on the table around a cluster of sauce bowls. This works particularly well if you are feeding a large crowd.

Serve the vegetables well chilled, but serve the sauces at room temperature for best flavor and aroma. Invite your guests to help themselves to a bit of everything, using fingers or chopsticks, as the occasion and mood suggest.

Leftover vegetables keep 2–4 days, refrigerated and sealed. Leftover sauce keeps indefinitely, bottled and refrigerated.

MENU SUGGESTIONS:

For a light lunch or dinner on diet days, this platter stands by itself. Or, for a cold meal or buffet, partner it with *Strange Flavor Eggplant* (page 295), *Tea and Spice Smoked Chicken* (page 158), and *Scallion and Ginger Explosion Shrimp* (page 233). As a prelude to a hot supper, most anything can follow. A light Johannisberg Riesling is a lovely accompaniment to the *crudités*.

Cold-Tossed Asparagus with Sesame Seeds

涼拌蘆筍

This dish of cool, crunchy, and lightly dressed asparagus nuggets is truly from the opposite side of the world as that which serves its asparagus long, limp, and clothed in butter or cream. It is a wonderfully easy way of cooking asparagus, with none of the fuss or calories we're used to in Western dining. ◆ Choose pencil-thin asparagus with firm, tight-closed tips and an overall smooth, full-fleshed, healthy look. Overly thin or very thick asparagus will not be as good. To store fresh asparagus, even for a few hours, stand them upright in the refrigerator in a bowl or measuring cup filled with an inch of cold water. The stalks respond to the water like a bunch of cut flowers. ◆ The asparagus takes 5 minutes to cut and 1–2 minutes to cook. It may be cooked a day in advance and sauced a few hours ahead of serving.

TECHNIQUE NOTES:
"Roll-cutting" is a classic Chinese method for cutting long, cylindrical vegetables. It exposes more surface area for fast cooking and a good penetration of seasonings and looks pretty besides. To roll-cut a spear of asparagus, first slice off the end with a 25° diagonal cut, not too sharp and not too blunt. Roll the stalk a quarter turn away from you, then cut on the diagonal about 1½ inches farther up the stem. Continue rolling and cutting on the diagonal until the entire stalk is cut into segments. Plan your cutting so at least 1 inch of stalk is left to support the tender tip.

Serves 2–3 as a cold vegetable course, 4–6 as part of a larger meal or an assortment of "Little Dishes."

INGREDIENTS:

> *1–1½ pounds fresh, pencil-thin asparagus, a scant ½ inch thick*

> *Dressing:*
> *1 tablespoon plus 2 teaspoons Chinese or Japanese sesame oil*
> *4 teaspoons brown or white sugar*
> *2 teaspoons white vinegar*
> *2 teaspoons thin (regular) soy sauce*
> *2 teaspoons untoasted white sesame seeds*

Pan-toasting the seeds:
Freshly toasted sesame seeds are always better than store-bought, and here's how to do it when you have only a small amount to toast: Add the seeds to a heavy, dry skillet. Set over medium heat and push the seeds around for several minutes until they turn a nutty, light brown. Regulate the heat so they neither scorch nor ooze too much oil. Scrape into a saucer to cool, stirring occasionally.

Roll-cutting and cooking the asparagus:
Bend each asparagus stalk near the base until the woody, whitish end snaps off. Discard the ends, then roll-cut the asparagus as described above in TECHNIQUE NOTES.

Station a metal colander in the sink, then bring a generous amount of unsalted water to a full boil over high heat. Drop the asparagus into the water for 1 minute if pencil-thin, 1½–2 minutes if thicker, no longer. Drain immediately in the colander and rush under cold running water until thoroughly chilled. Shake off excess water, then pat dry.

The asparagus may be cooked a day in advance. Spread on a large plate, seal airtight, and refrigerate until use.

Dressing the asparagus:
If you are working only an hour in advance, sauce the asparagus with brown sugar. If you have a few hours, use white sugar, which takes longer to penetrate but has a lighter taste.

Whisk the sesame oil, sugar, vinegar, and soy, stirring until smooth and slightly thick. Put the dressing aside to develop for 10 minutes, stir, then scrape over the asparagus and toss gently to mix. Toss again with all but ¼ teaspoon of the sesame seeds, seal airtight, and refrigerate 1–3 hours before serving, tossing occasionally.

Toss again just before serving and garnish with the remaining sesame seeds. Serve well chilled in a bowl of contrasting color to show off the deep asparagus green.

The asparagus is best within several hours of saucing. Leftovers quickly lose their sparkle.

MENU SUGGESTIONS:
As part of a cold menu, serve the asparagus with *Marbelized Tea Eggs* (page 325), *Orchid's Tangy Cool Noodles* (page 356), and *Scallion and Ginger Explosion Shrimp* (page 233). As part of a selection of "Little Dishes," serve it alongside *Soy-Dipped Red Radish Fans* (page 114). The asparagus is also excellent with cold poultry and cold *Saucy Potted Pork* (page 207).

| Carnelian Carrot Coins 滷紅蘿蔔 | This is one of the versatile, no-work dishes that can be done with master sauce—a pretty pile of oblong carrot coins, stained a deep color and rich flavor by several hours' steeping in the master brew. You may serve the carrots warm, at room temperature, or chilled as an edible garnish or a rich-tasting "Little Dish" to accompany most any kind of food. I like them best chilled, when they are at their flavor peak after a day's refrigeration and feel slippery on the |

tongue. ◆ Buy carrots that *smell* sweet when you puncture the skin with a fingernail. That is your assurance that there's a good carrot underneath, not wood. ◆ Cook the carrots up to 2 days in advance, if you like. The cutting takes only minutes, and the sauce does the rest.

TECHNIQUE NOTES:
The carrot coins must be cut properly to cook properly. The slices should be just over ¼ inch thick, so they have body to withstand the long steeping but are still thin enough to be penetrated by the sauce. Be careful also to cut them evenly thick, so both ends of the coin and all the individual slices cook to the same degree of doneness at the same time.

Yields about 2 cups carrot coins, enough to serve 2–3 as a light vegetable course, 4–6 as a "Little Dish" to accompany other foods.

INGREDIENTS:

> *½ pound sweet-smelling carrots, trimmed and peeled*
> *master sauce from making Master Sauce Chicken (page 153), to cover*

Cutting the carrots:
Cut the carrots on a sharp diagonal into oblong coins, 2 inches long and a bit over ¼ inch thick. Be sure to cut the coins so they are evenly thick at both ends. Don't throw away the odd-looking end slices. Steep them with the rest to enrich the sauce, then eat them yourself if you do not wish to serve them.

Steeping the coins:
Bring the sauce to a gentle simmer in a small, heavy pot that will hold the carrots snugly. (I use a small Chinese sand pot, illustrated on page 98, though any small, heavy pot will do.) Taste the sauce and adjust if required with a bit more water, soy, wine, or crushed golden rock sugar to achieve a rich and balanced blend. Go easy on the sugar. The carrots will imbue the sauce with their own natural sweetness.

Add the carrots, poke them under the sauce, then adjust the heat to maintain a slow simmer. Cover the pot and simmer 15 minutes. Turn off the heat, then let the carrots steep in the hot liquid for 2 hours. Remove the cover after 30 minutes, so the coins do not overcook in the concentrated heat.

Strain the sauce through several layers of wet cheesecloth, then cool, bottle, and refrigerate or freeze for future use. Gently nudge the carrots into a shallow bowl, taking care not to break them. Eat when tender and warm, or, for a richer flavor and a more interesting, firm texture, seal airtight and chill overnight.

Serve chilled carrots cold or at room temperature. Just before serving, invert the carrots into a shallow serving bowl so that the sauce that was on the bottom now glosses the top. For Western-style service, you may arrange the chilled coins in pretty fans on individual plates to highlight a main course. Or, use as a decorative garnish to rim a serving platter.

Leftover carrot coins keep 3–4 days, refrigerated and sealed airtight.

MENU SUGGESTIONS:
As part of a hot meal, the carrots make good accompaniments to *Cinnamon Bark Chicken* (page 162), *Tea and Spice Smoked Chicken* (page 158), *Fragrant Crispy Duck* (page 172), *Smoked Tea Duck* (page 169), *Steamed Whole Fish with Seared Scallions* (page 248) and *Clear-Steamed Flounder with White Pepper* (page 250). Try them as well with a cold poultry salad like *Ma-La Cold Chicken* (page 129) or *Cold Duck Salad with Two Sauces* (page 164), or a simple dish like *Old Egg* (page 332).

Master Sauce Mushrooms

滷花菇

Already lush-tasting Chinese black mushrooms become almost decadently so when steeped in rich master sauce. You should serve them as you would fresh truffles—whole, if you wish to be lavish, or cut into thin strips if you wish to be lavishly discreet. ◆ Chinese dried black mushrooms come in two varieties. The best for this dish are "flower mushrooms," the thick-capped sort that is plusher. You can spot them immediately by the white, flower-like lines that crack the surface of the black tops. Buy the largest, fattest caps your pocket can afford. ◆ This is a no-work way to bring luxury to a meal, something that may be done days in advance.

TECHNIQUE NOTES:
For this dish it is advisable to soak the dried mushrooms in *cold* water. Over several hours the caps will become soft and spongy, and the dusky taste will remain *inside* the

mushrooms. I most always use the "cold-soak" method for dried mushrooms, lily buds, and tree ears. The flavor and texture seem better in the end, and it gives me a way to work comfortably in advance. Once in the cold water, the mushrooms may be left overnight.

Count on 1–3 mushrooms per person, depending on size.

INGREDIENTS:

> *small, medium, or large Chinese dried black mushrooms, "flower" variety best (page 538)*
> *master sauce from making Master Sauce Chicken (page 153), to cover*

Soaking the mushrooms:
For best flavor, soak the mushrooms for several hours in cold water, overnight if you wish. If you are pressed for time, cover the mushrooms with hot water, cover the bowl, then soak about 20 minutes, until soft and spongy. Snip off the stems with scissors, then rinse the caps under running water to dislodge any sand trapped in the gills.

Steeping the caps:
Bring the sauce to a gentle simmer in a small heavy pot that will hold the mushrooms snugly. (I use a small Chinese sand pot, illustrated on page 98, though any small, heavy pot will do.) Taste and adjust the sauce if required, adding a bit more water, soy, wine, or crushed golden rock sugar to achieve a rich and balanced blend. Add the mushroom caps, stir, then adjust the heat to maintain a weak simmer. Cover and simmer 15 minutes. Turn off the heat, then let the caps steep in the covered pot for about 1 hour, longer if upon tasting them you find you want a richer taste. The steeping time will vary, depending upon the intensity of the sauce and the thickness of the caps.
   Remove the mushrooms to a small bowl. Strain, bottle, and refrigerate or freeze the sauce for future use.
   For best flavor and a wonderfully smooth texture, chill the mushrooms before serving, overnight if you wish. You may also eat them hot directly out of the pot, or tepid. To serve, cut them into strips, halves, or serve whole.
   The mushrooms will keep 2–3 days, sealed airtight and refrigerated.

MENU SUGGESTIONS:
Hot, the mushrooms are nice partners for *Tea and Spice Smoked Chicken* (page 158), *Smoked Tea Duck* (page 169), *Steamed Whole Fish with Seared Scallions* (page 248), and *Clear-Steamed Flounder with White Pepper* (page 250). Cold, they are good with *Master Sauce Chicken* (page 153), or *Saucy Potted Pork* (page 207) and an assortment of "Little Dishes" as part of a cold buffet.

Shantung Cold Eggplant with Sesame Sauce

涼拌茄子

For a quick, simple, and economical dish, you can not beat this common northern Chinese pairing of slippery cool eggplant and rich sesame sauce. It is especially good in summertime, when eggplants are plentiful and the urge to cook and chew is at low ebb. ◆ The long, slender variety of eggplant sold in Chinese and Japanese markets (page 543) is superior in this dish. The skin is tender, the flesh is sweet, and there are few seeds. If you cannot find it, choose small, firm, unblemished eggplant that feels heavy in your hand. ◆ You may cut the eggplant into chunks for serving, shred it into long, thin strips with a sharp knife or by hand, or purée it in the food processor. All three consistencies are traditional. I prefer the knife-cut strips with their slippery texture like "eggplant spaghetti." ◆ The eggplant and sauce may be prepared days in advance, and the dish assembled within minutes.

TECHNIQUE NOTES:
Chinese usually steam eggplant prior to inclusion in a cold dish. I like to bake it. The skin turns a bit crackly, and the flesh seems less water-prone. To stop the cooking and stiffen the flesh, slit the eggplant open and refrigerate it immediately after baking. Otherwise, an eggplant allowed to get watery will dilute a good sauce.

The Asian variety of eggplant, upon baking, will often exude a thick brown syrup as it cools. This eggplant "liqueur" is delicious, and you should include it in the dish. Western varieties, on the other hand, exude mostly water, and this should always be discarded.

Serves 2 as a main course, 3–5 as part of a multicourse meal, 6–8 as an hors d'oeuvre spread.

INGREDIENTS:

> 1½ pounds firm eggplant, slender Chinese or Japanese variety best
> 5–6 tablespoons Orchid's Spicy Sesame Sauce (page 471)
> 3–4 tablespoons fresh coriander leaves, or tender, young celery leaves, left
>   whole or coarsely or finely chopped

Baking the eggplant:
Pull off the leaves, then wash the eggplant and prick in several spots with the tines of a fork to release steam during baking. Bake in a heatproof dish in a preheated 450° oven until fork-tender, about 20–35 minutes depending on size. Turn the eggplant over midway through baking for even cooking and less liquid.

Remove from the oven, then immediately cut off the stem ends and slit the eggplant in half lengthwise to release the steam. Cut large eggplant lengthwise once or twice again, to yield long wedges about 1 inch wide. Chill cut side up, uncovered to allow the heat to escape, in the refrigerator until cold. Once cool, proceed to assemble the dish or seal the eggplant airtight and refrigerate up to 2 days.

Cutting and saucing the eggplant:
Peel Western eggplant entirely. Remove most of the peel from Asian eggplant, leaving on a bit for color if it clings.

For a chunky or shredded dish, cut the eggplant into ¾ inch cubes or shred by hand or with a sharp knife into long, thin strips. Place in a shallow bowl, top with a thick ribbon of sesame sauce, then garnish with the coriander or celery leaves to taste. Serve immediately after saucing and toss at the table. Have a bowl of sauce available for those who will want more.

To purée, cut the eggplant into chunks and add to the work bowl of a food processor fitted with the steel knife. Process until coarsely chopped, add the sauce, then process until nubbly or completely smooth, as desired. Taste, and add more sauce if the flavor of the eggplant requires it. Mound in a serving bowl and garnish with the chopped coriander or celery leaves just before serving. Serve immediately or, for fuller flavor, seal airtight and refrigerate 1–2 days. Serve at room temperature or slightly chilled, alone, with unsalted crackers, or with wedges of *Pan-Fried Scallion Bread* (page 435) or toasted pita bread.

Leftovers keep several days, sealed and refrigerated.

MENU SUGGESTIONS:
This dish is excellent in combination with other cold Chinese dishes such as *Tea and Spice Smoked Chicken* (page 158), *Orchid's Tangy Cool Noodles* (page 356), and *Marbelized Tea Eggs* (page 325). It is also a novel aside to grilled or broiled meats and poultry as part of a Western dinner. To partner the eggplant, choose a dry Gewürtztraminer.

Hunan Eggplant with Spicy Meat Sauce 湘味茄子

This is a spice lover's delight of soft shredded eggplant, nubbled with minced pork and redolent of hot chili and garlic. To eat it will put sweat on your brow—the unabashed joy of most Hunanese and Szechwanese who, living for much of the year in a hot and humid climate, look to the chili as a culinary sort of air-conditioning. The palate smolders and the body feels refreshed. It is a phenomenon known to Indians, Mexicans, and Chinese alike. ◆ True to Hunan taste, the eggplant is not at all oily, and the seasonings are well-balanced between fiery and sweet. A light yet wholesome and stimulating dish, it is excellent hot, tepid, or at room temperature. ◆ The eggplant may be cooked and shredded 1–2 days in advance of saucing. Completing the dish takes 5 minutes, which makes it ideal for a busy weekday night.

TECHNIQUE NOTES:
For cooking eggplant without making it watery or oily, and for the role of sesame oil in an eggplant stir-fry, see TECHNIQUE NOTES, page 295.

Serves 3–4 as a main course, 5–10 as part of a multicourse meal.

INGREDIENTS:

 1½ pounds firm eggplant, slender Chinese or Japanese variety recommended

Aromatics:
 4–8 large cloves garlic, stem end removed, lightly smashed and peeled
 1 walnut-size nugget fresh ginger
 1 medium whole scallion, cut into 1-inch lengths
 1 scant teaspoon Chinese salted black beans (not the variety seasoned with five-spice powder; page 561)

For stir-frying:
 2 tablespoons thin (regular) soy sauce
 1 teaspoon sugar
 2 tablespoons corn or peanut oil
 1½–2 tablespoons Chinese chili sauce (page 537)
 4–6 ounces ground pork butt
 1 tablespoon Chinese or Japanese sesame oil

Baking and shredding the eggplant:
Bake, peel, and shred the eggplant as directed on page 296. I prefer to tear the eggplant for this particular dish into long, thin shreds with my fingers, though you may use a cleaver or knife if you like.

The shredded eggplant may be sealed airtight and refrigerated 1–2 days prior to saucing. Bring to room temperature before stir-frying. If Western eggplant becomes watery in the refrigerator, drain the liquid before cooking.

Preparations:
Mince the garlic, ginger, and scallion in the work bowl of a food processor fitted with the steel knife, scraping down as necessary until fine. Add the black beans (do *not* soak or wash them), then process with 1 or 2 on-off turns until coarsely chopped. Scrape the seasonings into a dish. If you do not have a food processor, mince the garlic, ginger, and scallion by hand until fine. Chop the beans coarsely, then combine.

Combine the soy and sugar, stirring to dissolve the sugar.

This may be done hours in advance of stir-frying. Seal the aromatics airtight and refrigerate until use.

Stir-frying the dish:
Have the eggplant, the minced aromatics, the soy mixture, and the remaining ingredients all within easy reach of your stovetop. If you are serving the eggplant hot, put a serving dish of contrasting color in a low oven to warm.

Heat a wok or large, heavy skillet over high heat until hot enough to evaporate a bead of water on contact. Add the corn or peanut oil, swirl to glaze the pan, then reduce the heat to medium. When the oil is hot enough to sizzle one bit of the minced seasonings, scrape them into the pan. Adjust the heat so they sizzle without scorching, then stir gently until fully fragrant, about 20 seconds.

Add the chili sauce to the pan, stir 2–3 seconds to combine, then add the pork. Stir, mash, and toss to mix the meat with the seasonings and break it into tiny bits, adjusting the heat so it sizzles briskly without browning. When the pork is 90 percent gray, add the eggplant and stir to combine and heat the mixture through, about 30–45 seconds.

Add the soy and sugar, stir to blend, then reduce the heat to low and taste for the desired degree of hotness. (If you plan to serve the eggplant tepid or at room temperature, expect it to grow spicier as it sits, and don't overdo the chili. If it tastes spicy but not flavorful, add a dash of sugar.) When it is spiced to suit you, add the sesame oil, toss well to mix, then scrape the eggplant into the serving dish. Just before serving, toss lightly to redistribute the seasonings.

Leftovers keep 3–4 days, refrigerated and sealed airtight. Eat at room temperature, or resteam in a tightly covered dish until hot. The spiciness will grow, and peaks on the second day.

MENU SUGGESTIONS:
This is a wonderful accompaniment to *Orchid's Tangy Cool Noodles* (page 356) and *Scallion and Ginger Explosion Shrimp* (page 233) as part of a cold meal. Hot, it is an excellent simple meal served with *Everyday Chinese Rice* (page 400). Add *Steamed Whole Fish with Seared Scallions* (page 248) if another dish is needed. In a Western context, it is delicious served alongside grilled chicken or fish. To partner the spicy eggplant, choose a light Zinfandel.

<table>
<tr><td>

**Strange
Flavor
Eggplant**

怪味茄子
</td></tr>
</table>

In Chinese poetry and art criticism the word *kuai* can mean "odd" as in downright weird, or "strange" as in fascinating and unusual. In cooking, there is no such confusion. "Strange flavor" dishes are always extraordinary—spicy, subtle, sweet, tart, and tangy all at the same time, an ineffable blend of tastes. Usually, a strange flavor sauce has sesame paste as a component and is credited with a Szechwanese origin, but mine is clear and thin in a Shanghai mode. Instead of coating the eggplant, it permeates it. ◆ This is an extremely versatile dish, delicious hot or cold, shredded for presentation as a zesty vegetable or puréed for serving as a novel hors d'oeuvre spread with crackers. The complete lack of oiliness and the piquant flavor make it a great favorite. ◆ I prefer the elongated Chinese or Japanese eggplants (page 543), which are sweet and not watery, with a pleasantly edible skin. If unavailable, use the large Western variety and pick the smallest good-looking ones on the shelf. Chosen by Chinese standards, the skin should be unblemished and somewhat dull, and the plant should feel firm though not hard to the touch. ◆ The eggplant may be baked a day or two before saucing, and refrigerated another day before serving. The flavors become even fuller if the dish is made in advance.

TECHNIQUE NOTES:
Cooking eggplant in the oven eliminates the oiliness caused by stir-frying and the wateriness engendered by steaming. It is a Western technique I use gladly in the interest of a better dish.

When adding an assortment of minced condiments that includes red chili pepper to heated oil, add the pepper last. The oil will be somewhat cooled and tempered by the other ingredients, and the chili will be less likely to scorch.

Garnishing a dish with sesame oil just before it leaves the pan imparts aroma and luster. In the case of the eggplant, it also adds a pronounced flavor and a needed touch of oil, without which the eggplant tastes flat.

Yields about 2 cups, enough to serve 4–5 as a light vegetable course, 6–8 as part of a multicourse meal, 10–15 as an hors d'oeuvre spread with crackers.

INGREDIENTS:

1–1¼ pounds firm eggplant

Aromatics:
3–4 large cloves garlic, stem end removed, lightly smashed and peeled (to equal 1 tablespoon minced fresh garlic)
1 large walnut-size nugget fresh ginger (to equal 1 tablespoon minced ginger)
1 hefty whole scallion, cut into 1-inch lengths (to equal 3 tablespoons chopped scallion)
rounded ¼–½ teaspoon dried red chili flakes

Liquid seasonings:
2½–3 tablespoons thin (regular) soy sauce
2½–3 tablespoons packed light brown sugar
1 teaspoon unseasoned Chinese or Japanese rice vinegar
1 tablespoon hot water

2 tablespoons corn or peanut oil

1 teaspoon Chinese or Japanese sesame oil

To garnish:
1 tablespoon green scallion rings

Baking the eggplant:
Preheat the oven to 475° and set the rack in the middle of the oven. Tear off the leaves, rinse the eggplant, and pat dry. Prick in several places with a fork to act as steam vents during baking.

Bake the eggplant in a baking dish or on a baking sheet until it gives easily when you press it with a chopstick or spoon, about 20–40 minutes depending on size. Turn the eggplant over once midway through baking to insure even cooking. Remove to a plate and allow to cool. The eggplant will look like a deflated, wrinkled balloon.

Once cool, the eggplant may be sealed airtight and refrigerated for up to 2 days before saucing.

Cutting the eggplant and readying the sauce:
Discard the stem end and cut the eggplant in half lengthwise.

Peel large Western eggplant fully. The peel should tear off easily with your fingers. Asian eggplant can be peeled entirely, or you may leave on the bit of peel that inevitably clings to the flesh and is quite good tasting. Drain Western eggplant of any watery liquid, but reserve the thick, brown "liqueur" often exuded by Asian eggplant.

To purée the eggplant, cut it into large chunks, then process in a food processor or blender until completely smooth. For shreds, tear the eggplant into long, pencil-thin strips with your fingers. It is slower than slicing with a cleaver, but the texture is inimitable and the irregular contours drink up the sauce. Once puréed or shredded, the eggplant may be sealed airtight and refrigerated overnight. Bring to room temperature before saucing.

Mince the garlic, ginger, and scallion until fine in the work bowl of a food processor fitted with the steel knife, scraping down as necessary. Alternatively, mince the ingredients by hand. Put in a dish alongside the red pepper. Sealed airtight, the aromatics may be refrigerated for several hours.

Combine the soy, sugar, vinegar, and water, stirring to dissolve the sugar. Use the larger amount of soy sauce and sugar for Western eggplant.

Stir-frying the dish:
Have the eggplant and the remaining ingredients all within easy reach of your stovetop.

Heat a wok or medium-size, heavy skillet over high heat until hot enough to evaporate a bead of water on contact. Add the corn or peanut oil, swirl to glaze the pan, then lower the heat to medium. When the oil is hot enough to sizzle a bit of garlic, add the aromatics, nudging the chili flakes in last. Stir until fully fragrant, about 20–40 seconds, adjusting the heat so they foam without browning. When the fragrance is pronounced, stir the liquids and scrape them into the pan. Stir, wait for the liquid to boil around the edges, then add the eggplant and stir to combine it with the sauce and heat it through. Turn off the heat and taste. Adjust if required with a bit more sugar to bring the spiciness to the fore, then add the sesame oil and stir to combine. Scrape the eggplant into a serving bowl of contrasting color, then smooth the top with the spatula.

Serve the eggplant hot, tepid, at room temperature, or chilled, garnished with scallion. Left to sit for several hours or overnight, the flavors will enlarge and the

spiciness will become pronounced. Cover tightly and refrigerate once cool.
	Leftovers keep beautifully 3–4 days, sealed airtight and refrigerated.

MENU SUGGESTIONS:
This is an excellent opening to a hot dinner, paired with a Chenin Blanc. As part of a cold table, you might partner it with *Tea and Spice Smoked Chicken* (page 158), *Master Sauce Chicken* (page 153), *Scallion and Ginger Explosion Shrimp* (page 233), and *Orchid's Tangy Cool Noodles* (page 356). In a Western menu, it is a delicious accompaniment to unadorned broiled or grilled poultry or fish.

Dry-Fried Szechwan String Beans

乾煸四季豆

This is a stir-fry of *deep-fried* string beans, tossed with zesty condiments and bits of pork, then glazed with a sauce that one lets nearly evaporate in order to concentrate its flavor (this being what is known as dry-frying). It is one of the dishes for which Szechwan is famed—yet it hasn't a speck of chili in it. What makes it typically Szechwanese is the liberal use of dried and pickled condiments to create a pungency that moves one to eat more. ◆ Tender, young, and full-flavored beans are a prerequisite for this dish. Leathery Kentucky Wonders or overgrown and gnarled Chinese longbeans are simply not worth trying, and the otherwise lovely French *haricots verts* (which are now grown in Mexico) are here too delicate. The perfect bean should be tasty and tender enough to enjoy raw, yet possessed of enough body to withstand the deep-frying. Jersey beans are ideal, to praise my native state. ◆ This is a good dish hot, but is even better made in advance and served at room temperature when its flavors have had a chance to marry.

TECHNIQUE NOTES:
When deep-frying anything that cools the oil significantly (on account of its bulk or water content), it is crucial to allow the oil to regain its original high temperature before deep-frying the next batch. Oil used to fry even a scant half-pound of beans may require a full 5 minutes to climb back to 400°, depending on your stove. Be patient. If you rush the next batch, it will turn out greasy because the oil was too cool.

Serves 4 as a substantial vegetable course, 6–8 as part of a multicourse meal. For large parties, I go to the market and count out a loose fistful of beans per guest, then weigh and tally them with the recipe.

INGREDIENTS:

    1½ pounds fresh young string beans, or tender Chinese longbeans

  Condiments:
    2 rounded tablespoons dried shrimp (page 565)
    1 small walnut-size nugget fresh ginger
    2 ounces (6 tablespoons) Tientsin preserved vegetable (page 575)
    2 ounces ground pork butt

    4–6 cups corn or peanut oil, for deep-frying

Liquid seasonings:
1 tablespoon sugar
¾ teaspoon coarse kosher salt
¼ cup light, unsalted chicken stock or water

1 tablespoon well-aged Chinese black vinegar or balsamic vinegar (page 577)
1 teaspoon Chinese or Japanese sesame oil
1 tablespoon chopped green and white scallion

To garnish:
1 tablespoon freshly chopped scallion

Preparations:
Cut off the tips of the beans and cut longbeans into even lengths about 5 inches long. Rinse with cool water, then dry thoroughly to avoid spattering when fried.

Soak the shrimp in very hot tap water to cover until you can chew on one and enjoy its saltiness, about 15 minutes. Drain and pick through to discard any bits of shell.

Mince the ginger in the work bowl of a food processor fitted with the steel knife. Add shrimp and process with on-off turns until coarsely chopped. Add the preserved vegetable, process with 2 on-off turns to expose new surface, then scrape the mixture into a dish alongside the pork.

Alternatively, mince the ginger and coarsely chop the shrimp and preserved vegetable by hand.

The above may be done up to a day in advance of cooking. Seal the beans and condiments airtight and refrigerate. Bring to room temperature before cooking.

Deep-frying the beans:
Divide the beans into 2 equal batches and put each on a flat plate. Have the beans, cooking chopsticks or a long wooden spoon, a large Chinese mesh spoon, a bowl to hold the fried beans, and a large lid all within easy reach of your stovetop.

Heat a wok or a large, very deep, heavy skillet over high heat until hot. Add the oil, leaving 3–4 inches free at the top of the pot to accommodate bubbling. Heat the oil to the dense-haze stage, 400° on a deep-fry thermometer, when a thick haze is visible above the surface but the oil has not yet begun to smoke. Adjust the heat so the temperature does not climb, then test the oil with a single bean. It should come immediately to the surface surrounded by white bubbles.

Return the heat to high and slide the first plate of beans into the oil. Shield yourself from spatters by holding the pot lid several inches above the oil and angled away from you. Do not *cover* the pot. Give the beans a gentle stir to even them. After about 30 seconds, the bubbling will die down and you can put the lid aside.

Fry the beans over high heat for about 4 minutes or until thoroughly wrinkled, stirring occasionally. Remove them from the oil with the mesh spoon, hold briefly above the pot to drain, then transfer to the empty bowl or pot. If fried properly, the beans will look limp and pitiful.

Wait a full 3–4 minutes or longer for the oil to regain a temperature of 400°. Test again with a single bean, then repeat the process with the next batch. When both batches are fried, tip the bowl to drain off excess oil. The beans may be left uncovered at room temperature for several hours before continuing.

Once the oil cools, strain and bottle it for future use.

Stir-frying the beans:

Combine the sugar and salt with the stock, and leave the spoon in the bowl. Have the beans, the minced condiments, the combined liquids, and the remaining ingredients all within easy reach of your stovetop.

Heat a wok or large, heavy skillet over high heat until hot enough to evaporate a bead of water on contact. Add 2½ tablespoons of the deep-frying oil and swirl to coat the pan. When the oil is hot enough to sizzle a bit of ginger, add the minced mixture and pork. Stir-fry briskly, chopping and poking the pork to break it into tiny bits, adjusting the heat so it sizzles without scorching.

When the pork is 90 percent gray, give the liquids a stir and add them to the pan. Stir to blend, then raise the heat to bring the mixture to a simmer. Add the beans and toss to combine until most all the liquid has evaporated. Rapidly sprinkle in the vinegar, fold in the sesame oil and scallion, then turn off the heat.

Taste and adjust if needed with a bit more salt, sugar, or vinegar. The taste should be very zesty. When you have the taste you want, scrape the mixture into a large serving bowl or plate.

For best flavor, let the beans stand several hours at room temperature or refrigerate overnight once cool, stirring occasionally. Serve at room temperature, not cold, to enjoy the full flavor and aroma. Just before serving, garnish with a fresh sprinkling of scallion.

Leftovers keep beautifully, sealed airtight and refrigerated, for 3–4 days. Bring to room temperature before eating, stirring up the oils and seasonings from the bottom of the dish.

MENU SUGGESTIONS:

I love this dish in tandem with cold dishes such as *Orchid's Tangy Cool Noodles* (page 356), *Scallion and Ginger Explosion Shrimp* (page 233), *Master Sauce Chicken* (page 153), or *Tea and Spice Smoked Chicken* (page 158). It will also add zest to a simple dinner of *Hunan Pork Dumplings with Hot Sauce* (page 379), *Moslem-Style Beef or Lamb Pot Stickers* (page 384), or *Pan-Fried Meat Pies* (page 387). *Saucy Potted Pork* (page 207) and *Tea and Spice Smoked Fish* (page 256) are also dishes that mate well with the beans.

Spicy Buddha's Feast 羅漢齋

One of the classics of Chinese Buddhist cuisine is known as "Pure Meal of the Arhats"—pure meal being a euphemism for vegetarian dish, and arhats (or bodhisattvas as they are often called), referring to the bevy of Buddhas-on-earth who relinquished life in the upper realms in order to serve a nobler existence in the world of suffering below. In its standard form the dish includes soft ginko nuts, black mushrooms, tangles of hair-fine seaweed, and small wads of soy-seasoned wheat gluten, all in a purposefully mild and unscintillating brown sauce. Not much of a feast! This rendition is heretically different. It is very colorful and full-flavored, and also highly spiced—the path to my own culinary illumination being frequently strewn with chilies. ◆ This is a dish that makes broad use of canned and dried ingredients—all excellent and easily obtainable either in Oriental markets or through mail order (page 588). Once you have in stock the requisite cans and bags, all that is needed is one or two bright-looking fresh vegetables and the feast is on its way. Lest the list of ingredients daunt you, be assured that most things Buddhist are invitingly flexible.

Hence, one vegetable may be used instead of two, you may double the baby corn in the absence of straw mushrooms, or you may enliven the braised tofu with a shot of chili oil if the curried gluten is unavailable. The only rule is to mix dried, canned, and fresh ingredients in equal amounts, keeping it strictly vegetarian to please the Buddha. ◆ Preparations are simple and may be done a day or more ahead.

TECHNIQUE NOTES:
If there is one thing to remember here, it is to *taste*. The variables of canned and dried products are such that a bit of salt, a pinch of sugar, or that extra dash of soy or spice, is just what is needed to turn something bland into something lively.

For soaking bean threads to proper resiliency for a stir-fry, see TECHNIQUE NOTES, page 371.

Serves 3–4 as a main dish, 6–8 as part of a multicourse meal.

INGREDIENTS:

For the feast:
2 ounces bean threads (glass noodles) (page 533)
6 medium or 4 large Chinese dried black mushrooms (page 538)
4 ounces Chinese baby corn (page 531)
4 ounces Chinese straw mushrooms (page 555)
4 ounces "braised dried bean curd" (page 553)
5 ounces "curried braised gluten" (page 553)
2 squares (3–4 ounces) pressed tofu (page 576)
¾ pound fresh green vegetable—Chinese cabbage (page 536), snow peas or
  sugar snap peas, broccoli, zucchini, or any one in combination with the
  Chinese cabbage

For stir-frying:
about ¼ cup corn or peanut oil
¼ teaspoon coarse kosher salt
¼ teaspoon sugar
1½–2 tablespoons thin (regular) soy sauce
¾ cup liquid (about ½ cup water and ¼ cup curried canning juices to taste)

To garnish:
1½ teaspoon Chinese or Japanese sesame oil

Preparations:
Soak the bean threads in warm or hot tap water until rubber-band firm. Do not oversoak, lest they turn to mush when cooled. Drain, cut through the loop ends of the skein into 5-inch lengths, then cut and discard the rubber bands or strings holding the skein together.

Soak the black mushrooms in cold or hot water to cover until fully soft and spongy, 20 minutes to an hour. Drain, snip off and discard the stems, then rinse the caps under running water to dislodge any sand trapped in the gills. Cut the caps in half if you have more feasters than mushrooms.

Drain the canned corn and canned mushrooms. Rinse, then shake dry. Extra corn and mushrooms may be refrigerated up to 2 weeks, in water to cover. Change the water every 2–3 days.

Cut the "braised dried bean curd" against the grain into slices ¼-inch thick.

Drain the "curried braised gluten," retaining the canning liquid, then cut into slices ⅛–¼ inch thick. The remaining bean curd and gluten will keep up to 1 week, refrigerated and sealed airtight. Both make excellent, low-calorie snacks.

Holding a sharp, thin-bladed cleaver or knife parallel to the board, cut each slab of pressed tofu crosswise into slices ⅛-inch thick, anchoring it to the board with "flying fingers" (page 31). Stack the slices, then cut them lengthwise neatly into slivers ⅛-inch wide, using "curved knuckles" (page 32).

Combine all the above ingredients. They may be refrigerated up to 1½ days prior to stir-frying, sealed airtight. Bring to room temperature before cooking.

Slice the Chinese cabbage and/or one of the other vegetables as follows: Cut the cabbage crosswise into bands ¾–1 inch wide, then cut any very long bands in half. Remove the tips and top strings from snow peas and sugar snap peas. Cut the broccoli as directed on page 220, to make pretty use of the stems. Cut zucchini crosswise into rounds ¼ inch thick.

The cut vegetables may be refrigerated overnight in water-misted plastic bags. Bag cabbage and a second vegetable separately.

Stir-frying the dish:
About 10–15 minutes in advance of serving, have all the ingredients and a bowl to hold the vegetables within easy reach of your stovetop. Put a serving platter or bowl of contrasting color in a low oven to warm.

Heat a wok or large, heavy skillet over high heat until hot enough to evaporate a bead of water on contact. Add 1½ tablespoons oil if you are stir-frying two vegetables separately, or add 2½ tablespoons oil if you are cooking only one vegetable. Swirl to coat the pan, then reduce the heat to medium-high. When the oil is hot enough to sizzle one piece of vegetable, add the vegetables and stir-fry briskly to gloss with oil, adjusting the heat so it sizzles without scorching and dribbling in a bit more oil from the side if the pan becomes too dry. When evenly glossed, sprinkle with salt and sugar—half or the full amount, depending upon whether you are cooking one or two vegetables—then continue tossing briskly until the vegetable is almost cooked through, but still very crisp. (Snow peas and sugar peas will require about 15 seconds, zucchini about 30 seconds, and broccoli 1 minute.) Remove the vegetable to the waiting bowl and repeat with the second vegetable if you are using it.

Return the pan to medium-high heat, add 1½ tablespoons oil, then swirl to coat. Add the combined ingredients and toss briskly to mix. Sprinkle with 1½ tablespoons soy, toss to blend, then add the liquid. Raise the heat to bring the mixture to a simmer, stirring. Even the contents of the pan, adjust the heat to maintain a steady simmer, then cover the pan and steam-cook about 2 minutes, or until most of the liquid is evaporated. Reduce the heat to low and uncover the pan.

Stir, taste several noodles (it is the noodles that best absorb the seasonings), and adjust with a bit more soy and/or curried liquids if needed. Return the vegetables to the pan, toss to mix, then turn off the heat. Fold in the sesame oil and remove the mixture to the serving platter. Arrange several of the different items festively on top and serve.

Leftovers keep well 3–4 days, refrigerated and sealed airtight, and increase in spiciness. They are delicious at room temperature, or can be steamed in a covered bowl if you don't mind soft vegetables.

MENU SUGGESTIONS:
I typically serve this dish as a one-course meal. As part of a larger menu, pair it with *Pearl*

Balls (page 187), *Golden Egg Dumplings* (page 328), and *Steamed Whole Fish with Seared Scallions* (page 248). To partner the feast, choose a big-bodied Chenin Blanc, which will be an appropriate "silk curtain" backdrop for the boldness of the spice.

Baby Buddha's Feast

小羅漢齋

This is a pared-down version of the spicy "Big Buddha" on page 299, here limited to those ingredients which are tailor-made for a mandarin pancake (page 439). Fresh snow peas are especially tasty in this dish, but you may also use peeled and shredded broccoli stems, or slivered string beans, or thin ribbons cut from the inner leaves of a Chinese cabbage—most anything that is slightly crunchy and slim or supple enough to be cuddled inside the pancake. ◆ A special beauty of this filling is that it is equally delicious hot, tepid, or at room temperature. So for a mandarin pancake party, you have plenty of leeway to cook it when you please. It may be spiced up or toned down, but my own preference is for plenty of hotness as a foil for the pancake. ◆ All the preliminaries may be done a full day ahead. The actual stir-frying takes only minutes.

TECHNIQUE NOTES:
For soaking bean threads to proper resiliency for a stir-fry, see TECHNIQUE NOTES, page 371.

Serves 2 as a main course, 3–4 as part of a multicourse meal or mandarin pancake party.

INGREDIENTS:

> 3 large or 4–5 medium Chinese dried black mushrooms (page 538)
> 1 ounce bean threads (glass noodles) (page 533)
> 3–4 ounces pressed tofu (page 576)
> 5 ounces "curried braised gluten" (page 553), or "braised dried bean curd" (page 553), or equal parts of each
> ¼ pound fresh snow peas
> 2–3 tablespoons corn or peanut oil

Seasonings:
> ¼ teaspoon coarse kosher salt
> ¼ teaspoon sugar
> 1 tablespoon thin (regular) soy sauce
> ¼ cup water, seasoned to taste with the curried canning liquids or hot chili oil
> 1 scant teaspoon Chinese or Japanese sesame oil (or less, if using hot chili oil to season the dish)

Preparations:
Soak the mushrooms in cold or hot water to cover until soft and spongy, 20 minutes to an hour, depending on the temperature of the water and the thickness of the caps. Snip off and discard the stems, rinse the caps to dislodge any sand trapped in the gills, then cut the caps along their longest side into even strips ⅛-inch wide.

Soak the bean threads in hot tap water until rubber-band firm. Do not oversoak, lest they turn to mush when cooked. Drain, cut through the loop ends into 5-inch lengths, then cut and discard the rubber bands or strings holding them together.

Holding a sharp, thin-bladed cleaver or knife parallel to the board, anchor the pressed tofu with "flying fingers" (page 31) and cut the slab crosswise into slices ⅛-inch thick. Stack the slices, then cut lengthwise with "curved knuckles" (page 32) into long, even shreds ⅛-inch wide.

Drain the curried gluten, reserving the canning liquids. Cut the gluten and/or the braised bean curd into thin slivers ⅛-inch thick. Combine the mushrooms, bean threads, pressed tofu, gluten and/or bean curd. They may be sealed airtight and refrigerated overnight.

Remove the tips and top strings from the snow peas, then sliver them lengthwise into strips ⅛-inch wide. To store overnight, refrigerate in a misted plastic bag.

Stir-frying the feast:

Have all the ingredients and a bowl to hold the snow peas within easy reach of your stovetop. If serving the dish hot, put a platter of contrasting color in a low oven to warm.

Heat a wok or large, heavy skillet over high heat until hot enough to evaporate a bead of water on contact. Add 2 tablespoons oil, swirl to coat the pan, then reduce the heat to medium high. When the oil is hot enough to sizzle one sliver of snow pea, add the snow peas to the pan. Stir-fry briskly to glaze with oil, adjusting the heat so they sizzle without scorching. Sprinkle with the salt and sugar, toss briskly until 90 percent cooked through, about 15 seconds, then scrape the snow peas into the waiting bowl. They should still be very crisp.

Return the pan to medium-high heat, add ½ tablespoon oil, and swirl to glaze the bottom. Add the combined ingredients and toss briskly to mix. Sprinkle with soy, stir to blend, then add the seasoned water and raise the heat to bring the liquids to a simmer, stirring. Cover, simmer over moderate heat for 2–3 minutes, or until most of the liquid is evaporated, then turn off the heat.

Stir the mixture to redistribute the seasoning, then taste several noodles and adjust with a bit more soy or hot stuff if needed. (If you are serving the dish cold, remember the spiciness will intensify.) Fold in the vegetables with several quick stirs, fold in the sesame oil, then remove to the serving platter.

Serve hot, tepid, or at room temperature. Toss lightly just before serving and make the dish pretty by pulling several snow peas and black mushrooms to the top.

Leftovers keep beautifully, sealed and refrigerated, for 3–4 days. For best flavor, eat at room temperature.

MENU SUGGESTIONS:

For a Chinese party, serve this dish alongside *Cassia Blossom (Mu-Shu) Pork* (page 198), *Cold-Tossed Three Shreds* (page 303), and a tall pile of *Mandarin Pancakes* (page 439). For a light lunch, I find it delicious on its own, sometimes wrapped in lettuce leaves or on a bed of lightly dressed fresh greens. A big-bodied Chenin Blanc goes well.

Cold-Tossed Three Shreds

凉拌三絲

This is a salad-type dish of shredded cold vegetables and glass noodles, topped by a spicy peanut sauce and a healthy sprinkling of fresh coriander. It is delicious on its own as a zesty refresher in most any setting, but it has an extra practical beauty at a mandarin pancake party—with the pancakes and this cold filling done in advance, you are free to turn your attention to producing the perfect *mu-shu* pork. ◆ The peanut sauce and shredded vegetable may be prepared in advance. The coriander, lest it wilt, should be chopped at the last minute. If it is sweet red pepper season, add a fourth shred. The color and sweetness of the ripe pepper are irresistible here.

TECHNIQUE NOTES:
Sprinkling the carrots with salt and sugar does a dual job. It softens them by drawing out a bit of liquid, and it seasons them as well.

Serves 2 as a substantial salad course, 3–4 as part of a multicourse meal or mandarin pancake party.

INGREDIENTS:

> 1 ounce bean threads (glass noodles) (page 533)
> ¼ pound fresh bean sprouts (page 532)
> ¼ pound sweet-tasting carrots, trimmed and peeled (to yield 1 rounded cup shredded carrots)
> ¼ teaspoon coarse kosher salt
> ¼ teaspoon sugar
> 1 small red bell pepper (optional)

> To garnish:
> ½ bunch fresh coriander
> Spicy Szechwan Peanut Sauce (page 473)
> or
> Orchid's Spicy Sesame Sauce (page 471)
> or
> Sweet and Silky Sesame Sauce (page 472)

Preparations:
Soak the bean threads until soft and silken, as directed on page 533. Cut into 5-inch lengths, then cut and discard the rubber bands or strings binding the skein. Drain under cool water and shake dry. Once softened, the noodles may be bagged airtight and refrigerated overnight.

Blanch the bean sprouts in plain boiling water for 1 minute, then drain and rush under cold running water until chilled. Refrigerate covered with cold water until use, overnight if desired. Shortly before using, swish to dislodge and remove any green husks, drain, and spread on a dry kitchen towel.

Shred the carrots, toss with the salt and sugar, then let stand for 10–20 minutes at room temperature. Drain off excess liquid. If you are working in advance, the carrots may be sealed and refrigerated 1–2 hours. Toss and drain before using.

Core, seed and derib the bell pepper, then shred lengthwise into neat slivers ⅛-inch wide. To hold 1–2 hours, bag airtight and refrigerate in water-misted plastic.

Cut off and discard the lower third of the coriander stems, retaining the upper stems and leaves. Wash, then spin or pat dry. Once cleaned, the coriander may be refrigerated overnight in a water-misted plastic bag. Pat dry before chopping.

Assembling the salad:
Shortly before serving, pour the sauce into one or two small serving bowls. Arrange the vegetables prettily in rings or mounds of alternating color on a large platter. Chop the coriander coarsely or finely to taste. Sprinkle it lightly over the salad, use a bit to garnish the sauce bowls, then put what remains in a small serving bowl to be passed with the sauce.

Pass the sauce and salad separately, letting each guest choose and toss his or her own portion. Traditionally, the sauce gets rolled up in the pancake with the salad, but there are some confirmed dunkers who are best not thwarted.

Leftover sauce keeps indefinitely. Leftover salad looks jumbled but tastes fine, sealed airtight and refrigerated 1–2 days.

MENU SUGGESTIONS:
For a mandarin pancake party, serve with *Baby Buddha's Feast* (page 302), *Cassia Blossom (Mu-Shu) Pork* (page 198), and *Mandarin Pancakes* (page 439). The salad is also a good partner to cold *Tea and Spice Smoked Chicken* (page 158). In a Western meal, try it alongside grilled fish or in the company (maybe inside the bun?) of a barbecued hamburger.

Stir-Fried Spinach with Charred Garlic 炒菠菜

My all-time favorite meal in New York City's Chinatown (in a restaurant now defunct) was a pan-fried flounder so crisp that the bones were edible, and this slippery dish of garlic-tinged spinach. If you got there on a Tuesday night at about nine, the cook on duty would always char the garlic. If the garlic wasn't burnt, the dish had no panache. ◆ Loose, fresh spinach in clusters is best here. Avoid the bagged variety, if possible, and look for bunches of lively leaves atop thin, supple stems. ◆ This is an exceedingly easy dish to make that is good hot or cold. The spinach may be washed and blanched hours ahead of time, then stir-fried within minutes. If you're averse to charred garlic, you can knock several seconds off the cooking time.

TECHNIQUE NOTES:
The Chinese, with their eye for color and their interest in texture, would not think of discarding the stems or the pretty, pink root ends of spinach. If they are young and lithe as they should be, the stems are succulent. The tips, aside from being colorful, are crunchily sweet.

To cut spinach quickly, use scissors. First cut the leafy tops from the stems. If the leaves are large, cut them into broad bands about 2 inches wide. Next cut the stems into pieces about 2 inches long. Leave the star-like lower cluster of stems intact, but snip off the white, thick root that protrudes from the pink base. If the cluster is large, cut it lengthwise through the base into halves or fourths to make it manageable.

For blanching spinach prior to stir-frying, see TECHNIQUE NOTES, page 307.

Serves 2 as a vegetable with 1 or 2 other dishes, 3–4 as part of a larger, multicourse meal.

INGREDIENTS:

> *¾–1 pound fresh spinach with unblemished leaves, preferably with stems and pink root ends intact*

> *For stir-frying:*
> *1 tablespoon corn or peanut oil*
> *2–3 large cloves garlic, stem end removed, lightly smashed and peeled*
> *¼ teaspoon coarse kosher salt*
> *¼ teaspoon sugar, or a touch more to taste*

Preparations:

Discard any limp spinach leaves and any woody or straggly stems. Wash the spinach under cold running water, using your fingers to rub the area around each pink root end to clean it thoroughly. Cut with scissors as directed above in TECHNIQUE NOTES. If there are still spots of grit or sand, wash again.

Plunge the spinach into a generous amount of boiling unsalted water for 1 minute, then drain immediately in a colander and flush with cold water until chilled. Press down lightly to extract excess water. The spinach may be left at room temperature in the colander for several hours before stir-frying or refrigerated overnight, sealed airtight.

Stir-frying the spinach:

Have the spinach and stir-frying ingredients within easy reach of your stovetop. Put a shallow serving bowl of contrasting color in a low oven to warm. If you are a garlic lover, give the garlic an additional spank with the broad side of a cleaver or heavy knife to expose more surface area to season the oil. Fluff the spinach with your fingers to loosen the mass.

Heat a wok or large, heavy skillet over high heat until hot enough to evaporate a bead of water on contact. Add the oil and swirl to glaze the pan. Wait for the oil to smoke, reduce the heat to medium-high, and add the garlic. Toss and press it against the bottom of the pan—briefly until fragrant if you do not want it charred, or longer to brown it if you desire the full effect. Add the spinach and toss and poke for about 30 seconds to separate the mass and glaze it with the seasoned oil, adjusting the heat so it sizzles without scorching. Sprinkle with salt, stir to mix, then sprinkle with sugar to taste. Stir briefly to combine, then scrape the mixture into the heated bowl. Do not cook the spinach too slowly or over too low a heat, lest it get watery. It should be in and out of the pan within 1 minute.

Serve the spinach hot, tepid, or at room temperature. Leave the garlic in the bowl if you enjoy its slightly barbecued taste.

Leftovers may be sealed and refrigerated 1–2 days and are good at room temperature.

MENU SUGGESTIONS:

I like this vegetable best with simple dishes like *Steamed Whole Fish with Seared Scallions* (page 248), *Saucy Potted Pork* (page 207), *Hakka Stuffed Tofu* (page 343), *Mountain Stew* (page 254), and *Stir-Fried Spicy Clams in Black Bean Sauce* (page 269).

Stir-Fried
Spinach with
Fermented
Tofu

腐乳菠菜

One of the more conspicuous bottles on a Chinese grocer's shelf has floating in it tiny cubes of white or chili-peppered tofu. It is tofu that has been fermented to a creamy, cheese-like texture, and has a pungent, "high" aroma and a distinctive, sharp taste. If you are 100 percent Chinese, you will enjoy it by the chopstick-full, as an accompaniment to a morning bowl of steaming soupy rice. If you are more of a gradualist, you will appreciate it in its other role, as a spirited, light glaze for stir-fried greens. ◆ This is a dish of compelling tastes for adventuresome palates. It is very fresh, lively with the natural flavor of spinach, and—to my tongue, at least—extremely appealing. You needn't wait, however, for an adventurous meal with which to try it. This dish is best paired with simple, straightforward flavors, like those of steamed or pan-fried fish or grilled or roasted meats. ◆ For do-ahead ease, the spinach may be blanched hours in advance. The final cooking takes 1 minute, and the spinach is excellent hot or cold. For a more pungent taste add 1 extra teaspoon fermented tofu to the seasonings.

TECHNIQUE NOTES:
If you add raw spinach to a wok, the result will be a pool of bitter water and a soupy mass of green. The trick is to blanch the spinach before stir-frying it. The boiling water collapses the vegetable cells, expunging much of the water, removing the bitter taste, and leaving the spinach with a smooth and silky texture.

For buying and cutting fresh spinach for simple stir-frys, see page 305.

Serves 2 as a vegetable with 1 or 2 other dishes, 3–4 as part of a larger, multicourse meal.

INGREDIENTS:

> ¾ *pound fresh spinach with unblemished leaves, preferably with stems and*
> *pink root ends intact*

> *For stir-frying:*
> *1 tablespoon fermented tofu cubes with chili (page 575)*
> *1 tablespoon seasoned liquid from tofu bottle*
> *¼ teaspoon Chinese rice wine or quality, dry sherry*
> *½ teaspoon Chinese or Japanese sesame oil*
> *1 tablespoon corn or peanut oil*
> *1 medium clove garlic, stem end removed, lightly smashed and peeled*

Preparations:
Clean, cut, and blanch the spinach as directed on page 306.

Mash the tofu to a smooth consistency, then combine it with the seasoned liquid, wine, and sesame oil, stirring well to blend.

The blanched spinach and blended seasonings may be left at room temperature for several hours before stir-frying. Hold the spinach, uncovered, in a colander.

Stir-frying the spinach:
Have the spinach and remaining ingredients within easy reach of your stovetop. Put a shallow serving bowl of contrasting color in a low oven to warm. Fluff the spinach with your fingers to loosen the mass.

Heat a wok or large, heavy skillet over high heat until hot enough to evaporate a bead of water on contact. Add the corn or peanut oil, swirl to glaze the pan, then wait 3–4 seconds for the oil to heat. Add the garlic and toss it briskly for several seconds until fragrant, regulating the heat so it sizzles without scorching. Scatter the spinach into the pan and stir and poke it for 15–20 seconds, separating the mass and glazing the pieces evenly with the oil, adjusting the heat to maintain a brisk crackling. Pour the blended seasonings evenly on top, stir briskly to coat the spinach and evaporate most of the liquid, then scrape the mixture into the bowl. Do not cook the spinach too slowly or over too low a heat or it will get watery. It should be in and out of the pan within 1 minute.

Serve the spinach hot, tepid, at room temperature, or chilled. I like it best either very hot or very cold.

Leftovers keep 1–3 days, sealed airtight and refrigerated.

MENU SUGGESTIONS:
This is a good accompaniment to *Old Egg* (page 332), *Clear-Steamed Lobster with Scallion Oil* (page 278), *Clear-Steamed Flounder with White Pepper* (page 250), or a simple bowlful of *Ham and Egg Fried Rice* (page 405) or *Celery and Pork Thread Fried Rice* (page 406).

**Spinach
with
Glass
Noodles**

菠菜炒粉絲

This is one of those rare dishes that is exceedingly simple yet very special. Its charm is the play of texture and color between velvety green spinach and slippery glass noodles. It's an easy dish to make, with remarkable appeal. ◆ Like all Chinese spinach stir-frys, this one profits from the inclusion of the tender stems and rosy root ends. Most important, however, are lively and perfect spinach leaves. Wilted or battered leaves are not worth cooking here. ◆ The spinach may be cut, washed, and blanched a full day ahead. The final cooking takes only minutes.

TECHNIQUE NOTES:
For the appeal of spinach stems and roots in Chinese cooking and the method for cutting them, see TECHNIQUE NOTES, page 305. For blanching spinach as a preliminary to stir-frying, see TECHNIQUE NOTES, page 307.

Serves 2 as a substantial vegetable dish, 4 as part of a multicourse meal.

INGREDIENTS:

> 1½ *pounds fresh spinach with unblemished leaves, preferably with stems and pink root ends intact*
> 2 *ounces bean threads (glass noodles) (page 533)*
> 1 *cup rich, unsalted chicken stock*

For stir-frying:
> 3 *tablespoons corn or peanut oil*
> 1 *teaspoon coarse kosher salt*
> ½–1 *teaspoon sugar, depending on the tartness of the spinach*
> 2 *teaspoons Chinese or Japanese sesame oil*

Preparations:
Wash, cut, and blanch the spinach as described on page 306. If you are working in advance, refrigerate the spinach sealed airtight. Bring to room temperature before using.

Leave the rubber bands or strings binding the noodles in place, then put the noodles in hot tap water to cover until rubber-band firm, 1–3 minutes. Drain, cut into 4–5-inch lengths, then cut and discard the rubber bands or strings. Rinse the noodles in cool water and drain well, shaking to remove excess water. If you are working in advance, cover the noodles with cool water and drain thoroughly before using.

Cooking the noodles and stir-frying the spinach:
Have all the ingredients and a heatproof colander or large strainer within easy reach of your stovetop. Put a shallow serving bowl of contrasting color in a low oven to warm. Fluff the spinach to loosen the mass.

Combine the noodles and stock in a small saucepan. Bring to a simmer over moderate heat and cook very gently until the noodles turn soft and silky, 2–5 minutes.

Swish the noodles once or twice as they simmer and keep an eye on them lest they turn mushy. (In the course of simmering, the noodles will absorb most if not all of the stock.) Once silky, drain the noodles in the colander to remove excess stock, then proceed immediately to stir-fry the spinach.

Heat a wok or large, heavy skillet over high heat until hot enough to evaporate a bead of water on contact. Add the oil, swirl to glaze the pan, then reduce the heat to medium-high. When the oil is hot enough to sizzle a bit of spinach on contact, add the spinach and toss briskly to separate the leaves and gloss them with oil, about 15 seconds. Sprinkle with salt and sugar, then toss rapidly to combine and heat through, 30–40 seconds. Work quickly over crackling heat, lest the spinach get watery. Add the noodles and blend with rapid scooping motions until hot to the touch. Sprinkle in the sesame oil, stir 2 or 3 times to combine, then remove to the heated platter. Pause briefly to arrange the vegetable prettily, then serve.

Leftovers keep 2–3 days, sealed and refrigerated, and are tasty at room temperature.

MENU SUGGESTIONS:
There is hardly a more versatile dish than this in the whole of Chinese cooking. Try it with showy things like *Clear-Steamed Lobster with Scallion Oil* (page 278); homey dishes like *Saucy Potted Pork* (page 207); spicier foods like *Hunan Rice Crumb Pork* (page 200); and mild foods like *Silky Egg Custard with Baby Clams* (page 334). Stay away from very spicy dishes that would overwhelm its simple, clear flavor.

Stir-Fried Chinese Cabbage with Sweet Sausage

香腸炒白菜

White Chinese cabbage and red pork sausage are traditional partners in Chinese cooking. It is a yin-yang marriage of soft and solid textures, neutral and pronounced flavors, and contrasting colors and food types. Blanched separately then stir-fried together, the result is a very simple dish with a sweet, understated charm. ◆ What lifts this dish out of the ordinary is the use of the seasoned fat and steaming juices left over from cooking *Tea and Spice Smoked Chicken* (page 158) or *Cinnamon Bark Chicken* (page 162). If you do not have them, use plain chicken fat and chicken stock, and expect to add an extra touch of salt, *Roasted Szechwan Pepper-Salt* (page 476), or freshly ground pepper. ◆ You may blanch the cabbage and sausage hours or even a day in advance, then complete the stir-frying within 2 minutes.

TECHNIQUE NOTES:
Blanching the cabbage prior to stir-frying has three advantages here: It rids the vegetable of any natural bitterness; it partially cooks it, which means less oil, less time, and a cleaner taste in the end; and it gives a busy cook a means of preparing in advance, when the pressure of stir-frying might otherwise ruin a mood or a meal. It is a technique typically applied to spinach, less often to cabbage.

For stir-frying with chicken fat, see TECHNIQUE NOTES, page 311.

Serves 2–3 as a vegetable with 1 or 2 other dishes, 4–6 as part of a larger, multicourse meal.

INGREDIENTS:

3 ounces Chinese pork sausage (equal to 3 thin or 2 fatter sausages) (page 541)

1 pound very fresh Chinese cabbage leaves, cut from the dense, broad-leafed
   variety of Chinese cabbage that is pale white-green (page 536)

For stir-frying:
   1 tablespoon seasoned chicken fat or plain chicken fat (page 544)
   about ½ teaspoon coarse kosher salt, to taste
   ¼ teaspoon sugar
   3 tablespoons seasoned steaming juices, or rich, unsalted chicken stock
   a pinch or two Roasted Szechwan Pepper-Salt (page 476), or freshly ground
      pepper to taste

Preparations:

Slice the sausage into thin diagonal coins, 2 inches long and ⅛ inch thick. Simmer in
unsalted water to cover for 12 minutes, then drain and put aside.

Choose only very firm, full cabbage leaves at peak freshness. Wash and shake off
excess water. Stack the leaves with the curved side down, cut lengthwise through the
middle of the stack, then cut crosswise at 1½ inch intervals into large squares. (Cutting
the cabbage rib side down prevents it from splitting under the pressure of the knife.)

Blanch the cabbage in a generous amount of boiling unsalted water for 1–1½
minutes, until the thinner edges turn translucent. Drain immediately in a colander, then
rush under cold water until chilled. Press gently to remove excess water.

Once blanched, the sausage and cabbage may be left at room temperature for
several hours, or stored for up to 12 hours in the refrigerator. Bring to room temperature
before stir-frying.

Stir-frying the dish:

About 5–10 minutes in advance of serving, have the sausage, cabbage, and stir-frying
ingredients all within easy reach of your stovetop. Put a shallow serving bowl of contrasting color in a low oven to warm.

Heat a wok or large, heavy skillet over high heat until hot enough to evaporate a
bead of water on contact. Add the chicken fat, swirl to coat the pan, and reduce the heat if
necessary to keep the fat from smoking. When the oil is hot enough to sizzle one slice of
sausage, add the sausage coins and stir-fry briskly to coat and separate them. Add the
cabbage and stir-fry to glaze the pieces evenly with the oil, adjusting the heat so the
cabbage sizzles without scorching. Sprinkle with salt, toss to mix, then sprinkle with
sugar and toss briskly to combine. Add the steaming juices or stock, and raise the heat to
bring the liquids to a simmer, stirring. Cover the pan for about 20 seconds while the
contents bubble under the lid, then remove the cover, stir once or twice, and reduce the
heat to low. Taste and correct the seasonings as needed with a dash of salt, pepper-salt, or
pepper. The taste should be predominately fresh and sweet, with a hint of pepper to offset
the sausage. Scrape the mixture at once into the serving bowl and arrange several of the
sausage coins on top. The dish may be held at room temperature for 4–5 minutes before
serving, during which time the sausage grows appealingly chewy. Do not delay the serving further or it will harden.

Leftovers may be resteamed in a tightly covered bowl until hot. The coins and
cabbage are not as tasty as when first made, but the broth is extraordinary.

MENU SUGGESTIONS:
This is a versatile vegetable, useful where an understated touch of sweetness is desired. I like it best with very simple foods like *Old Egg* (page 332), *Clear-Steamed Flounder with White Pepper* (page 250), or *Tea and Spice Smoked Fish* (page 256). It is also a good complement to casseroles such as *Casseroled Chicken with Smoky Chestnuts* (page 156).

It took me years to bring myself to cook a plate of Chinese cabbage. My first week in Taiwan I ate virtually nothing but, being a panicky vegetarian who didn't have the vocabulary to order anything else. Then, I lived with a very old Chinese who couldn't chew worth a cabbage and would stir-fry the vegetable to a textureless, ignoble death. ◆ What changed my mind was literally the heart of a female cabbage. There it lay on the chopping block, one small cabbage in a ring of miniature "babies." (See TECHNIQUE NOTES, page 112, for the anatomy of Chinese cabbages.) I left the miniatures intact, cut the heart into thin coins, then concocted a dish to change my ways. It is delicate and delicious, a nice contrast of crisp vegetables and silken noodles. ◆ The leftover chicken fat and juices from making *Tea and Spice Smoked Chicken* (page 158) make this dish special. If you don't have them, use steam-rendered chicken fat (page 127) and a rich chicken stock, and spice it with a bit of *Roasted Szechwan Pepper-Salt*. ◆ From start to finish, this is a 15-minute dish.

TECHNIQUE NOTES:
Stir-frying with chicken fat turns of necessity into slow-paced sautéeing, owing to the delicacy of the fat and its tendency to smoke at low temperature. Do not raise the heat or try to hurry the process, lest the fat burn.

Serves 2 as a single vegetable, 3–4 as a small portion in a multicourse meal.

INGREDIENTS:

> ½ *pound Chinese cabbage heart (cut from a cabbage weighing 1½–2 pounds;*
> *to equal 1½ cups thin-sliced coins or wedges)*
> 1 *ounce bean threads (glass noodles) (page 533)*

> For stir-frying:
> 5–6 *teaspoons chicken fat, preferably rendered from a smoked chicken*
> ¼ *cup thin-cut green and white scallion rings*
> *scant 1 cup rich unsalted chicken stock, preferably the juices rendered from*
> *steaming a smoked chicken*
> *Roasted Szechwan Pepper-Salt (page 476), to taste (optional)*

Preparations:
Read about male and female cabbages in TECHNIQUE NOTES, page 112.

If the cabbage is a female, with tiny miniature cabbages arranged around the central core, pull off the miniature whole cabbages as you cut the core and put them aside. With a sharp cleaver or knife cut the base of the cabbage crosswise into thin disks, evenly ¹⁄₁₆ inch thick. As the leaves come free, stack them to the side, then continue slicing the base into thin disks and pulling off the whole baby cabbages. If once the entire heart is cut you don't have ½ pound thin disks and tiny whole cabbages, then cut the crispest ribs crosswise into narrow bands to make up the desired weight. Include also any flowers you may find at the core.

If the cabbage is a male, with only a single disk for the base, cut the base off ½ inch from the bottom, and cut it pie-fashion into wedges a scant ¼ inch wide. Stack the leaves that fall free to one side, then cut another ½-inch thick slice from the base and cut it into wedges. If once you have cut the entire heart you don't have ½ pound of wedges, then cut the firmest of the inner leaves crosswise into narrow bands to make up the desired weight.

Divide the usual 2-ounce package of bean threads in half by cutting through the loop ends of the skein with sturdy scissors and pulling away the required amount of noodles. Soak in hot tap water until rubber-band firm, drain and shake dry.

The cabbage and noodles may be prepared, bagged, and refrigerated a day in advance. Mist the cabbage lightly with water before storing.

Stir-frying the cabbage:
If you are using juices rendered from a smoked chicken, taste them for salt. If the taste is too strong, dilute the juices with enough unsalted chicken stock to make an appealing scant cup.

Have all the ingredients within easy reach of your stovetop. Put a shallow serving bowl of contrasting color in a low oven to warm. Reserve ½ tablespoon scallion rings as a garnish.

About 10 minutes before serving, heat a wok or large, heavy skillet over high heat until hot enough to sizzle a bead of water on contact. Reduce the heat to medium-low, add 4 teaspoons fat to the pan, and swirl to coat the bottom. When the fat is hot enough to gently sizzle one scallion ring—check after 3–4 seconds—add the scallions. Stir in small circles until fragrant, about 10 seconds, adjusting the heat so the scallions sizzle and the fat does not smoke. Add the cabbage, then toss several minutes just until translucent, adding a bit more fat if the pan gets too dry. Add the noodles, stir to combine, then add the stock and raise the heat to bring the liquid to a simmer, stirring. Cover and simmer gently for 1 minute, or until the noodles are slippery-smooth and there is only ¼ of the liquid left in the pan.

Turn off the heat, remove the cover, then taste and adjust with a pinch of pepper-salt if needed. Stir once or twice, remove to the heated serving bowl, and serve immediately, garnished with a sprinkling of the reserved scallion rings.

Eat this dish up. Like most things stir-fried with chicken fat, it is terrible cold.

MENU SUGGESTIONS:
This is an extremely versatile vegetable, especially good in the company of simple poultry and fish dishes such as *Paper-Wrapped Chicken* (page 150), *Tea and Spice Smoked Chicken* (page 158), *Steamed Whole Fish with Seared Scallions* (page 248), *Clear-Steamed Flounder with White Pepper* (page 250), and *Deep-Fried Shrimp Balls* (page 240). It also has a nice affinity for pork dishes—*Hunan Rice Crumb Pork* (page 200), *Saucy Potted Pork* (page 207), *Velvet Pork Pie with Szechwan Pickle* (page 189), *Crispy Pork Balls* (page 185). Do not hesitate to serve it in a Western setting, as an accompaniment to grilled, braised, or roasted meats, fish, or poultry.

<table>
<tr><td>

Brussels Sprouts with Black Sesame Seeds

炒小包心菜

</td><td>

This is a simple, colorful dish of interesting tastes and textures. The tiny cabbages are steamed just until tender, then tumbled in aromatic oil with a sprinkling of Smithfield ham and black sesame seeds. It is an unusual combination, with great taste appeal. ◆ This is a wonderful dish in which to use the seasoned fat left over from smoking or steaming chickens. If you don't have it and are using corn or peanut oil or a less salty ham, then add the extra

</td></tr>
</table>

roasted pepper-salt to offset the character of the cabbage. For best taste, use small Brussels sprouts, which are particularly sweet and delicate. ◆ The sprouts may be steamed hours in advance, then stir-fried within 1 minute. Hot or cold, they are unusually good.

TECHNIQUE NOTES:
Steaming the vegetable cooks it to tenderness. Stir-frying deepens the color and adds an appealing gloss and flavor.

INGREDIENTS:

¾ pound fresh, small or medium-size Brussels sprouts

For stir-frying:
1 tablespoon corn or peanut oil or seasoned chicken fat (page 544)
1½ tablespoons finely minced Smithfield ham (page 549)
rounded ½ teaspoon black sesame seeds (page 565)
¹⁄₁₆–¼ teaspoon Roasted Szechwan Pepper-Salt (page 476)
1 teaspoon Chinese rice wine or quality, dry sherry
1 teaspoon Chinese or Japanese sesame oil (omit if using seasoned fat)

Trimming and steaming the Brussels sprouts:
(For details on steaming and how to improvise a steamer, see page 60.)
Trim the hard stem ends off the Brussels sprouts, removing just enough to expose new flesh, and discard any faded outer leaves. Arrange in a single layer on a heatproof plate and steam over high heat just until tender, about 8–12 minutes depending on size, when the core can be pierced easily with the tip of a sharp knife. Do not oversteam. The cabbages lose most all of their appeal when mushy.
If you are not stir-frying them immediately, rush the sprouts under cold water until chilled to stop the cooking and set the color. Pat dry, then put aside for up to several hours at room temperature or covered overnight in the refrigerator. Bring to room temperature before stir-frying.

Stir-frying the dish:
Have the Brussels sprouts and the stir-frying ingredients all within easy reach of your stovetop. Put a shallow serving bowl of contrasting color in a low oven to warm.
Heat a wok or large, heavy skillet over moderate heat until hot enough to sizzle a bead of water on contact. Add the oil or fat and swirl to glaze the bottom of the pan. If you are using chicken fat, do not allow it to smoke. When the oil is hot enough to sizzle a single Brussels sprout, add the sprouts and stir gently to coat, about 20–30 seconds, adjusting the heat so they sizzle gently without scorching. Sprinkle the ham and sesame

seeds on top, stir to mix, then sprinkle with pepper-salt—sparsely if using seasoned fat and Smithfield ham, more liberally if using corn or peanut oil or a less salty ham. Toss to mix, splash with wine, toss, then fold in the sesame oil. Taste, adjust salt if required, then scrape the mixture into the heated bowl. The Brussels sprouts should be in and out of the pan within 1 minute.

Serve the Brussels sprouts hot, tepid or at room temperature. If serving them as part of a cold platter, you may wish to cut them in half and arrange them in a pattern. Otherwise, leave them whole, looking like a bowlful of carved jade.

Leftovers are excellent cold and will keep 2–3 days, refrigerated and tightly sealed.

MENU SUGGESTIONS:
The sprouts are particularly good with hot or cold poultry dishes like *Master Sauce Chicken* (page 153), *Tea and Spice Smoked Chicken* (page 158), and *Smoked Tea Duck* (page 169). Also with meaty dishes such as *Saucy Potted Pork* (page 207) and *Velvet Pork Pie with Szechwan Pickle* (page 189). As an accompaniment to fish, they will go nicely with *Clear-Steamed Flounder with White Pepper* (page 250) and *Tea and Spice Smoked Fish* (page 256).

| **Red Bell Pepper with Garlic and Coriander**
蒜爆紅椒 |

If every green bell pepper were a red bell pepper, I'd be a lot happier. The red pepper is the ripe fruit—clean, sweet, and clear-tasting, with none of the acrid beginnings or gaseous after-effects of the green. "If I were emperor of the universe" (as a friend of mine likes to say), I would make nine and a half out of every ten bell peppers red and save the green bit for an occasional garnish or for someone I didn't like. ◆ This, when I have firm, fresh, and wonderfully *red* bell peppers, is what I most like to do with them. It is a simple stir-fry of pepper cubes in garlic-infused oil, splashed lightly with soy and rice vinegar, then made colorful with fresh coriander. It is a dish of naturally sweet tastes that is good hot, tepid, or at room temperature. ◆ Preparations take only minutes.

TECHNIQUE NOTES:
Adding both salt and soy to a stir-fry is very common in Chinese cooking for reasons apart from taste. Here, the salt coaxes a bit of liquid from the peppers and heightens its natural flavor. The soy provides the liquid further needed to steam-cook the vegetable and a contrasting color to offset the red.

Serves 3–4 as a single vegetable, 6–8 as a small offering at a multicourse meal.

INGREDIENTS:

3 large, firm, unblemished red bell peppers (about 1¼ pounds)

For stir-frying:
1½–2 tablespoons corn or peanut oil
2–3 teaspoons finely minced fresh garlic
¼ teaspoon coarse kosher salt
2 teaspoons thin (regular) soy sauce
1 teaspoon unseasoned Chinese or Japanese rice vinegar
¼ cup loose-packed coarsely chopped fresh coriander leaves

To garnish:
½ teaspoon Chinese or Japanese sesame oil
a sprig or two of fresh coriander

Preparations:
Cut the peppers in half lengthwise. With a small sharp knife carefully remove the core, seeds, and any fleshy white ribs, and cut the peppers into cubes about 1 inch square. If you are not proceeding to cook them immediately, fleck lightly with water, bag airtight in plastic, and refrigerate for up to 8 hours. Pat dry before using. (In this sort of simple stir-fry, I much prefer to use the cut vegetable almost immediately. The juices which appear on the flesh as soon as it's cut seem too precious to lose.)

Mince the garlic and chop the coriander just before using.

Stir-frying the dish:
Have all the ingredients within easy reach of your stovetop. If you plan to serve the peppers hot, put a shallow serving bowl of contrasting color in a low oven to warm.

Heat a wok or large, heavy skillet over high heat until hot enough to sizzle a bead of water on contact. Add 1½ tablespoons oil, swirl to coat the pan, then reduce the heat to medium. When the oil is hot enough to sizzle one bit of garlic, add the garlic and stir gently until fragrant, about 5 seconds, adjusting the heat so it foams without browning. Add the pepper, then toss briskly to glaze with oil, regulating the heat so it sizzles without scorching. If the pan becomes very dry, dribble in a bit more oil from the side of the pan. Sprinkle with salt, then stir to combine.

When the peppers are evenly salted and hot to the touch, splash in the soy. Stir to mix, splash with vinegar, then stir to mix—all within seconds, lest the liquids evaporate. Sprinkle in the coriander, toss briefly to combine, then cover the pot. Remove it from the heat and let it sit for 1 minute to cook the peppers through from their own steam.

Uncover the pan, sprinkle the peppers with sesame oil, then stir two or three times to mix. Scrape the mixture into the serving bowl, turn some of the peppers prettily bright side up, and garnish with the sprigs of coriander.

Serve hot, tepid, or at room temperature. Stir before serving to redistribute the seasonings.

Leftovers stay tasty 1–2 days, refrigerated and tightly sealed. Eat at room temperature or slightly chilled and stir just before serving.

MENU SUGGESTIONS:
This colorful vegetable is a good partner for *Spicy Steamed Salmon with Young Ginger* (page 252), *Tofu and Salmon in Pepper Sauce* (page 346), *Tea and Spice Smoked Chicken* (page 158), *Master Sauce Chicken* (page 153), and *Smoked Tea Duck* (page 169). At room temperature, it is also excellent with cold poultry salads and cold fish.

Steamed Winter Melon with Ham

火腿蒸冬菇

This dish is neither a soup nor a vegetable, but something in between—a slightly soupy vegetable that I serve in a bowl to accompany rather splendid dishes like duck, which needs to be paired with delicate, unfatiguing morsels. It is an exceptionally pretty dish in its quiet way, very subtle and smooth on the tongue. ◆ Winter melon is a vegetable, not a fruit as one might expect. It looks a bit like a tallish green pumpkin from the outside, but the inner pulp is a pale white-green, like the finest jade. If you live in Asia, you usually see shoppers with a cross-slice of winter melon strung with a reed and dangling from their fingers. Or, if you shop in American Chinatown markets, the winter melon will be sold in a wedge, ideally cut on the spot to your specifications. I have recently seen it precut and sold supermarket-style in plastic wrap—often on the dry, downhill side of freshness—and that is a very sad thing. ♦ If fresh winter melon is unavailable, substitute very firm English cucumbers (the seedless variety with edible skins), cut neatly into coins ¼ inch thick. Cook them for a somewhat shorter time, about 15 minutes, or until a knife pierces them easily. ♦ This dish requires minimal preparation and little attention once it is in the steamer. It is ideal at a fancy dinner when you need something elegant but sparing of your energies.

TECHNIQUE NOTES:
Duck or chicken fat as the base for the sauce gives this dish a needed touch of richness. These fats are fragile and will burn at a lower temperature than most so heat them slowly and keep a close watch on the pan. For rendering fat quickly and simply, Chinese-style in a steamer, see page 127.

Serves 2–3 as a substantial vegetable dish, 3–5 as a smaller portion in a multicourse meal.

INGREDIENTS:

> *For steaming:*
> *1 pound fresh winter melon (weight before seeding and skinning)*
> *2–3 tablespoons finely minced Smithfield ham (page 549)*
> *⅓ cup rich, unsalted chicken stock*

> *For the sauce:*
> *1½ teaspoons duck or chicken fat*
> *2 tablespoons thin-cut green and white scallion rings*
> *coarse kosher salt, to taste*
> *1 teaspoon cornstarch dissolved in 1 tablespoon cold chicken stock*
> *⅛–¼ teaspoon freshly ground pepper, to taste*

Cutting the melon:
Seed the melon, scraping away any fibrous matter. With a sharp knife carefully trim off and discard the peel, cutting all the way down to the rind. (Winter melon is not a fruit melon like honeydew or cantaloupe, where the flavor diminishes as you near the rind.) Slice the pulp into domino-shape rectangles ¼-inch thick. The melon may be sealed airtight and refrigerated overnight. Bring to room temperature before steaming.

Steaming the melon:
(For details on steaming and how to improvise a steamer, see page 60.)
About 40–60 minutes prior to serving, choose a deep, heatproof bowl or Pyrex pie plate at least 1 inch smaller in diameter than your steamer. (If this will not be the serving dish, put one large or several smaller individual serving bowls in a low oven to warm.) Arrange a layer of melon slices evenly in the bottom of the bowl, then sprinkle with ham. Continue to build layers of melon sprinkled with ham, then pour the stock evenly on top.
Bring the water in the steaming vessel to a gushing boil over high heat. Add the bowl to the steaming rack, cover the steamer, then reduce the heat to medium-high and steam for 20 minutes. Midway through steaming, lift the lid partway and baste the melon with a bulb-top baster or shallow spoon. If the juices threaten to overflow the dish, re-

move some of them to a small bowl and reserve for the sauce. Quickly replace the lid and resume steaming.

Making the sauce:
At the end of 20 minutes, turn off the heat. Wait several minutes for the steam to subside, then lift the lid and transfer the juices surrounding the melon to an empty bowl. (If you do not have a bulb-top baster, hold the melon gently in place with a plate and tip the bowl to drain it.) Return the melon promptly to the steamer and replace the lid to keep it warm while you make the sauce.

Immediately heat a small, heavy skillet or saucepan over moderate heat until hot enough to sizzle a bead of water. Reduce the heat to low and add the fat. When the fat is hot enough to sizzle one ring of scallion, in about 3–4 seconds, add the scallions and stir gently until fragrant, about 10 seconds, adjusting the heat so the scallions sizzle mildly and the fat does not burn. Add the reserved steaming juices, stir, then raise the heat slightly to bring the mixture to a simmer. Reduce the heat to low, taste, and add salt as desired. Stir the cornstarch mixture to recombine, then add it to the pan. Stir until the liquids become glossy and slightly thick, about 15 seconds, then cover the pan and remove it from the heat.

Quickly transfer the melon slices to a serving bowl if necessary, then stir the sauce once and pour it evenly over the melon. Grind a bit of fresh pepper on top and serve at once. Chinese taste would traditionally insist upon white pepper, so as not to interfere with the pale color of the dish, but use what you like. I use a mixture of black and white peppercorns in a single mill, about 7–8 parts aromatic black to 2–3 parts spicy white.

Leftovers may be resteamed in a tightly covered bowl until hot and are tasty though rather mushy.

MENU SUGGESTIONS:
This delicate vegetable has a particular affinity to poultry dishes such as *Cinnamon Bark Chicken* (page 162), *Fragrant Crispy Duck* (page 172), and *Smoked Tea Duck* (page 169). With the winter melon and any of the above, serve *Flower Rolls* (page 415) for an elegant simple meal.

Steamed Cucumber with Cassia Blossoms

桂花蒸黄瓜

The simplicity of steamed foods can be dramatic, as this dish illustrates perfectly. It has an intriguing taste and is very pretty to look at—a cluster of jade-like circles, all a pale celadon. ◆ All you need are impeccably firm, fresh English cucumbers (the elongated seedless variety with edible skins), a bit of fine honey, and a sprinkling of smoked, finely minced ham. The cassia blossoms are a special embellishment, but you can do without them if the cucumbers and ham are exceptional. ◆ This is a dish that takes only minutes to prepare and steam. The only way to ruin it is to give it too much time.

TECHNIQUE NOTES:
For checking a steamer when every minute counts—as in the steaming of a fish or a delicate vegetable—don't dally. Lift the lid halfway *away* from you, blow the steam away to clear your view, then with your eye or a chopstick or knife, judge quickly for doneness. Once the dish is done, remove it swiftly from the steamer and serve it promptly.

Serves 2–3 as a light vegetable course, 4–6 as part of a multicourse meal.

INGREDIENTS:

> *1 very firm English cucumber, about a foot long*
> *about 1 tablespoon mild wild-flower-type honey or lavender honey*
> *½ teaspoon Chinese cassia blossoms (page 534) (optional)*
> *about 2 tablespoons finely minced Smithfield ham (page 549)*

Preparations:
About 15–20 minutes before serving, cut the cucumber into even coins a scant ½ inch thick. Be precise. They must be cut evenly to steam evenly, or one will be mushy while another remains hard.

Arrange the coins touching one another on one or two flat heatproof plates at least 1 inch smaller in diameter than your steamer. Leave at least an inch free at the rim of the plate to accommodate the juices that will collect during steaming. Use plates on which you can serve the cukes, to avoid having to transfer them once steamed and soft.

Mix the honey with the cassia blossoms to blend. Using your finger, smear the top of each coin with the honey mixture, lightly or more thickly to taste. Sprinkle a bit of ham on top of each coin. Proceed immediately to steam the dish.

Steaming the cucumbers:
(For details on steaming and how to improvise a steamer, see page 60.)

Bring the water in the steaming vessel to a gushing boil over high heat. Add the plate to the steaming rack, cover the steamer, then reduce the heat to medium-high. Steam the cucumbers for 8–10 minutes, until a knife pierces one coin easily. Serve immediately, surrounded by the steaming juices.

Eat this dish up. It loses everything upon cooling.

MENU SUGGESTIONS:
I like this delicate vegetable best with deep-fried poultry such as *Fragrant Crispy Duck* (page 172) and *Cinnamon Bark Chicken* (page 162), and with hot, smoked foods—*Tea and Spice Smoked Chicken* (page 158), *Smoked Tea Duck* (page 169), and *Tea and Spice Smoked Fish* (page 256). If you enjoy light meals of mostly steamed dishes, try it in the company of *Pearl Balls* (page 187).

Steamed Corn with Szechwan Pepper-Salt

椒鹽玉米

Corn, like the potato, is a New World vegetable that plays a minor but sweet part in Chinese cuisine. Grown predominately in northeast China, it is eaten straight from the cob by country folk or stripped into kernels for inclusion in soups and fritters. It was a boisterous favorite in our Chinese household, particularly for breakfast. ◆ This is a no-fuss, 10-minute vegetable that is a colorful accompaniment to most any Chinese meal, especially pretty if steamed on corn silk and served in a bamboo steamer. The requisite is to find the freshest corn possible, ideally picked just before cooking, when the natural sugars have not yet converted to starch. If you are not within sprinting or driving distance of a cornfield and must buy your corn a day old in the market, choose it carefully. Look for firm, unblemished ears with the husks and silk intact, that when pulled back reveal plump, perfect kernels.

TECHNIQUE NOTES:
If you are making pepper-salt especially for this dish, leave it rather coarse but still strain out the husks. The coarse grind and the bits of brown pepper are wonderful texture and color foils for the corn, and the bit of rusticity is in keeping with the dish.

I count 1½–2 large ears of corn per person for a simple, hearty meal, and ⅔–1 ear per person as part of a large, multicourse feast.

INGREDIENTS:

> *fresh as possible corn on the cob, ideally still in the husk*
> Roasted Szechwan Pepper-Salt (page 476)
> *sweet butter, at room temperature (optional)*

Preparations:
As much as 8 hours in advance of serving, remove the husk and silk from the corn. Trim and set aside some of the prettiest silk for lining the steamer. Bag the silk in plastic, cover the corn with a damp towel, and refrigerate if you are working in advance.

Just before steaming, cut off any cob or dry kernels at the ends of the ears, then chop the ears into 4-inch segments with a cleaver or heavy knife.

Oil the bottom of a metal or bamboo steamer basket with a thin film of corn or peanut oil. Spread the silk in a thin, even layer on top, then arrange the corn on the silk, leaving some space between the pieces.

Steaming the corn:
(For details on steaming and how to improvise a steamer, see page 60.)

Bring the water in the steaming vessel to a gushing boil over high heat. Add the corn to the steamer, cover tightly, and steam over medium-high heat about 8–10 minutes or until cooked to a nice firmness. Very young corn takes only minutes; mature ears take longer. Check so as not to overcook.

Serve the corn directly from the steamer with tongs, or transfer to a warm platter, silk and all. Invite the guests to roll the ears in butter and sprinkle them with pepper-salt.

Second helpings can be kept hot in the steamer, with the heat turned to the lowest setting. If left to cool, the kernels wrinkle.

Leftovers may be refrigerated once cool and make great eating for breakfast, re-steamed until hot.

MENU SUGGESTIONS:
For a very simple dinner, I serve this dish on its own alongside a bowl of *Moslem-Style Hot and Sour Soup* (page 450) or in the company of steamed fish—*Steamed Whole Fish with Seared Scallions* (page 248), *Clear-Steamed Flounder with White Pepper* (page 250), or *Clear-Steamed Lobster with Scallion Oil* (page 278). Try it also with *Tea and Spice Smoked Chicken* (page 158). In a Western setting, use it as you would any delicious ear of corn.

Eggs & Tofu

蛋豆腐

◆

◆

Most Chinese cookbooks written in English do not give separate attention to eggs and tofu. Eggs are usually lumped together quite naturally with poultry, and tofu is considered part of the vegetable realm. For me, however, they are foods that stand apart from other categories of Chinese edibles. Much like cheese in the West, eggs and tofu are given a distinct personality by the Chinese in contrast to other foods. They are neither meat protein nor vegetables, but a worthy category of their own. A waiter helping a family to order a meal will often say, "You don't have a tofu" or "How about an egg?" meaning that a dish made predominantly from one or the other is required to balance the beef, pork, poultry, fish, and vegetable dishes already ordered.

Eggs were everywhere in Taiwan. The large covered market near our house had a special "egg alley," bursting with crocks and trays of raw chicken, duck and quail eggs, strangely medicinal-looking duck eggs afloat in a clear salt or brown vinegar brine, and a bewildering variety of cured eggs coated variously in red and gray "muds," thick black ash or prickly mantles of gold and greenish straw—the latter being the so-called "hundred-year-old" or "thousand-year-old" eggs we speak about wide-eyed in the West, which are actually cured for only 2–4 months. On the corners and in front of every theater in the cold weather were the tea egg vendors, while in the warm weather the potted plants that filled every garden and nursery wore bumpy crowns of empty egg shells returning their calcium to the soil.

Tofu was also everywhere in sight. Each neighborhood had its own "factory," usually a small, dark wooden building heaped with curing trays, lined with pressing vats, and rimmed by a waiting line of youngsters who would rush the stuff to market. The markets housed the tofu sellers with their blocks of fresh white tofu and stacks of brown pressed tofu, alongside a mountain or bagful of deep-fried tofu cubes that smelled as savory as meat. Outside at night, the streets harbored the itinerant tofu vendors who peddled a particularly stinky variety whose message floated clear down the block.

Aside from their signs and smells, the years in Taiwan taught me to love eggs and tofu cooked the Chinese way, typically in tandem with highly seasoned and savory condiments for which they are a perfect foil. I have never been enamored of eggs in general, but tea eggs are too beautiful, crispy Hunan egg coins too delicious, and a Chinese soufflé with chives too comforting for me not to make them regularly. With tofu, I feel the same way. The almost tasteless white cubes with their soft, bouncy consistency repelled me when I was first served them. But now I know so many delightful ways to prepare tofu—whipped and seasoned in a vegetable salad, deep-fried then tumbled in a spicy-hot sauce, or stuffed with meat and sautéed with ginger threads and scallion—that it would be a real loss to cook without it.

TYPES OF FRESH TOFU   There is a bewildering variety of fresh tofu sold in America, made even more complex by the assortment of English names given to the product by various manufacturers. In general, the term given it is *tofu* (pronounced *doe-foo* in Chinese and *toe-foo* in Japanese), with the typical English names being bean curd, soybean curd, or bean cake.

The Japanese variety of tofu is extremely soft and silken and does not absorb other flavors readily. It is pleasant in soup, but it will fall apart in stir-frying, and I do not use it for Chinese cooking. If all that is available to you is this very soft variety, then you must weight it or drain it of excess water in order to make it appropriately firm. The method is very simple: First, cut the tofu carefully into cakes no more than 2 inches thick, if it was purchased in one large block. Fold a clean, dry, lint-free kitchen towel in half lengthwise, put the tofu in the center of one half of the towel, then bring the other half over the tofu so that it is sandwiched in between. Put a 2-pound weight on top of the towel, centered over the tofu (I use a small cutting board), then let the tofu drain until it has the firmness of a curd of cottage cheese, changing the towel for a dry one if necessary. The pressing time will vary anywhere from 30 to 90 minutes, depending upon the softness of the tofu when you began. To hurry the process, cut the tofu carefully into smaller rectangular slices a scant inch thick if the recipe permits it, then wrap and weight it as above.

Because of the weight loss in pressing, begin with a fourth more Japanese-style tofu if you are substituting it for the firmer Chinese tofu in the following recipes. For example, if the recipe calls for 12 ounces, then buy 16 ounces.

Far easier, if you have the choice, is to begin with *Chinese-style tofu*, which is generally firmer and more meaty in texture than the Japanese variety, in addition to being 25–35 percent richer in protein. The Chinese types range fully from a semiliquid curd called "tofu brains" in Chinese, to a quite firm, pillow-shape sort called "old tofu" *(lao-doe-foo)*, in reference to the comparatively long pressing. What is called for in the following recipes are the firmer among the Chinese types.

Firm Chinese-style tofu is sold several ways. In Chinatown markets, it is stacked neatly in large tubs of water or on large trays, typically in "cakes" that measure 3 inches square and about 1 inch thick, and what you choose will be bagged for you in plastic. In American markets and Chinatown supermarkets, tofu is packed in 1-pound sealed plastic tubs, in which one large block or 4 smaller, standard-size cakes are completely surrounded by water. Buy the firmest sort available. On the East Coast, a pillow shape typically indicates this variety. On the West Coast, the cakes are more consistently square, and I judge the firmness by feel, pressing my finger against the plastic coating on top of the packing tub if necessary. Firmer tofu will also look a bit different in texture from the softer varieties. The outer broad surfaces often have a creased or mat-like finish owing to the pressing, and the inner curd will show a slightly rough "grain" instead of a shiny-smooth surface.

If the Chinese-style tofu you purchase is not sufficiently firm to be cut neatly, then weight it as described above for 15–30 minutes, or until it is as firm as a curd of cottage cheese.

Do not be confused when shopping for fresh tofu by the ¼–½ inch-thick slabs of brown pressed tofu (called *doe-foo-gone*), which may be sold nearby. This is fresh tofu that has been pressed to the consistency of a solid Swiss cheese, then seasoned with a soy-based mixture that gives it its color. Pressed tofu is delicious shredded in stir-frys like *Spicy Buddha's Feast* (page 299). It is *not* a substitute for fresh tofu.

If fresh tofu is unavailable in your area, you can make your own quickly and easily with a tofu "kit," available in many health food stores and through The Soyfoods Center, P.O. Box 234, Lafayette, California 94549. The cost is minimal, the product is delicious, and to make it is great fun.

STORING FRESH TOFU   Tofu should be perfectly clean tasting and fresh smelling when you buy it, and to maintain it that way for a week to 10 days is a matter of keeping it fully covered with water, changing the water daily, and storing it in the refrigerator. I begin the freshness campaign by changing the water as soon as I bring the tofu home. Also, you want to be gentle when draining and resubmerging the tofu, so that it stays in a whole piece and doesn't break apart.

Freezing tofu will give it a pockmarked, slightly tough texture, which some people like but I find rather unpleasant. If I am faced with cooking it or throwing it out, then

I cook it with the long simmering method described on page 466, which transforms it into a form that can then be kept for another several days.

REFRESHING TOFU THAT IS ON THE WANE   If you suspect that your fresh tofu is beginning to sour, you can refresh it by simmering it in plain water to cover for 3–4 minutes. Some Chinese cooks regularly pour boiling water over tofu and let it sit for several minutes just before cooking it as an extra measure of freshness.

COAGULANTS IN FRESH TOFU   The proteins in liquid soy "milk" must be bound together to form tofu, in the same way as cheese, through the introduction of a coagulant. Inland Chinese tofu makers traditionally used quarry-mined gypsum, while coastal manufacturers used sea-extracted *nigari* (called bittern in the West).

I find tofu coagulated with *nigari* to be slightly sweeter and finer in taste, whereas gypsum-coagulated tofu often has an almost "smoky" quality. It is a fine point, which furthermore may hold true only for domestic American-manufactured tofu, and may have as much to do with the water as with the coagulant used, but it is nonetheless something I look for when buying tofu.

FURTHER INFORMATION ON TOFU   Tofu lovers and curious eaters and scholars alike should consult the extraordinary volume, *The Book of Tofu* (Ballantine paperback). Authors William Shurtleff and Akiko Aoyagi have researched tofu-making in depth in Japan and in Taiwan and have a lucid style that will only entreat you to eat more tofu!

AND A NOTE ON EGGS, REGARDING SIZE AND FRESHNESS   All the recipes in this book call for "large" eggs, which on today's supermarket shelves are usually the smallest of the lot. If you break one open, the yolk will measure a rounded tablespoon and the whites will measure 2 tablespoons. Egg size is quite important when you are using egg whites in a marinade or the whole egg in desserts, so be sure to measure out what you need if you are using a larger than "large" egg.

In Taiwan, we bought our eggs fresh from the market daily, newly plucked from the hen. In America, my prejudice for as-fresh-as-possible eggs holds firm, so I buy them as I need them and do not store them for any length of time except when making tea eggs (see below).

Marbelized Tea Eggs

茶葉蛋

As a child growing up on ballet and opera in America, intermission was synonymous with a carton of sticky orange drink. Later, as a young adult addicted to Peking opera in Taipei, intermission meant a chance to rush outside for a tea egg, snatched steaming from the portable kitchen of an itinerant vendor—a pail of richly scented, tea-brewed eggs set over a second pail of glowing coals, which at the opera's end was dismantled and carried to another busy corner. ◆ These extraordinary looking eggs are easy to make and absolutely stunning, the nicest magic one can work on a hard-boiled egg. Through an ingenious process of cracking the outer shell without removing it, the eggs acquire a batik-like finish of spidery brown lines, which makes them look dramatically like marble. ◆ For best flavor, tea eggs should be left untended in the brewing liquids 12–36 hours before eating, which is ideal in a busy week or when company is expected. Serve them tepid or cold, at the fanciest dinner, or for eating at work.

TECHNIQUE NOTES:

In my experience only relatively "old" eggs are guaranteed easy peelers. For them not to peel cleanly is a disaster for this dish, so my suggestion is to buy fresh eggs and store them uncovered in the refrigerator several days to a week before using. The eggs in the meantime will shrink slightly from the shell, and the Michelangelo results will justify the means.

The tea leaves, on the other hand, should be very fresh and pungent. Dowdy old leaves that are not fragrant contribute nothing.

Count on 1 egg per person at a smaller meal, ½ egg per person at a multicourse dinner.

INGREDIENTS:

> *6 medium or 8 large eggs*
> *1 teaspoon coarse kosher salt*

> *Steeping mixture:*
> *1 tablespoon thin (regular) soy sauce*
> *1 tablespoon black soy sauce*
> *¼ teaspoon coarse kosher salt*
> *2 whole star anise, broken into 16 individual points*

> *2 tablespoons black tea leaves plus one 2-inch length cinnamon stick, crumbled plus 1 thumb-size piece fresh or home-dried orange or tangerine peel, white pith removed*
> *or*
> *2 tablespoons cinnamon or orange-spiced black tea leaves*
> *or*
> *4 teaspoons Constant Comment spiced tea leaves*

Boiling and cracking the eggs:

Begin 12 hours to 1½ full days in advance of serving. Put the eggs and 1 teaspoon coarse kosher salt in a large, heavy saucepan. Cover with a generous amount of cold water, then bring to a near-boil over moderate heat. Reduce the heat to maintain a steady simmer, then cook uncovered for 20 minutes. Drain, then rush the eggs under cold water and let them sit in a cold bath until cool.

Using the back of a large, heavy spoon, tap a network of fine cracks over the surface of each egg, cradling the egg in your palm and turning it gently as you tap. Don't smash them; just a tinker's tap-tap will do. Should an egg lose half or all of its shell, don't worry. One partially or wholly dark egg on a platter of marbelized eggs will look quite beautiful.

Simmering the eggs in the tea mixture:

Return the eggs carefully to a heavy pot that will hold them snugly. Add the steeping ingredients and 3 cups cold water. Bring the mixture to a boil over high heat, stir near the top of the liquid to submerge the tea leaves, then reduce the heat to maintain a steaming, weak simmer. Cover the pot tightly and simmer 3 hours. Check periodically to see that the eggs remain almost covered and add water if needed. Do not add too much, lest you dilute the infusion. Swirl the pot several times while cooking to distribute the liquids over the eggs.

Steeping the eggs:
After 3 hours, turn off the heat. Let the eggs steep in the covered pot at room temperature for at least 8 hours, or for as long as 1½ days. The longer they sit, the richer the flavor and darker the color. The eggs may be eaten tepid, at room temperature, or chilled.

To chill before serving, discard the liquids (they cannot be reused), then refrigerate the unpeeled eggs in a shallow dish. Arrange them in a single layer if they are still tepid to prevent them from being squashed out of shape, then cover airtight with plastic wrap.

Just before serving, peel the eggs carefully, removing the shell and any membrane left clinging to the egg. Cut in half or into quarters if you wish, using a sharp knife and wiping it frequently to keep the eggs clean. Arrange the cut eggs in a pretty spiral pattern on a round platter, yolk side down, quarters joined to look like halves, and alternating darker and lighter eggs for the prettiest effect. Or, if the eggs are small or you wish to serve them whole, pile them prettily in a contrasting bowl, where they will look like a heap of elegant marble paperweights.

Store unpeeled eggs in their shells, refrigerated and tightly sealed. Store leftover peeled eggs in the refrigerator, sealed airtight. Tea eggs will keep 4–5 days.

MENU SUGGESTIONS:
As part of a cold table, present the tea eggs by themselves or in combination with the monochrome *Master Sauce Eggs* (page 327). Extend the menu by including *Orchid's Tangy Cool Noodles* (page 356), *Scallion and Ginger Explosion Shrimp* (page 233), *Carnelian Carrot Coins* (page 289), or *Dry-Fried Szechwan String Beans* (page 297). For a picnic, add *Sweet and Tangy Cucumber Pickles* (page 110) and *Soy-Dipped Red Radish Fans* (page 114). To partner the tea eggs and the cold dishes mentioned above, try a light red wine, such as a light Zinfandel or a Bardolino.

Master Sauce Eggs

滷蛋

This is the homey, deeply colored, and rich-tasting Chinese version of hard-boiled eggs. The cooked eggs are scored, plunked into a pot of hot master sauce (page 153), then left to steep untended for hours. It is a no-work dish, a simple way of transforming dull, everyday eggs into delicious golden orbs with a distinctive fragrance and taste. Even confirmed hard-boiled egg haters (like myself) enjoy them. ◆ The eggs are good warm or chilled, cut into quarters for salads, or left whole for a lunch box or a picnic hamper. You may do them days in advance for company, or enjoy their richness on your own over the course of a busy week.

TECHNIQUE NOTES:
Scoring the egg before steeping gives the flavorful sauce an entryway by which to penetrate and also decorates the egg. When scoring, cut almost down to, but not into, the yolk. Otherwise, the egg will come apart in the sauce.

For suggestions on easy peelers, see TECHNIQUE NOTES, page 326.

Serves 4–6 as luncheon fare, 8–12 as part of a multicourse meal.

INGREDIENTS:

> *4–6 medium or large eggs*
> *1 teaspoon coarse kosher salt*
> *master sauce from making Master Sauce Chicken (page 153), to cover*

Boiling and scoring the eggs:
Put the eggs and salt in the bottom of a heavy saucepan. Cover with cold water, then bring to a near-boil over moderate heat. Simmer 7 minutes. Drain, rush the eggs under cold water until cool, then shell.

Use a sharp thin-bladed knife to make 4 lengthwise gashes at even intervals around each egg, cutting from top to bottom, almost down to—but not into—the yolk.

Steeping the eggs in the sauce:
Bring the master sauce to a gentle simmer in a small heavy pot that will hold the eggs snugly. Taste the sauce, and adjust if required with a bit more water, soy, wine, or golden rock sugar. The sauce should taste rich and well-balanced.

Lower the scored eggs gently into the sauce. Adjust the heat to maintain a slow simmer, cover the pot, and simmer the eggs 20 minutes. Turn off the heat and let the eggs steep in the sauce 1–3 hours, or overnight. The longer they steep, the more intense the flavor and color will be. Swirl the pot occasionally while steeping to distribute the eggs in the sauce.

Remove the eggs carefully from the sauce. Strain the sauce through several layers of cheesecloth, then bottle and refrigerate or freeze for future use.

Serve the eggs tepid, at room temperature, or chilled. Leave them whole or cut them into halves or quarters to show off the pretty coloration.

Sealed and refrigerated, the eggs will keep 4–5 days.

MENU SUGGESTIONS:
Cold, these eggs are an excellent accompaniment to *Orchid's Tangy Cool Noodles* (page 356), *Cold-Tossed Asparagus with Sesame Seeds* (page 288), and *Soy-Dipped Red Radish Fans* (page 114). Served warm, they are good alongside *Stir-Fried Noodles with Chicken and Mushrooms* (page 367), or *Stir-Fried Spinach with Charred Garlic* (page 305).

Golden Egg Dumplings

蛋餃

These succulent, golden and brown dumplings from Peking always bring great pleasure to the eyes of my north Chinese friends. This is comforting food—juicy, tender, lush little pillows for the tongue. Often miniaturized in restaurants for inclusion in soups or hot pots, here they are in their homier presentation, as a main course or a flavorful companion to vegetables. ◆ This is a dish with wide appeal, perfect for entertaining or for bringing to a friend's. Prepare it a half or full day in advance. The flavor deepens and the texture becomes more interesting upon reheating.

TECHNIQUE NOTES:
To make folding the dumplings easier, put the filling on the half of the egg pancake nearest the side of the pan, so the pan braces the dumpling as you fold it closed. It is important to enclose the filling, but do not strive to make perfectly circular pancakes. The irregular, cloud-like edges are part of the dumplings' charm.

Yields about 25 dumplings, enough to serve 4–5 as a main course, 6–12 as part of a multicourse meal.

INGREDIENTS:

>   *To garnish the dumplings:*
>   >   *6 medium Chinese dried black mushrooms, "flower" variety recommended (page 538)*
>
>   *For the filling:*
>   >   *6 large water chestnuts, fresh best (page 578)*
>   >   *1 walnut-size nugget fresh ginger*
>   >   *1 thin whole scallion, cut into 1-inch lengths*
>   >   *6 ounces ground pork butt*
>   >   *1 tablespoon thin (regular) soy sauce*
>   >   *¼ teaspoon freshly ground black pepper*
>   >   *1 scant teaspoon Chinese or Japanese sesame oil*
>   >   *2 tablespoons light, unsalted chicken stock*
>   >   *6–7 large eggs*
>
>   >   *⅓–½ cup fresh corn or peanut oil, for pan-frying*
>
>   *To simmer the dumplings:*
>   >   *¾ cup light, unsalted chicken stock*
>   >   *1½ tablespoons thin (regular) soy sauce*
>   >   *1½ tablespoons Chinese rice wine or dry quality, sherry*
>   >   *1 scant teaspoon sugar*
>   >   *1 scant teaspoon coarse kosher salt*
>
>   *For reheating:*
>   >   *½ cup light, unsalted chicken stock*

Making the filling:
Soak the mushrooms in cold or hot water to cover until soft and spongy, 20 minutes to an hour. Snip off the stems with scissors, rinse the caps under cool water to dislodge any sand caught in the gills, then cut the caps into long strips ¼ inch wide. They may be sealed airtight and refrigerated overnight.

Peel fresh water chestnuts. Drain and blanch canned water chestnuts in plain boiling water to cover for 15 seconds, then chill under cold running water. Cut neatly into peppercorn-size bits.

Mince the ginger and scallion in the work bowl of a food processor fitted with the steel knife, scraping down as needed until fine. Add the pork, soy, pepper, sesame oil, and 2 tablespoons stock, then process with on-off turns to blend. Do not overprocess to a paste. Remove to a bowl and fold in the water chestnuts by hand to retain their texture. Alternatively, mince the ginger and scallion and mix the filling by hand, stirring in one direction until blended. The filling may be refrigerated up to a full day, with a piece of plastic wrap pressed directly on the surface.

To make the dumplings:
Beat the eggs until smooth but not frothy. Put the eggs, pork, and oil, a teaspoon, a cup of chilled water, a small spatula, some paper towels, and a ½ ounce ladle alongside your stovetop. Have a large plate nearby to hold the finished dumplings.

Heat a large, heavy skillet over high heat until hot enough to evaporate a bead of water on contact. Coat the bottom evenly with ¹⁄₁₆ inch oil. Turn the skillet, if necessary, so it sits flat on the burner and the oil is evenly distributed. Wait until the oil shimmers, then reduce the heat to medium. Test the oil. It must be hot enough to cause a dime-size drip of egg to puff with curly edges and be surrounded by tiny bubbles almost immediately on contact with the oil.

Use the ladle to pour 1 tablespoon of egg into the pan. As the egg sets, dip the teaspoon into the water, then scoop up about 2 teaspoons of pork and deposit it in one half of the pancake. While the egg is still a bit loose and will seal itself, use the spatula to fold it in half over the filling. Fry the bottom to a light golden brown, then flip the dumpling over and brown the other side. Transfer the finished dumpling to the waiting plate. Fry 3 or more dumplings at a time, as many as your pan and coordination permit, adding more oil as necessary, and adjusting the heat so the egg puffs instantly and the dumplings fry in a ring of tiny bubbles. Remove browned oil or burned bits with paper towels.

Arrange the finished dumplings in a single layer in a heavy 10–12 inch skillet, overlapping them slightly in a spiral pattern, beginning at the edge, and ending in the center of the pan. Combine the stock, soy, wine, sugar, and salt, and pour the liquids evenly over the dumplings. Scatter the mushroom strips on top.

Bring the liquids to a simmer over medium heat, reduce the heat to maintain a steady simmer, then cover and cook about 10 minutes, or until there is a scant ⅛ inch liquid left in the pan. Turn off the heat, move the pan to a cool burner and let the dumplings sit in the covered pot for several hours or overnight. Refrigerate if your kitchen is hot, and bring to room temperature prior to reheating.

Reheating the dumplings:
About 15 minutes before serving, put a serving platter of contrasting color in a low oven to warm, and add ½ cup unsalted stock to the pan with the dumplings. Bring the liquids to a simmer, cover, and simmer over low heat until most all of the liquid is absorbed. Transfer the dumplings to the heated platter in the same pretty spiral, sprinkle the mushrooms on top, then scrape any remaining pan juices over the dumplings.

Leftovers make wonderful breakfast fare, cold or reheated in a covered skillet with a bit of water, and served with a dab of mushroom soy sauce (page 569).

MENU SUGGESTIONS:
For a simple meal, serve the dumplings with any one of the fried rice dishes (pages 404 to 410). To expand the menu, add *Steamed Whole Fish with Seared Scallions* (page 248), *Clear-Steamed Flounder with White Pepper* (page 250), or *Spicy Steamed Salmon with Young Ginger* (page 252). If more of a vegetarian spirit is desired, pair the dumplings with *Chinese Cabbage Hearts with Glass Noodles* (page 311), *Spinach with Glass Noodles* (page 308), or *Stir-Fried Spinach with Fermented Tofu* (page 306). To accompany the egg dumplings, choose a Chardonnay.

Gold Coin Eggs

金錢蛋餅

Chinese enjoy money symbolism almost as much as nature symbolism in their food. For every "Cavorting Dragon and Playful Phoenix" (an unexpectedly mundane dish of shrimp and chicken), there is a *Gold Coin Shrimp Cake* (page 243), or a *Gold Coin Egg*. Springrolls thought to look like gold bars are standard at New Year's feasts, and ginko nuts are cherished for their likeness to silver *taels*, all in the same spirit. ◆ Of the "gold coin" family of dishes, this is the one least known in the West—a pan-fried heap of crusty, golden egg disks drizzled with a tangy Hunanese sauce. It is an immensely appealing dish, a wonderful novelty for brunch, or a zesty light choice for dinner. ◆ The eggs may be cooked a day in advance, then coated and fried within minutes. Be sure to present them on a round plate, in keeping with the gold coin motif.

TECHNIQUE NOTES:
When pan-frying small items such as egg coins, dumplings, or noodles in a skillet, ring them first along the outer edge of the pan (where the heat is less intense), then work in toward the center (where the pan is hottest). The pieces near the edge get a head start, and the whole panful then browns evenly.

The Chinese are not concerned about the exact time required to hard-boil an egg. The time varies from recipe to recipe, depending on the texture desired. One of my favorite writers on the subject of Chinese food, feisty Buwei Yang Chao, speaks of "hard-boiling eggs so long that they are soft again," and enjoins her readers to boil them for 1 hour! For easy peeling eggs, see TECHNIQUE NOTES, page 326.

Serves 3–4 as a main dish, 6–8 as part of a multicourse meal.

INGREDIENTS:

> *6 large or jumbo eggs*
> *1 teaspoon coarse kosher salt*
> *about 3 tablespoons cornstarch*
> *about ⅓ cup corn or peanut oil*

> For the sauce:
> *¼ teaspoon dried red chili flakes*
> *2½ tablespoons thin-cut green and white scallion rings*
> *½ teaspoon finely minced fresh ginger*
> *¼ cup hot water*
> *¼ teaspoon sugar*
> *2 teaspoons unseasoned Chinese or Japanese rice vinegar*
> *scant 2 teaspoons thin (regular) soy sauce*
> *1 teaspoon Chinese or Japanese sesame oil*

Boiling the eggs:
Put the eggs and salt in the bottom of a large heavy pot. Cover with a generous amount of cold water, then bring to a near-boil over moderate heat. Reduce the heat to maintain a gentle simmer, then cook for 25 minutes. Turn off the heat and let the eggs sit in the hot water for 10 minutes. Drain, run under cold water until cool, then peel.

You may hard-cook the eggs a day in advance. Seal airtight and refrigerate.

Coating the coins and readying the sauce:
About 30 minutes before serving, spread the cornstarch on a small plate. Have a large dry plate alongside. Holding the ends of the egg between your thumb and first finger (so as to keep the yolk in place), cut each egg into 5 evenly thick coins with a large sharp knife. Coat each egg coin fully in the cornstarch, pressing first one side then the other, and finally rolling the rim in the starch. Then put the coated coins aside on the plate.

Put the chili flakes, scallion, and ginger in a small dish. Combine the water, sugar, vinegar, soy, and sesame oil, stirring to dissolve the sugar. Line a baking sheet with a double thickness of paper towels. Put a round serving platter in a low oven to warm.

Pan-frying the coins:
Have the eggs, combined seasonings, the paper towel-lined tray, and the oil all within reach of your stovetop.

Heat a large, heavy skillet over high heat until hot enough to evaporate a bead of water on contact. (If your skillet is less than 12 inches in diameter, you must cook the eggs in two batches. In that case, raise the oven temperature to 250° so you can keep the first batch warm while you cook the second.) When the skillet is hot enough to sizzle a bead of water, coat the bottom evenly with ⅛ inch oil. Wait until the oil is hot enough to sizzle a pinch of cornstarch, about 20 seconds, then reduce the heat to medium. Quickly arrange the coins in the pan, close together but not touching one another, ringing them from the outside into the center of the pan. Adjust the heat so the oil sizzles merrily but not furiously.

When the egg coins are golden brown on one side (check the ones in the center of the pan first), turn them over with chopsticks, a small spatula, or a spatula-shaped cheese slicer. Once the second side is golden, remove the coins to the towel-lined tray and put the tray in the oven while you make the sauce.

Making the sauce:
Return the skillet to medium heat. If the bottom is not slick with oil, then add 1–2 teaspoons more oil. When the oil is hot enough to sizzle one bit of scallion, add the scallion and ginger, nudging the chili flakes in last, adjusting the heat so they foam without scorching. Stir until fully fragrant, about 10 seconds, then give the liquids a stir and add them to the pan. Stir once or twice to mix, then remove the pan from the heat.

Quickly arrange the egg coins on the heated platter, then pour the sauce evenly on top. Serve at once, while the coating is crisp. Leftovers are tasty cold, though not memorable.

MENU SUGGESTIONS:
For brunch, I like to pair these eggs with *Pan-Fried Scallion Breads* (page 435). For a fuller menu suitable for a light meal, add *Chinese Meatball Soup* (page 448) or *Szechwan Pork and Pickle Soup* (page 456), or *Spinach with Glass Noodles* (page 308).

Old
Egg

韭菜老蛋

Chinese do not have ovens, so the Chinese version of a soufflé is done on top of the stove in a heavy, covered pot. It is a dish with a country flavor and a rather dense, chewy consistency I find utterly delicious. "Old Egg" refers to the length of time the eggs take to puff up. It was a nickname given by Po-Fu, the head of our Chinese household, who liked to cook it on lazy, cold-weather nights. Ours was the only home in which I ever ate it, and the only recipe I have ever seen for anything like it comes from the book *How to Cook and Eat in Chinese*, by the delightful Buwei Yang Chao. My suspicion is that it is the invention of playful cooks, with no history behind it. ◆ *Old Egg* takes 2 minutes to put together and about 30 minutes to cook. All that is required is a small, heavy pot with a close-fitting lid (I use a cozy, 2-quart cast-iron Dutch oven bought in the hardware store) and a good book or a good companion with whom to while away the 30 minutes. In the place of Chinese chives, you may use green and white scallion rings or a scattering of tiny bay shrimp, cubed scallops, or picked-over bits of crab meat.

TECHNIQUE NOTES:
East is East and West is West when it comes to soufflés or what Mrs. Chao calls "grown eggs." The whites should not be whipped separately, the eggs should be only lightly beaten, and somehow the puff works better if you begin with cold eggs.

Serves 2 as a one-pot supper with a soup or starch alongside, 3–4 as part of a multi-course meal.

INGREDIENTS:

> *6 large chilled eggs, lightly beaten*
> *¼ cup rich, unsalted chicken stock*
> *2 ounces Chinese chives (page 538), cut into 1-inch lengths (to equal about 3 tablespoons), or 3 tablespoons green and white scallion rings, or ¼–⅓ cup bay shrimp, cubed scallops, or picked-over bits of crab meat*
> *1–2 teaspoons thin (regular) soy sauce, or part soy sauce and part coarse kosher salt if you are using fish and want a very light-colored mixture*
> *4–5 teaspoons corn or peanut oil*

Cooking Old Egg:
Just before cooking, beat together the eggs, stock, and chives or other seasoning. Add the soy slowly, tasting until you get the desired degree of saltiness.

Put a heavy, 2-quart pot over high heat until hot enough to evaporate a bead of water on contact. Add the oil, swirl to coat the bottom and sides fully (you may use an oil-soaked paper towel to complete the job), then reduce the heat to low. When the oil is hot enough to slowly bubble a drop of egg—about 30 seconds if you are using a properly heavy pot—swirl the pot, add the egg mixture, and cover the pot tightly.

Cook over low heat for 20–25 minutes, tightly covered. Only at the end of 20 minutes, peek quickly under the lid, lowering your eye to pot-level and raising the lid only the slightest bit lest the steam escape. To be fully cooked, the egg should be puffed to within ¾ inch of the top of the pot. If it is not fully puffed, shut the lid swiftly but gently and wait another 5 or 10 minutes.

When the egg is perfectly puffed, rush the pot to the table with the lid still in place. Call for the guests' attention, raise the lid, then admire it immediately as it sometimes sinks on the spot.

Cut into wedges as you would a pie and keep the pot covered for second helpings. The dish may stay swollen to the last, in which case you have made a remarkable Old Egg.

Leftovers are charming only if you like cold egg.

MENU SUGGESTIONS:
This dish is especially appealing for a light dinner, in the company of a simple stir-fry such as *Stir-Fried Chinese Cabbage with Sweet Sausage* (page 309) or *Spinach with Glass Noodles* (page 308). Or, try it alongside *Shanghai Vegetable Rice* (page 402) or *Celery and Pork Thread Fried Rice* (page 406), followed by *Chinese Meatball Soup* (page 448).

Silky
Egg Custard
with
Baby Clams
蛤蜊蒸蛋

This is an exceedingly light, delicate dish, whose charm is its simplicity. Known in Japan as *chawan mushi*, or "steamed thing in a tea
bowl," it is a very silky egg custard made with seasoned stock and
a sprinkling of cooked or marinated seafood or poultry, which is
steamed and served hot in individual cups. The steaming gives the
custard a slightly soft texture, unlike the firm baked custards to
which we are accustomed in the West, and I often serve it instead of
a soup to highlight its delicacy. ◆ The prettiness of this dish is mostly a matter of the
cups in which you steam it. I use small celadon or blue and white Chinese sauce bowls
and put a half-cup portion in each bowl. My friends the Lo's at whose table I first savored
this dish use glazed brown pottery crocks with lids. Variously, round or oval white
ramekins, pretty custard cups, or the special lidded *chawan mushi* cups sold through
Japanese importers will all dress up this custard. ◆ Preparations take only minutes.
While the custard steams, you can tend to the rest of the dinner or relax with your guests.

TECHNIQUE NOTES:
Steaming the custard overly long or at too high a temperature will cause it to separate.
The albumen in the eggs will shrink with too much heat and lose its ability to hold
liquids in suspension.

Skimming the mixture of froth insures that the custard will not have holes.
Straining it before steaming encourages a smooth, silky texture.

Serves 6–8, depending on the daintiness of the portion.

INGREDIENTS:

1 8–10-ounce can quality, whole baby clams, well-drained, juice reserved
4 large eggs, at room temperature
1¾ cups rich, unsalted chicken stock at room temperature plus ½ cup
  canning liquid or quality, bottled clam juice
2 teaspoons Chinese rice wine or quality, dry sherry
2 teaspoons thin (regular) soy sauce
about 1 teaspoon coarse kosher salt, to taste
sprinkling of freshly ground white pepper (optional)
4 teaspoons thin-cut green and white scallion rings or thin-cut rings of
  Chinese chives

Preparations:
Beat the eggs lightly, until thoroughly mixed but not frothy. Skim off any froth. Combine
the stock mixture, wine, and soy, then add to the eggs in a thin stream, stirring lightly to
blend. Add the salt gradually, stirring lightly and tasting, until you have added enough.
Add a dash of pepper, if desired. Be caring not to beat the mixture, as excess foam or
bubbles will result in a custard with holes.

Once blended, strain the egg mixture through a fine sieve to trap all the googly
egg bits.

Distribute the drained clams and the scallion rings or chives among the individual cups, then pour in the egg mixture to within ½ inch of the lip. Cover the cups with
their own lids or with aluminum foil to keep out condensation, then arrange them on a
large steaming rack.

Complete the preparations just before steaming the custards. Do not let the mixture sit.

Steaming the custards:

(For details on steaming and how to improvise a steamer, see page 60.)

Bring the water in the steaming vessel to a gushing boil over high heat, then reduce the heat to medium or thereabouts to maintain a steady, gentle steam. Add the steamer rack with the covered cups, cover the steamer, and steam the custard undisturbed for 20–25 minutes. Do not peek at the custard until the time is nearly up, and expect it to look soupy until the final minutes of steaming. The custard is done when a knife or toothpick inserted in the center comes out clean. Do not worry if it seems slightly loose; that is the character of the dish.

Serve the custard hot. I like to eat it with Chinese porcelain spoons, which, like the custard, feel deliciously slippery on the tongue.

MENU SUGGESTIONS:

This dish is best with other delicate dishes, like *Shanghai Vegetable Rice* (page 402), *Spinach with Glass Noodles* (page 308), or *Chinese Cabbage Hearts with Glass Noodles* (page 311). For a satisfying, light meal, serve the custard with either of the vegetables and *Steamed Buns with Minced Pork and Tree Ears* (page 429).

Pearl's Steamed Egg Custard

什錦蒸蛋

For one birthday lunch, my great comrade-in-chopsticks, Barbara Kafka, took me to a fancy New York City Chinese restaurant. There, amidst the high-tech furnishings and the thoroughly un-Chinese hush and fashionable gloom, we were served a splendid small meal. The highlight was this steamed egg custard, brought to the table in one large bowl—the old Chinese sort that resembles a cloud in shape, with an interior glaze of deep turquoise blue and a soupçon of soy on top to dramatize the golden custard. I felt, while eating it, like a Tang dynasty princess. ◆ This is a glorified version of the basic Chinese and Japanese steamed custard (page 334), that is even easier to make as it is served in one big bowl. The glory comes from the trimmings: slippery transparent noodles, slivers of black mushroom, strips of excellent roast pork or ham, with some peas or Chinese chives if you'd like a touch of green. ◆ Preparations are quick and simple. The presentation can be elegant, given the right bowl, demure lighting, and a fashionable hush.

TECHNIQUE NOTES:

The size and shape of the bowl used to steam the custard is in large part responsible for the timing and success of the dish. I use one about 4 inches deep and 7 inches wide. A 1½-quart Pyrex bowl is perfect, in lieu of something fancy.

For further pointers on successful steamed custards, see TECHNIQUE NOTES, page 334.

Serves 2–3 as a substantial dish, 4–6 as part of a multicourse meal.

INGREDIENTS:

6–8 medium Chinese dried black mushrooms, "flower" variety best (page 538)

1 ounce bean threads (glass noodles) (page 533)

⅓ cup sweet peas, blanched in unsalted water until tender if fresh, thoroughly defrosted if frozen, or 2 tablespoons chopped Chinese chives (page 538)

½ cup slivered Chinese roast pork (page 205) or quality, smoked or honey-cured ham

For the custard mixture:

4 large eggs, at room temperature

2¼ cups rich, unsalted chicken stock, at room temperature

2 teaspoons liquid chicken fat (page 544) (optional, but delicious)

1 tablespoon Chinese rice wine or quality, dry sherry

1 tablespoon thin (regular) soy sauce, or 2 teaspoons mushroom soy sauce (page 568)

about 1 teaspoon coarse kosher salt, to taste

To garnish:

1 teaspoon thin (regular) soy sauce

a sprinkling of green and white scallion rings or a cluster of whole fresh coriander leaves (optional)

Preparations:

Soak the dried mushrooms in cold or hot water to cover until soft and spongy, 20 minutes to an hour. Snip off the stems with scissors, rinse the caps to dislodge any sand trapped in the gills, then cut into slivers ⅛ inch thin.

Soak the bean threads in hot water until rubber-band firm, not mushy. Drain, rinse, and drain again. Cut into 2-inch lengths, then gently simmer the drained noodles and slivered mushrooms in 1 cup of the chicken stock until the noodles are silky-soft and transparent, about 2 minutes. Remove the pot from the heat promptly, and let the noodles and mushrooms cool in the stock.

Beat the eggs lightly, until thoroughly mixed but not frothy. Skim off and discard any froth. Combine the remaining 1¼ cup stock, chicken fat, wine, and soy, stirring lightly to blend, then add to the eggs in a thin stream, stirring lightly to combine. Bit by bit, add the stock used to poach the noodles, stirring gently, then gradually add the salt, stirring and tasting several times until you have added almost enough. Undersalt a bit, as the dish will be garnished with a sprinkling of soy. During the entire operation, take care not to beat the mixture or you will create bubbles that will undermine the final texture of the custard. Once blended, strain the egg mixture through a fine sieve to trap all the googly egg bits.

Scatter the mushrooms, noodles, peas and pork in the bottom of a deep, heatproof 1½-quart bowl. Pour the egg mixture to within ½ inch of the lip, then cover the bowl with aluminum foil to prevent condensation during steaming. Proceed immediately to steam the custard.

Steaming the custard:

(For details on steaming and how to improvise a steamer, see page 60.)

Bring the water in the steaming vessel to a gushing boil over high heat. Reduce the heat to medium or thereabouts to maintain a steady, gentle steam, then add the covered bowl to the steamer. Cover the steamer and steam the custard undisturbed for 25–30 minutes. It is done when a knife inserted about an inch down into the center of the custard comes out clean. The texture will be very tender, not firm.

Remove the bowl carefully from the steamer, then lift the foil straight up from the bowl to avoid adding any water that may have accumulated on the foil to the custard. Garnish with a sprinkling of soy, followed by the scallion rings or coriander.

Serve the custard at once. If the table is small and the group is a cozy one, give each guest a small heated bowl and a porcelain spoon and invite them to help themselves, Chinese style, directly from the serving bowl.

Leftovers may be rewarmed by steaming gently in a covered bowl.

MENU SUGGESTIONS:
As a light, one-dish meal, the custard is perfect with *Shanghai Vegetable Rice* (page 402) or *Everyday Chinese Rice* (page 400). For a more lavish menu, try it with *Steamed Whole Fish with Seared Scallions* (page 248) and *Shrimp, Leek, and Pine Nut Fried Rice* (page 408). To complement the custard, choose a fairly zesty, light red wine—a light red Bordeaux, a light California Pinot Noir, or a light California Gamay.

**Smooth
and Spicy
Tofu
Spread**

涼拌豆腐

Mashing chilled tofu with a light dressing of soy, sesame oil, and scallions is a common way to beat the heat in north China. This recipe takes the idea a few steps farther West, whipping the tofu to a thick purée in a food processor and seasoning it with a spicy blend of fresh vegetables. The result is a rich, flavorful spread, ideal with raw vegetables, crackers, or pita bread, and very much to contemporary Western tastes. ◆ For the purée to be perfectly thick, look for the firm variety of Chinese tofu (page 324). If you cannot find it, buy *three* cakes (12 ounces) of softer tofu, and weight them as described on page 323. ◆ This is an excellent way to break in a food processor. The recipe utilizes all of the blades and any slicing failures go into the purée. It is also a good choice for entertaining. Everything may be done in advance, and the finished platter made to look like a colorful, blooming flower.

TECHNIQUE NOTES:
To avoid a watery purée, even firm-style tofu must be drained of some of its water content so it can be flavored with liquid seasonings. Instead of weighting, drain firm tofu by cutting it into large cubes and spreading them cut side down on several layers of paper towels. Within 15 minutes, the towels will have absorbed the excess moisture.

Yields 1¾ cups, enough to serve 4–8 as part of a cold buffet or picnic, 12 as an hors d'oeuvre spread.

INGREDIENTS:

   8 *ounces* fresh white tofu, *firm Chinese style best (equal to 2 cakes, 3 inches square and 1 inch thick)*

Vegetables for the purée:
   6 *large, firm red radishes, trimmed*
   1 *medium carrot, trimmed and peeled*
   2 *medium whole scallions, cut into 1½-inch lengths*
   1 *small, overripe avocado*

Seasonings:
>   2 teaspoons thin (regular) soy sauce, or 1½ teaspoons mushroom soy sauce
>   (page 568)
>   1 tablespoon Chinese or Japanese sesame oil
>   ¼–½ teaspoon coarse kosher salt
>   ⅛ teaspoon sugar
>   ⅛–¼ teaspoon unseasoned Chinese or Japanese rice vinegar
>   ⅛–¼ teaspoon hot chili oil
>   freshly ground pepper to taste

Vegetable dippers (optional):
>   1 large, very firm cucumber, seedless variety preferred
>   2–3 thick carrots, trimmed and peeled

Preparations:
Drain or weight the tofu as described in TECHNIQUE NOTES. When firm and no longer watery, cut into large cubes if you have not already done so.

Slice the radishes into coins ⅛ inch thick, in a food processor or by hand. Put aside some large pretty slices to rim the purée and several smaller coins to garnish the top.

Shred the single carrot. Put about 10 pretty shreds aside for a garnish, along with several green scallion lengths.

Mash the avocado with a spoon until smooth.

Whipping the purée:
Mince the remaining radishes, carrots, and scallions in the work bowl of a food processor fitted with the steel knife, scraping down as necessary until coarse. Add the tofu and avocado, then process until smooth and thick, 15–30 seconds. Add the seasonings, process well to combine, then taste and adjust seasonings if needed. Tofu differs widely in taste, so play with the seasonings to get a taste you like. Be cautious about adding too much liquid, lest you spoil the thickness of the purée. If you do not have a food processor, mince the vegetables by hand, then whip and season the purée in a blender as described above.

Slicing the vegetable dippers:
Trim the cucumber and peel if needed. Cut into rounds between ⅛ and ¼ inch thick, in the food processor or by hand.

Cut the carrots on the diagonal into thin oblong coins, about 2 inches long and ⅛ inch thick. To dramatize their color, blanch in boiling unsalted water 5 seconds, drain and chill promptly in ice water, then pat dry.

Everything up to this point may be done up to a day in advance and refrigerated. Store the garnishes and the vegetable dippers wrapped separately in lightly misted plastic bags. Seal the tofu airtight, with a piece of plastic wrap pressed directly on the surface.

Serving the spread:
For a simple presentation, mound the purée in a bowl of contrasting color and garnish with scallion rings. Serve with a platter of vegetable dippers, unsalted crackers, or triangles of toasted pita bread, and invite everyone to help themselves.

For use as a delicious, portable sandwich, stuff the spread inside a round of pita bread and add some fresh vegetables for crunch.

Or, for those who like to decorate, mound the tofu in the center of a large platter and smooth the top of the purée with a spatula. Rim the purée with fresh vegetables, including the reserved radish coins, or unsalted crackers, or both. Garnish the top of the tofu with a pretty floral mosaic, pressing on overlapping trios of radish coins to make "plum bossoms," frilled scallions to make "branches" (page 563), scallion rings to form "leaves," and dots and shreds of carrot to form "stems," "pistils," or decorative swirls around the blossoms.

Leftover spread keeps well 2–3 days, refrigerated and tightly sealed. If the purée becomes watery, drain and reprocess until thick.

MENU SUGGESTIONS:
I usually present this dish on its own, as a light meal. As part of a cold table, team it with *Cold-Tossed Asparagus with Sesame Seeds* (page 288), or *Tea and Spice Smoked Chicken* (page 158), *Carnelian Carrot Coins* (page 289), and *Marbelized Tea Eggs* (page 325)—any or all.

| Caramelized Tofu Triangles 醬汁豆腐角 | A surprising number of people feel duty-bound to like tofu in its primal form—white, mushy, and tastelessly pure. For those who don't, here is tofu of another color, turned firm and chewy by a brief immersion in hot oil, then caramelized to a deep mahogany brown by a glaze of brown sugar and soy. ◆ This is one of the most appealing cold dishes I know. It is neither too sweet nor too pure—one of those |

engaging middles that draws people from both camps. Serve it as a novel appetizer, a light accompaniment to cold foods, or a bright-tasting midday munch. ◆ The triangles take only minutes to cook. You may do them hours or days in advance.

TECHNIQUE NOTES:
Caramelizing is (to me) a somewhat magical process. The sugar first turns dark, thick, and syrupy in a film of hot oil. Then, it must be diluted with a bit of water to make it *liquid* enough to coat the food. Finally, the liquid must be *evaporated* so the caramel will cling. In this last step it is important not to overcrowd the pan, otherwise the heaped-up triangles will generate too much steam and the caramel will refuse to thicken.

Yields 16 triangles, enough to serve 6–10 as part of a multicourse meal.

INGREDIENTS:

> *4 squares (1 pound) fresh white tofu, firm Chinese-style best (page 324)*
> *5–6 cups corn or peanut oil, for deep-frying*

> *For caramelizing the tofu:*
> *2 teaspoons black (thick) soy sauce*
> *1½ tablespoons thin (regular) soy sauce*
> *3–3½ tablespoons packed light brown sugar*
> *pinch five-spice powder (page 544) (optional)*
> *1 tablespoon corn or peanut oil*
> *3 tablespoons water*

Preparations:
If you are using a soft variety of tofu, weight it as directed on page 323. If you are

using a firm Chinese variety, no weighting is required.

Cut each square of tofu neatly across both diagonals, to yield 4 equal triangles per square, or 16 triangles in all. Stand the triangles on one of their cut ends on a tray lined with a triple thickness of paper towels, and leave them to drain for 15–30 minutes. You may leave them to drain overnight, if you wish, covered with plastic wrap and re-frigerated.

Deep-frying the triangles:
Have the triangles, a tray lined with a double thickness of dry paper towels, a pair of long chopsticks, a large lid, and a large Chinese mesh spoon all within easy reach of your stovetop.

Heat a wok or deep, heavy skillet over high heat until hot. Add the oil, leaving several inches at the top of the pot to accommodate bubbling. Heat to the light-haze stage, 375° on a deep-fry thermometer, when a bit of tofu bobs to the surface within 2 seconds. Slide the triangles gently into the oil, one by one in quick succession, so long as the bubbling continues, adding as many triangles as can float comfortably on the surface at one time. (I fry all 16 at once in my 14-inch wok.) Expect them to bubble rather furiously on account of their high water content and shield yourself from spatters with the lid. The tofu will at first stick together. After about 30 seconds, when the bubbling dies down, gently separate the triangles with the chopsticks or wooden spoons. Fry them until golden, about 4 minutes, turning them occasionally, then remove to the paper towel to drain. If you are frying the triangles in batches, remember to allow several minutes for the oil to regain its initial high (375°) temperature, and retest the oil before frying the second batch. Expect the triangles to shrivel a bit as they cool.

When the oil cools, strain, bottle, and refrigerate it for future use.

Caramelizing the triangles:
Combine the black soy, thin soy, brown sugar, and five-spice powder, if used, stirring until well blended. Taste and adjust for desired sweetness. Have the sugar mixture, tofu, oil, and water for caramelizing all within reach of your stovetop.

Heat a wok or large, heavy skillet over high heat until hot enough to sizzle a bead of water on contact. If your wok or pan is small and deep rather than broad and shallow caramelize the tofu in two batches and use only ½ the caramelizing ingredients for each batch.

Add the oil, swirl to coat the pan, then reduce the heat to medium. When the oil is hot enough to cause a drop of the sugar mixture to bubble, in several seconds, scrape the sugar mixture into the pan. Let it come to a simmer, then stir rapidly until it thickens in a full boil. Add the triangles, then toss briskly for about 2 minutes to glaze them evenly with the syrup. Do not allow the syrup to burn. Add the water to the bowl that held the sugar mixture, swish to reclaim the sugar clinging to it, then add the mixture to the pan. Raise the heat slightly to restore the bubbling, then continue to toss for 1–3 minutes, until there is only ⅛ inch syrup remaining in the bottom of the pan. Turn off the heat and let the triangles cool in the pan for about 10 minutes, tossing them every several minutes to distribute the syrup evenly. Scrape onto a plate to cool. If repeating with a second batch, wash the pan with hot water and dry before continuing.

For crisper triangles, let them cool completely on the plate, spread apart and uncovered. For a softer texture that will gradually absorb the syrup, put the triangles in a large, clean glass jar while they are still a bit warm, seal the jar, and rotate it occasionally to distribute the syrup.

The caramelized triangles may be refrigerated 1–2 days before serving. If you have cooled them on the plate, seal the plate airtight with plastic wrap.

Serve at room temperature, heaped in a shallow bowl or arranged in a pretty pinwheel on a flat serving plate.

Leftovers keep 4–5 days, refrigerated and tightly sealed.

MENU SUGGESTIONS:

For a refreshing cold meal, serve the triangles in the company of *Orchid's Tangy Cool Noodles* (page 356), *Tea and Spice Smoked Chicken* (page 158), *Dry-Fried Szechwan String Beans* (page 297), and *Soy-Dipped Red Radish Fans* (page 114). They are also excellent on their own as a midday snack.

Down-Home Hunan Tofu

家常豆腐

This Hunan-inspired dish of meaty, chili-zested tofu is far more to my liking than its well-known Szechwanese cousin, "Ma-Po Tofu." In this dish the tiny tofu cubes are first deep-fried to a firm golden brown, so they are resilient and not simply mushy when you bite down on them. The sauce is a spicy conspiracy of garlic, ginger, scallion, and chili, and the bits of meat and diced carrots or string beans contribute color, substance, and crunch. ◆ This is an easy dish to make, very hearty and satisfying for spice lovers. It takes 15–20 minutes to prepare and only 3–4 minutes to cook.

TECHNIQUE NOTES:

Black and white peppercorns *(Piper nigrum)*, called "foreign" or "barbarian pepper" in Chinese, have been a minor, "exotic" fixture on the Chinese spice shelf since their introduction in the eighth century. They are used when the cook desires a spicier, more strikingly pungent taste than that afforded by the native brown peppercorn *(Xanthoxylum piperitum)*, which is subtle and numbing as opposed to acrid.

For the clean taste of vegetables that are blanched prior to stir-frying, see TECHNIQUE NOTES, page 309.

Serves 2–3 as a main dish, 4–6 as part of a multicourse meal.

INGREDIENTS:

> 4 squares (1 pound) fresh white tofu, firm Chinese-style best (page 324)
> 3–4 cups corn or peanut oil, for deep-frying
> rounded ½ cup tiny fresh carrot cubes, diced string beans, or diced Chinese longbeans

Aromatics:
> 4–5 large cloves garlic, stem end removed, lightly smashed and peeled
> 1 large whole scallion, cut into 1-inch lengths
> 1 walnut-size nugget fresh ginger

> 3–4 tablespoons corn or peanut oil
> 6 ounces ground top round beef or ground pork butt
> 1–1½ tablespoons Chinese chili sauce (page 537)

Liquid seasonings:
> ½ cup rich, unsalted chicken stock

2 tablespoons thin (regular) soy sauce
1 tablespoon Chinese rice wine or quality, dry sherry

about ¼ teaspoon sugar
about ¼ teaspoon coarse kosher salt
1½ teaspoons cornstarch dissolved in 1½ tablespoons cold chicken stock
freshly ground pepper to taste

Preparations:
Weight soft tofu to drain it of excess water, as directed on page 323. Firm Chinese style tofu does not require weighting.

Cut the tofu neatly into small cubes ¼–½ inch square, then spread on a double thickness of paper towels to drain.

Blanch the diced vegetables in plain boiling water to cover, 20 seconds for carrots, 10 seconds for string beans or longbeans. Drain immediately, rush under cold water until chilled, then put aside to drain.

Mince the garlic, scallion, and ginger in the work bowl of a food processor fitted with the steel knife, scraping down as necessary until fine. Alternatively, mince by hand.

Combine the liquid seasonings.

Deep-frying the tofu:
Have the tofu cubes, a tray lined with a double thickness of dry paper towels, and a large Chinese mesh spoon within easy reach of your stovetop.

Heat a wok or large, heavy skillet over high heat until hot. Add the oil, then heat to the dense-haze stage, 400° on a deep-fry thermometer, when a cube of tofu bobs instantly to the surface with a crown of white bubbles. Gently scatter the cubes in the oil and fry 1–2 minutes until firm and golden, poking gently with the spoon to separate the cubes. Scoop from the oil and remove to the dry paper-towel drain. Shake the tray so the cubes turn and blot on all sides.

The above may all be done several hours in advance. Refrigerate the minced aromatics, sealed airtight, and leave the tofu on the paper towels at room temperature.

Once cool, strain, bottle, and refrigerate the oil for future frying.

Stir-frying the dish:
About 10 minutes in advance of serving, arrange the tofu, diced vegetables, meat, aromatics and liquid seasonings, and the remaining ingredients all within easy reach of your stovetop. Put a serving bowl with a lively color in a low oven to warm.

Heat a wok or large, heavy skillet over high heat until hot enough to evaporate a bead of water on contact. Add 3 tablespoons oil and swirl to coat the pan. When the oil is hot enough to sizzle a bit of garlic, add the minced aromatics and stir-fry until fully fragrant, about 30 seconds, adjusting the heat so they foam without browning. Add the meat and poke briskly to break up the clumps, adjusting the heat to maintain a merry sizzle and adding a bit more oil from the side of the pan if the meat is sticking. Toss just until the meat is 90 percent gray, then quickly fold in the chili sauce, add the vegetable, and stir to combine. Pour the liquid seasonings into the pan, add the cubed tofu, then stir very gently to mix. Raise the heat to bring the liquids to a simmer, taste, then add about ¼ teaspoon sugar to bring out the full, tangy spice of the chili, and salt to taste. Lower the heat to moderate, stir the cornstarch mixture to recombine and pour it evenly into the pan. Stir gently until the mixture turns glossy and slightly thick, about 30 seconds, then turn off the heat. Add freshly ground pepper to taste, stir gently to mix, then serve at once in the heated bowl.

Leftovers may be resteamed in a tightly covered bowl until hot, and will grow spicier in the process.

MENU SUGGESTIONS:
I love this dish for a simple supper, along with *Pan-Fried Scallion Breads* (page 435), or *Everyday Chinese Rice* (page 400). If a fuller menu is desired, add *Dry-Fried Szechwan String Beans* (page 297) or *Stir-Fried Spinach with Charred Garlic* (page 305). To cool off for dessert, try *Glacéed Orange Slices* (page 487). Choose a Côtes du Rhône, Zinfandel, or Petite Sirah to partner the tofu.

Hakka Stuffed Tofu

客家釀豆腐

Hakka means "guest people" in Chinese, and the name refers to a group of northern Chinese who were driven south in the wake of Tartar invasions in the fourth and ninth centuries and who re-established themselves in the mountainous regions of Canton and Fukien. To this day, the Hakka maintain a dialect, a way of dress, and a style of cooking that sets them apart from their southern neighbors. Hakka cooking, which is gutsier than Cantonese cooking and uses less oil and more pungent condiments, is particularly to my liking. It is for the most part earthy and simple, with a striking, clean taste. ◆ Stuffed pockets of tofu filled with a mixture of marinated pork are a famous Hakka specialty. In this version, the tofu is cut into smallish triangles, the stuffing is lightly spiced with dried shrimp and a bit of pepper, and the triangles are then pan-fried in a light, ginger-sparked sauce. It is a delicate, homey dish, ideal for a one-course dinner. ◆ Chinese cookbooks describe Hakka tofu as being especially tender and glossy owing to the mountain water from which it is made. That should be an inspiration to choose the tofu for this dish with care. It should be very fresh, sweet-tasting, and smooth, yet not so soft that it will fall apart when stuffed. Look for the firm Chinese style tofu made with *nigari* (page 325), ideally from a market that gets it daily. If all that is available is soft tofu, weight it as directed on page 323 until it can be cut without breaking. ◆ The filling may be made a night in advance, and the tofu may be stuffed hours before frying. The actual cooking takes about 10–12 minutes.

TECHNIQUE NOTES:
There are many ways to stuff a piece of tofu, and my way is called "the yawning mouth." The trick is to be careful that the "jaw" of the tofu triangle doesn't break while you are stuffing the mouth. Work the stuffing in gently with your fingers and cradle the tofu in your hand while you stuff it.

Serves 2–3 as a main course, 4–6 as part of a multicourse meal.

INGREDIENTS:

> 4 cakes fresh and firm Chinese-style tofu (page 324), each 3 inches square and
> 1½ inches thick (buy 5 or 6 cakes if they are smaller)

For the stuffing:
> 1 rounded tablespoon dried shrimp (page 565)
> 6 ounces ground pork butt
> 1 teaspoon finely minced fresh ginger
> 1 teaspoon finely minced green and white scallion
> 2 teaspoons thin (regular) soy sauce

1 tablespoon Chinese rice wine or quality, dry sherry
⅛ teaspoon freshly ground pepper
1 teaspoon cornstarch

1 cup rich, unsalted chicken stock
1 tablespoon thin (regular) soy sauce
6–8 tablespoons corn or peanut oil, for pan-frying
2 teaspoons fine julienne threads of fresh ginger, cut hair-thin
1 medium whole scallion, cut into 1½-inch lengths and shredded lengthwise
coarse kosher salt, to taste
1 teaspoon cornstarch dissolved in 1 tablespoon cold chicken stock

To garnish:
sprigs of fresh coriander

Making the stuffing:

Soak the dried shrimp in very hot tap water to cover until a single shrimp tastes pleasantly salty when you bite down on it, about 15 minutes. Drain, rinse, then discard any bits of clinging shell. Pat the shrimp dry and mince them finely, either in the work bowl of a food processor fitted with the steel knife or by hand.

In a medium bowl combine the minced shrimp, ginger, scallion, soy, wine, pepper, cornstarch and 1 tablespoon stock, stirring until well blended. Add the pork, then stir lightly in one direction to combine. Pick the pork up in your hand and throw it lightly 6 or 8 times against the side of the bowl to gently compact it. Transfer the pork to a bowl to hold it snugly, press a piece of plastic wrap directly on top of the pork to seal it airtight, and refrigerate until use, overnight if desired. Chilled, the stuffing will be easier to handle.

Cutting the tofu:

Cut each square of tofu into 4 triangles by cutting crosswise on the diagonal. Place the first triangle flat on your cutting surface, and then with a small sharp knife begin at the freshly cut pointed end (which used to be the center of the square) to cut out a V-shaped wedge to within ½ inch of what used to be the outside edge of the square. Make the wedge about ½ inch thick at the freshly cut pointed end, so that you have a nice open "mouth" ready to be filled with stuffing. Do not cut away too much, however. The idea is to stretch the opening and stuff it, not to throw away most of the tofu.

Once you have cut the tofu, proceed directly to stuff it.

Stuffing the tofu:

Pick up the first tofu triangle and cradle it in your palm. With your free fingers, scoop up 2–3 teaspoons filling, then gently begin to stuff it in the slit you have cut in the triangle. Work delicately to fill the slit so that the pointed "mouth" yawns wide open and the stuffing bulges gently on the sides, taking care not to stuff the filling in so far that you break the outer "jaw" and cause the triangle to split in two. (If this happens, gently press the triangle together again and fry it with the others. It may be less pretty in the end, but it will still taste fine.) When the mouth is yawning widely, smooth the outer bulge of filling with your finger and put the triangle aside on a plate, tofu side down so the filling is not touching. Repeat the process until all the triangles are stuffed. If you should have a bit of stuffing left over, roll it into tiny meatballs between wet palms and put them aside on the plate to be pan-fried with the tofu.

side view of yawning, stuffed tofu triangle

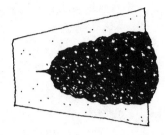

Once stuffed, the tofu may be refrigerated several hours before cooking, sealed airtight. Bring to room temperature before frying.

Pan-frying the tofu:
Combine the remaining stock and the soy. Blend the cornstarch mixture until smooth and leave the spoon in the bowl. Put all the ingredients within easy reach of your stovetop and put a shallow serving platter of contrasting color in a low oven to warm.

Heat a heavy, 12-inch skillet over high heat until hot enough to evaporate a bead of water on contact. Add 6 tablespoons oil, swirl to coat the bottom and sides of the skillet, then reduce the heat to medium-high. When the oil is hot enough to sizzle one triangle laid meat side down in the pan, quickly arrange all the triangles in the pan, working from the outside of the pan (which will be less hot) to the center (where it is the hottest), placing each of the triangles with one of their meaty sides touching the pan. Adjust the heat to maintain a merry sizzle without scorching the meat, then fry until the meat turns golden-brown, about 2–3 minutes.

When the first side is brown (check a triangle in the center of the pan), loosen the triangles with a small spatula or a spatula-shaped cheese slicer, and quickly turn them over to brown the second meaty side, beginning in the center and working towards the outside. Use your fingers or chopsticks to help turn the triangles over, whichever lets you work most quickly. Continue in the same manner to brown the second side, dribbling in a bit more oil from the side of the pan if needed to keep it lightly oiled.

Once the second side browns, detach the triangles with the spatula and lay them flat in the pan. Pour the stock on top, then raise the heat to bring the liquid to a simmer. Scatter the ginger and scallion threads evenly over the triangles, adjust the heat to maintain a bubbly simmer, then cover the pan and simmer until all but ⅓ of the liquid has been absorbed, about 3–4 minutes.

Turn off the heat, then quickly remove the triangles to the serving platter with the spatula, leaving the liquid behind in the pan. Taste the liquid and adjust with a bit of salt if required, then raise the heat to bring it to a simmer. Stir the cornstarch mixture to recombine, add it to the pan, and stir until the liquid turns glossy and slightly thick, about 15 seconds.

Pour the sauce evenly over the tofu. Garnish the top with several sprigs of coriander, then serve the dish at once.

Leftovers keep 2–3 days, refrigerated and sealed airtight. Steam in a shallow, covered dish over high heat until hot.

MENU SUGGESTIONS:
For a simple meal, serve the tofu with a light vegetable like *Spinach with Glass Noodles* (page 308), or something zestier like *Dry-Fried Szechwan String Beans* (page 297). If rice is desired, *Shanghai Vegetable Rice* (page 402) or *Ham and Egg Fried Rice* (page 405) would be my choice. To partner the tofu, pour a Pinot Noir or a French Burgundy.

Tofu and Salmon in Pepper Sauce

鮭魚豆腐

This is one of those fortuitous matings of excellent leftovers and excellent fresh things that results in a dish that no one has ever heard of—a simple stir-fry of steamed, poached, or baked fresh salmon with cubed tofu, slivered sweet pepper, and fresh coriander, left to bubble briefly in a peppery chicken stock. It was a dish first cooked when there was some leftover salmon in the icebox, and I have never been able to convince myself that it tastes as good if one starts with the uncooked fish. ♦ Given the cooked salmon, this is a quick and easy 10-minute dish, colorful and well balanced in a very Chinese way.

TECHNIQUE NOTES:
To steam a piece of salmon simply, put it on a heatproof plate and scatter a few pieces of slivered scallion and ginger on top, then drizzle it with a bit of Chinese rice wine or dry sherry. Steam over high heat until pale pink on the outside but still ruby within, about 6 minutes for a 1-inch steak. The scallion, ginger, and wine are the "de-fishers," and the steam traps all of the natural flavor right within the fish. The trick is to undercook it slightly, so that it will cook to perfection from its own heat once it has left the steamer.

Serves 2 as a main course, 3–4 as part of a multicourse meal.

INGREDIENTS:

> *½ pound fresh white tofu, firm Chinese-style preferable (page 324)*
> *6 ounces poached, steamed, or baked salmon, weight after removal of skin, bones and gelatinous bits*
> *2–3 tablespoons corn or peanut oil*
> *3 tablespoons thin-cut green and white scallion rings*
> *2–3 tablespoons coarsely chopped fresh coriander leaves*
> *⅓–½ cup finely slivered red bell pepper*
> *¾ cup rich, unsalted chicken stock*
> *about ½ teaspoon coarse kosher salt*
> *dash unseasoned Chinese or Japanese rice vinegar*
> *⅛–¼ teaspoon freshly ground black and white pepper*
> *1½ teaspoons cornstarch dissolved in 1 tablespoon cold chicken stock*

> *To garnish:*
> *fresh whole coriander leaves*

Preparations:
If you are working with exceedingly soft tofu that will not slice cleanly and hold its shape, then weight it as described on page 323. Take into account that the pressing will remove water weight and begin with an extra 2–4 ounces tofu.

   Cut the tofu into rectangular "mah-jongg tiles," about 1¼-inch long, ¾-inch wide and ⅜-inch thick. Ten minutes before cooking, cover them with boiling water to refresh the taste and velvetize the texture. Drain thoroughly just before using.

With your fingers or a blunt knife gently break the salmon into thick flakes along the natural grain. Do not mash it or flake it finely; it will taste better if left coarse.

Cut the scallion, coriander, and bell pepper just before using.

Stir-frying the dish:
Have all the ingredients within easy reach of your stovetop, and leave a spoon or chopstick in the cornstarch mixture. Put a shallow serving bowl of contrasting color in a low oven to warm.

Heat a wok or large, heavy skillet over high heat until hot enough to evaporate a bead of water on contact. Add 2 tablespoons oil, swirl to coat the pan, then reduce the heat to medium-high. When the oil is hot enough to sizzle a single scallion ring, add the scallion and stir-fry until fragrant, about 5–10 seconds, adjusting the heat to maintain a merry sizzle. Add the chopped coriander, stir gently for about 5 seconds to "explode" the coriander's aroma, then add the bell pepper to the pan. Toss briskly to combine, adjusting the heat to maintain a merry sizzle without scorching the pepper, and dribbling in a bit more oil from the side of the pan if needed to prevent sticking. When the bell pepper is glossy, in about 10–15 seconds, add the stock and stir to blend. Raise the heat to bring the mixture to a simmer, then slide the drained tofu into the pan. Swish gently to combine, cover, and simmer 1 minute to heat the tofu through.

Uncover the pot, scatter the salmon in the simmering brew, then swish for 10–15 seconds to mix. (Shake the pan rather than using a spoon or spatula to stir if the tofu is so soft that it is breaking apart.) Reduce the heat to low, taste, then add salt and a dash of vinegar as required. Sprinkle liberally with pepper and swish to combine. Stir the cornstarch mixture to recombine, add to the pan, then stir gently just until the sauce turns glossy and slightly thick. Immediately transfer the dish to the heated platter. Salting and seasoning the dish carefully in these last seconds is crucial to its success, but you must work quickly lest the mixture lose its savor.

Garnish with a pretty mound or sprinkling of fresh coriander leaves, then serve at once. Set the table with spoons, as this is a pleasantly soupy dish.

Leftovers are not at all good, so eat this dish up.

MENU SUGGESTIONS:
For a very pretty menu, serve the tofu with *Flower Rolls* (page 415) and *Red Bell Pepper with Garlic and Coriander* (page 314). *Everyday Chinese Rice* (page 400), *Ham and Egg Fried Rice* (page 405), or *Pan-Fried Scallion Breads* (page 435) could substitute for the steamed rolls, or *Stir-Fried Spinach with Fermented Tofu* (page 306) served in place of the bell pepper. *Mendocino Lemon Tart* (page 513) would follow nicely. To accompany tofu choose a California Chardonnay or a white Burgundy. Look for something with a fair amount of body, not astringent and not too aromatic.

Noodles, Dumplings, & Springrolls

麵餃子春捲

◆

◆

Noodles and dumplings enjoy a huge popularity in China, as might be expected in a country with an abundance of grains to make them, an inexhaustible population to shape them, and a philosophy of eating that emphasizes play and pleasure at the table. In the south, where the staple is rice, rice noodles and rice noodle-wrapped dumplings are prime teatime snacks. In the north, where wheat is the predominant starch, wheat and egg noodles and wheat flour-wrapped dumplings are everyday mealtime fare. They are variously steamed, boiled, pan-fried, deep-fried, and pulled from soups or dunked in dips. The range is limitless, and so too the Chinese enjoyment of them.

And me, I am a confessed noodle and dumpling addict. There is something about the slippery-smooth feel of the dough on my tongue and the wonderful shapes—long and narrow strands, broad ribbons, or little dough pockets and pouches holding treasures— that appeal to the child in me. In Taiwan, I was rarely as happy as when I would stop in a strange village during the daytime or stroll down the alleyway outside our home at night to find the noodle stand or dumpling cart that wafted the best smells and had gathered the plumpest crowd. And here in America, there is nothing better than assembling a crowd of friends in my own kitchen for a dinner of noodles or an afternoon of dumpling making followed by a night of eating. These are fun foods, easy foods, meant to be savored in good company or in a pleasurable solitude.

TYPES OF NOODLES FOR CHINESE DISHES   Specialty noodles such as bean threads and rice sticks are described in detail on pages 533 and 559, and for these there are no substitutes. Egg noodles, which are common in the West and are used in the majority of recipes in this chapter, raise more specific questions as to type and shape.

I vastly prefer *fresh Chinese egg noodles* to the dried Chinese variety. I will buy them fresh or frozen, preferring to get them fresh though I will store what I cannot use in the freezer if need be. Of the many widths available, I like best those that are exactly ¹⁄₁₆ inch thin before cooking. The yet thinner ones are a bit too delicate for a cold or pan-fried noodle dish (though they are superb in soup), while the thicker ones tend to overshadow the sauce and the trimmings. When buying fresh Chinese noodles, I make it a point to inspect them if I can through the wrapper and to feel their texture. They should not appear glued together in clumps and they should feel supple. Otherwise, the too-moist strands will not come apart in cooking or the too-brittle noodles will break up into bits. *Frozen Chinese egg noodles* should be thoroughly defrosted before cooking, sealed airtight in the bag in which they came against drying. Just before cooking, fluff in a colander and discard any wadded bits that do not separate into strands.

If fresh or frozen Chinese egg noodles are unavailable, *fresh Italian egg noodles* of a suitable thinness make a perfect substitute. *Tonnarelli* and *spaghettini* are often the names given ¹⁄₁₆-inch thin egg noodles. Do *not* get hair-thin *cappellini*, which will clump together in a wad in a Chinese dish.

When I do not have access to fresh egg noodles, I look for a Spanish or Italian variety of appropriately thin egg noodle called *fideos* or *fidellini*, available in supermarkets. In my experience, they are better-tasting than the Chinese dried varieties.

Japanese *soba*, or buckwheat noodles, I find to be too heavy to a Chinese taste. Moreover, their otherwise excellent, pronounced flavor overwhelms a Chinese sauce.

TYPES OF FLOURS AND DOUGHS FOR DUMPLING SKINS   See pages 397 to 398 for information on types of flour, how to measure it, and the texture of a properly made dough.

NOTES ON STORE-BOUGHT DUMPLING WRAPPERS AND SPRINGROLL SKINS Fresh noodle skins for wrapping dumplings and springrolls are widely and increasingly available in the refrigerator or freezer cases of most large Chinese groceries. When I can, I prefer to buy them directly at the noodle factory, where I know they are freshest. Otherwise, I look for a store with daily deliveries from the factory, or one with a steady turnover of merchandise. The point is, like all noodlestuffs, the fresher the dumpling or springroll wrapper the better it is. A fresh wrapper will feel supple, be easy to use, and taste best. An old wrapper will often be dry and will crack when shaped, and if the resulting dumpling or springroll wrapper doesn't fall apart when you shape it, it will often fall apart when cooked—in short, frustration and a mess.

Dumpling wrappers come in several shapes, thicknesses, and styles of packaging, usually a pound of wrappers to a package. My local noodle factory clearly labels their packages according to the type of dumpling for which the wrapper is best suited, but if the package does not include such helpful information, here is what to look for:

Pot-sticker skins are about 3½ inches round and exactly ¹⁄₁₆ inch thick when made in a factory. By Chinese standards this is a relatively thick skin, and it is designed to hold up through the process of pan-frying and steam-cooking and to lend to the hearty character of this northern Chinese dish. The package will often be labeled "kuo tieh skin" if it is made by a Chinese concern, or "gyoza skins" if a Japanese brand. I have found the Chinese-made wrappers to be superior, but I have sampled relatively few of the Japanese brands and if the Japanese sort is all that is available you should definitely try it.

Boiled dumpling skins are also about 3½ inches round but are ¹⁄₃₂ inch thin. This thinness is conducive to quick-cooking in water and gives the dumpling a certain delicacy. Homemade skins are typically made without eggs, but factory-made skins of this sort will often have eggs listed as one of the ingredients. The Chinese-made skins are often labeled "sue gow skin" (the Cantonese name) or "jyiao dz" or "jyiao tzu skin" (the mandarin name).

Shao-mai skins are yet a third type of 3½ inch round skin, thinner still than the two types above. Three *shao-mai* skins stacked one on top of the other are ¹⁄₁₆ inch thick, making each skin a scant ¹⁄₄₈ inch thin. Using a skin this thin gives the dumpling an unsurpassed delicacy and a beautiful translucent look. Cantonese in origin, the skins are typically made with an egg dough for a richer taste. They are often labeled "shu mai skins" or "su my wrapper" (reflecting the Cantonese pronunciation).

In the event that the round skins are not available, feel free to substitute 3½-inch square *won-ton skins* of the appropriate thickness. For a clean cut, use a sharp, 3½-inch round cookie cutter. If you must use scissors, first impress a circle on each wrapper with the top of a glass or a can so that you can cut accurately.

Springroll skins are paper-thin, 7–8 inch square or round wrappers, generally sold by the pound. They are shiny and not at all "doughy" looking, unlike the thick so-called egg roll wrappers that resemble fresh noodle dough. They are sold under various names— "Shanghai springroll wrappers," "lumpia wrappers," "*thin* eggroll wrappers"—so you must examine the package to be sure you are getting the appropriately thin type. Springroll skins are often frozen at the factory. They are typically sold in 1-pound heat-sealed bags, 30–35 wrappers per pound.

Dumpling and springroll skins are sometimes heat-sealed in plastic, and at other times are sold wrapped in a thick, white wax paper, depending on the factory. If you are buying them fresh, test the package with your fingers to check whether the skins are soft and supple; they should bend easily. If the skins are frozen, pick the heat-sealed over the paper-wrapped if you have the choice.

All dumpling and springroll skins keep well for up to a week in the refrigerator and for 1–2 months in the freezer, if properly wrapped. Heat-sealed plastic packages can be stored as is. For paper-wrapped skins, your best bet is to discard the paper, rewrap the skins in plastic wrap, then bag them airtight in a plastic bag before storing. Thinner skins should first be divided into parcels, unless you are planning a marathon dumpling party and need to use a hundred or more skins at one time.

Frozen wrappers must be thoroughly defrosted before using. Otherwise, they will not pull apart easily and will tear or break when shaped. Defrost them in the refrigerator, still in their airtight packaging. Exposure to the air will dry the dough and make it brittle.

AND A NOTE ON DIM SUM (WITH A LIST OF ALL THE DISHES IN THIS BOOK THAT FALL INTO THAT BRUNCHTIME CATEGORY) Noodles and dumplings are primary feature foods at *dim sum* tea houses where Chinese gather to eat a midmorning or early afternoon meal, drink tea, and enjoy all the goodies that are too tedious to make at home. *Dim sum* is a style of eating more than a specific category of food, and while not a topic for this book, many of the recipes included here could be banded together to make a gala *dim sum* brunch. For brunchtime Chinese cooks, here is the menu from which to choose:

all the *"Little Dishes"* (pages 103 to 121), excepting *Mongolian Stewed Garlic*, which might create an unsocial situation for the rest of the day
Ma-La Cold Chicken (page 129)
Cold Duck Salad with Two Sauces (page 164)
Crispy Pork Balls (page 185)
Curry Crescents (page 223)
Deep-Fried Shrimp Balls (page 240)
Gold Coin Shrimp Cakes (page 243)
Shrimp Rolls with Crisp Seaweed (page 241)
Spicy Shrimp Fritters (page 237)
Phoenix Tail Shrimp (page 235)
Walnut Chicken Slices (page 148)
Sesame Fish Slices (page 246)
Gold Coin Eggs (page 330)
Hakka Stuffed Tofu (page 343)
Moslem-Style Beef or Lamb Pot Stickers (page 384)
Hunan Pork Dumplings with Hot Sauce (page 379)
Shao Mai Dumplings (page 375)
Pan-Fried Meat Pies (page 387)
Baked Stuffed Buns (page 432)
Steamed Buns with Chicken and Black Mushrooms (page 425)
Steamed Buns with Minced Pork and Tree Ears (page 429)
Curried Vegetarian Buns (page 431)
Springrolls with Dijon Mustard Sauce (page 389)

And that's not all! Fried rice dishes, cold and hot noodle dishes, *Bong-Bong Chicken* (page 133), and *Pan-Fried Scallion Breads* (page 435) are all perfectly at home within this style of eating. It is hard to draw boundaries as to where street food ends and tea-house food begins and where the Cantonese custom of *dim sum* overlaps the northern Chinese love of dumplings and snack food at any time of day or night, and I won't try to do it here. Suffice it to say that *dim sum* (literally, "a bit of heart,"), can reasonably embrace anything small and munchable, anything that goes well with tea and most any food that sits nicely in a brunchtime belly.

Homemade Chinese Egg Noodles

蛋麵

It never would have occurred to me to make my own Chinese noodles. The fact of the matter is I have always chosen to live near sizable Chinatowns, where at least one factory and usually several churn out fresh noodles daily, expressly for noodle addicts such as myself. Even a finicky present-day Chinese cook would no more think of making his or her own noodles than a French person living within reach of a real French bakery would think of making his or her own *baguettes.* ◆ But what of those noodle-lovers who are deprived of a neighborhood noodle factory? Dried Chinese noodles have never seemed acceptable to me and while substitutes are available (page 351), here is a worthwhile option for making fresh Chinese-style egg noodles on one's own. The results are so good that the time seems well spent, so long as you have a pasta machine to speed you on your way. ◆ Homemade noodles may be cut and kept fresh a day in advance of cooking. You may also dry or freeze them, though I prefer to cook the noodles within 8 hours of cutting.

TECHNIQUE NOTES:
Chinese egg noodles are bouncy, extremely light-tasting, and silken in texture. Unlike Italian egg noodles, which are typically made from an exclusively egg and flour dough, Chinese egg noodles are made with more water than egg. They are noticeably lighter in color, milder in flavor, and rather refined and delicate as compared to more earthy and toothsome ones.

Also in contrast to the Italian practice, the Chinese habit is to roll out and dust noodles with sleek cornstarch instead of grainy flour. The cornstarch "patina" makes the dough pass much more smoothly through the rollers, and, once cut, the noodles stay supple longer—an advantage if you wish to hold them overnight before cooking. The final texture is very silky and smooth, not the sort to grip a sauce, as Italian taste requires, but a style that defines a slippery heap of noodles as a benign background for other tastes.

Yields 1½ pounds fresh noodles.

INGREDIENTS:

> *3 cups bread flour or all-purpose flour*
> *1 teaspoon coarse kosher salt*
> *2 large eggs*
> *about 9 tablespoons cold water*
> *⅛ teaspoon Chinese or Japanese sesame oil, or corn or peanut oil*
> *about ½ cup cornstarch, for rolling out and dusting the dough*

Making the dough:
If you have a food processor:
    (For details on dough-making in a food processor, see page 586).
    If you have a small capacity work bowl, divide the recipe in half and process 2 separate batches of dough, then knead them together by hand into one ball. If you have a large-capacity work bowl, then you may do the whole recipe at one time. Check manufacturer's instructions to be sure of bowl capacity.
    Put the flour and salt into the work bowl of a food processor fitted with the steel knife. Turn on and off twice to mix. Break the eggs into the work bowl, then process with 2 or 3 on-off turns to blend. With the machine running pour the water through the feed

tube in a thin, steady stream, stopping immediately when the dough begins to form a ball around the blade. Give the machine 2 or 3 seconds' "lag time" to incorporate the last water droplets and form a near-ball, then run the machine for 10 seconds to knead the dough. If necessary, add a bit more water until the dough comes together.

Remove the dough. It will be slightly sticky, though not wet. Knead by hand about 30 seconds, until smooth and fingertip-firm, and elastic enough so it springs back when you press it with your finger. If processed correctly in the machine, the dough will not stick to the board when kneaded. If it is sticking, then flour the board lightly.

Smooth the oil over the dough, seal airtight in plastic, then set aside to rest for 20 minutes to 3 hours at room temperature, or overnight in the refrigerator. Bring to room temperature before rolling out.

If you do not have a food processor:

Sift the flour and salt into a large mixing bowl. Make a deep well in the center of the flour, lightly beat the eggs with the water, then add to the well. With chopsticks or a wooden spoon, stir slowly at first from the center to incorporate the flour, then vigorously to form a firm dough, adding water by droplets if needed to bring the dough together. Turn out onto a lightly floured board, then knead by hand until fingertip-firm, smooth, and elastic enough so the dough bounces gently back when pressed with a finger, about 10 minutes.

Oil, seal, and let the dough rest as above.

Rolling out the dough with a pasta machine:

Cut the dough into 4 equal pieces and cover with a cloth against drying.

Remove and flatten the first piece with your palm or several rolls of a rolling pin into an approximate rectangle, about ¼ inch thick. Smooth cornstarch on both sides, then pass the dough through the widest roller setting. Fold the dough into thirds, folding one end towards the middle then the other end on top. Flatten firmly so the dough passes easily through the rollers without tearing. Smooth cornstarch on both sides, turn the dough 90° so it enters the rollers on an unfolded end, then feed it through the roller. Repeat folding, flattening, dusting, and rolling 2 or 3 more times at the same setting, until the dough is smooth and unwrinkled. These first run-throughs knead the dough. Hereafter, you will not need to fold or flatten it.

Turn the machine one notch to the next thinnest setting. Dust the dough on both sides with cornstarch, then pass it through the roller. Proceed to turn the machine down one notch, dust both sides of the dough with cornstarch, and send it through the rollers until you have a band that is either ⅛ inch thick (good for hearty pot-browned noodles) or 1/16 inch thick (good for cold noodles, soup noodles, stir-fried noodles, and more delicate pot-browned noodles). If one setting produces a too-thick result and the next one threatens to yield a too-thin result, run the dough through the wider setting *twice* and it will come out just right.

When the dough is as thin as you want it, spread it on a towel to dry, about 7–8 minutes on each side, or until the dough has firmed up slightly and will pass through the cutters with ease. (A terry towel works beautifully to speed the drying.)

As soon as one band is spread to dry, proceed to roll out the next piece of dough. If the first piece dries before the last piece is done, cover it with a towel to keep it supple.

Cutting the noodles:

The dough must be cut while supple but slightly firm to the touch. (Unlike flour-dusted dough, cornstarch-dusted dough will not get that slightly leathery feel, but it will feel firm.) Too wet, it will stick together and not cut cleanly. Too dry, it will crack and break when cut.

Fit the machine with the ⅛-inch cutting head, standard on most machines. (If you have a 1/16-inch head, you may use it instead.) Dust cornstarch on both sides of the first dough band, then send it through the cutter. If the metal teeth don't immediately grab and "bite" the dough on their own, gently press the dough into the cutter until it catches.

Stretch out the noodles in one long hank and use a sharp knife or cleaver to cut it crosswise in two, to yield noodles that are about 15 inches long. Toss the noodles on a cornstarch-dusted surface to coat the newly cut edges, then spread to dry on a terry towel-lined tray. Fluff occasionally, allowing the noodles to firm up at least 5–10 minutes before cooking.

Cut and dry the remaining dough.

Holding or storing the noodles prior to cooking:
The noodles may be left uncovered for about 1 hour before cooking. To hold them several hours to overnight, cover with plastic wrap or a towel to prevent them from drying out completely, and refrigerate if you wish, fluffing occasionally.

For longer storage, dry or freeze them. Either let them dry out completely on a cornstarch-dusted tray, coiling them if you like once half-dried, and pack them in a tin for an indefinite time. Or, leave them on a cornstarch-dusted tray for about 4 hours, fluffing occasionally, until they are supple yet firm and can be packed loosely into plastic bags without breaking or sticking together. Seal the bag airtight, and freeze up to 1 month. Fluff when thawed to separate the strands.

Cooking the noodles:
In an 8-quart pot, bring 4 quarts of unsalted water to a rolling boil over high heat. (Increase to 5½ quarts water for 2 pounds noodles.) Put a heatproof colander in the sink. Add the noodles to the pot, swish gently with chopsticks to separate, then cook until done but still toothy, adjusting the heat so the water merely simmers. (This will help you to not overcook them.) Fresh-made, 1/16-inch thin noodles require *only about 10 seconds to cook* once the water has returned to a simmer. Thicker or drier noodles will require longer. Taste often to check, pulling the strands from the water with chopsticks and biting into them.

When *almost* cooked, drain the noodles immediately and proceed as the recipe requires. Remember that the noodles will continue cooking en route to the colander and while they are being either chilled down or served up, so pluck them from the stove when still a bit undercooked.

Orchid's Tangy Cool Noodles

寶蘭涼麵

This is the quintessential Chinese cold noodle dish, a tangy northern-style blend of sweet, tart, and spicy tastes that has an astonishing popularity. It was the first Chinese dish I ever made, at a time when I had one tin pot in which to boil and store the noodles, and nothing big enough to toss them in but the kitchen sink. ◆ For economy, portability, and adaptability to any number of people or settings, "Orchid's" cannot be surpassed. Make them in advance. The flavors merge and enlarge as the noodles sit.

TECHNIQUE NOTES:
For the role of black soy sauce in a dressing for cold noodles, see TECHNIQUE NOTES, page 358.

Serves 6–8 as a luncheon-style dish with assorted "Little Dishes," 10–15 as part of a large buffet or multicourse meal.

INGREDIENTS:

> *1 pound long, ¹/₁₆-inch thin Chinese egg noodles, fresh or frozen (see page 351 for substitutes, and page 354 for making your own)*
>
> *Seasonings:*
> *3½ tablespoons Chinese or Japanese sesame oil*
> *3½ tablespoons black soy sauce*
> *1½ tablespoons well-aged Chinese black vinegar or balsamic vinegar (page 577)*
> *2 tablespoons sugar*
> *2 teaspoons coarse kosher salt*
> *½–1 tablespoon hot chili oil*
>
> *4 heaping tablespoons thin-cut green and white scallion rings*
>
> *To garnish:*
> *freshly cut scallion rings*

Cooking the noodles:
Fluff fresh or defrosted noodles in a colander to release any tangles. (Take care not to tear them. Long noodles in China are a metaphor for long life, and it is great fun to eat them that way.)

Bring a generous amount of unsalted water to a rolling boil over high heat. Add the noodles and swish with chopsticks to separate the strands. Put the colander in the sink. Cook the noodles until cooked but pleasantly firm to the bite, about 2–3 minutes for fresh store-bought noodles. Drain immediately in the colander and chill thoroughly under cold running water. Shake off excess water, then return the noodles to the clean dry pot or to a large bowl.

Saucing the noodles:
Blend the seasonings in a small bowl. Pour the sauce evenly over the noodles, using a handful of noodles to wipe the bowl clean so you don't lose any of the sugar. Toss gently with your hands to separate the noodles and distribute the sauce, then add the scallion rings and toss again to mix. Taste and adjust seasonings if necessary to achieve a tangy blend of sweet and hot flavors. Remember that the chili will grow more pronounced within a few hours, so err on the cautious side if you are not eating the noodles immediately.

For best flavor, cover and put aside for several hours at room temperature or store overnight in the refrigerator. Toss before eating to redistribute the seasonings. Serve at room temperature or slightly chilled, heaped in a bowl and garnished with a fresh sprinkling of scallion rings.

"*Orchid's*" lasts 4–5 days, sealed airtight and refrigerated. Flavor peaks in spiciness on the second day.

MENU SUGGESTIONS:
"Orchid's" are marvelous served alongside *Dry-Fried Szechwan String Beans* (page 297) and *Scallion and Ginger Explosion Shrimp* (page 233). To extend the menu, add *Sweet and Tangy Cucumber Pickles* (page 110), *Soy-Dipped Red Radish Fans* (page 114), *Marbelized Tea Eggs* (page 325), *Tea and Spice Smoked Chicken* (page 158), and *Strange Flavor Eggplant* (page 295)—any or all, depending on the size of the party.

| Peony
| Blossom
| Cold
| Noodles
| 牡丹涼麵

Lively with a chili-infused dressing, this dish with its tones of pale pink, green, ivory, and red is as pretty as a peony. It is very easy to make and very versatile—a cold luncheon, a supper on a summer's night, or the start of a special meal where something light and lively is needed are all settings in which these noodles shine. It is, after "Orchid's" (page 356), my favorite cold noodle dish. ◆ The noodles, oil, and trimmings may each be prepared in advance but should be tossed together just before serving lest their flavors and aromas dissipate. Be careful when shopping to get the freshest, whitest bean sprouts available. When blended with the noodles, they are almost invisible to the eye, and it is then that your tongue has the pleasure of discovering them. ◆ From start to finish, the noodles can be on the table in 30 minutes.

TECHNIQUE NOTES:
The more intensely salty black soy sauce gives you all the flavor and color of thin (regular) soy sauce with less liquid, making it ideal for cold noodle dishes where you want the sauce to cling to the noodles rather than lie in a puddle beneath them. Black soy sauce also has a slight molasses edge, which mates perfectly with the spunkier ingredients (vinegar, sugar, and chili oil or chili sauce) typically used to dress cold noodles.

Serves 4 as a main dish, 6–8 as part of a multicourse meal.

INGREDIENTS:

> ¾ pound long, ¹/₁₆-inch thin Chinese egg noodles, fresh or frozen (see page 351 for substitutes, and page 354 for making your own)
> 2½ teaspoons Chinese or Japanese sesame oil
> 1½ teaspoons coarse kosher salt

Trimmings:
> ¾ pound fresh bean sprouts (page 532)
> 1 cup thinly slivered cucumber or slivered and blanched fresh snow peas
> 1 cup thinly slivered, lightly smoked ham, Black Forest-style recommended (page 549)
> 1 cup firm red radishes, trimmed
> 1 medium carrot, trimmed and peeled
> ¼ cup freshly toasted chopped peanuts

Seasonings:
> 3 tablespoons Five-Flavor Oil (page 480)
> 1½ tablespoons black soy sauce

2 tablespoons unseasoned Chinese or Japanese rice vinegar
2 tablespoons sugar
1½–2 teaspoons Chinese chili sauce (page 536)

Preparations:
Cook the noodles as directed on page 357.

Once the noodles are drained and chilled, shake off the excess water, and toss them gently but thoroughly with the sesame oil and salt, tossing with your fingers to coat and separate each strand. Oiled, the noodles can be bagged airtight and refrigerated up to 2 days. Bring to room temperature before using.

As soon as possible after buying them, blanch the bean sprouts for 30 seconds in plain boiling water to cover, then drain and rush under cold water or plunge into ice water until chilled. (Blanching preserves the whiteness and removes the grassy taste.) Cover the sprouts with cold water and refrigerate until use, up to 2 days.

Mix the seasonings in a small bowl, stirring well to dissolve the sugar. Go light on the chili sauce if you are not familiar with its potency; you can always add more.

Just before assembling the dish, swish the bean sprouts to dislodge and remove any green seed cases, drain, then spread on a lint-free towel to blot up excess water. Shred the radishes and the carrot, in a food processor or by hand. (I like the carrots extra-fine for this dish, and shred them by hand with an inexpensive contraption sold in Japanese hardware stores, called "My-Ace"—a rectangular plastic box that can be fitted with different shredding and slicing blades. The package says it is guaranteed to "make your food more charming and delicious," and indeed, it does.)

Assembling the dish:
Shortly before serving, combine the noodles and bean sprouts in a large bowl, tossing with your hands and showering the noodles into the bowl to avoid breaking them. Add the seasonings, wiping the bowl clean with a handful of noodles to garner every bit of sugar, then gently toss to blend. Taste and adjust with an extra dab of chili sauce if required. The noodles should be very zesty in order to stand up to the trimmings when they are tossed together.

Mound the noodles on a large platter, then arrange the shredded radishes and carrot and the slivered cucumber and ham in heaps of alternating color around the noodles. Or, if the setting is such that you would like to assemble the dish on individual serving plates, then repeat the pattern on each plate. Garnish the top of the noodles with a sprinkling of peanuts and with a "scallion branch" if you like (see page 563).

Invite your guests to toss the noodles and trimmings together before eating to distribute them in the sauce. Traditionally, the tossing is left to the noodle eaters, and for the host to do it would be considered stealing the fun.

Leftovers keep nicely 1–2 days, sealed airtight and refrigerated, and grow spicier.

MENU SUGGESTIONS:
I typically serve this dish as a light meal on its own. It is also a good prelude to a hot meal of rather refined dishes like *Golden Egg Dumplings* (page 328), *Steamed Whole Fish with Seared Scallions* (page 248), and *Shrimp, Leek, and Pine Nut Fried Rice* (page 408). For a cold buffet, serve it alongside *Tea and Spice Smoked Chicken* (page 158) or *Strange Flavor Eggplant* (page 295). To partner the noodles, try a rosé with personality.

<table>
<tr><td>

**Don-
Don
Noodles**

担担麵

</td><td>

"Don-don" is Chinese onomatopoeia for "clap-clap" or "thunk-thunk"—the sound of the clapper announcing the vendor who peddled these noodles on the streets of Szechwan. True to the nature of real street food, there is no one "recipe" for *Don-Don Noodles*, only a multitude of tasty variations on a theme. The theme is a bowl of long, thin egg noodles, liberally topped with a spicy peanut or sesame-based sauce. Beyond that, the noodles may be hot or cold, and

</td></tr>
</table>

the sauce may be wild or tame, depending on which corner and from which vendor you buy it. ◆ This is my favorite version. The noodles are warm, the sauce is blazing. It is put together in minutes and is memorably satisfying. Make a lot of sauce. The noodles will beg for it. ◆ If you like to work in advance, you can cook the noodles without the carrots, undercook them slightly, then flush them with cold water to stop the cooking. Oil them as in the recipe, toss with the carrots, then bag and refrigerate up to 2 days. When you are ready to eat, simply steam the noodles over high heat until hot, about 10 minutes.

TECHNIQUE NOTES:

For most Chinese egg noodle dishes, I choose egg noodles that are ¹⁄₁₆ inch thin, possessed of enough body to stand up to the sauce, yet not so thick that the dressing becomes secondary. To cook them, I prefer the traditional Chinese method of using *unsalted* water, so that there is a good contrast between the typically fulsome sauce and the unseasoned noodles. In this recipe especially, the noodles should not compete with the topping.

Serves 2–3 as a main dish, 4–6 as part of a multicourse meal.

INGREDIENTS:

> *½ pound long, ¹⁄₁₆-inch thin Chinese egg noodles, fresh or frozen (see page 351
>   for substitutes, and page 354 for making your own)*
> *1–2 cups julienned or shredded carrots*
> *1 tablespoon Chinese or Japanese sesame oil*
> *1½ cups Spicy Szechwan Peanut Sauce (page 473)*

> *To garnish:*
> *coarsely chopped fresh coriander*

Preparations:

Put as many bowls as you have noodle eaters in a low oven to warm. Station a large heatproof colander in the sink. Put the sesame oil in the bottom of a large bowl suitable for tossing the noodles, then swirl the bowl to glaze it with the oil. If you lack one great big bowl, then divide the sesame oil between two medium bowls or stockpots. Have a pair of tongs or spaghetti forks alongside the bowl(s) ready to toss the noodles once they are done. Bring the sauce to room temperature, if chilled.

Cooking the noodles:

Bring a generous amount of plain water to a rolling boil over high heat. While the water is heating, fluff the noodles gently with your fingers to separate the strands. (Frozen noodles should be thoroughly defrosted in the bag, then fluffed like fresh before cooking.) Add the noodles to the boiling water, swish several times with chopsticks, then cook until the noodles look swollen and are firm but tender to the bite, about 2 minutes for fresh store-bought noodles. If you are serving the noodles directly, then add the shredded carrots to the pot after 1 minute, so they cook with the noodles. Drain immediately in the colander, then shake to remove excess water.

Add the drained noodles (and carrots) to the oiled bowl, then toss the noodles to glaze them evenly, lifting them up, and then showering them into the bowl repeatedly but gently so they do not break. Portion the noodles quickly into the heated bowls, and top each portion with a generous dollop of sauce. Garnish with a healthy sprinkling of coriander, for those who like it, then serve at once, accompanied by a bowl of extra sauce.

Invite each guest to toss his or her own noodles, as is customary in China where noodle eating is a participation sport.

Extra noodles may be kept warm in a regulation steamer or an improvised steamer (a covered colander set over a pot of simmering water), for those who want second helpings.

Cooled leftover noodles can be bagged and refrigerated for several days. Steam over high heat in a tightly covered bowl until hot. Leftover sauce keeps indefinitely.

MENU SUGGESTIONS:
This dish stands easily on its own for a simple lunch or supper with one of the "Little Dishes"—*Soy-Dipped Red Radish Fans* (page 114), *Sweet and Tangy Cucumber Pickles* (page 110), or *Sweet and Crunchy Red Bell Pepper Cubes* (page 115)—alongside. The noodles are also excellent partnered with simple barbecued meats and poultry.

The Five Heaps

五峰涼麵

Systems of interrelated fives pop up everywhere in Chinese culture. There are the Five Elements, the Five (Confucian) Relationships, the Five (Mythic) Emperors, the Five (Historic) Dynasties, the Five Colors, the Five Constant Virtues, the Five Flavors . . . So why not the Five Heaps? ◆ That is my playful nickname for one of my favorite warm-weather dishes—a mound of cold sesame-sauced noodles surrounded by five colorful piles of crisp vegetables. It is a thoroughly impromptu dish that may have four heaps or six depending on whim and the market, or no heaps at all if you prefer your noodles straight. ◆ This is a good, cheery dish for light eating alone, or an easy way to entertain company. It is also portable enough for a picnic or potluck dinner, and a dish that is certain to mix well with a variety of foods. Preparations may be done up to a day in advance, with only a few minutes needed to assemble the platter.

TECHNIQUE NOTES:
For choosing and cooking egg noodles for Chinese dishes, see TECHNIQUE NOTES, page 360.

Serves 2–3 as a main course, 4–6 as part of a multicourse meal.

INGREDIENTS:

½ pound long, thin Chinese egg noodles, fresh or frozen (see page 351 for substitutes and page 354 for making your own)

Sauce ingredients:
    2 tablespoons untoasted sesame seeds
    2 tablespoons Five-Flavor Oil (page 480)
    2 tablespoons Chinese sesame paste (page 565)
    2 tablespoons water
    1 tablespoon thin (regular) soy sauce
    2 teaspoons unseasoned Chinese or Japanese rice vinegar
    1½ teaspoons sugar
    scant ¼ teaspoon Roasted Szechwan Pepper-Salt (page 476)
    ¼–½ teaspoon chili oil (optional)

The five heaps:
    1 cup fresh bean sprouts
    1 cup of a crisp green (choose one):
        slivered fresh snow peas or sugar snap peas
        slivered string beans or Chinese longbeans, cut into 2-inch lengths
        slivered celery hearts and inner ribs, cut into 2-inch lengths
        slivered seedless cucumber
    1 cup julienned or shredded carrots
    1 cup shredded radishes
    1 cup (about 4 ounces) slivered Black Forest-type ham (page 549) or cooked chicken

To garnish:
    coarsely chopped fresh coriander

Preparing the noodles:
Cook the noodles as directed on page 357. Drain well, then toss with 1½ teaspoons of the premeasured Five-Flavor Oil. Once oiled, the noodles may be sealed airtight and refrigerated overnight. Bring to room temperature before saucing.

Toasting the seeds and mixing the sauce:
Toast the sesame seeds in a dry skillet over moderate heat, stirring until golden, about 5 minutes. Reserve 1 teaspoon of the toasted seeds for a garnish.

Add the remainder to the work bowl of a food processor fitted with the steel knife and process until coarsely ground. Scrape the seeds into a small dish, return the steel knife and the remaining sauce ingredients to the bowl, then process until homogenized. Taste and add chili oil if desired. The mixture should be very zesty and high-seasoned if it is to stand up to the noodles and the trimmings. Return the ground seeds to the work bowl, combine with several on-off turns, then scrape the sauce into a bowl. Seal airtight and let stand at room temperature, overnight if desired, to develop the flavors. Use the sauce at room temperature. Alternatively, crush all but 1 teaspoon of the sesame seeds in a mortar or blender. Combine the remaining sauce ingredients in a blender or by hand, then complete the sauce as above.

Preparing the five heaps:
Blanch the bean sprouts for 30 seconds in plain boiling water to cover. Drain, then rush under cold running water to stop the cooking. Cover with cold water and refrigerate until use.

Blanch snow peas, sugar snap peas, string beans, or longbeans until tender-crisp.

Test for timing with a single sliver. Drain, chill under cold water, and shake off excess water. Refrigerate, if desired, spread on a plate and sealed airtight. Pat dry before using.

The remaining vegetables and the coriander should be cut only shortly before serving.

Assembling the salad:

Just before serving, drain the bean sprouts and spread them on a lint-free towel to blot up excess water. Pour the sauce over the noodles, mixing well with your fingers to separate and coat the strands. Mound the noodles in the center of a large serving platter, then ring the noodles with the five heaps, alternating the colors for the prettiest effect. Sprinkle the reserved sesame seeds on top of the noodles, and serve.

Invite your guests to help themselves to a bit of everything and to toss the many heaps into one colorful heap in their bowls.

Leftovers keep 1–2 days, refrigerated and sealed airtight.

MENU SUGGESTIONS:

This dish is perfect on its own for a light meal. If you have not made chicken one of the five heaps, it is also excellent served alongside *Master Sauce Chicken* (page 153) or *Tea and Spice Smoked Chicken* (page 158). To extend the menu, try *Cold-Tossed Asparagus with Sesame Seeds* (page 288), *Soy-Dipped Red Radish Fans* (page 114), and *Master Sauce Eggs* (page 327) or *Marbelized Tea Eggs* (page 325). In a Western setting, the noodles are a novel accompaniment to simple grilled poultry and meat.

Hunan Noodles with Spicy Meat Sauce

炸醬麵

Noodles slathered with hearty sauces concocted from minced pork, bean pastes, and sometimes hoisin sauce are common in north China. This recipe takes us farther south into central China and the province of Hunan, for a spicy, lighter, and clearer-tasting variation on the same theme. The sparkle and spice is supplied by Chinese chili sauce, and there is lots of ginger, garlic, scallion, and pepper to give the noodles zip. Plus, there is enough pork to make it a complete meal in a bowl. ◆ This is a very simple dish to cook, even for a novice. Preparations may be completed a full day ahead, and the noodles served hot or tepid.

TECHNIQUE NOTES:

The cornstarch in the pork mixture binds the marinade to the meat, sealing the juices in, and giving the pork a special softness when it is cooked. The cornstarch also infiltrates the sauce and thickens it slightly, making the addition of any further cornstarch unnecessary.

The noodles are undercooked at the start so they can cook to doneness when combined with the sauce, absorbing its flavor as well as its heat.

Serves 4–6 as a main course, 8–12 as part of a multicourse meal.

INGREDIENTS:

   1½ pounds ground pork butt

   To marinate the pork:
      6 tablespoons thin (regular) soy sauce (read the cautionary note regarding brands on page 568)

4 tablespoons Chinese rice wine or quality, dry sherry
2 tablespoons cornstarch
2 teaspoons sugar
2 teaspoons Chinese or Japanese sesame oil
½ teaspoon freshly ground pepper

¾ pound ¹⁄₁₆ inch thin Chinese egg noodles, fresh or frozen (see page 351 for
    substitutes and page 354 for making your own)
1 tablespoon Chinese or Japanese sesame oil
1½ teaspoons coarse kosher salt

Aromatics:
    ½–¾ cup green and white scallion rings, cut a scant ¼ inch thick
    3 walnut-size nuggets fresh ginger
    8–10 large cloves garlic, stem end removed, lightly smashed and peeled
    1–1½ tablespoons Chinese chili sauce (page 536)

Sauce ingredients:
    2 cups rich, unsalted chicken stock
    4 tablespoons thin (regular) soy sauce
    1 teaspoon sugar
    ¼–½ teaspoon freshly ground pepper

¾–1 cup julienned carrots
3–4 tablespoons corn or peanut oil, for stir-frying

To garnish:
    coarsely chopped fresh coriander or fresh basil, cut into a chiffonade (page
        265)

Marinating the pork:
In the work bowl of a food processor fitted with the steel knife, blend the soy, wine, cornstarch, sugar, sesame oil, and black pepper until smooth. Distribute the pork around the blade (work in 2 batches if you have a processor with a small work bowl, using half the marinade and half the pork at a time), then combine with on-off turns. Do not over-process to a paste. If you do not have a food processor, stir the marinade ingredients in a large bowl until smooth and well-blended, add the pork, then stir well in one direction to combine. Pick up the pork in your hand and throw it lightly against the inside of the bowl 5 or 6 times to compact it.

Seal the mixture airtight with a piece of plastic film pressed directly on the surface of the pork, then marinate 1–3 hours at room temperature or overnight in the refrigerator. Bring to room temperature before using.

Parboiling the noodles:
Bring a generous amount of unsalted water to a rolling boil over high heat. Fluff the noodles to separate the strands and station a colander in the sink. (The remaining ¼ pound noodles, if you bought the noodles in the standard 1-pound bag, may be sealed airtight and frozen for future use.)

Add the noodles to the boiling water, then swish gently with chopsticks or a wooden spoon to separate the strands. Boil until tender but definitely firmer than you would want them if you were eating them directly—about 2 minutes, depending on the noodles. Taste frequently to be sure. Drain the noodles promptly in the colander and flush immediately with cold water until chilled. Shake to remove excess water, then toss gently with the sesame oil and salt, using your fingers to coat and separate the strands.

Coated, the noodles may be bagged airtight and refrigerated up to 2 days.

Other preparations:
Mince the ginger and garlic until fine, in a food processor fitted with the steel knife or by hand. Combine with the scallion rings and the chili sauce in a small bowl. (I like to cut the scallion rings by hand for this dish, to give them character and to add texture.) Seal the aromatics airtight and refrigerate until use, overnight if desired.

Combine the sauce ingredients, stirring to blend. If you are working a day in advance, seal airtight and refrigerate until use.

Cut carrots may be refrigerated overnight in a misted plastic bag. Coriander or basil should be cut just before serving.

Stir-frying the dish:
Have all the ingredients within easy reach of your stovetop, and put individual serving bowls in a low oven to warm.

Heat a wok or a large, deep, heavy skillet, or wide, heavy stockpot over high heat until hot enough to evaporate a bead of water on contact. Add the oil and swirl to glaze the pan. When the oil is hot enough to sizzle a single scallion ring on contact, add the aromatics and stir until fully fragrant, about 15 seconds, adjusting the heat so the mixture foams without browning. Add the pork, then poke, chop, and stir to break it into bits and sear it on all sides, adjusting the heat to maintain a merry sizzle so the fat content of the meat renders and helps to oil the pan. Dribble in a bit more oil from the side of the pan if needed to prevent sticking. When the meat is 90 percent gray, add the carrots and toss well to combine. Give the sauce mixture a stir and add it to the pan. Raise the heat to bring the mixture to a boil, stirring, then taste the sauce and adjust with more chili sauce or pepper if desired. It should be wildly spicy and zesty to stand up to the noodles and be true to Hunan taste.

Turn off the heat and add the noodles. Toss well but gently to combine, then cover the pot. Let stand 15–30 minutes to allow the noodles to absorb the flavors of the sauce and cook to doneness. If you like, they may be left in the covered pot for upwards of 2 hours, then served tepid.

Just before serving, toss to combine, portion into the heated bowls, and garnish with freshly cut coriander or basil.

Leftovers keep beautifully, 3–4 days, refrigerated and sealed airtight. To reheat, steam over high heat in a tightly covered bowl until hot. The noodles will be soft, but they are delicious nonetheless. Expect them to be even spicier.

MENU SUGGESTIONS:
I like this dish best on its own, with one or more of the crunchy "Little Dishes"—*Soy-Dipped Red Radish Fans* (page 114), *Sweet and Tangy Cucumber Pickles* (page 110), *Cold-Tossed Celery in Garlic Vinaigrette* (page 116), or *Sweet and Sour Green Tomato Pickle* (page 120). For a wine to serve alongside, choose a Côtes du Rhône or Chianti.

| Pot-Browned Noodles 煎麵 | Called "two-sides-brown" in Chinese, this is just about my favorite style of Chinese noodle dish—an inch-thick noodle "pillow," crunchy and brown on the outside and soft within, topped by a savory, saucy stir-fry of meat and vegetables. The texture appeals to me mightily, as does the cooking method. I relish the dramatic moment when one tosses the noodle pillow up in the air to flip it over, hoping that eternal split-second that it will land back neatly in the pan! (If |

your taste runs to greater surety, you may flip the noodles with a spatula. This dish is an easy one, and no unskilled flipper need fear it.) ♦ Below is the master recipe for the noodle pillow, plus a list of suggested toppings. These traditional choices aside, use your imagination for devising a topping. It needn't be fancy—a healthy splash of master sauce (page 153), the reheated leftovers from last night's *Saucy Potted Pork* (page 207), or a stir-fry of slivered vegetables bound together with a good dollop of top-quality oyster sauce are all fair game for a noodle pillow. Most any saucy stir-fry is compatible, as is a simple sprinkling of *Roasted Szechwan Pepper-Salt* (page 476). ♦ The noodles may be parboiled up to 2 days in advance. The frying, done just before serving, takes 15 minutes.

TECHNIQUE NOTES:
I know three tricks to successfully pan-fry pasta, whether you're browning noodles or the bottoms of Chinese dumplings to make pot stickers. First, use a heavy skillet—cast iron is ideal—with an even-heating, unwarped surface. Before using, fill it with ½ cup water and put it on the stovetop. If the water is deeper at one side, rotate the pan, switch it to another burner, or somehow balance it so the noodles fry evenly when the pan is glazed with oil. Second, swirl the pan once the oil has been added so the sides are glazed as well as the bottom. Otherwise, the dough will stick to the sides and you'll have a messy time detaching it. Third, when putting the noodles into the pan, start on the outside and work in toward the center. The center of a large skillet is typically hotter than the outer edge, and this will give the noodles or dumplings near the rim a necessary head start.

With a topping, serves 2 as a main dish, 4 as part of a multicourse meal.

INGREDIENTS:

> ½ pound long, ¹⁄₁₆ inch thin Chinese egg noodles, fresh best (see page 351 for
>   substitutes, and page 354 for making your own)
> 1½ teaspoons Chinese or Japanese sesame oil
> 1 teaspoon coarse kosher salt
> 6 tablespoons corn or peanut oil

> Toppings:
>   Four-Spice Pork with Spinach (page 191)
>   or
>   Capital Sauce Pork Ribbons (page 193)
>   or
>   Stir-Fried Beef with Silky Leeks (page 214)

Parboiling the noodles:
Boil the noodles until cooked but firm, as directed on page 357. Drain, then rush immediately under cold water until thoroughly chilled. Shake off excess water, and spread the

noodles evenly on a lint-free cloth. Roll the cloth up loosely, then gently pat the roll to dry the noodles, just as you would a sweater. Undo the roll and transfer the noodles to a large bowl. Toss gently but thoroughly with the sesame oil and salt, working with your fingers to lightly coat and separate each strand. Take care not to break the noodles.

Once oiled, the noodles may be bagged airtight in plastic and refrigerated, up to 2 days. Bring to room temperature before frying.

Frying the noodle pillow:
Heat a heavy 12–13-inch skillet over high heat until hot enough to evaporate a bead of water on contact. Add 5 tablespoons oil, swirl to coat the sides as well as the bottom of the pan, then arrange the skillet on the burner so the oil is evenly deep. Reduce the heat to medium.

When the oil is hot enough to sizzle one strand of noodle, coil the noodles evenly over the bottom of the pan, working from the outer edge toward the center. Press them down with a spatula, cover the pan, then cook until the underside of the noodles is nicely browned, 5–7 minutes.

Turn the noodles over like a pancake, flipping them in the air with a sharp jerk of the wrist if you're a practiced flipper, or with a spatula if you're not. Dribble the remaining 1 tablespoon oil in from the side of the pan and swirl the pan to distribute the oil underneath the noodles. Press the noodles down evenly with the spatula, cover, and cook until browned, 5–7 minutes.

While the second side is browning, stir-fry the topping so that the noodles and topping are done simultaneously.

Loosen the browned noodles with a spatula if necessary, then slip them out of the pan onto a large, heated platter. If the topping is not ready, the noodles may be held briefly in a 250° oven.

Mound the topping in the center of the noodle pillow, so an inch of noodles remains visible all around. Serve immediately, inviting your guests to pull the pillow apart with their chopsticks, Chinese-style, or use a knife if you wish to slice it like a pie.

Leftovers, in my opinion, are excellent at room temperature. Or you may warm them in an oven, covered tightly with foil.

MENU SUGGESTIONS:
Crowned with one of the suggested toppings, the noodle pillow makes a wonderful one-dish dinner, accompanied by a glass of good wine to complement the topping, and followed by fresh fruit and *Orange-Almond Coins* (page 495). If a soup is desired, *Soup of Many Mushrooms* (page 454) would be a versatile choice.

Stir-Fried Noodles with Chicken and Mushrooms

雞絲炒麵

When I left for Taiwan, what I knew as chow mein was a concoction of tinned, fried, and vaguely rancid brown noodles, topped with a taste-free chicken and celery sauce and served up proudly in high school and museum cafeterias. What naïveté! ◆ This is *real* chow mein, literally, "stir-fried noodles": thin egg noodles that are first boiled to cook them, then stir-fried to give them a special gloss and texture, and finally tumbled in a light sauce with a stir-fried variety of soft and crunchy accompaniments. It sounds complicated, but it is actually very easy, and the result is a one-dish dinner to make you forget all those high school lunches. ◆ Depending upon your mood, you may make the noodles soft or crispy-edged. Swift tossing over moderate heat in little oil yields a soft texture. Using more oil, higher heat, and pressing the noodles against the pan makes them crispy in spots. Both textures are compelling and equally traditional. ◆ All the preparations may be done in advance. The actual stir-frying, done just before eating, takes minutes.

TECHNIQUE NOTES:
Making chow mein involves two separate stir-frying steps—the meat and vegetables first, the noodles second—and necessitates working at top speed so the components stay crisp and savory. The trick is to get the meat and vegetables out of the pan when they are only 90 percent cooked, so they will cook to perfection when they are tossed with the noodles.

For the components of a velvet chicken marinade, see TECHNIQUE NOTES, page 145. For details on the velveting process, see TECHNIQUE NOTES and the recipe on page 137. Here, I like to velvet the chicken in water, both for ease and the lightness it gives the dish.

Serves 3–4 as a main dish, 5–8 as part of a multicourse meal.

INGREDIENTS:

> *½ pound ¹⁄₁₆ inch thin Chinese egg noodles, fresh or frozen (see page 351 for substitutes and page 354 for making your own)*
> *1½ teaspoons Chinese or Japanese sesame oil*
> *1 teaspoon coarse kosher salt*
> *½ pound skinned and boned fresh chicken breast, trimmed of all membranes, cartilage, and fat (weight after trimming; equal to about 1 pound with skin and bone in; see page 126 for easy, 5-minute boning)*

For marinating the chicken:
> *1 tablespoon egg white*
> *¾ teaspoon coarse kosher salt*
> *2 teaspoons Chinese rice wine or quality, dry sherry*
> *2 teaspoons cornstarch*

Vegetables:
> *4 large or 8 medium Chinese dried black mushrooms, "flower" variety recommended (page 538)*
> *2 tablespoons tree ears (page 576)*
> *¼ pound fresh young snow peas, strings removed, or 1 medium carrot, trimmed and peeled, or 8–10 ounces fresh broccoli stems and flowerets*

Aromatics:
> *1½ walnut-size nuggets fresh ginger*
> *4–6 large cloves garlic, stem ends removed, lightly smashed and peeled*
> *1–1½ teaspoons Chinese chili sauce (page 536) (optional)*

Sauce ingredients:
> *¼ cup rich, unsalted chicken stock*
> *2 tablespoons thin (regular) soy sauce*
> *1 tablespoon Chinese rice wine or quality, dry sherry*
> *½ teaspoon sugar*
> *¼ teaspoon coarse kosher salt*

> *2 teaspoons cornstarch dissolved in 1 tablespoon cold chicken stock*

4 cups water plus 2 teaspoons corn or peanut oil, for velveting
about ½ cup corn or peanut oil, for stir-frying

Cooking the noodles:
Cook and drain the noodles as directed on page 357. Toss well with 1½ teaspoons sesame oil and 1 teaspoon kosher salt, gently so as not to break the noodles. If working in advance, bag the noodles airtight in plastic and refrigerate up to 2 days. Bring to room temperature before stir-frying.

Shredding and marinating the chicken:
Chill and shred the chicken as described on page 146.

Whisk the marinade ingredients until smooth and thick and combine with the chicken, tossing well with your fingers to coat and separate the slivers. When the chicken is supple, seal airtight and refrigerate 4–24 hours, stirring occasionally. The longer the chicken marinates, the plumper and more tender it will be.

Other preparations:
Soak the mushrooms in cold or hot water to cover until fully soft and spongy, 20 minutes to an hour. Drain, snip off the stems with scissors, then rinse the caps to dislodge any sand trapped in the gills. Cut the caps into neat long slivers ⅛ inch wide.

Cover the tree ears with a generous amount of cool or warm water (they will expand greatly), and soak until supple, about 20 minutes. Drain, rinse well to remove grit, then discard any very tough or gelatinous bits. Rinse a second time and drain. Tear, if needed, into nickel-size pieces. Combine the tree ears and the slivered mushrooms.

Cut the snow peas on the diagonal into thin slivers a scant ¼ inch wide. Or, shred the carrot to yield 1½ cups shreds. Or, peel the broccoli stem of its woody outer bark and cut it crosswise on a diagonal into thin coins a scant ¼ inch thick, then stack several coins at a time and cut them lengthwise into slivers a scant ¼ inch wide. Cut the flowerets into small, dainty pieces the size of a marble. Altogether, you should have 1½–2 cups broccoli.

Mince the ginger and garlic in a food processor or by hand. Put aside on a small saucer, with the chili sauce if you are using it.

Stir the sauce ingredients to combine. Stir the cornstarch mixture to blend and leave the spoon in the bowl.

All the above may be done up to a full day in advance. Except for the cornstarch mixture, seal everything airtight and refrigerate, and bring to room temperature before cooking. The cut vegetables should be misted before bagging to keep them moist.

Velveting the chicken:
About 20–30 minutes before serving, bring the water for velveting to a near-simmer in a large saucepan, stir in the oil, and adjust the heat so the water does not boil. While it is heating, put a colander in the sink and a serving platter of contrasting color in a low oven to warm. Have all the ingredients for the dish and an extra plate to hold the vegetables within easy reach of your stovetop. Stir the chicken to loosen the pieces.

With the water at a superficial simmer—rolling but not quite bubbling on the surface—slide the chicken into the oil. Stir gently with chopsticks to separate the shreds, then drain the chicken into the colander as soon as it turns 90 percent white, in about 15–20 seconds. The chicken should be only part-cooked; if you are in any doubt, drain it sooner rather than later. Proceed immediately to the stir-frying.

Stir-frying the dish:

Put a wok or a large, deep, heavy skillet, or wide heavy stockpot over high heat until hot enough to evaporate a bead of water on contact. (You will need the roominess of a large wok or pot in which to tumble and shower the noodles.)

Add 4 tablespoons oil and swirl to coat the pan. When the oil is hot enough to sizzle a bit of ginger on contact, add the minced aromatics, nudging the chili sauce in last. Stir gently until fully aromatic, about 10 seconds, adjusting the heat so the mixture foams without browning. Add the snow peas, carrots, or broccoli, then toss briskly to glaze with oil, dribbling in a bit more oil from the side of the pan if it becomes too dry. When the vegetable is evenly glazed with oil, add the mushrooms and tree ears and toss briskly to mix, adjusting the heat to maintain a merry sizzle without scorching the vegetable. Toss a minute longer if you are using broccoli, until it is just tender-crisp, then add the chicken. Toss briskly to combine and heat the chicken through, about 10–15 seconds, then scrape the mixture onto the waiting plate. The vegetables and chicken should still be undercooked, so they will cook to perfection (not overdoneness) when combined with the noodles.

Quickly wipe the pan clean, then return it to high heat until hot enough to evaporate a bead of water on contact. Add 1½–3 tablespoons vegetable oil, depending upon whether you want soft or crisp noodles (more oil for crisper noodles), then swirl to glaze the pan. When the oil is hot enough to sizzle one strand of noodle on contact, shower them into the pan. Toss and shower them with rapid scooping motions, using one or two spatulas or spoons, to glaze them evenly with the oil and heat them through. For soft noodles, work over moderate heat and toss quickly and constantly. For crispy-edged noodles, raise the heat to medium-high and press the noodles repeatedly against the pan to brown them in spots. Dribble in a bit more oil from the side of the pan if they are sticking and lower the heat if the noodles begin to scorch.

When the noodles are hot and as crisp as desired, give the combined sauce ingredients a stir and add them to the pan. Toss gently to mix, then raise the heat to bring the liquids to a simmer. Stir the cornstarch mixture to recombine, then add it to the pan. Stir until the liquids turn glossy and slightly thick, about 20 seconds, then return the chicken and the vegetables to the pan. Toss and shower the noodles in large scooping motions to mix, then remove at once to the heated serving platter.

Serve at once, while hot and fragrant, pausing only to arrange things nicely on the platter with a few quick moves of chopsticks or tongs.

Leftovers keep 2–3 days and are very tasty (though not traditional) eaten at room temperature. Toss well before eating.

MENU SUGGESTIONS:

I like to serve this dish as a one-course supper, sometimes with *Sweet and Tangy Cucumber Pickles* (page 110) or one of the other crunchy "Little Dishes" on the side. If a soup is desired, try *Szechwan Pork and Pickle Soup* (page 456). To accompany the noodles, choose a Chardonnay.

Ants Climbing a Tree

螞蟻上樹

A justly famous, very spicy Szechwanese classic, so named because the dots of meat scattered throughout the noodles are thought to resemble ants. Think what you will of the name, but it is positive addiction for chili lovers and texture fiends. The little cubes of carrots, an untraditional touch, lend color and dash. ◆ Bean threads, the transparent "glass" noodles that wrap dutifully around one's tongue in submission, are here at their slinky, slippery best, stained and flavored temptingly by the sauce. They constitute the bulk of the dish and make it appealingly light. ◆ This is a simple enough dish for a beginner and a good choice for a quick, after-work dinner. All of the preparation, save the actual stir-frying, may be done in advance.

TECHNIQUE NOTES:

When soaking bean threads prior to inclusion in a stir-fry, it is important not to let them get too soft. Drain them while they are still rubber-band firm, and leave it to the cooking to turn them soft and supple.

Depending upon the brand of bean thread, you will need either warm or very hot tap water to turn them rubber-band firm. In general, brands from Taiwan (which I prefer) need only warm tap water, while brands from the People's Republic of China require very hot tap water. Anywhere from 30–60 seconds with the right temperature water is enough to turn them rubber-band firm, after which the noodles can be left in the water without softening further. If they remain wiry upon soaking, use hotter water.

Serves 2–3 as a main dish, 4–6 as part of a multicourse meal.

INGREDIENTS:

> *4 ounces bean threads (glass noodles) (page 533)*
> *½ cup tiny fresh carrot cubes*
> *½ pound ground pork butt*

> *For marinating the pork:*
> *2 tablespoons thin (regular) soy sauce*
> *2 tablespoons Chinese rice wine or quality, dry sherry*
> *1 teaspoon cornstarch*

> *Aromatics:*
> *2 tablespoons finely minced fresh ginger*
> *6–8 tablespoons thin-cut green and white scallion rings*
> *3–4 teaspoons Chinese chili sauce (page 536)*

> *⅔ cup rich, unsalted chicken stock*
> *1 tablespoon thin (regular) soy sauce*
> *coarse kosher salt, to taste*
> *about 5 tablespoons corn or peanut oil*
> *scant teaspoon Chinese or Japanese sesame oil*

Preparations:

Remove the outer wrapper from the noodles, but leave the rubber bands or strings binding them intact. Soak in warm or hot tap water, as described above in TECHNIQUE NOTES, until rubber-band firm. Once pliable, cut through the loop ends of the skein with scissors to cut the noodles into manageable lengths, then cut and discard the rubber bands or strings. Do not oversoak the noodles. Drain well. The noodles may be refrigerated covered with cool water or sealed airtight against drying overnight.

Blanch the diced carrots in simmering unsalted water only 1 minute, until tender-crisp. Drain and rush under cold water until chilled. If working in advance, cover with cold water and refrigerate, up to 2 days. Drain thoroughly before using.

Blend the soy, wine, and cornstarch until smooth, in the work bowl of a food processor fitted with the steel knife. Distribute the pork around the blade, then process with several on-off turns to blend. Alternatively, stir the marinade ingredients until smooth, then combine with the pork by hand, stirring in one direction until blended. Seal airtight and refrigerate until use, overnight if desired. Bring to room temperature before stir-frying.

Put the ginger, scallion, and chili sauce on a plate. Combine the stock and soy, taste, and add salt if required.

Stir-frying the dish:
About 10–15 minutes before serving, arrange all the ingredients within easy reach of your stovetop, and put a serving platter of contrasting color in a low oven to warm.

Heat a wok or a large, heavy skillet over high heat until hot enough to evaporate a bead of water on contact. Add the vegetable oil, and swirl to glaze the pan. When the oil is hot enough to sizzle one bit of ginger, add the scallion, ginger, and chili sauce, and stir until fragrant, about 10 seconds, adjusting the heat so the mixture foams without browning. Add the pork and stir briskly, tossing and chopping the meat to break it into tiny bits. Adjust the heat to maintain a merry sizzle, and dribble in a bit more oil from the side of the pan if the meat is sticking. When the pork is gray, add the stock mixture and bring the liquids to a simmer, stirring. Add the noodles, stir gently to coat, then add the carrots and stir to combine. Adjust the heat to maintain a gentle simmer and cover the pan.

Simmer until most of the liquid is evaporated, about 2–4 minutes, then remove the cover and turn off the heat. Stir the contents of the pan once or twice, sprinkle with sesame oil, and stir to combine.

Remove the mixture to the heated platter and serve at once, while the noodles are steaming, slippery, and fragrant.

Leftovers keep 2–3 days and are delightful at room temperature if you're a fan of cold noodles. If not, steam in a tightly covered bowl until hot.

MENU SUGGESTIONS:
An ideal partner for this dish is *Dry-Fried Szechwan String Beans* (page 297), for those who like the heat. A cooler choice would be *Stir-Fried Spinach with Fermented Tofu* (page 306), or *Stir-Fried Spinach with Charred Garlic* (page 305). In a Western setting, the noodles are an excellent side dish for simply cooked fish and poultry, and are ably partnered by a salad of fresh watercress or spinach dressed with a good oil and vinegar. To stand up to the spice of the noodles, choose a full-flavored Petite Sirah.

Star-
Country
Curried
Rice Noodles

星州炒米粉

I discovered this dish in a Cantonese restaurant and was as intrigued by the name as by the taste. "Star-Country" turns out to be Singapore, and what that has to do with the dish is unclear. Regardless, the soft texture of the thin rice noodles is wonderfully appealing, and the combination of plump shrimp and fruity-hot curry captivates me. ◆ This is a full-flavored, belly-warming dish, perfect for a one-dish supper. The preparation requires no skill and little time, and everything short of the actual stir-frying may be done in advance.

TECHNIQUE NOTES:
When cooking eggs for inclusion in a stir-fry, it is important not to overcook them. Work

over moderate heat so the eggs stay soft and get them out of the pan when they are only 90 percent set and still a bit runny. The eggs will continue to cook from their own heat after they leave the pan and will turn firmer still in the final stir-frying.

Also, if you do not have a wok (whose contours are perfect for this job), choose a skillet or omelet pan that will allow the egg to fill the pan ¼–⅜ inch deep. Too small a pan fills too deeply and the egg is hard to maneuver; too large a pan yields an egg pancake.

Serves 3–4 as a main dish, 5–8 as part of a multicourse meal.

INGREDIENTS:

> *½ pound small or medium fresh shrimp (for a note on "fresh" shrimp, see page 233)*

> *To marinate the shrimp:*
> *1 tablespoon egg white (from eggs below)*
> *2 teaspoons Chinese rice wine or quality, dry sherry*
> *1 tablespoon cornstarch*
> *½ teaspoon coarse kosher salt*
> *several grinds fresh pepper*

> *6 ounces ¹⁄₁₆ inch thin dry rice sticks, sold in flat wads (page 559)*
> *3 large eggs*
> *⅛ teaspoon coarse kosher salt*
> *several grinds fresh pepper*
> *4 medium whole scallions*

> *Sauce ingredients:*
> *⅔ cup rich, unsalted chicken stock*
> *2 tablespoons thin (regular) soy sauce*
> *2½ tablespoons curry paste (page 542)*
> *⅛ teaspoon sugar*

> *1½ teaspoons Chinese rice wine or quality, dry sherry*
> *1½ tablespoons finely minced Smithfield ham (optional)*
> *3 cups corn or peanut oil, for velveting and stir-frying*

> *To garnish:*
> *1 teaspoon Chinese or Japanese sesame oil*
> *freshly ground pepper to taste*
> *sprigs of fresh coriander (optional)*

Marinating the shrimp:
Shell and devein the shrimp, then rinse with cool water and pat dry. Blend the ingredients for marinating the shrimp until smooth and slightly thick. Scrape the marinade over the shrimp, toss to combine, then seal airtight and refrigerate 8–36 hours. The longer the shrimp marinates, the more marinade it will absorb and the more tender it will be.

Other preparations:
Cover the rice sticks with hot tap water and soak until supple, 5–10 minutes. Drain before using and shake to remove excess water.

Beat the eggs with the salt and pepper until combined but not frothy. Cut the scallions into 1-inch lengths, and cut the white and light green sections in half lengthwise. Stir the sauce ingredients to blend.

All the above may be done up to a full day in advance. Seal everything airtight and refrigerate, misting the scallions lightly before bagging to keep them crisp. Bring everything to room temperature before cooking.

Velveting the shrimp:
Have all the ingredients, a large Chinese mesh spoon, a bowl to hold the cooked eggs, and some paper towels all within easy reach of your stovetop. Put a serving platter of contrasting color in a low oven to warm. If you need to velvet the shrimp and stir-fry the noodles in one wok or large skillet, then have a heatproof bowl at hand in which to decant the hot oil.

About 20 minutes before serving, set a wok or a large, heavy skillet for velveting the shrimp over high heat until hot. Add the 3 cups oil, and heat to the slow-fry temperature, 275° on a deep-fry thermometer. Adjust the heat so the oil temperature does not rise, then stir the shrimp to loosen and slide them gently into the oil. Stir slowly with chopsticks or a wooden spoon until the shrimp turn 90 percent pinkish-white, about 15 seconds, then scoop them immediately from the oil with the mesh spoon or strainer and nest it on top of the bowl in which the shrimp marinated so they can drain. The shrimp should be only partially cooked, mostly white on the outside but raw within.

If you do not have another pot for stir-frying, then carefully decant the hot oil into the heatproof bowl. Otherwise, let the oil cool, undisturbed, and strain and bottle it later for future frying.

Stir-frying the eggs and the noodles:
As soon as the shrimp are velveted, set a wok or a *medium*-size, heavy skillet over high heat until hot enough to evaporate a bead of water on contact. Add 3 tablespoons of the frying oil, swirl to coat the pan, then reduce the heat to moderate. When the oil is hot enough to puff one drop of egg on contact, stir the egg mixture to recombine and add it to the pan. It should puff immediately. When the egg sets on the bottom, within seconds, gently push the cooked egg to the far side of the pan with a spatula, allowing the liquid egg to flow beneath and make contact with the hot metal. If you are using a flat skillet, tilt it to aid the flow. Continue pushing the cooked portion to the far side of the pan as it sets until the entire mixture is cooked but still very loose, adjusting the heat so the egg cooks swiftly but stays soft and does not brown. When it is 90 percent set, scrape the egg into the waiting bowl and break it into small bits with the spatula.

Wipe the wok clean with the paper towels and return it or a *large*, heavy skillet to high heat until hot enough to evaporate a bead of water on contact. Add 2 tablespoons of the frying oil and swirl to coat the pan. When the oil is hot enough to sizzle one scallion nugget, add the scallions and stir-fry briskly to coat with oil, adjusting the heat so they sizzle without scorching. When fully fragrant, in about 10 seconds, splash the wine into the pan, toss briskly several seconds, then remove the scallions swiftly to the bowl with the eggs.

Return the pot to the heat, stir the sauce mixture, and add it to the pan. Bring to a boil over high heat, add the drained noodles and the ham, if you are using it, and stir gently to blend. (The noodles will break into short lengths as you stir.) Adjust the heat to maintain a simmer, layer the velveted shrimp evenly on top of the noodles, and cover the pot. Cook until the liquids are absorbed, 2–4 minutes. Remove the cover, reduce the heat to low, and stir gently 2 or 3 times to redistribute the seasonings. Taste the mixture for curry and add a dab more if required. Return the eggs and scallions to the pan and toss gently to mix. Add the sesame oil and pepper to taste (I like lots), then toss gently to combine.

Slide the mixture onto the heated platter and pause to adjust a shrimp or piece of green scallion prettily here and there. Garnish if you like with a cluster of fresh coriander on top of the noodle mound, then serve.

Leftovers keep nicely 2–3 days, refrigerated and sealed airtight. Heat until hot in a tightly covered dish in either a steamer set over high heat or in a hot oven.

MENU SUGGESTIONS:
Alone, this dish is a satisfying and simple meal, followed if you wish by a light fruit dessert like *Glacéed Orange Slices* (page 487). For a fuller menu, try the noodles in the company of *Tea and Spice Smoked Chicken* (page 158) or *Red Bell Pepper with Garlic and Coriander* (page 314). To partner the noodles, try a big-bodied white wine—a white Rhône wine (Châteauneuf or Hermitage) or California Chardonnay—that is not too sweet or fruity.

Shao-Mai Dumplings

燒賣

These light yet meaty mouthfuls are to south China what pot stickers and *jyao-dz* are to north China—the standard way of pairing meat with pasta in a fun-to-eat miniature dumpling. *Shao-mai* means literally "to bake and to sell," but why *steamed* dumplings should be called "baked" is beyond my researches. Regardless, these little dumplings with their fluted edges and slightly peppery pork filling are better to eat than to ponder. ◆ *Shao-mai* fillings differ from area to area and from one *dim sum* tea house to another. My filling is more textured and spiced than most. The minced pork is littered with water chestnuts and crowned with tiny diced carrots, and there is enough ginger and black pepper to betray my north Chinese tastes. To complete the betrayal, I dab the dumplings with a garlic-soy dip—heresy in the south, but glorious on the tongue. ◆ Of all Chinese dumplings, these are perhaps the easiest to make. The filling may be mixed in a food processor, and the wrapper requires no special pleating or sealing. Because they are steamed and need no attention while cooking, *shao-mai* make perfect hors d'oeuvres while you're readying other dishes. ◆ The filling may be made a day in advance, and the dumplings shaped several hours before steaming.

TECHNIQUE NOTES:
In order to survive steaming with its upright shape intact, the wrapper must be so formed around the dumplings as to have a definite "waist." I use a four-finger approach, as follows: Using the thumb and third finger of both hands (pointing the second finger up and out of the way), bring the wrapper up and around the filling and press it to adhere to the pork in four equidistant places. Then lift, rotate, and poke the dumpling repeatedly with the same four fingers, until the wrapper is securely pleated around the filling and the dumpling has an "empire waist" about ⅔ up the side. Tap the dumpling lightly on the table, to insure it stands upright. To secure the waist, stand the dumpling in one palm

and gently squeeze the waist in a circle made of the thumb and first finger of your other hand. When the *shao-mai* is properly shaped, the filling should bulge about ¼ inch above the wrapper.

finished *shao-mai* dumpling, complete with empire waist and carrot crown, ready to be steamed

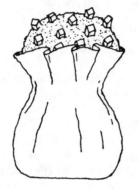

Makes about 30 dumplings, enough to serve 10–15 as an hors d'oeuvre, about 6–8 as part of a multicourse meal, or 4–5 as a more substantial accompaniment to soup or another dish.

INGREDIENTS:

> *about 30 shao-mai wrappers, 3 inches in diameter and no more than ¹⁄₃₂-inch thin, freshly bought from a Chinese noodle factory, stamped from thin won ton wrappers with a 3-inch cutter, or homemade (page 378)*

For the filling:
> *6–8 large water chestnuts, fresh best*
> *1½ walnut-size nuggets fresh ginger*
> *1 hefty or 2 thin whole scallions, cut into 1-inch lengths*
> *1 pound ground pork butt*
> *2 tablespoons thin (regular) soy sauce*
> *1 tablespoon Chinese rice wine or quality, dry sherry*
> *½ teaspoon coarse kosher salt*
> *2 teaspoons Chinese or Japanese sesame oil*
> *⅛ teaspoon freshly ground black pepper*

To garnish:
> *about 5 tablespoons tiny fresh carrot cubes, cut ⅛-inch square*
> *Garlic-Soy Dip (page 477)*

Making the filling:
Peel fresh water chestnuts. Blanch canned water chestnuts in plain boiling water for 15 seconds, then drain and rush under cold water until chilled. Chop the water chestnuts by hand to a neat, peppercorn-size dice.

Mince the ginger and scallion in the work bowl of a food processor fitted with the steel knife, scraping down as necessary until fine. Distribute the pork around the blade, add the remaining filling ingredients, then process with on-off turns to blend. Do not overprocess to a paste. (If you have a small capacity work bowl, divide the filling ingredients in half and process in two batches.) Scrape the mixture into a bowl, then stir in the water chestnuts by hand.

Alternatively, mince the ginger and scallion finely by hand, and combine with the remaining ingredients and the water chestnuts, stirring in one direction until well blended. Throw the mixture lightly against the side of the bowl 6 or 7 times to compact it.

The filling may be sealed airtight with a piece of plastic wrap pressed directly on the surface, and refrigerated several hours or overnight before using.

Shaping the dumplings:
Arrange the filling, the wrappers, a saucer with the carrots, and a tablespoon side by side on your work surface. Keep the wrappers covered as you work, lest they dry out. Line a baking sheet with silicon (no-stick) parchment paper if you are working in advance. Or, if you will be steaming the dumplings immediately, oil the rack of a bamboo steamer or the surface of a heatproof plate at least 1 inch smaller in diameter than your steamer with an even film of sesame oil, so the dumplings will not stick once steamed.

Fill and shape the dumplings one by one. Place 1 scant tablespoon filling in the center of the wrapper. Bring the wrapper up around the filling, as described above in TECHNIQUE NOTES, so it has a "waist." Then, turn the dumpling over and gently press the meat to the carrots so a crown of the tiny cubes will adhere to the top. Do not press so hard that the dumpling loses its waist, or it will collapse when steamed.

Put the finished dumplings on the baking sheet or steaming rack or plate, spacing them 1 inch apart. (See jacket photograph.)

The finished dumplings may be refrigerated on the parchment-lined sheet for several hours, sealed loosely but airtight. Bring to room temperature before steaming.

Steaming the dumplings:
(For details on steaming and how to improvise a steamer, see page 60.)
Bring the water in the steaming vessel to a gushing boil over high heat, then reduce the heat to medium to maintain a steady steam. (Too furious a steam will encourage the dumplings to collapse.) Add the dumplings to the steamer, cover, and steam 25 minutes. Turn off the heat and let the steam subside several minutes before slowly lifting the lid and removing the dumplings.

Dribble the top of each dumpling with ⅛–¼ teaspoon *Garlic-Soy Dip.* Serve immediately, directly from a bamboo steamer or transfer gently by hand to a heated serving platter. In my house this is finger food, meant to be popped into the mouth with only a cocktail napkin needed.

Leftover dumplings may be resteamed until hot, or are tasty snack food at room temperature.

MENU SUGGESTIONS:
I typically serve these dumplings as a single appetizer to begin a special meal, and accompany them with Champagne. For less grand occasions, serve them side by side with *Moslem-Style Hot and Sour Soup* (page 450) or *Soup of Many Mushrooms* (page 454). If you are hosting a *dim sum* brunch, the dumplings make an excellent trio with *Spicy Shrimp Fritters* (page 237) and *Springrolls with Dijon Mustard Sauce* (page 389).

| Homemade Shao-Mai Wrappers 燒賣皮 | *Shao-mai* wrappers—or "skins" as they are called in Chinese—are 3-inch round, extremely thin and supple fresh dough wrappers. They are typically stamped from the same egg and water dough used to make won ton skins and Chinese egg noodles, and one can often get good results by simply cutting a square won ton skin into a round *shao-mai* wrapper in those places where one is available and the other isn't. The thing to watch out for when improvising is thick- |

ness. A wrapper that is supple enough to embrace a *shao-mai* must be thin enough (about ⅟₃₂-inch) so that one can see a finger through it when held up to the light. ◆ I buy *shao-mai* skins at a Chinatown noodle factory where they are made fresh every day. If you need to make your own, here's how. With a food processor and pasta machine it's quite easy and simple. Without, the process is more tedious, but if that is the only route to eating *shao-mai*, then I'd say it's worth it.

TECHNIQUE NOTES:
For refrigerating or freezing homemade skins, be sure to dust both sides liberally with cornstarch before stacking. The satiny starch keeps the skins very supple and also prevents them from sticking together. As you unstack the wrappers to be filled and shaped, simply dust off the excess cornstarch with a clean pastry brush or paintbrush.

For more on the role of cornstarch in Chinese noodle-making, see TECHNIQUE NOTES, page 354.

Yields about 95 3-inch *shao-mai* wrappers. Divide the recipe in half if you want only enough wrappers for one batch of *shao-mai*.

INGREDIENTS:

   recipe for 1½ pounds egg noodle dough (page 354)

Preparations:
Make the dough, let it rest, then begin rolling it out in the pasta machine as described on page 355. Roll the dough for the wrappers even thinner than for noodles, to yield bands that are evenly about ⅟₃₂-inch thin. As the bands become awkwardly long, cut them in half, then continue rolling.

If you do not have a pasta machine, divide the dough evenly into 6–8 parts for a full recipe or 3–4 parts for a half recipe, and roll them out one at a time on a cornstarch-dusted board until the dough is evenly ⅟₃₂-inch thin. Do not stretch the dough as you work, and dust the top of the dough and the board with cornstarch as needed to prevent sticking. Check for evenness by running your fingers over the dough, and keep the un-rolled dough covered to prevent it from drying.

As you finish rolling out each piece, transfer it carefully, so as not to stretch it, to a terry towel. Let it air-dry for about 6–7 minutes on each side, until it has firmed up enough to be cut neatly without sticking. The drying time will vary, depending on the temperature and the draftiness of the room. Keep checking it with your fingers, lest it get too dry and become brittle.

Cutting the wrappers:
Smooth a thin layer of cornstarch over your work board with the palm of your hand. Transfer the first piece of dough to the board, covering the remaining pieces with a dry towel to prevent them from over-drying. Smooth a thin layer of cornstarch evenly on top

of the dough, then use a 3-inch round cutter to stamp out as many wrappers as possible from the sheet. (From a dough band rolled through a pasta machine, you will get more wrappers if you stagger them up and down the band than if you cut them neatly side by side all along one edge.) Dip the cutter in cornstarch if it is sticking to the dough.

If you are using the wrappers immediately or within the hour, transfer them in a single layer to a cornstarch-dusted surface and keep them covered with a dry towel.

To refrigerate or freeze, stack the rounds neatly on a large sheet of plastic wrap, dusting them liberally on both sides to prevent sticking. Then, dust the outside of the column (that is, around the circumference of the stacked wrappers), applying as much cornstarch as will stick. Bring the plastic wrap up and around the stack, smoothing and sealing it to form an airtight seal. Double seal the wrappers in an airtight plastic bag, and refrigerate 1–2 days or freeze up to 1 month. (Frozen wrappers are inevitably less perfect than fresh-made, so if you are going to the trouble of making them, try to use them fresh.)

Refrigerated wrappers may turn slightly gray if you have used unbleached flour, but will look and taste fine upon steaming. Frozen wrappers should be defrosted in the refrigerator and pulled apart as soon as supple to prevent sticking.

Hunan Pork Dumplings with Hot Sauce

湖南水餃

Everything in Hunan is on a grand scale—the dramatic variety and beauty of the terrain, the abundance of the harvest, the sheer spiciness and flavor of the food, and the expansive warmth of the Hunan personality. It is, in many ways, the Texas of China. Even the chopsticks, the bowls, and the dumplings of Hunan are enormous. ◆ For a dumpling-maker, bigger dumplings mean less work. For a dumpling eater, the bonus is a hearty mouthful as opposed to a polite nibble. I cast my vote on both counts and recommend it as a fine place to begin if you are new to making dumplings. ◆ In Hunan, these dumplings are traditionally boiled. You may, however, pan-fry them Peking-style, as directed on page 384. ◆ The dumplings may be shaped and refrigerated, or even flash-frozen, in advance. To boil them and serve them forth takes only minutes.

TECHNIQUE NOTES:
In contrast to steamed dumpling wrappers, the wrappers for water-boiled dumplings are made with *cold* water. The result is a sturdy, as opposed to a silky, dough that will withstand the hubbub of boiling.

When boiling the dumplings, the repeated addition of a cup of cold water stalls the vigorous boiling without significantly altering the cooking temperature of the water. The skins remain intact, and a minimum of flavor is leached by the water.

For the coarse-textured meat fillings common to northern- and central-style Chinese dumplings, see TECHNIQUE NOTES, page 384.

Yields about 2 dozen large dumplings, enough to serve 3–4 as a substantial main dish, 8–12 as part of a multicourse meal.

INGREDIENTS:

> *For the wrappers:*
> *2½ cups all-purpose flour*
> *about ¾ cup cold water*
> *additional flour, for rolling out the dough*

For the filling:
> ½ *pound crisp Chinese cabbage leaves, the variety that are evenly broad and a pale white-green (page 536)*
> 1 *teaspoon coarse kosher salt*
> ¾ *pound hand-chopped or coarsely ground pork butt*
> 1 *tablespoon finely minced fresh ginger*
> ¼ *cup coarsely chopped green and white scallion, or 3 tablespoons chopped Chinese chives*
> 1 *tablespoon thin (regular) soy sauce*
> 1 *tablespoon Chinese rice wine or quality, dry sherry*
> 1 *tablespoon Chinese or Japanese sesame oil*
> 1 *teaspoon coarse kosher salt*
> ¼ *teaspoon freshly ground pepper (optional)*

Sauce ingredients:
> ¼ *cup thin (regular) soy sauce*
> 2 *tablespoons white vinegar or unseasoned Chinese or Japanese rice vinegar*
> 2 *teaspoons Chinese or Japanese sesame oil*
> ½–¾ *teaspoon Chinese chili sauce (page 536), or substitute 1–2 teaspoons hot chili oil for the sesame oil above*
> ~~pinch sugar~~
> 2 *tablespoons thin-cut green and white scallion rings or coarsely chopped fresh coriander*

Making the dough:
If you have a food processor:
(For details on dough-making in a food processor, see page 586.)

Put the flour in the work bowl of a food processor fitted with the steel knife. With the machine running add the water in a thin stream through the feed tube just until the dough clumps in a near-ball around the blade. You may not use all the water or you may need a bit more, depending on the dryness of the flour. After a ball is formed, run the machine 10 seconds more to knead the dough.

Turn the dough out onto a lightly floured board and knead gently by hand about 30 seconds, until it is earlobe-soft and smooth, and will bounce gently back when pressed lightly with a finger. Dust the board only if the dough is sticking. When processed correctly it will need little or no additional flour.

Put the dough in a small bowl, seal airtight with plastic film, then set aside to rest 30 minutes at room temperature or overnight in the refrigerator. Bring to room temperature before rolling out.

If you do not have a food processor: Put the flour in a large mixing bowl. Stirring with chopsticks or a large spoon, combine it with enough water dribbled slowly into the bowl to form a stiff dough. Knead gently by hand on a lightly floured board 5–10 minutes, until earlobe-soft, smooth, and elastic enough to spring gently back when pressed lightly with a finger. Seal and let rest as above.

Making the filling:
Chop the cabbage until pea-size, sprinkle with 1 teaspoon kosher salt, and toss well to combine. Let stand for 10 minutes, drain, then squeeze firmly between your palms

or wring out enfolded in cheesecloth to remove excess moisture.

Scatter the cabbage in a large bowl, add the pork, then sprinkle the remaining filling ingredients on top. Stir briskly in one direction until well blended, with chopsticks or a fork, then throw the mixture lightly against the inside of the bowl 5 or 6 times to compact it. (This makes it cohesive enough to go inside the dumpling wrapper, but still loose and coarse enough to have a good texture.) For best flavor, seal the filling airtight with a piece of plastic pressed directly on the surface and let stand 30 minutes at room temperature or up to 24 hours in the refrigerator. Bring to room temperature before using.

Rolling out the dough and cutting the wrappers:

Remove the dough to a lightly floured board and knead gently with the heel of one hand just until smooth, about 10 seconds. Divide the dough into 3 equal pieces with a sharp knife. Roll out 1 piece at a time, keeping the remainder covered against drying.

Dust the board lightly, then press the first piece of dough into a flat disk and roll out to an even thinness of $\frac{1}{16}$ inch, dusting the dough and the board lightly as needed to prevent sticking. Put your eye level to the board and run your fingers over the dough to be sure it is evenly thin.

Use a sharp, floured $3\frac{1}{2}$ inch cutter to cut out as many dough rounds as possible, cutting them right next to one another to minimize scraps. Line up the wrappers on a lightly floured surface and cover them with a dry cloth. Squeeze the scraps into a ball and put aside with the remaining dough.

Fill and shape the first group of wrappers before you roll out the next piece of dough. When all 3 pieces have been rolled out and shaped into dumplings, gently knead the scraps together in a single ball on an unfloured board, then roll out and cut the last wrappers.

Filling and shaping the dumplings:

Line a baking sheet with silicon (no-stick) parchment paper to hold the finished dumplings. If you don't have the parchment, flour the baking sheet evenly to prevent the dumplings from sticking. Have the filling, a tablespoon, and the tray alongside the wrappers.

Fill one wrapper at a time, keeping the remaining covered. Put 1 level tablespoon of filling off-center in the wrapper, and nudge it with your finger into a half-moon shape, about 2 inches long, as illustrated below. You needn't be precise; shaping the filling simply makes the dumpling easier to seal. Pleat and press the dumpling closed as illustrated. When you are finished, the dumpling should be sealed tightly and prettily and should curve gracefully into an arc and rest flat on its smooth bottom.

Homemade wrappers are typically soft and moist, and you should have no problem sealing them. If, however, the dough has dried and will not adhere to itself (which is the case with store-bought wrappers), run a moist finger lightly around the edge of the circle before folding and pleating the dough. Do not use too much water, or the dough will turn soggy.

Transfer the finished dumpling to the tray, then cover with a dry cloth to prevent drying. Leave $\frac{3}{4}$ inch between the dumplings; they will spread a bit as they rest. Check midway to see if the dumplings are sticking to the paper or the sheet, and dust with additional flour if needed.

When all the dumplings are shaped, you may seal the tray airtight with plastic wrap or enfold it in a big bag from the cleaners and refrigerate the dumplings for several hours. Or, you may flash-freeze them on the tray until firm, bag airtight, and freeze for several weeks. Cook frozen dumplings when only partially thawed, while the dough is still firm. Cook refrigerated dumplings directly from the refrigerator.

Boiling the dumplings:
About 25 minutes before serving, put as many large bowls as you have dumpling eaters in a low oven to warm. Mix the sauce ingredients, and adjust to taste. The sauce should be high-seasoned and spicy.

Fill a 6–7-quart pot with 3 quarts cold unsalted water, cover, and bring to a rolling boil over high heat. Remove the cover, then quickly drop in the dumplings one by one. With chopsticks or a wooden spoon gently stir two or three times to separate the dumplings. Cover the pot and cook *only* until the water returns to a boil. Keep an eye on the lid to see when steam begins to escape, indicating the water is boiling.

Remove the cover, add 1 cup of cold water to the pot, and re-cover. When the water returns to a boil, remove the cover, pour in another cup of cold water, and replace the cover. Repeat this process once more, for a total of 3 cups of cold water. After the third cup, while you are waiting for the water to return to a boil, stir up the sauce and divide it evenly among the individual bowls.

When the water returns to a boil, turn off the heat and uncover the pot. Fish the dumplings from the water with a large Chinese mesh spoon, hold them briefly above the pot to drain, then transfer them swiftly and still dripping a bit of water to the bowls. If you have only a small spoon with which to retrieve the dumplings, transfer them in batches to a large metal colander.

Serve the dumplings at once, accompanied by small Chinese ladles or Western soup spoons, and let each participant toss his or her own dumplings in the sauce.

How to eat a Chinese dumpling:
Traditionally, one scoops a dumpling up on the spoon then steers all or a portion of it into one's mouth with chopsticks, keeping the spoon in readiness at the lips to retrieve what one can't or doesn't wish to bite off. Beware of the first bite! Boiled dumplings are delectably and dangerously juicy, and the hot liquid will squirt out embarrassingly if you are not gentle when you first bite down.

In most Chinese homes the poaching liquid is served up as a hot drink to follow the dumplings, often garnished with a soupçon of soy or chopped scallion, and sometimes profiting from the breakage of poorly sealed dumplings. Try it. It is tummy-soothing.

Cold leftover boiled dumplings are rather wretched, in my opinion, but there is rarely any trouble eating them up while they're hot.

THE ILLUSTRATED COMPLEAT DUMPLING: A STEP-BY-STEP GUIDE

Put filling off-center in wrapper, and nudge it into a half moon with your finger.

Fold wrapper exactly in half over filling. Pinch shut at midpoint.

Beginning to the right of the midpoint, make 3 tiny pleats on the *near* side of the wrapper only, folding the pleats *toward* the midpoint. After each pleat, pinch the dough to join the far, unpleated side of the wrapper. Pinch the extreme right corner of the arc closed. Now half the dumpling is sealed.

Repeat the process to the left of the midpoint, aiming the pleats the other way (that is, still pleating in the direction of the midpoint). Pinch the left corner closed. Then gently pinch all along the arc to insure it is sealed tightly and to thin the ridge of dough. The dumpling is now fully sealed.

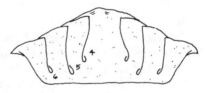

The finished dumpling, seen from an aerial view. It is pleated on one side, smooth on the other, curved prettily into an arc (on account of the pleating), and sitting flat on its bottom.

The genius of this method is that the dough is not overly thick at the top, having been pleated on only one side, and that the dumpling will stand upright on the tray or in the frying pan (if you are making pot stickers). Plus, it is beautiful to look at.

MENU SUGGESTIONS:
For a simple dinner, serve the dumplings alongside a bowl of *Moslem-Style Hot and Sour Soup* (page 450), or *Wine-Explosion Vegetable Chowder* (page 452). For a larger spread, add a selection of crisp "Little Dishes" (pages 103 to 121), plus *Bong-Bong Chicken* (page 133) or *Ma-La Cold Chicken* (page 129), and *Dry-Fried Szechwan String Beans* (page 297) or *Shantung Cold Eggplant with Sesame Sauce* (page 291).

Moslem-Style Beef or Lamb Pot Stickers

回式鍋貼

One of the pleasures of my last year in Taipei was living around the corner from a small Moslem restaurant, where in keeping with the dietary restrictions of the Chinese Moslems no pork was served. I went there regularly with Po-Fu, the family patriarch, who judged the place to have the best pan-fried dumplings in the city and in testimony to his feelings would down two dozen of them at a sitting. While he munched, I would watch the cook, a broad-faced Mongolian who wore an irrepressible grin and an oily knit cap whatever the weather and who for some reason chose to fry his dumplings out on the curb over a brazier, the smells undoubtedly a lure for prospective customers. ◆ To Chinese tastes, beef and lamb are rather rich and strong-tasting, best eaten in winter and best seasoned with liberal doses of soy, wine and ginger. Grated orange peel is also a favored seasoning for lamb in Mongolia, and it is excellent here in the lamb filling. If the weather is warmer or you are in a non-Moslem frame of mind, you may substitute the pork filling on page 379. ◆ Dumplings are a tedious business, even with a food processor to make the dough. Take heart that they freeze beautifully, and keep in mind also that it is traditional practice in China to invite your friends to a party that begins with pleating them and ends with eating them.

TECHNIQUE NOTES:

Pot stickers are the Chinese name for pan-fried dumplings, because, properly made, the crunchy bottoms will stick to the pot and you will need to release them with a spatula. No sticking usually means not enough crunch, but too much sticking means a mess. For best results, use a cast-iron pan (the traditional Chinese choice), and remember to heat it scorching-hot before adding the oil.

I like to steam-cook the dumplings in light, unsalted chicken stock instead of water, to give them an extra shot of flavor and color. The oil mixed with the stock remains in the pan after the liquid evaporates, and does the job of re-crisping the dumplings.

Meat fillings for northern-style dumplings are traditionally made with hand-chopped, rough-textured meat to give them substance. You can hack it yourself, ask the butcher to put the meat through the coarse blade of the grinder, or settle for the more easily purchased fine grind and mix the filling by hand. Don't use a food processor, which robs this filling of its character.

Makes about 4 dozen tiny dumplings, enough to serve 4–6 as a hearty meal with soup, 8–12 as part of a multicourse meal, or more as an appetizer.

INGREDIENTS:

> *For the wrappers:*
> *see recipe, page 378*
>
> *For the filling:*
> *¼ pound crisp Chinese cabbage leaves, the variety that are evenly broad and a pale white-green (page 536)*
> *½ teaspoon coarse kosher salt*
> *½ pound ground chuck plus ½ pound ground top round, or 1 pound ground lamb*

1 tablespoon finely minced fresh ginger for beef; 2 tablespoons for lamb

3 tablespoons minced green and white scallion or chopped Chinese chives (page 538)

2 tablespoons thin (regular) soy sauce

3 tablespoons Chinese rice wine or quality, dry sherry

1 tablespoon Chinese or Japanese sesame oil

½ teaspoon coarse kosher salt

⅛ teaspoon freshly ground pepper

¾ teaspoon grated fresh orange peel without any white pith, or soaked and minced home-dried orange or tangerine peel (page 557) for lamb filling only (optional)

about ½ cup corn or peanut oil, for pan-frying

about 2 cups light, unsalted hot chicken stock plus 2 tablespoons corn or peanut oil, for steam-cooking

Individual dipping sauce:

1 tablespoon thin (regular) soy sauce

2 teaspoons well-aged Chinese black vinegar or balsamic vinegar

¼ teaspoon finely minced fresh ginger

¼ teaspoon Chinese or Japanese sesame oil, or ⅛–¼ teaspoon hot chili oil

or

Garlic-Soy Dip (page 477) with a dash of hot chili oil to taste

Making the filling:

Chop the cabbage finely, sprinkle with ½ teaspoon kosher salt, and toss well to combine. Let stand 5 minutes, drain, then squeeze firmly between your palms or wring out in cheesecloth to remove excess moisture.

Scatter the cabbage in a large bowl, add the beef or lamb, and sprinkle the remaining filling ingredients on top. Stir briskly in one direction until well blended, with chopsticks or a fork, then throw the mixture lightly against the inside of the bowl 5 or 6 times to compact it. For best flavor, seal the mixture airtight with a piece of plastic film pressed directly on the surface and let stand 30 minutes at room temperature or several hours to overnight in the refrigerator. Bring to room temperature before using.

Making the dough, rolling it out, and filling and shaping the dumplings:

Follow the instructions on page 380; however, cut out 3-inch circles for the wrappers and use only 2 teaspoons filling per wrapper. Once shaped, the dumplings may be refrigerated or frozen as described on page 381. Pan-fry frozen dumplings when they are only partially thawed and the dough is still firm, and begin cooking at a somewhat lower heat so they thaw completely in the pan. Refrigerated dumplings should be cooked directly from the refrigerator.

Pan-frying and serving the dumplings:

For a full recipe, you will need to fry the dumplings in two batches, using a heavy 12-inch skillet, preferably made of cast iron, with a tight-fitting cover. (Or, if you have two pans and two cooks, you can fry them all at once.)

About 20 minutes before serving, mix the ingredients for the dipping sauce, taste and adjust to your liking, then place in small dip dishes or saucers alongside each place setting. Or, for hors d'oeuvre service, mix several batches in a small bowl. Put two round serving platters in a low oven to warm. Have the dumplings, the oil, the stock mixture, and the lid all within easy reach of your stovetop.

Heat the skillet over high heat until hot enough to evaporate a bead of water on contact. Add enough oil to coat the bottom with a scant ¼ inch oil, swirl the skillet to glaze it an inch up the sides, then adjust the skillet on the burner so that the oil is evenly deep. Reduce the heat to medium. When the oil is hot enough to foam a pinch of dry flour, pick up the dumplings by their tops and quickly arrange them smooth side down in the pan. Make concentric rings starting from the outside of the pan and working into the center, putting the dumplings directly next to and hugging one another. (The crowding will cause the dumplings to stick together in a pretty spiral when they are turned out onto the platter, which is the traditional presentation.) As you arrange the dumplings, adjust the heat so they sizzle mildly.

Once the dumplings are in place, raise the heat slightly to bring them to a merry sizzle and brown the bottoms. Check frequently, lifting them carefully with a spatula, and when the bottoms are evenly browned give the stock mixture a stir, and add enough to come halfway up the side of the dumplings. Expect the liquid to hiss loudly as soon as it is added.

Adjust the heat to maintain a simmer, and cover the pot. (These are the moments when the wrappers and filling will cook through and absorb the flavor of the stock.) After about 7 minutes, lift the lid to peek inside the pot, and when the stock is almost all absorbed remove the lid. Lift one dumpling with a spatula and check the bottom. If it is not crisp enough to "clink" against a fingernail, then continue to cook for a minute or so more. If there is not sufficient oil left after the steaming to crisp them, add a bit more oil from the side of the pan and swirl to distribute it under the dumplings.

When the bottoms are crisp, turn off the heat, move the pan off the burner, and loosen the bottoms of the dumplings with the spatula. Invert them onto the serving platter, browned bottoms up. If you have done the job well, they will cling in a spiral.

Eating pot stickers:
As soon as you have turned the dumplings out of the pan (and neatened them up if they did not emerge exactly as planned), rush them to the table. Part of the traditional fun is for the guests to pull them apart with their chopsticks, then, the eating begins: Pick a dumpling up with the help of chopsticks and a small Chinese porcelain spoon (a metal soup spoon will do, though it gets too hot to be perfect). Pick the dumpling up out of the spoon long enough to dunk its bottom in the dip, then return it to the spoon. Raise the spoon almost to your chin, use the chopsticks to complete the journey of the dumpling to your mouth, then after you have bitten off a neat half (carefully, so the steam and hot juices don't burn you), deposit the remaining half in the spoon until you are ready for the next bite.

Dumpling eating is designed to be fun and informal, so feel free to lose a dumpling here and there, splatter a bit of the dipping sauce if you have not perfected the art of dunking, and demand more dumplings in the spirit of a good party.

Cook only as many dumplings as will be eaten (which is usually more than you anticipate if you have assembled the appropriate audience). Cold pot stickers are beyond rewarming or at least beyond my taste.

MENU SUGGESTIONS:
The exertion required by pot stickers leads me to serve them with something simple and filling that can be done in advance, usually *Moslem-Style Hot and Sour Soup* (page 450),

Wine-Explosion Vegetable Chowder (page 452), or a platter of *Dry-Fried String Beans* (page 297). With any of the above, they make an excellent supper.

<table>
<tr><td>

**Pan-
Fried
Meat
Pies**

餡兒餅

</td><td>

This is the un-dumpling—a meat-stuffed dough wrapper that on account of its flat, disk-like shape is called in Chinese a "pie" *(bing)*, as opposed to a "dumpling" *(jyao)*. It has all the appeal of a pot sticker, but requires less fuss to cook. Here, you brown both sides of the tiny pies, flipping them over like pancakes. ◆ The filling for the pies has a particular tang, owing to the inclusion of "Szechwan preserved vegetable." It does for the stuffing what a good pickle does for a ham-

</td></tr>
</table>

burger, and in fact you can use some tasty chopped pickle if you can't find the Szechwan vegetable. ◆ The filling and dough are both made easily in a food processor. Make them a day ahead if you like, and the filling will be more flavorful and the dough easier to work with. Once shaped, the tiny pies may be refrigerated briefly or flash-frozen before frying.

TECHNIQUE NOTES:
For the method of sealing a dough-wrapper shut with tiny pleats, see page 428. Here, where the dough is not yeasted, a "belly" is not necessary.

Makes 20 small pies, enough to serve 4–5 as a hearty accompaniment to soup, 6–10 as part of a multicourse meal.

INGREDIENTS:

> *For the wrappers:*
> *see recipe, page 379*
>
> *For the filling:*
> *3 walnut-size knobs Szechwan preserved vegetable (page 571)*
> *1½ tablespoons thin (regular) soy sauce*
> *¼ teaspoon sugar*
> *¼ teaspoon coarse kosher salt*
> *1 tablespoon Chinese or Japanese sesame oil*
> *¾ pound ground top round*
>
> *For dipping:*
> *3 tablespoons well-aged Chinese black vinegar or balsamic vinegar*
> *1 teaspoon Chinese or Japanese sesame oil*
> *1 scant teaspoon finely minced fresh ginger or a cluster of hair-thin shreds of*
> *   fresh "young" ginger (page 548)*
>
> *about 6 tablespoons corn or peanut oil, for pan-frying*

Making the dough:
Follow directions on page 380.

Making the filling:
Rinse the preserved vegetable thoroughly, rubbing well with your fingers to remove the coating, then pat dry.

Mince the preserved vegetable in the work bowl of a food processor fitted with the steel knife, scraping down as necessary until fine, then add the remaining ingredients, distributing the beef evenly around the blade. Combine with on-off turns just until mixed. Do not overprocess.

Alternatively, mince the preserved vegetable finely, then combine with the remaining ingredients, stirring briskly in one direction until well blended, then throw the mixture lightly against the inside of the bowl 5 or 6 times to compact it.

For best flavor, seal the filling airtight with a piece of plastic wrap pressed directly on the surface, and set aside for 30 minutes at room temperature or overnight in the refrigerator. Bring to room temperature before using.

Shaping the pies:
Roll the dough into an evenly thick log 10 inches long on a lightly floured surface using lightly floured hands. Cut the log into 20 even pieces ½ inch thick. After each disk is cut, lay it cut-side down on a more generously floured corner of the board, then cover with a dry towel.

Divide the filling into 20 portions, each about 2½ teaspoons.

Flour the board lightly, press the first disk flat with your fingers, and roll it into a 3–3½-inch round. (A 10-inch secton cut from a broom handle or a 1–1¼-inch thick dowel is the perfect tool for this job.) Dust the board and the top of the wrapper lightly with flour if needed to prevent sticking, but do not use more than is necessary or the wrapper will not adhere to itself when pleated. Put a portion of the filling in the center, then pleat the wrapper shut and give it a final twist to seal, as described on page 428. Turn the dumpling sealed side down on the floured board, press lightly to flatten, then put the finished "pie" on a baking sheet lined with silicon (no-stick) parchment or sprinkled evenly with flour. Cover with a dry towel, and proceed to shape the remaining pies. Check midway to see if the pies are sticking to the paper or the sheet, and dust with additional flour if required.

Once shaped, the pies may be refrigerated for several hours before frying, sealed airtight. Or, you may flash-freeze them on the tray until firm, bag airtight, and freeze for several weeks. Refrigerated pies are best fried straight from the refrigerator. Frozen pies should be partially thawed on a floured tray, then cooked while the dough is still firm over a somewhat lower heat.

Pan-frying the pies:
About 15–20 minutes before serving, divide the ginger among as many small dip dishes as you have eaters or between 2 small sauce bowls. Mix the vinegar and sesame oil, then pour over the ginger. (The ginger will permeate the dip while you cook.) Put a serving platter of a color to contrast with the pies in a low oven to warm.

Heat a large, heavy skillet over high heat until hot enough to evaporate a bead of water on contact. Add enough oil to coat the bottom with a scant ¼ inch oil, swirl the skillet to glaze it an inch up the sides, then adjust the skillet on the burner so the oil is evenly deep. Reduce the heat to medium.

When the oil is hot enough to foam a pinch of dry flour, add as many pies as will fit in quick succession, working from the outside of the pan to the center, and leaving at least ⅛ inch between the pies to prevent them from sticking together. Adjust the heat so the oil sizzles merrily, not furiously, then cook, uncovered, until the bottoms are golden brown, about 3–4 minutes, checking frequently with a spatula to monitor the browning. Then, flip the pies over, beginning with the brownest ones first. Dribble in a bit more oil from the side of the pan if the pies are sticking and swirl the pan to distribute it under the pies. Brown the second side in the same manner, adjusting the heat to maintain a steady sizzle, so the dough browns in about 3–4 minutes and the filling has time to cook through.

Remove the pies to the hot platter, where they can rest for several minutes before being cool enough to eat. In the meantime, wipe the pan clean with paper towels and proceed to fry the next batch, knowing that if your guests finish the first pies before you are free, you can tuck away several of the next batch for yourself.

Leftover meat pies are beyond reviving. With that in mind, I always convince myself to eat more than I should.

MENU SUGGESTIONS:

For a simple supper, easy on the cook, serve pies with *Velvet Corn Soup* (page 460) or *Wine-Explosion Vegetable Chowder* (page 452). As part of a larger spread, try them alongside *Strange Flavor Eggplant* (page 295) or *Dry-Fried Szechwan String Beans* (page 297), *Master Sauce Chicken* (page 153) or *Ma-La Cold Chicken* (page 129), and an assortment of "Little Dishes" (pages 103 to 121).

Springrolls with Dijon Mustard Sauce

春捲

I used to stay up very late in Taiwan studying, and one of my favorite after-midnight occupations was to walk into the center of town to the stall of the springroll man, who set up shop at about 9 and stayed open till about 3 for late-night, hungry souls like me. The stall was cozy, the springrolls were crunchy, and they tasted much like these. ◆ What we call egg rolls in the West are called springrolls in Chinese. They are typically long and slender, and to the Chinese culinary imagination they resemble gold bars. Hence, they are a favorite food at New Year's time, which in the Chinese lunar calendar falls at the opening of spring, and are called springrolls. (Egg rolls are another Chinese dish, made of a filling that is rolled up, as one might expect, in a sheet of cooked egg.) ◆ For springrolls of the sort sold by the springroll man and eaten in north and central China, you need paper-thin wrappers (page 352). The thickish egg dough wrappers commonly used in Cantonese-American restaurants produce a crust with a thick, chewy character rather than a crisp and brittle one. If only the thick wrappers are available, try rolling them to a more palatable 1/16 inch thinness in a pasta machine. ◆ The filling may be made a full day in advance. Wrapping and frying the springrolls must be done only shortly before serving for them to be perfectly crisp and delicious.

TECHNIQUE NOTES:

When using paper-thin springroll skins, it is important to sliver the filling ingredients finely, keep the liquid seasonings at a minimum, and chill the filling thoroughly before wrapping. Bulky items will strain and conceivably break the wrapper, and too much liquid or heat from the filling will turn it soggy and tear it.

Yields about 30 4-inch long springrolls, enough to serve 5–6 as a meal alongside a hearty bowl of soup, 8–12 as part of a multicourse meal, or more as an appetizer or hors d'oeuvre.

INGREDIENTS:

   1 pound (equal to 30 or more) Shanghai-style springroll or lumpia wrappers (page 352)

For the filling:
    8 medium Chinese dried black mushrooms
    1 pound well-marbled pork butt, trimmed of any isolated pieces of fat (weight
        after trimming)
    2 tablespoons thin (regular) soy sauce
    1 tablespoon Chinese rice wine or quality dry sherry
    1 teaspoon Chinese or Japanese sesame oil
    1 tablespoon water
    1 tablespoon cornstarch
    ½ teaspoon sugar
    ¼ teaspoon freshly ground pepper
    2 cups fresh bean sprouts, or 3 packed cups slivered Chinese cabbage (page
        536)
    2 cups shredded carrots
    2 cups finely slivered fresh snow peas or peeled and slivered broccoli stems
    sprigs of fresh coriander, 2 or 3 for each springroll (optional)

For stir-frying the filling:
    about 6 tablespoons corn or peanut oil
    2 teaspoons coarse kosher salt
    ½ teaspoon sugar
    1 tablespoon Chinese rice wine or quality, dry sherry
    1 tablespoon mushroom soy sauce, or 2–3 teaspoons black soy sauce
    ¼ teaspoon freshly ground pepper
    1 teaspoon Chinese or Japanese sesame oil
    1 tablespoon cornstarch dissolved in 2 tablespoons cold water or cold chicken
        stock

    1 large egg, beaten until smooth
    4–5 cups corn or peanut oil, for deep-frying

For dipping:
    Dijon Mustard Sauce (page 475)

Preparing the filling ingredients:
Soak the mushrooms in cold or hot water to cover until fully soft and spongy, 20 minutes
to an hour. Drain, snip off the stems with scissors, then rinse the caps under cold water to
dislodge any sand trapped in the gills. Squeeze gently to remove excess water, and cut the
caps into slivers a scant ⅛ inch wide.
    Slice the pork against the grain into slices a scant ¼ inch thick, then cut the
slices against the grain into slivers a scant ¼ inch thin. If the slivers are very long, cut
them crosswise into 1½-inch lengths. In a bowl big enough to hold the pork, blend the
soy, wine, sesame oil, water, cornstarch, sugar, and pepper until smooth. Add the pork,
toss well with your fingers to coat and separate the slivers, then seal the mixture airtight
and put aside to marinate for 1–3 hours at room temperature or overnight in the refrigerator. Bring to room temperature before cooking.
    If you are using bean sprouts, blanch them in plain boiling water to cover for 30
seconds, drain, and refresh under cold running water until chilled. Leave covered with
cold water, refrigerated overnight if you wish. Just before using, drain and spread on a dry
kitchen towel to blot up excess water. If you are using Chinese cabbage, toss with ½
teaspoon coarse kosher salt. Let stand 15 minutes, then drain and press it gently between

your palms to remove excess water. Use at once. Combine the bean sprouts or cabbage with the mushrooms.

Stir-frying the filling:
Have the pork, vegetables, stir-frying ingredients, several damp paper towels, and a large plate or tray on which to spread the filling all within easy reach of your stovetop. Stir the pork to loosen the slivers.

Heat a wok or large, heavy skillet over high heat until hot enough to evaporate a bead of water on contact. Add 2½ tablespoons oil, swirl to coat the pan, then reduce the heat to medium-high. When the oil is hot enough to sizzle one shred of carrot, add the carrots and snow peas or broccoli, and toss briskly to glaze with oil, 10–15 seconds, adjusting the heat to maintain a merry sizzle without scorching the vegetable. Add the mushrooms and bean sprouts or cabbage, then toss briskly to combine, dribbling in a bit more oil from the side of the pan if the mixture is sticking. Sprinkle with salt and sugar, toss briskly to mix, then splash with the wine and toss several times to combine. Raise the heat several seconds to evaporate any liquid left in the pan, then scrape the vegetables onto the waiting plate. Work quickly so the green vegetable remains crispy and undercooked.

Wipe the pan clean with the damp towels, then return it to high heat. When hot enough to evaporate a bead of water on contact, add 3 tablespoons oil, swirl to coat the pan, and reduce the heat to medium-high. When the oil is hot enough to sizzle a single sliver of pork, add the meat to the pan and stir-fry briskly until 90 percent gray, adjusting the heat to maintain a merry sizzle. Return the vegetables to the pan, toss briskly to combine, then add the soy, sesame oil, and pepper. Toss to blend, reduce the heat to low, then quickly taste the mixture, and adjust if required. It should be flavorful and pleasantly peppery. Stir the cornstarch mixture to recombine, add it to the pan, then raise the heat to medium. Stir until the mixture becomes glossy and slightly thick, about 15 seconds, then scrape the filling onto the plate.

Spread the filling out so it cools quickly and the juices do not gather. If you are in a hurry, put the plate in the freezer. The filling must be completely cool before you proceed to shape the springrolls.

The cold filling may be sealed airtight and refrigerated overnight. Toss lightly before using to redistribute the seasonings.

Shaping the springrolls:
If you are using square wrappers that have brittle or torn edges, cut an even border from each side, so that you wind up with a 6-inch square. (Use a ruler to help you, as the wrapper must be perfectly square to fold correctly.) If you are using round wrappers, there is no need to cut them.

Have the wrappers, the beaten egg, an inch-wide pastry brush, the cold filling, the coriander, and a baking sheet lined up on your work surface. Stir the filling to redistribute the seasonings.

Gently pull the first wrapper free. If you are using square wrappers, place the wrapper pointed side toward you to make a diamond, as illustrated. Put 3 tablespoons filling in the lower third of the wrapper, then prod it into a rectangular shape with your fingers or chopsticks, leaving an inch of the wrapper showing at either end. (If you are using a wrapper that is larger than 6 inches square, you can use somewhat more filling.) Place a sprig or two of coriander on top of the filling. It will show through the wrapper and look very pretty when fried.

Dip the brush in the egg, then paint an inch-wide film of egg around the border of

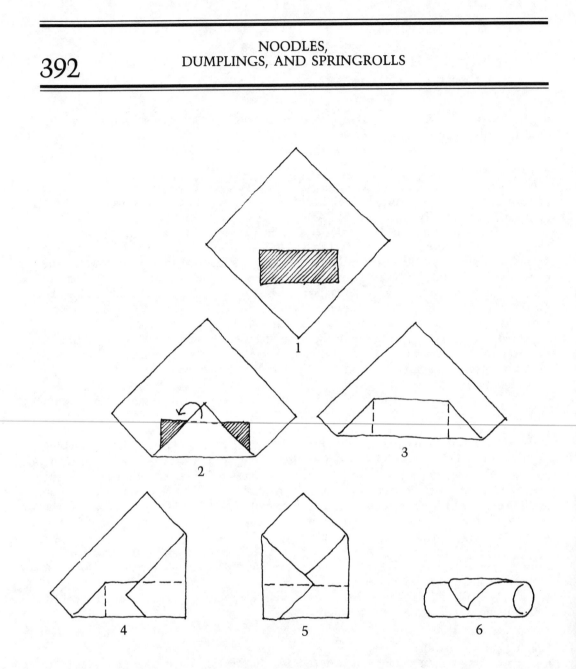

the wrapper. Bring the bottom of the wrapper up and over the filling, then roll the filling a single turn away from you, enclosing it in the wrapper. Do not roll too tightly or too loosely; the wrapper should hug the filling gently.

Paint a film of egg across the tubular roll, then bring the sides of the wrapper up and over the roll at right angles, so that it now resembles an open envelope. Be sure that the sides are at true right angles and not tilted outward, or the wrapper may open when fried.

Paint the "flap" of the envelope with a film of egg, then roll another turn or turn and a half away from you to complete the springroll shape. Place the springroll flap down on the baking sheet to insure the seal.

Once all the springrolls are made, proceed quickly to fry them, lest the wrappers get soggy. At most, refrigerate them for 1 hour, uncovered.

Frying and serving the springrolls:
Have the springrolls, a large Chinese mesh spoon, and a jelly-roll pan or baking sheet lined with a triple layer of paper towels all within easy reach of your stovetop. Put a serving platter of contrasting color in a low oven to warm, and ready the sauce in a small bowl.

Heat a wok or a large, heavy skillet over high heat until hot. Add oil to a depth of at least 1½ inches, and heat to the light-haze stage, 350° on a deep-fry thermometer, when the end of a springroll bubbles immediately when dipped in the oil. Slip the springrolls one by one into the oil, adjusting the heat to maintain a steady temperature so that each springroll comes to the surface within several seconds surrounded by a crown of white bubbles. Add as many springrolls as can float in one layer on the surface, frying in 2 batches if necessary. Fry until the springrolls turn golden and float high on the surface of the oil, turning them once or twice to insure even coloring, about 3–4 minutes in all. Remove immediately to the paper-towel drain, then shake the tray gently to blot up excess oil. Do not let the springrolls brown too darkly in the oil, as they will turn a shade darker from their own heat once they are on the tray.

For a second batch, allow sufficient time for the oil to regain its original temperature, and retest with an uncooked springroll. While the second batch fries, the first batch can be kept in a 250° oven on the paper towel drain. Do not hold them for more than 10 minutes, or they lose their fresh-fried taste.

Arrange the springrolls attractively on the platter, coriander side up. (The Chinese habit is to stack them like gold bars, in alternating layers.) Serve with the mustard sauce, inviting the guests to pick up a springroll with their fingers and dip it in the sauce. Bite down slowly; the springrolls are blazing hot.

If you are not a mustard fan, you may also serve the springrolls with the typical northern dipping sauce, a mixture of 1 tablespoon thin (regular) soy, 1½ teaspoons white or rice vinegar, and ¼ teaspoon sesame oil or sesame-based hot chili oil.

Leftover springrolls grow greasy with reheating, so eat them while they're fresh.

MENU SUGGESTIONS:
For a simple supper, serve the springrolls with a hearty soup, like *Moslem-Style Hot and Sour Soup* (page 450), or *Wine-Explosion Vegetable Chowder* (page 452) or the lighter *Soup of Many Mushrooms* (page 454). As an appetizer, serve them alone or paired with something quite different in texture, such as *Shao-Mai Dumplings* (page 375) or *Soy-Dipped Red Radish Fans* (page 114). Or, for a *dim sum* brunch, partner the springrolls with any of the steamed buns (pages 422 to 432), *Gold Coin Eggs* (page 330), and a colorful variety of "Little Dishes" (pages 103 to 121). To serve with the springrolls, try a California Johannisberg Riesling.

Rice, Breads, & Buns

米飯麵食

◆

◆

I t is a surprise for most people to learn that not all Chinese eat rice. North China is a wheat-growing plain, and the population of the entire northern half of the Chinese mainland is accustomed to a daily diet of millet, corn, or wheat-based dough stuffs. While rice may be omnipresent throughout South China and a fixture in Chinese restaurants in the West, one cannot appreciate the full character of Chinese cuisine without savoring a northern-style steamed bun, a pan-fried scallion bread, or the long, deep-fried wand of doughnut-like dough that is standard breakfast fare in Peking. Ancient Chinese civilization was rooted in this wheat-growing area, and like the tomb paintings that show dough making in progress and the long poems called *fu* that lyricize the dance of kneading, the breads and buns of the north capture a large part of the Chinese spirit.

In South China the landscape and tastes are different, and it is here that rice is the focus of the meal. The great mountains and broad, rugged plains of the north give way in the south to a gentler, sun- and water-drenched countryside, where paddy-grown rice is a prime agricultural pursuit. Rice has traditionally been used in the making of paper and wine, but its most important place is at the heart of a meal. It is eaten pure white and simply parboiled and/or steamed, with a mouthful taken plain before the meal as a palate cleanser and a symbol of grain's importance. Thereafter, the dishes traditionally accompany the rice and not the other way around, for in everyday Chinese eating the rice is the bulk of the meal and the dishes are seen as companion fare to help one eat more rice.

I have lived mostly among north Chinese, and so my own prejudices lie in that direction. I am a bread and bun lover to the core and if I am not serving noodles with a Chinese meal, then I am most often frying breads, steaming or baking buns, or accompanying some savory, saucy dish with a crusty "foreign" loaf. I find it immensely satisfying, and the novelty feeds my guests.

When it comes to plain white rice, however, I am a reluctant eater at best, and, while I have carefully concealed my heretical tastes from my Chinese friends, in the privacy of my own semi-Chinese home I regularly indulge my unforgivable appetite for kasha, bulgur, and stir-fried rice—all of which seem culturally "impure" compared to the plain white stuff. I can be passionate about these preparations as I can never be about plain steamed rice, and may the gods forgive me for heaping them in my bowl.

TYPES OF FLOUR   For everyday Chinese bread and bun-making, I use *all-purpose white flour*. I prefer the unbleached variety, having found it to yield a more tender product when the dough is fried or baked. If, however, you tend to refrigerate or freeze raw doughs before cooking them, you might be best off with the bleached variety. A raw dough made from bleached flour will stay pristinely white even after several days' refrigeration, whereas a raw dough made from unbleached flour will turn an unappealing (though harmless) gray.

A third to a half part *whole-wheat flour* may be incorporated into a white flour bread or bun dough, if you like. The results are rather interesting, too heavy and brown for Chinese tastes (Chinese insist upon whiteness in breads as well as in rice), but appealing if you are a cook with "whole foods" inclinations. When using whole-wheat flour, expect the rising and cooking times to be a bit longer.

Stone-ground flours, which include white and whole-wheat varieties, are made the old-fashioned way with millstones and seem to me to have more savor. When I used to be able to purchase them just a brisk walk away, I cooked with them regularly and loved the result. If you buy stone-ground flour, store it in the refrigerator or a cool place.

MEASURING FLOUR   I learned to make breads and buns in the restaurant kitchens of Chinese friends, where scales, measuring cups, and measuring spoons were unknown.

That is to say that I learned the look and *feel* of a properly made dough and knew from that how much water to add to the flour. I was taught that flour from different mills and in different seasons has a variable degree of absorbency and that I could never rely upon one precise formula if the heavens were to change or my location within them.

This means that a Chinese cook turning out wonderful breads and buns need not be at all fussy about measuring flour. I use a dry measuring cup (which has a circular rim; not the spouted variety designed for liquid measurement) and dip it into the flour, then sweep off the excess to give me an approximate amount. That is the beginning, and the rest is up to the senses.

For the dessert section of this book, my baking mentors suggest that the flour be measured by gently dropping or "fluffing" it into a dry measure cup with a spoon held several inches above the cup, and then sweeping off the excess. This gives a lighter weight than the "dip and sweep" method.

HOT AND COLD WATER DOUGHS   Non-yeasted Chinese wheat flour doughs fall into two categories: those made with cold water and those made with boiling water. Doughs made with boiling water have a special chewy quality and translucence, owing to the fact that the hot water "cooks" the flour and expands the starch molecules while the dough is being made. Boiling water doughs are typically used in recipes for steamed dumplings and mandarin pancakes, where their delicate character suits the nature of the dish. Cold water doughs are more often found with heartier fare—pan-fried dumplings, boiled dumplings, and northern breadstuffs with "bite." Chinese will often say that the more velvety hot water doughs typify the dumplings and *dim sum* pastries of the south, whereas the more robust cold water doughs belong to the north. In general, it is true, though to me it seems more a matter of cooking method: steamed things tend to begin with the translucent hot dough and boiled and fried things with the opaque cold water dough.

"FINGERTIP" AND "EARLOBE" DOUGHS   Half of the fun of dough-making is the *feel* of it, and most of the success of making good breads and buns rests with *getting* the feel. In my classes, I've come to distinguish between two textures of dough and find it extremely helpful to Chinese bread-makers-to-be.

"Fingertip" doughs are those with a smooth and rather firm texture, just like the feel of the tip of your index finger if you pinch it several times between the thumb and first finger of your other hand. This rather firm texture is typical of *yeasted* Chinese doughs.

"Earlobe" doughs are softer and seemingly without muscle. They are exactly the texture of your earlobe when you grasp it between your thumb and first finger. This smooth, soft texture is typical of *unyeasted* Chinese doughs, the sort used for making dumpling wrappers.

YEAST   Yeast is the magic fermenter, the kitchen activist that awakens the gluten in flour and causes it to swell and stretch in a network of gaseous pockets. Of the several sorts of yeast on the market, I prefer *active dry yeast,* a camel-colored, granulated powder that has a wonderful and distinctive smell. You can buy active dry yeast in bulk in health food stores, but I have taken to buying it in foil packets in the supermarket, where it should be kept in the refrigerator case and marked with a clear expiration date. Each of these packets contains 2 *teaspoons* yeast, not 1 tablespoon as many people suppose. When you bring yeast home, store it in the refrigerator and use it up within the date of expiration, while it is still strong and healthy.

TYPES OF RICE   The varieties of rice grown in China are even greater than those grown in the United States, with Chinese of different areas accustomed to eating rice that is variously long, short, flat, round, bright white, off-white, or even pink. This is heartening for Chinese cooks in America, for I take it to mean you can choose whichever sort of rice you like and still be within the range of authenticity.

According to The Rice Growers Association of California, the Chinese population of California favors *long-grain rice,* following the typical tastes of the average American rice eater. Grown in the Carolinas, it is less starchy than other white rices and the grains tend to stay firm and separate when cooked.

According to other researchers, Chinese in Asia favor a *shorter-grain rice* that is more absorbent and hence softer and moister when cooked. I share that taste, preferring a *short-grain rice* where it is available and a *medium-grain rice* where it is not. I find the thicker, stubby grains far more appealing and like the slightly creamy quality one gets from a shorter grain rice that is properly cooked. Most Americans who are used to long-grain rice use the same amount of water when cooking the short- and medium-grain varieties, and wind up with an unappealing mush. This has given short-grain rice a bad name, which is thoroughly undeserved.

Though it is getting scarcer owing to the average American preference, I am regularly able to find short-grain rice. On the East Coast, it is often sold under Spanish brand names. On the West Coast, my favorite variety is a California native called *pearl rice,* which is distributed throughout the Western states and in large cities like New York, Chicago, and Miami. The Japanese short-grain brands, such as Kokuho Rose and Blue Rose, are also excellent.

Italian Arborio rice, which is structurally similar to pearl rice though more expensive, tastes delicious, and I use it when a locally grown short-grain is unavailable. This rice is grown in northern Italy's Po River valley—a thoroughly Chinese-sounding place. (The Italians, parenthetically, are now importing California pearl rice.)

In all cases, I avoid *converted* (parboiled), *precooked* or *instant rice.* To me, they taste insipid, and the texture is disagreeably pasty.

Sweet rice (more accurately called *glutinous rice* and also called *sticky rice*), is an altogether different variety, taste and texture not to be confused with the ordinary table varieties listed above. Its use in China is restricted mostly to desserts and sweet snacks, stuffings, a few regional rice specialties, and as a decorative coating for certain foods. It is *not* the rice that a Chinese puts in the everyday bowl.

RINSING RICE   Chinese *always* rinse their ordinary table rice, and not once but several times, until the water runs nearly clear. It is a 3–5-minute ritual in most households, which signifies the beginning of preparation for a meal. Washing removes the dry and oily bran residue and the starchy polishing compounds that are a part of the common Asian milling process, as well as the bits of extraneous stuff, such as tiny stones or insects that typically populate a bag of Chinese market rice. The washing is also thought to tenderize the grains, and some families—my mentors, the Lo's, included—soak their rice for up to an hour before cooking to make it even more tender.

Here, in America, the issue is more complicated. In the past, rice was given a post-application of glucose and talc, and, while this practice has been made illegal (the asbestos in the talc having been deemed a carcinogen), some bags may still be on the market and one should pay careful attention to such a package that will specify that rinsing is necessary. Rice milled presently for the domestic American market is *not* coated at all and actually requires no rinsing, though the same chemists who patiently explained to me that there is no technical reason to rinse it *still* rinse their rice out of habit. Even if the package specifies "enriched," the household practice of everyone but a single vitamin-conscious home economist was to wash the grains, and hence wash all the nutrients away. Rice milled domestically for the Japanese market *is* coated, on the other hand, and does require rinsing. Being sophisticated rice-eaters, the Japanese demand that the rice be coated with cornstarch to inhibit the oily bran fraction left on the grains from going rancid and resulting in what they call "smelly" rice. Hence, Japanese brands must be rinsed if they are not to turn gummy from the cornstarch. So there, and it's pretty confusing!

I personally follow the Asian method of *repeated rinsing*, regardless of whether the rice is coated with talc, cornstarch, glucose, or nothing at all. I have found after a night of experimenting that the typical American habit of rinsing rice once briefly before cooking gives no perceptibly different result than if the rice is not rinsed at all, but the habit of my Chinese friends who rinse the rice several times—covering it with cold water, sloshing it around, then draining it repeatedly for about 3 minutes—makes an *enormous* difference in the final taste. As might be expected, the rice is less starchy for the lengthy bathing, but it is also and foremost strikingly clean, fresh, and light-tasting compared to rice that has been rinsed only once or not at all. The difference is dramatic, so as long as you are going to wash away the nutrients with a short rinsing, you might as well wash them away with a repeated rinsing and greatly improve the flavor of the rice.

Sweet (glutinous) rice is subject to the same conflicting opinions if one asks the American growers (not one of whom I spoke with had ever even cooked the grain!), but here my practice is thoroughly Chinese, necessary or not. I first sort through the rice and discard any unhulled or discolored grains and the occasional small stone, then wash the rice thoroughly with several rinsings of cool water. Next, I cover the rice with cold water and let it soak, anywhere from 1–24 hours, depending on convenience. The longer soaking does not seem to me to make any appreciable difference in the texture of the finished product, yet 1–2 hour's soaking *will* yield a greater tenderness.

**Everyday
Chinese
Rice**

白飯

According to one of my more reliable reference books, the average Chinese consumes a pound of rice a day (compared to the average American consumption of seven pounds a year). That's a lot of rice! Certainly it was the kind of consumption I saw all around me during my years in Asia, when several bowls of rice per meal was the habit of young and old, and the giant family rice cooker, the omnipresent rice bowls, and the luxuriant paddies outside my study window were all part of the daily scene. Rice is life in most of China, and its preparation is one of the day's most steady rhythms. ◆ The everyday Chinese rice bowl is filled with plain white rice, half-boiled and half-steamed, unseasoned by salt, oil, or stock. Brown rice is not eaten, not even by the poor, and seasonings are left to the other dishes one eats as an accompaniment to rice. The mainstay, the central part of the meal, has for centuries been the unadorned white bowlful. One Ching dynasty gourmet reportedly sent his maid scurrying to collect the dew from wild roses and cassia blossoms to infuse his rice—the modern equivalent, I suppose, to a squirt of orange flower water being added to the pot— but he was the exception in a tradition of simplicity. ◆ The Chinese have a standard method for cooking rice and, in Asia, a preference for short-grain rice. While short-grain rice is not the American favorite, it is absolutely delicious when cooked properly, and the thickish, slightly creamy grains are eager helpmates to spicy or saucy dishes—the ones that go best with rice. The method is simple, a matter of one heavy pot and a half hour of time from start to serving.

TECHNIQUE NOTES:
The Chinese (and Japanese) habit is to rinse rice repeatedly before cooking. The rice is put in a bowl or pail, covered with a generous amount of cold water, then stirred by hand until the water turns milky from the residue left by the milling process. It is immediately drained, then the process is repeated perhaps 5 or 6 times over the course of 3 or 4 minutes. Regardless of whether or not the rice has been coated in milling, the repeated rinsings over several minutes result in a perceptibly cleaner, lighter, fresher-tasting rice.

One cup raw rice yields 3½ cups cooked rice, generally enough to serve 3–4 Westerners. (In China, it would serve for a single person.)

INGREDIENTS:

> *1 cup short- or medium-grain white rice*
> *1½ cups cold water*
> *or*
> *1 cup long-grain white rice*
> *1¾ cups cold water*

if you are doubling the recipe:

> *2 cups short- or medium-grain white rice*
> *2½ cups cold water*
> *or*
> *2 cups long-grain white rice*
> *3 cups cold water*

Rinsing the rice:
Put the dry rice in a large bowl, cover generously with cold water, then stir the rice in circles with your hand for 10–15 seconds, or until the water turns milky white. Drain the rice immediately into a large sieve or colander, then return the rice to the bowl, cover again with cold water, and repeat the process. Do this 5 or 6 times, for a total of 3 to 4 minutes, by which time the rinsing water should be nearly clear. Stir with increased gentleness as you near the final rinsing, as the rice will absorb a bit of water in the process and be susceptible to breaking. Shake off any excess water, then proceed at once to cook the rice, or leave it to sit in the colander for up to an hour before cooking.

Cooking the rice:
If you are cooking a single cup of raw rice, use a heavy 2–2½-quart pot with a tight-fitting lid. If you are doubling the recipe, use a heavy 4–4½-quart lidded pot. The general rule with rice is to use a pot with more depth than breadth as you go to cook larger amounts, lest the water evaporate too quickly during the cooking.

Put the rinsed and well-drained rice in the pot, then add the appropriate amount of cold water for the grain and the amount of rice you are using. Do not bother to stir the rice, now or anytime during cooking. Bring the water to a rolling boil over high heat. When the big starchy bubbles climb nearly to the rim, in about 30 seconds, cover the pot at once with a tight-fitting lid and reduce the heat to low. What you want inside the pot is a slow, bubbly simmer, which requires either a low or moderately low setting depending on the stove. Check the simmer by putting your ear next to the pot and listening for the bubbling within, and by observing the tiny wisps of steam that should be escaping from around the lid. Do *not* uncover the pot.

Simmer the rice under the tight lid for 15 minutes, then move the pot off the heat, and let it sit undisturbed for 15–20 minutes. Do not open the lid even once; the rice is still at work within, absorbing the steam and plumping to tenderness. (Note that this "waiting" time is a bit longer for Chinese-style rice than is customarily given for American-style long-grain rice. The extra minutes mean extra tenderness and creaminess, which I personally like far better.)

When the waiting time is up, lift the lid, then gently fluff the rice with a fork, lifting the grains from the bottom and tossing gently to separate them. Serve the rice immediately, or let it sit in the covered pot where it will stay warm for another 15–20 minutes.

Holding, storing, and reheating rice:
In the course of an average Chinese meal, people refill their bowls several times. The covered pot will alone keep the rice warm for 15–20 minutes, but if you are anticipating extended service, then the rice may be kept warm for hours if it is placed in a covered bowl in a steamer and kept over low heat. The gentle steam keeps the rice hot without drying it, and the lid prevents extra moisture from creeping in and making the rice mushy.

Once cool, rice may be sealed and refrigerated several days. It is perfect for fried rice (page 404), or may be reheated by steaming in a covered bowl until hot. You may also, Western-fashion, reheat the rice in a foil-covered baking dish in a hot oven, but I like the steaming method better.

And a note on dry rice:
If you have followed the measurements and instructions given above carefully and the rice is not perfectly tender to the bite when you fluff it, then you may be using rice that is very old and therefore dry. You can rescue the first batch by sprinkling it with an extra tablespoon or so of water, then steaming it over moderately high heat in an open bowl until tender, about 10 minutes. If you use the same rice again, begin with a bit more water. Experience will quickly teach you just what you need for your rice, your stove, your pot and—most of all—your taste.

| Shanghai |
| Vegetable |
| Rice |
| |
| 菜飯 |

There is, for me, something extraordinary about Shanghai. Its people have a striking combination of beauty, intelligence, and strength. You can see it in the Isaac Stern film *From Mao to Mozart* and read about it in books by Emily Hahn. And the Shanghai dishes I have eaten feature a delicacy and a simplicity that is unique in my experience of Chinese food. ◆ This recipe was inspired by my Shanghai mentor and friend, Lucy Lo. True to the above, Lucy has a remarkable beauty and intellect, and this dish has about it a certain simple delicacy. It is unusual in the context of Chinese rice dishes: a mixture of crisp green cabbage, sweet sausage, and raw rice, which one sautées and seasons in the pot before adding the cooking liquid. The final effect is perhaps more reminiscent of a pilaf or risotto than it is of our standard notion of a bowl of Chinese rice. ◆ When you can find them, the miniature green cabbages that are 4–5 inches long are excellent in this dish. Otherwise, use the common Chinese cabbage that has an elongated head comprised of tightly wrapped, pale green-white leaves. The real requisite is short- or medium-grain rice (page 399). Without it, you lose the creaminess that is one of the most appealing features of this dish. ◆ Few recipes could be easier. Preparations take 10–15 minutes, then you simply wait 35 minutes for the rice to cook.

TECHNIQUE NOTES:
Steaming the sausage renders a delectable fat with which to sauté the rice. To add it to the dish cold would mean extra oil and a less tender sausage.

Serves 3–4 hearty rice eaters, 6–8 as a smaller portion in a multicourse meal.

INGREDIENTS:

> *3 ounces Chinese sweet pork sausage (equal to 3 thin or 2 fatter sausage)*
> *1 cup short- or medium-grain raw white rice*
> *½ pound trimmed Chinese cabbage—either miniature green cabbages (page 537), or the crisp inner leaves and heart of the elongated variety with evenly broad, pale leaves (page 537) (weight after trimming)*
> *about 1 tablespoon corn or peanut oil*
> *2¼ teaspoons coarse kosher salt*
> *2 teaspoons Chinese rice wine or quality, dry sherry (optional)*
> *1¾ cups cold water*

Preparations:
Slice the sausage on the diagonal into thin coins a scant ¼ inch thick. Put in a small heatproof saucer or bowl, then steam over high heat for 10 minutes, or until the fatty portion of the sausage is translucent and there is a pool of rendered fat in the bottom of the dish. Turn off the heat and leave the sausage in the steamer until you are ready to use it.

While the sausage is steaming, rinse the rice repeatedly as described on page 401. Leave the rice to drain in the sieve.

Cut the cabbage crosswise into bands ½ inch thick. If you are using miniature cabbages, separate the crisp ribs and leafy tops into two small bowls. If you are using the more common Chinese cabbage, use only the crisp inner ribs and core. Leave any baby cabbages you may find at the core uncut and slice any tender base pieces into wedges or thin coins.

Cooking the rice:
Have all the ingredients within easy reach of your stovetop. Put a serving bowl or individual rice bowls in a low oven to warm.

Choose a heavy, 2–2½-quart saucepan with a tight-fitting lid and set over high heat until hot enough to evaporate a bead of water on contact. While the pot is heating, drain the liquefied fat from the sausage into a ⅛-cup measure (equal to 2 tablespoons). Add enough corn or peanut oil to fill the measure.

Add the fat to the hot pot, swirl to glaze the bottom, then reduce the heat to medium-high. When the fat is hot enough to sizzle a piece of crisp cabbage, add the cabbage. (If you are using the baby cabbage and have a bowl of stems and one of leaves, add the stems at this point, toss for 15 seconds, then add the leaves.) Toss the cabbage with chopsticks or a wooden spoon to glaze the pieces with the oil, adjusting the heat so they sizzle without scorching. Sprinkle with salt, and continue to toss until the cabbage softens slightly and lessens in bulk, about 30 seconds. Sprinkle with wine, toss, then add the sausage to the pot and toss to combine. Add the drained rice, and toss well to mix the ingredients, and glaze the rice with the oil, about 1 minute.

Add the water to the pot, stir to combine, then raise the heat to bring the water to a full rolling boil, with large bubbles over the surface. Boil vigorously for a full 2 minutes, stir once or twice, then cover the pot. Reduce the heat to low (if you are work-ing on an electric stove, switch the pot to a low burner rather than wait the extra minutes for the coil to cool), and simmer the rice for 20 minutes. Do *not* open the lid. Check the simmer by putting your ear next to the pot (you can *hear* the mild bubbling within), and by watching the lid for wisps of steam.

After 20 minutes, remove the pot from the heat and let it sit undisturbed for 15 minutes. Do not lift the lid even a peek, or you will dispel the steam that is at work cooking the rice. At the end of the 15 minutes, remove the lid and fluff the rice gently with a fork or chopsticks.

Serve the rice immediately. Or, cover the pot and the rice will stay warm for another 10–15 minutes before the sausage grows chewy.

Leftover rice is delicious at room temperature. It may also be rewarmed by steam-ing in a covered pot over high heat until hot. (Steaming turns the fat in the sausage coins translucent and tender, which reheating in the oven will not do.)

MENU SUGGESTIONS:
This rice is best with delicately seasoned steamed and stir-fried dishes, like *Clear-Steamed Lobster with Scallion Oil* (page 278), *Pearl's Steamed Egg Custard* (page 335), and *Steamed Whole Fish with Seared Scallions* (page 248). It is also an excellent accom-paniment to *Master Sauce Chicken* (page 153), *Golden Egg Dumplings* (page 328), and *Hakka Stuffed Tofu* (page 343). Stick to milder dishes; it will be overwhelmed by any-thing very spicy or saucy.

Real
Fried
Rice,
Three Ways

炒飯

This is *not* the fried rice I ate ravenously as a kid in New Jersey—that exotic mound of dark brown stuff shaped with an ice-cream scoop and dotted with wisps of canned bean sprouts and cubes of roast pork (I thought it superb). This is *real* fried rice, left white, as the Chinese insist on (seasoned therefore with salt, not soy), and tossed to a fluffy mound with colorful, stir-fried bits of fresh meat and vegetables. It is altogether light and delicious, a pleasure to my adult tongue even while a blow to my childhood illusions. ◆ Fried rice in China is usually an unassuming and deeply satisfying bowlful, a way of using up last night's rice and creating a quick, nourishing snack or meal. Roadside stalls and vendors in bus stations and train depots sell fried rice as "fast food" and offer it up in the spirit of a snack. Occasionally it will appear on a restaurant menu, but it will then be brought to the table last in a succession of dishes, meant to follow and accompany the requisite plain rice and never to replace it. ◆ My own style is to eat fried rice either as a midnight snack or—tradition forgive me—as a replacement for unadorned white rice. Late at night, it is enormously comfort-ing. At mealtime, it should be paired with subtle flavors that will not override its delicate taste, or on occasion with stews to add some color to their brownness. ◆ Given the cold rice, which can be made days ahead, fried rice is a 10–20-minute dish depending upon how fast you chop.

| Ham and Egg Fried Rice 火腿蛋炒飯 | This is one of the most common and satisfying of northern-style fried rice dishes, a simple combination of cooked rice, cubed ham, sweet green peas, and fluffy bits of stir-fried egg. It is excellent as a one-bowl meal or as a colorful companion to a simple dish of fish or meat. ◆ Look for a very tender, tasty ham, one which is ready-to-eat and a bit on the sweet side. I look for it in a specialty market, where one can choose from among a wide variety and sample a snip- |

pet of each. ◆ Except for the 3–4-minute stir-frying, all may be done a day in advance.

TECHNIQUE NOTES:

Cold or cool rice is preferable to hot or still-warm rice for stir-frying. Cool rice breaks apart easily into individual grains and will not absorb oil.

For cooking eggs for inclusion in a stir-fry and the pan in which to do it, see TECHNIQUE NOTES, page 372.

Serves 2 as a one-bowl meal, 3–4 as a large bowlful, or 6–8 as a small portion in a multi-course meal.

INGREDIENTS:

> *3½ cups cold cooked rice (see below)*
> *2–3 ounces honey- or sugar-cured ham (to yield ½ cup cubed ham)*
> *½ cup fresh or frozen peas or baby lima beans*
> *2 large eggs, lightly beaten*
> *3½–4 tablespoons corn or peanut oil*
> *1–1¼ teaspoons coarse kosher salt*
> *3 tablespoons green and white scallion rings*

Preparations:

Cook the rice according to the directions on page 401. Fluff, let stand until cool, then seal airtight and refrigerate overnight. Or, if you wish to use the rice within the hour, spread it on a baking sheet and refrigerate, uncovered, until cool. Just before using, toss gently with your fingers to separate the grains.

Trim the ham of any skin or fat, then cut it into neat cubes about ¼ inch square.

Blanch fresh peas or lima beans in plain boiling water until tender, drain, and rush under cold water to stop the cooking. Frozen peas or lima beans should be thoroughly defrosted.

Preparations may be done a full day in advance. Seal the ingredients separately and refrigerate. Bring to room temperature before cooking.

Stir-frying the dish:

About 15–20 minutes before serving, put a large serving bowl or individual rice bowls in a low oven to warm. Have all the ingredients plus a medium-size bowl to hold the eggs within easy reach of your stovetop.

Heat a wok or a small, heavy skillet or omelet pan over high heat until hot enough to evaporate a bead of water on contact. Add 1½ tablespoons oil, swirl to coat the pan, then reduce the heat to moderate. When the oil is hot enough to puff one drop of the beaten egg on contact, add the eggs. If the oil is properly hot, they will swell and puff immediately. Give the mixture 3–4 seconds to set on the bottom, then gently push the cooked egg to the far side of the pan with a spatula, allowing the uncooked portion to flow underneath and puff on contact with the hot pan. (If you are using a flat skillet, hold the eggs in place once you have pushed them to the side, then tilt the skillet toward you to aid the flow of the liquid portion.) Continue pushing the cooked portion aside as soon as the bottom sets. When there is no more freely running egg, scrape the eggs promptly into the bowl and break into small bits. If you have cooked them correctly, they will be soft, a bit runny, and golden as opposed to brown.

Wipe the wok clean of any egg bits, then return it or a *large* heavy skillet to high heat, and heat until hot enough to evaporate a bead of water on contact. Add 2 tablespoons oil and swirl to coat the pan. When the oil is hot enough to sizzle a grain of rice on contact, add the rice and toss briskly to coat and separate each grain and heat the mixture through, about 2–3 minutes. Lower the heat immediately if the rice starts to scorch. If the rice is sticking, push it to one side and dribble in another 1–1½ teaspoons oil from the side of the pan. When hot, sprinkle the salt into the pan. Toss to combine, then add the ham and peas or lima beans. Toss to mix and heat the mixture through, about 30 seconds, then return the eggs to the pan and stir gently several times to combine. Add the scallions, and toss another 5–10 seconds until the eggs are hot.

Serve immediately for peak flavor. If the menu demands do-ahead cooking, fried rice can be kept warm for up to an hour, tightly covered, in either a steamer set over low heat or in a low oven.

Leftovers keep 3–4 days and may be reheated as above using high heat.

MENU SUGGESTIONS:
This is a very versatile dish, particularly appealing to me in the company of *Steamed Whole Fish with Seared Scallions* (page 248), *Clear-Steamed Flounder with White Pepper* (page 250), and *Stir-Fried Dancing Crab* (page 271). Fish aside, it is also good with *Hoisin-Explosion Chicken* (page 136), *Casseroled Chicken with Smoky Chestnuts* (page 156), and *Beef and Broccoli on a Bird's Nest* (page 219). In a Western setting, try it alongside any simple potted meat or poultry, or with poached fish.

Celery and Pork Thread Fried Rice

肉絲炒飯

Fried rice is one of my favorite midnight indulgences and rarely has it ever tasted so good as when prepared one wintry night by my Chinese friends, the Hu's, in the kitchen of their restaurant. The crowds were gone, the cooks were beat, and everyone was warmed by this simple snack. ◆ All that is needed is what was on hand—a bit of fresh pork butt, a few stalks from the tender heart of the celery, and a mound of colorful carrot cubes. The splash of wine is mine, a flourish to lend savor to the bowl. ◆ Preparations take only 5–10 minutes, given cold rice. For peak flavor, work on your feet about 13 hours rolling hundred of springrolls and chopping until your cleaver seems a part of your hand, then sink down in a chair with a warm bowl and ready chopsticks.

TECHNIQUE NOTES:
For cold or cool rice as the basis of stir-fried rice, see page 405.

Serves 2 as a one-bowl meal, 3–4 as a large bowlful, or 6–8 as a small portion in a multi-course meal.

INGREDIENTS:

> 3½ cups cold cooked rice (see below)
> ¼ pound trimmed pork loin
> 1 large carrot, trimmed and peeled (to yield ⅔ cup tiny diced carrot)
> 2 inner stalks of celery plus the heart (to equal ½ cup thin slices)
> 2–2½ tablespoons corn or peanut oil
> 2–2½ teaspoons Chinese rice wine or quality, dry sherry
> 1–1¼ teaspoons coarse kosher salt
> 3 tablespoons thin-cut green and white scallion rings

Preparations:

Cook the rice as directed on page 401. Fluff, let stand until cool, then seal airtight and refrigerate overnight. Or, for use within the hour, spread the rice on a baking sheet and refrigerate, uncovered, until cool.

Slice the pork evenly into slices a scant ¼ inch thick, then shred them against the grain into slivers a scant ¼ inch thick. Cut any overly long slivers into 1-inch lengths. For precision shredding, chill the meat in the freezer, wrapped airtight, just until rigid enough to slice neatly.

Cut the carrot lengthwise into sticks a scant ¼ inch thick, then grasp the sticks together and cut them crosswise into tiny cubes a scant ¼ inch square.

Cut the celery stalks and heart on a slight diagonal into comma-shaped slices ⅛ inch thin. Include some pale, tender leaves from the heart; they will lend a pretty look and a nice texture to the dish.

Preparations may be done several hours in advance of cooking. Seal the ingredients separately, airtight, and store in the refrigerator.

Stir-frying the dish:

About 15 minutes before serving, put a large serving bowl or individual rice bowls in a low oven to warm. Have all the ingredients within easy reach of your stovetop. Gently break the rice into individual grains with your fingers.

Heat a wok or a large, heavy skillet over high heat until hot enough to evaporate a bead of water on contact. Add the oil, swirl to coat the pan, then reduce the heat to medium-high. When the oil is hot enough to sizzle one carrot cube, add the carrots and toss briskly to glaze with oil and heat them through, about 15 seconds. Next, add the celery to the pan, and toss several seconds to combine, adjusting the heat so it sizzles without scorching. Add the pork, and continue to toss until the meat is 90 percent gray. Sprinkle the wine at once into the pan, wait a brief second for it to "explode" in a fragrant hiss, then add the rice. Toss briskly to coat and separate the grains and combine the mixture, dribbling in a bit more oil from the side of the pan if needed to prevent sticking and lowering the heat if the rice begins to scorch. Once hot, sprinkle with salt, toss to combine, then taste and adjust with a bit more salt if required. Add the scallions, toss to combine, and remove the mixture at once to the heated bowl(s).

Fried rice is best served immediately. If the menu demands you cook in advance, cover the rice and keep it warm in a steamer set over low heat or in a low oven. Or, if you have cooked the rice in a heavy pot, remove it from the heat and cover it tightly; the heat of the metal will keep the rice warm for about 20 minutes.

Leftovers keep 3–4 days. Reheat, covered tightly, in a steamer set over high heat or in a hot oven.

MENU SUGGESTIONS:
For a simple dinner, try the rice with *Scallion and Ginger Explosion Shrimp* (page 233), or *Spicy Steamed Salmon with Young Ginger* (page 252). For a fuller menu, add *Stir-Fried Spinach with Fermented Tofu* (page 306) or *Dry-Fried Szechwan String Beans* (page 297). In a Western menu, use it most anywhere you would like a lightly seasoned rice.

Shrimp, Leek, and Pine Nut Fried Rice

蝦仁炒飯

This is a dish of my own devising, one which combines the northern Chinese taste for leeks, the eastern penchant for pine nuts, and the southern Chinese liking for shrimp with fried rice. It would prove baffling to a food historian, but I think it delicious. ◆ Unlike the more homey fried rice recipes above, this is a rather grand bowlful owing to the relative expense of the ingredients and the care required to prepare them. Use only short- or medium-grain rice; its plump shape and creamy texture mate perfectly with the shrimp and the pine nuts. ◆ If possible, marinate the shrimp 12–24 hours to give them time to absorb the seasonings. With preparations done, stir-frying the rice takes only 10–15 minutes.

TECHNIQUE NOTES:
Deep-frying marinated shrimp in warm oil prior to stir-frying "cooks" the exterior, protects the delicate flesh from the high heat of stir-frying, and eliminates any problem of the shrimp sticking to the pan. It is an extra step well worth the results. The shrimp becomes so velvety and succulent that people mistake it for lobster. For the roles of the different ingredients in a "velvet" marinade, see TECHNIQUE NOTES, page 145.

For cold rice as the basis of stir-fried rice, see page 405.

Serves 2–3 as a one-bowl meal, 4–5 as a large bowlful, or 6–8 as a small portion in a multicourse meal.

INGREDIENTS:

> 3½ cups cold cooked rice, short- or medium-grain best
> 3 large eggs
> ½ pound small or medium-size fresh shrimp (for a note on "fresh" shrimp, see page 233)

> To marinate the shrimp:
> 1 tablespoon egg white
> 2 teaspoons Chinese rice wine or quality, dry sherry
> ½ teaspoon coarse kosher salt
> .1 tablespoon cornstarch

> ½ pound tender, young leeks (to yield ⅔ cup thinly sliced leeks)
> ½ cup pine nuts
> 3–4 cups fresh corn or peanut oil, for velveting the shrimp

> To stir-fry the leeks:
> ⅛ teaspoon coarse kosher salt
> ⅛ teaspoon sugar
> 1½ teaspoons Chinese rice wine or quality, dry sherry

> about 1 teaspoon coarse kosher salt

Preparations:

Cook the rice as directed on page 401. Fluff, let stand until cool, then seal airtight and refrigerate overnight. Or, for use within the hour, spread the rice on a baking sheet and refrigerate, uncovered, until cool.

Separate one of the eggs and measure out 1 tablespoon egg white for the shrimp. Lightly beat the yolk and remaining white together with 2 whole eggs, then seal airtight and refrigerate until use, overnight if desired.

Shell and devein the shrimp, rinse, then pat dry. Combine the reserved egg white, wine, salt, and cornstarch in a small bowl, whisking until smooth and slightly thick. Add the shrimp, toss well with your fingers to coat, then seal airtight and refrigerate at least 3–6 hours so the shrimp absorb the marinade. For best results, refrigerate a full 24 hours. Bring to room temperature before cooking.

Trim the leeks of their stems and green tops, leaving only 1 inch of the more tender, light green neck. Cut in half lengthwise, and discard the outer layer of leek if it is, as typically, tough, wilted, or discolored. Slice the leeks crosswise into thin half-moons, a scant ¼ inch thick. Rinse thoroughly in a large bowl of cold water, stirring to dislodge dirt, then drain and rinse again. Shake off excess water and put aside until use, sealed airtight and refrigerated, overnight if you like.

Toasting the pine nuts and velveting the shrimp:

An hour to 30 minutes before stir-frying the rice, spread the pine nuts on a heavy jelly-roll pan or doubled baking sheets (to prevent browning the bottoms of the nuts), and toast in a preheated 300° oven until fragrant and only lightly speckled with brown, about 4–5 minutes. Transfer the nuts to a shallow dish.

About 15–20 minutes in advance of stir-frying, assemble all the ingredients within easy reach of your stovetop. Have an extra bowl and a large Chinese mesh spoon or metal sieve that will nest directly on top of the bowl nearby. Put a large serving bowl or individual rice bowls in a low oven to warm.

Heat a wok or deep, heavy skillet over high heat until hot enough to evaporate a bead of water on contact. Add the oil for velveting, then heat to the slow-fry stage, 275° on a deep-fry thermometer, reducing the heat to medium or low once it has reached 200° to prevent it from climbing too quickly. When the oil reaches 275°, turn off the heat and slide the shrimp into the oil. They will sink to the bottom and bubble gently. Nudge the shrimp gently with chopsticks to keep them afloat and separate until they turn 90 percent pinkish-white, about 15–20 seconds, then scoop them immediately from the oil in one movement with the mesh spoon or sieve. Hold the shrimp briefly above the oil to drain, then put the spoon or sieve atop the waiting bowl to let them drain further. They will look mottled, and the inside will be raw.

Proceed immediately to stir-fry the rice. If you must use the deep-frying pot, then very carefully drain the oil into a heatproof bowl or pot. Use the hot oil for stir-frying. When the remainder cools, it may be strained and bottled for future use.

Stir-frying the dish:

Have an extra bowl nearby to hold the eggs and beat them lightly to recombine.

Heat a wok or a medium-size, heavy skillet or omelet pan over high heat until hot enough to evaporate a bead of water on contact. Add 2½ tablespoons oil, swirl to coat the pan, then reduce the heat to moderate. When the oil is hot enough to puff a drop of egg on contact, add the eggs. Allow several seconds for them to puff and swell and the bottom to set, then gently push the cooked egg to the far side of the pan, tilting the pan toward you if needed so the uncooked, liquid portion flows beneath and comes in contact with the pan. Repeat the process until there is no liquid egg left to flow, then immediately scrape the egg into the bowl and break it into bits. It should be soft, slightly runny, and golden. (If you cooked it to 100 percent doneness, then you cooked it too long. If it has browned, then the heat was too high.)

Wipe the wok clean of any egg bits, then return it or a *large*, heavy skillet to high heat until hot enough to evaporate a bead of water on contact. Add 2½ tablespoons oil, swirl to coat the pan, then reduce the heat to medium-high. When the oil is hot enough to sizzle one piece of leek, add the leeks. Stir-fry briskly to coat them with the oil, adjusting the heat so they sizzle merrily without scorching. When evenly glazed, sprinkle with ⅛ teaspoon salt and sugar, then toss until they turn supple and soft, about 30 seconds. Add the shrimp, stir several times to mix, then sprinkle in the wine. Pause a split second to allow the alcohol to "explode" in a fragrant hiss, toss to blend, then add the rice to the pan. Toss briskly to combine and heat the rice through, about 2 minutes, lowering the heat if the rice starts to scorch and pushing the rice to one side and dribbling in a bit more oil from the side of the pan if necessary to prevent sticking. Once hot, reduce the heat to low and season the rice carefully with salt, keeping it on the light side to show off the richness of the pine nuts. When the taste is right, return the eggs to the pan and toss gently to combine, then sprinkle in the pine nuts and toss 5–10 seconds to mix, until the mixture is heated through.

For best flavor, serve immediately. If the rice must be held, cover it tightly and place it in a steamer set over low heat or in a low oven. If it was cooked in a heavy pot, the pot may be taken off the heat and covered tightly and the rice will stay warm for about 20 minutes.

Leftovers will keep 3–4 days, refrigerated and sealed airtight. Reheat, covered tightly, in a steamer set over high heat or in a hot oven.

MENU SUGGESTIONS:
Try this particular fried rice with delicate dishes like *Paper-Wrapped Chicken* (page 150), *Clear-Steamed Flounder with White Pepper* (page 250), and *Golden Egg Dumplings* (page 328). Or, treat it as a main dish and pair it with a delicate vegetable like *Steamed Cucumber with Cassia Blossoms* (page 317).

Everyday Chinese Bread

饅頭

While much of the Chinese population picks up a rice bowl with every meal, Chinese of the northernmost provinces, including the citizens of Peking, pick up an oblong-shaped bun of steamed dough. It is in every way the equivalent of rice—white, plain, soft, with an overtone of sweet freshness. ♦ Just like bread on a Western table, these buns appear variously at the beginning or somewhere in the middle of a northern Chinese meal, often after a bowl of noodles or dumplings, when the stir-fried and potted dishes begin to emerge from the kitchen and a good sopper-upper is needed. For this purpose they are delicious, either steamed, as is traditional, or deep-fried after steaming, which is my own preference. Either way they are homey and satisfying without being heavy and a perfect partner to any good sauce or soup. ♦ The individual loaves are extremely simple to make. They may be done in several hours or leisurely over the course of a day and may be refrigerated or frozen before serving with no loss of flavor or texture.

TECHNIQUE NOTES:
For the hows and whys of yeast, baking powder, and Chinese steamed doughs, see the introductory pages of this chapter and TECHNIQUE NOTES, page 415.

Makes 12 individual breads, enough to serve 6–8 alongside a hearty bowl of soup, or 10–12 as part of a multicourse meal in place of rice.

INGREDIENTS:

> *1 recipe steamed bread dough (page 415)*
> *3–5 cups corn or peanut oil, if you wish to deep-fry the breads*

Making the dough:
Follow the directions on pages 416 to 417 for proofing the yeast and making the dough, letting it rise and punching it down, and incorporating the baking powder.

Shaping the breads:
Have cut 12 rectangular paper bases for the loaves, each 4 inches long and 2½ inches wide. If you do not have silicon (no-stick) parchment, use greased parchment or greased wax paper. Put them greased side up on one or two baking sheets with at least 1½ inches between them, then put the sheet(s) and a second dry towel alongside your work surface.

Divide the dough into two even pieces with a sharp knife. On a lightly floured board roll and thump each piece with your palms into a smooth log 6 inches long. Then cut each log crosswise at 1-inch intervals into 6 pieces, for a total of 12 pieces in all. Put the pieces cut side down on a floured corner of the board, and keep them covered while you shape the breads.

To shape each loaf, take a piece of the dough between your palms and roll, push, and smooth it into an oblong shape about 3 inches long. If it is too elastic to shape easily, then cover the dough and let it rest 5–10 minutes. Once shaped and smoothed, center the bread on a paper base and cover it with the towel. Repeat the process until all the loaves are shaped and covered.

Letting the loaves rise:
Let the loaves rise until about double in bulk, when a loaf feels light and airy in your palm and a finger mark pressed into the dough does not spring quickly back, anywhere from 35 minutes to 1½ hours, depending on the temperature of the room. If you wish to stall the rising, you can put the breads in the refrigerator or even the freezer, so long as they are sealed airtight against drying.

At this point the breads may be flash-frozen, sealed airtight on the baking sheet until firm, then bagged airtight and frozen for several weeks. Steam directly from the freezer as directed below, allowing an extra 10 minutes' steaming time.

Steaming the breads:
(For details on steaming and how to improvise a steamer, see page 60.)

If you are using a Chinese bamboo or metal steamer, then transfer the loaves on their paper bases directly to the steaming tier. If you are improvising a steamer, then transfer to a flat, heatproof plate at least 1 inch smaller in diameter than your steaming vessel. Leave 1–1½ inches between the loaves.

To steam the whole batch at once, use two steamers or two steaming tiers, so long as they are deep enough to accommodate the height of the loaves plus 1 inch for expansion. If you are using *metal* tiers, stretch a fine-woven piece of cheesecloth or flour sacking beneath the top tier to absorb condensation and inhibit water from dripping on the loaves below.

Bring the water in the steaming vessel to a gushing boil over high heat, put the loaves in place, then reduce the heat to medium-high to maintain a strong, steady steam. (For double-decker tiers, check to see that the steam gushes clear up through the top tier. Then there is no need to reverse tiers during steaming.) Cover the steamer and steam the breads for 15 minutes. Turn off the heat, then let the steam subside for 5 minutes before lifting the cover slowly away from you, lest a blast of cold air cause the tops of the loaves to wrinkle.

At this point the loaves may be served, kept warm in the steamer for an hour over low heat, deep-fried, or left to cool for refrigerating or freezing.

If you are storing newly steamed loaves or leftover steamed loaves, be sure they are thoroughly cool, then bag airtight for storage. Resteam on paper squares over medium-high heat until hot, 10–20 minutes, depending on whether they go into the steamer at room temperature or frozen. Leftover steamed loaves are incredibly durable, and may be refrigerated or frozen then resteamed one or more times with no flavor or texture loss.

The deep-frying alternative:

To deep-fry the loaves, take them directly from the steamer, still warm, for best results. Refrigerated or frozen loaves should be plumped in the steamer before frying.

Discard the paper, then fry and drain the loaves as described on page 422. Serve whole, brought to the table heaped in a bamboo steamer or towel-lined basket, or on a heated platter of contrasting color.

Deep-fried loaves are best freshly made; they grow oily with reheating.

MENU SUGGESTIONS:

Steamed or fried, this bread goes happily with saucy stir-frys and stews, wherever a sopper-upper is needed. Deep-fry them when the accompanying dish—a tofu dish, for instance—would profit from the addition of extra texture and color.

New Year's Bread Wheel

紅棗饅頭

Chinese New Year is a warm, very family-centered time, when the doors of the house are thrown open to welcome anyone who even might be considered kin—which in the average extended Chinese family means that the cook has to expect a horde for every meal. My restaurateur friends, the Hu's, count their hordes in the hundreds, and in their restaurant and their home they make this special bread a feature of the holiday. The shape is symbolic of wholeness and continuity, and the red jujubes that garnish the top mimic the Eight Trigrams of Chinese philosophy—an edible reminder of change at the turning of the new year. ◆ Festivity aside, this is a very simple bread to make. There is no special shaping involved, and there is little to do but watch the bread rise. Instead of using jujubes, you might like to knead ½ cup of minced ham and ½ cup of minced green and white scallion bits into the bread, and instead of steaming it you might put the bread in the oven and bake it until golden. Neither is traditional but both are delicious, and I think the gods would not mind. ◆ As with all steamed bread doughs, you may shorten the process to several hours or stretch it out over a day. The bread may be steamed in advance and also freezes beautifully.

TECHNIQUE NOTES:
For notes on yeast, baking powder, and the proper feel of a steamed Chinese bread dough, see TECHNIQUE NOTES, page 415. If you are a newcomer to bread making, read carefully the introductory pages of this chapter.

Makes 1 round bread about 9 inches in diameter, enough to serve 8 as part of a multi-course meal, or 4–6 as a large wedge alongside a single dish or bowl of soup.

INGREDIENTS:

> *1 recipe steamed bread dough (page 415)*
> *8 soft, pitted Chinese jujubes (page 550)*
> *or*
> *½ cup coarsely minced honey- or sugar-cured ham and ½ cup minced green and white scallion*

Making the dough:
Follow the directions on pages 416 to 417 for proofing the yeast and making the dough, letting it rise and punching it down, and incorporating the baking powder.

Shaping the bread wheel:
Shape the kneaded dough into a round loaf. If you are adding the ham and scallion, combine them in a small bowl, then sprinkle a third of the mixture at a time on the board and work it into the dough as you knead it.

    Dust the board lightly with flour, then use a rolling pin to roll the loaf into a 9-inch round. If the dough is very elastic and keeps springing back, then cover it with a dry towel for 5–10 minutes and let it rest to allow the gluten to relax.

    If you are garnishing the top with jujubes, take a small, sharp knife and make two parallel slashes about 1½ inches long and ⅜ inch deep an inch in from the perimeter of the loaf, aiming the slash marks toward the center of the loaf. Use the tip of the knife to cut through at the base of the slash marks to join them, so that you can poke a finger through and carefully lift up a band of dough. Press your finger down to make a hollow for the jujube, then slip it under the band of dough so it is held in place on top of the bread as illustrated. Continue slashing the bread, making a space with your finger, and inserting a jujube beneath the dough band at 7 more regular intervals around the loaf.

finished loaf

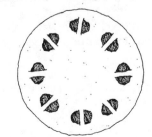

Letting the bread wheel rise:
Transfer the bread wheel to a baking sheet lined with a 9½–10-inch circle of silicon no-stick parchment paper. Alternatively, use a greased circle of plain parchment or a greased circle of wax paper.

Center the bread on the paper, then cover with a dry kitchen towel. Let rise until almost double in bulk, when the dough feels very light and a finger mark pressed into the dough does not spring back, about 40 minutes to 1½ hours, depending on the temperature of the room.

At this point, the dough may be flash-frozen, sealed airtight on the baking sheet until firm, then bagged airtight and frozen for several weeks. Steam directly from the freezer or while cold and firm as directed below, allowing an extra 15–20 minutes' steaming time.

Steaming and serving the bread wheels:
(For details on steaming and how to improvise a steamer, see page 60.)

Transfer the bread on its paper round directly to a bamboo or metal steaming tier. For an improvised steamer, transfer the bread and paper to a flat, heatproof plate at least 1 inch smaller in diameter than your steaming vessel.

Bring the water to a gushing boil over high heat, put the bread in place, then reduce the heat to medium-high to maintain a strong, steady steam. Cover the steamer and steam the bread for 20 minutes.

Turn off the heat and wait 5 minutes for the steam to subside before lifting the cover. Lift the cover slowly away from you to prevent a sudden draft of cold air that could cause the bread to wrinkle.

Discard the paper and slice the bread into 8 wedges with a long, serrated knife, centering a jujube in each slice. Restore the loaf to its original shape and serve in a bamboo steamer or on a heated platter of contrasting color. If you need to hold the bread before serving, leave it in the steamer over low heat for up to an hour; it will taste equally good.

The baking alternative:
After the bread has risen, brush the top and sides lightly and evenly with a wash. For a soft blonde crust, use corn or peanut oil or melted butter. For a firmer, golden crust, use a mixture of 1 large egg beaten with 1 tablespoon milk or cream. Bake the bread on the paper-lined baking sheet in the lower third of a preheated 350° oven until the bottom of the loaf sounds with a hollow thump when tapped with a finger, about 30–40 minutes. Rotate the baking sheet midway through baking to insure even coloring. If you wish a softer textured bread more in keeping with Chinese dishes, set a pan of boiling water on the floor of the oven to gently steam the bread as it bakes.

Leftover steamed bread may be bagged airtight once cool, then refrigerated or frozen. Resteam on paper squares over medium-high heat until hot, about 10 minutes for room temperature bread, 20 minutes for bread steamed directly from the freezer. Steamed breads are incredibly resilient and may go from the freezer to the steamer and back again with no perceptible damage to flavor or texture.

MENU SUGGESTIONS:
The round loaf is a festive accompaniment to casseroled dishes like *Garlic-Stewed Sparerib Nuggets* (page 202), and *Casseroled Chicken with Smoky Chestnuts* (page 156) and

hearty soups like *Wine-Explosion Country Vegetable Chowder* (page 452) and *Moslem-Style Hot and Sour Soup* (page 450)—dishes one can cook easily and in quantity when expecting a crowd. Try it also with *Hot and Sour Hunan Chicken* (page 142), *Saucy Potted Pork* (page 207), or something with an equally abundant sauce that invites dunking.

Flower Rolls

葱肉花捲

These steamed rolls with their petal-like layers are a traditional fancy bread in north China. They typically accompany the great banquet duck dishes, and are set around the platter as a pretty frame for the bird. I love them with duck—the plush bread is the perfect balance for any oil—but I like the rolls also with homey stir-frys and soups, most anytime I'm feeling festive and want to "dress up" the meal. ◆ Flower rolls appear in a wide variety of shapes, mostly depending on the habit or whimsy of the cook. I like to make a double-decker flower and usually heighten the flavor and color by adding some minced scallion and ham. For plainer moods or less agile hands, you may leave out the trimmings and do single, smaller flowers. ◆ A food processor makes quick work of forming the dough. Once shaped, the rolls may be flash-frozen, and once steamed they may be resteamed with no discernible loss of texture. Like all steamed breads, they are remarkably durable, and are a practical contribution to any grand meal.

TECHNIQUE NOTES:
Yeast and baking powder are traditional companions in Chinese steamed doughs. The baking powder is always kneaded in just prior to shaping, to give an extra jolt of height over and above the yeast. According to the six-foot, two-hundred-pound Shantung cook who taught me Chinese bread making, yeast makes the dough expand *(fa)*, while baking powder gives it lift *(tee)*.

It is extremely important that the dough be *fingertip firm* when shaped. If it is too soft (like your earlobe), then the flowers will collapse in a dismal heap and the dough will not cook through. If in doubt with Chinese yeasted doughs, always make them firmer.

Makes 12 piggyback flower rolls. I usually count on 1 or 2 per person, depending on the appetite of the guests and the size of the meal.

INGREDIENTS:

> *Steamed bread dough:*
> 1 teaspoon active dry yeast
> 2½ teaspoons sugar
> 1 cup plus 2 tablespoons warm (100–105°) water, in a spouted liquid
>   measuring cup
> 3½ cups (1 pound) all-purpose flour
> ½ teaspoon Chinese or Japanese sesame oil
> 1 teaspoon double-acting baking powder
> additional flour, for kneading and rolling out the dough

Seasonings:
> 2½ teaspoons Chinese or Japanese sesame oil
> 1½ teaspoons coarse kosher salt
> ½ cup coarsely minced honey- or sugar-cured ham
> scant ½ cup finely chopped green and white scallion

Proofing the yeast and making the dough:
Begin at least 3–4 hours in advance of serving. I like to begin 6–8 hours in advance, in order to let the dough rise in a cool spot, a slower process that gives the bread a better crumb and a lighter texture.

Add the yeast and sugar to the warm water, stirring to dissolve the yeast. Put aside in a warm (70–85°), draft-free spot for about 10 minutes, by which time there should be a thick foam on top. No foam means that the yeast is not fresh or that the water was either too hot or too cold, in which case you must begin again.

If you have a food processor:
(For details on making dough in a food processor, see page 586).

Put the flour into the work bowl fitted with a steel knife. With the machine running, add the yeasted liquid through the feed tube in a thin, steady stream, pushing the foam in first with your finger or a spoon. Stop adding liquid when the dough begins to mass lumpily around the blade, then give the machine 2–3 seconds' "lag time" to incorporate the last water droplets and cause the dough to form a ball. If a ball does not form, add water in droplets until the dough comes together. You may need a bit more or less water than called for, all depending on the dryness of the flour, so have some extra warm water alongside in case you need it. Continue to run the machine for 30 seconds after the dough comes together. (It may jump and make noises of complaint, but hold it and yourself steady, and pay it no mind.) Remove the dough promptly to a lightly floured board, and knead by hand for about 3 minutes, until the dough is smooth, shiny, and fingertip firm, and will bounce slowly but surely back when you make a fingertip impression in the dough. If you have processed the dough correctly, it will not stick to the board after the initial seconds of kneading and require little or no extra flour. If it is too wet and is sticking, then dust the board with flour as required, and knead several minutes longer to incorporate the flour and produce a firm, shiny, and bouncy dough.

If you do not have a food processor:
Put the flour in a large bowl, then add the yeasted liquid in a thin stream, stirring first with chopsticks or a wooden spoon and finally with your hand until a stiff, lumpy dough is formed. Add extra water in droplets if the flour requires it to cohere. Press into a mass, turn out onto a lightly floured board, then knead vigorously for 10–15 minutes, until the dough is smooth, elastic, and fingertip firm, and bounces slowly but surely back when you make an impression in it with your finger. While kneading, dust the board with flour as required to prevent the dough from sticking.

Letting the dough rise and punching it down:
Put the sesame oil in a large bowl fully three times the size of the dough. Add the dough and turn it to coat both itself and the inside of the bowl with a thin film of oil. Seal the bowl airtight with plastic wrap, and let the dough rise until double in bulk. For a relatively fast rising that will take 1–2 hours, put the dough in a warm (70–85°) room, or in the oven with the pilot on. For a slower rise that will produce a better crumb, put the dough in a cooler place (the basement, a cool room, or even the refrigerator), and let it rise slowly over 3–5 hours. While the dough is rising, proceed to cut out and grease any

paper bases that may be called for when it is time to shape the dough.

When the dough is double its original bulk, and a fingertip impression does *not* spring back, use your fist to punch it repeatedly and reduce it to a near pancake. At this point the bowl may be resealed and the dough given a second rising and a second punching down. The second rising is not necessary, but it will yield a distinctly lighter bread.

Incorporating the baking powder:

Turn the punched-down dough out onto a board dusting with the baking powder. (If the powder is lumpy, crush it with several rolls of a rolling pin, then smooth it over the board.) Knead vigorously 4–5 minutes, incorporating the baking powder and restoring the dough to its original smooth, fingertip-firm state, dusting the board with flour as required to prevent sticking. When the dough is elastic enough so a fingertip impression bounces back slowly, transfer the dough to a lightly floured corner of the board and cover it with a clean, dry towel. Proceed immediately to make final arrangements for shaping, so the dough will be waiting no longer than 5–10 minutes.

Shaping the flower rolls:

Have cut a 3-inch by 2-inch rectangular paper base for each roll: 12 bases for piggyback rolls or 24 bases for single rolls. If you do not have silicon (no-stick) parchment, use greased parchment or greased wax paper. Arrange the paper greased side up on one or two baking sheets, leaving 2 inches between them. Put the sheet(s), the seasonings, a long ruler, an oiled chopstick, and a second dry towel alongside your work surface.

Sprinkle the board more generously with flour, then roll out the dough into an evenly thick rectangle 24 inches long and 10 inches wide. This is not as hard as it sounds, given some good rolling, occasional pulling, and help from the ruler to measure and square the sides. If the dough is frustratingly elastic, cover it with the towel and let it rest several minutes before attacking it anew. As you roll out the rectangle, check occasionally to see if it is sticking, and brush flour underneath as required.

Use joined fingers to smooth the sesame oil evenly over the top of the dough, clear to the edges. Repeat an even sprinkling of salt, ham, and scallion. If you are not adding ham and scallion, do not use salt, and you will have made the standard, sweet flower rolls that are the choice of most cooks.

Beginning at the long side closest to you, roll the dough away from you into a long cylinder, just as you would roll up a carpet. Do not roll too loosely; the layers should hug one another. Keep the ends even and tug at the dough as needed to keep the sides straight and the corners squared. When the long jelly roll is formed, pinch the top seam shut. Measure the length and roll it evenly back and forth if needed to stretch it to its original 24 inches.

With an eye to the ruler, use a sharp knife to cut the log crosswise into 24 pieces, each 1 inch wide. As you cut, move every other piece an inch above its neighbor or the slices will stick together.

For double flowers, put one piece of dough directly on top of another, piggyback fashion, seam side down, smooth sides touching, and cut sides open, as illustrated. Shape one double flower entirely before piggybacking the next, or they will topple.

For both double and single flowers, press the thinner half of the oiled chopstick lengthwise across the top of the dough as illustrated, so the cut ends flare up and the layers open. Press the chopstick firmly enough so the layers spread apart, but not so hard that you flatten the dough clear against the board.

Slide the chopstick out of the pleat it has formed, then accentuate the flower shape as follows: Pick up the dough by its smooth, rounded ends (not the cut sides), then pull the ends down until they meet underneath the roll. Pinch the ends together to join them. As you pull the ends down and pinch them together, the cut sides of the single or double flower will flare further, and the rather flat flower will become round. Put the finished flower pinched side down on the paper base, then cover with the dry towel. Continue to shape the flowers, placing them 2 inches apart on the baking sheet.

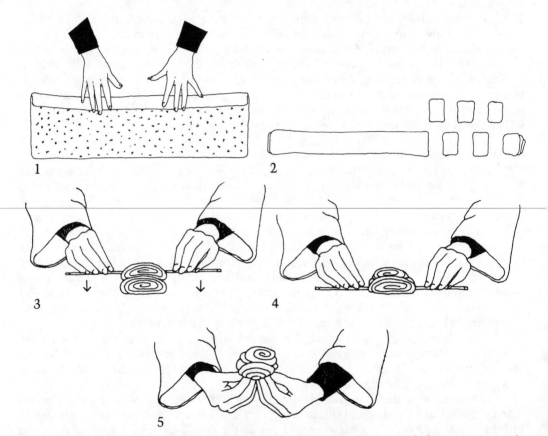

Leave the covered rolls to rise for about 30 minutes, or until they spring gently back when poked with a finger. If you are not ready to steam them, they may be flash-frozen on the baking sheet, then bagged airtight and kept frozen for several weeks. Steam as directed below, either directly from the freezer or while cold and firm, lengthening the steaming time by about 10 minutes.

Steaming and serving the flower rolls:
(For details on steaming and how to improvise a steamer, see page 60.)

Transfer the rolls on their paper bases to a bamboo or metal steaming tier, leaving 2 inches between them for expansion. If you are improvising a steamer, transfer the paper and rolls to a flat plate at least 1 inch smaller in diameter than your steaming vessel.

Bring the water to a gushing boil over high heat, reduce the heat to medium-high to maintain a strong, steady steam, then put the rolls in place and cover the steamer. Steam for 12–15 minutes.

Discard the paper and serve the rolls in a bamboo steamer or on a heated platter of contrasting color. Extra rolls may be kept warm in the steamer over low heat for up to an hour, with no harm to texture or flavor.

Leftover flower rolls should be left to cool, then bagged airtight for refrigerating or freezing. (The dough freezes perfectly, though the ham and scallion lose their zest.) To rewarm, steam on paper squares over medium-high heat until hot, about 10 minutes if the rolls are at room temperature, or 20 minutes if you steam them directly from the freezer.

MENU SUGGESTIONS:
The classic partners to these rolls are *Cinnamon Bark Chicken* (page 162), *Fragrant Crispy Duck* (page 172), and *Smoked Tea Duck* (page 169). They are also lovely with *Steamed Whole Fish with Seared Scallions* (page 248), *Clear-Steamed Flounder with White Pepper* (page 250), and *Tofu and Salmon in Pepper Sauce* (page 346).

| Silver and Gold Thread Rolls 銀絲捲 | Being a bread lover at heart, I sampled every type of steamed, fried, and occasionally baked bread I could find during my two years in Taiwan. This was my favorite: an oblong loaf of steamed bread, tinged with sweetness and fashioned so ingeniously that it came apart in a skein of soft, thickish "threads" when pulled. Served white and freshly steamed, it was known as a "silver thread roll." Deep-fried until golden (the way I like it best), it became a "gold thread |

roll." ◆ The process of kneading, shaping, and steaming this bread is a leisurely one, with several hours in between while the dough rests and you can too. The food processor does an excellent, fast job of kneading, and more good news is that the rolls may be steamed days in advance of serving and freeze beautifully. For the pleasure of sopping up a perfect Chinese sauce with a perfect wedge of Chinese bread, the effort to me is worth every minute. ◆ If your fingers are not nimble or time is at a premium, you can buy tiny, individual loaves in the refrigerator or freezer section of many large Chinese markets, where they are bagged by the dozen and sold as Peking Steamed Bread or *yin-sz-jwan*, and then take them home and steam or fry as directed below. They are not half as good as homemade, but the taste may inspire you to cook them for yourself.

TECHNIQUE NOTES:
The "threads" inside the rolls are formed by stretching a layer of shredded dough over a layer of smooth dough, and then rolling them in a jelly roll with the shreds trapped within. The shreds must be stretched very slowly so that they remain a tight set of neighboring bands, and the double layers must be rolled with sufficient tightness. Otherwise, when the bread is steamed and cut open there will be large gaps where there should be bread.

Newcomers to working with yeasted doughs should read TECHNIQUE NOTES, page 433, and the notes on "fingertip" and "earlobe" doughs and yeast on page 398.

Makes 2 small oblong loaves, enough to feed 2 passionate bread eaters as a sopper-upper for sauce or soup, 3–4 in place of rice to accompany a simple meal, or 5–6 as a slice of novelty in a multicourse dinner.

INGREDIENTS:

> ¾ *teaspoon active dry yeast*
> 2 *tablespoons sugar*
> ½ *cup plus 2 tablespoons warm water (100–105°, baby bottle temperature), in*
> *a spouted liquid measuring cup*
> 2 *cups all-purpose flour*
> *about 4 teaspoons Chinese or Japanese sesame oil*
> *additional flour, for kneading and rolling out the dough*
> 3–4 *cups corn or peanut oil, for frying Gold Thread Rolls*

Making the dough:
Follow the instructions on pages 416 to 417 for proofing the yeast and making the dough, letting it rise, and punching it down, using the proportions of ingredients specified above.

Shaping the dough:
Turn the punched down dough out onto a lightly floured board, then knead vigorously for 3–4 minutes until shiny and elastic, dusting the board as required to prevent the dough from sticking.

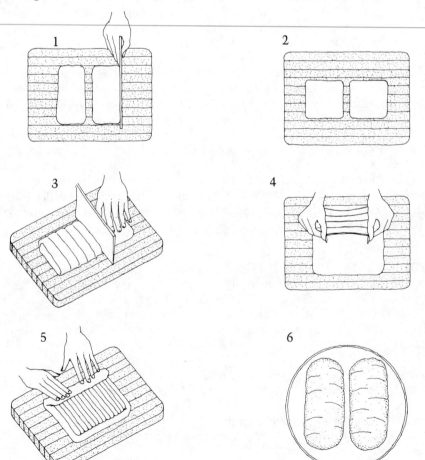

With a sharp knife divide the dough into four equal portions. Put two pieces aside cut side down on a lightly floured surface and cover with a dry towel. With the help of a ruler to measure and square the sides, roll the first two pieces into rectangles, each 4 inches wide and 8 inches long, dusting the board lightly if the dough sticks. Spread a thin film of sesame oil evenly over the top, then fold each rectangle towards you in half, to yield two 4-inch squares. Spread again with oil, then fold each square toward you in half again, to yield two rectangles, each 2 inches wide and 4 inches long. Cover with a dry towel and let the dough rest.

Roll out the two remaining pieces into 6-inch squares, using the ruler to measure and square the sides, and dusting the board as necessary to prevent sticking.

With a sharp knife, shred each of the oiled and folded rectangles crosswise into bands ¼ inch wide, cutting through to the board and leaving the shreds side by side, as illustrated, so they wind up looking like two rubber rafts.

Working with one raft and one smooth square at a time, pick up one half of the shreds, grasping them by their folded sides, then very gently stretch them until they are about 5½ inches long. (If the dough is too elastic to stretch easily, cover the shreds and let the gluten relax 5–10 minutes.) Place them over the bottom half of the smooth square, then anchor them to the square by pressing along the edges of the shreds, as illustrated. Grasp, stretch, and anchor the remaining shreds so the first square is covered, then repeat the process with the remaining two pieces of dough. You should now have two squares of dough covered with shreds.

Beginning at one of the anchored edges, roll each square securely into a jelly roll, as illustrated. Pinch the ends and bottom seams shut, then place each loaf seam side down on an 8-inch by 3-inch rectangle of silicon (no-stick) parchment paper, greased parchment, or greased wax paper.

Giving the loaves a final rising:
Transfer the loaves and the paper bases to a baking sheet, then cover with a clean, dry towel and let rise until swollen and springy to the touch, 30–60 minutes depending on the warmth of the spot. (Be sure the loaves are draft-free during the final rising, or they will have an odd, tough crust when steamed.)

Steaming the loaves to make *Silver Thread Rolls*:
(For details on steaming and how to improvise a steamer, see page 60.)
Bring the water in the steaming vessel to a gushing boil over high heat, then reduce the heat to medium-high to maintain a strong, steady steam. Transfer the loaves on their paper bases directly to a bamboo or metal steaming tier (or to a flat plate 1 inch smaller than your steamer if you are improvising), leaving 3 inches between them for expansion. Put the loaves in position, cover the steamer, and steam the loaves for 30 minutes without lifting the cover. Turn off the heat, let the steam subside for 5 minutes, and lift the cover slowly away from you, lest a sudden draft of cold air cause the loaves to wrinkle.

Discard the paper and cut the loaves into thick slices for serving. If you are not ready to serve them, the loaves may be left in the steamer over low heat for 30–60 minutes. Or, they may be put aside to cool and then refrigerated several days or frozen for up to a month, wrapped airtight.

Reheat refrigerated or frozen rolls by steaming on a paper base over high heat until hot, about 10–20 minutes. Frozen rolls may be steamed directly from the freezer. Leftovers may be refrozen a second time, provided they are left to cool entirely and then wrapped airtight.

Deep-frying *Silver Thread Loaves* to make *Gold Thread Loaves*:
During the final 10 minutes of steaming, heat a wok or heavy skillet over high heat until hot, then add the oil and heat to the light-haze stage, 375° on a deep-fry thermometer. Adjust the heat so the temperature does not rise. Put a baking sheet lined with a double layer of paper towels and a Chinese mesh spoon and cooking chopsticks within easy reach of your stovetop.

Remove the bread from the steamer, discard the paper, and cut each loaf cross-wise in half for a total of four pieces. Test the oil with one crumb of the steamed dough. If the oil is properly hot, it will rise to the surface within 2–3 seconds wearing a crown of tiny white bubbles.

Fry the loaves until golden, about 2 minutes, turning them once or twice to color them evenly. Fry all four at once if they have room to float on the surface, or fry in two batches and retest the oil before the second batch. Do not let them get too brown, as they will continue to darken from their own heat after leaving the oil. Remove the bread to the paper towel-lined tray, blot the top of excess oil, then cut into wedges ¾ inch thick. Serve promptly, in a bamboo steamer, a basket, or arranged on a heated platter of contrasting color.

Gold Thread Rolls are best freshly fried. They grow oily if reheated.

MENU SUGGESTIONS:
I love these rolls most anywhere there is a thin, tart, and spicy sauce that needs sopping up. *Strange Flavor Fish* (page 259), *Tung-An Chicken* (page 140), and *Hot and Sour Hunan Chicken* (page 142) all fit the bill. They are equally good with *Steamed Whole Fish with Seared Scallions* (page 248), *Casseroled Chicken with Smoky Chestnuts* (page 156), *Saucy Potted Pork* (page 207), *Mountain Stew* (page 254), and in place of noodles in *Wine-Simmered Duck* (page 166).

Chinese Steamed Buns, Three Ways

蒸包

Steamed pork buns, usually unspeakably sweet and gooey on the inside, are a regular fixture of Cantonese-style Chinese eating in America. In China, the same steamed bun dough is found throughout the country, stuffed with something different as one travels from province to province and eats of the imagination of different cooks. What follows is a trio of excellent fillings, each unique in character and fairly novel to the Western experience of Chinese food, plus specific instructions on the hows and whys of the dough. ◆ Steamed buns are extremely easy to make once you have the knack and may be put together leisurely days in advance if you like, and then resteamed with no appreciable loss of flavor or texture. A food processor mixes the dough with speed and skill, and the time needed for the dough to rise gives the cook time for other things. ◆ I personally like to make the filling a full day in advance of beginning the dough and leave it in the refrigerator to marinate or develop in flavor. The dough itself I prefer to make 6–12 hours before steaming, to let it rise slowly in a cool place and let it rise twice, in the interest of a lighter texture and finer crumb. This is perfect for the cook *and* for the buns if you like to stretch things out. If, however, you need to be speedy, you can put steamed buns on the table within 3–4 hours and they will still taste delicious.

TECHNIQUE NOTES:
Chinese bun making is one of those tactile, instinctive arts that has never, to my knowledge, been elucidated worth a penny in writing. The result is scores of would-be bun

makers who either can't get their buns to rise in the first place, or who, when they put the buns in the steamer, are shocked to retrieve them 30 minutes later looking as if they'd been the victims of a big rainstorm! I too have suffered at the mercy of bad recipes, pooped yeast, improperly kneaded dough, and storms inside the steamer, and this is what I can pass on in the way of tips:

◆ The dough must be fully *fingertip-firm*, bouncy, and elastic when you are done kneading it and are ready to shape it. If it is too soft and wet, it will turn gummy in the steamer. Err on the firm side if in doubt.

◆ You may vary the amount of sugar in the dough to taste, anywhere from 2 teaspoons to 3 tablespoons. Less sweet is a northern Chinse taste, more sweet is southern Chinese taste and specifically Cantonese in style, but the amount of sugar will not affect the texture of the dough.

◆ A richer dough, favored by Cantonese cooks for the most part, may be had by substituting 1 cup warm milk for 1 cup of the warm water called for in the recipe. In that case, proof the yeast and sugar in the remaining 2 tablespoons warm water, then add the milk to the dough after you have added the water mixture. Another Cantonese-style addition for richness's sake is to cut 1 tablespoon soft lard (home-rendered or store-bought processed) into the flour before adding the liquid. Without them, you will still get a good-tasting dough.

◆ Active dry yeast that is good and fresh (check the expiration date on the package) and double-acting baking powder are both helpmates in producing a high-rising dough. The baking powder must be kneaded in at the end, just before shaping the buns.

◆ Longer rising in a cool place and two risings result in a perceptibly lighter dough with a finer texture. This is something I learned in *dim sum* tea house kitchens, where doughs are typically left to rise overnight.

◆ The filling must be thoroughly cool and not liquidy, and the dough must be firm yet not dry, if the pleats are to stay securely shut and the bun is to hold its shape during the rising and steaming.

◆ You must leave a thickish nickel-size "belly" (as it is called in Chinese) in the center of each dough wrapper when you are rolling it out. The way to achieve this is to roll from the outer perimeter of the circle toward the center (without rolling clear into the center), turning the wrapper after each roll. This puffy belly makes the smooth side of the bun equal in thickness to the pleated side, and insures that when the dough is stretched around the filling it does not become so thin that it will burst during rising or steaming.

◆ To roll the wrapper with greatest ease and speed, use an inch-thick dowel 10 inches long. This enables you to roll with one hand on the top of the dowel, freeing your other hand to turn the wrapper after each roll, as illustrated on page 427. Your hand on the dowel gives you maximum control, so you don't roll over the belly. The dowel is a standard item in *dim sum* kitchens, occasionally sold in Chinese or Japanese hardware stores. For a perfect substitute, go to a hardware or lumber store where they will cut a 10-inch segment from an unfinished, inch-thick dowel or broomstick.

◆ Resist the natural temptation to stuff the bun too full! About 2–2½ tablespoons is the usual limit. If you stretch the dough too much to accommodate the filling or have filling popping out as you pleat it shut, it will burst open most every time. If filling seeps out when you are almost done pleating, spoon it out rather than try to force it in.

◆ The amount of filling that will fit neatly into a bun is variable, depending upon the compactness of the filling, the character of the dough, and the cook's agility in pleating. Chinese cookbook practice is generally to say "divide the filling into X number of portions," and that's one route. Another is to say, as I've done here, begin with 2 tablespoons and see whether that's too much or too little. Extra filling can be eaten up by the bun maker as a reward for hard labor, and extra dough can be shaped into 1 or more small loaves and either steamed or baked for a morning bun.

♦ The pleats must be tiny to hold well and be pretty. The traditional method is to pleat ½ inch of dough precisely in half to form a small pleat ¼ inch wide. The pleats should build out accordion-style in a straight line from your thumb; your thumb never moves and the pleat is pressed into place by your first finger. Study the illustration on page 427 and practice with a piece of material before you try making a bun.

♦ When you have gone as far as you can and the end of your thumb is preventing the dough from pleating entirely shut, you will be left with a small fluted hole like the top of a volcano. Close the hole by pinching it between your thumb and your bent first finger (just like you would chuck someone's cheek), then secure the closure by twisting the dough into a tiny "topknot" in the same direction as you have been pleating (which is *opposite* the direction that the pleats will be facing.)

♦ The buns may be left to rise and steam pleated side up, or they may be overturned if you like. Northern and central Chinese seem to favor steaming and presenting the buns pleated side up. The southern style is to turn them over, smooth face to the world.

♦ After shaping, the buns should be placed on small squares of silicon (no-stick) parchment paper or lightly greased plain parchment or greased wax paper to rise and steam. Otherwise, they will stick to the baking sheet, the steamer, or ungreased paper, and be a mess to remove in one piece. Use solid vegetable shortening to grease the paper.

♦ Steam the buns over moderately high heat, high enough to create a steady gush of steam, then turn off the heat and let the steam subside for 5 minutes before slowly lifting the steamer lid. If you lift the lid immediately and hit the buns with a gush of cold air, they will collapse or wrinkle.

♦ Steam the buns in such a manner that there is no condensation dripping down on them. You may use a bamboo steamer, which absorbs condensation, a single-tier metal steamer with a dome-shaped lid, or stack several metal tiers on top of one another if you stretch a finely woven cotton cloth (like a fine cheesecloth or flour sacking) tautly between each one to asborb the water that drips from the metal. Water raining down during steaming will result in a water-logged, beached bun.

♦ If you are short on steaming space, you should steam the buns in several batches, then return them in a pile to the steamer and let them heat through just prior to serving. When uncooked, they must be steamed in one layer with 1½ inches between them, but once steamed they will reheat perfectly in a pile without sticking.

♦ You may choose to *bake* any bun that is designed to be steamed. The texture, of course, will be different, but the taste is thoroughly good.

For baked buns:

The topknot must be securely twisted shut and the buns are best left to rise and bake *smooth side up* to insure that the bun stays closed and the filling does not dry out. Just prior to baking, brush the smooth tops and sides of the buns with a mixture of 1 beaten egg plus 1 teaspoon water or milk (and ½–1½ teaspoons sugar, if you like, for sweeter, meaty fillings). Bake in the center of a preheated 350° oven for 20–25 minutes, until golden, spacing the buns 1½–2 inches apart on heavy-duty or doubled baking sheets, each bun atop its parchment or greased paper square. Rotate the tray after 10 minutes to insure even baking and have a pan of boiling water in the bottom of the oven (or mist the oven walls periodically with a flower mister) to create steam and prevent the buns from drying out.

◆ Excess dough may be shaped into a round, left to rise, and then steamed or baked off as a miniature bread. Brush with beaten egg (see above) if baking.

<table>
<tr><td>

**Steamed Buns
with Chicken
and Black
Mushrooms**

雞肉冬菇包

</td><td>

The filling for these unusual buns is at once sweet and savory, a combination of plump cubes of marinated chicken and bits of dusky Chinese black mushrooms, bound in a light sauce. It is delicious on its own as a hot stir-fry and very special as a filling for buns. ◆ For best flavor, the chicken should be left to marinate a full 24 hours before cooking to absorb the marinade entirely. If black mushrooms are unavailable, you may chop fresh white mushrooms or chan-

</td></tr>
</table>

terelles and use a tablespoon less stock to account for their juices. ◆ The filling may be cooked a day in advance or while the dough is undergoing its first rising. The buns themselves may be steamed days ahead, then resteamed before serving.

TECHNIQUE NOTES:
For every trick I know to making successful steamed buns, see TECHNIQUE NOTES, page 422.

For velveting chicken to give it a plush, juicy texture, see TECHNIQUE NOTES, page 137.

Makes 20 buns, each about 2½ inches in diameter, enough to serve 4–6 as a hearty meal with soup, 8–10 for brunch or as part of a multicourse meal.

INGREDIENTS:

> *1 recipe steamed bread dough (page 415)*

> *For the filling:*
> *1 pound skinned and boned fresh chicken breast, cut by hand to a tiny ¼-inch dice (see page 126 for directions on easy, 5-minute boning)*
> *2 large egg whites*
> *2 tablespoons Chinese rice wine or quality, dry sherry*
> *2 teaspoons coarse kosher salt*
> *2 tablespoons cornstarch*
> *6 medium Chinese dried black mushrooms*
> *½ cup ¼-inch dice bamboo shoots (page 531; use only if white and clean tasting)*
> *1½–2 tablespoons minced scallion, white and light green parts only*
> *1 tablespoon thin (regular) soy sauce*
> *1 tablespoon sugar*
> *¼ teaspoon freshly ground pepper*
> *1½ teaspoons Chinese or Japanese sesame oil*
> *2 tablespoons cornstarch dissolved in ½ cup cold chicken stock*
> *3–4 cups fresh corn or peanut oil*
> *or*
> *4 cups water plus 2 teaspoons corn or peanut oil*

> *Individual dipping sauce (optional):*
> *2–3 teaspoons thin (regular) soy sauce*
> *1 teaspoon white vinegar*
> *¼ teaspoon Chinese or Japanese sesame oil or sesame-based hot chili oil*
> *a sprinkling of green scallion rings*

Preparations for the filling:
In a food processor fitted with the steel knife or in a blender, blend the egg whites, wine, salt, and cornstarch until thoroughly smooth and thick, 30–60 seconds. Toss well with the chicken, stirring with your fingers, seal airtight, and refrigerate 8–24 hours to allow the chicken to absorb the marinade. The longer it marinates, the more tender and juicy it will be. Bring to room temperature before cooking.

While the chicken is marinating, soak the mushrooms in cold or hot water to cover until soft and spongy, 20 minutes to an hour. Drain, snip off the stems with scissors, then rinse the caps to dislodge any sand trapped in the gills. Squeeze gently to remove excess water, then mince the caps. Minced, they may be sealed airtight and refrigerated overnight. If you are using fresh mushrooms, brush clean and chop just prior to cooking.

If you are using bamboo shoots, blanch them in plain simmering water to cover for 15 seconds, then drain and flush with cold water until chilled. Seal airtight, and refrigerate until use.

Velveting the chicken and stir-frying the filling:
Combine the soy, sugar, pepper, and sesame oil. In a second bowl, stir the cornstarch mixture until smooth and leave the spoon in the bowl. Have all the ingredients for the filling within easy reach of your stovetop.

Stir the chicken to loosen the pieces, then velvet it in oil or water as described on page 139. Diced chicken will turn 90 percent white in as little as 10 seconds, so be prepared to remove it swiftly, sooner rather than later if in doubt. If the chicken is only 70 percent white, it will still be better than if you have cooked it too long. As soon as the chicken is velveted, proceed to stir-fry the filling.

Heat a wok or heavy skillet over high heat until hot enough to evaporate a bead of water on contact. Add 1½ tablespoons oil, swirl to coat the pan, then reduce the heat to medium-high. When the oil is hot enough to sizzle one bit of scallion on contact, add the scallion and stir several seconds until foamy and fragrant, adjusting the heat so it sizzles without scorching. Add the mushrooms and the bamboo shoots if you are using them and stir to gloss and combine, about 15 seconds. Adjust the heat to maintain a merry sizzle and dribble in a bit more oil from the side of the pan if needed to prevent sticking. When the mixture is fragrant, add the chicken and toss briskly several times to mix. Add the seasonings, stir two or three times to blend, then give the cornstarch mixture a quick stir to recombine it and add it to the pan. Stir just until the mixture becomes glossy and slightly thick, about 5–10 seconds, then turn off the heat. Remove the mixture to a shallow bowl if you are working well in advance, or spread it on a plate if you want to cool it quickly in the refrigerator or the freezer. It must be thoroughly cool when you start to shape the buns.

Cooled, the filling may be sealed airtight and refrigerated overnight. If you are not working in advance, make the filling while the dough is first rising, and chill it quickly as above.

Making the dough:
Follow the instructions on pages 416 to 417 for proofing the yeast and making the dough, letting it rise and punching it down, and incorporating the baking powder.

Shaping the buns:
Have ready twenty 2-inch square paper bases for the buns. If you do not have silicon (no-stick) parchment, use greased parchment or greased wax paper. Arrange the squares

greased side up on two baking sheets. Put the sheets, the cool filling, two dry, lint-free towels, and a ruler alongside your work surface. Stir the filling to redistribute the seasonings.

With a sharp knife, divide the dough into two equal parts. Return one piece, cut side down, to the floured corner, and cover. Dust the board lightly with flour, and with your palms roll the other piece of dough into a smooth, even cylinder 10 inches long. Eying the ruler, cut the cylinder into 10 inch-thick slices, then set the slices cut side down on a floured surface and cover with a dry towel. Repeat with the remaining piece of dough. If your kitchen is warm or you are new to bun making and work slowly, transfer half the slices to a floured baking sheet, cover, and refrigerate to stall the yeast.

Remove the first slice from under the towel, dust both cut sides with flour, then flatten it with joined fingers. Rolling the dowel with one hand, roll from the outer edge *almost* into the center of the dough. Turn the dough a notch with your free hand, then roll again *almost* into the center of the dough. Repeat until you have a round dough wrapper 4½ inches in diameter, with evenly thin edges and a puffy, nickel-size belly in the center of the dough. If you roll with your *right* hand, your left hand should turn the dough a notch counterclockwise after each roll, as illustrated. If you roll with your *left* hand, your right hand should turn the dough clockwise after each roll.

Place about 2 tablespoons filling in the center of the dough round, mounding it so it stays humped in the center. If you are right-handed, grasp the edge of the dough round farthest away from you between the end of your right thumb and first finger, thumb on

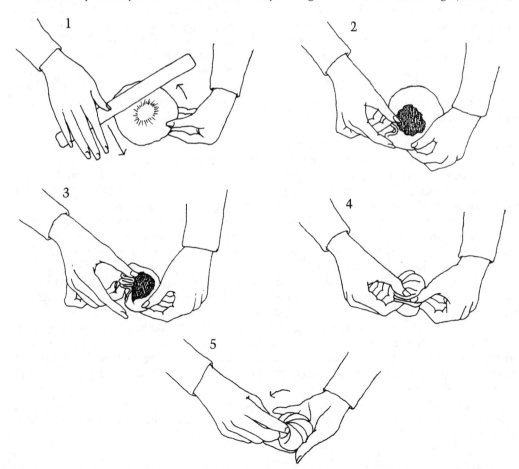

the inside positioned ½ inch below the edge of the dough. The job of your thumb will be to stay in place as an anchor during the pleating. The job of your first finger will be to move away from your thumb to catch the pleat, then move back toward the thumb to press the pleat into place. As the pleats build out from the thumb, it and the first finger will be separated by an increasingly thick accordion of dough. With your right hand in position, it is the job of the left hand to bring the dough to the right hand to be pleated. (If you are left-handed, read all this in reverse, as well as what follows.)

To begin pleating, grasp the edge of the dough round ½ inch to the left of your stationary thumb between your left thumb and first finger, here again with the thumb on the inside grasping the dough ½ inch down from the edge (so the resulting pleats are neither too shallow nor too deep). Bring the half-inch of dough over to the right thumb and index finger in an even fold, then straighten out your right finger briefly in order for it to catch the pleat before tacking it down against the stationary thumb. If the dough is properly firm, not too dry and not too moist, it will pleat securely.

When the pleat is secured, move your left thumb and first finger another half inch farther along the edge of the dough and bring the next bit of dough over to form the next pleat, with your right finger catching and tacking it down as before. Repeat the process, with the pleats building out from your thumb in a straight line, like a pushed-together accordion. As you pleat, the bun will turn clockwise on its own and the top will pleat shut around your stationary thumb.

With the trapped thumb doing the lifting, put the bun on your free palm. Extract the thumb, pinch together the open top of the bun, and twist it firmly closed in a topknot in a counterclockwise direction, as illustrated. (Remember, if you are a lefty, you will be proceeding in reverse.) At this point, the bun is shaped, a job that takes only 1 minute when you are proficient, in spite of the long-winded explanation!

Put the finished bun on the paper square, and cover with a dry towel. Continue to roll, fill, pleat, and twist the buns shut, one by one, in the same manner. As each is done, put it on a paper square on the baking sheet, keeping the buns covered and spaced 2 inches apart from one another.

Giving the buns a final rising and steaming the buns:
(For details on steaming and how to improvise a steamer, see page 60.)

Let the buns rise under the towel until the dough is springy to the touch, 30–60 minutes, depending on the temperature of the room. During the final minutes of rising, bring the water in your steaming vessel to a gushing boil over high heat.

Transfer the risen buns still on their paper squares to a steaming rack, spaced 1–1½ inches apart. (If you are forced to work in batches, place the remaining buns, now covered loosely but airtight in plastic, in the refrigerator or even the freezer to halt their rising.) Station the rack in place, reduce the heat to medium-high to maintain a strong, steady steam, then cover the steamer and steam the buns for 15 minutes. Turn off the heat and let the steam subside for 5 minutes, then remove the lid slowly, so the buns do not collapse with the sudden gush of cold air.

Serve the buns immediately, or hold them in the steamer set over low heat for up to 1 hour. Just before serving, mix a small dish of dip sauce for each person present, combining the soy, vinegar, sesame oil or chili oil to taste, and garnish with a sprinkling of scallion. Discard the paper, and serve the buns in the bamboo steamer or on a heated platter of contrasting color.

Leftover steamed buns may be left to cool, then sealed airtight and refrigerated several days. To rewarm, steam on paper squares over medium-high heat until hot, about 15 minutes.

The baking alternative:
Once the buns have risen, you may bake them instead of steaming them. Follow directions for applying an egg wash and baking on page 414.

Leftover baked buns may be sealed airtight in foil and reheated in a hot oven. They are OK, but not as good as rejuvenated steamed buns, the second time around.

MENU SUGGESTIONS:
I enjoy these buns most in the company of soup—*Wine-Explosion Vegetable Chowder* (page 452), *Moslem-Style Hot and Sour Soup* (page 450), *Soup of Many Mushrooms* (page 454), or a good minestrone. As part of a *dim sum* brunch, serve the buns with an assortment of crunchy "Little Dishes" (pages 103 to 121), and partnered by *Springrolls with Dijon Mustard Sauce* (page 389), or *Spicy Shrimp Fritters* (page 237).

Steamed Buns with Minced Pork and Tree Ears

木耳肉包

Small steamed buns, fluted on the top and stuffed with a mixture of seasoned ground pork, are a favorite in northern and central China. The variations on the seasonings are limitless, but the traditional way to steam and serve them is in a bamboo steamer lined with a large blanched cabbage leaf, which one can munch on after the buns are gone. In the unlikely event that there are any buns left over, you can pan-fry the bottoms brown, add some light stock or water to the skillet to steam-cook them through, then serve them up as a close cousin to pot stickers (page 384). ◆ This filling is easily put together and does not need to be cooked before the buns are stuffed. Making and shaping the dough may be done in as few as 3 hours or as many as 8 to 10, depending upon whether you want to give it a quick, warm rise or a slower, cool one.

TECHNIQUE NOTES:
For every trick I know to making successful steamed buns, see TECHNIQUE NOTES, page 422.

Makes 20 buns, each about 2½ inches in diameter, enough to serve 4–6 as a hearty meal with soup, 8–10 for brunch or as part of a multicourse meal.

INGREDIENTS:

> *1 recipe steamed bun dough (page 415)*

> *For the filling:*
> *⅛ cup tree ears (page 576)*
> *2 medium whole scallions, or 1 small whole scallion and 2 tablespoons coarsely chopped fresh coriander*
> *1 walnut-size nugget fresh ginger*
> *1 pound pork butt, cubed*
> *seasonings:*
> *2½ tablespoons thin (regular) soy sauce*
> *2 tablespoons Chinese rice wine or quality, dry sherry*
> *2½ tablespoons Chinese or Japanese sesame oil, or 2 tablespoons sesame oil*

and 1–1½ teaspoons sesame-based hot chili oil
½ teaspoon coarse kosher salt
¼ teaspoon freshly ground pepper
¼ cup unsalted chicken stock

Individual dipping sauce (optional):
2 teaspoons thin (regular) soy sauce
¾ teaspoon well-aged Chinese black vinegar or balsamic vinegar
¼ teaspoon Chinese or Japanese sesame oil
a small clump of fresh ginger slivers cut hair-thin, "young" ginger (page 548)
especially delicious
or
Garlic-Soy Dip (page 477)

Making the filling:

Cover the tree ears with 1 cup cool or warm water, and soak until supple, about 20 minutes. Drain, swish repeatedly in ample cool water to loosen grit, then drain and repeat. Pick over and discard any unchewable or gelatinous bits, rinse a final time, and shake to remove excess water. Cleaned, the tree ears may be sealed airtight and refrigerated overnight.

Cut the scallions into 1-inch lengths, add with the ginger to the work bowl of a food processor fitted with the steel knife, and process until finely minced, scraping down as needed. Add the tree ears and the coriander if using it, then process until chopped. Add the cubed pork and the seasonings, and process with on-off turns until the mixture is blended but still rather coarse. Do not overprocess to a paste. The filling will taste best if it has some texture.

Alternatively, mince the scallions and ginger finely by hand. Chop the coriander and tree ears into peppercorn-size bits, then chop the pork with one or two equally weighted knives until the size of tiny peas. Put the pork in a large bowl and scatter the scallion, ginger, and seasonings on top. With chopsticks or a fork, stir briskly in one direction until blended, then pick up the mixture with your hand and throw it lightly against the side of the bowl 6–8 times to compact it.

Seal the filling airtight with a film of plastic wrap placed directly on the surface, and refrigerate until use, overnight if desired. If you are not working in advance, make the filling while the dough is first rising.

Making the dough, and shaping and steaming the buns:
Follow the directions on pages 426 to 428. Extend the steaming time to 20 minutes.

Shortly before serving, mix the soy, vinegar, and sesame oil in individual dip dishes. Scatter the ginger threads on top, and let stand 5–10 minutes for the ginger to infuse the liquids.

MENU SUGGESTIONS:
For a simple and satisfying meal, try these buns in the company of *Stir-Fried Spinach with Charred Garlic* (page 305) or *Dry-Fried Szechwan String Beans* (page 297), or *Soup of Many Mushrooms* (page 454) or *Wine-Explosion Vegetable Chowder* (page 452). For a fuller menu, serve both the vegetable and the soup. Or, for a different mood, serve the buns with *Steamed Whole Fish with Seared Scallions* (page 248). As part of a *dim sum* brunch, pair them with *Spicy Shrimp Fritters* (page 237) or *Deep-Fried Shrimp Balls* (page 240).

<table>
<tr><td>

Curried Vegetarian Buns

咖喱素包
</td></tr>
</table>

My first week in Taipei was a nightmare. A typhoon was in full gale, I was a vegetarian and unprepared for the fact that Chinese do like to throw a teeny bit of meat in most everything, and I had been living on a diet of stir-fried cabbage and black mushrooms because that was all I could order in Chinese. Enter my friend from Brooklyn, Harvey, who somehow sniffed his way through the typhoon and the strange city to a tiny vegetarian restaurant. At the top of a long flight of stairs we sat down to a rickety table and I ate my first steamed buns. They were spicy, beautifully green inside, and aromatic of spinach, and I think they were like these. ◆ You have to be a spice-lover to enjoy these buns, though if your tongue is a bit shy you can increase the quantity of spinach and decrease the amount of curried gluten, one of those few very wonderful things that comes from a can. Given the can and the fresh spinach, the filling may be blended in minutes. Making the dough and shaping the buns may be done in 3 hours or stretched over a long day, depending on whether you let the dough rise in a warm spot or a cool one. Once steamed, the buns may be refrigerated and resteamed days later. They will still be very tasty, and if anything even spicier.

TECHNIQUE NOTES:
For every trick I know to making successful steamed buns, see TECHNIQUE NOTES, page 422.

Makes 20 buns about 2½ inches in diameter, enough to serve 4–6 as a hearty meal with soup, 8–10 for brunch or as part of a multicourse meal.

INGREDIENTS:

    1 recipe steamed bun dough (page 415)

For the filling:
    1 ounce bean threads (glass noodles) (page 533)
    6 medium Chinese dried black mushrooms (page 538)
    ¾ pound fresh spinach with leaves and stems
    one 10-ounce can curried gluten (page 553)
    seasonings:
    3–4 teaspoons thin (regular) soy sauce
    ½ teaspoon coarse kosher salt
    ⅛ teaspoon sugar
    ½ teaspoon Chinese or Japanese sesame oil

Individual dipping sauce (optional):
    1 tablespoon thin (regular) soy sauce
    ¼ teaspoon Chinese or Japanese sesame oil
    pinch finely minced coriander

Making the filling:
Soak the noodles in warm or hot tap water to cover, until rubber-band firm, not mushy. (If you are planning to bake the buns, soak the noodles until fully soft and silken.) The temperature of the water required will vary with the noodles; try hotter water if they remain wire-like after 30 seconds. Drain, rinse, shake off excess water, and chop into small bits ¼ inch long.

Soak the mushrooms in cold or hot water to cover until fully soft and spongy, about 20 minutes to an hour. Snip off the stems with scissors, rinse the caps to dislodge any sand trapped in the gills, and squeeze gently to remove excess water.

Divide the spinach leaves from the stems, and cut the stems into 1-inch lengths. Pump the leaves and stems up and down in a large bowl of cold water to clean, then drain and repeat if necessary. Blanch in plain boiling water to cover for 1 minute, drain promptly, and rush under cold water until chilled. Squeeze the spinach firmly to remove all excess liquid, squeezing by the fistful wrapped in cheesecloth for best results.

Extract the gluten from the can, leaving behind the canning liquids and sediment. Blot the gluten with a paper towel if there is a lot of oil still clinging to the surface.

Add the mushrooms to the work bowl of a food processor fitted with the steel knife and process until minced, scraping down as necessary. Add the gluten and process with on-off turns until pea-size. Chop the spinach roughly by hand, and distribute it around the steel knife. Sprinkle the seasonings on top, then process with several on-off turns to combine. Do not overprocess to a paste. Alternately, mince the mushrooms, gluten, and spinach by hand until fine, then combine with the seasonings.

Stir the chopped noodles into the gluten mixture. Taste, and adjust if required with a dash more soy or sesame oil. The filling should be spicy, and not wet.

The filling may be sealed airtight and refrigerated overnight. Be forewarned (or gladdened) that it grows spicier as it sits. If you are not working in advance, make the filling while the dough is rising. Stir before using to redistribute the seasonings.

Making the dough and shaping and steaming the buns:
Follow the directions on pages 426 to 428. Steam the buns for 15–20 minutes, and mix the dipping sauce just before serving, putting an extra pinch of coriander on top of each sauce dish. Owing to the compactness of the filling you can use about 2½ tablespoons of filling per bun.

Do not be dismayed if the buns become stained upon steaming. It is just the curried gluten looking out at you from the inside.

MENU SUGGESTIONS:
I like to serve these buns in the simple company of one other dish like *Dry-Fried Szechwan String Beans* (page 297) *or Steamed Corn with Szechwan Pepper-Salt* (page 318). For a soup to partner the buns, try *Soup of Many Mushrooms* (page 454), *Chinese Meatball Soup* (page 448), or your very best split-pea or lentil soup. As part of a *dim sum* brunch, pair the buns with *Gold Coin Eggs* (page 330).

Baked Stuffed Buns

葱肉燒餅

Stuffed buns, bought at tea houses, specialty shops, or from street vendors, are the familiar snack food of China, and from region to region one finds different stuffings, different techniques for wrapping the dough around the filling, and the occasional bun that is baked instead of steamed. This is one such baked bun: a small puff of honey-glazed dough that is filled with either minced ham or minced roast pork and topped by a crusty layer of sesame seeds. They are terrifically good with soup or as a tea snack, and are wonderful for brunch. ◆ Each filling recipe is good for one batch of dough. Thus, you can either halve each filling and make eleven buns of each type, or choose one filling and make all twenty-two buns alike. I typically take the former route and use black sesame seeds and white sesame seeds to "color code" the different fillings. ◆ The fillings may be made a day in advance of shaping the buns and the buns may be half-baked a day in advance of serving. It is altogether a simple preparation, one I was able to tackle successfully before I had ever baked bread.

TECHNIQUE NOTES:
Several explanations if you are new to working with yeasted doughs: Sugar and warm water are friendly to yeast. In their presence, yeast will bubble up and become alive. A draft-free environment is friendly to a rising dough. Exposed to drafts, the unbaked dough will crack and stiffen and lose its smooth texture. Letting a yeasted dough rise in a cool place will take more time but produce a finer crumb. You should try both a warm and a cool rising to judge the difference for yourself.

For the Chinese techniques of rolling out a circle of dough with a belly and pleating a bun shut with a topknot, and for some other hints on bun making applicable to steamed buns, see TECHNIQUE NOTES, page 422.

Makes 20 buns, each about 2½ inches in diameter, enough to serve 4–6 as a hearty meal with soup, 8–10 for brunch or as part of a multicourse meal.

Ham and scallion filling (for 20 buns):
  ¾ pound very flavorful honey or sugar-cured ham, with some soft fat left on
  4–5 medium whole scallions
  thin (regular) soy sauce to taste

Roast pork filling (for 20 buns):
  ¾ pound very flavorful Chinese roast pork, with some soft fat left on (see page 205 for making your own)
  1¼ to 1½ cups loosely packed fresh coriander leaves and upper stems
  about 4 teaspoons unseasoned Chinese or Japanese rice vinegar

  1 recipe steamed bread dough (page 415)

For the topping:
  1 tablespoon honey dissolved in 1 tablespoon boiling water
  ½ cup untoasted white or black sesame seeds, or ¼ cup of each to color code the different fillings

Dipping sauce (optional):
  mustard sauce of your choice (page 475 and 476)
  or
  Garlic-Soy Dip (page 477)
  or
  thin (regular) soy sauce mixed with a dash of sesame oil and rice vinegar to taste, garnished with chopped scallions

Making ham and scallion filling:
Cube the ham, cut the scallions into 1-inch lengths, and mince coarsely in the work bowl of a food processor fitted with the steel knife, using on-off turns. Or, mince by hand. Toss in a bowl with soy to taste, adding 2–3 teaspoons finely minced fresh lard if the ham is dry. Seal airtight and refrigerate until use, overnight if desired. The flavors will develop as the mixture sits. Bring to room temperature before using. If you are not working in advance, make the filling while the dough is first rising.

Making the roast pork filling:
Cube the pork, chop the coriander coarsely, and mince until coarse in the work bowl of a food processor fitted with the steel knife, using on-off turns. Or, mince by hand. Toss in a bowl with vinegar to taste, adding 2–3 teaspoons finely minced fresh lard if the pork is dry. If the pork needs it, also add a dash of soy. Seal airtight and refrigerate until use, overnight if desired. The flavors will enlarge as the mixture sits. Bring to room temperature before using. If you are not working in advance, make the filling while the dough is first rising.

Making the dough:
Follow the instructions on pages 416 to 417 for proofing the yeast and making the dough, letting it rise and punching it down, and incorporating the baking powder.

Filling and shaping the buns:
Line two baking sheets each with a layer of silicon (no-stick) parchment, or parchment or wax paper greased lightly with solid vegetable shortening. Put the honey mixture in one shallow saucer, and the sesame seeds in one or two others (two if you're using both black and white seeds). Put the saucers, baking sheets, 2–3 dry kitchen towels, and the fillings alongside your work surface.

Roll out the dough and shape and fill the buns as described on page 426, beginning with rolling a 10-inch log of dough and ending with twisting the first bun shut in a topknot. Up to this point, the baked bun is made exactly as if it were a steamed bun.

When the first bun is shaped, place it pleated side up on the board, and press gently with joined fingers to flatten it slightly. Dip the smooth underside of the bun into the honey mixture, then press the wet dough into the sesame seeds so the face of the bun is completely encrusted. Turn the bun seed side up on the parchment-lined baking sheet, then cover with the towel to prevent drying.

Continue to shape, fill, seal, and coat each bun in the same manner, putting the finished buns about 1½ inches apart on the baking sheet. Be certain the buns are fully covered with the dry towel, then leave them to rise for 30–60 minutes, or until they look proudly round on top and the dough on the side springs back slowly when pressed lightly with your finger.

While the buns are rising, preheat the oven to 350°. Put a shallow pan of boiling water on the bottom of the oven, so the buns will bake in a steamy environment and not become too dry.

Baking the buns:
Bake the buns on the parchment-lined sheets in the center section of the oven until lightly golden, 20–25 minutes. Midway through baking, rotate the trays front to back and top to bottom to insure even browning.

Transfer the baked buns to a heated platter of contrasting color, a pretty tray, or a basket. Serve hot, accompanied by your choice of dipping sauce.

Leftovers are excellent for breakfast or snacks. Seal airtight in tin foil and rewarm in a hot oven.

MENU SUGGESTIONS:
These buns are a wonderful addition to a *dim sum* brunch, served alongside *Sweet and Tangy Cucumber Pickles* (page 110), or in the rustic company of *Old Egg* (page 332) or in the more elegant company of your favorite omelet. For a light Chinese meal, I enjoy them

with *Wine-Explosion Vegetable Chowder* (page 452). They are also perfect with one-bowl meals such as *Peppery Soup Noodles with Shrimp Balls* (page 463).

<table>
<tr><td>

**Pan-
Fried
Scallion
Breads**

葱油餅

</td><td>

Scallion breads are one of those superb combinations of dough, seasonings, and grease—oil or shortening in polite culinary language—that promise instant addiction. Like a buttered bagel or a good pizza dough, these savory flatbreads have a universal appeal. They are eaten at mealtimes and in-between times, and are excellent for brunch. ◆ Throughout northern and central China, one finds scallion breads variously thick or thin, bready or crisp, fried in new oil or

</td></tr>
</table>

old. My favorites were made by an old man on a tiny burner in a Taipei alleyway. They were thick and rather chewy, and one could take them home wrapped in a sheet of yesterday's newspaper, the oil and the scallions making a fragrant stain on the newsprint. ◆ These scallion breads are like his. They are easy to make, fun to shape, and take only minutes to cook. Use all the dough for a single, giant scallion bread and the result will be a thick, pie-shaped flatbread you can really chew on. Divide the dough into two equal parts, and you will have smaller, thinner breads more traditional in size. Another choice can be made with the grease: I have tried everything from lard to duck fat, and sesame oil and *schmaltz* are the winners on my tongue. ◆ With a food processor you can make, shape, and cook the dough within an hour. The dough itself may be made a day in advance of shaping.

TECHNIQUE NOTES:
The spiral in which the dough is coiled is named a "snail shape" in Chinese, and it is the basis for many flaky or puffy pan-fried pastries. It is this air-trapping shape, plus the oiling of the dough before rolling it up, that creates the special interior layering of the bread. To coil easily and cook to a tender consistency, the dough must be *earlobe-soft*. Pinch your earlobe to know the right texture. For more on dough textures and hot and cold water doughs, see page 398.

Old-time Chinese cooks insist on shaking the pan while the bread is frying. The shaking encourages steam, which helps to puff the dough, and it's great fun besides.

Makes one 10-inch or two 8-inch flatbreads, enough to serve 4–5 people generously, or 6–8 as part of a multicourse meal. When there are only 2 of us, I cut the recipe in half and make one 8-inch bread.

INGREDIENTS:

> *Cold water dough:*
> *1 cup all-purpose flour*
> *2 teaspoons double-acting baking powder*
> *⅓ cup cold water*

> *Hot water dough:*
> *1 cup all-purpose flour*
> *1 teaspoon coarse kosher salt*
> *⅓ cup boiling water*

> *additional flour, for kneading and rolling out the dough*
> *¼ teaspoon Chinese or Japanese sesame oil*

Seasonings:
   1½ teaspoons Chinese or Japanese sesame oil, or rendered chicken fat (page 127)
   1½ teaspoons coarse kosher salt
   2–3 medium whole scallions, cut into thin green and white rings

   about ½ cup fresh corn or peanut oil, for pan-frying

Making the dough:
If you have a food processor:
   (For details on making dough in a food processor, see page 586.)
   Put 1 cup flour and the baking powder into the work bowl fitted with the steel knife. With the machine running add the cold water through the feed tube in a thin steady stream, just until the dough begins to mass lumpily around the blade. Give the machine 2–3 seconds' "lag time" to incorporate the last water droplets and form a ball. If no ball forms, then add several drops more water until the dough comes together. You may need a bit more or less than ⅓ cup water, all depending on the dryness of the flour.
   Stop the machine as soon as a ball forms and remove the dough. (Typically, there will be one large ball and several smaller "blobs," and you should remove them all.) Return the blade to the work bowl, add 1 cup flour and 1 teaspoon coarse kosher salt, and repeat the process using ⅓ cup boiling water. The water must have been boiling just before use or it will not be hot enough to cook the flour as it should.
   Stop the machine as soon as the hot water dough coheres in a ball, and return the cold water dough to the work bowl. Process the two doughs together for 15 seconds, remove the dough to a lightly floured board, and knead it gently with the heel of your hand for 1–2 minutes, until it is smooth and earlobe-soft, and elastic enough so it springs gently back when pressed lightly with a finger. If you have processed the dough correctly, it should not stick to the board. If it is sticking, then dust the board lightly with flour as required and gently knead the dough until it is smooth and no longer sticks. Be wary of adding too much flour and making a stiff dough. The dough must be earlobe-soft or it will be tough when cooked.
   If you do not have a food processor:
   Combine 1 cup flour and the baking powder in a mixing bowl. Add the cold water in a thin stream, stirring with chopsticks or a wooden spoon until the mixture comes together in a lumpy mass, adding extra water in droplets if required to make the flour cohere. Remove the cold water dough, add the next cup flour and the salt, then repeat the process with boiling water. Knead the two doughs together gently for about 10 minutes until smooth, earlobe-soft, and elastic enough so a fingertip impression bounces very slowly back. Add flour to the board as required to prevent the dough from sticking, but avoid working too much into the dough lest it become too stiff.
   Put the sesame oil in a small bowl, add the dough, then turn the dough so that both it and the inside of the bowl are coated with a thin film of oil. Cover the bowl with a dry towel and put the dough aside to rest for 30 minutes–2 hours at room temperature, or overnight in the refrigerator if more convenient. Seal the dough airtight with plastic wrap once cool, and bring to room temperature before shaping.

Shaping the breads:
Turn the soft, rested dough onto a lightly floured board, and knead gently until smooth, dusting the board lightly if the dough is sticking. If you are making 2 breads, divide the dough evenly into 2 pieces with a sharp knife and form each piece into a smooth ball. Put

one ball aside on a lightly floured surface, covered with a dry towel, while you shape the other.

Flour the board lightly, then roll out the dough into a circle a scant ¼ inch thick for one giant bread, or ⅛ inch thick for two smaller breads. Dust the board and the top of the bread a second time if the dough is sticking and do not worry if the final shape is not perfectly circular. Spread the sesame oil or chicken fat evenly over the top with your fingers, then sprinkle the salt and scallions evenly over the oil. Remember to divide the seasonings in half if you are making two breads. (If you are using chicken fat, steam it until liquid, then let it cool before using until only mildly warm, not hot, to the touch.)

1

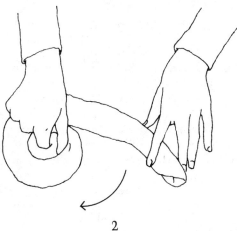

2

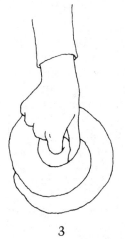

3

Roll the dough up like a carpet, neither too tight nor too loose, and pinch the top seam shut. Place the cylinder seam side down, then grasp one end of the dough gently between your thumb and first finger to anchor it to the board. This is the "head" end. Next grasp the other, the "tail" end, of the cylinder with your other hand and wind this neatly around the head into a coiling, flat spiral, as illustrated. The coils of dough should be touching at every point, so there are no holes in the spiral. Finally, tuck the tail end under the spiral. Extract your pinned fingers by pressing down gently on the dough around them with your free hand so that the coil remains in place on the board.

Press gently on the snail with your palms and joined fingers to flatten it a bit, then roll out the dough until it is about 10–11 inches in diameter for one giant bread, or about 7–8 inches in diameter for two smaller breads. Roll gently so you do not burst the layers of dough, though it is almost inevitable that a few scallions will pop through. If the dough does not roll out easily, cover it with a dry towel and let it rest for 5–10 minutes. This is an especially useful tactic when you are needing to form a second snail or when you must wait extra minutes for the company to arrive.

Once rolled to the appropriate thickness, I like to cook the bread almost immediately. For a softer texture, put the coil aside on a lightly floured surface, covered with a dry towel, for up to 30 minutes, then roll it out fully just before cooking.

Once rolled out, the scallion breads may be flash-frozen on a baking sheet until firm, sealed airtight in heavy-duty foil, and frozen for several weeks. Partially defrost in the refrigerator, and pan-fry while still thoroughly cold and firm, for a slightly longer time and over a somewhat lower heat. They turn out quite well, though not as perfectly as fresh.

Pan-frying the breads:
Choose a heavy, 12-inch skillet if you are frying one giant bread. Use a heavy, 10–12-inch skillet for smaller breads and fry them in two batches or simultaneously in two heavy pans. Do not use a lightweight pan. It will scorch the bread or toughen the crust before the inside can cook through.

Heat the skillet over high heat until hot enough to evaporate a bead of water on contact. Add enough oil to coat the bottom evenly with ⅛ inch oil, swirl to coat the lower sides, then reduce the heat to medium. Adjust the pan on the burner so the oil is evenly deep. When the oil is hot enough to foam a pinch of dry flour, add the scallion bread, adjusting the heat so the bubbles sizzle slowly around it. Cover the pan, then cook over moderately low heat until the bottom of the bread is golden brown, occasionally shaking the pan back and forth to encourage the steam that will puff the bread. The bottom may take anywhere from 2–5 minutes to brown, depending on the thickness of the bread and the sort of pan you use. Check frequently, and do not let it scorch.

When evenly golden, flip the bread over. If the pan is very dry, dribble in a bit more oil from the side, then shake the pan gently to distribute the oil under the bread. Cover, reduce the heat slightly, and cook for 3–5 minutes more, shaking the pan occasionally. Check the bottom, and, if it is not yet golden, raise the heat slightly and replace the cover. Check the bread at 30-second intervals so you can catch it when perfectly golden and not overcooked.

Slide the bread onto a cutting surface, and cut it into pie-shaped wedges. Transfer to a heated round serving plate of contrasting color, the wedges pushed together to look like an intact bread, and garnish with a few scallion rings. Do not blot off the excess oil clinging to the bread. It contributes to the flavor like butter on a bun.

If you are frying a second scallion bread, wipe the skillet clean, reheat the pan, and begin with fresh oil.

Leftovers grow slightly oily when reheated in a hot oven, but I devour them nonetheless.

MENU SUGGESTIONS:
I enjoy this bread most with hearty soups—*Wine-Explosion Vegetable Chowder* (page 452), *Moslem-Style Hot and Sour Soup* (page 450), or *Peppery Soup Noodles with Shrimp Balls* (page 463)—or with Szechwanese or Hunanese stir-frys. In the latter category *Hot and Sour Hunan Chicken* (page 142), *Down-Home Hunan Tofu* (page 341), *Hunan Eggplant with Spicy Meat Sauce* (page 293), and *Szechwan-Hunan Pork Threads* (page 195) all come to mind. For brunch, try scallion breads with *Gold Coin Eggs* (page 330).

Mandarin Pancakes

薄餅

In Chinese, the name for these supple, flour and water crepes is "thin bing" (*bing* meaning "round, flat thing"). We call them mandarin pancakes in English because they are a feature of north and central China as opposed to the south, and because pancakes as we know them are also thin-round-flat things. The job of the Chinese pancake is to embrace a filling—usually something sultry and steaming, and less often something cool and spicy. Four fillings are given in these pages (pages 193, 198, 302, and 303), and any two, three, or even four of them plus a platter of *Mandarin Pancakes* is grand enough for a party.

TECHNIQUE NOTES:
I had a damnable time trying to master *Mandarin Pancakes* to my satisfaction, and have subsequently discovered that there's a whole fraternity out there of unsuccessful pancake makers all about ready to throw in the towel. Take heart! These tricks, however untraditional, produce a perfectly beautiful pancake:

First, roll out the dough to a meticulously even ⅛ inch thickness, then cut out 3-inch circles as the start of the pancake. This yields, at least in my hands, far more precise results than the traditional method of rolling the dough into a log and pinching off estimated equal amounts.

Second, oil the tops of *both* circles that will comprise the sandwiched-together pair. The standard instructions to oil only one of the two typically results in either too *little* oil being used (so they will not come apart once cooked), or too *much* oil (which tends to make them slither apart in rolling).

Third, roll the paired pancakes out until they are evenly ¹⁄₁₆ inch thin (consult a ruler!), never minding the diameter. A thick mandarin pancake is a flabby mandarin pancake, and as uninviting a piece of dough as you can chew. The finished pancake should be so beautifully thin (¹⁄₃₂ inch thin, once it is separated) that you can almost see and feel the filling through it.

Fourth (and final in this bag of tricks), cook the pancakes with an attention to how they *feel* and not to how they look, pulling them from the pan while they are still very supple. If you watch the clock or wait for the much-discussed brown dots to appear, it's likely you'll overcook them to brittleness.

For words about boiling-water doughs, see page 398.

And *another* word on mandarin pancakes: I've sometimes heard and often read that the reason mandarin pancakes are cooked in pairs is to make the cooking go twice as *fast*. As far as I know, traditional Chinese cooks never did anything in the interest of speed—or at least it wasn't their first thought! My guess is that the pancakes are rolled in pairs so that each one becomes twice as *thin* as it could be otherwise and are then cooked in pairs so the one side dry-cooks while the other side (in the middle of the sandwich) steam-cooks, producing a supple pancake with a dual texture.

Yields 20–22 single pancakes.

INGREDIENTS:

> 2 cups all-purpose flour
> ¾ cup boiling water
> 1–2 tablespoons Chinese or Japanese sesame oil
> about 1 cup flour, for rolling out and dusting the dough

Making the dough:
If you have a food processor:
  (For details on making dough in a food processor, see page 586.)
  Put the flour into the work bowl fitted with the steel knife. With the machine running add the water through the feed tube in a thin stream, just until the dough begins to mass lumpily around the blade. Give the machine 2–3 seconds' "lag time" to incorporate the last water droplets and form a near-ball. If a ball does not form, add water in droplets until the dough comes together. You may not use all the water or you may need a bit more, all depending on the dryness of the flour; have extra boiling water alongside the machine in case. As soon as a ball forms, stop the machine.
  Remove the dough to a board—the big lump and the bits as well—then knead gently with the heel of your hand for about 4–5 minutes, until the dough is earlobe-soft and smooth and elastic enough so it springs gently back when pressed lightly with a finger. Flour the board lightly only if necessary to prevent sticking.
  Press the dough into a thick disk. Cover with a damp tea towel, and let rest 15–30 minutes. If you wish to hold it overnight, dust the disk with flour, bag airtight in plastic, and refrigerate. Bring to room temperature before rolling out.
  If you do not have a food processor:
  Put the flour in a large bowl, and add the boiling water in a thin stream, stirring with chopsticks or a wooden spoon until the flour masses together in a lumpy dough. Add extra boiling water in droplets if required to make the flour damp enough so it will cohere when pressed with your fingers. Turn out onto a lightly floured board, and knead with the heel of your hand until earlobe-soft and smooth, and elastic enough so that a light fingertip impression springs gently back, about 10 minutes. Flour the board only as necessary to prevent sticking, lest the dough become too stiff.
  Press into a disk, cover with a damp tea towel, and let rest 15–30 minutes. To hold overnight, dust with flour, bag airtight, and refrigerate. Bring to room temperature before using.

Rolling out the dough, and cutting and pairing the pancakes:
On a floured surface roll the rested dough into a circle evenly ⅛-inch thin, paying more attention to thickness than to shape. Dust the board and the top of the dough lightly with flour as needed. To check for even thinness, look with your eye level to the board and then run your fingers lightly over the dough.
  With a sharp, 3-inch round cutter, cut out as many circles as possible, spacing them touching one another to minimize scraps. Gently remove the cut circles to a floured surface and cover with a dry towel. Knead the scraps briefly into a ball, seal airtight in plastic, and let the ball rest while you oil the first batch of circles.

Using your fingers, spread a very thin film of oil evenly over the top of each circle and around the edge. The dough should look dully glazed and not oily. Too little oil and the pancakes won't pull apart once cooked; too much oil and they will ooze and slide apart when rolled out. If this is your first time making *Mandarin Pancakes*, oil one or two pairs, then flatten and cook the pancakes as described below. That will tell you for certain just how much oil is required.

Match the circles in pairs, putting one circle on top of the other, oiled sides together and edges matching exactly. Put a dry towel over the paired circles. Roll out the scrap ball, and repeat cutting out circles, oiling and pairing them, and rolling out scraps until all the dough is used up. (On a lucky day, you will come out with an even number of circles.) Proceed immediately to roll out and cook the pancakes.

Thinning and pan-cooking the pancakes:

Put the first paired "sandwich" on a lightly floured board. Press the dough gently in several places with your fingers to firm the seal and anchor the pancakes together, then roll out to a circular shape evenly 1/16-inch thin. Make your first rolls from the center to set the shape, then roll to insure even thinness. Be careful not to make the edge thinner or thicker than the middle. Dust the board and the top of the pancake as necessary to prevent sticking and blot up any oozing oil. At the very beginning, feel free to turn it over once or twice to roll both sides and better align the edges. Once the pancake becomes thin, do not flip it lest you stretch it.

Transfer the thinned pancake without stretching it to a flour-dusted surface, and cover with a dry towel. Roll out 3–5 pairs in the same manner, or as many as your work surface can hold. (As you become proficient in pancake making, you will find yourself rolling out one pair while another cooks in the pan, but if this is your first try don't do it. Until you get the feel, it is necessary to keep your attention undivided on the pan.)

Put a *heavy* dry skillet at least 8 inches in diameter over medium-low heat. Cast iron, Calphalon, or some slightly porous surface that has absorbed a bit of oil works best. Have a heatproof luncheon-size plate and a dry towel within easy reach of your stovetop.

Check the pan after a minute with a drop of water. It should sizzle slowly. If it doesn't, raise the heat to medium and repeat the test in 10 seconds. What you want is a hot, not a scorching, pan.

When the metal is properly hot, put the first pancake in the pan and cook until it puffs from the steam that builds up inside, about 45 seconds, raising the heat very slightly if it does not begin to puff within 30 seconds. When the pancake is puffy and the bottom is dry but still supple, flip the pancake over. (I use my well-worn fingertips. Otherwise, use a wooden spatula.) Cook the second side for a shorter time, about 30 seconds, until it too has puffed and dried somewhat but still feels very supple. Do not worry at this point about waiting around for the brown speckles that *Mandarin Pancakes* are supposed to have. The first pancakes often don't have them, and even if you wind up with none once the pan has tempered, that's perfectly OK.

As soon as your fingers tell you it is done, remove the pancake to the waiting plate, and gently pull it apart, beginning at the edge. (Usually one edge opens a bit on its own to show you where to start.) Stack the two single pancakes one directly on top of the other, oiled sides up, then cover closely with the towel to prevent drying.

Slip the next pancake into the pan and repeat the process, adjusting the heat so the dough puffs quickly—within 10–15 seconds—and cooks to supple doneness in about 15–30 seconds more. As the pan tempers, the pancakes will cook a bit more quickly, but be on your guard lest it get too hot. Typically, the first side takes 45–60 seconds, and the second side takes 30–45 seconds to cook to proper doneness.

Continue cooking, separating, stacking, and covering the pancakes until all are done. If you have one that feels a bit dry as you pull it apart, put it in the middle of the stack so it will soften from the steam of its neighbors.

When all the pancakes are pan-cooked, proceed immediately to steam them.

Steaming the pancakes:
(For details on steaming and how to improvise a steamer, see page 60.)

Bring the water in the steaming vessel to a gushing boil over high heat. Reduce the heat to medium to maintain a steady, gentle steam, then take the towel off the pancakes and add the plate to the steaming rack. Cover the steamer and steam the pancakes for 10 minutes, until piping hot.

Once steamed, the pancakes may be served immediately. Bring them in one stack to the table, covered with a towel to keep them warm, or serve only part at a time, keeping the remainder hot in the steamer over low heat for up to 1 hour. If you wish something fancier than a stack, fold the pancakes, oiled side in, into quarters before steaming, and arrange them in an overlapping swirl on the plate.

Storing the pancakes:
If you are not serving the pancakes immediately after steaming, let them come fully to room temperature, covered with a cloth against drying. For refrigerating 3–4 days, bag airtight in plastic. For freezing, wrap airtight in plastic wrap, then seal again in foil. Defrost in the refrigerator before resteaming.

To reheat, steam the pancakes as above, for about 10 minutes until hot.

How to eat a *Mandarin Pancake*:
Serve or take a pancake with fingers or chopsticks (the latter being more acceptable if deftness allows). Place it flat, oiled side up on your palm or plate (either being acceptable). Put a dollop of filling in the middle of the pancake, then put the pancake on your plate if it isn't there already. Using chopsticks and fingers in equal measure, bring two sides of the wrapper up and over the filling to form a tube, then bring the remaining ends over to seal the tube shut. Clamping one end shut with chopsticks and the other end with fingers (the choice is up to you which end to clamp with which), steer the package neatly to your mouth and bite off what can be comfortably chewed, tipping the tube slightly upwards in the aftermath as it is now without an end.

Note: It is not acceptable, according to my vast table-watching experience, to tear the original pancake in two in order to create two bite-size bundles. One must cope with the open end as best one can!

MENU SUGGESTIONS:
To fill the pancakes, try *Cassia Blossom (Mu-Shu) Pork* (page 198), *Szechwan-Hunan Pork Threads* (page 195), *Baby Buddha's Feast* (page 302), and *Cold-Tossed Three Shreds* (page 303)—any or all, depending on the size of the party.

Soups:
Light
&
Hearty

湯

◆

◆

Soup is the universal soother, in China as well as the rest of the world. Thick or thin, simple or complex, it is the comforting and (in China) always-hot bowlful that warms the spirit and makes the food slide down. In a Chinese meal, soup typically comes at the end of the eating when the belly needs soothing, although in the informality of a Chinese home it is often brought out somewhat earlier, and then sipped between bitefuls or spooned over rice.

I have eaten Chinese soups in at least three settings, and the style of the soup and the implements with which one ate it changed accordingly. The first, which is the way I like soup best, is the simple huge bowlful that contains a whole meal—the thick vegetable chowder or the pint of real chicken stock crammed with a dozen won ton, which I relished at roadside stalls in Taiwan and which sated me, body and soul, for the rest of the day. This was the sort of soup one ate with a chipped spoon and hearty slurping, occasionally with the aid of chopsticks and preferably with one's elbows atop the table in a posture that spelled business.

The second sort was the everyday soup eaten with lunch and dinner at home, a demure soup served in a simple, small rice bowl, meant to provide a footnote to the meal. Here, one drank the soup directly from the bowl, with deep sighs if not hearty slurps.

Of the third sort of soup, I have had precious little experience. These are the painstaking banquet soups of China—the soups made from the nests of a little bird called a swift, soups made from shark's fins, and various sweet and rare soups made from nuts and gelatinous fungi—and though I have eaten them in proper form with a straight back and genteel sips from their delicate, prettily patterned bowls, they have never appealed to me half as much as the more homely and homey sorts.

Left to my own desires, I rarely serve soup with a Chinese meal, and if I do it is a very simple one whose color and taste are in harmony with the season and the other dishes. Mostly, I like to eat soup *instead* of a meal, along with a steamed bun or a wedge of hot scallion bread and a good companion to join me in the pleasure.

What follows is an assortment of soups for different moods. There are light soups to serve as a beverage-like companion to dinner; hearty, toe-warming soups in need of only a platter of springrolls or a dozen dumplings to quell even a grand hunger; casseroled soups of several large things bound in little bits of rich broth, which are like multicourse meals in a bowl. So, whether you're wanting to sip soup from a cup, churn it in a 10-gallon pot when company is coming, or sit down to a cozy sand pot of soup by yourself, there should be a soup here for you.

TYPES OF CHICKEN STOCK   In any good cook's world, there are of course two kinds of chicken stock: good and bad. *Good chicken stock* has a genuine, fresh flavor that smacks of chicken, a light, clean bouquet, and a clear golden look. The best is homemade over a long, slow heat with a treasure load of bones and a few feet thrown in to make a pleasant gel. Only a few canned chicken stocks can even hint at this flavor. When I move to a new area, I buy several different brands and taste them carefully and then pick the best so I can have something decent in an emergency. *Bad chicken stock* has a sour or salty taste or no genuinely "chickeny" taste at all. It is either homemade stock that has gone bad, or canned or powdered sorts that were made cheaply or with too heavy an addition of ersatz flavorings, colorings, and preservatives. It will not be a suitable background—in color, taste, or aroma—for the light play of light ingredients that is typical of Chinese soups.

In the world of a Chinese cook, there are two other types of chicken stock, both belonging to the "good" guys. The first is what I have called *"light chicken stock."* This is a light-tasting, clear broth that is subtle in flavor. It is the sort of stock that goes into sauces for most stir-frys and which is the little hint of chicken or fragrant goodness in thousands of Chinese dishes. In my kitchen, it is usually made by reducing the poaching liquids from "no-poach" or water-chilled chicken, or by a simple brewing of a small potful of bones. Most canned stocks fall into this "light" category. On the other hand, there is *"rich chicken stock,"* which is much more intensely flavored and colored than the first sort. This is a stock which TASTES richly of chicken and has a compellingly chickeny aroma—the kind most of our grandmothers made (and some of us still make) by reducing a large potful of meaty bones and chicken parts over many hours. This is the stuff of most of the soups in this chapter. It is also a large contributor to mild-mannered stir-frys and casseroles, those that for instance use tofu, where the rich background is needed to make a simpler food shine. This taste, so far as I know, can never come from a can.

Always, you will hear me calling for *"unsalted* chicken stock." A Chinese cook typically does not salt the stock until it is considered in combination with other foods. Ginger and scallion alone are there to contribute the background flavors to the stock, and the salting where necessary is a matter of tasting or knowing the individual dish and *then* judging what it requires. This gives you as the cook far more freedom in developing the flavor of a dish than if you begin with a stock that is already salted. You also have the additional freedom of reducing a stock, if you wish, even after you have made and stored it, for you will then be concentrating only flavor, not salt.

**Chinese
Chicken
Stock**

雞湯

Making a good Chinese-style chicken stock is a remarkably easy, economic affair, well within the reach of anyone having a large pot, a not-too-large pile of chicken bones and parts, one hefty scallion, and a few coins of ginger. You don't even need time or energy, as the stock cooks conveniently on its own. Accumulating the bones, scallion, and ginger is also easy. Simply save the trimmings from boning chicken breasts or preparing a whole chicken (page 126), and freeze them along with the occasional leftover scallion or bit of ginger. Then, when your freezer is full, it's time to make stock. ◆ The role of such a simple stock in Chinese cooking is to enhance stir-fry sauces and to provide a light-colored, clear-tasting base for soups. Lacking carrots and onion skins, which are the keys to a Western stock's deep golden color, Chinese chicken stock is a pale blonde. Seasoned only with scallion and ginger, it has a fresh, clean quality that one cannot duplicate otherwise. ◆ Making the stock requires about 3 hours of no-hands cooking while the liquids simmer gently on the stove. The cooking may be interrupted at any point, which makes the stock-making easier still. Once strained, it keeps indefinitely in the freezer.

TECHNIQUE NOTES:
As I learned in a Mongolian kitchen (which is where a good Jewish girl like me had to go to learn how to make chicken soup), there is a simple, straightforward route to producing a clear stock: Don't stir it and don't boil it. Once you have removed the nasty-looking scum that rises to the surface and have established a steady, slow simmer, ignore the stock. Walk away and leave it alone, and it will turn crystal clear.

Yields about 2 quarts (7–8 cups) stock.

INGREDIENTS:

> *3–3½ pounds chicken bones, with some meat left clinging to them, including*
> *necks and backs and a chicken foot or two, with any loose fat removed*
> *3–4 quarter-size slices fresh ginger*
> *1 hefty or 2 thin whole scallions, cut into 3-inch lengths*
> *3–4 Szechwan peppercorns (optional)*

Preparations:
Rinse the bones with cool water to remove any blood.

With a thick-bladed heavy cleaver especially designed for chopping bones, break the bones partway or clear through into plum-size hunks to expose the marrow and enrich the stock. Whack with authority, so the bones break cleanly without shattering. Chop necks and feet into pieces as well.

Lightly smash the ginger and scallion with the blunt handle end or broad side of the cleaver, to release their juices.

Brewing the stock:
Put the bones into a heavy 6-quart non-aluminum stockpot. The bones should fill the pot only ⅓–½ way. Add cold water to come within 1 inch of the top of the pot, then set the pot over high heat. Bring the liquids to a near-boil, then reduce the heat to maintain a steady simmer.

After 5–10 minutes, when a thick foam has risen to the surface, use a large shallow spoon to skim off and discard the scum. Continue skimming for 4–5 minutes, when it no longer clusters thickly on the surface. Add the ginger, scallion, and Szechwan peppercorns, and reduce the heat to maintain a weak simmer, with bubbles rising lazily to the top of the pot.

Simmer the stock undisturbed for 3–4 hours, or until the liquids are reduced by about half and are ½–1 inch below the bones. Do not stir the stock while it is simmering and do not let it boil.

The simmering process may be interrupted at any point, and the stock left uncovered on the stove for up to 12 hours. To hold it more than a few hours in warm weather, refrigerate the stock in its pot. When ready to continue, bring the liquid slowly to a simmer over low heat. Be sure not to let it boil, lest the clarity of the stock be ruined.

Straining the stock:
Once the bones are poking above the liquid, turn off the heat and leave the pot to sit undisturbed for 30 minutes or more, so the impurities will coagulate on the surface or sink to the bottom.

Line a large strainer or colander with a triple layer of damp cheesecloth (wetting the cloth expands the fibers, making it a finer trap through which to strain things), and set it securely over a large pot or bowl.

Push the thin, congealed surface greases gently to one side, then very gently ladle the stock into the strainer. Tilt the pot slowly as you ladle and disturb the bones as little as possible. When you near the bottom of the pot, hold the bones in place with an overturned plate or a small pot lid, then pour the last of the clear liquid through the strainer. Discard the sediment-filled liquid and the ginger, scallion, and bones.

Reducing the stock:

If the bones were neither meaty nor ample enough to produce a rich-tasting liquid, then return it to a non-aluminum pot and simmer it until the water content is reduced and the flavor is as concentrated as you want. This reduction can be done immediately after straining the stock or at any later time.

Storing the stock:

Refrigerate or briefly freeze the stock until the fat rises and hardens on the surface. Scrape off the fat and refrigerate some or all of it for use in stir-frying Chinese cabbage (page 311) or making *Scallion Breads* (page 435). Divide the stock into convenient portions and refrigerate it 4–5 days or store it indefinitely in the freezer. Stock that begins to sour in the refrigerator can be rescued by slowly bringing to a boil and simmering 5–10 minutes. Stock that is defrosted and only partially used up may be refrozen. Frozen light stock can also be added to the stockpot when a new batch of bones is set to brew, if you want to make a richer stock than you have either gotten or are likely to get.

| Chinese
| Meatball
| Soup

粉絲肉丸湯

This is an exceedingly light soup, with a pretty look and a very pleasant flavor. The tiny meatballs float in chicken stock alongside the silvery noodles and fluffy greens, and the only surprise is the discovery of crunchy water chestnuts when you bite down on a meatball. Preparations are quick and simple and will not daunt even a noncook. ◆ If you can find them fresh, by all means add the long and slender *enokitake* mushrooms to the soup. They are a perfect foil for the noodles and are graceful to look at and lovely to eat. ◆ From start to finish, this is a 30-minute soup. If you like, the meatball mixture may be made a day ahead.

TECHNIQUE NOTES:

Adding the uncooked meatballs to cold stock as they are shaped, then cooking the meatballs while the stock is brought to a simmer is a good example of the economy of the Chinese kitchen. Everything happens in one pot and not a drop of flavor is lost.

Serves 2–3 as a large bowlful, 4–6 as a smaller portion in a multicourse meal.

INGREDIENTS:

For the meatballs:
4 large water chestnuts, fresh best (page 578)
½ pound ground pork butt
2 teaspoons finely minced fresh ginger
2 teaspoons finely minced green and white scallion
1 large egg, lightly beaten
1 tablespoon thin (regular) soy sauce
1 tablespoon Chinese rice wine or quality, dry sherry
½ teaspoon coarse kosher salt
½ teaspoon sugar
several grinds fresh pepper
1 tablespoon cornstarch dissolved in 2 tablespoons cold chicken stock
scant teaspoon Chinese or Japanese sesame oil

2 ounces bean threads (glass noodles) (page 533)
1 bunch fresh watercress with smooth, lively leaves, or 6 ounces very fresh
    spinach leaves
3 ounces fresh enokitake mushrooms (optional)
4½ cups rich, unsalted chicken stock (see page 446 for making your own)
1½ tablespoons thin (regular) soy sauce
Roasted Szechwan Pepper-Salt (page 476), or coarse kosher salt and freshly
    ground pepper to taste

Preparations:
Peel fresh water chestnuts, and cut into a neat, peppercorn-size dice. If you are using
canned water chestnuts, blanch them in plain boiling water for 15 seconds, drain immediately, and refresh under cold water before dicing.

In a bowl large enough to mix the pork put the water chestnuts, pork, and remaining meatball ingredients. Mix lightly with a fork or chopsticks, stirring in one direction until well blended, then throw the mixture lightly against the inside of the bowl 5–6
times to firm the filling. Seal airtight, with a piece of plastic film pressed directly on the
surface of the meat. If you are working in advance, refrigerate the meat until use, overnight if you wish. Bring to room temperature before making the meatballs.

Leave the rubber bands or strings binding the noodles in place, put the noodles in
a bowl, and cover with hot tap water. Soak briefly until rubber-band firm, then cut the
noodles into 4–5-inch lengths with scissors. Cut loose and discard the rubber bands or
strings, rinse the noodles in a colander with cool water, and put aside to drain.

Cut the watercress above the string that joins the bunch and discard the lower
stems. Sift through the upper sprigs, discarding any discolored leaves. If you are using
spinach, discard any discolored leaves or bits of stem, and cut any large leaves crosswise
into bands 1½ inches thick, leaving the smaller leaves whole. Pump the watercress or
spinach up and down in cold water to clean it, then shake off excess water. Blanch in
plain boiling water to cover for 10 seconds, drain immediately, and rush under cold water
to stop the cooking. Drain, squeeze gently to remove excess water, then put the vegetable
aside on a plate. If you are working in advance, seal airtight and refrigerate, overnight if
you wish.

Completing the soup:
About 20 minutes before serving, cut off the spongy root cluster that joins the mushrooms and pull the mushrooms gently apart in small bunches.

Put the noodles in a small pot with 1 cup of the stock. Bring the stock to a
simmer over moderate heat and simmer the noodles gently until silky, about 2 minutes.
Remove the pot from the heat.

Combine the remaining stock and the soy sauce in a small, non-aluminum stockpot. Put the pot on the stove, with the meat mixture, a tablespoon, and a bowl of cool
water alongside. Put the soup bowls in a low oven to warm.

Dip your palms and the spoon into the water. Scoop up 1 tablespoon of the meat
mixture with the spoon, then toss it lightly between your wet palms to form a small,
walnut-size meatball. Drop the meatball into the cold stock mixture, then repeat the
process until the meat mixture is used up, wetting the spoon and your hands as needed to
keep the meat from sticking.

Add to the pot whatever stock was not absorbed by the noodles, then bring the
liquid to a near-boil over moderate heat. Skim the surface of foam, reduce the heat to

maintain a gentle simmer, then cover the pot and simmer 5 minutes.

In the last minutes of simmering, portion the noodles and the watercress or spinach among the individual bowls.

At the end of 5 minutes, turn off the heat. Add the mushrooms to the pot and stir gently once or twice to mix. Taste the soup and adjust as required with pepper-salt or kosher salt and fresh pepper. Ladle the soup into bowls, portioning the meatballs among them, then fluff the noodles and greens gently with chopsticks to float them in the soup. Serve at once.

Leftovers keep 2–3 days and may be reheated by steaming in a covered bowl, or by reheating over moderate heat until hot.

MENU SUGGESTIONS:
For a simple supper, try this soup in the company of *Pan-Fried Scallion Breads* (page 435). For a fuller menu, serve it with any of the steamed fish dishes (pages 248, 250, and 252) and *Ham and Egg Fried Rice* (page 405) or *Everyday Chinese Rice* (page 400). It is a very versatile soup, compatible with many cuisines.

Moslem-Style Hot and Sour Soup
回式酸辣湯

The fathers in my life have always been absent on Friday nights. My real father was a fiend for poker, and Po-fu, my adopted Chinese father, was addicted to a weekly shot of mah-jongg. The one advantage of their absence was an evening of special eating. In my American childhood I wolfed down enough potato chips and pretzels to last the week, secretly and under the covers. In Taiwan, I scampered off in full view and with full approval to enlist "take out" at our neighborhood Moslem restaurant. My order was always the same—a half-gallon of hot and sour soup and enough pot stickers (page 384) for the household. Never, not once, was it less than the-best-soup-I-have-ever-eaten. ◆ I transported the soup in Po-fu's swank, insulated ice bucket, molded clear up to the lid in imitation of a Shang dynasty bronze. Perhaps that is why I can never get it to taste quite the same. This, then, is not *the* best but the *second* best hot and sour soup I have ever eaten. ◆ Rich and thick, and marvelously peppery and vinegary, this is the soup that has warmed north and central China for centuries. What makes it Moslem is that it uses chicken broth and beef and shuns pork, which is otherwise the favored meat of China. ◆ Everything may be done in advance except the final stirring together of the soup, which takes minutes.

TECHNIQUE NOTES:
Shredding the meat *against* the grain makes it decidedly more tender. Each shred is then a chain of meaty bits rather than one long, sinewy muscle.

Marinating the meat, for even 5 minutes, changes its texture remarkably. It becomes plush and slippery on account of the cornstarch and oil, which create an impenetrable flavor seal for the beef when it enters the hot stock. As for the soy, wine, and sugar, their job is to enrich the taste and balance what the Chinese perceive as the strong, odiferous character of beef.

Serves 4 as a large bowlful, 6–8 as a smaller portion in a multicourse meal.

INGREDIENTS:

    3 tablespoons tree ears (page 576)

25 lily buds (page 552)
6 medium Chinese dried black mushrooms, "flower" variety recommended
   (page 538)
6 ounces well-trimmed round steak (weight after trimming)

To marinate the beef:
2 teaspoons thin (regular) soy sauce
1 teaspoon Chinese rice wine or quality, dry sherry
¼ teaspoon sugar
1 teaspoon cornstarch
¼ teaspoon Chinese or Japanese sesame oil
1 teaspoon water
several grinds fresh pepper

2 cakes (½ pound) fresh white tofu, firm variety best (page 323)
4 cups rich, unsalted chicken stock (see page 446 for making your own)
2 tablespoons thin (regular) soy sauce
3 tablespoons cornstarch dissolved in ¼ cup cold chicken stock
¼ cup unseasoned Chinese or Japanese rice vinegar
1 teaspoon freshly ground pepper
1 large egg, lightly beaten

To garnish:
1 teaspoon Chinese or Japanese sesame oil
2–3 tablespoons thin-sliced green and white scallion rings

Preparations:
In separate bowls, soak the tree ears and lily buds in cool or warm water to cover until
supple, about 20 minutes. Cover tree ears generously, with about 2 cups water, to allow
for expansion. In a third bowl, cover the mushrooms with cold or hot water and soak
until soft and spongy, 20 minutes to an hour. All three items may be left to soak overnight with no loss of flavor.

Drain the tree ears, swish well in an ample amount of cool water to dislodge grit,
then drain and repeat. Pick over and discard any unchewable or overly gelatinous bits,
then tear the tree ears if needed into quarter- or nickel-size pieces.

Drain the lily buds and snip off the hard stem ends. Cut them in half crosswise.

Drain the mushrooms, snip off the stems, then rinse to dislodge any sand trapped
in the gills. Cut the caps into thin slivers ⅛ inch wide. Combine with the drained tree
ears and lily buds.

Cut the beef crosswise against the grain into slices a scant ¼ inch wide, then cut
lengthwise against the grain into long shreds a scant ¼ inch thick. Cut the shreds
crosswise into 1½–2-inch lengths. (Partially freezing the meat before shredding is not
necessary here, as it usually is in a stir-fry. The liquid medium of a soup is not as demanding of even slices, and the slight irregularity of the slivers is charming in a soup.)

Mix the marinade ingredients until smooth, then toss well with the beef. Mari-
nate for 30 minutes at room temperature or overnight in the refrigerator, sealed airtight.
Stir once with your fingers midway through the marinating to redistribute the seasonings.
Bring to room temperature before cooking.

Holding a sharp knife parallel to the board, cut the tofu through the middle into
slabs ¼ inch thick, then stack the slabs and shred them into slivers ¼ inch wide. Cut

carefully, so the tofu does not break. Refrigerate several hours or overnight if desired, covered with cool water. Drain before using.

Making the soup:
About 10–15 minues before serving, combine the soy with the cornstarch mixture and leave the spoon in the bowl. Combine the vinegar and the pepper, and stir the meat to loosen the slivers. Have all the ingredients within easy reach of your stovetop. Put the soup bowls in a low oven to warm.

Bring the stock to a steaming near-simmer over medium heat in a 4–5-quart non-aluminum pot. Add the tree ears, lily buds, and black mushrooms, then slip the tofu gently into the pot. Swish once or twice gently to mix, cover, then cook until the stock boils. Add the beef, swish gently several times to mix, then reduce the heat to maintain a low simmer. Cover the pot and simmer 2 minutes.

Remove the cover, stir the cornstarch mixture to recombine, then pour it evenly into the soup. Stir gently until the liquid becomes glossy and slightly thick, 15–20 seconds. Add the vinegar and pepper, stir gently to blend, then turn off the heat.

Immediately add the egg to the soup in a thin stream, stirring gently as you pour it so it comes to the surface in chiffony wisps. Taste, and adjust with more vinegar and pepper, if desired. The taste should be vibrant and sharp—very hot and very sour. Work quickly, so the vinegar bite does not dissipate.

Stir in the sesame oil, then portion the soup into the heated bowls and garnish each with a thick sprinkling of scallion. Serve immediately.

The soup will keep nicely in the refrigerator for several days and can be frozen with great success. If necessary, respark with a bit more vinegar after reheating.

MENU SUGGESTIONS:
I love this soup as the centerpiece of a meal, partnered with *Moslem-Style Beef or Lamb Pot Stickers* (page 384) or *Pan-Fried Meat Pies* (page 387) or *Springrolls with Dijon Mustard Sauce* (page 389). *Pan-Fried Scallion Breads* (page 435) are also wonderful with the soup, as are any of the steamed buns (pages 425 to 429). If you are a real spice lover, serve the soup with a meal centered on a spicy chicken or pork dish, such as *Hot and Sour Hunan Chicken* (page 142) or *Hunan Rice Crumb Pork* (page 200).

Wine-Explosion Vegetable Chowder

酒爆玉米羹

Most of the Chinese soups we find in the West are the clear, thin sort called *tong* in Chinese. Here is a different soup altogether. Known as *keng*, or chowder in English, it is a thick, rich, hearty brew that in ancient north China comprised the main part of a meal. What Confucius ate six nights of the week was probably a *gung*. ◆ This particular *gung* is a New World soup, full of the colors and flavors of tomatoes, corn, and white mushrooms, all relative newcomers—by Confucian standards—to Chinese cooking. It is a soup with a remarkable popularity, even among those who otherwise don't like corn soups. While it is superb in the months when the ingredients are garden-fresh, I like it even better in winter as a warming one-bowl meal. ◆ This soup is fast, dramatic, and fun to make. The flavors enlarge upon sitting, so you may make it a morning or full day in advance. It also freezes well. Some of the texture of the greens is lost, but none of the flavor.

TECHNIQUE NOTES:

"Exploding" wine in heated oil as the first step in making a soup is a classic Chinese technique, seemingly unique to China. Its nearest counterpart is the French technique of deglazing a pan. The alcohol and water dissipate immediately upon contact with the heat, and the oil glaze traps the wine essence as a flavoring for the soup. The result is a soup that tastes not of alcohol, but of the essence of the wine. It is a subtle but discernible touch, quintessentially Chinese, and one which requires the very best rice wine or sherry you can muster.

For the technique of weaving threads of egg white into soup, see TECHNIQUE NOTES, page 460.

Serves 4–5 as a large bowlful, 8–10 as a smaller portion in a multicourse meal.

INGREDIENTS:

> *¾–1 pound sweet-smelling fresh tomatoes (or an equal amount of quality, unsalted whole canned tomatoes)*
> *7 large or 13 medium fresh white mushrooms, stems intact*
> *2 ounces bright green, crisp vegetable (choose one): fresh snow peas or sugar snap peas, fresh or frozen green peas, or tender string beans or Chinese longbeans*
> *2 tablespoons corn or peanut oil*
> *2 tablespoons Chinese rice wine or quality, dry sherry*
> *5½ cups rich, unsalted chicken stock (see page 446 for making your own)*
> *17 ounces quality cream-style corn*
> *4 tablespoons cornstarch dissolved in 6 tablespoons cold chicken stock*
> *1 large egg white*
> *sugar and salt as required*
> *2 ounces lightly smoked or flavorful honey- or sugar-cured ham, coarsely minced*

Preparing the vegetables:

Plunge fresh tomatoes briefly in boiling water just until the skin splits, remove with a Chinese mesh spoon or slotted spoon, and let cool. Peel and core, retaining the juices. Cut fresh or canned tomatoes into quarters and chop coarsely, in the food processor using on-off turns, or by hand. Retain the liquids.

Clean the mushrooms by bobbing them and rubbing them gently in a bowl of cold water. Cut off only the ragged or brown base of the stems, then put the mushrooms on their sides and cut into thin umbrella-shaped slices ¹⁄₁₆ inch thick.

String snow peas or sugar snap peas and cut on the diagonal into slivers a scant ¼ inch thin. Defrost frozen peas. Cut off the tips of string beans or longbeans, then cut on the diagonal into 1¼-inch lengths.

The cut vegetables may be sealed and refrigerated overnight. Seal the green vegetable in lightly misted plastic.

Making the soup:

About 10–15 minutes before serving, assemble all the ingredients within easy reach of your stovetop, and put individual soup bowls in a low oven to warm.

Heat a heavy non-aluminum stockpot over medium-high heat until hot enough to evaporate a bead of water on contact. Add the oil, swirl to glaze the bottom of the pot, then heat until a bead of wine added to the pot "explodes" in a sizzle. Add the wine, allow only 1 second for it to explode in a fragrant hiss, then immediately add the stock to capture the wine essence. Bring the stock to a boil, then add the tomatoes, mushrooms, and corn. Cook over moderate heat, stirring constantly, until the mixture returns to a boil. Do not increase the heat or cease stirring, lest the soup scorch. Reduce the heat to maintain a steady simmer, then add the green vegetable. Simmer about 2–3 minutes for snow peas or peas, 4 minutes for beans, stirring constantly until the vegetable is cooked but quite crisp. It will continue to cook while you finish and serve the soup.

Taste the soup, and add salt and sugar as needed. Store-bought tomatoes, especially, will require sugar to restore the natural sweetness bred out of them. Do not hesitate to add it. Otherwise, the soup will lack sparkle and taste flat.

Reduce the heat to low. Stir the cornstarch mixture to recombine, then add it to the pot in a steady stream, stirring slowly for about 2 minutes until the soup turns glossy and thick. Turn off the heat. With a fork or chopsticks beat the egg white with quick, light strokes just to break the gel. It will froth a bit, but do not beat to a foam. Holding it about 6 inches above the surface of the soup, add the egg white in a very thin, steady stream. Stir gently once midway, and again when finished to bring the lacy threads to the surface.

Serve immediately, garnishing each bowl with a sprinkling of ham. Or, cover the pot and serve 1–4 hours later, when the vegetables are no longer crisp but the soup is even deeper in flavor.

Leftovers keep nicely 4–5 days, refrigerated, or may be frozen. Reheat in a heavy pot over medium heat, stirring frequently.

MENU SUGGESTIONS:
I enjoy this soup most as a one-bowl meal, in the company of something like *Baked Stuffed Buns* (page 432), *Pan-Fried Scallion Breads* (page 435), or *Steamed Buns with Chicken and Black Mushrooms* (page 425). To accompany a full dinner, it is especially good with simple poultry dishes like *Master Sauce Chicken* (page 153), and is robust enough to stand up to a spicy dish like *Szechwan Rice Crumb Beef* (page 221).

Soup of Many Mushrooms

什菇湯

Whereas a mushroom soup in the West is typically a hearty affair, rich and filling, a mushroom soup in China is delicate and light. The stock is clear and the mushrooms float in strips on the top, garnished with a sprinkling of green. It is a simple bowlful, meant to be sipped throughout the meal as a beverage, or drunk at meal's end to settle and soothe (though you may serve it as an opener if you like, in the spirit of a good consommé.) ◆ I like to make this soup when some particularly fresh or interesting mushrooms catch my eye. The more exotic varieties found increasingly in our markets are wonderful—the elongated *enokitake*, thick-capped *shiitake*, trumpet-like *chanterelles*, or smooth oyster mushrooms (which the Chinese call "abalone mushroom"). Even the common button sort is pretty, if it is exceedingly white and fresh. I enjoy using at least two varieties if possible, and, if I am wanting additional body, I add some slivered fresh pork to the pot. ◆ The soup is simple to prepare and takes only minutes to cook. Its flavor develops beautifully if done several hours in advance, and it is also excellent made a day ahead.

TECHNIQUE NOTES:
This is a good example of a "stir-fried soup," the everyday, home-style soup of China. The

solid ingredients are first stir-fried in a modicum of oil, then the stock is poured on top and the soup brought to a simmer. It is a method that gives savor to even the simplest of soups.

Serves 3–4 as a substantial bowlful, 5–6 as a smaller portion in a multicourse meal.

INGREDIENTS:

> *8–10 large Chinese dried black mushrooms, preferably the thick-capped
> "flower" variety (page 539)*
> *½ pound fresh mushrooms (choose one or two varieties from what is freshest
> and most interesting in your market): white button mushrooms, enokitake,
> chanterelles, fresh shiitake, fresh oyster mushrooms, all excellent*
> *3½ cups rich, unsalted chicken stock (see page 446 for making your own)*
> *½–¾ cup fresh green peas, or defrosted frozen peas*
> *2–4 tablespoons corn or peanut oil*
> *1 teaspoon Chinese or Japanese sesame oil*
> *2 teaspoons finely minced shallots*
> *1 tablespoon finely chopped scallions, light green and white parts only*
> *1 tablespoon Chinese rice wine or quality, dry sherry*
> *1 or 2 pinches sugar*
> *coarse kosher salt to taste*

Optional:

> *6 ounces well-trimmed pork butt or pork loin (weight after trimming)*
> *2½ teaspoons thin (regular) soy sauce*
> *1 teaspoon Chinese rice wine or quality, dry sherry*
> *2½ teaspoons cornstarch*
> *⅛ teaspoon sugar*
> *¼ teaspoon Chinese or Japanese sesame oil*

Preparations:
Soak the dried mushrooms in 3 cups cold or hot water to cover until soft and spongy, 20 minutes to an hour. (You will get maximum flavor if the mushrooms are soaked in cold water several hours or overnight.) Snip off the stems with scissors, strain the soaking liquid to eliminate any sand, then put the stems and the strained liquid aside. Rinse the caps thoroughly to dislodge any sand trapped in the gills, then slice them into long slivers ¹⁄₁₆ inch thick.

Clean fresh mushrooms if required: Brush button mushrooms or bob them briefly in cool water; brush, wipe, or briefly rinse *chanterelles* (they are fragile, so avoid rinsing if you can); wipe *shiitake*. *Enokitake* do not require cleaning. Trim off and reserve the browned or ragged base of the stem, and cut button mushrooms into ¹⁄₁₆-inch thin umbrella-like slices. Reserve any trimmings from *chanterelles*, and cut them into thin slivers that will accentuate their pretty curves. Snip off and reserve *shiitake* stems, and cut the caps into long slivers ¹⁄₁₆ inch thin. Cut off and reserve the spongy base of *enokitake* where they are joined together, and gently separate the mushrooms into small groups. Cut off the base of oyster mushrooms if spongy or dry, reserve, and leave the smaller mushroom clusters intact.

Add the mushroom trimmings to the stems and strained liquid reserved from soaking black mushrooms. Bring to a boil in a small saucepan, simmer until reduced by half, then strain through several layers of wet cheesecloth. You will need 1 cup deeply flavored liquid. If you have more than 1 cup and the taste is pale, reduce it further.

If you are adding pork to the soup, cut it crosswise against the grain into thin slices ⅛ inch thick. Shred the slices against the grain into slivers ⅛ inch wide, then cut long slivers crosswise into 1¼-inch lengths. Blend the soy, wine, cornstarch, sugar, and sesame oil until smooth, and toss well with the pork. Seal airtight and refrigerate 30 minutes or overnight.

Making the soup:
Combine the slivered dried black mushrooms, chicken stock, and 1 cup reduced mushroom liquids in a 2–2½-quart non-aluminum saucepan. Bring to a simmer, add fresh peas if you are using them, and cover the pot. Reduce the heat to low and keep the stock at a very gentle simmer while you stir-fry the fresh mushrooms.

Proceed immediately to heat a wok or a large, heavy skillet over high heat until hot enough to evaporate a bead of water on contact. Add 2 tablespoons corn or peanut oil and 1 teaspoon sesame oil, swirl to coat the pan, and reduce the heat to medium to avoid burning the sesame oil. When the oil is hot enough to sizzle a bit of scallion, add the shallots and the scallion. Stir gently until fragrant, 10–15 seconds, adjusting the heat to maintain a merry sizzle without browning the shallots. When fully fragrant, add the wine, let the alcohol "explode" in a fragrant hiss, then immediately add the fresh mushrooms. Stir-fry about 4–5 minutes, or until soft, dribbling in more oil if necessary from the side of the pan. Use only as much oil as the mushrooms absorb; there should be no extra left in the pan.

When the mushrooms are soft, add them to the stock. Raise the heat to bring the mixture to a near-boil, then adjust to maintain a steady simmer. Cover, and simmer 5 minutes. Reduce the heat to low and taste the soup. Add the sugar, then season carefully with salt to bring out the full mushroom flavor. If you are working a day in advance, turn off the heat, let the soup cool under a cover, then refrigerate overnight.

Just before serving, return the soup to a simmer over moderate heat. If you are adding pork, stir the shreds with your fingers to loosen them, and slide them into the simmering stock. Stir gently until the meat turns gray, about 15 seconds. If you are adding defrosted peas, slide them in last, then stir several seconds to heat them through.

Serve the soup in heated bowls, portioning the many mushrooms evenly between them.

Leftovers keep beautifully 4–5 days and grow even richer with reheating.

MENU SUGGESTIONS:
This is a very versatile soup, which accompanies beef, pork, and vegetarian dishes with equal ease. On its own, the soup is excellent with *Pan-Fried Scallion Breads* (page 435), *Steamed Buns with Chicken and Black Mushrooms* (page 425) or *Steamed Buns with Minced Pork and Tree Ears* (page 429). In a Western setting, try it with grilled, thinly sliced steak.

Szechwan Pork and Pickle Soup
榨菜肉絲湯

One of Szechwan's most common soups, and to my mind one of her most charming, is this peppery, light blend of soft shredded pork, crunchy Szechwan pickle, and slippery glass noodles. The pickle, actually knobs of cabbage root preserved in a chili-type paste that one rinses off before using, lends an irresistible spice to the soup. It is clean and refreshing and unassumingly simple, the kind of soup for which China is best known. ◆ Cooking the soup takes only 3 minutes. The preparations do not take much longer and may be done a day ahead. For the time spent and eating pleasure gained, it is one of my favorite soups.

TECHNIQUE NOTES:
Marinating the shredded pork before adding it to the broth is a distinctive touch that results in a subtly seasoned meat and an enriched soup. The cornstarch, which binds the flavor to the meat and protects each shred, both velvetizes the pork and gives just the right touch of body to the broth.

Serves 2–3 as a main course soup, 4–6 as a rice bowl-size portion in a multicourse meal.

INGREDIENTS:

¼ *pound well-trimmed pork butt or loin (weight after trimming)*

To marinate the pork:
2 *teaspoons thin (regular) soy sauce*
2 *teaspoons Chinese rice wine or quality, dry sherry*
1 *teaspoon cornstarch*
pinch sugar
⅛ *teaspoon freshly ground black pepper*
¼ *teaspoon Chinese or Japanese sesame oil*

2 *ounces Szechwan preserved vegetable (page 571)*
2 *ounces bean threads (glass noodles) (page 533)*
3½ *cups light, unsalted chicken stock (see page 446 for making your own)*
about ½ teaspoon thin (regular) soy sauce
about ⅛ teaspoon freshly ground black pepper

To garnish:
a heaping tablespoon thin-cut green and white scallion rings

Preparations:
Cut the pork crosswise against the grain into thin slices a scant ¼ inch thick. Shred the slices against the grain into slivers a scant ¼ inch wide. Cut long slivers into 1½-inch lengths. Blend the marinade ingredients until smooth and combine with the pork, stirring with your fingers to coat and separate each shred. Seal the pork airtight, then refrigerate 30 minutes or overnight to set the marinade and swell the pork with its flavors.

Rinse the preserved vegetable under cool water, rubbing to remove the reddish coating from the knobs. Pat dry, then slice into matchstick shreds about ⅛ inch thin and 1¼ inches long. (You should have ⅓ cup shreds.)

Soak the noodles in warm or hot tap water to cover until rubber-band firm, about 30 seconds, the timing and water temperature to depend on the noodles. Do not let them get mushy. With scissors, cut the noodles through the loop ends of the skein, into 4–5-inch lengths. Cut and discard the rubber bands or strings, then drain and rinse the noodles.

The pickle and noodles may be refrigerated overnight.

Making the soup:
Have all the ingredients within easy reach of your stovetop. Put a large serving bowl or several individual soup bowls in a low oven to warm.

About 5–10 minutes before serving, bring the stock in a heavy saucepan to a steaming near-simmer over moderate heat. Add the pickle, stir to disperse the threads, then let it sit under cover for 1 minute to infuse the broth with its peppery flavor. Uncover the pot, raise the heat to maintain a gentle simmer, then stir the pork shreds to loosen them and slide them into the soup. Stir once or twice to scatter the shreds, and simmer until the meat turns gray, about 20 seconds. Add the drained noodles, stir to blend, and simmer the soup gently for 2 minutes more.

Add the soy and pepper to the pot, stir to combine, then taste the soup carefully and adjust as required to get a zesty, invigorating taste. Scatter in the scallion rings and turn off the heat.

Ladle the soup into warm bowls, using chopsticks or tongs to portion the slippery noodles and the pork shreds between them. Serve at once.

The Chinese style is to eat the noodles and pork with chopsticks, then sip the broth directly from the bowl—a fine way to enjoy the aroma and treat your lips to the peppery taste.

This soup does not reheat well. It is best made just before serving and then eaten up on the spot. Leftovers, if you have them, are best reheated by steaming in a covered bowl.

MENU SUGGESTIONS:
For a soup-centered meal, I love this soup in the company of *Moslem-Style Beef or Lamb Pot Stickers* (page 384), *Pan-Fried Scallion Breads* (page 435), or *Steamed Buns with Chicken and Black Mushrooms* (page 425). As part of a fuller menu, I typically include it where another spicy, light dish is the focus, such as *Down-Home Hunan Tofu* (page 341), or *Stir-Fried Noodles with Chicken and Mushrooms* (page 367).

Floral Chicken Soup

翡翠雞片湯

The inspiration for this soup came from one of my favorite books, *Chinese Gastronomy*, written by Hsiang Ju Lin and Tsuifeng Lin in collaboration with the grand old man of Chinese letters in America, Lin Yutang. The book is an extraordinary record of the food and culture of China, and most of its recipes describe dishes that are as delicate and refined as this one. ◆ The soup combines an excellent chicken stock, preferably homemade, with tender watercress and a seasoned chicken purée that one steams in a bowl and slices into "petals" before adding to the soup. You may also steam the purée in brioche molds, tartlet tins, or barquette tins, and unmold them whole to make them appear as "flowers." Either way, it is a very pretty soup with a refreshing taste, ideal for a dressed up dinner. ◆ Preparations are simple and may be completed several hours in advance.

TECHNIQUE NOTES:
Blanching watercress prior to inclusion in a soup, purée, or stir-fry rids it of its acrid taste and highlights the refreshing side of its flavor. Blanching also deepens the color dramatically and prevents the plant from becoming watery when cooked.

Serves 3–4 as a substantial bowlful, 5–6 as a smaller portion in a multicourse meal.

INGREDIENTS:

2 bunches (12 ounces) fresh watercress, with lively unblemished leaves

For the purée:
  ¼ *pound skinned and boned fresh chicken breast, trimmed of all membranes,*
    cartilage, and tendons (weight after trimming; equal to about ½ pound
    with skin on and bone in; for easy, 5-minute boning, see page 126)
  ¼ *teaspoon finely minced fresh ginger*
  1½ *teaspoons steam-rendered, cool chicken fat (page 127)*
  2 *teaspoons Chinese rice wine or quality, dry sherry*
  1 *large egg white, beaten to a froth*
  ½ *teaspoon coarse kosher salt*

  additional chicken fat, for greasing molds
  6 *cups rich, unsalted chicken stock (see page 446 for making your own)*
  coarse kosher salt or Roasted Szechwan Pepper-Salt (page 476) to taste

Preparations:
Cut the watercress above the band holding each bunch together and discard the lower stems. Sort through and pinch off any thick stems and wilted or discolored leaves. Pump gently in cool water to clean, drain, and shake off excess water. Put aside ⅔ of the prettiest, most tender pieces. Take the remaining ⅓, strip the stems of leaves, and discard the stems. Blanch the larger pile of watercress and the smaller pile of leaves separately in plain boiling water to cover for 10 seconds, drain promptly, and rush under cold water to cool. Press gently to remove excess water, then set aside in the original 2 piles. The watercress may be blanched a day in advance and refrigerated, sealed airtight. Bring to room temperature before making the soup.

Cut the chicken into chunks, then add the chicken and the small pile of watercress leaves to the work bowl of a food processor fitted with the steel knife. Add the remaining purée ingredients to the work bowl, process with on-off turns to chop, then let the machine run to achieve a purée. If you do not have a food processor, mince the chicken and the watercress leaves finely by hand, then chop with one or two equally weighted knives to reduce to a paste. Blend in a bowl with the remaining purée ingredients, stirring briskly in one direction until combined.

The purée may be sealed airtight with plastic film pressed directly on the surface and refrigerated overnight. Bring to room temperature before steaming.

Steaming the purée and making the soup:
(For details on steaming and how to improvise a steamer, see page 60).

Evenly grease the inside of a 1-cup rice bowl, four ¼-cup brioche molds, or six ⅛-cup tartlet tins with a generous film of chicken fat. Pack the purée firmly into the bowl or molds, leveling the top with a spatula and smoothing the edges neatly.

About 20–30 minutes in advance of serving, bring the water in the steaming vessel to a gushing boil over high heat. Add the bowl or molds to the steaming rack, cover the steamer, then steam the purée over medium-high heat about 15 minutes for a single bowl or 10 minutes for ½-cup or smaller molds, until a toothpick inserted in the center comes out clean. Do not be alarmed if there is a bit of liquid floating on the top of the purée when you check it for doneness.

While the purée is steaming, put a large tureen or individual soup bowls in a low oven to warm. Bring the stock to a simmer in a non-aluminum saucepan, and season with kosher salt or pepper-salt to taste. Cover the pot and keep the stock at a gentle simmer.

Remove the bowl or molds from the steamer, and invert to unmold. If you have steamed the purée in a ricebowl, slice it pie-fashion into wedge-like "petals" ⅛ inch thin.

Fluff the watercress to loosen, and portion it between the heated bowls. Put the petals or smaller molded "flowers" on top. Ladle the soup into the bowls, pull up a piece of watercress here and there with chopsticks if needed, then serve at once.

This soup is best freshly made. Leftovers can be reheated by steaming in a covered bowl, but will taste faded by comparison.

MENU SUGGESTIONS:
This soup is particularly nice in the context of a light meal, such as one including *Golden Egg Dumplings* (page 328) or *Steamed Whole Fish with Seared Scallions* (page 248), along with *Shanghai Vegetable Rice* (page 402).

Velvet Corn Soup

玉米湯

Creamed corn is not one of my favorites—far from it!—but I am mad about this soup. It is luxuriant, simple, and classically Chinese, and is an especially good partner to chicken and duck. ◆ The only caution is to be sure to buy an excellent brand of creamed corn, one that tastes good and sweet and falls nicely (not paste-like) from the spoon. (The Del Monte people make the best in my experience, but your experience may find a better one still.) Of course, you can set about making your own by shucking fresh ears and adding a bit of cream or milk, but I, for one, find the canned variety just fine. ◆ This is a soup that takes only minutes to prepare and remains great-tasting for days.

TECHNIQUE NOTES:
A favorite Chinese trick is to weave beaten whole eggs or egg whites into a soup, the first to form broad, fluffy bands, and the second to form lacy, thin "threads." I favor the delicate threads, which one makes by adding the egg whites to the soup in a thin, steady stream from a bowl or cup (helpfully one with a spout) held several inches above the pot. When almost all added, give a few gentle stirs and the threads float upward to glamorize the brew. The egg whites must be beaten enough so that the gel is broken and they don't plop ungracefully into the pot (where they will form thick ribbons), yet not so much that they turn foamy and bunch on top of the soup.

For "exploding" wine as a preliminary to soup-making, see TECHNIQUE NOTES, page 453.

With the ham, serves 2–3 as a substantial bowlful, 4–5 as a rice bowl-size portion. With the crab, serves 3–4 as a larger bowlful, 6–8 in a rice bowl.

INGREDIENTS:

> 6 tablespoons coarsely chopped ham, honey- or sugar-cured or lightly smoked, or ½ pound picked-over crab meat, preferably fresh (to garner a safe ½ pound meat, begin with a 1½–2 pound crab)
> 2 large egg whites
> 2 tablespoons corn or peanut oil
> 2–3 tablespoons chopped green and white scallion
> 1½ teaspoons finely minced "young" ginger (page 548), or 1 teaspoon minced fresh ginger
> 2 tablespoons Chinese rice wine or quality, dry sherry
> 4 cups rich, unsalted chicken stock (see page 446 for making your own)

17 ounces quality, cream-style corn
about 1 teaspoon coarse kosher salt, to taste
1 tablespoon cornstarch dissolved in 2 tablespoons cold chicken stock

To garnish:
   a bit of freshly chopped coriander or scallion for each bowl

Preparing the crab:
If you are beginning with a whole, live crab, either plunge it into unsalted boiling water for 1 minute or steam it for 5 minutes, until it stops moving. Clean as described in TECHNIQUE NOTES on page 272, crack it, and extract all the meat. Pick over the meat carefully, then put aside ½ pound. If you are using frozen crab, defrost it, break it into coarse bits, and pick over carefully to remove shells and cartilage. The crab may be prepared up to a day in advance. Seal airtight, refrigerate, and bring to room temperature before cooking.

Making the soup:
About 10–15 minutes before serving, put individual soup bowls in a low oven to warm. Have all the ingredients within easy reach of your stovetop.

   Set a heavy, non-aluminum stockpot over high heat until hot enough to evaporate a bead of water. Add the oil to the pot, swirl to coat the bottom, then reduce the heat to medium-high. When the oil is hot enough to sizzle a bit of scallion, add the scallion and ginger, adjusting the heat so they sizzle without scorching. When fully fragrant, about 10–15 seconds, add the ham or crab. Stir briskly to combine, about 10 seconds, then add the wine. Wait a split second for it to "explode" in an aromatic hiss, then toss the meat briskly several times and immediately add the stock. Stir to blend, add the corn, and stir again. Bring the mixture to a near-boil over moderate heat. Stir frequently and watch that the heat does not climb too high, lest the corn burn.

   Reduce the heat to low, taste, and add salt as required. Stir the cornstarch mixture to recombine it, pour it evenly into the soup, and stir gently for about 1 minute until the mixture becomes glossy and slightly thick. Turn off the heat. Beat the egg whites lightly with a fork or chopsticks to break the gel. They will froth a bit, but do not beat to a foam. Add them to the soup in a thin, steady stream, pouring from a stationary spot about 6 inches above the pot. Stir gently once midway, then again after all the egg whites have been added, to bring the lacy threads to the surface.

   Serve at once, ladling the soup into the heated bowls and garnishing each with a sprinkling of coriander or chopped scallion. Or, cover the pot and keep the soup warm over the lowest possible heat. It will keep nicely this way for an hour, if you need to cook in advance.

   Leftovers keep well 4–5 days, refrigerated, and also survive freezing in remarkably good shape. Rewarm in a heavy pot over moderately low heat, stirring frequently.

MENU SUGGESTIONS:
This is the classic partner to elegant poultry dishes such as *Fragrant Crispy Duck* (page 172), *Cinnamon Bark Chicken* (page 162), *Smoked Tea Duck* (page 169), and *Birthday Duck* (page 175). It is also good with delicate fish and shellfish dishes like *Clear-Steamed Flounder with White Pepper* (page 250), and *Clear-Steamed Crab with Ginger* (page 274). For a simple, soup-centered meal, try it with *Steamed Buns with Chicken and Black Mushrooms* (page 425), *Pan-Fried Scallion Breads* (page 435), or *Flower Rolls* (page 415).

**Smoked
Chicken
Noodle
Soup**

燻雞湯

This is a simple soup for two, a happy invention occasioned by left-overs. It is colorful and flavorsome to be sure, but it is the sort of thing one eats with a good friend, when there is the wish to feel cozy and a bit of smoked chicken in the ice box. ◆ The base for the soup is the steaming juices from making *Tea and Spice Smoked Chicken* (page 158) and it is nice if you can save some of the chicken and its smoky skin and a spoonful of the jellied liquid left behind on the serving platter to add their luster to the pot. Everything else is easily obtained—something fresh and green (watercress or ribbons of fresh spinach), a hill of slivered carrots to contrast, strips of dried or fresh mushrooms on occasion (fresh *shiitake, enokitake* or *chanterelles* are all wonderful), and always a silvery heap of transparent bean threads.

TECHNIQUE NOTES:
Thin, quickly-cooked Chinese soups made of various fresh vegetables proceed in much the same way as a stir-fry. What is firmest and will take longest to cook goes into the pot first. Softer things follow. It is ideal to serve the soup when at least one item is still crisp.

Serves 2 cozily, 3 if you're sharing.

INGREDIENTS:

> *1 ounce bean threads (glass noodles) (page 533)*
> *1 bunch fresh watercress with lively, unblemished leaves*
> *1 small carrot, trimmed and peeled*
> *2 ounces interesting fresh mushrooms (shiitake, enokitake, or chanterelles, if available), or 4 medium Chinese dried black mushrooms*
> *2–3 ounces leftover Tea and Spice Smoked Chicken (page 158) or other good-tasting smoked chicken*
> *several thumb-size pieces smoked chicken skin*
> *¾ cup reserved steaming liquids from Tea and Spice Smoked Chicken*
> *1½ cups rich, unsalted chicken stock (see page 446 for making your own)*
> *coarse kosher salt and freshly ground pepper, or Roasted Szechwan Pepper-Salt (page 476) to taste*
> *2 teaspoons jellied juices reserved from the smoked chicken serving platter, or 1 teaspoon chicken fat from the steaming smoked chicken*

> *To garnish:*
> *1 tablespoon green and white scallion rings*

Preparations:
Cover the noodles with very hot or simmering water, and soak until soft and silky. The temperature and timing will vary with the noodles; use hotter water if they don't turn silken within 1 minute. Once soft, cut into manageable lengths if you have not already done so, drain, and set aside.

Cut the watercress above the band holding the bunch together and discard the lower stems. Sort through and pinch off any thick stems and wilted or discarded leaves. Pump gently in cool water to clean, drain, and shake off excess water. Blanch in unsalted boiling water to cover for 5 seconds, drain immediately, and rush under cold water to cool. Press gently to extract excess water and set aside.

Cut the carrot on the diagonal into thin coins ⅛ inch thick. Stack the coins, spread the stack like a row of steps, then shred the coins lengthwise into slivers ⅛ inch thin.

Prepare fresh mushrooms or dried mushrooms as described on page 455, but do not reserve the trimmings or soaking liquid.

Slice the smoked chicken against the grain into long slivers ⅛ inch thin.

Preparations may be done hours in advance. Seal the ingredients airtight, refrigerate, and bring to room temperature before using.

Making the soup:
About 10 minutes before serving, put individual soup bowls in a low oven to warm and fluff the watercress to loosen. Combine the reserved steaming liquids, the chicken stock, and the smoked chicken skin in a large, non-aluminum saucepan, and bring to a boil over medium-high heat. Reduce the heat to maintain a steady simmer, then add the carrots and mushrooms. Cover and simmer for about 2 minutes, or until the carrots are tender-crisp. Add the noodles and simmer for 30 seconds more. Turn the heat to low, taste the soup, then adjust with salt and pepper or *Roasted Szechwan Pepper-Salt* to taste. Discard the chicken skin, then add the shredded chicken, and stir to heat it through. Add the jellied juices or the chicken fat, and stir until combined.

Divide the watercress among the bowls and ladle the soup on top, using chopsticks or tongs to portion the noodles between them. Garnish with scallion rings and perhaps a last flourish of pepper.

This is already a soup of leftovers, and it should not be left over.

MENU SUGGESTIONS:
I am partial to this soup in a very simple setting, with *Pan-Fried Scallion Breads* (page 435), or *Flower Rolls* (page 415), served alongside. As part of a larger meal, the mood should still be simple, with the soup to accompany something like *Hakka Stuffed Tofu* (page 343), or *Clear-Steamed Flounder with White Pepper* (page 250).

Peppery Soup Noodles with Shrimp Balls 蝦球湯麵

Soup noodles are the great wayfarer's snack and street food of China—a meal in a bowl, combining the slippery fun of noodles and the warm nourishment of soup. Travelers record the soup noodles they had in this or that province, students nearly always live on soup noodles from a favorite stall, and my favorite Chinese detective hero, Judge Dee, almost never solves a murder without downing a bowl of soup noodles somewhere along the way. (Judge Dee, a famous Tang dynasty magistrate, was immortalized in English by Robert van Gulik. There are more than a dozen Judge Dee thrillers in print, all of them positively addictive.) ◆ Here in the province of California, where there are few noodle stalls on the streets, I bring soup noodles to the dinner table. They make a wonderful one-bowl meal. This version, with shrimp balls, greens, egg noodles, and a rich broth afloat with ham, carrots, and pepper, is one I particularly enjoy. ◆ Preparation may be started a day in advance. Final preparations and cooking take less than an hour.

TECHNIQUE NOTES:
Deep-frying and then steaming the shrimp balls comprises one of the plays on texture for which Chinese cooking is best known. Frying turns the shrimp balls golden and sets the skin with an interesting texture. Steaming cooks them through and makes the middle very tender and juicy, at the same time enriching a liquid that will be added to the stock.

Serves 4 as a hearty, one-bowl meal, or 6–8 as a less majestic bowlful.

INGREDIENTS:

> 1 recipe shrimp paste (page 244)
> ½ pound fresh or frozen Chinese egg noodles, ¹⁄₁₆ inch thin (see page 351 for
>   substitutes, or page 354 for making your own)
> 2 teaspoons Chinese or Japanese sesame oil
> 1½ teaspoons coarse kosher salt
> 2 cups fresh, washed greens (choose one):
>   miniature green Chinese cabbages (page 537), cut crosswise into bands ½
>   inch thick
>   small snow peas, strings removed
>   slender string beans or Chinese longbeans, cut into 2-inch lengths
>   tiny broccoli flowerets and/or peeled and slivered broccoli stems
>   unblemished spinach leaves, cut crosswise into 1-inch bands, or tender
>   sprigs of fresh watercress
> 4–6 cups corn or peanut oil, for deep-frying
> 6 cups rich, unsalted chicken stock (see page 446 for making your own)
> 1½ tablespoons thin (regular) soy sauce
> 2 tablespoons Chinese rice wine or quality, dry sherry
> ¼ cup finely shredded Smithfield ham
> ¼ cup julienned fresh carrots
> Roasted Szechwan Pepper-Salt (page 476), or coarse kosher salt and freshly
>   ground white pepper to taste

Preparations:
Prepare the shrimp purée as described on page 244. If you are working in advance, seal airtight with a piece of plastic film pressed directly on the surface and refrigerate until use, overnight if desired. Bring to room temperature before frying.

Cook, drain, and water-chill the noodles as described on page 356. They will simmer an additional 2 minutes in the soup, so drain them when they are still a trifle underdone. Shake off excess water and toss gently with 2 teaspoons sesame oil and 1½ teaspoons kosher salt, using your hands to coat and separate each strand. Oiled, the noodles may be bagged airtight and refrigerated 1–2 days. Bring to room temperature before using.

Blanch the greens in plain boiling water to cover until deep green and tender-crisp. Probable times are snow peas 10 seconds, string beans 20 seconds, longbeans 30 seconds and broccoli 15–20 seconds. Test to be sure. Miniature cabbages, spinach, and watercress should be blanched only 5 seconds. When done, drain promptly and plunge immediately under cold water to stop the cooking. Lightly pat the firmer vegetables dry. Gently press the spinach and watercress between your palms to extract excess moisture. If you are working more than several hours in advance, set the vegetables aside on a plate, seal airtight, and refrigerate, overnight if desired. Bring to room temperature and drain off any liquids before using.

Deep-frying and steaming the shrimp balls:
(For details on steaming and how to improvise a steamer, see page 60.)

About an hour before serving, shape, deep-fry and drain the shrimp balls as described on page 240. However, remove the shrimp balls from the oil when they are only *lightly* golden, about 1½ minutes. Frying gives color and texture and will not cook them through.

Once drained, transfer the shrimp balls in one layer to a Pyrex pie plate or heat-proof quiche plate at least 1 inch smaller in diameter than your steamer. Combine the stock with the soy and wine, then add enough to the plate to come ⅓ of the way up the shrimp balls. If your steamer is not big enough to hold the single plate, then steam the shrimp balls on two tiers or in two batches, and divide the stock mixture in half.

Bring the water for steaming to a gushing boil over high heat, put the shrimp balls in place, and reduce the heat to medium-high to maintain a strong, steady steam. Cover, and steam the shrimp balls for 15 minutes. Remove them carefully from the steamer, if you like first siphoning off the juices with a bulb-top baster. Do not lose a drop.

Simmering the soup noodles and assembling the soup:
While the shrimp balls steam, put 4 large soup bowls or 6–8 rice bowls in a low oven to warm. Put the remaining stock in a non-aluminum pot large enough to accommodate the noodles and steaming juices. Cover the pot and set the heat to low.

When the shrimp balls are done, add the steaming juices to the stockpot and stir to blend. Bring the liquids to a simmer, then add the noodles, carrots, and ham. Poke the noodles under the liquid, stir gently to mix, then adjust the heat to maintain a gentle simmer. Cover the pot and simmer for 2 minutes. While the soup is simmering, divide the shrimp balls and greens among the bowls, clustering them to one side to leave room for the noodles and fluffing the spinach or watercress to loosen.

As soon as the 2 minutes are up, remove the pot from the heat. Taste the stock and adjust with pepper-salt or kosher salt and freshly ground pepper to taste. Using chopsticks or tongs, portion the noodles among the bowls, nesting them in the empty corner between the shrimp balls and the greens. Then pour the soup gently on top.

Serve at once. This is an "eating soup," and chopsticks and small Chinese ladles (or soup spoons if you like) are the traditional utensils with which to retrieve the goods and sip from the bowl.

Leftovers may be resteamed in a covered bowl until hot, but this soup is best freshly made.

MENU SUGGESTIONS:
I typically present this soup as a one-bowl meal, with nothing else added. If your appetite is bigger or the menu needs filling, try *Springrolls with Dijon Mustard Sauce* (page 389). For serving as a lesser soup in a larger meal, plan a *dim sum* assortment—*Shao-Mai Dumplings* (page 375), *Steamed Buns with Chicken and Black Mushrooms* (page 425), plus a trio of contrasting "Little Dishes" (pages 103 to 121).

Honeycomb Tofu Soup 燉豆腐湯	For special show-off dinners, the elderly but always playful head of our Chinese household, Po-fu, would make this soup. It was the traditional ploy of the Chinese gourmet, starring something thoroughly unpretentious and inexpensive as a contrast to an otherwise lavish meal. Other cooks might have bought shark's fins or busied themselves carving a winter melon. Po-fu cooked tofu. ◆ Underneath its apparent simplicity, this is a very special soup. The tofu is sim-

mered lengthily to transform its texture into a meaty honeycomb, and the chicken is likewise marinated for hours to turn it velvety and plush. A rich homemade stock is a must, for without it the tofu tastes bland. ◆ Preparations may be completed a day in advance, then the soup heated and served within minutes.

TECHNIQUE NOTES:
Simmering solid tofu produces a change in the protein structure, whereby its water content is driven out and the proteins form a lacy network that makes the tofu look like a sponge. The texture is soft and appealingly chewy, and the honeycomb sops up other flavors readily. It is not at all like frozen tofu, which is tough by comparison.

Serves 4 as a substantial bowlful, 6–8 as a rice bowl-size portion in a multicourse meal.

INGREDIENTS:

> 3 cakes (¾ pound) fresh white tofu, a medium-firm Chinese variety best (see page 575 for details on types of tofu)
> 9 cups rich, unsalted chicken stock (see page 446 for making your own)
> ½ pound skinless and boneless fresh chicken breast (weight after removal of cartilage, membranes, and tendons)

> To marinate the chicken:
> 1 tablespoon egg white
> 1 teaspoon coarse kosher salt
> 1 tablespoon Chinese rice wine or quality, dry sherry
> 1½ teaspoons cornstarch
>
> ½ pound unblemished fresh spinach leaves without stems
> ¼ cup finely slivered Smithfield ham
> Roasted Szechwan Pepper-Salt (page 476) or coarse kosher salt, to taste

Cooking the tofu to a honeycomb:
Put the tofu in a heavy saucepan. Add cold water to cover and bring to a boil over high heat. Reduce the heat to maintain a lively simmer, cover the pot, and simmer the tofu for 10 minutes. While it is simmering, bring the chicken stock to a lively simmer in a heavy, non-aluminum saucepan or stockpot that will permit the tofu to tumble freely about.

After 10 minutes, remove the tofu carefully with a Chinese mesh spoon or a large metal sieve to cradle it gently without breaking it. Rinse briefly with cool water to remove any scum, then transfer it to the simmering stock. Cover and simmer for 1 hour, checking periodically to insure a lively simmer and to turn the tofu over gently.

Hold the tofu above the stock to drain, and spread the cakes on a large plate. Let cool for several minutes, then neatly cut off the outer skin if it is tough. (This will differ depending on the tofu.) Slice each cake crosswise into rectangular slices ¼ inch thick, then cut the slices crosswise into rectangles about 1 inch long.

Strain the stock through wet cheesecloth to remove any impurities. If you are working in advance, refrigerate the stock and tofu separately, spreading the tofu in a single layer on a plate, sealed airtight. Otherwise, return the stock and tofu to the pot, and cover.

Other preparations:
While the tofu is simmering or before, complete the remaining preparations.

Holding your knife parallel to the board, cut the chicken into slices about ¼ inch thick. With the broad side of a cleaver, spank the slices to make them evenly about ⅛ inch thin, then shred the meat crosswise against the grain into slivers about ⅛ inch wide. Cut long slivers into 1½-inch lengths. Stir the marinade ingredients briskly until smooth, scrape over the chicken, then toss with your fingers to coat each shred. Seal airtight, and refrigerate 30 minutes to 24 hours. The longer the chicken marinates, the plumper and tastier it will be.

Tear large spinach leaves into coarse pieces. Leave small leaves whole. Pump gently in cool water to clean, then shake off excess water. Blanch in plain boiling water to cover for 5 seconds, drain promptly, and rush under cold water until cool. Press gently to extract excess water. If you are working in advance, spread the leaves on a plate, seal airtight, and refrigerate. Bring to room temperature before using.

Making the soup:
Have all the ingredients within easy reach of your stovetop. Put individual soup bowls in a low oven to warm.

Combine the tofu, ham, and chicken stock in a non-aluminum stockpot, cover, and bring to a lively simmer over moderately high heat. Reduce the heat to maintain a slow, steady simmer, stir the chicken with your fingers, and gently slide it into the pot. Swish several times to separate the shreds, then turn off the heat. Taste the soup, and adjust with pepper-salt or salt if required. Add the spinach and stir once or twice to disperse the leaves.

Serve immediately.

Leftovers keep nicely and may be rewarmed in a covered pot over moderate heat.

MENU SUGGESTIONS:
This soup mates nicely with classic dishes like *Golden Egg Dumplings* (page 328) and *Steamed Whole Fish with Seared Scallions* (page 248). As the focus of a light meal, pair it with *Baked Stuffed Buns* (page 432), *Shao-Mai Dumplings* (page 375), or *Pan-Fried Scallion Breads* (page 435).

Sauces, Seasonings, & Oils

調味品

◆

◆

T his is a small chapter, devoted to the jars, bottles, and bowlfuls of aromatic and saucy stuff that fill my refrigerator and cupboard and populate the countertop when cooking gets underway. They are the "enhancers" of a Chinese dish, the spirit if not the soul, and every bit as important to the flavor of *real* Chinese cooking as salt, pepper, and olive oil is to the seasoning of Western foods. Just as most Americans require a bottle of ketchup and mustard in the kitchen, northern Chinese need their sesame sauces, Cantonese need their mustard sauces, and Szechwanese feel life to be painfully dull without a good, spicy peanut sauce close at hand. For the most part, they are simple concoctions, which one variously sprinkles, dabs, dribbles, or spreads over food. Yet they are the signature marks of real Chinese cuisine, without which an otherwise authentic and well-prepared dish tastes "nude." For me, to send a plate of deep-fried shrimp balls to the table without a dip dish of *Roasted Szechwan Pepper-Salt* is like serving an undressed salad at the end of a Western meal. It's unfinished, incomplete, and downright depressing.

All the care we associate with the making of hot sauces in the West, in China goes into the making of cold sauces, seasoned oils, and sweet and sour sauce (the latter being the single stock sauce that is used hot). The trickery is not a matter of technique so much as ingredients, with each restaurant or gourmand's household guarding their ingredient lists jealously. My ingredient list is public; please note the brands specified in the glossary. If you are using different brands, expect that you will need to adjust the final blends carefully to achieve a proper balance. Sauces require fine tuning, and what you want is a vibrant orchestration of tastes—a mixing of sweet and sour, tart and spicy, smooth and zesty in every spoonful. If a Chinese sauce tastes of only one thing, it is not a good Chinese sauce.

While an average Chinese home cook would mix a cold sauce or roast some pepper-salt close to the time of making a dish, I've adopted the restaurant custom of making these staples in quantity and having them on hand when I need them. It's a real time-saver and the nut and mustard sauces, in particular, get better as they sit. For some of the other items—the pepper-salt and the oils—the appropriate care must be taken so that they store without spoiling or fading, usually nothing more complicated than an airtight bottle and a cool cupboard.

Their Chinese uses aside, these sauces, spices, and oils are wonderfully versatile. I have yet to meet an omelet that wasn't happy for a sprinkling of *Roasted Szechwan Pepper-Salt* or a grilled fish that would wince when eaten with a dab of *Coriandered Dijon Mustard Sauce* or *Spicy Szechwan Peanut Sauce*. Similarly, a raw carrot is better for a dunking in a Chinese sesame sauce, and a salad of simple greens is delicious dressed with *Five-Flavor Oil* and a bit of good rice vinegar. For a creative cook, here then is a small shelf-full of treasures.

Orchid's Spicy Sesame Sauce

寶蘭芝麻醬

Sesame sauces of varying degrees of sweetness and spiciness are a prominent feature of northern, and to a lesser extent, central Chinese cooking. The base is always the dark brown and keenly aromatic paste ground from toasted sesame seeds. As to the spicing, garlic, scallion, ginger, vinegar, and sweeteners are all used in sesame sauces to give each its special taste. ◆ This blend is my favorite, a sleeping tiger—a sauce that is sweet to begin and spicy on the way down, mellowed by the addition of honey and sparked by fresh coriander, garlic, and hot chili oil. Apart from its Chinese uses, it is excellent to have on hand when some cold chicken, grilled fish, or sliced roast beef needs dressing.

TECHNIQUE NOTES:

The magic transformation of a cold Chinese sauce from a group of ingredients to a *blend* of tastes happens not in the mixing but in the resting that follows. After everything is whirled together and beaten up, the sugar needs time to dissolve, the chili needs time to bloom, and the garlic and coriander require an hour or so to infiltrate every corner of the mixture. It is like a group of strangers at a party who need time to get things going. Remember in particular that chili is the shy guy—the one who requires time to come forth—and begin with the smaller amount if you are hesitant.

Yields ⅔ cup.

INGREDIENTS:

> 3 large cloves garlic, stem end removed, lightly smashed and peeled
> 2 tablespoons chopped fresh coriander leaves and upper stems
> 3 tablespoons Chinese sesame paste, drained of oil (page 565)
> 1 tablespoon Chinese or Japanese sesame oil
> 2 tablespoons plus 2 teaspoons thin (regular) soy sauce
> 1 tablespoon plus 1 teaspoon Chinese rice wine or quality, dry sherry
> 2 teaspoons unseasoned Chinese or Japanese rice vinegar
> 1 tablespoon plus 1 teaspoon wild-flower honey
> ¾–1 teaspoon hot chili oil
> about ⅛ teaspoon Roasted Szechwan Pepper-Salt (page 476), to taste

Mince the garlic and coriander until fine in the work bowl of a food processor fitted with the steel knife. Add the remaining ingredients and process until thoroughly homogenized, about 1 minute, scraping down the bowl once or twice.

If you do not have a food processor, mince the garlic and coriander finely, then combine with the remaining ingredients in a blender or whisk by hand until thoroughly thick and smooth.

For best flavor, set aside to develop at room temperature several hours or overnight, sealed airtight. Use at room temperature for full flavor and aroma.

Store the sauce in a clean, airtight bottle in the refrigerator, where it will keep indefinitely. Reblend before using and add a bit of water if the sauce thickens beyond the point where it falls in smooth ribbons from a spoon.

USED IN:

Ma-La Cold Chicken (page 129), *Bong-Bong Chicken* (page 133), *Chinese Crudités* (page 284), *Shantung Cold Eggplant with Sesame Sauce* (page 291), and *Cold-Tossed Three Shreds* (page 303).

Sweet and Silky Sesame Sauce

蜂蜜芝麻醬

This is an especially versatile sauce—a silky, rich sesame blend without the stamp of garlic or coriander. It is more northern and less Szechwanese than the preceding sauce, with a more pronounced sweetness and a more subtle spiciness. ♦ This is the one to choose for foods or people that would be overwhelmed by a hotter blend.

TECHNIQUE NOTES:

For letting the flavors of a cold Chinese sauce come to fullness, see TECHNIQUE NOTES, above.

Yields ½ cup.

INGREDIENTS:

> 2½ tablespoons Chinese sesame paste, drained of oil (page 565)
> 1 tablespoon plus 1 teaspoon Chinese or Japanese sesame oil
> 1 tablespoon thin (regular) soy sauce
> 1 tablespoon black soy sauce
> 1 tablespoon plus 1 teaspoon wild-flower honey
> 1 teaspoon hoisin sauce
> ¾–1 teaspoon hot chili oil
> about 2 teaspoons warm water, as required for a ribbony consistency

Add all the ingredients except the water to the work bowl of a food processor fitted with the steel knife. Process until completely smooth and emulsified, scraping down as necessary. Gradually add water as required to obtain a silky sauce that will fall in overlapping ribbons from a spatula, processing to blend.

Alternatively, mix the ingredients in a blender, or by hand until smooth and well blended.

For best flavor, put aside for several hours at room temperature or refrigerate overnight in a clean, airtight jar. Use at room temperature for full flavor and aroma.

Sealed and refrigerated, the sauce keeps indefinitely. If it thickens, blend with additional water as required.

USED IN:
Ma-La Cold Chicken (page 129), *Bong-Bong Chicken* (page 133), *Cold Duck Salad with Two Sauces* (page 164), *Chinese Crudités* (page 284), and *Cold-Tossed Three Shreds* (page 303).

> **Spicy Szechwan Peanut Sauce**
> 四川花生醬

This is a classic Szechwanese peanut sauce. The texture is thin, the flavor nutty and garlicky, and the bite mild to ferocious, depending on how much hot chili oil you use. It is splendid with noodles, cold poultry and cold vegetables, and in the Western realm with most anything you might put on a grill. Try it with French fries, it's delicious! ◆ To make a good peanut sauce, you need a first-rate peanut butter. If I am not making my own, I use only "pure" peanut butter made from roasted peanuts with no seasonings added, ideally with the red skin ground in for color and extra bite. Walnut Acres and Arrowhead Mills' Deaf Smith are two excellent brands.

TECHNIQUE NOTES:
For the blossoming power of cold Chinese sauces, see TECHNIQUE NOTES, page 472.

Yields 1½ cups.

INGREDIENTS:

> about 10 large cloves garlic, stem end removed, lightly smashed and peeled
> about ⅔ bunch fresh coriander leaves and upper stems
> ½ cup unseasoned peanut butter (for making your own, Chinese-style, see
>   page 474)

½ cup plus 1 tablespoon thin (regular) soy sauce (read the cautionary note
regarding brands on page 568)
5 tablespoons sugar
½ teaspoon Chinese rice wine or quality, dry sherry
1–2 tablespoons hot chili oil

Mince the garlic and coriander separately in the work bowl of a food processor fitted with the steel knife, scraping down as needed until fine. Measure to obtain 2 packed tablespoons garlic and 3 packed tablespoons coriander. Return the measured garlic and coriander to the work bowl, add the remaining ingredients, and process 1 minute until homogenized, pausing once or twice to scrape down the bowl.

Alternatively, mince the garlic and coriander finely by hand, pack in tablespoons to measure, then blend with the remaining ingredients until smooth and well combined, in a blender or by hand.

Seal the sauce airtight and set it aside at room temperature for 1 hour or overnight in the refrigerator to give the flavors a chance to develop. The chili taste will enlarge during this time, so go easy at the start if you are at all hesitant. You can always add more. Bring to room temperature before using, and stir briskly or reprocess to mix.

Store the sauce in a clean, airtight jar in the refrigerator. It keeps indefinitely.

USED IN:
Bong-Bong Chicken (page 133), *Chinese Crudités* (page 284), *Cold-Tossed Three Shreds* (page 303), and *Don-Don Noodles* (page 360).

**Chinese-
Style
Peanut
Butter**

中式花生醬

While Western cooks are accustomed to roasting nuts, Chinese cooks typically fry them. It is quick and easy, and the nuts are never dry. In a peanut butter, the fried nuts contribute an inimitable taste. ◆ Use peanuts still in their red jackets. The butter will have a slight, wonderful spice of bitterness and will require no further seasoning. This flavorful "bitterness" is the quality of *ku*, one of the hallowed Five Flavors of classic Chinese cuisine.

TECHNIQUE NOTES:
For shallow-frying nuts, see TECHNIQUE NOTES, page 107.

Yields a rounded ½ cup.

INGREDIENTS:

1 cup raw, unblemished red-skinned peanuts
3 cups fresh corn or peanut oil, or oil for frying nuts (page 84)

Frying the nuts:
Have a large Chinese mesh spoon and a large plate alongside your stovetop.

Heat a wok or heavy skillet over moderate heat until hot. Add the oil, then heat to the slow-fry stage, 275° on a deep-fry thermometer, when the oil is swirling actively but still relatively warm. Lower the heat or turn it off so the temperature does not climb.

Add the nuts to the oil. They will barely bubble. Fry 5–7 minutes, stirring occasionally, until the nuts turn pale gold, adjusting the heat so they fry at a constant temperature. Scoop the nuts from the oil with the spoon and transfer them without draining to the plate. The extra oil clinging to the nuts will be used in blending the butter.

Let the nuts cool 5 minutes. Once the oil cools, strain and bottle it for future frying.

Grinding the peanut butter:
Scrape the nuts and excess oil on the plate into the work bowl of a food processor fitted with the steel knife. Run the machine for 1 minute. Scrape down the bowl, then process for an additional minute. For a creamier texture, continue processing for 15–30 seconds more.

Refrigerate the peanut butter in a clean, airtight jar. It will keep 2 weeks or longer.

USED IN:
Spicy Szechwan Peanut Sauce (page 473).

I loathe most Chinese mustard sauces, with their raw, strong bite. The culprit is dry mustard, which is almost always harsh and bitter. Here instead is a smooth and tingly East-meets-West mustard sauce, flavored by sesame oil and Dijon mustard. It is a superb garnish for an endless variety of foods, from hot Chinese meatballs to Jewish corned-beef-on-rye. ◆ I use Maille brand unflavored Dijon mustard, which has a full rich taste that is neither spicy nor vinegary. You may need to go to a specialty store to find it, but the taste is well worth the trip. Do not use the more widely available Grey Poupon, or any of the extra-strong imported blends. They will not work well in this recipe.

TECHNIQUE NOTES:
Sea salt works perfectly in this East-West blend. Its flavor accentuates the character of the mustard in a way that kosher salt does not. It is a fine point, but if you have it on hand then try it.

Yields 1 cup.

INGREDIENTS:

> *½ cup mild, unflavored Dijon mustard—Maille, Dessaux, and Amora brands*
>   *recommended, in that order*
> *½ cup Chinese or Japanese sesame oil*
> *2 tablespoons unseasoned Chinese or Japanese rice vinegar*
> *1 tablespoon plus 1 teaspoon Chinese rice wine or quality, dry sherry*
> *fine sea salt, to taste*

Blend the ingredients until thoroughly emulsified, in the work bowl of a food processor fitted with the steel knife, in a blender, or by hand. Taste and adjust with salt. Let mellow several hours at room temperature or refrigerate overnight in a clean, airtight jar. Use at room temperature for best taste and bouquet.

Store airtight in the refrigerator. The sauce will keep indefinitely. For best consistency, whisk or return briefly to the processor or blender before each use.

USED IN:
Ma-La Cold Chicken (page 129), *Coriandered Chicken Salad with Mustard Sauce* (page

131), *Cold Duck Salad with Two Sauces* (page 164), *Crispy Pork Balls* (page 185), *Shrimp Rolls with Crisp Seaweed* (page 241), *Chinese Crudités* (page 284), *Springrolls with Dijon Mustard Sauce* (page 389), and *Baked Stuffed Buns* (page 432).

Coriandered Mustard Sauce

香菜芥末醬

This is a "flavored" mustard, made simply by adding finely chopped fresh coriander to *Dijon Mustard Sauce.* It would hardly seem mentionable as a separate sauce, except that with the addition of coriander the mustard sauce has a striking affinity to fish and shell-fish. I therefore keep both blends on hand, the plain and the fla-vored. ◆ A curious feature of this sauce is that it tastes perfectly all right to people who otherwise cannot tolerate the flavor or smell of fresh coriander. I do not know why this is so, but note it as a curiosity.

TECHNIQUE NOTES:
For letting cold sauces made with coriander develop, see TECHNIQUE NOTES, page 472.

Yields 1 rounded cup.

INGREDIENTS:

> 1 cup Dijon Mustard Sauce (page 475)
> ¼–⅓ cup coarsely chopped fresh coriander leaves and upper stems

Put the mustard sauce and coriander in the work bowl of a food processor fitted with the steel knife and process until the coriander is fine, scraping down as needed. Alternatively, mince the coriander finely by hand, and whisk thoroughly to blend.
Put the sauce aside to develop, store it, and use it like the unflavored sauce. It too will keep indefinitely.

USED IN:
Crispy Pork Balls (page 185), *Spicy Shrimp Fritters* (page 237), *Deep-Fried Shrimp Balls* (page 240), *Shrimp Rolls with Crisp Seaweed* (page 241), cold *Tea and Spice Smoked Fish* (page 256), *Chinese Crudités* (page 284), and *Baked Stuffed Buns* (page 432).

Roasted Szechwan Pepper-Salt

花椒鹽

This is the salt and pepper of China, and how much more interesting than our own! The salt acquires a depth of flavor during roasting that mates beautifully with the numbing tingle of the fragrant flower pep-per. Visually, it is like the prettiest of sand beaches, a study of pale browns, golds, and off-whites. Its Chinese use is primarily as a dip-ping salt to cut the rich oiliness of deep-fried foods. In a Western kitchen, use it as a subtle all-purpose seasoning—for omelettes, roasts, vegetables, salads, or your own deep-fried specialties. ◆ Chinese favor a high ratio of salt in the mixture. I cut it back to let the pepper come through. For extra dimen-sion and punch, you may add some fruity black peppercorns (Tellicherry recommended) to the mix.

TECHNIQUE NOTES:
Avoid roasting the salt in a wok or pan with a prized patina. The salt will absorb the oil.

Instead, use a dry, medium or heavy skillet. Also, do not use sea salt or regular table salt in this mixture, even in reduced proportions. It has an acrid, strident taste here, which overwhelms the peppercorns.

Yields ½ cup.

INGREDIENTS:

> *¼ cup Szechwan brown peppercorns (page 571)*
> *½ cup coarse kosher salt*
> *½ teaspoon whole black peppercorns (optional)*

Combine the salt and peppercorns in a dry, heavy skillet. Stir over moderate heat until the salt turns off-white and the peppercorns are fragrant, about 5 minutes. The peppercorns will smoke. Do not let them scorch.

Scrape the hot mixture into the work bowl of a food processor fitted with the steel knife, then process for 1 minute until fine. Alternatively, pound to a fine consistency with a mortar and pestle.

Strain the mixture through a fine sieve to remove the peppercorn husks, then store in an airtight bottle, away from light, heat, and moisture.

Use sparingly. A mere pinch or sprinkle is the right approach, as the mixture is very pungent.

Sprinkle foods with pepper-salt before serving them, and/or serve the mixture in tiny dip dishes alongside each place setting or in a dip dish nestled on the serving platter.

The pepper-salt remains good so long as it is keenly aromatic, several months if you store it correctly.

USED IN:
Walnut Chicken Slices (page 148), *Cinnamon Bark Chicken* (page 162), *Fragrant Crispy Duck* (page 172), *Phoenix Tail Shrimp* (page 235), *Spicy Shrimp Fritters* (page 237), *Deep-Fried Shrimp Balls* (page 240), *Shrimp Rolls with Crisp Seaweed* (page 241), and *Steamed Corn with Szechwan Pepper-Salt* (page 318) as a dipping salt, and in numerous other dishes as a seasoning.

Garlic-Soy Dip 蒜頭醬油	This is a simple, sprightly dressing that gives a flavorful nudge to understated foods. ◆ It mates particularly well with steamed pork, and with a whole variety of pork-filled dumplings, meatballs, and buns. ◆ Like all Chinese vinegar-soy dips, this should be mixed soon before eating and used sparingly.

TECHNIQUE NOTES:
Even in this small amount, the garlic must be very firm and fresh. Discard any green at the core of the clove, and when you chop the garlic, leave it a bit nubbly for your tongue.

Enough to dress about 25 dumplings or meatballs. For buns, make a single recipe for every 5 buns served.

INGREDIENTS:

> *1½ tablespoons thin (regular) soy sauce*
> *1 scant tablespoon white vinegar*
> *¼ teaspoon Chinese or Japanese sesame oil*
> *pinch sugar*
> *1 teaspoon finely chopped fresh garlic*

Mix the liquid ingredients and the sugar. Add the garlic and stir to blend. Let stand 5–10 minutes before using to give the garlic time to permeate the soy.

Dribble ⅛ teaspoon over individual dumplings or meatballs. For serving in a shallow dip dish, garnish with a few green scallion rings. Use sparingly.

Make fresh each time.

USED IN:
Pearl Balls (page 187), *Shao-Mai Dumplings* (page 375), *Moslem-Style Beef or Lamb Pot Stickers* (page 384), *Steamed Buns with Minced Pork and Tree Ears* (page 429), and *Baked Stuffed Buns* (page 432).

Sweet and Sour Dipping Sauce
甜酸醬

I was sorely tempted to call this *Un-Sweet and Sour Dipping Sauce*, to separate it from the candy-like concoctions that prevail in every bad Chinese restaurant. The base is the classic mix of sugar and vinegar, but an initial infusion of garlic and ginger in the oil dampens the sweetness and enlarges the tang, and also dots the sauce with bits of gold and white. Light in taste, it is also light in consistency. There is just enough cornstarch to bind it, no more. ◆ This is a refreshing, "cooling" dip for any number of hors d'oeuvre-type foods, from tiny meatballs to deep-fried slices of fish. It is easily made within minutes, and will keep nicely on the stove until it is needed. You may also make it days in advance.

TECHNIQUE NOTES:
Sautéing the aromatics in heated oil, before adding the sauce liquids, cooks the aromatics and infuses the oil, resulting in a substantially more fulsome "mellow" sauce than if you were to plunk them in raw.

Yields about ½ cup, enough for dipping 25–30 pieces of food.

INGREDIENTS:

> *Liquid Seasonings:*
> *1½ tablespoons unseasoned Chinese or Japanese rice vinegar*
> *2 tablespoons sugar*
> *1 tablespoon quality ketchup*
> *1 teaspoon thin (regular) soy sauce*
> *¼ cup water*
>
> *1 tablespoon corn or peanut oil*
> *1½ teaspoons finely minced fresh garlic*

1 teaspoon finely minced fresh ginger
1 teaspoon cornstarch dissolved in 1 tablespoon cold water

Combine the liquid seasonings, stirring well to dissolve the sugar. Put them and the remaining ingredients within easy reach of your stovetop.

Heat a small, heavy saucepan over high heat until hot. Add the oil, and swirl to glaze the bottom of the pot. When the oil is hot enough to sizzle one bit of garlic, add the garlic and ginger and stir gently until fragrant, 10–15 seconds, adjusting the heat so they sizzle gently without browning. Add the combined liquids, stir to blend, then raise the heat to bring the mixture to a bubbly simmer, stirring. Reduce the heat to medium-low, stir the cornstarch mixture to recombine it, and add it to the pan. Stir until the mixture thickens and becomes glossy, about 20 seconds. Turn off the heat and cover the pot to keep the sauce warm.

The sauce may remain in the pot until you are ready to serve it. If it cools, reheat over a low heat, stirring.

The sauce may be made up to several days in advance. Let it come to room temperature, seal airtight, and refrigerate. Reheat as above before serving.

USED IN:
Crispy Pork Balls (page 185), *Phoenix Tail Shrimp* (page 235), *Sesame Fish Slices* (page 246), and *Sesame Scallop Balls* (page 267).

Homemade Hot Chili Oil 紅辣油

Vegetable oil infused with the color and fire of hot red chili peppers is a staple seasoning throughout north and central China. It is used mainly in cold dishes or as part of a dipping sauce for dumplings or springrolls, but occasionally is sprinkled on top of a stir-fry as it exits from the wok. Some people I know insist on carrying a bottle of chili oil with them most everywhere they go and putting it on most everything they eat, but I am more of a spice-loving moderate. "A little dab 'll do you," as they used to say in the Bryl-Creem commercials, and that's my cautionary word on hot chili oil. ◆ When quality sesame-based hot chili oil (page 536) is unavailable, or when the price you need to pay for it is painful, here is an easy way to make your own. The process takes only minutes, and the only equipment required is a small heavy pot, a mesh strainer, and a square of cheesecloth. The result is a beautifully bronze and fiery oil, with a scent of sesame and the ability to enliven a wide variety of foods. ◆ Please note that this is *not* a cooking oil. It is a seasoning oil, meant to be used sparingly. Once made, it will keep indefinitely in a cool place without paling in either color or flavor.

TECHNIQUE NOTES:
For infusing aromatic seasonings in oil, see TECHNIQUE NOTES, page 480.

Yields 1 cup.

INGREDIENTS:

⅓ cup Chinese or Japanese sesame oil
⅔ cup fresh corn or peanut oil
1 tablespoon dried red chili flakes

Infusing the oil:
Combine the sesame oil and corn or peanut oil in a small, heavy saucepan. Heat over medium heat for several minutes, until several chili flakes foam instantly without blackening when added to the oil. When the test flakes foam, add the tablespoon of chili flakes to the oil, remove the pot from the heat, and cover the pot.

If the test flakes blacken, turn off the heat and let the oil cool somewhat. Test with a few more flakes until the oil temperature is low enough for them to foam without burning, then proceed as above to add the flakes and cover the pot. Burned flakes produce bitter oil.

Let the oil sit overnight or until cool.

Straining and storing the oil:
Strain the oil through a mesh strainer lined with dry cheesecloth to extract the flakes.

Store in a clean glass jar, away from light and heat. A cool, dark cupboard is best. If you must refrigerate the oil, allow it to come to room temperature before using. Stored properly, the oil will keep indefinitely.

USED IN:
Numerous recipes throughout this book.

Five-Flavor Oil

五味油

Seasoning oils—oils infused with aromatics and oils pressed from the fragrant, toasted sesame seed—have traditionally played a large part in refined Chinese cuisine. Caring cooks have always made chili oil, ginger oil, fagara oil (infused with Szechwan brown peppercorns), and even orange peel oil in the pursuit of aroma and a special subtlety of taste. ◆ This is an oil that combines five fragrances—scallion, ginger, Szechwan peppercorn, chili, and sesame—in an amber-auburn blend. The depth of color and spice will depend on the amount of chili you use. ◆ Very versatile, it is a superb dressing for cold noodles, dumplings, cold meat and vegetable salads, or a lunchtime bowl of crisp, tossed greens. You may combine it freely with rice vinegar or Western wine vinegar, and with soy sauce, salt, or *Roasted Szechwan Pepper-Salt* (page 476). ◆ Note that this is *not* a cooking oil. The delicacy of flavor would be ruined by reheating, though you may use it freshly made and warm.

TECHNIQUE NOTES:
For a successful infusion, the oil must be hot enough to extract the flavor and color of the seasonings, yet not so hot as to cause them to burn. To safeguard against burning, use a heavy pot and heat a single bit or two of chili along with the oil, so you can see precisely the moment at which it will sizzle without blackening.

Yields 1 cup.

INGREDIENTS:

> *1 hefty or 2 medium whole scallions, cut into 1½-inch lengths*
> *7 quarter-size slices fresh ginger*
> *1 teaspoon dried red chili flakes*
> *2 teaspoons Szechwan brown peppercorns*
> *¾ cup corn or peanut oil*
> *¼ cup Chinese or Japanese sesame oil*

Infusing the oil:
Smash the scallion and ginger lightly with the broad side of a cleaver or the blunt handle of a heavy knife to bring their oils to the surface. Combine the scallion, ginger, chili flakes, and peppercorns in a small dish and put within reach of your stovetop.

Combine the corn or peanut oil and sesame oil in a small, heavy saucepan. Stir with a chopstick or wooden spoon to blend, then add 1 or 2 chili flakes to the oil. Heat over moderate heat until the flakes sizzle merrily surrounded by a ring of white bubbles. Let sizzle 5 seconds, then turn off the heat and remove the pan to a cool burner. Immediately add the combined seasonings. Stir once or twice to blend, then cover the pot loosely to allow the steam to escape. The mixture will continue to sizzle from the heat of the pan about 10 minutes more.

If you overheat the oil and the seasonings burn, begin again with fresh ingredients. Otherwise, the oil will be bitter.

Straining and storing the oil:
For full flavor and rich color, cover the pot completely once the sizzling has stopped, and let the oil stand overnight to a full day at room temperature. Filter the oil through a strainer lined with several layers of dry cheesecloth, and discard the seasonings.

Bottle the oil in an immaculately clean glass jar and store in the refrigerator or in a cool, dark place. Use at room temperature.

USED IN:
Peony Blossom Cold Noodles (page 358), and *The Five Heaps* (page 361), and most any time you'd like to replace hot chili oil or sesame oil in a soy-based dipping sauce.

East-
West
Desserts

甜
食

◆

◆

C hinese desserts, or the lack of them, are unfathomable to a Westerner. Traditional Chinese banquet sweets such as "Eight-Jewel Rice," "Almond Float," "Sweet Peanut Soup," and "Candied Bananas" stun most Western dessert fans with their cloying sweetness, while the typical fresh fruit ending to a casual Chinese meal leaves us feeling robbed. We are used to a special, light, and crafted touch of sweetness at the end of a meal, and no number of canned litchis or fortune cookies—the Chinese-American restaurant solution to the Western sweet-tooth problem—will fill that gap.

This, then is a heretical chapter: a treasury of excellent *sorbets*, ice creams, fresh fruit, and baked desserts that satisfy with sweetness and yet will not overwhelm the flavor orchestration of an otherwise traditional Chinese meal. Some are based on classic Chinese sources—centuries-old novels, dramas, and poems, filled with suggestive-sounding sweets that inspired me to recipes. Others are the result of "field work," namely a cook's normal business of tasting, eating, and discovering wonderful food in restaurants, at the tables of friends, or in desultory walks through old cookbooks. A few were even winners at my annual birthday party, a bring-a-dessert marathon that is a multinational event.

Whatever the origin, I trust in their good taste and deliciousness and suspect they will go beyond the lesser efforts of the fortune cookie-makers and the nobler efforts of perhaps the first conceiver of an East-West dessert, Mr. M. Sing Au, who in his 1936 jewel, *The Chinese Cookbook*, set forth the following prescription for a "Mandarin Grapefruit Salad":

Boil one-half pound bean sprouts and drain in cold water. Chop two slices pineapple, two grapefruit and two bananas into small pieces. Mix all with French dressing flavored with Chinese [soy] sauce. Place on lettuce leaves and top with whipped cream.

May the following be an improvement!

Cassia Blossom Steamed Pears 桂花蒸梨

This thoroughly modern dessert of steamed, chilled pears filled with an intriguing honey and Cognac syrup dates back to the ninth century. Then, in the golden age of the Tang dynasty, it was already common to combine the "cool"-natured pear with the "warming" qualities of cassia, honey, and wine. According to the same yin-yang culinary rule, the soon-to-be velvety pear was frequently stuffed with nuts or bits of chewy dried fruit to offer a nice contrast of texture. ◆ This, in my opinion, is authentic Chinese dessert cooking at its finest. It deserves the prettiest pears, an excellent, subtle honey, and a trip to Chinatown to search for cassia blossoms or a wait while you order them (page 588). If you must have them tonight, put a slip of cinnamon bark in the core of each pear, then extract it prior to serving. The bark is a near-relative to the blossom and will imbue the filling with an appropriate spice. ◆ I find rock-hard Anjous give the best results. The hard fruit has had no chance to grow grainy or sandy, and holds up best to the heat. Choose chubby, squat pears that are easy to fill and flat-bottomed ones that will not topple when steamed. A 7–8-ounce pear will do for a dainty dessert, or an 8–12-ounce pear for a more substantial one. I usually opt for the bigger size, which is easier to fill. ◆ For peak flavor, make the pears 12 hours to 2 days in advance, and chill thoroughly before serving. With the incitement to make them in advance and their elegant presentation, this is a superb dessert for entertaining.

TECHNIQUE NOTES:
Wallowing a hole in a hard pear is a tricky business. The best tool I know is a trough-shaped zucchini corer, with a cylindrical apple corer as a second choice. Use the corer to pull out a narrow plug from the middle of the pear, then follow up with some deft knife work, or use the zucchini corer to widen the excavation evenly from top to bottom. Be careful not to cut through the bottom of the fruit.

Letting the pears sit in the covered steamer after the heat has been turned off prevents their skins from wrinkling. It is the same principle one observes when making steamed breads and buns.

Serve 1 pear per person.

INGREDIENTS:

> *4 large or 6 smaller hard, green, unblemished Anjou pears (to equal 3 pounds)*
>
> *To fill the pears:*
> *6 tablespoons wild-flower honey*
> *2 rounded tablespoons white raisins*
> *1 rounded teaspoon cassia blossoms (page 535) or as many thin slips of*
> *fragrant cinnamon bark as you have pears, or several drops orange-flower*
> *water for each pear*
> *1½ tablespoons Cognac*

Coring and stuffing the pears:
Combine the honey, raisins, cassia blossoms, and Cognac. Stir well to blend, then put the mixture aside to plump the raisins and develop the flavors.

Neatly slice off the top of each pear about 1 inch from the stem end, in a straight line so the top will not slide off during steaming. Leave stems and leaves intact, for decoration. Put each cap alongside its pear, to match them up properly later on.

Core the pears with a sturdy fruit corer and a knife if needed, as described above in TECHNIQUE NOTES. Be careful not to cut through the bottom and to leave ¼–½ inch of solid pear at the base. Make the gouged-out column as wide as possible, while leaving a ¼–½-inch wide rim of pear around the top of the hole. Do not worry about losing a lot of pear. The filling is as scrumptious as the fruit, so eat the trimmings in good conscience.

Pour an equal amount of the honey mixture into each pear, portioning the raisins evenly among them. Replace the tops, and adjust for an invisible fit.

Steaming the pears:
(For details on steaming and how to improvise a steamer, see page 60.)

Stand the pears close together in a Pyrex pie plate or heatproof quiche plate at least 1 inch smaller than the diameter of your steamer. Or, steam the pears in individual bowls if your steamer can accommodate them. The pears will render a lot of juice, so choose bowls at least 2 inches deep.

Choose the largest possible vessel to fit under your steamer, to avoid having to refill it frequently during the lengthy steaming. Fill with water to come 1 inch below the steamer tray or rack, then bring the water to a gushing boil over high heat. Cover the pears tightly once the steam begins to gush, reduce the heat to medium, then steam the pears 45 minutes–2 hours, until the fruit feels soft to the touch. While steaming, check periodically to replace any lids that slip off and replenish the steamer with boiling water as required. When checking the pears, lift the lid slowly and as little as possible so a sudden change in temperature will not wrinkle the skin.

When the pears feel soft turn off the heat and let them sit in the covered steamer for 10 minutes. Then lift the lid and remove the juices from around the pears with a clean bulb-top baster. Take the pears from the steamer and let them cool in the plate for 20 minutes, while the juices cool separately to prevent them from overcooking.

For best flavor, surround the pears with the juices once cool, seal airtight, and refrigerate 1–2 days before serving.

Serve the pears well chilled. Stand them upright in individual bowls or in stem goblets, caps on and surrounded by the sweet juices. Garnish, if desired, with a sprig of tiny white flowers or green leaves to offset the gold of the fruit. Don't be distressed if the skin has wrinkled after all. It is forgotten with the first bite of pear.

Sealed and stored in the refrigerator, the pears will keep upwards of a week without losing their flavor.

MENU SUGGESTIONS:
This is a delicate, very special dessert, best used to end a meal of classic dishes like *Pearl Balls* (page 185), *Steamed Whole Fish with Seared Scallions* (page 248), *Birthday Duck* (page 175), and *Golden Egg Dumplings* (page 328). Light, sweet dessert wines—like a sweet California Johannisberg Riesling—that might be overwhelmed by a conventional Western dessert, are perfect with the pears.

Glacéed Orange Slices

糖汁橘片

Oranges with their round shape, scarlet-gold color, and sweet flavor are the canonical fruit of China. They are placed on every altar, however humble or grand, and are regularly profferred up at the conclusion of a Chinese meal, typically sectioned into eighths and fanned out on a platter like a giant russet chrysanthemum. To be truthful, I grew quite sick of them in Taiwan and found myself wishing they could be "dressed up" a bit. ◆ This is the answer to my wish, a dessert known in French as *oranges glacées*, here done with far less sugar than is usual and with a splurge of liqueur to heighten the flavor of the fruit. Decorated with amber slivers of candied peel, it is a thoroughly pretty dessert, perfect for entertaining. ◆ The success of the dessert rests on finding very sweet and juicy navel oranges. If they are full of juice, they will feel heavy in your hand (a good way to judge any citrus fruit). ◆ Preparations are simple, and doing the dish in advance will only better it.

TECHNIQUE NOTES:
To make the dessert look particularly beautiful, I give each cross-section of orange the look of a scallop-edged flower by removing all the pith and branch-like veins by hand, so that the orange stays contained in its own shapely membrane. Typically, the pith and membrane are cut away with a knife, leaving the orange either round or vaguely octagonal. My method takes three times as long, but I like the result.

INGREDIENTS:

6 large, very sweet, heavy-in-the-hand navel oranges (about ¾ pound each)
⅓ cup water
⅓–½ cup sugar, depending on the sweetness of the oranges
about 3 tablespoons quality Cognac or Grand Marnier

Preparing the peel:
Wash the oranges. With a vegetable peeler, remove the peel from 4 of them (or all 6 if you're a fan of glacéed peel and would like to have extra). Work carefully so you take off only the minimum amount of white pith and aim for broad, long strips.

Put the peel orange side down and cut or scrape away any trace of white pith, then cut the peel into long julienne strips $\frac{1}{16}$ inch thin.

Bring water to cover to boil in a small saucepan and simmer the peel 12–15 minutes to make it tender and less bitter. Drain, rush under cold water to stop the cooking, and set aside to drain.

Candying the peel:
Put $\frac{1}{3}$ cup water and the sugar in a small, heavy saucepan. Bring the liquid to a boil over moderately high heat, swirling the pot gently until the mixture is 100 percent clear, indicating the sugar has dissolved. Cover the pot, then let the mixture boil for 1 minute while the steam washes the sugar crystals from the side of the pot. Remove the cover, wait about 30 seconds for the bubbles to thicken, then add the peel to the syrup. Swirl gently to coat the threads and boil 1–2 minutes until the syrup thickens slightly. Remove the pan from the heat and let the mixture cool. The peel will turn a beautifully translucent red-gold. The syrup should be light, not thick and sticky. If you have overdone the boiling and let too much of the water evaporate, simply stir a bit of water into the mixture if it is still very hot. Otherwise, return the pot to the stove and stir in water to thin the syrup over a low heat.

Peeling and slicing the oranges:
Use your fingernails and/or a small, sharp knife to remove *all* the white pith from the oranges, including the white, branch-like veins along the side of each segment. The end result will be prettiest if you can do this without slicing through the translucent membrane that surrounds each segment, though if you're in a hurry or less patient you can do a speedy job by slicing off the pith and the membrane in one swoop.

Lay each orange on its side, slice off the ends, then cut the remainder into even round slices about $\frac{3}{8}$ inch thick. Using a tweezer or the point of a small knife, remove any seeds and white pith from the center of each slice, taking care to keep the slices whole. Put a layer of slices side by side in a broad, shallow bowl (either the serving bowl or a big glass pie plate). Using your fingers, smooth a thin film of liqueur over the top of each slice, then scatter a bit of peel on top of that, taking only that syrup which clings to the peel. Continue to build the layers of orange, smear them with liqueur, and scatter peel on top until you've used up all the oranges and dressed the top layer with a pretty crown of peel. Squeeze the juice from the end slices over the dessert, using cheesecloth or a sieve to trap any seeds or pulp, then discard the pulp. Taste the combined liquids in the bowl and add a bit more syrup if you like a sweeter taste.

Seal airtight and refrigerate at least 2 hours before serving. While chilling, use a clean bulb-top baster or spoon to occasionally ladle the juices in the bowl over the top of the dessert.

Serve chilled in a large serving bowl of contrasting color or arranged on individual chilled plates, topped by a bit of juice and a tangle of peel, and accompanied by a cookie.

The oranges keep perfectly for about a week in the refrigerator, sealed airtight. Leftover peel and syrup may be refrigerated indefinitely and are delicious on ice creams or in compotes of dried and fresh fruit.

MENU SUGGESTIONS:
The oranges are a particularly welcome ending to meals of richer foods like *Smoked Tea Duck* (page 169), *Fragrant Crispy Duck* (page 172), or *Master Sauce Chicken* (page 153). They are also very good with mildly seasoned pork dishes, like *Pearl Balls* (page 187) or *Golden Egg Dumplings* (page 328). Given a fancier menu, this is a wonderful dessert to serve alongside a rich French Sauterne. The effect is a lovely balance of sharp orange and sweet liqueur.

| Cassia-
Cognac
Strawberries

桂花草莓 | Had Chinese cooks of classic times known our familiar wild or wood strawberry *(Fragaria vesca)*, they would have loved it, both for its felicitous red color and its multitude of tiny seeds (the word for "seeds" in Chinese being a homonym for much-desired "sons"). Here, to make up for lost centuries, is a simple, Cognac-laced dish of fresh strawberries, turned smooth and a blazing ruby by a light honey syrup. It is a very pretty dish that can be prepared in min- |

utes. ◆ The main requirement is superbly ripe berries. Judge them by smell. Ripe, luscious strawberries always *smell* sweet, while a good color can often mask a lifeless fruit. Cassia blossoms, should you find them, are a distinctive touch, but the berries will be delicious without them. ◆ The strawberries should macerate 4–6 hours to reach their flavor peak. If they were quite firm to begin, they can be held longer before serving. If they were on the other hand very ripe, they should be eaten quickly.

TECHNIQUE NOTES:
Macerating strawberries with sugar and wine, as is common in Western desserts, tends to turn them a dull red-brown. For a reason I have not been able to discover, honey produces the opposite effect, heightening the color to a bright ruby red. In addition, the syrup acquires a particular softness that is not possible with sugar.

Yields 2 cups, enough to serve 3–4 as a light dessert with cookies.

INGREDIENTS:

> *1 pint sweet-smelling, firm strawberries*
>
> *To macerate the berries:*
> *2 tablespoons wild-flower honey*
> *2 teaspoons Cognac*
> *⅛ teaspoon cassia blossoms (page 535)*

Preparing the strawberries:
Spray the berries briefly with cool water, then put aside to drain on paper towels. Hull the berries with the point of a small knife, making a neat incision around the stem and cutting away any portions that are white or green. Extract the pithy "finger" in the center of the berry.

    Transfer the berries to an immaculately clean glass jar with a tight-fitting lid. (The jar permits you to evenly macerate the berries without touching them, which is important once they soften.)

Macerating the strawberries:
Combine the honey, Cognac, and cassia blossoms, stirring until smooth. Scrape the mixture over the berries, seal the jar tightly, then rotate it gently to distribute the syrup. Lay the jar on its side, and prop it up if it is leaking. Rotate the jar a few turns every 15 minutes for an hour. The liquids will triple and the berries will turn a burning red.

For best flavor, refrigerate the berries 3–5 hours, rotating the jar occasionally.

Serve the berries at room temperature or slightly chilled, in a shallow bowl of contrasting color, with the syrup spooned on top. If you are serving a simple vanilla ice cream, they make a nice accompaniment.

Leftover berries may be refrigerated. Firm berries will hold 2–3 days.

MENU SUGGESTIONS:
The berries follow nicely in the wake of light and flavorful dishes such as *Lettuce-Wrapped Spicy Chicken* (page 145), *Cassia Blossom (Mu-Shu) Pork* (page 198), and *Spicy Steamed Salmon with Young Ginger* (page 252). They are good company for most any classic dessert wine—a French Sauterne, California late harvest Johannisberg Riesling, or German Auslese.

Caramelized Apple Slices with Armagnac

焦糖蘋果片

If you have ever attempted the Chinese restaurant dessert of caramelized apple wedges, whereby the already-tired cook runs to the stove, batters and deep-fries the apples, simultaneously caramelizes the sugar, coats the apples, prepares ice water, and sprints to the table before the apples cool and the water warms, then you will *doubly* appreciate this luxurious, leisurely alternative. It is the recipe of my French-cooking friend, Michael James, whose desserts have always impressed me with their elegance and their clean, unsweet flavors. In my opinion, it is better than the original, which if done in authentic Chinese-style must be made with starchy yams! ◆ Armagnac is a district in southwest France, which like Cognac to the north gives its name to a distinctive type of brandy. For lack of a high-quality Armagnac (the cheaper blends can be harsh), substitute a good-quality Cognac or Calvados. ◆ The apples may be caramelized a full day in advance. The dessert can then be finished in 15 minutes once the meal has ended, if you wish to eat it hot, or several hours in advance if it is more convenient to serve it warm.

TECHNIQUE NOTES:
Three separate processes conspire to make this a dish of savory, closely bound essences, rather than one of so-so apples sloshed with cream. *Deglazing* the baking pan reclaims the caramelized fruit juices and puts them back into the dessert. *Flambéing* the brandy removes the harsh alcohol and concentrates the brandy flavor and aroma. *Reducing* the cream evaporates the superficial liquid, causing it to cling to the fruit without smothering it. For the Chinese technique of "wine-explosion," which is akin to flambéing but used at the other end of the meal, see TECHNIQUE NOTES, page 453.

Serves 6–8.

INGREDIENTS:

> *4 pounds firm, crisp, well-flavored apples that will hold their shape during baking—Greening, Granny Smith, Pippin recommended*

¼ pound sweet butter
⅔ cup sugar
½ cup highest quality Armagnac, Cognac, or a good Calvados
¾ cup heavy (whipping) cream

To garnish:
powdered confectioners' sugar in a shaker or sieve

Cutting and caramelizing the apples:
Preheat the oven to 400°. Adjust 2 racks to divide the oven evenly into thirds. Grease 2 large baking sheets with half the butter.

Peel the apples, halve them lengthwise, then remove the stems and cores. Slice neatly into wedges ¼ inch thick. Arrange the slices on the baking sheets in a single layer. Sprinkle evenly with the sugar, then dot with the remaining butter.

Bake the apples for 20–30 minutes, stirring occasionally, until tender and nicely caramelized. Rotate the sheets back to front and top to bottom in the oven once midway through baking to insure even browning. Do not worry if some of the bits become quite dark; they will inspire a rich flavor. Do not, however, let the sugar burn.

Deglazing the pan:
Remove the apples to a large oval gratin dish (you may substitute a 9 × 13 rectangular pan), or to individual porcelain gratin dishes, spreading them in a not too thick layer. Put the baking sheets over low heat until the sugar softens, sprinkle with a few tablespoons of the Armagnac, then scrape up any good (that is, not blackened) caramel with a wooden spoon or spatula. The alcohol will evaporate while you scrape up the sugar. Pour the deglazing juices over the apples.

The apples may be kept at room temperature for 2–3 hours, loosely covered, before completing the dessert. Or, seal and refrigerate them once cool, for up to 24 hours. Bring to room temperature before finishing.

Flambéing the brandy and reducing the cream:
As much as 2 hours before finishing the dessert, warm the Armagnac in a small heavy saucepan over low heat. Do not let it boil. When the brandy is well heated and fragrant, avert your face and put a match near the surface to set it alight. When the flame is nearly out, signaling that most of the alcohol has evaporated, add the cream, stir to combine, and bring to a simmer over moderately low heat. Allow the cream to reduce to about ½ cup. Keep a close eye on it, and do not let it boil.

Finishing the dessert:
To serve the apples hot, finish them just before serving. To serve warm, finish them just before sitting down to dinner, up to 2 hours in advance.

Preheat the oven to 450° and set the rack in the middle of the oven. Rewarm the cream, if necessary, and pour it over the apples. Bake 10–15 minutes, until the apples are hot. Remove the apples from the oven, raise the heat to ignite the broiler, and set the broiler rack close to the flame or coil.

Sprinkle the apples with 1–2 tablespoons of the powdered sugar, then run the dish under the broiler to brown it lightly. For a final touch, dust the edges of the dessert with a pretty hemline of powdered sugar.

Serve immediately, portioning the apples onto warm serving plates if you have baked them in the large dish.

Or, if you are serving them warm, remove the apples to a rack in a warm corner of the kitchen for up to 2 hours. Do not hold them longer; they are not good cold.

MENU SUGGESTIONS:
This is a "big affair" dessert, best in the company of distinctive dishes with mild flavors, like *Birthday Duck* (page 175), *Pearl Balls* (page 187), *Shrimp, Leek and Pine Nut Fried Rice* (page 408), *Clear-Steamed Flounder with White Pepper* (page 250), and *Clear-Steamed Lobster with Scallion Oil* (page 278). It goes well with most all the fancy duck and chicken dishes—*Cinnamon Bark Chicken* (page 162), hot *Tea and Spice Smoked Chicken* (page 158), *Smoked Tea Duck* (page 169), and *Fragrant Crispy Duck* (page 172). For a dessert wine, look to a rich German Auslese or Spätlese.

Shansi Drunken Jujubes

山西醉棗

Jujubes in their semi-dried form are a date-like fruit, which when plopped in liquor and left to soak up its flavor become plush, plump, and "drunk." They are pleasantly intoxicating nibbles with tea, or can be served as an elegant dessert, arranged in a stem glass with a dollop of *crème Chantilly* on top. ◆ This recipe originated in Shansi province in north China, an area famed for its large, honey-sweet jujubes and a strong, locally brewed white liquor. In Taiwan, we steeped the jujubes in homemade litchi wine. Here, in America, I find Cognac and golden rock sugar make the best blend and result in a syrup that is as good as the fruit. ◆ For this recipe, use only soft, moist, pitted red jujubes, available in large Chinese markets and by mail order boxed in cellophane and labeled red dates without stone. Dried prunes make a good substitute. Do not use black jujubes (which are smoked), or the small, hard, red jujubes sold in plastic bags. ◆ Cover the fruit with brandy at least 2 weeks before eating.

TECHNIQUE NOTES:
One week in brandy turns the jujubes soft but harshly intoxicating. After two weeks, the flavor mellows to a rich, subtle fullness, and the syrup becomes smooth, sweet, and pleasantly thick. Longer, and they get better still.

Count on 1–2 jujubes per person with tea, 3–4 as a dessert with *crème Chantilly*.

INGREDIENTS:

> moist, pitted red jujubes (page 550)
> Cognac to cover
> 1 teaspoon crushed golden rock sugar (page 570) for each ½ cup Cognac

Steeping the jujubes:
Put the jujubes in a clean glass jar with a tight-fitting lid. Remove any cardboard lining the lid, and replace it with several thicknesses of plastic film if necessary for a tight fit. Add Cognac to cover and the crushed rock sugar, then twist the lid securely shut. Rotate the bottle to distribute the mixture, and put aside in a cool, dark place for 2 weeks, rotating the bottle occasionally to distribute the liquids. In the course of 2 weeks the fruit will swell, the sugar will dissolve, and the syrup will thicken perceptibly.

Serving the jujubes:
To serve alone with tea, present the jujubes whole in a small dish, speared with tooth-

picks, and glossed with a bit of the syrup. Or, for an elegant dessert, serve the jujubes and some of the syrup in individual stemmed glasses or on pretty, individual plates, garnished with a dollop of *crème Chantilly* (chilled heavy cream whipped to very soft peaks, with sugar and a touch of vanilla or Cognac to taste).

Leftover syrup is a fine beginning for more drunken jujubes, prunes, or golden raisins. It is also an excellent topping on its own for ice creams, waffles, or intoxicating pancakes.

MENU SUGGESTIONS:
I like these liqueur-soaked fruits best at midday or late at night, with a cup of green or Jasmine tea. To follow a meal, any of the wine-rich dishes such as *Master Sauce Chicken* (page 153), *Casseroled Chicken with Smoky Chestnuts* (page 156), *Wine-Simmered Duck* (page 166), or *Saucy Potted Pork* (page 207) if served in simple company would stand up well to such a dessert. The combination of cream, sugar, and alcohol would make a normal dessert wine seem thin by comparison, so if you want a wine to partner the jujubes try an old, rich Oloroso.

General Yang's Western Ocean Wafers
楊士西洋餅

At the close of the eighteenth century, the Chinese poet-epicure, Yuan Mei, recorded this recipe for a Western Ocean (that is, European) cookie made in the household of one General Yang:

Mix an egg white and some flour to a paste. Forge a pair of metal scissors with two metal discs at the ends, each the size of a small plate. When you close the scissors, there should be less than 1/10 inch between the discs. Heat over a fierce fire [with some batter in between the discs] . . . In a moment, the wafer will be done—white as snow and lustrous as glazed paper. On top, add a powdering of frosted sugar and pine nuts.

It sounded to me like the general was baking a version of *tuiles*—the crisp, nut-sprinkled French wafers that are curled after baking to resemble roof tiles. So I asked my cookie friend Oona to develop a recipe using rice flour, which seemed more appropriately Chinese. The result was a perfectly delicious cookie-wafer, a lovely partner for many of our other "Western Ocean" desserts. Extra-crisp, lightly sweet, and rich with the scent of almonds, they are an elegantly simple ending to many Chinese meals. ♦ You may serve them flat, like the general did, or curl them into graceful arcs. (In imitation, naturally, of *Chinese* roof tiles.) Or, roll them more tightly into a cigarette to hold a home-made fortune. Sprinkle with sliced almonds for a delicate, crispy garnish, or use pine nuts for a smooth and luxurious taste. ♦ *Tuiles* should be baked no longer than 12 hours in advance. Bake them in the oven. No special scissors required!

TECHNIQUE NOTES:
If you wish to curl the cookies, you must move quickly while they are still warm and pliable. If they cool and crisp before you can get to them, set the baking sheet on the oven door or on a warm burner and they will soften again.

Yields about 3 dozen 3-inch cookies.

INGREDIENTS:

For the cookie batter:
4 tablespoons (½ stick) sweet butter
½ cup sugar
2 large egg whites
⅓ cup rice flour (plain, non-glutinous variety)
⅓ cup ground almonds (requires 1⅓ ounces almonds; use blanched nuts if you want a whiter cookie)
½ teaspoon pure vanilla extract
¼ teaspoon pure almond extract

To garnish:
¼ cup sliced almonds
or
⅓ cup pine nuts

Preparations:
Preheat the oven to 425° and set the rack in the middle level. Butter 2 baking sheets. If you are using non-stick sheets, butter them lightly.

To grind the almonds, add them to the dry work bowl of a food processor fitted with the steel knife. Process together with 1 tablespoon of the premeasured flour until finely ground. (The flour will prevent the nuts from turning to nut butter.) Put the mixture aside.

Cream the butter and sugar in the food processor, or with a mixer, or by hand. When fluffy, add the egg whites, and process briefly to combine. Add the flour, ground almonds, and vanilla and almond extracts. Process 5–10 seconds, just until homogenized.

Baking the cookies:
Line up your equipment: the batter, the buttered baking sheets, a teaspoon measure, a tablespoon, a wide metal spatula, a rolling pin or wooden spoon if you are curling the cookies, and a cooling rack.

Prepare and bake only one sheet at a time. Drop the batter by slightly rounded teaspoons onto the first sheet, then use the back of the tablespoon to spread the batter into 3-inch rounds, evenly ⅛–1/16 inch thick. Leave about 2 inches between the cookies. Lightly sprinkle several sliced almonds or pine nuts on top of each cookie. Do not press them into the batter.

Bake 3–5 minutes, until there is a thin brown rim ⅛–¼ inch wide around each cookie. Use the spatula to lift the cookies one by one from the sheet, moving quickly to shape them while they are still warm and pliable. For flat wafers, remove directly to the rack to cool. For gentle arcs, drape the cookies over a rolling pin. For cigarette rolls to hold fortunes, turn the cookie upside down on your work surface, then roll around the handle of a wooden spoon or cylindrical cookie mold. Once crisp, gently dislodge the cookies from the molds and remove to the rack to cool. Fortunes should be inserted after the cookies have cooled completely. If you have trouble with cookies crisping before you can remove them from the baking sheet, see above, in TECHNIQUE NOTES.

For best taste and texture, bake shortly before serving. Be diligent to guard *tuiles* airtight against moisture, as they will rapidly become limp in a damp or warm kitchen. Store airtight in a tin, freeze, or hold in a 100° warming oven until ready to serve, to insure that they will be crisp.

Serve the cookies as a crisp aside to ice cream, *sorbet*, or fresh fruit, or arrange the cookies on a plate as a sweet touch with tea.

Leftover batter keeps well 2 days, sealed airtight and refrigerated.

MENU SUGGESTIONS:

These cookies are lovely served alongside *Glacéed Orange Slices* (page 487), *Fresh Ginger Ice Cream* (page 496), *Mandarin Orange Ice Cream* (page 498), *Pear and Jasmine Tea Sorbet* (page 500), or *Persimmon Sorbet* (page 502). Their delicate texture makes them most appropriate for meals of rather "dressy" foods, such as those that star a whole chicken or duck or fish. For a wine to accompany the cookies, look to a light, sweet dessert wine, like a California sweet Johannisberg Riesling.

Orange-Almond Coins

橘味杏仁餅

Though one rarely thinks of butter in a Chinese context, shortbreads, pastries, and sugar cookies made with or fried in butter were an "exotic" luxury item on Chinese tables as early as the ninth century, when the cosmopolitan Chinese of the Tang dynasty were also toasting one another with grape wines and cooling off with *sorbets* made from mare's milk and fruit juices. ◆ I like to think that the quintessential luxury almond cookie resembled these buttery cookie miniatures inspired by my pastry friend, Flo Braker. They are quarter-size melt-in-your-mouthers, just the type of thing you would imagine a Tang poet might enjoy. ◆ These cookies are extremely easy to make. The dough refrigerates and freezes beautifully, and once baked, the cookies will keep for 2 weeks or more. For best flavor, make the dough a day in advance to give the orange peel time to permeate.

TECHNIQUE NOTES:

No need to spend time skinning almonds for this cookie! Unblanched almonds give an unusual charm—an interesting, lightly flecked patina and the hint of another flavor to balance the sweetness.

To prevent the bottom of the cookies from browning, bake them on a doubled baking sheet, that is, two sheets sandwiched together.

Yields 8 dozen quarter-size cookies.

INGREDIENTS:

> *For the dough:*
> 1½ teaspoons freshly grated orange rind, no white pith included, or 1½
>   teaspoons finely minced, home-dried orange peel (page 557), soaked in warm
>   water for about 10 minutes until supple and patted dry before mincing
> 4 ounces (⅔ cup) unblanched whole amonds
> ½ cup plus 1 tablespoon sugar
> 2 cups all-purpose flour
> pinch salt
> ½ pound well-chilled sweet butter, cut into small cubes
> ½ teaspoon orange-flower water

Making the dough:

Add the orange rind, nuts, and sugar to the work bowl of a food processor fitted with the steel knife. Process until the nuts are very finely ground. Add the flour and salt, and process 2–3 seconds to mix. Distribute the cubed butter evenly around the blade, sprinkle the orange-flower water on top, and process until the dough forms a near-ball. Do not overprocess.

Press the dough together with your hands, seal airtight with plastic wrap, then refrigerate 12–24 hours before baking for best flavor. Part or all of the dough may be frozen, sealed airtight and then bagged in plastic. Defrost in the refrigerator before using and shape when cold.

Baking the cookies:
Preheat the oven to 325° and set the rack in the lower third of the oven. Line a doubled baking sheet with parchment paper.

Using 1½ teaspoons of dough, roll a ball the size of a large marble between your palms, and put it on the paper. Do not flatten or press it; these are domed cookies. Repeat until you fill the entire sheet, leaving an inch between the cookies.

Bake one sheet at a time for 15–20 minutes, rotating the sheet after 8 minutes to insure even baking. When perfectly done, the cookies will be pale blonde (not brown), and the dough will look a bit dry. Remove to a rack to cool completely.

Once cool, the cookies may be stored at room temperature in an airtight tin. Do not refrigerate. They will keep 2 weeks or longer and grow a bit softer in the tin.

MENU SUGGESTIONS:
These cookies are particularly good in combination with *Mandarin Orange Ice Cream* (page 498), *Persimmon Sorbet* (page 502), *and Glacéed Orange Slices* (page 487). They are very versatile and would be appreciated after a hearty meal of spicy foods, where I would serve them in the company of fresh fruit, or after a dinner of delicate dishes. They are also lovely partners to *Cassia-Cognac Strawberries* (page 489). If you would like to accompany the cookies with wine, choose a light and sweet dessert wine such as a California sweet Johannisberg Riesling.

Fresh Ginger Ice Cream

薑味冰淇淋

In spite of the fact that the Chinese were the first of the world's peoples to have ice technology, and ice-chilled fruits and fruit juices were fashionable throughout Chinese history, ice cream as such never took hold of the Chinese imagination. Even in periods when mare's milk and cow's milk were blended with fruits or aromatics and plunged into ice pits to chill as a sort of Chinese *frappe*, it was considered unhealthy to eat thoroughly iced things. It was left to Chinese in the West to add ice cream to a Chinese menu, where one usually finds it cloyingly creamy, lumpy with ice, and a poor partner to even a hope-filled fortune cookie. ◆ This is a very different ice cream altogether. It is very refreshing and pleasantly spicy, with a pale color and silky texture that give it a special elegance. The invention of my good cook-friend Mary Jane Drinkwater, it is a dessert I never tire of serving or eating. ◆ The ice cream mixture may be made 1–2 days in advance of freezing, which gives the flavors time to blossom and marry. If you're a ginger lover like me, you'll want to use the larger amount of fresh ginger. If you're an ice-cream lover, double the recipe.

TECHNIQUE NOTES:
The acid content of fresh ginger can be high enough to cause milk to curdle. If you want its dazzle in a cream dessert, the trick is to first make a sweet syrup of sugar, water, and

minced fresh ginger, and then add this neutralized mixture to the milk.

Yields about 1½ pints.

INGREDIENTS:

For the ginger syrup:
⅓ *cup water*
¼ *cup sugar*
2½–3 *packed tablespoons food-processor-minced or grated, peeled fresh ginger*

Milk mixture:
1 *cup whole milk*
2 *tablespoons sugar*
2 *teaspoons finely minced ginger in syrup (page 548), drained before mincing*

Custard mixture:
3 *large egg yolks*
¼ *cup sugar*
1 *cup heavy (whipping) cream*
½–¾ *teaspoon freshly squeezed, strained lemon juice*

Preparing the mixture for freezing:
To make the syrup, heat the water and ¼ cup sugar in a small saucepan over medium heat, stirring to dissolve the sugar. When the sugar is dissolved, add the fresh ginger. Stir to disperse, then bring the mixture to a boil over medium-high heat. Reduce the heat and simmer the syrup uncovered for 5 minutes. Remove the pan from the heat.

In another pan combine the milk, 2 tablespoons sugar, and the minced preserved ginger. Stir over medium heat until the milk comes to a scalding temperature, just short of a simmer, then remove the pan from the heat. Scrape the fresh ginger syrup into the milk mixture, and stir well to blend. Cover and steep 20 minutes to infuse the milk.

In a small bowl beat the egg yolks and ¼ cup sugar until the mixture is pale yellow, thick, and falls in ribbons from the beater.

Put the heavy cream in a medium-size bowl. Nest the cream bowl in a larger one lined with ice cubes and place a large, fine mesh strainer alongside.

When the steeping time is up, bring the milk mixture to scalding again, stirring. Slowly add ¼ of the scalded milk to the egg mixture, whisking constantly to temper the eggs, then pour the egg mixture back into the remaining milk, continuing to whisk. Cook over moderate heat, whisking slowly but steadily, until the mixture reaches the custard stage, thick enough to coat and cling to the back of a spoon, 180° on an instant-reading thermometer. Do not let the mixture boil lest the eggs scramble.

Immediately pour the custard through the strainer and into the bowl of cream set over ice. Scrape the pot clean, then slowly stir the liquid trapped in the strainer in order to coax it through the mesh. Press firmly and repeatedly on the ginger to extract all the liquid, then finally scrape the bottom of the strainer to claim every last drop for the cream. Discard the ginger solids. Allow the cream mixture to cool completely, stirring occasionally.

Once cool, the mixture may be sealed airtight and refrigerated 1–2 days before freezing.

Freezing the cream:
Just before freezing, adjust the mixture with ½–¾ teaspoon fresh lemon juice, stirring and

tasting after every several drops just until the ginger flavor is perceptibly heightened by the lemon.

Freeze in an ice-cream maker according to the manufacturer's instructions, or freeze in a shallow tray and beat with a food processor, as described on page 501. The food-processor product is dense and rich, akin to a frozen cream.

When the freezing process is completed, pack the ice cream into a clean plastic container, poking deep into the mixture, then pressing it with a spoon or spatula to eliminate any air bubbles. Press a piece of plastic wrap directly on the surface of the ice cream to prevent the formation of ice crystals, then return the mixture to the freezer for at least 2 hours to firm up and "ripen."

If frozen solid, allow the ice cream to soften slightly in the refrigerator before serving. For the full flavor and bouquet, it should be eaten slightly soft.

Serve the ice cream unadorned in well-chilled goblets or bowls.

The ginger flavor is keenest the first 24 hours. It is still sprightly after 2 days, but then begins gradually to fade.

MENU SUGGESTIONS:

This ice cream is excellent on its own or in the company of *Mandarin Orange Ice Cream* (below) or either of the cookies (pages 493 to 495). I use it with all sorts of menus, from big affair meals to casual meals of informal, spicy foods. About my only hesitation is to serve it after gingery dishes or foods dressed with a peanut or sesame sauce. A top-quality Jasmine tea, a green tea like Dragon Well, or a combination of Dragon Well and Baby Chrysanthemum tea is a perfect accompaniment to the ice cream. Tea is thoroughly refreshing, whereas a sweet dessert wine would be helpless against such creaminess.

Mandarin Orange Ice Cream

橘子冰淇淋

This is an unusual ice cream with a satiny texture and a strong citrus-sweet flavor, made from the juice and skin of fresh tangerines. Garnished with a pretty tangle of glacéed peel, it makes a festive dessert, in keeping with our Western association of tangerines and Christmas (when a full half of the tangerine crop reaches the market), and the Chinese association of the whole orange family with good fortune and prosperity. The recipe comes from Mary Jane Drinkwater, who went through about 30 pounds of tangerines to get it just right. ◆ Though the nomenclature gets pretty confusing, tangerines, mandarin oranges, tangelos and Clementines generally refer to the same thing—a loose-skinned orange native to China (hence the name mandarins), first introduced to Europe in the eighteenth century, and marketed through the Moroccan seaport of Tangiers (where they acquired the name tangerines). Ideal for this recipe is the especially sweet variety called the Honey Tangerine (once called the Murcott orange!). Whatever variety you use, it is the flavor of the juice that is most important, and, if it doesn't taste intense, then begin with 1½ cups of juice and simmer it down to a more potent 1 cup and do not worry if the juice separates upon simmering. ◆ If you wish to work in advance, the ice-cream mixture may be made 1–2 days in advance of freezing. Once frozen, it stays flavorful for up to 1 week.

TECHNIQUE NOTES:

When ice cream recipes call for milk, half-and-half, or heavy cream, or a combination, what is being played with is the butterfat content, the thing that to a large extent gives ice cream its body and texture. In the context of a Chinese dinner, the butterfat content is extremely important, as you want to end an oil-based meal with refreshment and not with a cream-coated tongue. Thus, our recipes purposely never call for all heavy cream.

Yields about 1 quart.

INGREDIENTS:

For the infusion:
   1 cup half-and-half
   ⅜ cup sugar
   ¼ cup finely chopped fresh tangerine peel, all traces of white pith removed

For the ice cream custard:
   3 large egg yolks
   ⅜ cup sugar
   ¾ cup heavy (whipping) cream

Flavorings:
   1 cup very flavorful, freshly squeezed, strained tangerine juice
   1½–2 tablespoons Mandarine Napoleon liqueur
   about ¼ teaspoon freshly squeezed, strained lemon juice

Optional garnish:
   thin slivers of glacéed tangerine peel (follow method for glacéed orange peel
      on page 488)

To make the infusion:
Wash the tangerines, then remove the skin with a vegetable peeler in as broad pieces as possible. Spread the strips of skin orange side down, slice or scrape away all traces of white pith, then chop the peel. You will need ¼ cup.

   Combine the chopped peel, half-and-half, and ⅜ cup sugar in a small, non-aluminum saucepan. Bring to scalding over medium-high heat, stirring gently to dissolve the sugar, until there is a thick rim of tiny bubbles all around the edge of the pot. Turn off the heat, cover the pot, and let the mixture steep for 20–30 minutes, or until cool. Don't worry if the mixture appears to have curdled.

Making the custard:
Put the heavy cream into a medium-size bowl, then set the bowl into a larger bowl lined with ice. Put a fine-mesh strainer alongside.

   Using a wire whisk or a mixer, beat the yolks with ⅜ cup sugar until the mixture is pale yellow, fluffy, and falls in broad ribbons from the beater.

   Stir the half-and-half mixture, then bring to scalding again over medium heat. When scalding, add ¼ of the half-and-half mixture to the yolk mixture, whisking constantly to prevent the eggs from scrambling. Then, immediately pour the tempered yolk mixture back into the pot, whisking all the while. Cook over medium heat, whisking, until the mixture coats the back of a spoon, 180° on an instant-reading thermometer.

   Pour the custard through the strainer and into the cream, pressing down on the peel to extract all the liquid. Scrape the underside of the strainer clean and discard the peel. Stir to combine the custard with the cream.

Flavoring the ice cream:
Add the tangerine juice to the cream mixture, stirring to blend. Add liqueur to taste (no

more than 2 tablespoons, lest the alcohol prevent the ice cream from freezing), and stir. Add the lemon juice several dropfuls at a time, stirring and tasting after each addition just until the tangerine flavor is perceptibly heightened.

At this point the mixture may be refrigerated before freezing, up to 2 days if you like, sealed airtight. Don't worry if the mixture separates; just stir to recombine before freezing.

Freezing the ice cream:
Freeze in an ice-cream maker according to manufacturer's instructions, or in a tray with the aid of a food processor as described on page 501.

Remove the soft ice cream to a clean plastic container, pack it down, and press a sheet of plastic wrap directly over the surface to prevent the formation of ice crystals. Return it to the freezer for several hours to "ripen" and develop its flavors.

Transfer the ice cream to the refrigerator 15–30 minutes before serving if it is very firm, so that it will be slightly soft and full-flavored when eaten. Scoop onto chilled plates or into small chilled bowls, then decorate if you like with a bit of glacéed peel.

This ice cream keeps well for a week, with only a slight diminishing of flavor. Store with plastic wrap pressed directly on the surface.

MENU SUGGESTIONS:
This ice cream is superb on its own, or may be served in the company of *Fresh Ginger Ice Cream* (page 496) or either of the cookies (pages 493 to 495). It is equally good with dressy hot foods, informal cold foods, and spicy dishes, and just about the only time I'd hesitate to serve it would be on the heels of a peanut or sesame sauce or a dish flavored with orange peel. A distinctive Jasmine tea that is subtly perfumed, or a refreshing green tea such as a top-quality Dragon Well, is a wonderful partner for the ice cream. Do not try a dessert wine, which is unable to penetrate the creaminess of the dessert and would be left unappreciated.

Pear and Jasmine Tea Sorbet

香梨冰淇淋

This is a *sorbet* of great subtlety. The color is a very pale blonde, and the flavor is evocatively pear-like, with a refreshing aftertaste of Jasmine tea. It is a delicate, quietly romantic dessert, inspired by a recipe uncovered by San Francisco cook and Francophile Donna Nordin on one of her *nouvelle cuisine* food trips through France. ◆ To be perfect for a *sorbet*, pears should be long past the point where you can pick them up and slice them prettily in your hand. In other words, they should be ripe, soft, and smelling lushly like pears. The tea should be the best quality Jasmine you can find, and it too should have a strong and wonderful smell. Old tea or underripe pears just won't *taste* if they lack aroma. ◆ Making the *sorbet* is extremely quick and simple and may be done in either an ice-cream maker or in shallow trays with the aid of a food processor. Moreover, the *sorbet* mixture may be made in advance, and kept refrigerated until you are ready to freeze it.

TECHNIQUE NOTES:
When I have the time, I like to use "the sunshine method" to brew the tea. Combine the tea leaves with 1¾ cups cold water in a clean glass jar, seal the jar, then let it sit in the sun for several hours or overnight at room temperature. The resulting brew tastes especially clean and clear, with almost no trace of the tannin common to hot water brewing. It is, in fact, the very same method I use for softening Chinese dried black mushrooms, tree ears, and the like.

The addition of lemon juice to a *sorbet* or ice cream serves to heighten and enlarge the flavor of the sweetened mixture. It is a purposeful pairing of sugar and acid, a great example of culinary yin and yang.

Yields about 1½ pints, depending upon the method and the machine used for freezing (machine-made *sorbets* are airier, hand-whipped *sorbets* are denser, and one machine varies from the next).

INGREDIENTS:

> *For the tea:*
> > 2–3 tablespoons fragrant, dry Jasmine tea leaves (use the greater amount for
> > less pungent leaves)
> > 1¾ cup water
>
> *For the pear mixture:*
> > 1–1¼ pounds sweet-smelling, very ripe pears (to yield 2 cups chopped pears)
> > ¼ cup freshly squeezed, strained fresh lemon juice
> > ⅓ cup sugar, superfine if available for fast dissolving
> > 1½–2 tablespoons eau-de-vie de Poire William or other quality white pear
> > liqueur (optional)

Preparations:

Brew the tea. If you have time, use "the sunshine method," described above in TECHNIQUE NOTES. Otherwise, bring 1¾ cup water to a rolling boil, turn off the heat, and let the water sit for 30 seconds (this will lessen the effect of the tannin released in brewing). Pour the water over the dry tea leaves, cover, and steep for 20 minutes, or until cool. Stir, strain the tea, and measure out 1½ cups. The brew should be very strong.

Put the lemon juice in a bowl, then peel, core, and dice the pears, adding them to the bowl and tossing them in the juice as you work to prevent discoloration. You should have 2 cups chopped pears.

Combine the pears, lemon juice, tea, and ⅓ cup sugar in a small, non-aluminum saucepan. Bring to a boil over medium heat, stirring to dissolve the sugar. Reduce the heat to maintain a steady simmer, then cook 12–15 minutes, until the pears turn translucent and soft and the liquids are reduced, concentrating the flavors. Turn off the heat, remove the mixture to a food processor fitted with the steel knife or to a blender, then purée until thoroughly smooth, working in batches if necessary. While still warm, taste and adjust with more sugar or lemon juice to achieve a full, lively flavor. The mixture should be on the too-sweet side when you taste it at room temperature, or it will not be sweet enough once frozen. Stir to dissolve any additional sugar, then seal and refrigerate it until cold before freezing. It may be left in the refrigerator for up to 2 days.

Freezing the *sorbet*:

Just before freezing, stir the mixture and add pear liqueur to taste. Do not add more than 2 tablespoons, lest the alcohol inhibit the freezing process.

If you have an ice-cream maker or *sorbetière*, freeze the mixture according to manufacturer's instructions. Once frozen, transfer the *sorbet* to a clean plastic container, pack it down, then press a piece of plastic film directly over the surface to prevent air contact and the formation of ice crystals. Let the sorbet "ripen" in the freezer for about 2 hours to bring the flavors to fullness. About 20–30 minutes before serving, put the container in the refrigerator so the *sorbet* will be slightly soft and fully aromatic when eaten.

Or, if you have a food processor and not an ice-cream maker, pour the mixture into a shallow pan or tray (an 8-inch cake pan or 2 ice cube trays with the dividers removed is ideal). Press plastic film directly on the surface of the purée to make it airtight, and freeze until the mixture is thick, slushy, and fully ¾ frozen, turning the freezer down to its lowest setting if you wish to hurry the process. Remove the part-frozen mixture in hunks to a food processor fitted with the steel knife, working in batches if necessary, and process until smooth and fluffy. Immediately return the mixture to the tray(s), seal airtight as before, and freeze at least 3–4 hours to allow the flavors to develop. Serve slightly soft for best flavor. If the mixture has frozen solid during the ripening time, then whip it in the food processor just before serving.

Serve on chilled plates or in chilled bowls or goblets.

The delicacy of this *sorbet* makes it short-lived. Eat it within 24 hours of freezing to enjoy it at its peak.

MENU SUGGESTIONS:
This *sorbet* goes best with other delicate foods—milder dishes like *Paper-Wrapped Chicken* (page 150), *Gold Coin Shrimp Cakes* (page 243), or any of the clear-steamed fish (pages 250, 274, and 278), or spicier dishes like *Lettuce-Wrapped Spicy Chicken* (page 145), *Spicy Steamed Salmon with Young Ginger* (page 252), or *Stir-Fried Spicy Scallops with Orange Peel* (page 263). For a cold luncheon, try the *sorbet* after *Tea and Spice Smoked Fish* (page 256). For a tea to follow the *sorbet*, brew a light mixture of Dragon Well and Baby Chrysanthemum teas, with a single chrysanthemum afloat in each cup.

Persimmon Sorbet

柿子冰淇淋

In her charming autobiography, *The Mandarin Way*, Cecilia Chiang recalls Chinese New Year in Peking, when her mother would bury fresh persimmons in the snowdrifts outside their home and then serve up the frozen fruit with a spoon as a sort of instant *sorbet*. This recipe, from my cook and writer friend, Jane Helsel, goes a step beyond the snowdrift method to produce a wonderfully festive *sorbet* with a glorious color and the texture of ice cream. ◆ For the *sorbet* to be successful, the persimmons must be overly ripe—soft and squishy all over, with a mottled look reminiscent of an overripe tomato. A less ripe fruit will be tannic and bitter instead of sweet. To insure overripeness, buy the persimmons a week or two before making the *sorbet* and leave them out in a warm place to soften. If you need to hasten the process, put them in a brown paper bag and let the gases exuded by the fruit hurry them along. ◆ Persimmon pulp freezes perfectly, so you are wise to buy them in the season when they are plentiful and store them for the persimmonless months ahead. Let the fruit turn overly ripe, purée the pulp with a bit of lemon juice to keep it from darkening, then freeze it in an airtight container with a piece of plastic film pressed directly on top. ◆ As with most all *sorbets* and ice creams, you may blend the mixture up to 2 days in advance of freezing and should prepare to freeze it 6–12 hours before serving.

TECHNIQUE NOTES:
Many *sorbets* are a combination of puréed fruit and a so-called "simple syrup," made by boiling sugar and water together until they form a clear, slightly thick liquid. The syrup, a mixture of one part sugar and one part water, is very easy to blend with the fruit purée, and contributes to the exceedingly smooth, ice-free texture of the finished *sorbet*. If you make *sorbet* often, make the syrup in quantity; it will keep indefinitely in the refrigerator.

Yields about 1 quart.

INGREDIENTS:

> *4 very large, overripe American persimmons, or enough to yield 2 cups purée*
> *¾ cup water*
> *¾ cup sugar, superfine if available (for fast dissolving)*
> *4–4½ tablespoons freshly squeezed, strained lemon juice*

Making the syrup:

Combine the water and sugar in a small, heavy saucepan. Bring to a boil over medium heat, stirring until the sugar dissolves and the mixture is entirely clear. Let simmer undisturbed for 3–4 minutes, uncovered, then remove the pot from the heat and let the syrup cool before using.

The syrup may be made well in advance of making the *sorbet*. Stored in a clean glass jar in the refrigerator, it will keep indefinitely.

Making the fruit mixture:

Slit the persimmons in half, then squeeze or scoop out the pulp. Using a flexible spatula, press the pulp through a fine sieve to remove any seeds, fibers, or gelatinous bits of pulp. Purée the pulp until thoroughly smooth in a food processor fitted with the steel knife or in a blender or food mill. Put aside 2 level cups purée. Extra purée may be blended with a bit of lemon juice to prevent discoloration, then frozen for future use.

Combine 2 cups purée with 1¼ cups syrup and 4 tablespoons lemon juice, stirring well to blend. Taste, then continue to add lemon juice by the drop just until the mixture peaks in a lively, sweet flavor. Remember that the mixture should taste *too* sweet at room temperature if it is to be just sweet enough when frozen.

If you wish to delay the freezing, the mixture may be sealed airtight and refrigerated 1–2 days. Stir well before using and taste to see if more lemon juice is needed.

Freezing the *sorbet:*

Freeze in an ice-cream maker or *sorbetière* according to manufacturer's instructions. Or, if you do not have an ice-cream maker, freeze the *sorbet* in a shallow tray and whip it to smoothness in a food processor, as described on page 502. Once "frozen," pack the mixture into a small container, rap it on a counter several times to dislodge any air bubbles that might cause the mixture to crystallize, then seal airtight with a piece of plastic film pressed directly on the surface. Place in the freezer for about 2 hours so the flavors ripen and the texture firms before serving.

For best flavor, serve the *sorbet* slightly soft. If it has frozen too hard, put it in the refrigerator to soften 15–30 minutes before serving.

Serve in chilled bowls or goblets that will show off the pumpkin color of the *sorbet*.

Leftover *sorbet* will keep for about 2 days in the freezer before the flavors fade noticeably. Seal airtight before freezing, with a sheet of plastic film pressed directly on the surface.

MENU SUGGESTIONS:

Given the festiveness of persimmon season, this *sorbet* seems especially appropriate for a meal featuring a "dressy" poultry dish such as *Cinnamon Bark Chicken* (page 162), *Smoked Tea Duck* (page 169), or *Birthday Duck* (page 175). If you save and freeze the pulp, it is also a lovely visual ending to a meal during salmon season, which stars *Spicy*

Steamed Salmon with Young Ginger (page 252) or *Tofu and Salmon in Pepper Sauce* (page 346). A quality Jasmine tea with a subtle as opposed to a cloying fragrance is especially nice in the wake of the *sorbet*. Brew it on the mild side, with a single jasmine flower placed in the bottom of each cup.

Ginger-Infused Crème Caramel

薑味布丁

When I first came to California, I was fortunate enough to meet the young cook-entrepreneurs Michael James and Billy Cross and be invited by them to cook a luncheon for the great French chef Michel Guérard and his students at their elegant cooking school at the Robert Mondavi Winery. The setting was one of crystal goblets, great wines, and extraordinary table settings, and I was beside myself to think of a dessert that would be an appropriate salute to the grandeur of the chef and the spiffiness of the occasion. ◆ This was the answer, a small and silken plateau of crème caramel, with the refreshing taste of fresh ginger woven through the caramel and the custard. The idea began with a recipe in a cooking magazine that didn't work at all and which my pastry friend Oona then worked and reworked until it came out just right. The reward was a kiss from the bemused M. Guérard, and a dessert which I down untiringly. For a special meal, Chinese or otherwise, it is a delicious and novel ending. ◆ This is a simple dessert to make, which requires more attention than time. Once made, it may be refrigerated several days before serving.

TECHNIQUE NOTES:
If you are new to caramelizing sugar for use in a custard mold, there are several things to know that will make the going easier: Use a small and heavy, preferably silver-colored pot. If the pot is too wide, the water will evaporate too quickly; if it is thin, it may result in the sugar burning; and if it is a black or dark-colored pot, you cannot gauge the color change without having to dip a spoon in and out of the pot and risk the sugar crystallizing. Also, do not stir the sugar mixture while it is caramelizing or you will give the crystals a chance to form. To sidestep the usual anticrystallization technique of running a wet brush around the top of the pot, simply cover the pot for the first minutes of boiling and let the condensation from the lid wash the crystals from the sides.

Serves 6 if you use ½-cup molds, or 8 if you use ⅓-cup molds.

INGREDIENTS:

> *For the caramel:*
>   *10 slices of peeled fresh ginger, with the diameter of a quarter and the*
>   *thinness of a dime*
>   *1 cup water*
>   *½ cup sugar*
>
> *For the custard:*
>   *2 cups milk*
>   *½ cup sugar*
>   *4 large egg yolks plus 2 large whole eggs*

Making the caramel:
Line up the custard cups within easy reach of your stovetop.

Combine the ginger and water in a small, heavy saucepan. Bring to a boil over high heat, then boil until the liquid is reduced by about one half. Strain through a fine sieve into a heatproof measuring cup, then put the ginger coins aside for use in the custard.

Rinse the pan to remove any trace of ginger, then return it to the stove. Add ½ cup sugar to the pan, then add ⅓ cup of the ginger water. Any remaining ginger water can be thrown away. Over low heat, gently swirl the pot until the liquid is clear, indicating the sugar has melted. Raise the heat to high and bring the mixture to a boil without stirring. Cover the pot for 1–1½ minutes to allow the condensation to wash down any sugar crystals from the sides of the pan. Then remove the lid and continue to boil the mixture until it turns amber with a touch of red. (This is not the rich mahogany color one often sees with crème caramel, but more of an amber-gold.)

As soon as it turns red-amber, quickly portion the liquid among the custard cups, pouring directly from the pot into the molds. If the caramel is the proper consistency, it will solidify almost immediately. (Note that for this rendition that you do not need to twirl or invert the cups to line them with the caramel. A top glaze is all that is needed for it to drip prettily down the sides when the custard is unmolded.)

Put the cups open side up on a rack to cool. If you are working in advance, you may refrigerate the cups overnight, covered with a sheet of plastic film. Bring to room temperature before filling.

If you are not continuing immediately, seal the ginger coins airtight and put them aside. You must use the blanched coins for making the custard or the milk is likely to curdle.

Making the custard:

Preheat the oven to 325° and put the rack in the middle level. Put the custard cups open side up in a baking pan and ready a fine-mesh strainer over a 3–4-cup spouted measuring cup or a spouted bowl to make filling the custard cups easier.

Put ¼ cup sugar, the egg yolks, and whole eggs in a medium-size bowl, and stir gently with a whisk to combine. Do not beat the mixture or cause bubbles to form, which will undermine the smooth texture of the custard.

Combine the milk, ¼ cup sugar, and the reserved ginger coins in a small, heavy saucepan. Cook over low heat, stirring gently to dissolve the sugar, until the milk is scalded, and there is a ring of fine bubbles all around the edge.

Remove the pan from the heat and pour several tablespoons of the scalded liquid into the egg mixture in a thin stream, whisking gently. When combined, add the remaining liquid in a thin stream, continuing to whisk gently to blend the mixture. Do not whisk vigorously or too much. You want as few bubbles as possible.

Pour the mixture gently through the strainer to omit the particles of coagulated egg. Then gently pour the custard into the cups, dividing the liquid evenly among them. Let stand several seconds, then skim off any foam on the top. Proceed immediately to bake the custards.

Baking the custards:

Fill the baking pan with enough warm water to come ⅔ of the way up the sides of the molds. Transfer the pan carefully to the preheated oven and bake the custards for 25–35 minutes, or until a sharp, thin knife inserted at the *edge* of the mold comes out with a thick, curdlike coating and the top of the custard feels waterbed-bouncy when pressed lightly with a finger. At no time during the baking should the water be allowed to boil. Add some ice cubes to the pan if it appears to need cooling. If the custard is cooked too long or at too high a heat, it will crack and become watery.

When done, remove the molds from the bath and transfer them to a rack to cool at room temperature.

Once cool, the custard may be refrigerated for several days before unmolding and serving, with a piece of plastic film sealing the open cups. For best texture, refrigerate for at least 3–4 hours after coming to room temperature.

Unmolding the custards:
Unmold the custards just before serving. You will need a sharp knife with a thin, straight blade long enough to go down to the bottom of the cup, and 6 or 8 pretty serving plates.

To unmold, slip the knife to the bottom of the cup, then run it just once around the custard, keeping the blade pressed against the side of the cup and working smoothly so as not to injure the profile of the custard. Keeping the knife in place, invert the cup halfway over the plate, then press the knife very gently toward the center of the custard to break the vacuum seal. Expect the caramel to seep up to the edge of the cup as you do this. Put the knife down, cover the cup with the plate, then invert the custard onto the center of the plate.

If the custard does not slip out at once, then tilt the mold back to expose the open end, gently reinsert the knife at the edge of the cup, slide it to the bottom and again press gently toward the center to break the seal.

If perfectly cooked, the custard will bulge slightly when unmolded and the texture will be silky smooth.

Serve the custard with a spoon and, if you are in the mood, with a sliver of good crystallized ginger, and a violet or some other small and pretty flower alongside.

MENU SUGGESTIONS:
I usually serve this dessert at the end of a meal of classic dishes featuring either a steamed fish (pages 248 to 252) or an elegant dish like *Stir-Fried Spicy Scallops with Orange Peel* (page 263). Very spicy or saucy dishes would not prepare you for its delicacy. The custard is light enough to be served very successfully with a sweet Johannisberg Riesling.

Walnut-Apricot Tart

核桃杏子塔

Walnuts and apricots figure in Chinese feasts from antiquity. In addition to their culinary attributes, ground walnuts were favored as a remedy for baldness, and apricots were thought to cure disorders of the heart. Bald heads and faint hearts aside, most everyone will enjoy this moist and nubbly fruit and nut dessert, the creation of Berkeley chef Diane Dexter. It is a deep tart filled with a light mixture of crushed nuts on a thin base of orange and lemon-zested puréed apricots. It is a beautiful-looking dessert, dusted lightly with powdered sugar and adorned, if you wish, with crystalline, sugar-dipped walnut halves. The yin-yang blend of sweet-tart flavors and nut and fruit textures make it one of my favorite conclusions to a Chinese meal. ◆ For best flavor, the tart should be made 12–24 hours in advance, so that the fragrant walnut essence has time to permeate the tart. The crust may be shaped and the apricot filling made weeks in advance. From start to finish, the food processor makes this a simple preparation.

TECHNIQUE NOTES:
Fruit peels, like nuts, are rich in aromatic oils. To capture the essential oils of the lemon and orange peel, grate them directly into the puréed apricots, rather than onto a plate.

Aerated beaten egg whites add volume and lightness to the filling. For best results, warm the whites slightly before beating, add a pinch of salt to stabilize them, and use an immaculately clean bowl and whisk. To warm the whites, either put the whole eggs in a bowl of warm-hot water before separating them, or put the whites in a cup, then put the cup in a bowl of warm-hot water.

For firming a crust in the freezer prior to baking, see TECHNIQUE NOTES, page 514.

Serves 8.

INGREDIENTS:

For the crust:
  2 tablespoons finely ground walnuts (see below)
  1 cup all-purpose flour
  1 tablespoon sugar
  6 tablespoons room temperature sweet butter, cut into cubes
  1 large egg yolk
  1 tablespoon dark rum, Myers's preferred
  1 teaspoon pure vanilla extract

Apricot base:
  packed ⅓ cup dried apricots
  ⅛ teaspoon grated fresh orange peel
  ⅛ teaspoon grated fresh lemon peel
  sugar to taste

Walnut filling:
  ½ cup sugar
  3 tablespoons room temperature sweet butter, cut into cubes
  3 large egg yolks
  1 cup finely chopped walnuts
  1 teaspoon pure vanilla extract
  3 tablespoons dark rum, Myers's preferred
  3 large egg whites, slightly warmer than room temperature
  pinch salt

To garnish:
  plain powdered confectioners' sugar, in a shaker or sieve
  8 Crystalline Walnut Halves (recipe on page 509) (optional)

Making the dough:
In the dry work bowl of a food processor fitted with the steel knife, process 1¼ cups walnuts until coarsely chopped. Filter through a sieve to obtain 2 tablespoons finely ground nuts for the crust, then put aside 1 cup chopped nuts for the filling. Do not fine-chop them at this time.

Return the steel knife and the 2 tablespoons ground nuts to the work bowl. Add the flour, sugar, and butter, then process to a paste, scraping down as necessary. Add the egg yolk, rum, and vanilla, and process with several on-off turns, just until the liquids are incorporated. Do not overprocess. Remove the dough from the work bowl and pat into a smooth ball.

Alternatively, blend the ground nuts, flour, sugar, and butter to a paste by hand. Beat the yolk, rum, and vanilla to combine, then add to the flour mixture and work lightly until smooth. Pat into a ball.

At this point, the dough may be refrigerated several days or frozen, wrapped in wax paper, then sealed airtight in a plastic bag. Bring to room temperature before shaping.

Shaping the crust:
Press the dough into a 2-inch-deep removable-bottom tart pan 9 inches in diameter, or into a 9-inch springform pan. Use the same method described on page 511, but make the bottom and sides of the tart evenly ⅛ inch thick. The walls should be a very even 2 inches high. When the crust is well shaped, use the tines of a fork or the blunt side of a knife to tap gently around the top of the crust to give it a pretty scored edge.

Refrigerate the crust for 1 hour or freeze it for 30 minutes before baking, loosely covered. To freeze it longer, wrap airtight once firm, and bake directly from the freezer.

Baking the crust:
Preheat the oven to 375° and set the rack in the middle of the oven.

Bake the crust until lightly browned, about 20 minutes. Turn once midway through baking to insure even browning. At the same time prick the bottom several times with the point of a knife if it has swollen in one or more bubbles.

Remove the crust to a rack to cool completely. It may be left at room temperature up to 12 hours before filling, and must be thoroughly cool when filled.

Making the apricot base:
Put the dried apricots in a small, heavy saucepan. Add water to cover, then bring to a simmer. Cook uncovered over low heat until soft, stirring occasionally, about 10–15 minutes. Drain the apricots, retaining the liquids.

Add the apricots to the work bowl of a food processor fitted with the steel knife. Process until smooth, scraping down as necessary. Bit by bit, add enough of the cooking liquid to obtain a smooth, easily spreadable, jam-like consistency, processing after each addition to incorporate the liquid. Using the small holes on a hand grater, grate the orange and lemon zest directly into the work bowl on top of the purée, then process to blend. Be careful not to grate any of the white pith. Slowly add sugar to taste, processing to combine and tasting until you achieve the right balance of sparkly and tart tastes. Scrape the purée into a bowl to cool.

If you do not have a food processor make and season the purée in a blender.

Once cool, the apricot mixture may be refrigerated for up to 2 weeks, sealed airtight. Bring to room temperature before using. If the mixture has thickened, blend in a bit more water as needed to obtain an easily spreadable consistency.

Making the walnut filling:
Cream the sugar and butter in the work bowl of a food processor fitted with the steel knife, scraping down as needed until smooth. Add the yolks, and process to blend. Add the walnuts, vanilla, and rum, then process to combine until the nuts are peppercorn-size. Do not overprocess; the nuts should be nubbly. Scrape the filling into a bowl.

If you do not have a food processor, blend the filling in a mixer or by hand, chopping the nuts peppercorn-size before adding them to the bowl.

Put the warmed egg whites in a large, non-aluminum bowl with a pinch of salt, then whisk by hand until the whites form soft, thick peaks. Fold the beaten whites carefully into the walnut mixture until well incorporated. Use the filling promptly.

Assembling and baking the tart:

Preheat the oven to 350° and adjust the rack to the middle of the oven. Spread the apricot mixture evenly ⅛ inch thin over the bottom of the cooled pastry shell, using a flexible rubber spatula or the back of a soup spoon. Pour the walnut filling into the shell. It will come almost to the top.

Bake until set, about 30–40 minutes, when a wooden skewer or the point of a sharp knife comes out clean when inserted into the center of the tart. Rotate the tart once midway through baking to insure even coloring.

When the center is firm and set, remove the tart to a rack to cool completely. Once entirely cool, remove the outer ring. Cover loosely, then let the tart stand at room temperature 12–14 hours before serving to allow the nut and fruit flavors to permeate the tart.

Garnishing the tart:

As much as 3 hours in advance of serving, dust the tart lightly with powdered sugar, entirely over the top or just around the edges, as you wish. If you are adding the crystalline walnuts, space them round side up evenly around the tart, about 1 inch in from the edge.

To serve, slip the tart still on its metal base onto a large serving platter, lined with a doily if you like. Do not remove the base, lest the fragile crust break. Present the tart whole, then slice it at the table, centering a walnut in each slice.

Leftovers keep beautifully for several days. Store at room temperature, loosely covered.

Crystalline Walnut Halves

糖核桃

INGREDIENTS:

- *8 perfect walnut halves*
- *½ cup sugar*
- *3 tablespoons water*
- *2 teaspoons light corn syrup*

Put the sugar, water, and corn syrup in a small, heavy saucepan with a silver-colored interior (so you can watch the mixture darkening as it caramelizes). Set over medium-high heat, stir several times to dissolve the sugar, then bring the mixture to a boil without stirring.

When the thickly boiling mixture turns brown at the edges, swirl the pan gently to even it. Just before it becomes a nutty brown, remove the pan from the heat (the mixture will continue to darken a bit from the heat of the pan). Let the mixture cool somewhat, until it stops boiling and thickens slightly.

One by one, spear the walnut halves with a toothpick and dunk them into the hot caramel, swirling the nut on the pick to coat it evenly. Remove to lightly greased wax paper or parchment paper to cool. Repeat until all the nuts are glazed.

When the nuts are thoroughly cool, transfer them to a wax paper or parchment paper-lined airtight tin. Left at room temperature, they will keep up to one week.

MENU SUGGESTIONS:

The character and look of this tart make it more appropriate for a "dressy" than an informal meal. I like it best on the heels of mildly seasoned or lightly spicy foods, where the taste buds are still alert to appreciate the complexity of the tart's flavors. It is especially nice in a menu that includes one dish with a sweet and tart accent—*Birthday Duck* (page 175), *Sesame Scallop Balls* (page 267), *Sesame Fish Slices* (page 246), or *Phoenix Tail Shrimp* (page 235)—though the remaining dishes should be purposefully unsweet and untart. Most dessert wines will partner this dessert nicely and will not be overwhelmed by the subtle sweetness of the tart.

Yin-Yang Kiwi Banana Tart

陰陽塔

To end a Chinese meal on a deliciously philosophical note, here is a stunning fresh fruit tart, with a jewel-like topping of lightly glazed kiwi and banana slices arranged in the Chinese symbol of yin and yang. It is a dessert whose flavors and textures convey the yin-yang message perfectly. The citric jade-green kiwi (native to central China) and the rich blonde banana (from the south) are delightful complementary opposites. Likewise, the sturdy shortbread crust and the soft, almondy filling are dramatically different yet harmonious. This dessert tastes as good as it looks, with a fruity flavor that is thoroughly appealing after Chinese food. ◆ The tart is extremely easy to assemble and need not intimidate even a beginner. The crust and filling are made in minutes in the food processor, and may be baked half a day in advance. Several hours or just before serving, the fruit is arranged on top with no need to cook it. ◆ The recipe is a conspiracy of two good yin-yang friends. The tart is Oona Aven's invention, and the food-processor method for making your own almond paste which follows comes from the wonderful kitchen of Rosemary Manell. ◆ For the tart to be picture-perfect, the fruit must be firm yet ripe. The kiwis should yield slightly to the touch like a ripe peach, and the banana skin should show no trace of green. If one or the other fruit is not available, the tart may be constructed entirely with kiwi or banana and still mesh beautifully with a Chinese meal.

TECHNIQUE NOTES:
To prevent shrinkage, the dough must be rolled out quickly, shaped in the pan carefully, then put in the freezer to firm it thoroughly before baking. While rolling it out, do not flip or dangle the dough. When shaping it in the pan, do not poke the dough enthusiastically with your fingers, but rather let it fall softly into place, then mold it gently with your fingertips. The gluten in wheat dough is elastic, and will bounce back and shrink if stretched.

The thin lacquer of warm apricot jam used to glaze fruit tarts is ingenious. It adheres the fruit to the tart, gives it dazzle and a note of citric sweetness, and forms an airtight acidic shield to prevent discoloration. Apricot jam is the traditional choice, but passion fruit jam (I use one made with Grand Marnier by Scott of Scotland) is, to my tongue, even more delicious.

Serves 8–10.

INGREDIENTS:

For the crust:
1¼ cups all-purpose flour
¼ pound well-chilled or frozen sweet butter, cut into large cubes
1 large egg, lightly beaten
1 teaspoon pure vanilla extract
¼ teaspoon pure almond extract

For the filling:
  ⅓ cup sugar
  4 tablespoons room temperature sweet butter, cut into small cubes
  4 ounces almond paste (recipe on page 513)
  2 large eggs
  2 teaspoons dark rum, Myers's recommended
  ¼ teaspoon pure almond extract

For the yin-yang topping:
  ½ cup passion fruit or apricot jam, pressed through a sieve to remove bits of peel and pulp if necessary
  3 large or 4 small kiwis, firm but yielding slightly to the touch
  2 medium bananas, moderately speckled with no green at the tips

To make the dough:
Add the flour and cold cubed butter to the work bowl of a food processor fitted with the steel knife. Process with on-off turns until the mixture resembles coarse meal. Combine the egg and vanilla and almond extracts. With the machine running pour the liquids through the feed tube in a steady stream, stopping the machine immediately when the dough forms a near-ball around the blade. Do not overprocess.

If you do not have a food processor, cut the butter into the flour until pea-size. Make a well in the center, add the liquids, then push the flour from the sides into the center with a fork or spatula. Work with the fingertips until the dough comes together in a homogeneous mass.

Press the dough into a flat disk. Wrap airtight in plastic and chill thoroughly before rolling out. The dough may be refrigerated for several days, or double-wrapped and frozen. Defrost in the refrigerator and roll out when very cold.

Rolling out the dough and shaping the crust:
Roll out the dough on a lightly floured board to form an 11–12-inch circle, evenly ⅛ inch thick. For even results, roll in one direction out from the center—not back and forth—rotating the dough ¼ turn with every few rolls of the pin. Roll quickly and deftly, so the dough remains well chilled and is not overworked. Flour the board and the top of the dough as necessary to prevent sticking; however, use a minimum of flour lest you alter the final texture of the dough.

Transfer the dough to a 9-inch removable-bottom tart pan using one of two methods: Fold the dough into halves or fourths, then lift it into the center of the pan and gently unfold it. Or, reverse-roll the dough loosely over the pin, then unroll it out lightly over the top of the pan, taking care to center it. Lift the edges of the dough to help it fall gently into place in the pan, then pat lightly to shape it without pushing or stretching. Press the rippled dough into the sides of the pan to form smooth walls that are evenly ⅜ inch thick. The dough should extend evenly ⅛ inch above the sides of the pan, to allow for shrinkage when baked. You will have a few tablespoons of excess dough. Sprinkle them with sugar and bake them off as cookies when you bake the crust.

Freeze the dough, loosely covered, for 30 minutes before baking. You may freeze it longer, if you like. Seal airtight once firm, and bake directly from the freezer.

Partially baking the crust:
Preheat the oven to 350°, and set the rack in the middle of the oven. Weight the crust by

lining it with a sheet of foil, filling it with raw rice, beans or weights, then drawing the foil up around the weights.

Bake about 10 minutes, until the sides look dry and no longer shiny. Remove the weights and the foil, prick the bottom of the crust in several places with the tines of a fork and bake for about 10 minutes more, until the bottom loses its shine and the crust is pale golden-blond. Do not expect it to brown.

Remove the pan to a rack. The hot crust may be filled immediately, or left at room temperature for up to 8 hours before filling.

Making the almond filling:

Put the sugar, cubed butter, and almond paste in the work bowl of a food processor fitted with the steel knife, and process until well combined and creamed. Add 1 egg to the work bowl, process to combine, then add the second egg and process until smooth. Add the rum and almond extract, then process until incorporated. Use the filling immediately.

Baking the filling in the crust:

Preheat the oven to 350° and set the rack in the middle of the oven. Pour the filling into the partially baked shell.

Bake 25–30 minutes, until evenly browned, turning the tart after 15 minutes to insure even coloring. While baking, the filling will puff up like a soufflé.

Remove the tart to a rack to cool completely. As it cools, the filling will sink back down level with the crust. When entirely cool, remove the outer ring from the pan by centering the tart on your palm or a heavy can.

The tart may be left 8–12 hours at room temperature before adding the fruit topping.

Slicing the fruit and glazing the tart:

Finish the tart no more than 2–3 hours before serving, lest the fruit wilt.

Melt the jam in a small heavy pot over low heat until liquid. Cover the pot to keep the jam liquid while you cut the fruit.

With a small sharp knife peel the kiwis and cut off the ends. Slice into even rounds ⅜ inch thick. Peel the banana, remove any fibrous strings, then slice on a slight diagonal into oblongs 1–1¼ inches long and ⅜ inch thick, to match the kiwis. Once the banana is cut, work quickly to apply the glaze.

Using a 1–2-inch-wide pastry brush, spread the top of the tart with a very thin, even film of warm jam, to act as a "glue" for the fruit. Return the lid to the pot to keep the jam warm and liquid. Arrange the fruit slices in a slightly overlapping ring around the outside of the tart, using the kiwi slices around the first half, then completing the circle with banana. Arrange another ring of overlapping fruit slices inside the first, then fill in the center of the tart, placing the kiwi and banana in the yin-yang pattern, as shown on page 16. Do not forget to slip a slice of kiwi into the banana half of the tart, and vice versa.

When the pattern is complete and the tart is entirely covered with fruit, brush the tops and sides of each fruit slice with a thin, even glaze of jam and also brush the uppermost edge of the tart shell.

For maximum beauty, serve the tart within several hours of completing it. You may leave it uncovered before serving, or cover it with a domed lid.

To serve, slide the tart carefully off its metal base and onto a flat serving plate. If you feel hesitant, simply center it base and all on a doily-lined plate. Present the yin-yang intact, then slice a thin wedge of the yin banana and a matching wedge of the yang kiwi for each guest.

Leftover tart remains tasty for 2 days; however, its good looks quickly fade. Store at room temperature, sealed loosely but airtight with plastic wrap.

Homemade Almond Paste

杏仁泥

Yields about 10 ounces.
INGREDIENTS:
>   *6 ounces (about 1 cup) blanched almonds (see below)*
>   *½ cup sugar*
>   *1 teaspoon freshly squeezed, strained lemon juice*
>   *¼ teaspoon pure almond extract*
>   *2–3 teaspoons boiling water*

To blanch brown-skinned almonds, cover the nuts with boiling water and let them stand 5 minutes. Drain, then quickly slip the skin from the nuts. Dry between paper towels, spread on a jelly-roll pan or baking sheet, and put in a preheated 250° oven for about 15 minutes until hot and dry to the touch, shaking the pan occasionally to turn the nuts.

Put the almonds in the work bowl of a food processor fitted with the steel knife, and process until coarsely chopped. Add the sugar, then grind as fine as possible. With the machine running, add the lemon juice, almond extract, and 2 teaspoons boiling water through the feed tube, then stop the machine. If the mixture will not press into a mass with a spatula, then sprinkle with the additional water and process with one or two on-off turns to blend.

The result is a soft, crumbly, not overly sweet mixture. Use it immediately or press into a tight mass, seal airtight, and freeze. Defrost before using. What isn't used for the tart refreezes perfectly.

MENU SUGGESTIONS:
The character and beauty of this tart make it most appropriate at the end of a meal of rather subtle tastes. A "classic" menu of *Pearl Balls* (page 187) or *Shao Mai Dumplings* (page 375), followed by *Steamed Whole Fish with Seared Scallions* (page 248) and *Shrimp, Leek, and Pine Nut Fried Rice* (page 408) would indicate the mood best suited to the dessert. To accompany the tart, choose a dessert wine with body, such as a French Sauterne or a heavier Auslese, namely a Rhine Auslese as opposed to a Moselle Auslese.

Mendocino Lemon Tart

檸檬塔

Mendocino is a picturesque spot on the north Califorrnia coast, where the cliffs drop steeply to the sea, and the mist rushing over the weather-worn trees reminds me of Japan. In a corner of the town is a charming rose-ringed Victorian house, my friend Margaret's Café Beaujolais. It is there one can find extraordinary desserts, including this smooth and tangy lemon tart. ◆ This is a simple, foolproof dessert, perfect for beginners. The rich, cookie-type crust is made in minutes in a food processor, then pressed into place by hand. The filling, a smooth lemon curd, requires nothing more than an arm to beat it. You may garnish the tart with plain or fancy nuts or whipped cream rosettes, all depending on your mood and the style of the occasion. ◆ The recipe will make one 9-inch tart. The crust may be frozen. The lemon curd may be refrigerated for 2 weeks, or frozen for a longer period if you like, with no loss of flavor or texture. Frozen lemon curd should be defrosted in the refrigerator, then beaten 2–3 seconds in a food processor, or thoroughly with a wire whisk before using. before using.

TECHNIQUE NOTES:

If your lemons are the least bit old or hard, put them in a preheated 150° oven for 10–20 minutes. Even the hardest ones will soften and become easy to juice.

Cooking in the top of a double boiler provides a gentle, indirect heat. Do not let the water touch the bottom of the pan or rise above a steaming near-simmer. Otherwise, you risk curdling the eggs.

Freezing the crust partially or fully before baking minimizes shrinkage. It also, by firming the butter, contributes to a flakier crust with a more pronounced layering.

Serves 8–10.

INGREDIENTS:

> *For the crust:*
> 1 cup all-purpose flour
> 1 tablespoon sugar
> medium-grated zest of 1 lemon (use box grater; do not grate any of the white
>   pith)
> ¼ pound room temperature sweet butter, cut into large cubes
> pinch salt

> *For the lemon curd:*
> 3 whole large eggs
> 3 large yolks
> medium-grated zest of 1 lemon (use box grater; do not grate any of the white
>   pith)
> ½ cup freshly squeezed, strained lemon juice
> ⅔ cup plus 2 teaspoons sugar
> ¼ teaspoon salt
> ¼ pound room temperature sweet butter, cubed

> *To garnish:*
> freshly toasted sliced almonds
> or
> Crystalline Walnut Halves (page 509)
> or
> about ½ cup chilled heavy (whipping) cream, whipped to stiff peaks with
>   powdered confectioners' sugar and pure vanilla extract to taste

Making the dough:

Add the flour, sugar, and lemon zest to the dry work bowl of a food processor fitted with the steel knife. Process 5 seconds to mix. Distribute ½ of the butter cubes evenly on top of the flour mixture, turn on the machine, and drop the remaining cubes one by one through the feed tube. Process about 20–30 seconds, until well blended. The dough will look crumbly. It will not form a ball around the blade.

If you do not have a food processor, blend the ingredients in a mixer or by hand until crumbly and well combined.

Press the dough into a compact ball. At this point the dough may be refrigerated or frozen, wrapped in wax paper, then sealed airtight. The dough should be soft and at room temperature when you shape the crust.

Pressing the dough into the pan:
Use a 9-inch removable-bottom tart pan.

Begin with a big wad of dough to form the wall and the outer rim of the base. Use your thumb to press the dough into the side of the pan, turning the pan as you go, removing most of the excess from the top, and pressing on a slight diagonal, so after one full turn you have the wall and the outer rim pressed into place. Go around again, if necessary, to even the dough. The wall should be evenly 3/16 of an inch thick, becoming slightly thicker where it slopes to meet the base, and should bulge 1/8 inch above the pan to allow for shrinkage during baking. Then use the flat of your fingers to press the remaining dough into the bottom of the pan, to form an even base 3/16 inch thick. The whole process will take 10 minutes or less once you get the hang of it.

Chill the crust in the freezer, loosely covered, for a full 30 minutes before baking. For longer freezing, seal airtight once firm, then bake directly from the freezer without defrosting.

Baking the crust:
Bake the crust on the middle level of a preheated 375° oven for about 20 minutes, until pale golden, rotating the pan after 10 minutes to insure even browning.

Remove to a rack, then let the crust cool completely in the pan. Once cooled, it may be kept at room temperature several hours before filling.

Cooking and chilling the lemon curd:
Beat the whole eggs and the egg yolks until combined.

In the top of a double boiler over very low heat, combine the grated zest, lemon juice, sugar, and salt. Add the beaten eggs, then whisk gently for 15 minutes, until the mixture is thick enough to coat a spoon. Add the butter, stir to melt, then remove the pot from the heat.

Strain the mixture through a sieve to remove the bits of zest and coagulated egg. Chill uncovered in the refrigerator for 4 hours, until thoroughly cold and thick. To hasten the process, you may chill the lemon curd in the freezer for 1–2 hours, but be diligent about stirring it up from the bottom every 15 minutes, so it does not begin to freeze.

Assembling the tart:
Just before serving, remove the metal collar from the tart pan by centering it on your palm or the top of a large can. Leave the fragile crust on the metal base and put it on a doily-lined serving plate. Fill the shell evenly with lemon curd to come 1/8–3/16 inch below the top of the crust, then smooth the top lightly with a spatula. Garnish with a border of sliced toasted almonds, *Crystalline Walnut Halves*, or whipped cream rosettes pressed from a pastry bag fitted with a star tip.

Slice the tart at the table, or—Café Beaujolais-style—serve each slice on an individual doily-lined plate, with a fresh tea rose alongside.

Eat the tart promptly. It quickly wilts.

MENU SUGGESTIONS:
This tart is zesty and simple enough to follow a "dressy" meal of mildly seasoned foods or an informal meal of lightly spiced dishes with equal ease. It is especially good when served on the heels of deep-fried foods and smoked foods, when the lemony taste of the tart is wonderfully refreshing. For the same reason, it is a very good ending to a meal featuring fish. To serve alongside the tart, try a California Angelica, which is reappearing again long after its popularity in the nineteenth century.

Crunchy Almond Tart

杏仁塔

My first Chinese dessert, once I had progressed beyond the fortune cookie years, was a plump, almond-stuffed mooncake bought en route to a samurai film in New York City's Chinatown. (A mooncake is a deceptively pretty, crust-enclosed pastry baked especially in celebration of the Chinese Moon Festival.) Somewhere between the lopping off of the enemies' heads and the spearing of them on long poles in a triumphant parade, I downed a bite of the mooncake. (Shamefacedly, I confess ravenous hunger in times of terror.) The doughy crust and the paralyzingly sweet filling were infinitely more shocking than the movie, to one brought up tenderly in the land of Jewish pastry. ◆ I have eaten all types and qualities of almond mooncakes since that time, but none would I trade for this delicious almond tart. It comes from the Café Beaujolais in Mendocino and is a thin, crispy, caramelized bed of sliced almonds in a rich, flaky crust. With its intriguingly crunchy texture and striking almond taste, it is wonderfully suited for a Chinese meal. ◆ This is a tart even a novice can make. The crust is blended within seconds in a food processor and may be frozen long before baking. The filling is combined in 2 minutes with a spoon, then put aside for 30 minutes to thicken. ◆ For extra ease, you may bake the tart 12 hours before serving. It should be baked at least 1–2 hours in advance.

TECHNIQUE NOTES:
Warming the cream for the filling, then putting the filling in a warm place is a passive way to dissolve the sugar and cause the mixture to thicken a bit. Beating the liquids would introduce air into the filling and increase its volume, resulting in a creamy instead of a crunchy tart.

When baking, the top of the tart should caramelize to a very dark, glossy brown. If one side browns before the other, cover it with a piece of foil to prevent it from darkening further.

Serves 8.

INGREDIENTS:

For the crust:
1⅓ cups all-purpose flour
⅛ teaspoon salt
1 tablespoon plus 1 teaspoon sugar
10 tablespoons (6 ounces) room temperature sweet butter, cut into 5 cubes
4 teaspoons water
1 teaspoon pure vanilla extract

For the filling:
¾ cup heavy (whipping) cream
¾ cup sugar
pinch salt
1 tablespoon Grand Marnier
⅛ teaspoon pure almond extract
1 cup untoasted sliced almonds

Making the dough:
Add the flour, salt, and sugar to the work bowl of a food processor fitted with the steel knife. Process with 1–2 turns to combine. Distribute the butter evenly on top of the flour

mixture, sprinkle the water and vanilla on top, then process just until the mixture masses around the side of the work bowl and stop the machine promptly. Do not wait for the dough to form a ball around the blade.

If you do not have a food processor, blend the ingredients in a mixer or by hand, until crumbly and well combined.

Press the dough into a compact ball. At this point, it may be refrigerated or frozen, wrapped in wax paper, then sealed airtight in a plastic bag. Bring to room temperature before shaping.

Pressing the dough into the pan:
Reserving 2 teaspoons dough, press the soft dough into a 9-inch removable-bottom tart pan, as directed on page 515. Then chill the crust in the freezer, loosely covered, for a full 30 minutes before baking. For longer freezing, seal airtight once firm, then bake directly from the freezer without defrosting.

Baking the crust:
Bake the crust on the middle level of a preheated 400° oven for about 30 minutes, until light golden brown. Rotate the pan after 15 minutes to insure even browning, and at the same time, prick the bottom of the crust once or twice with a fork if it has swollen in a bulge.

Remove the pan to a rack and let the crust cool completely in the pan. Cooled, it may be left at room temperature for several hours. Use the reserved dough to patch any cracks, lest the tart caramelize to the pan.

Making the filling:
Anywhere from 2–12 hours in advance of serving, make the filling and bake the tart.

Warm the cream in a small heavy pot over low heat until warm to the touch. Combine the cream, sugar, salt, Grand Marnier, and almond extract, stirring gently to combine. Carefully fold in the almonds, so they do not break. Set the mixture aside in a warm spot, uncovered, for 30 minutes to thicken slightly. Do not put it in a *hot* place; an oven with a lit pilot is sufficient.

Baking the tart:
Preheat the oven to 400° and set the rack in the upper third of the oven. To catch drippings, lay a piece of foil beneath the rack or put the tart pan on a baking sheet.

Carefully stir up the filling to redistribute the almonds, then pour it into the cool pastry shell. Smooth gently with a spatula or the back of a spoon to distribute the almonds evenly.

Bake the tart for 30–40 minutes, until evenly caramelized and a dark, glossy brown. Rotate the tart after 15 minutes to insure even cooking, and thereafter as necessary to insure even caramelization, covering any prematurely browned portions with foil. Watch the tart *like a hawk* (says Margaret) in the final minutes of cooking. Several minutes too long in the oven will turn it from the desired deep, dark brown to an overcooked black.

Remove the tart from the oven, then promptly disengage the sides of the pan by centering the tart on a mitted hand or the top of a large heavy can. If the caramelized sugar has bound portions of the pastry wall to the pan, then use the point of a small knife to carefully separate them. Transfer the tart to a rack to cool, still on its metal base.

Serve the tart at room temperature when it will be firm and crunchy, or while it is still slightly warm and soft. Transfer it still on the base to a serving plate, lined with a doily if you like.

Leftovers may be covered and stored at room temperature. They will be softer but still good a day after baking.

MENU SUGGESTIONS:
This is an extremely versatile dessert, good with a meal of mild or spicy foods, and suitable for a fancy dinner or an informal buffet. Like a Chinese mooncake, it even has a place at a *dim sum* brunch. This tart is a good partner for a French Sauterne—a "fat" wine with body—or with a glass of Madeira, sweet sherry, or California Angelica.

Steamed Banana Cake with Chinese Jujubes

香樵蒸糕

In the realm of traditional Chinese tea snacks and brunch eating, there is a wide variety of steamed, flour-based concoctions called *gao* or "cakes." Made variously of wheat or rice flour, with or without eggs or leaveners, they range in flavor from savory to cloyingly sweet and in texture from feather-light to leaden. The unifying factor is that they are all steamed as opposed to baked and are served with or between meals with tea—never as a dessert. ◆ This is a teatime cake I "invented" one day in Taiwan, when in a fit of craving for sweets I dumped a favorite banana bread batter into the greased pail of our large family rice cooker. Well-endowed with walnuts and contraband raisins from the PX and topped with a pretty mosaic of date-like jujubes, the cake was a huge success. Moist, fragrant, and lightly spiced, it is my annual Chinese New Year's gift to my older Chinese friends, who praise it unceasingly as a "real" Chinese cake. ◆ For lack of a 10-cup rice cooker, steam the cake in a large deep pot outfitted with a high-legged trivet (page 66) or a wide, open-ended tin can on which to place the cake mold. I use a rice cooker pail 8 inches in diameter and 4 inches deep, available in Chinese hardware stores. Substitute any 8-inch-wide, 2–3-quart baking dish or pudding mold. The batter must come only ⅔ to the top, to allow for expansion during steaming. ◆ For best flavor, use black, soft, overripe bananas. I like to put the more presentable store-bought ones in the freezer, where the skin turns black and the pulp acquires a marvelous, liqueur-like edge. I leave them there for months and use them when the cake craving hits.

TECHNIQUE NOTES:
Presteaming the jujubes and raisins plumps and lightens them, and prevents them from sinking into the batter. Coating the walnuts and the plumped raisins in a bit of dry flour achieves the same end.

Covering the cake mold tightly during steaming keeps the moisture from invading the batter, resulting in a moist yet strikingly light cake. Without the cover, the texture turns densely pudding-like. You can play with the texture by varying the tightness of the seal, but as you loosen the seal expect the cake to need longer to steam.

Serves 10–12.

INGREDIENTS:

To garnish:
7 moist, pitted red jujubes (page 550)

For the batter:
¼ cup dark raisins
1 cup broken walnut meats
1½ teaspoons all-purpose flour
¼ teaspoon ground allspice
2 cups sifted all-purpose flour
1½ teaspoons double-acting baking powder
1 teaspoon baking soda
½ teaspoon sea salt
1 teaspoon ground cinnamon
½ teaspoon ground nutmeg
½ teaspoon ground cloves
1 cup whole milk
1 tablespoon white vinegar
2 medium, soft, and blackened bananas, peeled and mashed
2 teaspoons pure vanilla extract
¼ pound room temperature sweet butter, cut into cubes
¼ cup packed light brown sugar
⅔–¾ cup white sugar
2 large eggs

Preparations:
(For details on steaming and how to improvise a steamer, see page 60.)
Steam the jujubes and raisins in a heatproof bowl over medium-high heat until plump and soft, about 10 minutes. Turn off the heat and remove the raisins, leaving the jujubes in the steamer. Let the raisins cool a bit, then toss them with the walnuts in a mixture of 1½ teaspoons flour and the allspice to coat. Put aside.

Choose an 8-inch round cake pan, soufflé dish, or pudding mold that is 3½–4 inches deep. Cut out a circle of waxed paper to fit the bottom. Grease one side of the paper and the bottom and sides of the pan, then put the paper in the pan, greased side up. If you want a sweet, glossy edge to the cake, sprinkle 2 tablespoons sugar into the pan, then rotate and tap it to dust the bottom and sides evenly, adding more sugar if required. Otherwise, dust the mold with flour in the same manner.

Making the batter:
Sift together the sifted flour, baking powder, baking soda, salt, cinnamon, nutmeg, and cloves.

Combine the milk and vinegar, then put aside at room temperature for about 10 minutes, until curdled. In the work bowl of a food processor fitted with the steel knife, combine the curdled milk, banana, and vanilla. Process 1 minute, scrape down, then process another full minute until thick and smooth. Scrape the mixture into a bowl.

Return the blade to the bowl, add the butter and sugar, and process until creamed, scraping down as needed. Add the eggs, then process for about 1 minute until the mixture is satiny, scraping down once or twice. Remove to a large bowl.

If you do not have a food processor, combine the milk mixture and cream the butter in a mixer or by hand.

Add half the flour mixture and half the milk mixture alternately to the creamed ingredients, stirring after each addition until well blended. Add the remaining flour and liquids, stirring after each addition, then stir until smooth. Fold in the floured walnuts and raisins, scrape the batter into the prepared pan, then shake the pan gently once or twice to even the top.

Remove the plumped jujubes from the steamer and cut them in half lengthwise. Arrange round side up evenly around the top of the cake, reserving 1 for the center. Place them gently on top of the batter. Do not press or they will sink when steamed.

Cover the pan with a greased sheet of heavy-duty tin foil, tenting the foil slightly if the pan is less than 4 inches high to allow for expansion during steaming. Press the foil tightly around the sides of the mold. Secure it with string for a light-textured cake, or leave it untied for a moister consistency.

Steaming the cake:

Center the pan on a high trivet in a large deep pot at least 1 inch larger in diameter than the cake pan, to permit a good circulation of steam. Fill with boiling water to come within 1 inch of the pan, then bring to a gushing boil over high heat. Cover the pot tightly, reduce the heat to medium, and steam the cake for 1½–1¾ hours, until a dry bamboo skewer inserted into the center comes out relatively clean. (It will not be as clean as with a baked cake, but the clinging bits should look cooked, not pudding-like.) Check occasionally and replenish with boiling water if required, lifting the lid as little as possible to maintain a constant steam.

Unmolding the cake:

Turn off the heat and let the steam subside for 5 minutes before removing the cake from the covered steamer. Transfer the pan to a rack, remove the foil, then let the cake cool undisturbed for 30 minutes. As it cools, it will deflate and shrink from the sides of the pan.

Run a knife around the edge of the mold, then invert the cake onto a plate. Peel off the wax paper, then quickly invert the cake, jujube side up, onto a serving platter. If flour is clinging to the sides, dust it off with a pastry brush.

Serve the cake warm or cool. Cut into thin wedges, centering a jujube in each slice.

Leftovers keep upwards of a week, sealed airtight and refrigerated. They may be wrapped in foil, steamed about 10 minutes, and served warm, if you like.

MENU SUGGESTIONS:

This is a perfect cake for a Chinese brunch or to serve alongside a cup of Jasmine, green, or Oolong tea at any time of day or night. It is very well suited for cold Chinese meals and will follow nicely on the heels of simple, potted dishes like *Casseroled Chicken with Smoky Chestnuts* (page 156) or *Mountain Stew* (page 254). If you would like to serve wine with the cake, try a slightly sweet California Gewürztraminer with residual sugar.

Wine & Tea

酒與茶

In the West we sometimes drink to accompany food and sometimes just for conviviality. "The Chinese," explains Lin Yutang, a twentieth-century writer, "have not developed the nicety of serving different drinks with different courses of food." They drink for fun. Wine is nothing but an excuse for a good time, he tells us without apology, for jokes and noisy games punctuated every so often by a dish. He admits, too, that in China choice of wine is limited, and almost none of it would fit our own definition: a beverage made from the fermented juice of freshly gathered grapes.

The rice wine of Shaohsing is invested with as much myth and romance as we have generated over the centuries in our tales of Falernian, Hermitage, Vintage Port, and old Bordeaux—the unique quality of Jian Lake water in which the rice is first steeped and steamed before fermentation, the antiquity of the yeast, continually present for more than two thousand years, the wine's alleged restorative properties and its more evident capacity to inspire the poets and scholars for which Shaohsing is equally distinguished.

But myth and romance do not adequately substitute for the enormous range of subtle variation possible in wines made from grapes. Had such wines been available to them, the Chinese, who allowed few civilized pleasures to slip past them, would doubtless have mastered the art of matching them to their food centuries ago. We are in the fortunate position of having both Chinese food and Western wines, and lack of traditional associations between them should present creative opportunities rather than obstacles.

Isn't it odd, though, how often those opportunities are wasted? Those who should know better tell us that "Chinese food" needs tea, beer, or white wine, miserably dull and condescendingly omnibus advice that nobody would think of giving in connection with "French food," "Italian food," or, indeed, any other European food. One respected gastronomic guidebook says dismissingly, and without further explanation, "Chinese food needs spicy white wine." Yet even if we ignore regional variations and specialties, Chinese food is at least as delicate, as diverse, and as imaginatively constructed as any other, and therefore deserves at least as much care and sensibility in matching to wine. A consensus of opinion on wine and food partnerships that work well together has to be based on harmonies, contrasts, and affinities that apply equally to wine and *any* food. True, Chinese food is designed to sparkle on the palate in a way that could tease attention from an accompanying great Bordeaux, but most French food is designed to do the same. Shallots, garlic, tarragon, and reductions of all kinds are not the ingredients of bland fare. That is why we prefer a simple *filet de boeuf* or plain lamb chops with such a wine.

Chinese cooking, to a greater extent than Western, is based on harmony, contrast, and affinity within the dish itself, however, and an accompanying wine must conform to that balance or provide, in taste terms, a silken backdrop for it. We tend to match wine to the principal ingredient, be it fish, lamb, chicken, or whatever, and then take its presence into consideration when planning sauce or garnish. A Chinese dish, on the other hand, constructed, like a good perfume, with evanescent top note, sustaining bottom note, and middle substance, must be thought of as a whole, or the wine becomes an intrusion.

I once made the mistake of assuming that an aromatic wine was needed for a chicken dish tangy with lemon and musky with green coriander. But they were just two notes in a chord that contained many others, and the grapey quality of the Rhine wine I chose could not have been more irrelevant, more out of place. The dish needed a wine solid enough not to be overwhelmed by its piquancy, but restrained enough not to impose. A good Chablis, or a young Meursault, perhaps, would have been a far better choice. I had a similar experience with marinated and stir-fried hoisin lamb. A fruity young Beaujolais that I had imagined would go well with its spicy-sweetness seemed to be frivolously out of place. A Beune, fortunately to hand, made a more dignified and a more compatible partner.

It is steamed dishes, in my experience, that allow the greatest latitude, however. A young Saar wine with a crisp Riesling bouquet and flavor that would have added an unnecessary and unwelcome baroque flourish to most dishes was excellent with steamed chicken; a richly flavored 1979 Saint-Veran added dimension to steamed crab; and, unbelievable though it might seem, I have rarely enjoyed a bottle of my limited stock of 1959 Château Lynch-Bages as much as when it accompanied Hunan-style steamed salmon with ginger threads and black beans (page 252). But then ginger and garlic, I have discovered, add scale to a dish, and make possible, even obligatory, a wine of more pronounced character than might otherwise be the case. When allied to beef or lamb they require the support of a robust red: Burgundy from a year like 1972 or 1979; Hermitage or Saint-Joseph from the northern Rhône; California Petite Sirah; or perhaps vigorous Brunello di Montalcino. With chicken or fish they make full-bodied, flavory white or light, fruity red equally acceptable. The breadth that ginger will add to fish, in particular, provides an answer to those California Chardonnays of such intense fruitiness that they distort or overwhelm most other foods.

If you are serving more than one wine with a Chinese meal, the usual caution is needed with sequence. The first wine should not steal the thunder of the second: a light wine should precede a full-bodied one, young before old (unless the latter is fading and might then seem to be thin), and dry before any wine that might have residual sugar. But though we normally prepare the palate for one wine by serving another, unfamiliar combinations with Chinese food are certain to reveal surprising nuances in wines thought to be old acquaintances. Helen Kan of San Francisco once remarked that Western wines brought out flavors new to her in dishes she had eaten all her life. The reverse is also true, and who knows what further hidden charm a favorite simple rosé might disclose when matched to a lettuce-wrapped spicy chicken?

—GERALD ASHER

On
Tea

茶

Tea in China means contemplation, relaxation, and renewal. One grasps the warm cup and sniffs the fragrant leaves as a tonic, to soothe the spirit and quiet the mind. The water used for brewing should be fetched from a calm mountain stream. The atmosphere should be simple and still. The company, if one is not alone, should be conducive to reflective ease. Or so the early Chinese writers on tea would like us to learn. "One drinks tea to forget the world's noise," writes a sixteenth-century Chinese gentleman in his "Essay on Boiling Spring Water." "It is not for those who eat rich food and dress in silk pyjamas!"

Tea as such is the opposite of wine in China, a drink in which the Chinese indulged with equal pleasure but viewed quite differently. Tea was *yin* and wine was *yang* to the traditional Chinese mind, a pair of complementary opposites that were compatible in the larger scheme of one's life or in the fullness of one's day, but which were in definite conflict in a single setting or a single mood. Whereas wine was yang—full of fire and warmth, radiating aggressive cheer and best drunk in boisterous company to the accompaniment of good food and lively games—tea was at the opposite pole of the cosmos. Tea was yin—cooling in its effect, inspiring of purity and quietude, best drunk in the companionship of mannered friends or in the solitude of a moonlit garden. Tea was never taken with food, but was left instead for those moments in between meals. One needed a certain introspection to appreciate the "flavor echo" of a cup of tea properly brewed. Noisy streets, crying infants, hot-headed persons, and quarreling servants—several of the many "Things and Places to Keep Away from When Drinking Tea," recorded by one scholar of a previous age—were taboo in the mood and the setting assigned to tea.

The beginnings of tea in China are poetically obscure. Orthodox Confucian mythology credits its discovery to the shadowy culture hero, Shen-nung, who presides over the birth of Chinese civilization like some omnipresent giant. As the story goes, the great Shen-nung was boiling up the water for his dinner when some tea leaves blew into the pot on the heels of a fortuitous wind, causing the first kettle of tea instead of the anticipated dinner. A conflicting tale, promulgated by the Zen sect that sprouted in China after the introduction of Buddhism from India, credits the invention or discovery of tea to the Zen patriarch, Bodhidarma. It was five years after the great monk had committed himself to a cave to watch the wall in front of him unceasingly in silent meditation, when he was overcome by hunger and reached out to grab a tea branch and nibble on the leaves, a snack that roused him to wakefulness almost immediately. According to another story, the sleepy sage cut off his eyelids in order to keep them from closing, and there on the ground where the lids fell grew a tea plant to help him stay awake.

From that beginning it was not inconceivable that tea in China remained primarily a medicinal drink until well into the sixth century. Those needing to stay awake for meditative purposes, or those in search of "a remedy for noxious body gases and a cure for lethargy" all looked to the restorative powers of tea. Early records say that newly picked tea leaves were plucked, pressed into cakes, and then roasted dry. The sickly recipient would break a bit off, pound it to a powder, then brew it in water along with some orange peel, ginger, or onion, depending on what the doctor ordered. If the tea in those times was anything like the herbal tonics prescribed by acupuncturists today, then it is a sure bet that early tea-drinkers quaffed the drink quickly with their noses pinched shut and gasped wide-eyed in the aftermath.

More gentle times for tea and tea-drinkers came at the turn of the seventh century, when the patron saint of tea merchants, Lu Yu, published his celebrated *Classic of Tea (Ch'a Ching)*. Lu prescribed which water was best for brewing (springwater first, river water second, well water third), elaborated on the twenty-four implements required to brew and drink a cup of tea (the double-dozen scheme giving his work a mystical Taoist cast), and decreed that the best tea leaves for drinking should "curl like the dewlap of a bullock, crease like the boot of a Tartar horseman, unfold like the mist rising from a ravine, and soften gently like fine earth after it is swept by rain." With one book, he thus inspired centuries of tea-drinking for pleasure, centuries of porcelain manufacture to provide the necessary accoutrements, and centuries of prose, poetry, and painting devoted to tea.

The refinement of tea-drinking in China, which began with Lu Yu, reached its apex in the succeeding Sung dynasty (960–1278 A.D.). Tea drinkers stopped using salt to flavor their tea, and the pressed tea cake became unfashionable. Whipped tea was in vogue, the dried leaves first ground to a powder and then whipped into hot water with a delicately crafted bamboo whisk. Teahouses sprouted in large cities, where groups with different interests could gather in between meals and business to sip tea, share a newly purchased blend, and consider pet birds, the fine points of painting, or dominoes. Porcelain manufacturers rose to the occasion of tea's new social status with the most beautiful tea ware ever seen in China—tea bowls of pale celadon green, crackle-glaze ivory, or sea-blue with a rich splotch of purple like a luscious plum. The Confucian officials in their mansions remarked that "the delicate bitterness of tea resembled the aftertaste of good counsel," while the Zen monks gathering in their monasteries for rituals of prayer involving tea were sowing the seeds for the tea ceremony that was to be exported to Japan and become one of that country's highest arts.

Tea times were good in the Sung. However, with the invasion of the Mongols from the north and the establishment of the Yuan dynasty, the increasing refinement of tea and the cult that was growing around it suffered a blow from which it never recovered. Tea remained a gentlemanly preoccupation of poets and philosophers and wove a strong thread through the fabric of everyday Chinese life. Meetings began with an offer of tea and ended with the raising of an empty cup, strangers and dear ones alike were greeted with a cup of tea at the door of any shop or any home, and teahouses continued to flourish on the streets while tea parties were a constant happening in the gardens of literati. But the Chinese artistry surrounding tea had reached its zenith, and the perfection of the tea ritual was to occur in Japan. In China, tea remained along with food, wine, and good company one of the pleasures of life to which anyone had access. Instead of a ritual, it became a regular punctuation mark of everyday living, a retreat to a teacup instead of to a temple.

By the time I was living an everyday Chinese life (straight from a background of tea bags and tepid water), the preparation and drinking of tea in Taiwan was a casual matter but for a few old-fashioned people. At school, a giant kettle constantly bubbled to replenish the cups of teachers and students who were never without them. Exchanging my shoes for a pair of slippers and accepting a cup of tea were things I came unconsciously to expect upon entering anyone's home. Tea shops selling colorful tins of tea were on most every corner, and when one wasn't busy eating one was usually sipping tea. But twentieth-century life had imposed itself upon tea-drinkers. No one collected snow water for tea and then sealed it in a crock to be buried underground for five years to mellow before drinking—the habit of a fastidious nun in China's best-loved novel, *Dream of the Red Chamber*. No one journeyed to mountain springs and returned home to paint scrolls or write poems with friends who gathered to celebrate the special water with a tea party in a luxuriously appointed garden—the occasion of innumerable paintings and poems from Sung times on. No person of power sent ladies-in-waiting at nightfall to plant a sachet of tea in each closing lotus blossom and then to retrieve the scented tea the following morning once the flowers had opened, as was the practice of one empress. And so far as I know, no woman was sent a tea plant by her in-laws upon her engagement, a custom that traditionally symbolized fidelity to the future husband and his family, as a tea plant would not grow if it were transferred to other ground.

Still, I was fortunate with tea as with food to live among Chinese people who cared greatly about what they put in their bellies. Po-fu, the old man with whom I lived, blended his own teas in unusual combinations. His "yin-yang cup," as I called it, was a mixture of acrid green Dragon Well tea leaves and sweet, white baby chrysanthemums. When the boiling water was poured over the mixture in his big covered teacup, the green leaves would unfurl on the bottom while the tiny round flowers would bloom and float to the top. It tasted refreshingly bitter and soothingly floral all at the same time, a signature mark of the man who had conceived it. Together we would sample teas at the city's most traditional tea shop, where one long red couch was provided for the leisurely tastings, and a bevy of serious attendants pulled the requested teas one by one from their giant pewter urns—all overseen by the bustling, fat proprietor, and spied on covertly by the skinny man in a back room who painted birds and flowers on the small canisters which one could buy with the tea.

The Lo's, as well, my mentors in tea and other tastes when I returned from Asia, made of tea a ritual of caring. It was they who taught me that different types of tea should be brewed with different temperatures of water and that black teas brewed with vigorously boiling water are delicious, but that green teas require water that has come down from a boil if they are not to taste tannic and bitter. They showed me how to brew fine tea to a strong, uniform strength, and only then to dilute it with freshly boiled water if a weaker tea were desired, much as one would choose to drink an excellent whiskey with water or ice cubes, as opposed to pouring a whiskey that had been diluted in the brewing process. I was taught also that when pouring tea from a pot I should first fill the cups halfway and then reverse the order of pouring so that each full cup was of equal strength.

Aside from the techniques of brewing tea, I learned from the Lo's something of the atmosphere in which tea was best drunk. Their tea service was always pristine and plain: a grouping of white porcelain cups, occasionally alongside an unadorned white porcelain teapot if the leaves were not to be brewed directly in the cups. The simplicity of the service in a very definite way underscored the taste of the tea. Teas sent from China or Hong Kong and deemed very special would result in a gathering of tea drinkers or presents of the tea to their friends. Tea was variously a casual welcome to their home, an occasion for sharing a poem or a new idea, or simply a warm accompaniment to easy silence. In such an atmosphere, tea was always a pleasure, and occasionally a revelation.

In my own home, tea-drinking is a simple, important part of each day. Much to the amazement of most people who visit, I have no kettle and no teapot. I use an old enamel pot for boiling the tea water, a pot used solely for tea and whose open face tells me the temperature of the water as it climbs from the first stage of "fish eyes and crab's foam," meaning the tiny bubbles that cluster on the bottom of the pot, to the second stage of a lively simmer and "crystal beads in a rolling fountain," finally to the "billowing waves," which mark a vigorous boil. To brew the tea, I use individual teacups, each with a lid that keeps the water hot, thus forcing the leaves to sink. Unlike one Chinese poet of antiquity who was buried with his teapot, and a generation of elderly northern Chinese with teeth stained brown from tannin who carried their teapots on their person, I give all my affection to my teacups. There are big brown ones to begin the morning in earnest, smaller and lighter-colored cups for the tea-drinking moments of midday, and pale celadon ones embossed with cranes and clouds to sip from contemplatively in the evening.

To each cup I add a small portion of tea: a level teaspoon of dry leaves to a large 10-ounce cup, a touch more or less depending on my mood and the freshness of the tea. Then I cover the leaves with the appropriate temperature water, cover the cup to let the tea steep quietly for three or four minutes, and then gratefully if not always contemplatively drink it down. When I reach the bottom third of the cup and the taste of the tea on my tongue is decidedly strong, I fill it again to the brim with newly boiled water. This "second pouring" is always a bit better than the first, the leaves somehow cleansed of their impurities and the drinker feeling purer in the wake of the first cup.

If the drinking of tea is one of my greatest pleasures, then the purchase of tea is one of my greatest adventures. I buy perhaps fifty or more small tins and boxes of Chinese tea each year in order to sample what is new on the market and what is new to my tongue. Chinese stores are constantly receiving shipments of new types and brands of teas, packaged in marvelous boxes and tins, while specialty coffee and tea shops are popping up everywhere, all fair game for those who wish to sniff and sample the extraordinary range of Chinese teas and Chinese-style blends. There is a huge variety to acquaint oneself with: The black teas—fermented, bold, and full-bodied, often called the "red wines" of tea. The green teas—unfermented, evocative, and strikingly clean on the tongue, considered the "white wines" of tea. And the intermediate class of semi-fermented teas, including the brisk and refreshing Oolongs, the densely smoked Lapsang Souchongs, and the extended family of Pouchongs scented with Chinese orchid, gardenia, or jasmine blossoms. Discovering and sampling all the many varieties and grades, one can exercise the passion of a wine collector with one important difference: Teas in general, except for certain black teas, which are like fine burgundies, do not age well. Even stored as they should be, in an airtight glass or metal container, kept away from light, heat, and moisture, they will quickly fade in aroma and taste. They must be bought and drunk while they are richly fragrant, which means one must buy in small quantities and store tea with special care.

Getting to know good tea is to cultivate a certain discretion. One learns as one sips that each variety or blend of tea has its own special mood. Finding the time of day, season of the year, and changes of the heart that best accompany each cup and bring it to fullness is the pleasure of connoisseurship. In the morning, I will choose a smooth black tea if I am already awake or a blend of green tea and toasted rice if I need a more gentle rousing. At midday, I like a semi-fermented tea like the hearty Water Goddess or invigorating Oolong. Early evening with its quietude requires a lightly scented Jasmine or a mild and soothing green tea. Late at night it is Po-fu's yin-yang cup that seems perfect, with its mixture of bitterness and perfume an appropriate accompaniment to reflection on the day. Summertime brings out the best in green tea, winter suggests black, while the turning seasons seem best suited to the Oolongs and the Pouchangs. Or so my taste would have it, though one's taste, like one's age, changes.

As to the water for brewing tea, it must have a good flavor. Tap water that tastes oddly of chemicals, "old" water that has been heated once already, or water that is flat from having been boiled too long and consequently robbed of its oxygen are all to be avoided. As you drink better and better teas, you will need to provide better and better water. Perhaps like so many Chinese poets, a hike to the mountains is in order to capture some water from a clear-flowing stream. Or, like the nun in the novel, you might trap some snow or rainwater in a crock and then seal and bury it underground. Possibly there is a friend nearby who has some extraordinary water and who will send you a jugful if you send a servant with a poem. . . .

With the perfect tea and the perfect water, all that is left to find is the appropriate moment for drinking tea. Consider the suggestions of one old Chinese gentleman who centuries ago conceived what he thought were the "Proper Moments for Drinking Tea":

When one's heart and hands are idle.
Tired after reading poetry.
Engaged in conversation deep at night.
With charming friends and slender concubines.
In a painted boat near a small wooden bridge.
In a pavilion overlooking lotus flowers on a summer day.
After a feast is over and the guests are gone.

And to his suggestions I would add my own:

When the writing of a book has reached its end,
and one is ready to still one's mind.

Glossary
of
Ingredients

材料

I am a firm believer that one cannot cook well without good ingredients, and that one cannot cook good *Chinese* food without certain very *specific*, quality ingredients. The problem for a non-Chinese-speaking cook or someone who is new to Chinese cooking is immense. English names on labels are thoroughly confusing and inconsistent, quality Chinese ingredients are often very difficult to find even in well-stocked Oriental groceries, and the market is fairly flooded with "imitation" Chinese ingredients wearing reassuring English labels that make us think we're getting something good. How to remedy this?

What I have tried to do below is to give as clear an indication as possible of what *I* use in my kitchen to cook the recipes in this book. I have gone beyond the usual information found in Chinese cookbooks to provide brand names, Chinese characters, mandarin and Cantonese pronunciations, all the English names applied to an ingredient, and descriptions of packaging, measurements, and weights—in other words, everything you will need to pull that particular item from a shelf where it may well be surrounded by a half-dozen similar products of inferior quality or strikingly different taste. In many cuisines, there may not be such a problem. But in the Chinese case, where the same cabbage is called by two different names depending on which province you are from, or a sauce that goes by the same name is one thing in Hunan and another thing in Peking, it is impossible to work through the maze of available products without a clear guide. Some people might wonder whether brands change and whether new products supplant the old and of course they do. However, I have seen this happen only a few times in the past several years with the influx of goods from the People's Republic of China. Ninety-nine times out of a hundred, a good thing remains a good thing, and a new item is an additional goodie rather than a replacement.

I have also indicated below how to store these ingredients, and what type of shelf life you can expect. For the most part, you can count on needing nothing more than a shelf in a closed cupboard for storage and can look forward to a product lasting for years. That is comforting when you are faced with your first "grown-up size" bottle of soy sauce and are wondering how you will ever use it up. Well, you will!

To make this as useful a guide as I've intended it to be, I heartily suggest that you make one or two photocopies of this glossary. Put one in your car or your pocket, so that it will be handy for shopping. Then if you can't find what you need, the Chinese or Japanese grocer to whom you show the characters will be able to spot it for you in an instant. (The characters in the recipe titles can serve the same purpose. If a certain recipe calls for a special ingredient, trace the Chinese characters for the recipe title on your shopping list. Many recipes have a classic constellation of ingredients, and your grocer may know by the name of the dish just what ingredients you will need.) As for the second copy, use it if you are required to mail order for ingredients. Then no one can justifiably send you a brand you don't want or a product you can't use. It is a streak of missionary zeal on my part, I know, but I can't help thinking that the sooner we educate ourselves as to what's truly good out there in the world of Chinese ingredients the sooner we'll see fewer imitation sauces and weak-kneed black beans dressed up in pretty packages.

A note on revolutions and tongue twisters:

If you are a newspaper reader keeping up with current events or a reader of books on China, you will probably note that my transliteration of mandarin and Cantonese sounds in the glossary does *not* follow any of the standard romanization systems for Chinese language now in use in the West. Those systems are designed according to linguistic principles and leave the hapless English speaker faced with the formidable task of pronouncing something like "xiao"! What I am offering should be more readily pronounceable to an English tongue and, hopefully, more readily understood by a Chinese ear, which seems to me to be the point. Keep in mind as you glance at the entries that a group of letters clustered together forms one syllable. Therefore, *yuan* is not *yoo-an* but *yuan*, and Mao is not *may-o* (which might be more appropriate to a cookbook) but *mao*— one short burst of sound.

Know, in any event, that it is probably not the sounds but the *Chinese characters* printed below that will be your best tool for communication. Your Chinese grocer will be able to tell at a glance what you want, regardless of the dialect he or she speaks, and the characters may also be quickly recognized if your grocer is Japanese or Korean.

A

ABALONE MUSHROOMS, SEE MUSHROOMS

AJITSUKE NORI, SEE LAVER

ANISE, SEE STAR ANISE

B

BABY CORN
(玉米筍 *mandarin: yoo-mee-swun; Cantonese: yook-my-son*)
Also called "young corn" or "baby young corn" on the label, these 2–3-inch tiny yellow corns come in 15-ounce cans (8-ounce drained weight), packed in lightly salted water. Maypride markets the larger length, about 18 to a can. Companion packs a smaller variety, about 30 to a can, and the tiny corns can be somewhat uneven in quality. Other packers may include broken, fibrous, or overgrown corns in their cans, so buy one can and check it before buying several.

To use, drain and rinse the corn with cool water to wash off the traces of salt. Unused corn may be covered with cool water and refrigerated a week or more. Change the water every 3 days.

Baby corn has a lovely sweet fragrance and taste, and an irresistible eat-the-whole-cob texture. They are usable in stir-frys and soups or make intriguing crudités or garnishes for cold salads.

BAMBOO SHOOTS
(竹筍 *mandarin: jew-swun; Cantonese: jook-son*)
These crunchy shoots with their mild, refreshing taste are extraordinary when fresh. Like endive, they become bitter when taken from the ground, and thus far I have never sampled a fresh bamboo shoot that has been shipped from overseas with its taste intact.

Canned bamboo shoots are either white, crisp, and thoroughly clean-tasting, or yellow, limp, and smelling hideously like a biology lab, or something dull and in between (this according to an inch-thick stack of labels and tasting notes I have accumulated over the years). In my experience, only three particular cans are worth buying: Ma

Ling Bamboo Shoots, packed in a 1-pound 3½-ounce can with a green label (drained weight 12⅝ ounces) are large, crisp shoots that taste very good. Companion Winter Bamboo Shoots In Water, packed in the same size can with a blue label, are again large, clean-tasting, and crisp. Companion Giant Bamboo Shoots Stripped In Water (Chinglish for "bamboo strips in water") come in the same large, blue can and are very good, though not as good as the other two.

Before using, drain the shoots and rinse well with cool water, cleaning them of any white residue you may find in the interior ridges. As a preliminary to stir-frying to remove any tinny taste, blanch canned bamboo shoots in plain boiling water to cover for 10–15 seconds, drain promptly, and rush under cold water until chilled. Unused shoots may be covered with cool water and refrigerated up to 2 weeks. Change the water every 3 days.

BEAN SPROUTS
(绿豆芽 *mandarin: loo-doe-ya; Cantonese: sai-dao-nga*)

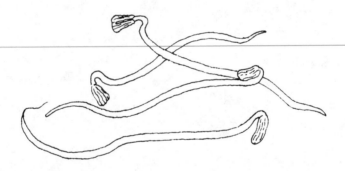

More properly called mung bean sprouts, these are the deliciously crispy, white-gold sprouts grown from dried and soaked green mung beans. At their best, they will be pure white-gold and erect, without a trace of limpness or brown. The sort you buy in a store is often 1½–2 inches long (a bit longer than if you sprout the beans at home), with a thread-like tail and often a pair of tiny yellow "horns" growing from the burst seed case. They are best bought loose from a store that has them delivered fresh daily, or directly from the tofu factory that produces them. Do not confuse mung bean sprouts with the thicker soybean sprouts grown from large yellow soybeans. You will know instantly which is which by looking at the "head" of the sprout.

If you are not using bean sprouts within a few hours of buying them, blanch them as soon as possible in plain boiling water to cover for 30 seconds, drain, and rush immediately under ice water or icy tap water to stop the cooking. Then cover with cold water and refrigerate until use, up to 5–6 days, changing the water daily. Blanching preserves the color and removes the slightly acrid taste of bean sprouts while doing nothing to harm their texture.

It was traditional in Chinese households that could afford a bevy of servants to have them pluck the tails and heads from bean sprouts before cooking. I have experimented on several occasions and discover that it takes about an hour to pluck what it takes five minutes to eat. It is not worth it.

To grow your own bean sprouts, soak ¼ cup dry mung beans in cool water to cover overnight. Drain, then transfer to a clean, wide-mouth jar. Cover the open end of the jar with two layers of cheesecloth held in place with a rubber band, then lay the jar on its side in a warmish dark place, tilted down for good drainage. Rinse the beans 2 or 3 times a day, running warm water into the jar through the cheesecloth, giving the beans a swirl, then tilting them to drain. Make sure the top is open to the air and if you don't have a dark spot, then cover the jar (except for the mouth) with a towel. In 3–5 days, you should have a jarful of about 5 cups sprouts, 1½–2 inches long.

BEAN THREADS
(粉絲 *mandarin: fun-szz; Cantonese: foon-see*)

Called by a host of lyric or irrelevant or misleading names in English, including glass noodles, cellophane noodles, silver noodles, Chinese vermicelli, transparent noodles, and long rice, these are dry, ¹⁄₃₂-inch thin, white or semiclear noodles made from mung bean starch. While still wet, the noodles are hung on bamboo poles to dry partway, then are folded into skeins to dry completely before packaging. Typically, the skeins are 5–6 inches long and weigh 2–3 ounces, though fatter, longer skeins weighing up to 8 ounces are occasionally sold in Chinatown markets. Skeins from Taiwan and Thailand generally weigh 2 ounces, and are packaged in cellophane, with red or pink rubber bands binding the skein; they can be purchased 8 skeins to a 1-pound net bag. Skeins from the People's Republic of China are usually bound with string and packaged in small plastic bags sealed with a ribbon.

In my experience, the thinner and more delicate brands from the PRC and the somewhat thicker Thai brands both stick together in clumps upon soaking, so I generally buy the Taiwan brands. In soups or cold salads, however, where the thinner sort made in the PRC has an unbeatable delicacy and glassy look, I call upon my patience and settle for carefully picking apart the clumps.

Depending upon the country of origin, bean threads require soaking in either warm or hot water to reach the desired consistency. When you want *rubber-band-firm* bean threads that will be cooked to further softness in stir-frying, soak the Taiwan brands in warm tap water and the PRC brands in very hot water. In about 30 seconds, they should be rubber band-like and may sit in the water without softening further. When you want *soft and silky* noodles, appropriate for soups or cold salads, cover the Taiwan brands with very hot tap water and the PRC brands with simmering water. Generally, 15–30 seconds will do the job, then the noodles should be drained. Do not let them become mushy.

To cut bean threads that need soaking into manageable lengths, put them in to soak still wearing their rubber bands or strings. Once they have softened to the rubber-band stage, use scissors to cut through the loop ends of the skein—in most cases, that will cut them into the desired length—then cut through the bands or strings binding the skein and discard them.

To cut bean threads that will be deep-fried in their *dry* form, use strong scissors to cut through the loop ends of the skein, cut the bands binding the skein, then pull the individual strands apart inside a large paper bag to keep them from flying about. Cutting bean threads while dry is something you will also have to do for those recipes which call for less than 2 ounces, making it necessary to divide a skein in half or into thirds before soaking.

Dry bean threads keep indefinitely at room temperature. Soaked bean threads may be drained and refrigerated up to 3 days and may require a new bath in warm or hot tap water if they have firmed during refrigeration.

BLACK BEANS, SEE SALTED BLACK BEANS

BLACK MUSHROOMS, SEE CHINESE DRIED BLACK MUSHROOMS

BLACK SOY SAUCE, SEE SOY SAUCE

BLACK VINEGAR, SEE VINEGAR

BROWN SUGAR, SEE SUGAR

C

CABBAGE, SEE CHINESE CABBAGE

CASSIA BARK

(桂皮 *mandarin: gway-pee; Cantonese: gwai-pay)*

Cassia bark *(Cinnamomum cassia)* is often called "false cinnamon" or, in cookbooks, "Chinese seasoning stick" or "Chinese cinnamon." Native to China, it is the thick, inner bark of an evergreen of the laurel family, a tree that figures largely in Chinese poetry because of its aroma and the mythic association of the cassia tree with the moon. Thicker and stronger in flavor than the cinnamon sticks common to Western kitchens, cassia bark is also a ruddier brown, with a pungent smell that reminds me of the candies called "red hots." It is sold in Chinese groceries and pharmacies, either in bulk or packaged in small plastic pouches. Judge it by smell, the more pungent the better. The shape, which varies from thick, woody slabs to thin shards, is not an issue so long as the fragrance is pronounced.

Store cassia bark as you would any spice, in an airtight jar away from light, heat, and moisture. As long as it smells strong and good, it will do its job, either scenting and flavoring stews and sauces or providing a fragrant smoke over which to smoke foods.

If the Chinese variety of cassia bark is unavailable, use very pungent cinnamon stick in a slightly larger amount. The flavor will be less intriguing perhaps, but fine.

CASSIA BLOSSOMS

(桂花 mandarin: gway-hwa; Cantonese: gwai-fa)

Also called "cassia buds" and less frequently "honey laurel" and "sweet olive" in English, these are the delicate, five-petaled yellow flowers—the dried, unripe fruits—of the cassia tree. Highly aromatic and possessed of a flavor that is simultaneously salty and sweet tasting on the tongue, they are a feature of refined Chinese sweets. Cecelia Chiang, in her fascinating autobiography *The Mandarin Way* recalls that her father had Cognac-steeped cassia blossoms added to his tobacco. Culinary uses are equally lyric.

The very best way to buy these flowers is preserved in a thick, sugary jam, which coats them like honey in clusters. Cassia Blossom Jam (桂花醬 *mandarin: gway-hwa-jyang; Cantonese: gwai-fa-jyeung*) will keep indefinitely under refrigeration, unlike the blossoms packed in bottles of sugar water, which tend to ferment. I know presently of only two sources for the jam (pages 588 and 589). If you buy the water-packed variety, look for bubbles in the jar, which could indicate fermentation. Both varieties are found in the refrigerator case of the grocery and should be refrigerated at home.

Pick through the buds to eliminate tiny twigs before using and drain the water-packed sort.

If cassia blossoms are unavailable, you can try a mixture of a wild-flower honey and orange-blossom water to achieve a somewhat similar, though hardly as celestial, effect.

CELLOPHANE NOODLES, SEE BEAN THREADS

CHANTERELLES, SEE MUSHROOMS

CHESTNUTS, DRIED

(栗子乾 mandarin: lee-dzz-gone; Cantonese: lut-gee-gawn)

These pungent, smoky, dried chestnuts are a feature of northern-style Chinese foods. Found bagged in cellophane in Chinese markets, they should be judged by their smell and whether they are still whole or shattered.

To use, cover with boiling water, cover the bowl to retain the heat, and soak 3 hours or overnight. The chestnuts will soften, though they must be cooked to soften further. Before using, pick out the bits of red skin from between the folds of the nut with a toothpick, a bamboo skewer, or the point of a small knife.

To store, keep in an airtight container at room temperature, away from light, heat, and moisture. They keep indefinitely.

CHILI FLAKES, DRIED RED

(辣椒末 mandarin: la-jyao-maw; Cantonese: la-jyew-muh)

I use these flakes, also called dried red pepper flakes, for their convenience and good taste in place of the whole dried red chilis one often sees in Chinese dishes. Someone who is not Chinese and has not been brought up to avoid the fiery devils when eating will inevitably swallow or bite down on one whole, then suffer the painful consequences. I *always* use the flakes, whether I am serving in broad daylight or at a candlelight dinner.

Look for cherry-red flakes that are evenly cut, neither powdery nor ragged. The brands I favor are either from Thailand or ones that are labeled with the word Szechwan, which you will find packaged airtight in plastic pouches and sold in Oriental markets. In addition to being fiery, they are flavorful and almost sweet. Avoid the darker-colored Spanish label varieties, which do not look pretty and can taste bitter when cooked in a Chinese dish. Also avoid the canned or bottled flakes sold in supermarkets or gourmet shops, which are usually half as pungent at twice the price. Properly "fresh" dried red chili flakes should be so strong smelling that one whiff makes you draw back.

Store as you would any dry spice, in an airtight bottle at room temperature, away from light, heat, and moisture. When they lose their strong, eye-tearing smell, not for many months if stored properly, it is time to throw them away.

CHILI OIL

(辣油 *mandarin: la-yo; Cantonese: la-yao)*
Also called hot oil, red pepper oil, and hot chili oil in English, this is the red and spicy oil made from an infusion of spicy red peppers in either vegetable or sesame oil. I use the sort made with sesame oil, called "Aji Oil" in Japanese (辣蘇油 *mandarin: la-ma-yo; Cantonese: la-ma-yao)*, which has a fragrance and depth in addition to being hot. The best bottled brands, packed by the Japanese firm Kadoya under the name Aji Oil and by the Japanese firm Iwai's under the name Sesame Chili Oil (Chima Rayu), are excellent though expensive. I have never found a Chinese brand to compete with them, though I am always looking. You can make an excellent chili oil at home (page 479) if you have a good Chinese or Japanese sesame oil to begin with.

Chili oil keeps indefinitely in the bottle, stored in a coolish place away from light and heat. I prefer a cool cupboard to the refrigerator, which forces you to bring the oil to room temperature before using it if you want the best of its flavor and smell.

CHINESE CABBAGE

(大白菜 *mandarin: da-bye-tsai, or Tyen-jin-bye-tsai; Cantonese: die-bok choy)*

Calling something Chinese cabbage is about as meaningless as a cook calling something lettuce, which is to say that there are at least a dozen varieties of common Chinese cabbage and each of them tastes, looks, and cooks differently. It is not, alas, merely a matter of a sloppy or an unspecific English name. The name given to the very same cabbage will change from one area of China to the next, which means that the only way to separate one cabbage from its cousin is to describe what it looks like.

The type of Chinese cabbage that I use 90 percent of the time is an oblong head 6–10 inches long, of evenly broad leaves wrapped tightly around one another. The broad rib is surrounded by a skirt of thin, crinkly leaf, which is sometimes tinged with a bit of green. The taste is light, fresh, and delicate, and not at all cabbagy. The perfume is similarly mild, clean, and slightly sweet. I use the outer leaves for general stir-frying, and save the inner leaves and hearts for pickles or more delicate dishes.

You will find this cabbage by its look, not the name given to it, which changes from store to store and from one Chinese speaker to the next. I have seen it, as well as several other varieties, marketed as white cabbage, Napa cabbage, Chinese cabbage, and bok choy, the latter being a general designation which will at least get you to the cabbage shelf.

A perfect head of what I am calling *Chinese cabbage* in spite of my tirade should feel firm when you press it between your hands, and should be very white in color, not green. Dots of black on the ribs do not affect the taste. My grocers say it is a mark of heavy rainfall, but I haven't been able to verify this intriguing bit of information.

If the head is perfect to begin with, it will keep for up to a month in the refrigerator, sealed airtight in plastic wrap. Discard the outer leaves as they soften and brown, then reseal the head with fresh wrap.

Another variety of Chinese cabbage that I love to use is what I call *Miniature Green Chinese Cabbage* (青梗菜 *mandarin: ching-gong-tsai; Cantonese: ching-gong-choy*). A common trade name is baby bok choy.

Very different in appearance from the white Chinese cabbage above, it is a loose, bulbous cluster of light green stems topped by oval, grass-colored leaves, the whole plant measuring anywhere from 3–3½ inches for the real babies to about 6 inches for the more mature plant. The stalks should be perky and smooth, and the leaves should be lively and unblemished. Like most fresh vegetables in a Chinese market, it will be heaped in a more or less neat stack alongside the other cabbages. It has almost no smell, just a very clean and slightly grassy aroma, and the taste is wonderfully refreshing, with just a touch of acridness to give it character.

If the head is perfect when you buy it, it will keep for a week or more in the refrigerator, sealed in a plastic bag with the bag puffed balloon-like around it to keep the leaves from squashing and releasing the juices that hasten spoilage.

CHINESE CHILI SAUCE
(辣椒醬 mandarin: la-jyao-jyang; Cantonese: la-jyew-jyeung)
This is a very spicy, slightly fruity chili sauce made from spicy red chilis, salt, and soybeans or a potato-like tuber, with a bit of vinegar thrown in. It is a condiment I vastly prefer to hot bean paste, both for its loose, light texture and its full-bodied taste. I have for years used Szechwan brand, which comes in a tuna fish-like can with a black label with crossed red chilis stamped on it like a crest. Recently, I have discovered a bottled variety by Koon Yick Wah Kee, which is very tasty and spiked with lemon. In contrast to dried chili flakes, hot chili sauce provides a fuller (not necessarily spicier) flavor in a semiliquid base.

After opening, store chili sauce in a clean airtight bottle at room temperature or in the refrigerator, whichever you prefer. Nothing, so far as I know, can kill it.

CHINESE CHIVES

(韭菜 *mandarin: jyo-tsai; Cantonese: gao-choy*)
Often called garlic chives *(Allium tuberosum)*, this member of the lily family has a

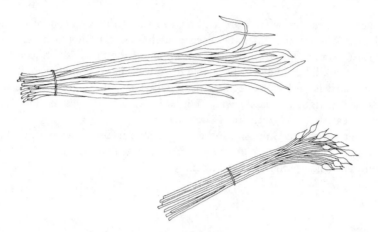

striking garlicky taste, which some call delicate and others call strong. Unlike our Western chives, the long and slender bright green leaves are flat, and in summer are topped by tiny, white bulbous flower heads that are edible. If harvested while the leaves are thin and slender, the taste is wonderfully delicate. Left in the ground too long and harvested when the leaves are over ⅛ inch thick, the taste and aroma become pronounced and a bit overwhelming.

Chinese chives are sold by the bunch, bound by a rubber band, and are recognizable by the narrow, tapered leaves that range from 6–9 inches in length. The leaves should be erect and unblemished when you buy them. Store as you would Western chives, refrigerated in a plastic bag. They will keep for about 1 week.

Chinese chives are exceedingly easy to grow. Seeds are available from many suppliers (page 592).

CHINESE DRIED BLACK MUSHROOMS

(冬菇 *mandarin: doong-goo; Cantonese: doong-goo*)

I have called these dried black mushrooms "Chinese" to distinguish them from other dried black or brown mushrooms frequently seen in specialty stores, but they are in fact common to Japan and Korea as well as to China. "Dried Oriental mushroom" or "*shiitake*," the Japanese name, might be as good or better for buying purposes than the name I have chosen, all referring to a dried and wrinkled "black" mushroom *(Lentinus edodes)*, with a cap that can be brown-black, gray, or even tan, and an underside of fawn-colored gills. The caps range in width from 1 inch or less (small) to 1¼ inches (medium) to 1¾ inches (large) and even upwards of 2¼ inches (giant). They are typically bagged by size, with or without stems, and are always expensive relative to other Chinese staples. In my kitchen, I am generally using medium or large mushrooms.

There are two types to distinguish between for cooking purposes. The first is what is usually called in Chinese *"fragrant mushroom"* (香菇 *mandarin: hsiang-goo; Cantonese: hung-goo*). The cap is rather flat, thin, and unbroken in color. This is the less expensive variety, prized more for its taste and dusky aroma than for its texture. Hence it is frequently chopped or thinly slivered.

In contrast is what is usually called *"flower mushroom"* in Chinese (花菇 *mandarin: hwa-goo; Cantonese: fa-goo*), a thicker cap with clefts and fissures that show up as white-tan lines against the dark color of the cap. The texture of this variety is plush and velvety upon soaking, and one accordingly pays a higher price. "Flower mushrooms" are typically left whole to show them off, or variously cut into halves or quarters.

I keep both sorts on hand, buying them in 8- or 16-ounce plastic bags to get a better buy, though a 4-ounce bag will be a less imposing investment if you are new to Chinese cooking and not yet hooked on black mushrooms. They keep for years, stored airtight in a plastic bag and kept like flour, in a dark and somewhat cool place.

Black mushrooms must be softened until supple before using, in water to cover. The best flavor is had by soaking 1–2 hours or overnight in cold water, though a faster job can be done with very hot tap water in 15–30 minutes, the exact time to depend on the thickness of the caps. Once soft, snip off the woody stems with a scissors, then rinse the caps under cool running water to remove any sand trapped in the gills (the thicker "flower mushrooms" will more often be sandy than the thinner "fragrant mushrooms"). If you like, you can strain and save the soaking liquid and stems, then simmer them down when convenient to potent *reduced black mushroom stock*, which can be an interesting addition to soups and stir-frys.

For information on *fresh* black mushrooms, see *Mushrooms.*

CHINESE EGG NOODLES, FRESH

(新鮮蛋麵 mandarin: hseen-hsyen-don-myen; Cantonese: san-seen-dan-meen)
Fresh Chinese egg noodles are a wheat and egg-based noodle typically dusted with cornstarch as opposed to flour during processing, giving them a lightness and a silken texture as well as a certain "bounce." Packaged in 1-pound plastic bags or wax-paper wrappers, they are usually kept in the refrigerator or freezer case of an Oriental grocery, where you will find them oftentimes in 3 or 4 different thicknesses. In all of the recipes in this book, I call for noodles which are ¹⁄₁₆ *inch thin*, on the thin end of the Chinese noodle spectrum but still not the very thinnest.

For the freshest noodles, go directly to the Chinatown factory where they are made (if you are within reach of a sizable Chinatown), where you will also find a wide range of dumpling and springroll wrappers. If you are not buying direct from the factory, check that the package feels supple, indicating that the noodles are fresh and not dried out. Frozen noodles are perfectly satisfactory if they were fresh when frozen.

Fresh noodles keep up to 1 week in the refrigerator, or may be frozen for a month or more. Defrost until supple before using, then fluff in a colander before cooking. For further information, including possible substitutes, see page 351.

CHINESE LONGBEANS
(長梗豆 mandarin: ching-gong-doe; Cantonese: ching-gong-dao)

These approximately foot-long, stringless green beans *(Vigna sinensis* var. *sesquipedalis)* are one of the most colorful items in a Chinese vegetable market. Bound in a long hank and left to flop over the shelf, they look like the colorful ponytail of some Jolly Green Giantess. Variously called yard-long beans, cow beans, *haricots baguette,* Chinese green beans, and (for a reason I can't comprehend) asparagus beans, they are sweet and tender when thin and have a wonderful shape and texture for stir-frying, something like our own best string beans but with a bit more crunch and body.

Longbeans should be smooth-skinned, uniformly green, and a scant ¼ inch across when you buy them. Yellowed, irregularly bumpy, wrinkled or thicker beans are usually signs that they were left too long before harvesting. Thinner means younger, which usually means best. To use, simply cut into 3-inch lengths, all but the hard base end, and cook and store as you would Western string beans.

Longbeans have their own special character, but you may use any sweet, tender string bean in its place. To judge either a long bean or a string bean for sweetness, simply nibble on one. If you have a garden and want to grow longbeans for yourself, see page 592.

CHINESE PARSLEY, SEE CORIANDER

CHINESE RICE WINE
(紹興酒 mandarin: Shao-Hsing-jyo; Cantonese: Siew-Hing jao)
This is the staple cooking and drinking wine of China, brewed from rice and water and generically called "yellow wine" (黃酒 *mandarin: hwang-jyou; Cantonese: wong-jao).* A prized variety, and the one I use in cooking, is manufactured as it has been for centuries in the city of Shao-Hsing—south of Hangchou in the central coastal province of Chekiang—and is called Shao-Hsing Wine. The brand I use is Pagoda blue label Shao Hsing Hua Tiao Chiew, the color of the label denoting an alcohol content of 17 percent. The wine itself is deep golden-brown in color, rich in aroma, and tastes pleasantly nutty, sweet, and smooth. If I cannot find this particular brand, I look for either the staple Taiwan brand that comes in a 21-fluid-ounce clear glass bottle with square sides and a black and red Chinese label, or a decidedly good quality dry sherry with a rich aroma and taste.

Be certain to avoid using Japanese *sake,* which is an altogether different taste, *mirin,* which is sweetened and almost syrupy Japanese cooking wine, and anything produced in the West and labeled something like Chinese cooking wine. These last are invariably pale in color, fragrance, and taste, with their only distinction being their price.

Genuine Chinese rice wine or a good-quality dry sherry substitute may be kept at room temperature, best out of direct sunlight. I keep my bottle stopped with a convenient spouted pour top, available cheaply in liquor stores.

CHINESE SAUSAGE

(香腸 *mandarin: hsyang-chong; Cantonese: lop-chong)*

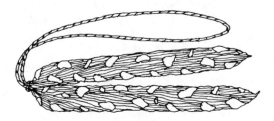

Generally sold in strings of two, each sausage measuring about 6 inches in length, ¾ inch across, and weighing 1½ ounces, these sausages lend a unique color, sweetness, and richness to a dish. Unlike our Western sausages, they are hard to the feel and very bumpy in profile, because they are dried as a preservative and are made with pieces of firm pork fat. The most common variety is pork sausage, which is sweet and rosy. However, there is also a popular sausage made from duck liver, which is dark and rich. You will also occasionally see beef sausage and extra-lean pork sausage. The standard pork variety is my favorite, both for the way it complements the vegetable and rice dishes in which I most frequently use it and for its own good taste.

I am extremely picky about Chinese sausages, finding many of them tasting painfully of chemicals. There are two factories, one on the East Coast and one on the West, which make excellent sausage and will mail order (pages 588 and 590). Short of mail order, trust your own tongue to find a brand with a clean, sweet, full-bodied taste.

Chinese sausages keep for weeks in the refrigerator and months in the freezer, wrapped airtight. Cut into thin diagonal coins and steam until the fat turns translucent and soft before using. If the fat is objectionable, blanch the coins to soften them prior to stir-frying.

COARSE KOSHER SALT, SEE SALT

CORIANDER

(香菜，芫茜 *mandarin: hsyang-tsai or yen-hsee; Cantonese: yoon-sai)*

Known in English as Chinese parsley or by its Spanish name, *cilantro,* coriander (*Coriandrum sativum)* is a staple of Chinese cooking. The leaves and stems are flatter and more delicate than our common curly parsley and smaller than Italian parsley, with a taste and odor all their own. Some people find the smell simply awful and liken the taste to soap. For others, it is a lovely aroma and a refreshing, stimulating flavor. Check among your guests before serving it raw, although finely minced and mixed into a sesame, peanut, or mustard sauce or blended into a filling it seems to be less a source of argument. (One of the complainers must have given the plant its Latin name, which is derived from the Greek for fetid bedbug. However, East is East and West is West—the Chinese name means "fragrant plant.")

When buying coriander, look for supple stems, lively, unblemished leaves, and a clean, pronounced smell. Once home, I find it keeps nicely for 1 week refrigerated in a water-flecked plastic bag ballooned out before sealing to give the fragile leaves an airy pillow. Some people store it like parsley, in a glass of water, though it seems to me to diminish the aroma.

CORNSTARCH

(太白粉 mandarin: tie-bye-fun; Cantonese: tie-bok-foon, or ling-foon)
Cornstarch is on occasion the great offender in Chinese cooking in the West—creating the gloppy sauces for which Cantonese-American restaurant cooking and inexperienced Chinese cooks are often known. Used in the right measure, it performs at least three important jobs in a Chinese kitchen. One, it binds the liquid ingredients of a marinade to each other and to the meat, poultry, or fish being marinated. Two, it protects fragile food against the heat of the pan or the oil, often creating a crispy coating around it. Third (and least used in my own kitchen), cornstarch thickens a sauce so that it clings lightly to the food, a feat it can achieve agreeably enough if it is used in moderate amounts.

In China, the most common binder starch is made from water caltrops *(Trapa bicornis)*, the horn-shaped seed of a water plant, and a mixture of water chestnut flour, tapioca flour, and the starch of potato-like tubers. The effect is essentially the same as cornstarch, though not the misuse.

Cornstarch must be dissolved in approximately twice its amount of cold liquid before it is added and cooked into a sauce. It will separate from the cold liquid and sink to the bottom of the mixing bowl within a minute or so of mixing, so it is a good idea to train yourself to leave the spoon in the bowl, ready for easy remixing when you are poised at the stove.

Chinese cookbooks are frequently misleading when they say "cook until the cornstarch turns clear." A sauce to which a cornstarch mixture has been added will *never* turn clear. It will go from opaque to *glossy* once the starch molecules have absorbed their share of the hot liquid and thickened the sauce by swelling, but it is not in the nature of the ingredient to turn clear. Do not fear that you will miss the change; it is very apparent when it happens, so long as you keep your eye on the pot.

CURRIED GLUTEN, SEE MOCK MEAT

CURRY PASTE

(咖哩醬 mandarin: jya-lee-jyang; Cantonese: ga-lay-jyeung)
This is a very spicy, fruity, oil-based mixture made hot by chilies, golden by tumeric, and aromatic by the presence of a dozen fragrant spices. It is a lovely seasoning, a world away from the raw taste of curry powder. I use the same brand we used in Taiwan, Daw Sen's curry paste, packaged in Calcutta in bottles of various sizes, all of which wear tattered

cellophane wrappers and a smattering of sawdust hiding the beautifully florid label. It is commonly found in Chinese groceries, an import in the sixth century along with Buddhism, that has earned its place alongside the bottles of hoisin sauce and chili sauce. If you cannot find Daw Sen's, then turn to a gourmet specialty shop for a bottle of Subahdar brand Brindal Pickle, which is also very good.

Curry paste is indestructible and immortal. I keep it capped in a cupboard.

D

DRIED BLACK MUSHROOMS, SEE CHINESE DRIED BLACK MUSHROOMS

DRIED CHESTNUTS, SEE CHESTNUTS

DRIED SHRIMP, SEE SHRIMP

E

EGG NOODLES, SEE CHINESE EGG NOODLES

EGGPLANT, CHINESE AND JAPANESE
(中國茄子 *mandarin: Jung-gwo-chyeh-dzz; Cantonese: Joong-gwok-keh-gee)*

In comparison to large Western eggplant and even the smaller, bulbous Italian variety, Chinese and Japanese eggplants are decidedly sweet and tender, with a noticeable lack of seeds and a pleasantly edible skin. The Japanese variety is generally 4–6 inches long and 2 inches across at the thickest point and is either purple-black or pure white in color. The pulp is slightly green when baked. The Chinese variety is longer, thinner, and paler in color: it measures about 6–9 inches long and evenly 1 inch across, with a pale lavender or blue-amethyst skin and a flesh that is white when baked. Given my choice, I prefer the Chinese to the Japanese variety, and the Asian sort to the Western. If you know a supplier who carries Japanese eggplant, it is worth trying to get them to stock Chinese eggplant.

Asians typically choose eggplants with an attention to a dull skin, not a shiny one, in the belief that a very shiny skin indicates a plant too long on the vine. I look for a firm, not hard, plant with a smooth, unblemished skin, and pay only secondary attention to its sheen. If I must resort to buying Western eggplant for a Chinese dish, then I look for a small specimen that feels heavy in the hand and firm though not hard to the touch.

Asian eggplants, if they are perfectly fresh and firm when purchased, will keep for up to 2 weeks in the refrigerator, bagged in plastic. If they should soften a bit, they will still be good for the recipes in this book.

To purchase seeds for growing Chinese eggplant, see page 592.

EGGS, FRESH

This seemed a good place to mention that I use grade AA *large* eggs, which most always contain 1 tablespoon of yolk and 2 tablespoons of white. It is particularly important to use this size egg or to measure out the appropriate amount of egg white from a larger egg when you are marinating poultry, fish, or seafood as the first step in "velveting" (see TECHNIQUE NOTES, page 145). More egg white will result in a coating that hangs from the food like a piece of extra skin.

ENOKITAKE, SEE MUSHROOMS

F

FATS, CHICKEN AND DUCK

This seemed the appropriate place to mention the small plastic containers of home-rendered chicken and duck fat that I keep in my freezer and use in cooking. One sort is that which I render, Chinese-style, by steaming the fresh, cubed fat sacs I garner from chicken and ducks that I have bought whole (page 127). The other sort is the fat that drips off a well-seasoned bird during steaming and which is made extremely tasty by salt, Szechwan pepper, and occasionally minced orange peel (pages 158, 162, 169, and 172).

Duck fat I find generally too rich and use only occasionally. Chicken fat, on the other hand, has a very appealing and light taste on my tongue, and I use it happily (and sparingly) to give a glossy dressing-up to a simple stir-fry of Chinese cabbage or bean threads or tofu, those foods that by virtue of their plainness are a good foil for a dab of tasty, liquid fat.

FERMENTED TOFU, SEE TOFU

FIVE-SPICE POWDER

(五香粉 *mandarin: woo-hsyang-fun; Cantonese: ng-heung-foon*)
This is a variable mixture of five or seven spices, which typically include star anise, fennel, Szechwan peppercorns, clove, and cinnamon, all ground to powder ranging in color from tan to brown or amber. There seem to be two general types on the market: the first that is finely ground, highly aromatic, and well balanced in smell and taste, and a second that is coarser, darker, and smells and tastes too strongly of cheap spice, much like a bad perfume. Even for the recipes in this book, where its use is an accent to only a small number of dishes, you should shop for the finer variety and judge it with your nose or your eye. Do not be concerned with packaging; the grimiest plastic packet on a Chinatown shelf frequently holds a treasure.

Five-spice powder is like any dry spice: It should be stored in an airtight, preferably glass container, away from light, heat, and moisture, and will remain good so long as it smells pungent and strong.

(Parenthically, just as I mentioned systems of interrelated fives in the introduction to the recipe for *The Five Heaps* [page 361], five-spice powder is likely the ancestor of a pseudo-pharmaceutical concoction, predicated on the proper yin-yang balance of flavors and meant to exemplify the Five Tastes [sweet, sour, bitter, pungent, and salty]. The Five Tastes were, in turn, predicated on the Five Elements [earth, wood, fire, metal, and water], which makes this a very cosmic powder indeed.)

G

GARLIC
(大蒜 mandarin: da-swan; Cantonese: die-syoon)

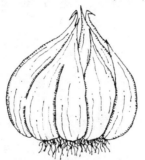

Fresh garlic *(Allium sativum)* is fresh garlic the world around—that hard, white bulb with its papery outer skin and its tough inner skin protecting a pungent flesh—"the stinking rose" that has caused great schisms between herbalists and country folk who believe in its magic powers and more up-tight sorts who fear its various potencies. In China, where food and medicine were tightly interwoven, garlic was considered simultaneously a tonic and a seasoning, scorned only by religious groups like the Buddhists who considered it one of the five impure things to eat (literally, The Five Chaoses). It is especially prevalent in northern and central Chinese cooking, the regional cuisines I like best, and is revered for its "warming" qualities.

Garlic should be literally rock-hard when you buy it, each individual clove feeling like a marble to your fingers when you squeeze the densely packed head. I usually look for small heads with a purple blush to the skin that seem to have a particular sweetness, though firmness is a priority over size. To separate the cloves from the head, simply rap the head pointed side down on a counter, repeatedly or with some force if the head is properly firm. Or, better still if you will be using the whole head, pull off the outer papery layers and put the head in a bowl of cold water for about 10 minutes, then pat it dry. The cloves will come apart easily, and as you cut off the stem end and spank the clove with the side of a cleaver or knife to split and dislodge the peel, the knife and your fingers will not be covered with the sticky stuff that makes peeling garlic such an irritating task.

By calling for a large clove of garlic I mean a *large* clove of garlic, one that would fill up the bowl of a teaspoon measure if it were plopped in whole. I am not at all shy about garlic in combination with other balancing aromatics like ginger, scallion, and chili, and I use *lots.* My attitude when it comes to most if not all of the recipes in this book is that when in doubt use *more.*

Garlic should be used within an hour or less of mincing and should be sealed airtight and refrigerated to stall oxidation until use. If the recipe calls for you to combine it with ginger, scallion, and chili—my own culinary Gang of Four—then its keeping powers after mincing extend considerably if you seal the four of them side by side or mix them lightly and then refrigerate until use.

Store garlic in a dry, room temperature or slightly cool spot, exposed to the air. I keep mine in a big glazed bowl on an airy counter in the kitchen, where it stays hard for months if it was rock-hard to begin with. Do not use garlic when it gets soft. Also, when the cloves have a green sheath at the core, taste the sheath and discard it before mincing the clove if bitter. Sometimes it is bitter and at other times it is simply pungent and clean-tasting, so nibble on a bit to be sure.

It should go without saying that dehydrated garlic or garlic powder has no place in a Chinese kitchen. You want the real stuff, bought in a fashion where you can test its firmness by clenching it in your fist, preferably not dolled up in a hermetically sealed box.

GINGER, FRESH

(生薑 *mandarin: sheng-jyang; Cantonese: sang-gung)*

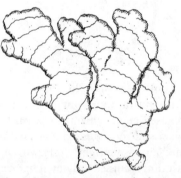

Fresh ginger *(Zingiber officinale)* is a mainstay of Chinese cooking. Ginger and scallion, soy sauce and rice wine, two yin-yang complementary pairs of seasonings, are the very foundation of Chinese cuisine. One cannot cook *real* Chinese food without fresh ginger, and I do not think I am overstating the case.

Finding fresh ginger is no longer the problem it was even five years ago in a Western market. Erroneously called "gingerroot" (for the antler-like horns or "hands" are in fact an underground rhizome or stem and not a root), fresh ginger pops up in every other suburban supermarket. The problem is to find it at its fresh best. Fresh ginger should be rock-hard, with a smooth, thin, tannish skin pulled tautly over the bulb, and only then will the gold inner flesh (which is sometimes tinged at the edge with green) be properly spicy-clean on the tongue. If the skin is shriveled and the bulb is soft or badly scarred, then the flesh will be weak-tasting. If you are forced to buy a wrinkled piece, one that has lost much of the vital moisture that gives ginger its spunk, then plan to use *more* of it than the recipe suggests.

When ginger is properly fresh and the skin duly taut and smooth, there is no need to peel it, except if you are slivering it finely for a topping and want a clean uniformity of color. Articles in cooking magazines typically call for one to peel ginger and sometimes even blanch it. That is a waste of time. For everyday mincing and chopping, simply slice off the scarred tips where the horn broke and healed itself over with a thick skin, and that is all. If you are using a shrivelled, over-the-hill piece of ginger, then by all means cut away the skin that will be tough and virtually tasteless. Otherwise, don't peel.

The matter of storing fresh ginger is also a question on which you are likely to see some interesting and conflicting suggestions. My method is very simple. First I take the fresh root and put it in a small, absorbent brown paper bag (not the waxed kind). Then I stash that inside a plastic bag, which I press around the paper bag and seal airtight. Finally, the package goes into the refrigerator, and every week or so as I use the ginger I check to see if the paper bag is moist. When it is, I exchange it for a dry paper bag. Stored in this manner, with the paper bag to absorb the moisture and keep the ginger from rotting, and the plastic bag to hold enough moisture in so that the ginger does not dry out, a perfectly rock-hard piece of ginger will last for months in the refrigerator. You may need to cut away bits of mold and use increasingly more of the flesh as the ginger ages and loses its punch, but that is all. It is a logical method, in fact, a modern translation of the traditional way in which Chinese cooks kept and grew their ginger: in a clay pot covered with a good-draining sandy soil, which kept in moisture yet allowed the air to flow through.

Another method of storing ginger is to peel it (this prevents clouding) and put it in a scrupulously clean glass jar topped with Chinese rice wine or dry sherry. You will then have a gingered wine and "drunk" ginger, which are both useful for cooking. I prefer fresh ginger in most cases and for me it is always available, but if you live in a region where ginger is rare, then you may want to preserve it in this manner. The amount used in recipes remains the same. However, adjust a sauce slightly to account for the extra wine in a recipe where wine is already a feature.

Freezing fresh ginger is another often-mentioned solution for storage. It weakens the flavor enormously and I don't recommend it, preferring the sherry method in its place if you must store it in a way other than the double-bag trick detailed above.

Whatever way you choose, remember that perfectly fresh ginger adds enormously to a dish. To my way of thinking, if you have to make longer or more frequent trips to get it, a picture-perfect piece of fresh ginger is always worth it in the end.

Giving measurements for fresh ginger in a cookbook is difficult, and I have tried to provide measurements that mean something: calling for a "quarter-size slice of fresh ginger" where you're meant to bruise it and add it whole to a sauce; calling for tablespoons and teaspoons when it's easiest to mince ginger by hand; and in some recipes that use a food processor specifying "a walnut-size nugget" or "a large walnut-size nugget" of ginger. By a large walnut, I mean a hunk the size of a large walnut in its shell. If you were to mince it, a walnut-size nugget would amount to a tablespoon or so, and a large walnut-size nugget would be about 1½ tablespoons. Know, however, that ginger is like garlic, or at least that my attitude toward it is the same. Namely, that more is generally better when you are in doubt. In the case of a steamed fish, where one is sprinkling raw slivers on top, there might be some hesitancy to splurge with the ginger and wind up with too much "bite," but at most other times I play rather freely and do not hesitate to add more if the spirit, my nose, the weather, or the condition of the ginger moves me.

GINGER, YOUNG

(嫩薑 , 子薑 mandarin: noon-jyang, or dzz-jyang; Cantonese: noon-gung, or gee-gung)

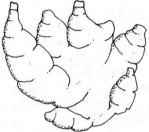

This is a variety of fresh ginger that is pulled from the ground several months earlier than the common variety of fresh ginger, and accordingly has a thinner skin and a more delicate-tasting flesh. Whereas the more common, "old" ginger has a tan-brown skin and a deep gold flesh, so-called "young" or "tender" ginger has a semi-translucent pale yellow skin (with pale green and pink shoots typically showing at the top), and a pale gold flesh. The young variety has few if any fibers. It is especially prized in combination with fish and beef on account of its compellingly clean fragrance and light taste.

Young ginger should be stored in the same way as the more mature type. It needn't be peeled, and you may wish to slice the shoots into thin disks and add them to stir-frys. This tender ginger is a remarkable treat and should be bought and used lavishly during the two times of the year when it is available for 4–6 weeks, then peeled and stored in rice wine or sherry for the leaner months. Because the taste is mild, you may wish to use more young ginger in a recipe calling for the mature variety.

GINGER IN SYRUP

(蜜羌子, 糖薑 mandarin: mee-jyang-dzz, or tong-jyang; Cantonese: toong-gung)

This addictive confection is knobs of candied young ginger (sometimes called *stem ginger* on account of the shoots mentioned above). They are peeled and then poached repeatedly in a sugar syrup until the syrup penetrates the flesh, sweetening and softening the knobs. It is wonderful in ice cream (page 496) or slivered on top of ice cream for a touch of spice. I like to nibble on a bit with a cup of green tea; it is a remarkably refreshing combination.

You can make syrup ginger on your own, but it is hardly worth it when you can buy the excellent brand made by Tung Chun Soy & Canning Company. It is sold in a fetching green-glazed crock and priced cheaply in Chinatown markets though often expensively in specialty stores. The crock is sexagonal and of ancient design, with each of the panels molded with a picture of one of The Six Friends of Winter (the number of friends changes but the motif is a traditional one)—those plants like plum, bamboo, and pine that bloom in the cold and symbolize the stalwartness of the Confucian gentleman in times of political or personal stress. It is something to ponder while you munch on the ginger. The empty crock, by the way, is a perfect holder for chopsticks.

GLASS NOODLES, SEE BEAN THREADS

GLUTEN, SEE MOCK MEAT

GLUTINOUS RICE, SEE SWEET RICE

GOLDEN ROCK SUGAR, SEE SUGAR

GREEN ONIONS, SEE SCALLIONS

H

HAM

(火腿 mandarin: hwo-tway; Cantonese: fwo-toy)
I mainly use two sorts of ham in my kitchen, one the densely smoked and salty *Smithfield ham*, and the other a lightly smoked and ready-to-eat *Black Forest ham*. A third sort, a *honey- or sugar-cured ham*, I use less frequently.

The *Smithfield ham* I use *uncooked*, the lean part finely slivered or minced into dishes either as a garnish or a salty seasoning (sometimes both). The fatty portion I mince and include as a richly flavored, salted fat mainly in steaming fish. In this way it most approximates the famous smoked Yunnan ham of China, which is unavailable here. Smithfield ham is sold cut into cross-slices about 1 inch thick in most larger Chinese markets, bagged in plastic so you can inspect its condition. It should be free of mold and superficial oil when you purchase it and should be refrigerated promptly when you get home. If mold should appear, you can scrape or wash it away, then safely eat what is beneath. As you use Smithfield ham, store the scraps of fat in a plastic bag in the refrigerator and keep the bone. They are invaluable as seasonings, and the bone is especially good in soup. Once bought and refrigerated, the ham will keep for a year or more.

If you cannot get Smithfield (which can be mail ordered in slices; page 588), use prosciutto or Westphalian ham, which are similar enough to Smithfield, though each has its own special character. Whichever the ham, nibble a bit of it before cooking to know how much salt it will be contributing to the dish, then adjust accordingly. All the recipes in this book that call for Smithfield have taken its saltiness into account. (And, a note to those who might wonder about eating "uncooked" ham: USDA inspection regulations require that hams be heated to an internal temperature of at least 137° during the smoking and curing process, which is sufficient to kill the Trichina parasite that has made us, as a nation, so wary of undercooking pork.)

For dishes where I do not want the intensity of flavor of a Smithfield and am looking for a full-flavored ham with character that I can sliver and chew on comfortably—say, as part of a cold noodle dish—I turn to a *Black Forest ham*. This is a small, ready-to-eat ham, which is very lean, very deep in color, and lightly smoked. It is likely to be the most flavorful ham in the case of a good specialty shop or delicatessen, and is head and shoulders above most all of the honey- and sugar-cured varieties for depth of flavor. Buy it in small quantities for almost immediate use, as its flavor will fade like any cold cut if kept more than a few days.

For fried rice and buns, where Black Forest hams are generally too lean, I use the best *sugar- or honey-cured ham* I can find. This, like the above, you must sample to know what you are getting.

HOISIN SAUCE

(海鮮醬 mandarin: hi-hsyen-jyang; Cantonese: hoi-seem-jyeung)
The name of this sauce in Chinese means literally "sea-freshness sauce," which is as enigmatic as the name "fish-flavor" applied to a certain style of Szechwan-Hunan dish (page 195). So far as I can tell, it belongs to a family of sauces made from fermented wheat or soybean bases, which can be variously sweet or salty, thick or thin.

I use a widely distributed brand, Koon Chun, that is jam-like in consistency and on the sweet side (though the label says it contains vinegar, chili, garlic, and sesame). Indeed, it is rather a spicy-fruity concoction that I find perfectly acceptable when thinned with a bit of wine and smoothed with a bit of sesame oil.

Hoisin sauce will keep indefinitely in a cool cupboard or the refrigerator, sealed airtight against drying.

HOME-DRIED ORANGE OR TANGERINE PEEL, SEE ORANGE AND TANGERINE PEEL

HONEY

(蜂蜜 mandarin: fung-mee; Cantonese: fung-mup)
Chinese honey flavored variously with blossoms and jujubes is increasingly available in Chinese markets, in crocks and bottles to delight the collector and with rich tastes that are intriguing and novel to honey lovers. Because quality and availability have thus far been inconsistent, I use local *wild-flower honey* for those Chinese dishes such as steamed pears (page 485) where it is an ingredient. I prefer the "uncooked" variety, which seems to me to have a better flavor. I avoid stronger honeys such as buckwheat and more characteristic honeys like orange blossom, especially when the honey is to be paired with Chinese cassia blossoms and would mask or distort their delicate taste.

HOT CHILI OIL, SEE CHILI OIL

J

JUJUBES

(紅棗 mandarin: hoong-dzao; Cantonese: hung-jo)
Jujubes, a glossy fruit with a dark-rust to blood-red skin, are an ancient Chinese fruit, which when dried become wrinkled and resemble dates. Called variously Chinese dates, red dates or black dates, depending on their color, and dried Oriental dates, they are typically used in Chinese sweets and appreciated for their felicitous color, sweet taste, and smooth texture. I do *not* use the hard, dried Chinese jujubes that are commonly sold

in cellophane bags in Chinese markets, which are reddish, about the size of an olive, and have the pits left in. Instead, I use *soft, pitted red jujubes* that are manufactured in the People's Republic of China by Polar Bear Brand and sold in ¼-pound cellophane-coated boxes, labeled Red Dates Without Stone (無核紅棗 *mandarin: woo-huh-hoong-dzao; Cantonese: moe-what-hung-jo*). There are many boxed varieties currently on the market, but so far as I know this is the only one *without sugar*. The jujubes are ready-to-eat and terribly sweet as is, and are lovely when steamed in a cake (page 518) or bread (page 412). There is no substitute for this particular kind.

Store the soft, pitted sort in an airtight container at room temperature, and they will keep indefinitely.

L

LARD
(猪油 *mandarin: jew-yo; Cantonese: jyew-yao*)
This in my kitchen means the pure white, firm, unseasoned, and odorless fresh fat from the back of the pig. In butcher shops you should ask for fat back or fresh pork fat, which the butcher will often sell you gratis. If you have difficulty locating a source, ask a friend or call a specialty shop that makes pâté, for lard is a staple in any kitchen where it is made. For smaller amounts, trim the pure white fat from a pork chop. Do *not* use salt back or salt pork, which are seasoned.

Lard was the traditional cooking fat of China and was used for both deep-frying and stir-frying. It is the reason why you find, in many of the old Chinese cookbooks, the stern admonishment to eat a dish up because it will not be good cold. One of lard's disadvantages (to counter the wonderful crispness and flavor it imparts) is that unlike vegetable oils, it congeals and is unappetizing when cold.

Lard's job, ironic as it seems given our Western associations with this product, is to make things light and/or crisp. It is a standard ingredient in Chinese shrimp pastes and *dim sum*-type pastry doughs, and there is no substitute. For use in the shrimp mixtures or to add a bit of emollience to a steamed fish, you do not need to render the lard. For Chinese pastry doughs, you must first render it to a liquid, cutting the solid stuff into cubes and then either steaming it or heating it slowly over the stove. Then, let it solidify to a smooth, firm mass before using. Some cooks who work more extensively with lard prefer the fine *leaf lard*, often called caul fat or net fat, that wraps the kidneys of the pig and has a finer texture when rendered. *Processed lard*, to me, has an unappealing aftertaste, and I avoid using it.

Fresh lard may be kept indefinitely in the freezer, cut into small blocks and bagged for easy use, then taken directly from the freezer for mincing.

LAVER
(紫菜 *mandarin: dzz-tsai; Cantonese: gee-choy*)
When fresh, this is a rosy purple variety of seaweed *(Porphyra umbilicalis)* that grows in flaps, fronds, and branches and is typically boiled in Ireland and England. In China and Japan, it is dried and pressed into brittle, thin, olive-purple sheets that earn it the Chinese name of "purple vegetable." To be crisp and tasty, it must either be deep-fried or toasted over a flame. Then it has a wonderful flavor, slightly reminiscent of good bacon.

For flame-toasting and crumbling into a simple soup, I use the plain laver sold in folded sheets in elongated, rectangular cellophane packages in Chinese and Japanese markets, usually labeled Dried Laver and/or by its Japanese name, *nori*. For wrapping around shrimp rolls (page 241), I prefer the precut and seasoned laver that is a Japanese specialty called *ajitsuke nori*. True to the Japanese love of packaging and austere cleanliness, these small rectangular strips are wrapped several to an individual bag, put on a larger tray with a packet of demoisturizer, then the whole thing is packed in a large, rectangular cellophane pouch. Opening the package takes longer than it does to eat the *nori*! The brand I like is Hanabishi's Flavored Sea-Weeds (*sic*) Wafers: Ajitsuke Nori, in a colorful red, white, and blue package. If you cannot find the seasoned variety, use the plain sort and make up for the plainer taste with an extra dusting of Roasted Szechwan Pepper-Salt or a light brushing with Five-Flavor Oil after the shrimp rolls are cooked.

Laver keeps indefinitely, sealed airtight at room temperature, away from light, heat, and moisture. So long as it smells distinctly seaweedy, it is good.

LILY BUDS
(金針 mandarin: jin-jun; Cantonese: gum-jum).

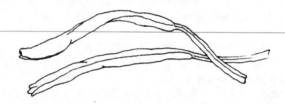

These are unopened dried tiger lillies *(Lilium lancifolium)*—the gold or orange lilies that grow in many American gardens—which are dried by the Chinese and used as a texture element and gentle taste in several classic dishes, most notably hot and sour soup (page 450) and *mu-shu* pork (page 198). The flowers dry to a dark brown blushed with gold and measure about 4 inches long and about ⅛ inch wide (slightly broader at the tip), hence the Chinese name, "golden needles." The flowers, typically called lily buds in English, are sold in a large tangle, bagged in cellophane. When dry, they have a distinctive, powerful smell. (Once, when vacationing at a hot-springs in the middle of Taiwan, I was stranded in a tiny village owing to the collapse of a rope bridge that hung breathtakingly across an immense chasm and was the only way from the village into the town. The village depended entirely on the hot springs and the cultivation of lily buds, so I alternately bathed and ate the flowers for one very long week. It took me years before I could eat another and not associate their smell with a sulfurous bath!)

To use lily buds, soak them in warm or cool water to cover until fully supple, 20–30 minutes usually, depending upon the temperature of the water. Drain, rinse, then snip off any knobby stem ends with scissors (sometimes the flower-plucker has done the job for you). Then, the bud is alternatively shredded, cut in half lengthwise, or used whole.

Lily buds keep forever, sealed in a jar or an airtight cellophane bag at room temperature, away from light, heat, and moisture. So long as they are on the soft side and smelly, they are good. (By the way, the smell goes away once they are soaked, leaving only a pale, floral scent.)

LONGBEANS, SEE CHINESE LONGBEANS

M

MALTOSE

(麥芽糖 mandarin: my-ya-tong; Cantonese: ma-nga-toong)

Maltose is a type of malt sugar, an ancient sweetener in China made primarily from barley. Unlike malt extract and malt syrups in the West, every Chinese sort of maltose that I have seen is beautifully pale gold in color, not brown. It is ferociously sticky and hard and must be plied out of its jar with a sturdy spoon dipped in boiling water and then diluted with boiling water to be used. All the trouble is worth it. Maltose has a richness and a balanced, mild sweetness that makes it unique.

Several varieties of maltose are available in Chinese groceries. The best, in my experience, are Tungoon Genuine Maltose that comes in a squat brown crock with a cinemagraphic label, and Butterfly Brand Maltose, packed in an equally attractive white crock with a label that is almost as good. Once the maltose is gone, the crocks make wonderful pencil or brush holders.

I have tried using some of the excellent whole food-type malt syrups in place of the maltose, but the final taste and coating action is not the same.

MOCK MEAT

(麵筋 mandarin: myen-jin; Cantonese: ming-gun)

"Mock meat" is a catch-all and, I admit, not terribly attractive name for a variety of products made variously from wheat gluten and soybeans that are flavored and fashioned to resemble meat. I came to know them well when I was living in Taiwan for about nine months as a very emotional vegetarian and would be regularly taken to Buddhist vegetarian restaurants by Chinese friends who didn't know how else to feed me. What I ate there was simply wonderful, a world away from the heavy, poorly flavored gluten and soybean products one often finds sold in whole food stores (which are becoming increasingly better, however).

Of the many canned preparations available on the shelves of Chinese groceries, two are excellent. One is a mild soybean product called Braised Dried Bean Curd on the blue label (紅燜素鶏 *mandarin: hoong-mun-soo-gee; Cantonese: hung-mun-sew-guy*), which is packaged by Companion brand in a tuna-fish size 8-ounce can. The Chinese name translates "red-cooked vegetarian chicken," and there is indeed the very pleasant texture of potted poultry to the light yet very satisfying stuff. Sliced thinly and tossed with a bit of soy sauce or along with vegetables in *Spicy Buddha's Feast* (page 299), it is delicious.

The other can that finds its way into my kitchen without complaint is another product packaged by Companion, called Curry Chai Chi Jou (Curry Bruised Gluten) (咖喱齋雞肉 *mandarin: jya-lee-jai-gee-row; Cantonese: gah-lay-dzai-jyew-yo*). The name translates literally as "curried Buddhist chicken," and this is indeed a curried product, very spicy and wonderfully full-flavored. The base is wheat gluten, the texture is quite firm, and the 10-ounce can is wrapped by a bright gold label that I suspect is meant to signify curry. If you cannot find the Companion brand, Longevity brand makes a very similar gluten product called Curry Vegetarian Mock Duck Meat (咖喱齋鴨 *mandarin: jya-lee-jai-ya; Cantonese: gah-lay-dzai-gna*). For the same taste but a softer texture, look for Curried Mock Abalone (咖喱齋鮑魚 *mandarin: jya-lee-jai-bao-yoo; Cantonese: gah-lay-dzai-bow-yoo*) made by Companion and Longevity and canned in the same fashion. Either one is delicious, stir-fried into *Spicy Buddha's Feast*, used in a stir-fry of fresh vegetables, or simply eaten plain on a slab of hot buttered bread. For those who like spicy, light foods, it is a wonderful thing to have on hand.

Let me stress that I have never found any similar product, even by the same brand, that is satisfactory. In my experience, *only* these four items are excellent. They are widely marketed and available by mail order.

Once opened, either product will keep up to 1 week in the refrigerator. Braised Dried Bean Curd does not need to be drained. For curried gluten, discard the sediment at the bottom of the can and store the curried liquid separate from the gluten; the liquid is the first to sour and the sediment hastens the process.

MONOSODIUM GLUTAMATE (MSG)

(味精 mandarin: way-jing; Cantonese: may-jing)

Let me say immediately that *I don't use MSG* to those who, like me, tend to judge a Chinese cookbook by whether or not MSG appears in the ingredients list. No, I don't use it, but I am so frequently asked about MSG that I thought it deserved a mention here.

Variously called by its Japanese name *aji-no-moto*, by its Vietnamese name, *ve-tsin*, or by the brand name Accent, or various English names such as taste powder, flavor enhancer, or Chinese salt, MSG is a common item in most every Chinese kitchen. It would not be thought refined if one did not use it. It would merely be thought strange. I am thought a bit strange by many of my Chinese friends, because to my tongue food does not need it.

Originally made from dried fermented wheat gluten and often made at home, MSG as such was isolated in the early twentieth century from seatangle *(Laminaria japonica)* by a Japanese chemist. Since then the tiny, white crystals with their ability to heighten the natural salts and sugars in food have become popular in restaurant, hotel, and home kitchens worldwide.

I do not know why the headaches, tingles, and numbness associated with eating foods made with MSG in Chinese restaurants do not seem to occur in other situations where MSG is used. It might be the amount that is used, or the fact that things like stock are often left to stand long after the MSG has been added. I do not know. Arguments are vociferous and continuous on the subject.

Whereas a pinch of MSG is ritual in Chinese homes and restaurants where I have eaten with pleasure for years and where no one ever feels a ripple of a headache, it is not necessary to use it if your goal is wonderful-tasting Chinese food. Freshness of the primary ingredient is all-important, and, beyond that, whatever seasonings you choose should be a helpmate and not a source of concern.

To my tongue, MSG leaves a faint aftertaste and has a slight tinniness. It tastes to me like fine table salt, and for me one is as objectionable as the other. So no, I do not use it.

MUSHROOMS, FRESH AND CANNED

While Chinese dried black mushrooms are without question the most important mushroom in Chinese cooking, there are other varieties of mushrooms that are used by Chinese cooks. Even more valued by me than the several Chinese canned sorts available here are the marvelous mushrooms not native to China but which can be purchased fresh and are wonderful in Chinese-style dishes. What follows is an introduction:

Abalone Mushrooms/Oyster Mushrooms (鮑魚菇 *mandarin: bao-yoo-goo; Cantonese: bow-yoo-goo*). These pearl gray mushrooms have a mild taste, smooth texture, and a shape reminiscent of an oyster, owing somewhat to the stem that grows from the side. While called oyster mushrooms in English *(Pleurotus ostreatus)*, the Chinese call them "abalone mushrooms." The canned sort, in my opinion, are hardly worth using. Fortunately, they are increasingly available fresh in both Western and Chinese markets. Included in stir-frys and soups, they are delicious.

Straw Mushrooms (草菇 *mandarin: tsao-goo; Cantonese: tso-goo*). Sometimes called padi-straw mushroom or umbrella mushroom in English, this small, brown mushroom with its phallic shape *(Volvariella volvacea)* is commonly grown in China on beds of rice straw, hence the name. They are widely available canned and provide a pleasant slippery texture to stir-fried dishes and soups, contributing only a mild taste. The best are less than an inch small and are peeled before canning. Companion is a good brand. These mushrooms are also available dried, but I find them overwhelming in flavor and smell.

Enokitake is the Japanese name for a type of mushroom that in Chinese is called "golden needle mushroom" (金針菇 *mandarin: jin-jun-goo; Cantonese: gum-jum-goo*), a slender and exceedingly delicate mushroom comprised of a slender cream-colored stalk about 5 inches long and $1/16$ inch thick, topped by a tiny umbrella-like cap. The canned variety is so eclipsed by the fresh that I have introduced them here with their Japanese name, under which they are marketed, put first. You will find fresh *enokitake* both in Oriental and Western markets, packed in 3-ounce plastic pouches, kept in refrigerated cases. Once home, they will keep 4–6 days before browning, but my practice is to use them immediately. Mild in flavor and aroma, they are a lovely addition to soups, with no preparation required except to cut off the spongy base of the stems.

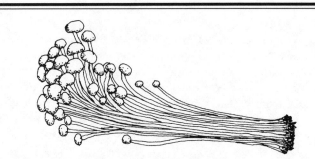

Shiitake is again the Japanese name for a mushroom that has been widely marketed in the West in recent years, also under the name black forest mushroom and forest mushroom. It is nothing other than the Chinese dried black mushroom in its fresh form *(Pasania cuspidata)*, looking like a disk of dark brown velvet with an underbelly of light fawn. It is a wonderful addition to stir-frys and soups, though not a replacement for the dried caps. The dried mushrooms have a more concentrated essence, and the two are more like separate species than variations on a theme.

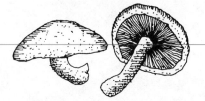

Chanterelles *(Catharellus cibarius)*, also called *girolles*, is a fresh mushroom unknown in China so far as I am aware, but which is wonderful slivered and included in Chinese-style stir-frys and soups. It is a curving trumpet of pretty apricot-gold, common in deciduous woods, and often brought to my kitchen by jogger friends. To clean it requires a damp towel, a fine brush, and much patience (for to dunk the mushroom under water and scrub it, as one might like, is to destroy it). The taste is inimitable. Lightly stir-fried into a dish of glass noodles poached in chicken stock with some slips of winter melon or cucumber added, it is a mushroom to delight a Chinese (and any other) palate.

MUSHROOM SOY SAUCE, SEE SOY SAUCE

N

NOODLES, SEE BEAN THREADS, EGG NOODLES, AND RICE STICKS

NORI, SEE LAVER

O

OIL, CORN AND PEANUT

What a Chinese cook needs from a cooking oil is one that will heat to a high temperature (frequently up to 400°) without burning and will not impart a characteristic smell or taste to foods. It is important also that the oil be light and not greasy, and to my mind that it be economical as well.

My everyday cooking oil is Mazola *corn oil*. I buy it in 1 gallon plastic containers, typically in Chinese groceries where it is sold a few dollars below the average supermarket price. I like the light, clean taste of corn oil on my tongue and find that it heats without foaming and seems to stay cleaner during repeated deep-frying. When I am ready to throw out frying oil that has turned from gold to brown, the plastic container is a perfect receptacle.

I use *peanut oil* as a second choice. It is available in several good brands, Planters which one sees most everywhere, and also in Chinese brands such as Panther and Tung Ming, equally good for Chinese purposes. The expense of peanut oil and what seems to me its stronger, more oily taste is what leads me to choose it second. This makes me atypical among Chinese cooks who for the most part seem to prefer it, though I suspect this is a matter of habit as much as taste, peanuts in China being far more plentiful than corn.

As for *cottonseed oil* and *soybean oil*, often used in Chinese restaurant kitchens in the West, I have not had much experience with them. My general impression is that what is on the market is poorly processed and overly oily in taste. What I have sampled does not perform as well or taste as good as quality corn or peanut oil.

If you are shopping in Chinese markets where the number of oil types and brands is great, one word of caution: buy the smallest container available and try it out at home, first by heating it to 400° and then by frying a piece of bread at 350°. The smell and look of the oil as it heats is a good index of its character and the refinement of the processing. The bread will tell you what it tastes like. Oil that foams, has a chemical smell, or blankets the food with a strong or specific taste is not appropriate for Chinese cooking.

For recycling oil used in deep- or shallow-frying, and for the meaning of the designation *"fresh oil"* that appears in some recipes, see pages 82 and 84.

Corn and peanut oil are *cooking* oils. For information on *seasoning* oils, see *Sesame Oil, Chinese and Japanese*, and *Chili Oil*.

ORANGE AND TANGERINE PEEL, HOME-DRIED

(陳皮 *mandarin: chun-pee; Cantonese: chun-pay*)

Chinese groceries typically carry one or more brands of dried orange or tangerine peel, which are meant to be softened in water and then used in stir-frying, particularly for some of the spicy specialties from Szechwan and Hunan. Over the years, I've found that using the store-bought product, frequently seasoned with salt and sugar, isn't half as satisfying as drying my own. The taste and color are wonderful, the process is simple, and you can't beat the price.

To make home-dried orange or tangerine peel, first wash the fruit well. Slice it into eighths, then separate the peel from the edible fruit (eating the fruit while you work, of course). Place the peel white side up on a cutting surface, anchoring it to the board with your fingertips, then hold a sharp knife parallel to the board and cut off the layer of white pith with a small back and forth sawing motion. Cut clear down to the orange skin to remove every bit of the bitter white and expose the oil sacs on the rind. Some people scrape off the pith, but I find the sawing movement quicker. Finally, put the rind cut side up on a rack, then let it sit 2–3 days until curled and fairly dry. (It will still be flexible, neither brittle nor moist to the touch.) At that point, store the peel in an airtight plastic or glass container, where it will stay fragrant for many months. Replenishing the supply is easy. Just eat another orange.

The difference between the orange and the tangerine peel is minuscule, and I use them interchangeably when smoking foods or seasoning stir-frys. The only instance where I definitely want tangerine peel is for *Mandarin Orange Ice Cream* (page 498), and then I am usually using the peel fresh from the fruit.

When a recipe calls for minced or slivered orange or tangerine peel, simply cover the home-dried peel with warm water and let soak until supple, about 10 minutes. One slice of peel from a large orange that has been sectioned into eighths is what I have called "a thumb-size piece." Where measurements are important, I have indicated teaspoons and tablespoons. Where they are not, I have given the more general visual reference to your thumb. When in doubt, use more.

OYSTER MUSHROOMS, SEE MUSHROOMS

OYSTER SAUCE
(蠔油 mandarin: how-yo; Cantonese: ho-yao)
This Cantonese-style seasoning is packaged under many brands, each of them very different in taste and texture. The very best, to my taste, is made by Hop Sing Lung Oyster Sauce Company, and comes in a 14-ounce bottle with a colorful picture of China's favorite mythological beast (a cross between a dragon, a lion, and a horse) on a small label around the neck of the bottle. It is the *only* oyster sauce I have tasted that is properly rich, flavorful, and gelatinous. You pay for what you get relative to other Chinese oyster sauces, but it is worth every penny.

I keep oyster sauce in the refrigerator, where it keeps indefinitely.

P

PEPPER, BLACK AND WHITE
(胡椒 mandarin: hoo-jyao; Cantonese: hoo-jyew)
Black and white peppercorns *(Piper nigrum)* were an early import to China from the tropics and were especially in vogue during the Tang dynasty, when their presence in an exotic "foreign" meat dish was as *de rigueur* as our serving chutney with a curry. Black pepper became a part of many northern dishes, while white pepper was the visual choice for light-colored foods such as shrimp pastes and fish stews. "Foreign pepper" or "barbarian pepper" as it is called in Chinese never supplanted the aromatic brown pepper in Chinese kitchens (see below, *Szechwan Brown Peppercorns*), but it has remained a nice flourish associated with certain foods.

In my own kitchen, a peppermill filled with fresh peppercorns is an important item, kept within arm's reach of the stove. I buy peppercorns in small specialty spice stores where one can smell them before buying, just like choosing from among different roasts of coffee beans. Tellicherry and Lampong are varieties I especially enjoy. To a peppermill filled with 8 or 9 parts black peppercorns, I'll add 1 or 2 parts white for a variety of spice and color.

Using fresh whole peppercorns is essential, to my way of cooking and thinking. The preground variety inevitably tastes dead or lackluster in comparison, and you also don't get the textural qualities that can be had with peppercorns you grind yourself from a mill.

PINE NUTS

(松子 mandarin: soong-dzz; Cantonese: song-gee)
Pine nuts are indigenous to China, although the more plump and sweet sort from Korea was an early import. Strewn on special tea cakes or dipped in honey and then fried as a special nibble, pine nuts are also a feature of eastern Chinese cuisine, where they are used to garnish fish and poultry dishes.

I much prefer the smaller, round-tipped Mediterranean pine nuts to the larger, triangular variety presently imported from Taiwan. The European sort is rich and sweet, whereas the other tastes grassy.

R

RICE

(米 mandarin: mee; Cantonese: my)
For detailed information on types of rice and the difference between short- and medium-grain versus long-grain rice, see page 399.

When shopping for rice, you are best off using your eyes to discern which grain is which. Medium- or short-grained rice is short, oval, and plump. Long-grain rice is oblong and slim, with relatively pointed ends. If you are ordering rice by mail (page 588) be sure to specify that you want short- or medium-grain *regular* rice (page 399) and not the sweet or glutinous variety of rice that belongs to the family of short-grained rice but is entirely different in texture and use (see *Sweet Rice* below).

RICE STICKS

(米粉 mandarin: mee-fun; Cantonese: my-foon)

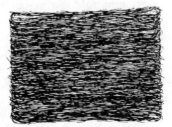

These are 1/16 inch thin, dry white noodles made from rice flour, usually called rice sticks and sometimes called rice vermicelli to distinguish them from the broader, ribbon-like fresh rice noodles often carried in Chinese groceries. They are sold typically in 1-pound cellophane bags, three or four loose, broad wads to the bag. In contrast to bean threads, rice sticks are decidedly off-white and opaque and are wavy as opposed to straight. When soaked, they turn white, as opposed to transparent. When cooked, they lose their body and break into short lengths. Consequently, there is no need to cut rice sticks; they will break into bits on their own.

Dry rice sticks can be fried in 400° oil to puff up in a nest in the same manner as bean threads. They have a slightly more delicate, brittle character than the bean threads when fried, though they will absorb more readily any discoloring impurity in the frying oil.

To soak rice sticks for use in stir-frying, cover the required amount with warm tap water until supple, about 10–15 minutes. Hotter water cooks the rice sticks to a significant degree, to be avoided when the recipe calls for them to be simmered further in a sauce. Once supple, rice sticks may be left in the (now cool) soaking water until use, overnight if you like. Drain well before using.

RICE VINEGAR, CHINESE OR JAPANESE, SEE VINEGAR

RICE WINE, SEE CHINESE RICE WINE

S

SALT

(▩ mandarin: yen; Cantonese: yim)
The history of salt mines and salt monopolies in China is enough to fill a volume (as I'm sure it already has, on more than one occasion), but suffice it to say here that salt was important to Chinese cooking from early times, both as a preservative and a seasoning. Various sorts of salt were known and used, and the Tang poet, Li Po, likened one type of salt mined inland to flowers gleaming white like snow.

I am extremely fussy about salt, liking only certain types in the company of other Chinese seasonings, and being very particular about the amount used. Unlike most native Chinese cookbook writers who salt their dishes to accompany bland white rice, I salt food to be eaten on its own or in the company of a flavorful starch, whether it be fried rice, steamed or panfried breads, or noodles. I do not have the taste for that much salt and do not think it necessary.

I use only *coarse kosher salt* in my Chinese cooking, the traditional kind sold in a 3-pound box. It is a pure, distinctly mild-tasting salt with a flavor that balances well with other Chinese seasonings like soy sauce, rice wine, ginger, and scallion. Let me emphasize that the *taste* of coarse kosher salt has nothing to do with its coarseness. If you grind it finely, it will still taste the same and that taste will be far milder and different from other types of salt. Coarse kosher salt is available in large supermarkets, often on a shelf with other Jewish ingredients, and can be found increasingly in specialty shops. It is *half as salty* as fine table salt or fine or coarse sea salt, so if the amounts given in recipes look large, it is probably because you are accustomed to using saltier salts. In recent months, a "gourmet blend" of what I call "c.k. salt" has appeared on the market. This is *not* what I use. Its taste is repellent.

Fine table salt is something I *never* use. In Chinese foods, it contributes too sharp and salty a taste, moreover one that does not merge well with the usual Chinese constellation of seasonings. The additives put into a box of fine table salt make it unpalatable to my tongue. Especially when salting vegetables for "Little Dishes" (pages 103 to 121), fine table salt will ruin the flavor of the dish.

Sea salt in both its coarse and fine textures is a salt I enjoy, though *not* in Chinese foods. It has an assertive character of its own, which again does not mesh well with standard Chinese seasonings. I use it in pastry doughs and in *Dijon Mustard Sauce* (page 475), but never in stir-frying or in seasoning Chinese dishes. It, too, is twice as salty as coarse kosher salt, so if you insist on using it instead of coarse kosher salt begin with only *half* as much as the recipe calls for.

Lest I sound tyrannical, the only way to know for yourself the character of different salts is to taste them side by side, first on their own in a small saucer and then, if you want to experiment further, cooked in the same dish. I do this regularly in my classes, and it is always a revelation to my students. It proves the point that some salts are pleasant backgrounds, while others are overriding tastes, and that the character of a salt will change when it is used in different cuisines. In this way it is very much like wine. One must choose what works best in a certain context.

SALTED BLACK BEANS

(豆豉 mandarin: doe-jrr; Cantonese: dao-see)
According to Bill Shurtleff at The Soyfoods Center (see the entry for *Soyfoods* below), this fermented, salted, soft black soybean is the oldest recorded soyfood in history, the noble ancestor of *miso* and soy sauce. It is a rather remarkable new look at a humble black bean, which I have always thrown unthinkingly into sauces and scattered on top of steaming fish and until recently did not even realize was a soybean. Soybeans, I know now, can wear black seed coats as well as yellow ones.

Packaged in heavy plastic bags and typically labeled Salted Black Beans, this popular Chinese seasoning is also known as Chinese black beans, salted beans, fermented black beans, and occasionally ginger black beans. The process is generally the same for all brands: boiling or simmering black soybeans until soft, inoculating them with an *Aspergillus oryzae* mold, then covering them with a brining solution for six months, with shreds of ginger or orange peel or a dash of five-spice powder occasionally added to season the beans in the final soaking stage.

I prefer salted black beans that are seasoned with ginger and avoid the sort seasoned with five-spice powder. The latter is very strong-tasting and if used for the preceding recipes will destroy the balance of flavors. If they are all you have on hand and there is no time to purchase a new bag, then wash the beans in cool water to remove the five-spice flavor, and add a bit more salt to the dish to make up for what was washed away.

When shopping for salted black beans, you will need to look at the list of ingredients to tell which sort is which, as the label on the package invariably reads Salted Black Bean. If you are looking for the variety seasoned with ginger, you will see the tiny, black tufts of ginger scattered throughout the beans. I use Mee Chun brand, widely distributed in several size bags.

Salted black beans should feel soft and supple through the bag when you buy them. Once opened, store them in an airtight container at room temperature, away from light, heat, and moisture. They keep indefinitely.

As you may already have noted in the recipes, *I do not wash salted black beans,* as is common. It is a practice I have never understood and to which the only actual answer I was ever given was that of a very old Chinese man, who looked at me quizzically from beneath his bushy brows and said, "Why, it's to make them less black!" It does not make sense to me to wash them when you are adding salt to the dish anyway (which is the consistent practice of the bean washers, so far as I have observed). So I simply save myself the extra step and count in their saltiness when I am calculating the other seasonings for a dish. The old man forgive me, all the recipes in this book are based on *unwashed* beans, which will not taste salty once cooked but will indeed be very black!

SAUSAGE, SEE CHINESE SAUSAGE

SCALLIONS
(葱 *mandarin: tsoong; Cantonese: toong*)

Also commonly called green onions, scallions are as common to Chinese cooking as yellow onions (called "Western scallions" in Chinese) are to European and American cooking. They form a complementary seasoning pair along with fresh ginger (scallion being *yin*, and ginger being *yang*), and are also often used in the company of garlic and red chili (two other *yang* foods).

Except in shrimp purées, where the traditional practice is to use only the white part of the scallion (a color prejudice to which I do not always adhere), scallions are almost always used *whole*, that is from the white bulb clear up to the top of the green stalks. The only thing that is discarded is the bearded, tough root tip and any wilted greens or bedraggled stalk ends.

In many recipes in this book, I have distinguished between thin, medium, and hefty whole scallions. *Thin* means a bit thinner than the average pencil; *medium* means a bit thicker than the average pencil; and *hefty* means the width of two pencils if you put them side by side (about ½ inch across). This is a general index and not a firm measurement, so if in doubt (as I frequently say also regarding garlic and ginger), use *more*.

When buying scallions, look for a smooth, unblemished bulb and perky, erect stalks. If you are forced to buy wilted scallions, trim them carefully and use more than the recipe calls for to make up for the loss of pungency. Store scallions unwashed and untrimmed, in a lightly misted airtight plastic bag in the refrigerator. They will keep 1–2 weeks if they were perfect to begin. As the outer layers grow wilted and wet, discard them, wipe the scallion dry, then return it to the bag.

Scallions are easy to clean: simply pull off and discard the outermost layer, which is usually wilted or tough relative to the rest, then rinse them briefly with cool water or wipe with a damp towel.

Scallion brushes can be made from the white and light green part of the scallion. Using a small, sharp knife, hold the trimmed scallion length in your hand, then cut upwards from the middle of the scallion, rotating it a notch clockwise after each cut so that the upper portion is completely fringed. Turn the scallion length upside down, then repeat the process to fringe the end you've left whole, cutting from the center of the stalk upward but leaving ¼–½ inch uncut in the very center of the stalk. Then put the cut scallion in a bowl of ice water and watch the ends curl back. They will curl within minutes if the scallions were perfectly fresh, and then should be drained and the excess water shaken off before using. If you are working in advance, pop the brushes into a plastic bag, seal it in a "balloon" to keep them from crushing, and refrigerate until use.

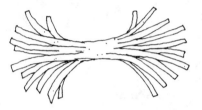

It should be mentioned that the only place where scallion brushes and scallion lengths are eaten raw is in the area of Shantung, the northeastern province not far from Peking. Just as garlic is credited with magic powers in the West, the Chinese commonly say that it is by eating raw scallion that the people of Shantung grow so tall.

Scallion spider chrysanthemums were taught to me by my student, Catherine Kunkle, who frills these garnishes with a thin sewing needle. Start with the white portion of a long, medium or hefty scallion, trimmed of the hairy beard but with the root end left intact to hold the flower together. Hold the scallion by the root end in one hand, then use the needle to cut upwards from the root to the top of the scallion length, making gashes about halfway through the scallion and turning it a tiny notch clockwise after each cut so that it is fringed delicately all around. What you are doing, in short, is making half a scallion brush. If you want a tightly curled flower, use the ice water method above. For a looser look, put them into a water-misted plastic bag sealed in a "balloon" and refrigerate several hours or overnight.

Scallion branches are much more my style. They can be made in seconds from a lively green stalk of scallion, cut about 2½ inches long. Put the piece of stalk flat on your cutting surface, then use the point of a thin-bladed cleaver or the point of a small, sharp knife (whichever is in your hand), and make a long cut 1/16 inch in from the side of the stalk, running from ¼ inch above the base clear through the top. As you complete the cut, the freed sliver of scallion will curl off to the side. Continue cutting at ⅛-inch intervals until you reach the other side. Then give the cut stalk a shake. If it was perfectly fresh, the limbs will curl outwards prettily. Scallion branches can be bagged in lightly misted plastic and refrigerated until use, overnight if you like. For a dainty garnish make them smaller, starting out with a 1½-inch stalk.

SESAME OIL, CHINESE AND JAPANESE

(蔴油 *mandarin: ma-yo; Cantonese: ma-yao*)

Sesame oil in China and Japan is generally pressed from *toasted* sesame seeds, hence it is dark brown in color and very rich in flavor and aroma. This toasted sesame oil burns at a low temperature, so it is foremost a *seasoning oil* and not a cooking oil, altogether different from the light golden sesame oils of the Middle East and the "cold-pressed" sesame oils marketed in whole foods stores. These oils are *not* interchangeable. Chinese and Japanese sesame oil is used as a garnish for a hot stir-fry or soup, a component of a cold sauce, or an ingredient in a seasoned oil. Its job is to add flavor, color, gloss and aroma, and its personality is pronounced.

I judge Chinese and Japanese sesame oils by their color and fragrance, the richer the better. A good sesame oil smells so lushly aromatic you could wear it as an exotic perfume. Kadoya, a Japanese brand, is the best I have found thus far. Dynasty, also a Japanese brand, markets a red label sesame oil that is my second choice. (Dynasty yellow label is less aromatic.) Smell Dynasty sesame oil before buying if possible; it is sometimes burned in processing. Other than these two there are few brands which are even satisfactory.

opened, which leads me to suspect that the container is in part the culprit, and to advise you to never buy Chinese or Japanese sesame oil unless it is packed in a glass bottle or can. If forced to buy oil in plastic, unscrew the top if possible and smell the oil before you buy it; then you will know what you are getting. Rancid or poor grade sesame oil smells offensive or indifferent.

Store sesame oil in a relatively cool place away from light and heat, where it will keep perfectly for many months. If you store it in the refrigerator for lack of a cool cupboard, then let it come to room temperature before using. If you buy sesame oil in bulk, use an emptied and clean brown wine bottle to hold what you need for everyday cooking and top it with a liquor pour-spout.

When shopping for dark brown Chinese or Japanese sesame oil, do not confuse it with *black sesame oil*, which is a thick, black oil used occasionally in Chinese confections. You see it rarely and it is clearly labeled, but be on guard nonetheless.

SESAME PASTE
(芝蔴醬 mandarin: jrr-ma-jyang; Cantonese: gee-ma-jyoong)
Just like Chinese and Japanese sesame oil, Chinese sesame paste is made from *toasted* sesame seeds, and is a thoroughly different product from Middle Eastern tahini or sesame pastes sold in whole foods stores. The Chinese paste is dark brown in color, very aromatic and strong in flavor, and has the consistency of cement that is just about to harden. A layer of oil typically floats on top of the paste and keeps it moist.

I use Lan Chi brand Sesame Seed Paste, which is widely distributed in an 8-ounce bottle with a pink and white label. White Horse brand is also good. Before using, decant the oil into a small bowl, then dig out the paste you need with a sturdy small spoon or blunt knife. Return a thin layer of oil to the bottle to keep the remaining paste moist, then seal the bottle and keep it at room temperature, away from light and heat where it will keep indefinitely.

The oil that floats on the top of the sesame paste is *not* the equivalent of a top-quality Chinese or Japanese sesame oil. I discard it.

SESAME SEEDS, WHITE AND BLACK
(白芝蔴，黑芝蔴 mandarin: bye-jrr-ma and hay-jrr-ma; Cantonese: bok-gee-ma and hut-gee-ma)
White and black sesame seeds are a common garnish in Chinese cooking, where they are used for their color, taste, and crunch. The white seeds should be hulled when you buy them. For use as a garnish without further cooking, they must be toasted briefly in a dry skillet over low heat, stirred until golden. The black seeds may be toasted if you like—it brings their aromatic oil to the surface—but it is not necessary.

White and black sesame seeds are available in Oriental groceries, in small plastic pouches weighing from 2 to 4 ounces. They are a far better buy than the tiny bottles of sesame seeds one gets on a spice shelf in a supermarket, and are usually fresher. If you cannot buy sesame seeds in an Oriental market, purchase them in bulk at a whole foods store where you can first sniff the seeds for freshness. Buy the whitest (actually pale, pale golden) white sesame seeds you can find, and be watchful for packages that contain chaff or a lot of discolored seeds. Black sesame seeds should also look clean in the package; they are often sold as "black *goma*" under a Japanese label.

I store sesame seeds in airtight containers in the refrigerator or freezer, which is a good policy for any nut or seed with an oil content that is likely to go rancid.

(Parenthetically, I have searched without result to find a distinction between white sesame seeds and black sesame seeds that would give a clue as to how or if they are botanically different. The black seeds are black through and through, which sheds no light on the subject.)

SHERRY, DRY, SEE CHINESE RICE WINE

SHIITAKE, SEE MUSHROOMS

SHRIMP, DRIED
(蝦米 mandarin: hsya-mee; Cantonese: ha-my)
These tiny dried shrimp, called "shrimp kernels" in Chinese, have a salty, concentrated taste. Ranging in size from a mere ¼ inch to an inch long, they also have a keen odor that one can smell right through the cellophane bags in which they are sold, usually

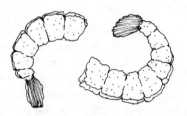

about two cups to a bag. Dried shrimp are used variously in soups and stir-fried dishes, where they function both as a highly seasoned condiment and a chewy texture food.

I look for dried shrimp that are nearly an inch long, unbroken, and carefully cleaned. They are usually the most expensive, but are best in flavor and do not necessitate a careful sifting through after soaking to pick off the tiny legs and bits of shell. Stored in an airtight bottle at room temperature, kept away from light, heat and moisture, they last indefinitely.

Dried shrimp must be soaked in hot tap water to cover before using. The soaking rids the shrimp of most of their salt, and softens them to a chewy consistency. Gauge when pleasantly salty by biting down on one shrimp, anywhere from 15–25 minutes depending on the size of the shrimp and the temperature of the water. Drain and rinse before using. Do not oversoak to blandness. The salty taste of the shrimp is always, in the preceding recipes, counted into the seasonings for the dish.

SMITHFIELD HAM, SEE HAM

SNOW PEAS

(雪豆 *mandarin: shweh-doe; Cantonese: shwut-dao*)

Often called Chinese pea pods, pea pods, Chinese sugar peas, sugar peas, or by their French name *mange tout* (which means, "eat it all"), these boat-shaped edible pea pods with their sweet, crisp taste have become perhaps the best-known and loved of all Chinese vegetables. They are wonderfully easy to grow—all you need are a few stakes, some string, and a finger with which to dig a little hole in the ground—and provide early summer satisfaction for even a first-time gardener. They can be planted before most anything else and flourish when the weather is brisk, hence the Chinese name "snow pea." Seeds are widely available, or may be ordered through the mail (page 588).

If you buy snow peas in the market, look for crisp, unblemished pods with a thin skin. When left too long on the vine they turn tough, and when held for too long in the store they turn limp. Limp snow peas can sometimes be revived by refrigerating in a water-misted plastic bag, assuming they are not too far gone, and a limp pea is to be chosen over a tough pea if you have no choice.

Snow peas should be strung before using by pinching off each tip end of the pea pod and drawing it slowly back to release the top string. Immature, perfectly picked peas will not have any string to speak of. For a fancy touch, use the tip of a sharp knife or small scissors to cut a V-shaped notch from each end of the snow pea after the strings have been removed. It's a nice way to cover up the fact that the tips were broken off, and is lovely in a simple stir-fry where the snow peas are the star.

Sugar snap peas, developed in recent years, are wonderful substitutes for snow peas when a recipe calls for using them whole, though they are more difficult to shred without the little peas escaping.

Frozen snow peas are to be avoided at all costs. When a substitute is needed, choose something equally fresh, green and crisp, like peeled broccoli stems or fresh and sweet string beans.

SOYFOODS

This is a category of foods that includes, among many other soybean-based products, fresh tofu, pressed tofu, fermented tofu, Companion brand's Red-Cooked Vegetarian Chicken (discussed under the heading *Mock Meat*), "salted black beans," and "soy sauce," all from the list above. I highlight the category here as a bow to Bill Shurtleff and Akiko Aoyagi, who through their researches and writings have done much in a few short years to improve the availability of soyfoods in America. Part of their work is to achieve a meaningful standardization of soyfood names, so that long-winded entries such as mine—which are designed primarily to get you to pick the right product from the shelf— will no longer be necessary. In their perfect world, the name bean curd will be forgotten and tofu will be used exclusively, and misleading names like salted black beans will be called soy nuggets or soft black soybeans (a topic now under discussion). Vegetarian chicken will be called Buddha's chicken, that is, if the arms of the Chinese manufacturers can successfully be twisted. It is a noble program, already well under way, which will allow those who shop for Chinese ingredients and who cannot read Chinese to select exactly what they want based on a clear English label.

If you are interested in soyfoods and the intricacies of the processes and history behind them, I refer you to Shurtleff's and Aoyagi's books, *The Book of Tofu* (Ballantine edition) and *History of Soybeans and Soyfoods* (available through The Soyfoods Center, P.O. Box 234, Lafayette, California 94549). The latter was not available at the time of my writing, but I look forward eagerly to reading it.

SOY SAUCE
(醬油 *mandarin: jyang-yo; Cantonese: jyoong-yao)*

No matter how skillful your deft fingers may be, you cannot make good chop-suey and other Oriental dishes with inferior sauce. It is absolutely necessary to use the best chop-suey sauce (soy) to get the tang of the Orient.

So reads a passage from a 1930's volume called *Oriental "Show-You" Recipes* printed in Indiana and containing recipes like "La Tempura No. 1." I support the feelings of its author (perhaps the ancestor of the Kikkoman factory in Wisconsin?) wholeheartedly. One cannot cook good Chinese food without a good soy sauce, "good" meaning one whose flavor and texture is appropriate to the dish being made.

Soy sauce and soy sauce-related products appear on American shelves wearing such different names on the outside and containing such different tastes within that to say something is soy sauce will mean just about as much to a discerning cook as saying that something is wine will mean to a discerning drinker. Japanese soy sauces (called *shoyu* in Japanese, hence the name of the book quoted above) and Chinese soy sauces are remarkably different in taste. The former are rather sweet to my tongue and the latter are decidedly salty. What is marketed as *tamari* usually tastes to me quite metallic, while the synthetic soy sauces that my mother (innocently) used to buy are chemical aberrations that hardly deserve the name.

The process behind most of these products is generally the same: cooked soybeans and usually some proportion of wheat are injected with an *Aspergillus* mold, left to grow for several days, then mixed with a briny solution and put in fermenting tanks for 6–24 months, after which the raw liquid is drained off. The differences arise from the amount of wheat used in the original mixture, the length of fermentation, and the temperature control or lack of it, and the purity of ingredients versus the presence of chemicals and additives.

My everyday soy sauce is *Kikkoman soy sauce*, produced in their factory in Wisconsin and available most everywhere in red and black tins or bottles with a red, blue, and yellow label. Kikkoman, to my tongue, is a wonderful middle ground between the sweeter Japanese-made soy sauces that are excellent in Japanese dishes but that I find do not mesh well with Chinese seasonings, and the saltier Chinese soy sauces that are simply too salty for my taste. If you are particularly sensitive to salt, Kikkoman also makes what they call Milder Soy Sauce, in which the salt is reduced from about 15 percent to about 9 percent. It tastes quite good. Unlike the regular Kikkoman that I use, it is a preservative-free soy sauce and must be kept in the refrigerator.

Kikkoman is what I call *thin (regular) soy sauce (*生抽 *mandarin: sheng-cho; Cantonese: sen-chao)* and what some people call light soy sauce, although both terms can be confusing. Thin soy sauce means a soy sauce that is thin in consistency, appropriate for liquid sauces and cooking where you want to inject liquid as well as color and taste. Thin also refers to the light flavor, which is fulsome but devoid of seasonings such as molasses or sugar that are featured in other styles of soy sauce, including black soy sauce below.

CAUTION: If you are substituting a Chinese brand soy sauce such as Superior or Koon Chun, use *less* than is called for in my recipes, as the Chinese brands are *distinctly saltier* than Kikkoman, a fact which becomes apparent, especially when used in large amounts. In recipes calling for ¼ cup or more, decrease the amount initially by 2 teaspoons for every ¼ cup, then taste to determine whether you need to add more. Be particularly careful with stews and casseroles, where the liquids will reduce during cooking.

On no account consider using the chemical supermarket brands of soy sauces that are labeled with pseudo-Chinese names like La Choy or Chun King. They are synthetically produced from hydrolized vegetable protein and contain additives like corn syrup and caramel. In other words, they don't taste good, and at any rate bear little resemblance to real soy sauce.

*Black Soy Sauce (*老頭抽 *mandarin: lao-toe-cho; Cantonese: low-toe-chao)* is the other sauce that features regularly in my cooking. The brand I use is Koon Chun, which comes in a 21-ounce bottle with a red, blue, and yellow label, and is widely available in Chinese markets. "Black soy sauce" is the name on the label; the Chinese name means literally "old-head soy," referring to (I think) a longer period of fermentation and/or a reduction of the liquid drained from the fermentation vat. So-called black soy sauce is not any blacker or thicker than thin soy sauce, but it is far *saltier* and contains a hint of molasses to further deepen its flavor.

Black soy sauce is used in those dishes where one wants the color and flavor of soy sauce *without* the liquid content of thin soy sauce, for instance in cold noodle dishes, occasional cold sauces, and stews, where a reduced mixture will better coat and cling to the food, or where an already liquid sauce will profit from a strong jolt of color and taste. The molasses flavor is also prized. It is a soy sauce that I use in a finite number of dishes, but for those it is irreplaceable. There are no substitutes.

Black soy sauce and thin soy sauce may be kept at room temperature, ideally sealed airtight and stored away from direct light and heat. Occasionally black soy sauce as it nears the end of the bottle will seem to crystallize, but the flavor of the liquid portion is unaffected. To my knowledge, both soy sauces will keep indefinitely without any change in taste.

Mushroom Soy Sauce (蘑菇醬油 *mandarin: maw-goo-jyang-yo; Cantonese: mo-goo-jyoong-yao*) is a flavored soy sauce, something between thin soy sauce and black soy sauce in saltiness. The brand I like best is Pearl River Bridge, which is made specifically with straw mushrooms, and is classified in Chinese as black soy sauce (草菇老豆 *mandarin: tsao-goo-lao-cho; Cantonese: tso-goo-low-chao*), owing to a touch of sugar that is included in the mixture. It is delicious sprinkled into a stir-fry of meat or vegetables. Use sparingly, and store as above.

STAR ANISE
(八角 mandarin: bah-jyao; Cantonese: baht-gook)

Star anise *(Illicium verum)*, also called Chinese anise, is a member of the magnolia family and the product of a small evergreen native to southwest China. The Chinese name, literally "eight points," refers to the hard, star-like brown pod, each point of which holds a glossy brown seed. Both the pod and the seed are used. The whole pod is very pretty in a dish, and I like to use it as a garnish. Break into individual points if less than eight are required, or when greater permeation of flavor is wanted.

Star anise is available in all Chinese markets, typically bagged in small cellophane pouches. You should be able to smell it through the wrapper—a licorice-like aroma that is reminiscent of, though stronger than, Western anise (to which star anise is botanically unrelated).

Store star anise in an airtight glass jar kept at room temperature, away from light, heat, and moisture. So long as it is fragrant it is good, and if properly stored will last a year or more.

SUGAR

Sugar is widely used in Chinese cooking, not just one variety or color but several. Sweet is one of the classic Five Flavors of Chinese cooking, and precisely because it is used in balance with the other four, and hence used in moderation, sugar has never been a problem to the health of the average Chinese. A regular diet of sweet desserts and sweet drinks is unknown in the traditional Chinese home. If a sweet and sour dish is served it is more likely to be tart than sweet, or at least such was the case in my northern and central Chinese homes, though a Cantonese taste for sweetness is far more pronounced.

Not only is sugar used in moderation, but it is used quite consciously as a *balance* to other seasonings. Sugar used properly modulates the taste of soy sauce, enhances the flavor of vinegar, and brings a fullness to the taste of hot chili, things you can taste for yourself if you mix a little in a saucer with soy sauce or vinegar or a chili-based sauce. It is not that the addition of sugar makes these things taste *sweet*, it simply brings them to fullness and, if the constellation of seasonings is correct, brings them to balance. Chinese food that is made without that small amount of sugar is considered imbalanced and therefore unhealthy to an educated Chinese palate. The Five Flavors must all be present, and the rigorous exclusion of any one of them destroys the harmony and, to a Chinese way of thinking, the healthfulness of a dish.

I use three types of sugar in my kitchen, each to different effect.

White Sugar (糖 *mandarin: tong; Cantonese: toong*) I use mostly in small amounts, typically in marinades or sauces to balance soy sauce or vinegar. Whereas I do not like sweet soy sauces or sweet vinegars, sugar cooked in combination with an unsweet soy sauce or a sharp, full-flavored vinegar enhances their tastes.

Brown Sugar (黄糖 *mandarin: hwong-tong; Cantonese: hwong-toong*) I use to sauce eggplant and to marinate beef for hearty northern-style dishes, where the extra depth of molasses seems to best complement the food. Here again, it is used to balance soy sauce and vinegar, whose own flavors are quite intense and are best partnered by the richer sugar. I usually mix light brown sugar and dark brown sugar in a single canister.

Golden Rock Sugar (黄冰糖 *mandarin: hwong-bing-tong; Cantonese: hwong-bing-toong*) is a type of sugar used widely in north China, primarily in potted dishes and in particular with poultry. It has a unique, mild sweetness not unlike maltose, and is made with a combination of white sugar, unrefined brown sugar and honey. Sold in Chinese markets many times under the label Yellow Rock Sugar, it takes the form of large, irregular nuggets that are rock-hard, pale gold in color, and packed in 1-pound plastic bags. Do not confuse it with the darker "slab sugar" that is sold in thin, rectangular blocks, and has a different taste.

Golden rock sugar must be broken into small bits before it is added to a sauce. Do *not* attempt this in a food processor. The best approach, I find, is to wrap several nuggets at a time in a heavy, lint-free cloth, and go at them with a large hammer. I like to get all the banging over with in one session, and then store the bits in an airtight container at room temperature, ready to use without further banging. Kept away from light, heat and moisture, this sugar keeps forever.

In addition to its characteristic sweetness, golden rock sugar imparts a special sheen to things that are stewed with it. It is this glazing effect that is hardest to duplicate. Amber sugar crystals, an expensive, English-made sugar product, and white sugar in combination with wild-flower honey will give you something of the taste, but there is no real substitute for either the flavor or the sheen.

SWEET RICE

(糯米 *mandarin: naw-mee; Cantonese: naw-my*)
Often called glutinous rice or sticky rice, but marketed widely in America under the name sweet rice, this is an altogether different type of rice than the short-, medium-, or

long-grain rice that Chinese eat every day. In contrast to everyday rice, which is 15–26 percent amylose (that feature of the starch chemistry that keeps the grains separate), so-called sweet rice has no amylose whatsoever and is 100 percent amylopectin, which in layman's terms means it sticks together! Rather than call it sticky rice, the packers chose to label it sweet rice. The sweetness is not much more pronounced than any good-quality, fresh, short-grain rice, but in stickiness it is a standout.

Sweet rice is easily recognizable. The grains are small, oval, and starkly white, as opposed to the nearly translucent grains of regular short-grain rice. Sweet rice is coated with glucose and starch after milling to retard rancidity, and must be rinsed thoroughly and repeatedly until the water runs clear. It must also be soaked before using, anywhere from 2 hours to overnight, covered with cold water. In addition to removing the milling starch, soaking softens the kernel and is the customary preliminary to cooking, much the same as soaking beans.

Sweet rice is a dressy rice in China, used as a coating for steamed meatballs (page 187) or in stuffings or desserts bound mostly for a banquet table. If you were to cook it plain, it must be soaked overnight, steamed in a thin layer on wet cheesecloth for 60 minutes, and sprinkled midway through steaming with a light shower of water. If you boil sweet rice it becomes decidedly oily, and there is in fact a dish called Greasy Rice that calls purposely for it to be boiled.

SZECHWAN BROWN PEPPERCORNS
(花椒 mandarin: hwa-jyao; Cantonese: fa-jyew)

Szechwan brown peppercorns *(Xanthoxylum piperitum)* are altogether different in look, smell, and taste from our familiar Western white and black peppercorns. Often called *fagara*, Chinese pepper, Szechwan pepper, wild pepper, brown pepper, or "flower pepper" (the literal translation of its common Chinese name), these hollow brown peppercorns are keenly aromatic when whole, and have a pleasantly numbing, as opposed to a spicy or biting, effect. At one time in China it was fashionable to make sachets from Szechwan peppercorns and present them as a token of affection—an idea that I find almost as appealing as cooking with them.

Szechwan brown peppercorns are available in most any Chinese grocery, bagged in small plastic pouches or larger heavy plastic bags weighing up to 8 ounces, and costing a fraction of the price you will pay in a Western gourmet shop. Like star anise, the fragrance of the spice should be clearly discernible through the thinner plastic bag, and the more pronounced the smell, the surer your guarantee of flavor.

Once opened, the peppercorns should be sealed in an airtight jar or tea tin, and kept at room temperature, away from light, heat and moisture. So long as they are fragrant they are good, which will be for many months if stored properly.

In many recipes, the first step to using Szechwan brown peppercorns is to heat them in a dry skillet to release their aromatic oils. Be forewarned that they will smoke as they grow hot. The trick is to use a medium- or heavyweight skillet and keep the heat low so they do not burn.

SZECHWAN PRESERVED VEGETABLE
(四川榨菜 mandarin: Szz-chwan-jah-tsai; Cantonese: Say-chwoon-dza-choy)

This is a delightfully crunchy pickled vegetable, with a crisp and refreshing salty aftertaste, something like a good kosher pickle. It is regularly canned under the name Szechuen Preserved Vegetable or Preserved Szechwan Mustard, and may sometimes be found in Chinese markets sold loose in 2-foot high, brown-glazed crocks. The appearance of the vegetable—which is neither mustard nor kohlrabi as is often said, but rather the knobby root end of a leafy green cabbage—is somewhat forbidding. It is covered by a thick, red paste that smells as bad as it looks.

To use the preserved vegetable, rinse off the paste under cool running water, rubbing the knobby contours to clean them thoroughly. Then shred or mince as the recipe requires. Unused knobs should be stored unwashed in an airtight bottle, in a cool place or in the refrigerator, away from light, heat and moisture. Wash just before using. It will keep indefinitely, which is after all the *raison d'être* of a preserved vegetable.

If you cannot find the sort sold loose in the crock, which is both tender and crisp, a good canned brand is what Companion calls Preserved Szechwan Mustard.

T

TANGERINE PEEL, SEE ORANGE AND TANGERINE PEEL, HOME-DRIED

TEA, CHINESE

(茶 *mandarin: cha; Cantonese: cha*)

Chinese teas are traditionally divided into three main categories: *fermented black teas* (sometimes called "red" teas); *unfermented green teas;* and *semi-fermented teas* (sometimes called "brown" teas, to distinguish them from the black and the green). All three types are made from the leaves of the tea plant *(Camellia sinensis)*, an evergreen shrub native to China and India with leathery green leaves that have a serrated edge and a sharp, tapered point. Left uncut, the shrub becomes a tree. Tea cultivation, however, involves pruning the shrubs repeatedly to a height of 3 or 4 feet, to encourage the new shoots called "flushes" that bear two tender small leaves and one tiny, unopened bud and are used for the finest grade of tea.

In the production of *black tea*, the newly plucked tea leaves are first withered naturally or with the introduction of heated air to make the leaves pliable. They are next rolled to gently break open the cells where the juices are stored (traditionally, this was accomplished by people treading on the leaves, reminiscent of grapes being crushed). As the juices are released to the air, oxidation begins and the leaves are left to ferment until they turn a bright copper. The final step is a drying or firing that halts oxidation by drying the leaves and turns them black. Tea that undergoes this process is typically strong-tasting, full-bodied, and has an earthy, foresty aroma.

In the production of *green tea*, the leaves are steamed or heated soon after plucking to render them soft and to stop fermentation. They are then rolled and dried alternately until they become crisp and assume their characteristic rolled or twisted shape. The leaves remain green in color. They have a pungent, grassy smell, and a uniquely clean, cooling taste.

Semi-fermented teas are treated to the same process as black teas; however, the withering and fermentation periods are shortened. The result is a greenish-brown leaf with a taste and aroma somewhere in between those of black and green teas.

For brewing Chinese teas: In general, black teas should be brewed with water that has just been brought to a full boil. Green teas require a more gentle treatment so as not to release the tannin in the leaf at a temperature that would bring forth its bitterness and overwhelm its aroma. Consequently, when brewing green tea, bring the water to a full boil then turn off the heat and let the water stand for 2–3 minutes. Pour water over the leaves to cover, then cover the vessel in which they are steeping. Wait 2 minutes more, then pour the remainder of the water over the leaves. This same treatment applies to the more delicate Jasmine and scented teas. Gutsier Oolongs can typically stand freshly boiled water. Experiment by infusing the same tea in different temperatures of water to best understand how it is affected. The results are as interesting as a good wine tasting.

When measuring tea leaves, start with a general measure of 1 *level* teaspoon per 10 ounces (1¼ cups) water. If you are brewing in a pot, do *not* add an extra teaspoonful for the pot. On the contrary, *decrease* the amount per 10 ounces, as the concentration of heat in the pot will result in a stronger brew. If the potful is brewed too strong, then fill the cups only partway and top with freshly boiled water to the brim. Also, if the tea is of good quality, empty the pot only one half or two thirds of the way, then fill to the brim with freshly boiled water and enjoy a second pouring, which with a fine Chinese tea, is more intriguingly flavored than the first.

Use a scrupulously clean porcelain or earthenware or glass pot for Chinese teas. Do not use silver or metal pots for brewing, and do not use aluminum kettles to boil the water. The character of the metal will taint the taste of the tea, particularly green teas. Warm the pot or the cup with boiling water prior to brewing, so the temperature of the brewing water is not lowered by a cold vessel.

Varieties of Chinese teas are myriad, but here are some I particularly enjoy and drink every day. Buy the best grade you can, judging quality by aroma and the integrity of the leaf.

Rose Black or Litchi Black (玫瑰紅茶, 荔枝紅茶 *mandarin: may-gway-hoong-cha, or lee-jrr-hoong-cha; Cantonese: moy-gwoy-hong-cha, or lai-gee-hong-cha*). These are the keenly aromatic blacks I use mostly for smoking foods. Sometimes labeled in English as Rose Congou and Litchi Congou. They are made from an infusion of rose petals or litchi fruit and black tea, which impregnates the leaves with a heady perfume. I use the widely available Ying Mee Tea Company brand, which comes in a colorful 5-ounce box with pictures of mountains or birds on flowering branches, wrapped airtight in clear cellophane. Perfectly delicious for drinking if you enjoy strongly scented teas.

Toasted Rice Tea (玄米茶 *mandarin: hswan-mee-cha; Cantonese: sao-my-cha*). Marketed widely by Japanese firms under its Japanese name *Genmai Cha*, this is a mixture of flat, rolled green tea leaves and mostly brown grains of roasted rice, with an occasional white, popcorn-like grain that burst open in the roasting. The tea is typically a coarse-grade green tea made from large leaves (called *bancha* in Japanese), and what is available here is a poor grade inclusive of twigs and stems. Nonetheless, it is delicious, and well worth fishing out the little twigs. The rice gives the tea a wonderful, nutty flavor that makes it a pleasant accompaniment to breakfast. It is very soothing, and toasted rice brewed on its own as a tea is a traditional stomach settler in China. Best brewed in individual cups with boiling water, and best to catch and eat the rice before it sinks!

Water Goddess Tea (水仙茶 *mandarin: shway-hsyen-cha; Cantonese: soy-seen-cha*). This is my favorite semi-fermented tea, also called Water Nymph, with a richer flavor and more depth of color and aroma than a standard Oolong tea. (Parenthetically, Oolong means "black dragon," and dragons, like water nymphs, live in the water, making them perfect candidates for tea names.) This tea can be properly brewed with boiling water. An excellent brand currently on the market from the People's Republic of China comes with individually wrapped packets inside a rectangular metal tin. The tin is predominantly green and gold and has a painting of one of China's Five Sacred Mountains on the top.

Jasmine (香片茶 *mandarin: hsyang-pyen-cha; Cantonese: heung-peen-cha*). This variety of tea, called "fragrant petal" in Chinese, is well known in the West. It can be as cloying as a bad perfume or absolutely heavenly, all depending on the grade. A good grade will have a slightly twisted, small, and slender Oolong-type leaf, and will smell evocative—pleasantly floral and slightly grassy at the same time. The best grade Jasmines do *not* have the flowers included with the leaves; they are strained out once the leaves have been infused. To get both the flavor and the visual beauty, I buy a top grade imported Chinese Jasmine for the scented leaves, and a top grade English Jasmine for the whole Jasmine flowers. I discard the English tea (which has never, in my experience, been able to hold a candle to the Chinese import), and put a single flower in each teacup before I brew the tea. Chuan-Shang Tea Company's Jasmine tea, available through mail order (page 588), is the best I have yet tasted.

Chrysanthemum (菊花茶 *mandarin: jyew-hwa-cha; Cantonese: gook-fa-cha*). This is not a leaf tea at all, but a tea that one brews from tiny, dried white chrysanthemums. The taste is wonderfully refreshing, and slightly sweet. The flowers bloom and float in the water, which makes it the prettiest cupful or potful one can imagine. A perfect tea for a *dim sum* brunch, also lovely in combination with Dragon Well tea. Brew with boiling water. In the summertime, Chinese enjoy this tea made with rock sugar and chilled slightly before drinking.

Chrysanthemum tea is seen more frequently now in large Chinese markets, but the grades are often quite poor. A choice grade should have a pleasantly floral aroma, and each flower should be intact. Chuan-Shang Tea Company in Taipei packages tiny baby chrysanthemums available through mail order (page 588). Packs of larger, sweeter chrysanthemums are available in many Chinese markets.

Dragon Well (龍井茶 *mandarin: loong-jeeng-cha; Cantonese: loong-jang-cha*). This is my favorite variety of green tea, named after a famous spring in the vicinity of Hangchow. The leaves have a decidedly grassy smell, and are flat, rolled, and slender like a spear, usually with a tuft of light green at one end of the leaves. This is a volatile tea, with a refreshing slight bitterness and must be brewed carefully with water that has come down in temperature from a full boil, as described above.

It is difficult to find a truly good grade of Dragon Well on the current market. The best I have drunk is again packaged by Chuan-Shang Tea Company and is available through mail order (page 588).

As a final word on tea, the Westerner who is used to buying tea bags and popular commercial teas will in no way be prepared for the expense of buying a top-grade Chinese tea. It is by no means prohibitive, but fine tea like fine wine has its price. The best policy is to buy in small amounts, so the tea does not have a chance to fade and you have the opportunity and the extra pennies to sample and drink more.

TEA MELON, SEE WHITE CUCUMBER IN SYRUP

THIN SOY SAUCE, SEE SOY SAUCE

TIENTSIN PRESERVED VEGETABLE
(天津冬菜 *mandarin: Tyen-jin-doong-tsai; Cantonese: Teen-joon-doong-choy*)

This is a shredded, salted, preserved cabbage that is crunchy and keenly aromatic. The cabbage is called winter cabbage and is grown primarily in the area around Tientsin, south of Peking, hence the Chinese name is quite specifically "Tientsin winter cabbage," though the translation on the label is confusingly vague. To add to the confusion, the dish in which this condiment is best known is *Dry-Fried Szechwan String Beans* (page 297).

The brand I like best is widely distributed, marketed in an attractive, squat crock with a rich brown glaze. There is a red, white, and blue label over the mouth of the crock and also a banner on the side that has nothing in English save the words Tientsin Preserved Vegetables. In traditional style, the crock is sealed with a heavy paper "lid," which must be cut through and then pulled off. To store the cabbage, simply seal the crock with a square or two of tin foil held in place with a thick rubber band, then keep it at room temperature away from light, heat, and moisture. It will keep forever, like any respectable preserved vegetable.

This ingredient does *not* need to be rinsed before using. Its salty character is a part of any dish that calls for it, and will be balanced by the other seasonings. Also note that *Tientsin* Preserved Vegetable is *not* the same thing as *Szechwan* Preserved Vegetable, which is discussed above.

TOFU, FERMENTED
(豆腐乳 *mandarin: doe-foo-roo; Cantonese: foo-yoo*)
These are bottled cubes of mold-fermented tofu afloat in a briny liquid, which you will recognize more by look than by name. They have an almost cheesy taste when mashed to a smooth consistency and added to a stir-fry of vegetables, and their aroma is pleasantly, to my nose, pronounced. I prefer the sort seasoned with hot chili flakes, which you can easily spot by the flakes floating in the bottle. My bottle is labeled Pepper Bean Cake (辣椒腐乳 *mandarin: la-jyao-foo-roo; Cantonese: la-jyew-foo-yoo*) and is made by Quong Hop.

Fermented tofu will keep for years. Refrigerate after opening. The liquid will get murky and the cubes will lose their shape, but the taste is still fine. Do not decant the liquid, as it is used along with the tofu cubes to mash them to a paste.

TOFU, FRESH
(豆腐 *mandarin: doe-foo; Cantonese: dao-foo*)
Increasingly packaged under the name tofu (pronounced *toe-foo* in Japanese), and less frequently under the name bean curd, soybean curd, and bean cake, this is the protein-rich, low-calorie food made from soy milk solidified by a coagulant that has fed the Chinese nation for centuries. The Chinese varieties are generally sold in small cakes, about 3–3½ inches square and 1–1½ inches thick, floating in water—either in a large

open tub or tall can if you are buying them at the factory or an outlet, or sealed in a small container weighing about a pound if you are buying them in a store. The color is always pure white. The shape will be square-edged if it is the softer Chinese sort, or round-edged like a pillow if it is the firmer, denser Chinese variety called "old tofu" in Chinese (老豆腐 *mandarin: lao-doe-foo, Cantonese: yao-dao-foo*). Either variety is preferable for the recipes in this book to the Japanese sort, which is beautifully silky but tends to fall apart when subjected to the hubbub of Chinese cooking.

For details on storage and pressing softer tofu to a firmer consistency, see page 324.

TOFU, PRESSED
(豆腐乾 mandarin: doe-foo-gone; Cantonese: dao-foo-gawn)
Press the fresh, white cake of tofu with a weight, season it with soy sauce (and occasionally cinnamon or star anise), and you have the brown compact cake with a texture like muenster cheese that is frequently shredded and included in vegetarian stir-frys such as *Buddha's Feast* (page 299). You must hunt for a truly good-tasting brand. Avoid the very dark, ¼-inch thin sort that is typically sold in Cantonese markets in sealed plastic bags of 6–8 squares. It is usually heavily seasoned with five-spice powder and is lacking in flavor and unpleasantly hard. Search instead for a small market that has thicker and sometimes smaller cakes of a caramel color that smell savory and taste delicious when you bite into them. This homestyle sort is most often found loose and stacked on a tray in a Chinese market or packaged informally in small baggies. In the San Francisco area, there is a luscious variety called Savory Baked Tofu, manufactured by Quong Hop and sold mainly in whole food stores. See if you can get your local dealer to stock it, as well as Quong Hop's firm fresh tofu.

Pressed tofu keeps for a week or more, refrigerated. When it goes bad, it will have a sour smell and a slimy feel. When it is just about to turn and feels a bit slick, it may still be used if first rinsed with cool water.

To make your own pressed tofu, press a cake of fresh tofu under weights as described on page 324 until it is ⅜–½ inch thick, then soak 8–24 hours in a mixture of 1 part thin soy sauce and 3 parts light, unsalted chicken stock or water to cover. Bring the mixture to a simmer before covering the tofu, and season it if you like with a bit of five-spice powder, a few points of star anise, a slip of orange or tangerine peel scraped clean of white pith, and/or a dash of sesame oil.

TREE EARS
(木耳 mandarin: moo-er; Cantonese: maw-yee)

Also called wood ears, cloud ears, Jew's ears, and dried black fungus in English, this rubbery but crunchy, saucer-shaped fungus *(Auricularia polytricha)* is habitually dried for use in Chinese cooking. It is tasteless, but nonetheless valued for its rich, brown-black color and its intriguing texture. It is typically paired with golden needles, and featured in the well-known dishes hot and sour soup (page 450) and *mu-shu* pork (page 198).

There are two types of tree ears found in Chinese markets. The type to get is fortunately also the most common, thumb nail-size, irregular bits of blackness without any sheen, bagged in plastic, about 2 ounces per bag. The sort to avoid is called "white-backed black tree ear" in Chinese, and has a relatively shiny black "belly" and a fuzzy-looking, light tan "back." The latter are huge and tough once soaked and look more like something to resole a jogging shoe than to put in a bowl of soup.

Tree ears must be soaked and thoroughly cleaned before using. Cover generously with warm or cool water—about 1 cup water for each 2 tablespoons tree ears—then soak until supple, 20–30 minutes. Drain, then swish repeatedly in a large bowl of water to dislodge all the foresty bits that are trapped in the irregular folds of the fungus. Drain, swish, and drain again. Pinch off any unchewable or overly gelatinous bits, but do not remove the extra-crunchy folds that give the tree ears character. Once clean, cover with cool water until use, overnight if you like, and drain thoroughly before using.

Most Chinese cookbooks call for the tree ears to be broken into small bits before using. I like to leave them at least nickel size, so that my tongue and eye can enjoy their irregular, wavy charm.

V

VINEGAR
(醋 mandarin: tsoo; Cantonese: tso)
I love vinegar, as do most Chinese, who throughout the course of their rich culinary history have made vinegar variously from rice, wheat, peaches, and grapes, flavoring them on occasion with peach blossoms and kumquat leaves. I use many types when I cook, and am always tasting new brands. Unfortunately, as my generous pile of labels and tasting notes attests, there are few high-quality Chinese vinegars currently available in American markets.

Rice Vinegar (白米醋 *mandarin: bye-mee-tsoo; Cantonese: bok-my-tso*). Called "white rice vinegar" in Chinese, this is a white to golden vinegar with a sharp, clean taste, lighter in character and more full-flavored than a distilled Western white vinegar, and not as sweet as cider vinegar. "Refreshing" and "pleasantly tangy" are two phrases which crop up repeatedly in my notes, but seem an inadequate description for the charm of this vinegar.

The Chinese brands I have sampled are a bit on the harsh side. My customary brand is Marukan, a Japanese product. Be sure to buy the *unseasoned* sort that is bottled with a *green* label. Another excellent brand is Mitsukan, again a Japanese make.

I use rice vinegar more and more, increasingly to the exclusion of Western white vinegar. It is excellent in Western salads, paired with a dash of sesame oil.

Well-Aged Chinese Black Vinegar: There are a variety of terms in Chinese to describe dark vinegar, a vinegar with a distinctive dark color and depth of flavor that is made from a fermented rice base. A lighter dark vinegar will be called red vinegar (紅醋 *mandarin: hoong-tsoo; Cantonese: hong-tso*), while a more deeply colored and fla-vored dark vinegar will be called black vinegar (黑醋 *mandarin: hey-tsoo; Cantonese: hut-tso*). The best and most richly flavored of the dark vinegars are known as Chekiang, Chen-jung, or Chenkong vinegar (鎮江醋 *mandarin: Jen-jyang-tsoo; Cantonese: Chen-goong-tso*) all being transliterations of the name of the central coastal province long fa-mous for their production.

To find here a quality, well-aged Chinese black vinegar with a strong but good flavor is as difficult as finding dragon's teeth. I have found only one brand that appeals to me, Narcissus brand Black Vinegar, Yongchun Laocu (水仙花牌永春老醋), whose Chinese name means "aged vinegar from Yongchun," which is a city in Chekiang. This particular brand appears on the market in spurts, as it has for years, and is easier to get mail order than to find on one's own. It is good in combination with other Chinese seasonings, though it is rather harsh when tasted alone.

A perfectly good substitute is *balsamic vinegar*, which is an Italian aged vinegar very similar in character to Chekiang vinegar but with a touch more sweetness. I use a reasonably priced brand, produced in Modena by Federzoni Elio and Company, which comes in a 17-ounce bottle with an olive-green label and is available in large specialty shops and through mail order (page 588). If you are using balsamic vinegar in any of the preceding recipes, decrease slightly the amount of sugar called for, then adjust further if required.

As with oils, I am always sampling new brands as they appear and suggest that you do the same. The vinegar situation has remained the same for years, but I keep looking hopefully for the next good one to appear.

Cider Vinegar and White Vinegar: These are the vinegars with which I first learned to make Chinese pickles in the kitchen of my mentors, the Lo's, and I still like them for this purpose. They are rather sweet and harsh, respectively, but their assertive tastes are in keeping with the character of pickled vegetables. For the same reason, you will usually see white vinegar used in hot and sour-style dishes, where it is the nature of the dish to be bold and gutsy, not refined.

W

WATER CHESTNUT POWDER
(馬蹄粉 *mandarin: ma-tee-fun; Cantonese: ma-tie-foon*)
This is the dry starch or flour of fresh water chestnuts, which is a bright white and feels very smooth, soft and "squeaky" between your fingers, like a fine talc or chalk. It is frequently used in combination with cornstarch to coat foods that are to be first steamed and then deep-fried. The powder cools after steaming into an opaque shell, which when deep-fried becomes golden and delicately crisp.

Water chestnut powder is boxed by Companion brand and widely distributed. Store like any flour, in a cool spot away from light, heat, and moisture.

WATER CHESTNUTS
(馬蹄, 荸薺 *mandarin: ma-tee, and bee-gee; Cantonese: ma-tie*)

There is hardly anything quite like a fresh water chestnut! Sweet and juicy and wonderfully crisp, it is as far from a canned water chestnut as a canned green bean is from a garden-picked Jersey string bean or a French *haricot vert*. From the outside, fresh water chestnuts look a bit like a chestnut, but have a black outer peel and a slightly pointy, tufted top. They are usually dull to muddy when they appear in the markets, plucked directly from their marshy beds and often crated in a hemp-lined box. They have become quite common in San Francisco and New York City markets and will survive mailing nicely if you have a friend who will send you some.

Fresh water chestnuts should be judged by their firmness. When you pinch one all around with your fingers, it should be literally rock-hard. Soft spots mean bad spots and a wrinkled exterior means a mealy or sour water chestnut. Once bought, they will keep for up to 2 weeks refrigerated in a plastic bag, if they were perfectly rock-hard to begin. Wash clean with cool water just before using, then peel with a sharp paring knife (or with a cleaver if you'd like to show off in the traditional manner, rolling the water chestnut toward you with one hand as you slice off the skin in short pieces with the blade of the cleaver held angled away from you in the other hand). Pare away any dark gold or brown spots, though the peeled water chestnut needn't be perfectly white. Then slice into coins, stack the coins neatly, and cut lengthwise and crosswise into neat, square bits the size of a peppercorn, so you can enjoy their texture with your tongue. Mincing water chestnuts, as many Chinese cookbooks call for you to do, is absolutely ridiculous. That would be like mashing a crisp apple to a pulp before eating it.

If you cannot get fresh water chestnuts, use *jicama*, a large and bulbous tuber with a tan skin and a white, crisp flesh that is much like a fresh water chestnut though not quite as sweet or starchy. It is typically sold in Mexican markets and increasingly in Chinatown markets. Jicama (pronounced HICK-a-ma) must be peeled before using. A level ½ cup diced jicama will equal 6–8 large fresh water chestnuts. What doesn't go into the Chinese dish will taste great in a salad.

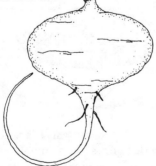

Canned water chestnuts have little to recommend them but the occasional crunch, once you have been spoiled by the fresh. The only satisfactory brand I have yet come across is Ma Ling, which packs whole peeled water chestnuts in an 8-ounce can with a navy blue label. After draining, blanch briefly in plain boiling water for about 15 seconds, then drain and rush immediately under cold water until chilled. Blanching removes any traces of the tinny taste from the can, though it will not restore the natural sweetness to the water chestnut. The best you can hope for is a neutral, clean taste and a good crunch when you bite down.

Canned water chestnuts are much smaller than fresh water chestnuts. Generally, 2–3 canned water chestnuts equal 1 large, fresh water chestnut. For a more specific measurement applicable to many of the recipes, remember that ½ cup diced water chestnuts equals 6–8 large, fresh water chestnuts.

Parenthetically, if you look up water chestnuts in a botanical book to see what they look like, there may be some confusion. The sort of water chestnut referred to above is the round tuber of a sedge *(Eleocharis tuberosa)*, with a layered black skin that prompts southern Chinese to call it by the name "horse's hoof." There is something else frequently called a water chestnut, sometimes called a caltrop *(Trapa bicornis)*, which is another inhabitant of Chinese marshes and lakes. It is a two-horned fruit with a seed in each horn (in Chinese called *ling* 菱), that has a smooth, hard black shell and looks a bit like a play moustache.

WHITE CUCUMBER IN SYRUP
(甜茶瓜 mandarin: tyen-cha-gwa; Cantonese: teen-cha-gwa)
This is the common English term given to a crisp, small, cucumber-type melon that is called in Chinese by the far more poetic name "tea melon." It is packed and preserved in a sugar syrup and is a beautiful translucent white-gold. Finely slivered, it is a delicious garnish for cold poultry and fish salads and is used regularly as such by the Cantonese.

The best brands I have found are Mei Chun and Tung Chun, both packed in clear glass jars. More frequently seen canned brands have no sparkle whatsoever. Opened, the tea melon will keep indefinitely in the refrigerator, covered with the packing syrup.

WINE, SEE CHINESE RICE WINE

WINTER MELON
(冬瓜 mandarin: doong-gwa; Cantonese: doong-gwa)

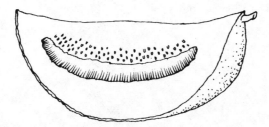

Surprisingly, given the English name, this is a vegetable and not a fruit, a member of the vegetable gourd family that grows like a pumpkin *(Benincasa hispida)*. From the outside, it is a bit more tall than wide, covered by a silver-green skin. On the inside, the flesh is white and pulpy with a network of pumpkin-like seeds that the Chinese love to dry, season, and crack between their teeth with a dexterity that gives rise to envy (and piles of empty shells). Once cooked, typically steamed or poached in a soup, the flesh turns translucent and delicately sweet. It has the character of a steamed cucumber, which is a reasonable replacement if fresh winter melon is unavailable.

Fresh winter melon should look juicy and plump when you buy it. Ideally, it will be cut to order, as is the practice in all traditional Chinese markets. To use, cut off all the green rind, so there is no trace of green on the flesh, and cut away the fibrous portion including the seeds. If you purchase a small, whole winter melon, it is traditional to cut off the top and scoop the melon out, then carve the exterior with a dragon chasing a sun (or a phoenix chasing a dragon, or flowers, or good luck Chinese characters, as you will). As a final step the cubed flesh is put back into the hollow shell with a rich stock and some ham, then the soup is steamed inside the melon and served up for a grand occasion.

WOOD EARS, SEE TREE EARS

A Food Processor in a Chinese Kitchen

食物切拌器

It would be lovely to think that a single machine could do all or even most of the work for a Chinese (or any other) cook, but it simply is not so. There are many things that a food processor *can* do splendidly in a Chinese kitchen, but there are a far greater number of things that it *cannot* do at all, or will do at only a ridiculous expense of time and effort. ◆ Here is an outline of the talents and foibles of the machine as I see them, keyed to those ingredients and tasks most likely to confront the Chinese cook. There is also a MAYBE, which may be translated into a CAN or CANNOT depending upon your own habits and tastes for precision.

CAN DO

◆ A food processor can mince raw fish, shellfish, poultry, or meat to a smooth paste with incredible speed and uniformity. No two cleavers can fly faster and produce such excellent results. This puts a lot of *dim sum* specialties within easy reach of a home cook.

◆ A food processor can process ¼–⅓ cup or more of garlic, ginger, scallion, and coriander to a fine mince, together or separately, with several turns of the blade and scrapings down of the work bowl. It is well worth it when the recipe calls for other processor tasks to mince even the smaller amount by machine.

◆ A food processor can blend ingredients like soy sauce, cornstarch, and wine for a marinade, then simultaneously fine-polish ground meat and mix it with the marinade with several on-off turns. It is effective and a real time-saver, when compared to whack-mincing and combining by hand.

◆ A food processor can whip a velvet marinade (the egg white, cornstarch, salt and wine partnership that forms a protective coating for chicken and fish) to unsurpassed thickness and lightness. There is no better way to blend cornstarch and liquids to a homogenized consistency.

◆ A food processor can make doughs for Chinese noodles, breads, buns, and dumpling wrappers with speed and skill. It eliminates the tedium of mixing and kneading by hand and produces a very good product.

◆ A food processor can mix the sesame, peanut, and mustard sauces that accompany Chinese cold salads with super-speed. It produces a beautifully homogenized sauce in seconds and will restore with equal speed any sauce that separates upon storing.

CANNOT DO

◆ A food processor cannot cut scallions into rings or shreds as neatly, quickly, and precisely as can be accomplished with a Chinese cleaver or with a sharp Western knife.

◆ A food processor cannot shred ginger to the hair-fine shreds that many Chinese dishes require.

◆ A food processor cannot chop water chestnuts to the type of tiny, precision square dice that is pretty to look at and joyful in the mouth.

◆ A food processor cannot be a time-saver for mincing small amounts, such as three cloves of garlic or one nugget of ginger, when that is the only mincing chore the recipe requires. I have given teaspoon and tablespoon measurements when it makes sense to mince them by hand.

◆ A food processor cannot dice a vegetable neatly without a ridiculous amount of manipulation. It is easily and precisely done by hand once you understand the simple rules (page 35).

◆ A food processor cannot shred raw meat as uniformly as stir-frying demands. Unevenly cut things will not cook evenly when stir-fried, and it is silly to start with the cards stacked against you. Hand-shredding meat with a cleaver or very sharp knife is the only way to get the precision that is needed, and it is easily and efficiently done once you know the simple rules (page 33).

◆ A food processor cannot shred cooked meat with enough uniformity and good looks to make it worthy of a Chinese cold salad. If finger-shredding seems too laborious in those recipes where it is suggested, turn to a cleaver or sharp knife where you can accomplish the job quickly and still control the size and grain of the shreds.

◆ A food processor cannot coarse-chop fresh coriander for a garnish and have it look beautiful. The plant is too delicate not to be torn to ugly shreds by the blade. Several cuts with a cleaver or sharp knife will do the job in seconds, with finesse.

MAYBE

◆ A food processor *can* chop nuts coarsely or more finely for coating deep-fried foods and garnishing stir-frys and cold salads. However, the nuts (walnuts especially) tend to become oily, and the machine produces a lot of nutty "dust" that requires careful sifting through a colander if it is not to dirty up the frying oil or muddy the tastes and textures of the foods. If I need a pound or more of nuts for a coating, then it sometimes seems worthwhile to process the nuts by machine, sift them carefully, then bag and freeze the dust for baking. On the other hand, if I need nuts for garnishing, I always chop them by hand. The clean, sharp contours of hand-cut nuts are, to me, far too appealing to sacrifice. If you are less fussy, you may coarse-chop the nuts for garnishing by machine, so long as you are careful to sift them free of all dust.

Food Processor Techniques and Tricks 切拌器用法

MINCING AROMATICS
In the everyday cooking of north and central China—those cuisines I like best—a Chinese cook spends inordinate amounts of time mincing aromatic condiments like scallion, ginger, garlic, and coriander. To throw them in the work bowl fitted with the steel knife and let the processor do the work is a pleasure, particularly when there's a great quantity of one thing to mince, or the need to mince several things together. One needs only to occasionally scrape the bowl down with a spatula to redistribute the contents, and an otherwise big job is accomplished in seconds.

◆ To mince evenly, aromatics should be cut before processing into "bite-size" pieces, that is, into *walnut- or marble-size hunks* or into 1–1½-inch lengths. The work bowl is exactly like the human mouth. It chews with greatest efficiency things that are already precut. When you are processing a cupful or more of food you can begin with larger pieces, but for processing ½ cup or less, you are wise to start with things cut small.

◆ On-off turns, where the machine is activated for only a split second, are the best way to control the size of the mince. Let the machine run freely only if you want a near-purée, or if you are mincing fresh ginger, which is sufficiently hard that the blade needs more than several seconds to chop it. On-off turns are the best way to proceed through the stages of coarse-chopping, fine-chopping, coarse-mincing, and fine-mincing to get exactly the texture you want.

◆   Your *ears* will tell you when you need to scrape down the work bowl. When the whirling of the knife has flung everything onto the walls of the bowl, you will hear only a quiet hum, indicating that it is cutting only air. That is the time to scrape down the bowl. I use this trick often, whenever I am fine-mincing a large quantity in the work bowl and want to turn my eyes elsewhere to accomplish another task.

◆   You can mince different ingredients in the work bowl at the same time. Scallion lengths and ginger nuggets, as examples, will mince together to a uniform nubble, in spite of their comparatively different shapes and textures. When the difference is pronounced—fresh ginger and raw shrimp, for example—mince the *harder* ingredient first before adding the softer ingredient to the bowl.

◆   Machine-minced ginger has a discernibly longer shelf life than if minced by hand, perhaps because of the greater liquids that exude in the processor. This means that if you are cooking over two day's time, you can machine-mince a large amount of ginger on the first day, and refrigerate it sealed airtight for use on day two. (Garlic is a more volatile thing. Only when it is being mixed with chili sauce, ginger, and scallion as part of a set of aromatics for a spicy stir-fry is the oxidation that happens otherwise retarded.)

POLISHING RAW MEATS

Chopping and polishing raw meats is another major preoccupation of an everyday Chinese cook. Meats are most often bought uncut and then whack-minced (page 39) until coarse at home. Meat bought preground is also whack-minced briefly to expose new surface area and to "polish" the texture to a special smoothness. The food processor does not chop meat to my satisfaction, but it will polish ground meat nicely so long as you are careful not to overprocess the meat to a paste.

◆   Polishing ground meat generally requires only 2–3 on-off turns. To avoid over-processing it to a paste, process only ¼–½ pound at one time. As extra insurance, divide the meat into fourths around the blade rather than lumping it all in one corner of the bowl, so that the first sweep of the knife cuts it all.

PURÉEING RAW MEATS, POULTRY AND FISH

Puréeing uncooked meats, poultry, and fish to a smooth paste is what the food processor does best. No control over the machine is necessary, except for an occasional scraping down of the work bowl to redistribute the contents.

◆   When processing raw pork to a near- or smooth paste, the steel knife will leave intact the long, thin white filaments that run through the meat. Do not bother fishing these out. They are totally undetectable (melted?) once cooked.

◆   Unless they are very black and ugly, intestinal veins on raw shrimp do not need to be laboriously extracted prior to processing. The machine will purée the veins as thoroughly as the flesh, and they are invisible on the palate.

◆   Before puréeing meat or fish, blend any liquid ingredients and/or mince any solid aromatics needed to accompany the purée in the work bowl. *Then* add the meat and proceed to purée and season it in one step.

CHOPPING AND GRINDING NUTS

Chopping or mincing nuts to coat or garnish other foods is accomplished in a food processor with on-off turns. Puréeing nuts to a butter is done by letting the machine run freely. When grinding nuts for desserts, sugar is added to the work bowl so they will not turn to paste.

◆ To best control texture when chopping or mincing, process nuts in small amounts (½ cup–1 cup at a time), using on-off turns. Do not overprocess or the nuts will become oily and eventually turn to nut butter.

◆ If you are using machine-chopped nuts as a garnish or a coating for other foods, shake them heartily in a colander after processing to sift out all the nutty "dust" that processing creates. Otherwise it will clog up the workings and the textures and taste of your dish. Once sifted out, the dust may be bagged and frozen for use in baking or nut butters.

BLENDING MARINADES, CORNSTARCH COATINGS, AND SAUCES

In this realm of kitchen whippery, the food processor is a good notch above a blender, a whisk, a wooden spoon, or a pair of chopsticks for sheer churning power. You can walk away from the machine and do something else while it runs, returning to the bowl just once or twice to redistribute the mixture.

I use the *steel knife* to blend everything, even liquids. Some food processors come with a plastic blade designed especially for blending, but I find that the steel knife sits lower in the bowl and does the better job.

◆ When blending liquid ingredients like soy sauce and wine together with dry things like cornstarch and pepper, add the dry things to the work bowl *last*. Otherwise they tend to stick to the bottom of the bowl. Furthermore, sprinkle the dry things around the *sides* of the blade. If plunked on top of the knob, they will cling there and not incorporate.

◆ Cornstarch mixtures must be blended *immediately* before using, though you may put the ingredients in the work bowl and give them a preliminary blending in advance. Cornstarch will separate from liquid if it is given any opportunity to sit around, and the mixture when you use it must be smooth and lump-free.

◆ Peanut, sesame, and mustard sauces may separate upon storing owing to their oil content and can be restored to homogeneity with 10–15 seconds' continuous processing. Reprocessing is also a good way to "stir up" sauces that have thickened after refrigeration and that may require the addition of water to restore their free-flowing consistency.

SHREDDING VEGETABLES

The shredding disk will shred carrots and radishes for cold Chinese salads and noodle dishes with great finesse, so long as you are careful to weed through the work bowl and extract any unprocessed bits.

◆ Stack carrots for shredding on their sides in the feed tube, rather than standing them upright. This produces a *long* shred, ideal for salads and noodles. Putting the plastic pusher alongside the carrot as you cut it will indicate exactly the length of segment that will fit neatly in the tube.

◆ Shred carrots or radishes *just before* they are needed, unless the recipe states that they can be tossed and "sealed" with oil prior to using. The uncoated shred oxidizes quickly on contact with air, turning dry and unappealing and losing much of its natural sweetness.

◆ When you are shredding more than one feed tube's worth of food, there is a great trick for reducing the number of slabs left unshredded on top of the disk. Shred the first feed tubeful only partway, leaving ⅓–¼ of the original batch still in the tube. Fill the tube to the top with more of whatever needs shredding, then continue to process—only partway if there is still more to be shredded, or plunging the pusher clear down to the disk when it comes to the last batch. With this system, only the final batch will leave slabs clinging to the blade.

DOUGH MAKING

Chinese-style doughs, whether they are yeasted or unyeasted, may be mixed in a food processor with excellent results. The principles for processing both types are the same: Put the flour (along with salt and cubed fat, if the recipe calls for it) in the dry work bowl. Start the machine. Then add just so much water (sometimes with yeast and sugar dissolved in it) through the feed tube in a thin stream as required to cause the flour to cohere in a lumpy mass around the blade. Making a food processor Chinese dough is exactly that simple.

Some recipes will call for a dough to be extracted from the work bowl as soon as it masses together in a lumpy near-ball. Other recipes will require it to be left in the bowl and spin around the blade in a ball for 10 seconds or more. It all depends upon whether you want the wheat gluten (the "flour muscle," as it is called in Chinese) to develop the molecular bonds that comprise an elastic, bouncy dough, the property that is developed with kneading.

♦ Once the flour is added to the bowl, one or two on-off turns will serve to aerate it, as well as to mix it with any salt or fat.

♦ A spouted liquid measuring cup is a great help when adding liquids through the feed tube. It does a neat, efficient job.

♦ Begin with more liquid than the recipe suggests in the spouted cap or placed alongside, so that extra is at hand if the dryness of the flour requires it. For yeasted doughs where the initial dissolving is done in a precise amount of water, station an extra cup of plain warm water alongside the machine.

♦ Pour the water through the feed tube in a thin, steady stream—neither a trickle nor a gush, but someplace pleasantly in between. If you pour too slowly, the gluten may become overworked as the dough begins to cohere. If you pour too quickly, you can overlook the moment when the dough begins to mass together, and thus wind up with a gooey dough.

♦ Keep in mind that the machine has a *lag time*, and that the water droplets need 2–3 seconds from the time they leave the cup in order to be incorporated into the flour. So, as soon as you see the dough starting to mass around the blade, *stop* the water flow. Wait 2–3 seconds. If it does not come together in a near-ball, then add several droplets more and wait again. If you continue pouring water up to the very moment when the dough forms a ball, then the dough will be too wet.

♦ Feel free to stop the machine *at any time* during the dough-making process. If you need to consult the recipe, catch your breath, or get more water, the dough will wait without injury as long as the machine is turned *off*.

♦ If you have added too much water and the dough is gooey, sprinkle the top evenly with about 1 tablespoon of flour, then run the machine only 2–3 seconds to incorporate it. Check the texture and if it is still conspicuously wet, then repeat the process with another tablespoon of flour. If still no luck, remove the dough to a floured board and knead in gently whatever is required by hand.

♦ Do not overprocess the dough, either when correcting the texture or when kneading it in the machine. If you run the machine too long, the dough ball falls apart and adheres to the bowl in a strange, sticky mass. (In the event that this happens, pry the dough from the bowl, let it rest in a lump under a dry towel for about five minutes, then knead gently by hand to see if it will again come together.)

◆ To extract a sticky dough from the processor, use lightly floured hands.

◆ In my experience, a properly processed Chinese-style dough is soft and slightly sticky to the touch, but dry enough to be taken from the bowl and kneaded on a lightly floured board without sticking. That's my test.

◆ If the dough is sticking to the board, do not return it to the machine. Scrape the board clean, flour it lightly, and continue to knead by hand, dusting the board with flour whenever the dough sticks. The idea is to allow the dough to absorb as much flour as is required to prevent it from being tacky, while not adding too much lest it lose its softness and become overly stiff.

I travel widely to teach Chinese cooking, to little towns and big cities where I don't know the local shops, and the first thing I do when I arrive in need of good ingredients or special tools is exactly what *you* should do if your cupboard is bare of Chinese essentials or you are in need of a particular item, and you don't know where to go.

♦ First, call the local cooking school to find out about the local shopping scene, namely, who carries Chinese goods and how to get there. If you do not know the name of a cooking school in the neighborhood, then call one or more of the local specialty food shops or kitchenware shops to find out where one might be. If no answer is forthcoming, then write or call the International Association of Cooking Schools, 1001 Connecticut Avenue NW, Suite 800, Washington, D.C. 20036, telephone (202) 293-7716. They will be able to supply you with the name of a cooking school, a Chinese cooking expert in the vicinity, or a list of suppliers who may be able to help you.

♦ If you have not done so already, contact the nearest Chinese cook, or a good cook or caterer of any persuasion. Cooks are continually discovering or hearing about resources for specialty foods and equipment, even if they themselves don't use them.

♦ If there is no help forthcoming from any of the local cooks, gourmet shops, or specialty retailers, then call or visit the closest Chinese restaurant. The food may be mediocre or worse and communication may be a problem, but if the restaurateurs are using products that you want to use, then *they* will know where to get them.

Lest, however, I leave you high and dry with no specific resources to turn to, there are several areas of the country with which I am comfortably familiar and have shopped in for many years on the hunt for things Chinese. Where I haven't hunted personally, I have gleaned recommendations from other teachers, so I don't leave a big gap in the middle of the land.

What follows is a listing of several suppliers in each area that I know for a fact will either have what you are looking for if you arrive on foot, or will be able to mail order what you need. One source in particular, Orient Delight Market in Mountain View, California, and its sister store (it *is* literally run by the sister), Mandarin Delight Market in San Francisco, will ship or sell every brand of foodstuff or tool mentioned in this book.

SAN FRANCISCO

ORIENT DELIGHT MARKET 865 East El Camino Real, Mountain View, California 94040 (415) 969-4288

> This wonderfully well-stocked market is the primary mail order source, brand-specific, for this cookbook. They have supplied me for years with specialty items I could find nowhere else. If you are in the area, take advantage of all the fresh food that cannot be shipped. What can be mailed includes Smithfield ham, Chinese sausages, cassia blossoms in jam, and Chinese teas (including Chuan-Shang Tea Company's teas), in addition to tools and nonperishable foodstuffs. Catalog available. Address any inquiries to the manager, Robert Yin.

THE CHINESE GROCER 209 Post Street at Grant Avenue, San Francisco, California 94108 (415) 982-0125 (800) 227-3320

> This is the oldest established mail order center for exclusively Chinese goods, with an excellent track record for promptness and reliability. Special cooking stoves available, also decorative kitchenware. Catalog available.

THE YING COMPANY 1120 Stockton Street, San Francisco, California 94133 (415) 982-2188

A specialty shop devoted to essential kitchenware: woks, metal steamers, Chinese mesh spoons, Chinese sand pots, in all sizes. Restaurant service (plates, platters, cups, tea pots) also available. Write with specific measurements for mail order, and address all inquiries to Jeannie Fung. An excellent shop to walk into if you're in the neighborhood.

MANDARIN DELIGHT MARKET 1024 Stockton Street, San Francisco, California 94108 (415) 781-4650

A small market with a remarkably well-chosen stock, which has been my supplier for years. The only other place in the country I know of that carries cassia blossoms in jam. Mail order done through the sister store in Mountain View (see Orient Delight Market above), but walk on in if you are visiting. Address any inquiries to Wendy Chang.

NEW HONG KONG NOODLE COMPANY 847 Pacific Avenue, San Francisco, California 94133 (415) 433-1886

If you are in the area or coming through with an empty suitcase, this is the most impressive selection of noodles, dumpling wrappers, and springroll wrappers I have ever seen under one roof. Everything made fresh daily, heat-sealed in heavy plastic, and all items freeze well. They will not mail, but they will fill your suitcase.

JAPAN FOOD CORPORATION 445 Kaufman Court, South San Francisco, California 94080

The major supplier of Oriental foods in the United States. Will send upon request specific information on stores or suppliers with mail order departments in your city.

LOS ANGELES

YEE SING CHONG COMPANY, INC. 966 North Hill Street, Los Angeles, California 90012 (213) 626-9619

Right in the heart of L.A. Chinatown, this is the store I shop in when I give classes in the area. A grand supermarket, with everything from cans and bottles to woks and snow peas.

PORTLAND

ANZEN JAPANESE FOODS & IMPORTS 736 North East Union Avenue, Portland, Oregon 97232 (503) 233-5111

This is an excellent, well-stocked grocery with a full array of Chinese and Japanese foodstuffs.

DAE HAN 9970 South West Beaverton Highway, Beaverton, Oregon 97005 (503) 646-7127

This store carries everything that is missing at Anzen. In addition to a good selection of nonperishable foodstuffs, there is a good assortment of Chinese cookware.

NEW YORK CITY

KAM MAN FOOD PRODUCTS, INC. 200 Canal Street, New York, New York 10013 (212) 571-0330/0331

If you can get there in person, this is *the* store to begin your shopping in New York City's Chinatown. On the street floor is a deli, a butcher, and rows of everything from Kadoya oils to noodles and breadstuffs and cassia blossoms in water. Downstairs are cans and bottles, woks and sand pots. They have almost everything I use. For mail order, write and request specific items and quantity (include clippings from the photo-copied glossary).

KAM KUO 7 Mott Street, New York, New York 10013 (212) 349-3097

The little sister-store to Kam Man, with less of a stock, but including items that they may be out of or are no longer carrying at Kam Man. Same mail order policy applies here as at Kam Man.

MING JAN SAUSAGE CO. 54 Mulberry Street, New York, New York 10013 (212) 349-1696

A small, immaculate factory and smokehouse, with sausages (pork or duck's liver), Chinese-style bacon, and dry salted ducks hanging in various postures from the ceiling. Will mail order, prepaid.

DEAN & DeLUCA 121 Prince Street, New York, New York 10012 (212) 254-7774

A thoroughly unlikely source for a Chinese cookbook, except that they stock the best crystallized ginger I have ever eaten (spicy and sharp!), and they will mail order it as well as Monari brand balsamic vinegar.

WALNUT ACRES Penns Creek, Pennsylvania 17862 (717) 837-0601

Another unlikely source, but these folks make wonderful food, including the best-tasting peanut butter I have ever had, and they will mail order short-grain rice. Catalog available.

CHICAGO

ORIENTAL FOOD MARKET & COOKING SCHOOL 2801 West Howard, Chicago, Illinois 60645 (312) 274-2826

A full selection of nonperishable foodstuffs and basic equipment if you're in the area. Mail order catalog does not give brands, so call or write with specifics.

STAR MARKET 3349 North Clark Street, Chicago, Illinois 60657 (312) 472-0599/2184

A Japanese-owned store with a large stock of canned and bottled goods. Write with specific requests for mail order.

WOKS 'N' THINGS 2234 South Wentworth Avenue, Chicago, Illinois 60616 (312) 842-0701

According to my student Margaret Miller, who sent me snapshots of this impressive-looking store, it is "the best source of Chinese cooks' supply in the Midwest." From what I can see in the picture, they have the right woks, steamers, Chinese mesh spoons, and such in all sizes.

MIAMI

THE RED ROAD MARKET 4016 Red Road, Miami, Florida 33155 (305) 661-1726
A large gourmet grocery with a big Oriental foods selection. According to my student Sara Sharpe, owner Stanley Harris will get anything you want.

KEESAN IMPORTS 9252 Bird Road, Miami, Florida 33165 (305) 552-7196
The best Oriental specialty market in the area, reports Sara. Primarily nonperishable foodstuffs.

BON APPETIT 359 Miracle Mile, Coral Gables, Florida 33134 (305) 443-6241
A wide selection of basic Chinese cookware, including bamboo and metal steamers, woks, and cleavers. Owner Mickey Finkle will order on request what he doesn't have in stock.

BOSTON

MING'S MARKET 85-91 Essex Street, Boston, Massachusetts 02111 (617) 482-8805
My fellow cook Nina Simonds tells me that this is the best Chinese market in the Boston area, and one of the best Chinese markets period. A large import operation, Ming's has a full line of fresh and nonperishable foodstuffs and their own Chinese butcher. Chinese cookware of all sorts, including steamers.

AKRON

THE DRAGON TRADING COMPANY 943 Dopler, Akron, Ohio 44303 (216) 836-8877
A real treasure where you'd least expect it, says Nina. An impressive selection of fresh and nonperishable Chinese items, and an assortment of basic Chinese cookware. Address inquires to Emily Uy.

FORT WORTH

QUEEN'S FRESH PRODUCE 5714 Locke Avenue, Fort Worth, Texas 76116 (817) 731-6105
My student Pat Brooks reports that Queen's has the best specialty Asian produce in town, including fresh water chestnuts. The friendly Japanese owner, "Scott," stocks a full array of dry and canned goods, noodles and Chinese sausage, and will order anything you need.

THE VIETNAM-LAOS GROCERY 33-26 East Lancaster, Fort Worth, Texas 76103 (817) 535-0536
This store has an extensive selection of dry and canned goods, plus some basic cooking equipment.

VIETNAM MARKET 3913 East Belknap, Fort Worth, Texas 76111 (817) 838-9101
Here you'll find what you'll find above, plus a bit more.

AUSTIN

THE ORIENTAL MARKET 502 Pampas Street, Austin, Texas 78752 (512) 453-9058

> Cooking teacher Sara Aleshire tells me that this store has a huge selection of canned, bottled, and dry goods, in addition to a full selection of cookware including steamers, mesh spoons, and chopping blocks. There are noodles and dumpling wrappers, and the Thai owner, Chai, keeps the shelves filled with his own, homegrown organic vegetables.

HOUSTON

CHINATOWN SUPERMARKET 1806 Polk Street, Houston, Texas 77003 (713) 225-9312

> This market carries the full array: canned, bottled, and dry goods, fresh noodles, Chinese sausage, fresh produce, and basic Chinese cookware.

DALLAS

JUNG'S ORIENTAL FOOD 2519 North Fitzhugh, Dallas, Texas 75204 (214) 827-7653

> A major supplier, with a full stock of perishable and nonperishable items, as well as steamers, woks, teas, and institutional-size tubs of soy sauce and cans of oil.

⊕

GROWING YOUR OWN

This is a list of suppliers who stock seeds for Chinese vegetables, plus a book on the subject that has won my heart.

STOKES SEEDS, INC. 737 Main Street Box 548, Buffalo, New York 14240

> Seeds for Chinese cabbage, snow peas, mung beans, and Chinese broccoli. Catalog available.

MELLINGER'S 2310 West South Range Road, North Lima, Ohio 44452

> To look at the picture of these people in their catalog makes you want to buy their seeds. Chinese cabbage, winter melon, longbeans, Chinese chives, Chinese celery, Chinese spinach, snow peas, and coriander (listed as *cilantro*) all available. Following the list of Chinese seeds, there is the quote, "They conquer who believe they can."

TSANG & MA INTERNATIONAL P.O.B. 294, Belmont, California 94002

> These people have never been known to answer correspondence, but their large selection of Chinese vegetable seeds is sold widely in Chinese stores.

BETTER VEGETABLE GARDENS THE CHINESE WAY: PETER CHAN'S RAISED-BED SYSTEM by Peter Chan and Spenser Gill

> This book made me journey to Portland to meet Peter and see his garden. All three— the book, the man, and the garden—are inspiring. Even if you never intend to pop a seed in the earth, this is great reading. Write directly to the publisher, Graphic Arts Center Publishing Company, 2000 North West Wilson, Portland, Oregon 97209.

Barbara Tropp was born and raised in suburban New Jersey, in a town of one Chinese restaurant. For no discernible reason, she was smitten with Chinese things at an early age and decided to study the Chinese language. She graduated in 1970 from Barnard College of Columbia University with honors in Oriental Studies, and then received a Woodrow Wilson Fellowship to continue graduate work at Princeton University in Chinese literature and art history. During the course of her graduate studies, she lived in Taiwan for two years as an adopted child in two Chinese homes, both headed by superb traditional cooks. In Taiwan, she learned to eat.

Ms. Tropp returned to Princeton in 1973. Hungry, and out of homesickness for Asia, she taught herself how to cook. In 1978, she decided to stop work on her thesis (a helplessly obscure topic in Tang dynasty poetics) and start work on a cookbook.

Ms. Tropp now teaches Chinese cooking across the country and writes about Chinese cuisine for several national magazines. She lives in San Francisco and is usually found in Chinatown.

Ms. Tropp speaks, reads, and writes Chinese. She wrote the characters for the divider pages of this cookbook, copying the calligraphic style of her first (and well-worn) Chinese dictionary.